UNDERSTANDING THE MIDDLE AGES

THE TRANSFORMATION OF IDEAS
AND ATTITUDES
IN THE MEDIEVAL WORLD

Harald Kleinschmidt

GW00724508

THE BOYDELL PRESS

First published 2000
The Boydell Press, Woodbridge
Reprinted in paperback 2003, 2008

Transferred to digital printing

ISBN 978-0-85115-949-2

The Boydell Press is an imprint of Boydell & Brewer Ltd
PO Box 9, Woodbridge, Suffolk IP12 3DF, UK
and of Boydell & Brewer Inc.
668 Mt Hope Avenue, Rochester, NY 14620, USA
website: www.boydellandbrewer.com

A CiP catalogue record for this book is available
from the British Library

Library of Congress Catalog Card Number: 00-023627

This publication is printed on acid-free paper

Contents

List of Illustrations

Abbreviations

AAWG	Abhandlungen der Akademie der Wissenschaften in Göttingen, Philologisch–Historische Klasse, Dritte Folge
BAR	British Archaeological Reports
CCCM	Corpvs Christianorum. Continvatio mediaevalis
CCSL	Corpvs Christianorvm. Series Latina
CSEL	Corpvs scriptorvm ecclesiasticorvm Latinorvm
MGH	*Monumenta Germaniae Historica.*
AA	*Monumenta Germaniae Historica. Auctores antiquissimi*
Capit.	*Monumenta Germaniae Historica. Capitularia regum Francorum*
Concilia	*Monumenta Germaniae Historica. Concilia*
Const.	*Monumenta Germaniae Historica. Constitutiones et acta publica imperatorum et regum*
DD F I	*Monumenta Germaniae Historica. Die Urkunden Friedrichs I.*
DD Karol. I	*Monumenta Germaniae Historica. Die Urkunden Pippins, Karlmanns und Karls des Großen*
DD Otto II	*Monumenta Germaniae Historica. Die Urkunden Otto des II.*
DD Otto III	*Monumenta Germaniae Historica. Die Urkunden Otto des III.*
Epp.	*Monumenta Germaniae Historica. Epistolae (in Quart)*
Epp. Karol.	*Monumenta Germaniae Historica. Epistolae Karolini aevi*
Epp. sel.	*Monumenta Germaniae Historica. Epistolae selectae*
Fontes iuris Germ. ant.	*Monumenta Germaniae Historica, Fontes iuris Germanici antiqui in usum scholarum separatim editi*
Fontes iuris Germ. Ant. N.S.	*Monumenta Germaniae Historica. Fontes iuris Germanici antiqui,* Nova Series
Libelli de lite	*Monumenta Germaniae Historica. Libelli de lite imperatorum et pontificum*
LL	*Monumenta Germaniae Historica. Leges (in Folio)*
LL.nat. Germ.	*Monumenta Germaniae Historica. Leges nationum Germanicarum*
Poetae Lat.	*Monumenta Germaniae Historica. Poetae Latini medii aevi*
SS	*Monumenta Germaniae Historica. Scriptores (in Folio)*
SS rer. Germ.	*Monumenta Germaniae Historica. Scriptores rerum Germanicarum in usum scholarum separatim editi*

SS rer. Germ. N.S.	*Monumenta Germaniae Historica. Scriptores rerum Germanicarum,* Nova Series
SS rer. Lang.	*Monumenta Germaniae Historica. Scriptores rerum Langobardicarum et Italicarum saec. VI–IX*
SS rer. Merov.	*Moumenta Germaniae Historica. Scriptores rerum Merovingicarum*
PG	*Jean-Pierre Migne, ed., Patrologiae cursus completus. Series Graeca*
PL	*Jean-Pierre Migne, ed., Patrologiae cursus completus. Series Latina*
VIÖG	Veröffentlichungen des Instituts für Österreichische Geschichtsforschung
VMPIG	Veröffentlichungen des Max-Planck-Instituts für Geschichte
VSWG	Vierteljahrschrift für Sozial- und Wirtschaftsgeschichte
VuF	Vorträge und Forschungen, herausgegeben vom Konstanzer Arbeitskreis für Mittelalterliche Geschichte

Chronological Table

312	Emperor Constantine wins a battle against his co-emperor Maxentius and converts to Christianity
325	First ecumenical council at Nicaea
c. 370	An allied force of Anglians and Swabians wins a battle at the Fifeldor (Eider) against the Myrgings and the Myrgings migrate to Britain
395	Death of Emperor Theodosius I; division of the Roman Empire
410	Sack of Rome by warriors under the leadership of Alaric, King of the Visigoths; Emperor Honorius announces that Britons will have to defend themselves
c. 410	Foundation of monasteries at Marseilles and Lérins
418	Visigoths settle in Aquitaine with Toulouse as their centre
429	Vandals take control of the Roman province of Africa
443	Burgundians take control of areas in the western Alps
449	The date given by Bede for the migration of Saxons, Angles and *Iutae* to Britain
451	Defeat of Attila, King of the Huns, near Châlons-sur-Marne
476	End of Roman imperial rule in the city of Rome
477	The date given in the Anglo-Saxon Chronicle for the migration of Saxons under Aelle to Britain
481	Julius Nepos, the last Roman emperor who had occupied the imperial throne in Rome, dies
481–511	Clovis King of the Franks
483–577	St Brendan, founds several monasteries in Ireland
493	Theoderic, King of the Ostrogoths, takes control of parts of Italy
495	The date given in the Anglo-Saxon Chronicle for the migration of Saxons under Cerdic to Britain
c. 496	Clovis, King of the Franks, converts to Catholicism after victory over Alamans
507	Clovis defeats Visigoths in the battle of Vouglé; the Visigoths move on to Spain
508	In Tours, Clovis receives imperial honours from Emperor Anastasius
511–34	Theuderic King of the Franks
524	Boethius, a Roman senator, sentenced to death because of his opposition to Theoderic

529	Foundation by St Benedict of a monastery on Montecassino
526	Theoderic dies
527–65	Justinian Roman Emperor in Byzantium
531	A Frankish army under King Theuderic defeats King Irminfrid of the Thuringians and destroys their kingdom
534	Promulgation of a code of laws by Emperor Justinian
534–48	Theudebert King of the Franks
535	Byzantine troops defeat Vandals in Africa
535	Byzantine troops march into Italy against Ostrogoths
542	Outbreak of an epidemic of bubonic plague
547	Date of the accession of Ida, the first recorded king of Bernicia in Britain
554	Byzantine troops take control of Italy
559	Date of the accession of Aelle, the first recorded king of Deira in Britain
560–616	Ethelbert King of Kent
568	Lombards settle in northern Italy
587	King Reccared of the Visigoths converts to Catholicism
590	Columbanus, a Catholic missionary from Ireland, and his companions arrive in Gaul
590–604	Pope Gregory I
596	St Augustine of Canterbury arrives from Rome and begins Catholic mission in Kent
612	Columbanus founds a monastery at Bobbio
616–40	Eadbald King of Kent
635	Aidan, a missionary from Ireland, arrives at Lindisfarne at the request of King Oswald of Northumbria
638	Arabs take control of Jerusalem
664	The synod of Whitby settles disputes between Irish and Roman Catholic missionaries
669	Wilfrid becomes Bishop of York
672	Perctarit, King of the Lombards, converts to Catholicism
685–88	Caedwalla, King of the West Saxons, abdicates and dies in Rome 689
688–726	Ine, King of the West Saxons, rules together with his father, Coenred, for some time, abdicates and dies in Rome in or after 726
690–725	Wihtred King of Kent
697	Arabs take control over Carthage
711	Arab-led troops appear in the Iberian peninsula
719	Winfrith-Boniface receives a papal mandate to become a missionary in areas north of the Alps
722	Winfrith-Boniface appointed Bishop by Pope Gregory II
732	Defeat of Arab-led troops by the Frankish *Majordomus* Charles Martel in the battle of Tours and Poitiers

744	Sturmi becomes the first abbot of the monastery founded by St Boniface at Fulda
751	Pippin III deposes the last of the descendants of Clovis and has himself elected king of the Franks
754	Pippin seeks support from Pope Stephen II to consolidate his position as king of the Franks
768–814	Charlemagne, son of Pippin III, King of the Franks
772–805	Charlemagne fights a series of campaigns against Saxons
774	Charlemagne becomes also King of the Lombards
791–842	King Alfonso II of Asturias, propagates the supposed identification of a late Roman mausoleum as the grave of Apostle James the Elder (dec. c. 44) at a place subsequently named Santiago de Compostela; from the tenth century, the place attracts pilgrims from all over Europe
793	Lindisfarne sacked by Vikings
800	Charlemagne receives an imperial crown in Rome from Pope Leo III (795–816)
812	Disputes between Charlemagne and the Roman emperors in Byzantium end
814	Foundation of the bishopric of Halberstadt
814–40	Louis the Pious, son of Charlemagne, King of the Franks
827	Arab troops take control of parts of Sicily
840	Vikings establish themselves in Ireland and found Dublin
840–77	Charles the Bald, youngest son of Louis the Pious, King of the Franks and Emperor
843	Charles the Bald and his two brothers divide the Frankish kingdom among themselves in the Treaty of Verdun
855–70	Edmund King of East Anglia
858–67	Pope Nicholas I
860	Vikings from Kiev attack Constantinople
865	The Viking 'Great Army' moves into England
871–99	Alfred King of Wessex
876	Byzantine troops begin a series of campaigns against Arabs in Sicily
898–923	Charles the Simple King of the Franks
899	Hungarian raids in Italy
899–924	Edward the Elder King of the West Saxons
910	Duke William the Pious founds Cluny
911	Conrad I elected as King by representatives of political groups in the Frankish kingdom east of the Rhine; King Charles the Simple grants parts of Normandy to the Viking leader Rollo
919–36	Henry I, Duke of the Saxons, succeeds Conrad as King
920–23	Duke Robert of Neustria elected against King Charles the Simple
c. 922	Henry I authorises the building of fortifications against Hungarians in his kingdom

933	Henry I defeats Hungarians at Riade
936–73	Otto I, son of Henry I, succeeds his father as King
953–54	Otto I's son, Duke Liudolf, revolts against his father, dies 957
955	Otto I defeats Hungarians on the Lechfeld near Augsburg
957/9–75	Edgar King of England
962	Otto I crowned emperor by Pope John XII in Rome
965	Brun, youngest son of Otto I, dies as archbishop of Cologne and Duke of Lorraine
968	Otto I founds the archbishopric of Magdeburg
973–83	Otto II succeeds his father Otto I as king and emperor
982	Otto defeated by Arab troops at Cotrone
983–1002	Otto III (born 980) succeeds his father as king and emperor under the regencies of his mother Theophanu and his grandmother Adelheid
987–96	Hugh Capet, grandson of King Robert, King of the Franks
996–1021	al-Hakim Khalif of Baghdad
996–1031	Robert II King of the Franks in succession to his father Hugh Capet
999–1003	Pope Sylvester II (Gerbert of Aurillac) teacher of Emperor Otto III
1000	Otto III visits Gniezno in Poland and promotes the foundation of an archbishopric there; King Stephen of Hungary establishes a series of bishoprics; King Olaf of Sweden accepts Catholicism
c. 1000	Vikings cross the northern Atlantic and reach America which they call Vinland
1002–24	Emperor Henry II
1007	Henry II establishes a bishopric at Bamberg
1009/10	The Church of the Holy Sepulchre in Jerusalem demolished
1016	Vikings appear in Sicily
1016–35	King Cnut succeeds as King of England, becomes also King of Denmark and King of Norway
1024–39	Emperor Conrad II
1039–56	Emperor Henry III
1056–1105	Emperor Henry IV
1059	Papal election decree
1066	King Harold of England defeats King Harald Hardrada of Norway in the Battle of Stamford Bridge and is defeated in the Battle of Hastings by Duke William of Normandy who becomes King of England
1066–87	William the Conqueror King of England
1071	Saxon revolt against Henry IV; Byzantine troops defeated by Turkish troops in the Battle of Manzikert
1073–85	Pope Gregory VII
1076	Gregory VII excommunicates Emperor Henry IV

1077	Henry IV visits Gregory VII at Canossa who lifts the ban from the emperor
1087–1100	William II King of England
1088–99	Pope Urban II
1095	Urban II demands a crusade against Muslims in Palestine at a council in Clermont-Ferrand
1097–99	First Crusade against Muslims in Palestine
1099	Jerusalem conquered by crusaders
1100–1135	Henry I King of England
1106–25	Emperor Henry V
1122	Concordate signed at Worms between Emperor Henry V and Pope Calixtus II
1130	Roger II crowned King of Sicily
1135–1154	Stephen King of England
1140	Abelard condemned by a council at Sens
1146	St Bernard of Clairvaux supports demands for another crusade
1147	Pope Eugene III issues a bill which encourages crusades against Slavs and against Muslims in Spain
1147–49	Second Crusade against Muslims in Palestine
1152	King Louis VII of France (1137–80) divorces his wife, Eleanor of Aquitaine, who soon afterwards marries Henry, son of Duke Geoffrey of Anjou
1152–90	Frederick I German King and (since 1155) Roman Emperor
1154–89	Henry of Aquitaine King of England as Henry II
1156	Frederick restores Bavaria to Duke Henry the Lion of Saxony (1129/30–95); Henry Jasimirgott (1141–77), the former Duke of Bavaria, becomes Duke of Austria
1157	The empire styled Holy Roman Empire for the first time
1168	Henry the Lion marries Mathilda, daughter of King Henry II of England
1180	Henry the Lion is deprived of his duchies
1180–1223	Philip II August King of France
1187	Sultan Saladin (Salah-ed-Din) conquers Jerusalem from the crusaders
1188	The sons of Henry II of England rebel against their father
1189–92	Third Crusade against Muslims in Palestine
1189–99	Richard Lionheart, King of England
1190	Emperor Frederick I dies during the Third Crusade before reaching Palestine; at the time of the siege of Acre, the Ordo domus S. Mariae Teutonicorum (Teutonic Order) in Jerusalem is established for the care of injured; it begins its conquest of Prussia in 1226
1190–97	Henry VI succeeds his father Frederick I as Emperor, prepares another crusade, but dies before the crusade gets on its way

1198	War in the empire between rival parties supporting three candidates for the imperial succession: Philip of Swabia, brother of Henry VI; Frederick II, son of Henry VI; and Otto of Brunswick, son of Henry the Lion
1198–1216	Pope Innocent III
1199–1216	John Lackland King of England
c. 1200	Groups of mainly German settlers migrate eastward beyond a line from Schwerin to Dresden into areas inhabited by Slavic population groups
1204	Fourth Crusade; crusaders conquer Byzantium, expell the Roman emperors from the city and establish a new Latin Empire
1209–29	Crusades against Albigensians in southern France
1210	St Francis receives approval from the pope for his mendicant monastic order
1212–50	Frederick II German King and Roman Emperor
1214	Philip II August defeats a coalition of Plantagenet and Imperial troops in the battle of Bouvines
1216	Papal approval for the foundation of the Order of the Preachers (Dominicans)
1216–72	Henry III King of England
c. 1225–74	St Thomas Aquinas
1226–70	Louis IX, King of France; dies during a crusade.
1227–41	Pope Gregory IX
1228–29	Frederick II leads the Fifth Crusade as an excommunicated emperor
1229	Frederick II crowned King of Jerusalem
1230	Unification of the kingdoms of León and Castile
1237–42	Mongols reach Hungary, Poland and the Adriatic Sea
1244	Jerusalem reverts to Muslim rule
1245–73	Succession crisis in the Roman Empire of the Occident
1254	Union of towns and aristocrats in the Rhineland in support of King William of Holland (1252–56)
1261	End of the Latin Empire in Byzantium
1268	Charles of Anjou, King of Sicily (1265–82), defeats Conradin, the last descendant of Frederick II, in the battle of Tagliacozzo
1269–95	Journey of the Polo family to East Asia
1272–1307	Edward I King of England
1273–91	Rudolf of Habsburg German king and King of the Romans
1282	'Sicilian Vespers': Charles of Anjou (1265–82) expelled from Sicily, Peter III of Aragón takes his place as King of Sicily (1282–85)
1282–84	Edward I conquers Wales
1285–1314	Philip IV the Fair King of France

1291	Acre, the last stronghold of the crusaders in Palestine, taken over by Muslims; the Swiss cantons of Schwyz, Unterwalden and Uri conclude a perpetual union against the Habsburg lords
1302	A mounted French army under Philip the Fair defeated by Flemish infantry forces in the Battle of Kortrijk
1306–29	Robert I King of Scotland
1307–27	Edward II King of England
1309–77	Papacy in Avignon
1310–13	Emperor Henry VII (1308–13) leads an expedition to Italy; dies in its course
1313–75	Giovanni Boccaccio, writes his *Novellae* 1349–51
1314	Edward II defeated by Scottish troops under Robert I of Scotland at the battle of Bannockburn
1315	The Swiss defend their autonomy against Duke Frederick of Austria (1314–30) in the Battle of Morgarten
1322–28	Charles IV King of France
1327–77	Edward III King of England
1328–50	Philip VI King of France
1337–1492	'Hundred Years War'
1338	Declaration of Rhense renounces the right of the pope to approve of a candidate elected as German king and king of the Romans
1340	Edward III, King of England (1327–77), assumes the title King of France
c. 1343–c.1400	Geoffrey Chaucer, writes his fragment *Canterbury Tales* c. 1393–1400
1346	English troops defeat their French counterpart at Crécy
1346–78	Charles IV Roman Emperor
1347	English forces conquer Calais
1347–50	The Black Death in Europe
1350–64	John II King of France
1354	Turkish conquest of Gallipoli
1356	English victory at Poitiers
1358	Jacquerie (peasant rising) in France
1360	Treaty of Brétigny through which Edward III renounces his claims to the French throne
1363–1404	Philip the Bold, Duke of Burgundy, becomes Count of Flanders and Artois in 1384, Duke of Limburg in 1396
1364–80	Charles V King of France
1372	French–Castilian naval victory over the English fleet at La Rochelle
1377–99	Richard II King of England
1378–1417	Great Schism of the Catholic Church
1380–1422	Charles VI King of France
1381	Great English Rising

1387	Thessalonica comes under Ottoman Turkish control
1389	A mixed southern Slav army defeated by an Ottoman Turkish force in Kosovo
1397	Norway, Sweden and Denmark establish a union at Kalmar
1399–1413	Henry IV King of England
1404–19	John the Fearless Duke of Burgundy
1413–22	Henry V King of England
1415	English victory at Agincourt; Ceuta conquered by Portuguese forces
1419–36	Wars and crusades against Hussites in Bohemia
1419–67	Philip the Good Duke of Burgundy
1422–61	Charles VII King of France
1422–72	Henry VI King of England
1423–54	Wars between Milan, Florence and other principalities in Italy
1428	Joan of Arc begins her campaign against English troops in France
1431	Joan of Arc sentenced to death and burnt
1438	The Pragmatic Sanction of Bourges confers on the king powers over the Catholic Church in France
1440–93	Emperor Frederick III
1453	Constantinople conquered by a Turkish army under Sultan Mehmed II (1451–81); English troops withdraw from France except for the town of Calais
1454	Peace of Lodi ends Italian wars
1458–64	Pope Pius II
1458–71	George of Podiebrad King of Bohemia
1461–83	Louis XI King of France
1462	Cape Verde islands colonised by Portuguese
1467–77	Charles the Bold Duke of Burgundy
1473	In Trier Charles the Bold and Emperor Frederick III negotiate the conditions of Charles's succession as emperor
1474–75	Charles the Bold besieges Neuss
1476	Swiss infantry armies defeat Charles the Bold at Grandson and Murten
1477	Charles the Bold dies in the battle of Nancy against Swiss infantry forces
1477–82	Mary, daughter of Charles the Bold, Duchess of Burgundy, married to Maximilian, son of Emperor Frederick III
1480–81	Turkish occupation of Otranto on the Italian mainland
1487	Bartholomew Dias rounds the southern tip of Africa
1492	The last Muslim emirs of Granada withdraw peacefully from the city; Jews expelled from Spain
1492–93	First voyage of Christopher Columbus
1493–1519	Maximilian I Roman King and Emperor Elect
1494–95	Charles VIII, King of France (1483–98), invades Italy

1495   An Imperial Diet meeting at Worms attempts major reforms of the Roman Empire under the leadership of Maximilian I

1497–99 Vasco da Gama sails around Africa and reaches Calicut in southwest India

Introduction

Europe is a geographical concept without boundaries towards Asia
and an historical concept with changing boundaries

— Edgar Morin[1]

This book is about concepts. Concepts are abstractions from the world of
tangible realities. We use them to facilitate our own reconstructions of these
realities as the subject matter of our thoughts and in order to give meaning to
the words which we need for their expression. The meaningful interconnection between reconstructions of realities, language and concepts has been
referred to as the semiotic triangle, which implies that concepts need to be
defined as a part of this semiotic triangle.[2] Defining is the process of marking
the logical boundaries of concepts.

Here begins the problem for the historian. For, as Edgar Morin (b. 1921),
the research director of the renowned *Centre National de Recherches Scientifiques*, made explicit, it may be difficult to establish these logical boundaries.
In some cases, the definitions may be vague and elusive rather than precise.
Moreover, in a large number of cases, concepts have a history of their own,
that is, their logical boundaries, once established, move in time and, consequently, are specific to groups, places and periods. There are various possibilities to tackle the problems of conceptual history. One possibility is to
scrutinise written sources for changes of definitions of concepts. This method
leads to good results in cases where concepts are explicitly defined in writing.
Another possibility is to search for the actions into which concepts were
translated and to investigate the changing patterns of actions at times, places
and within groups. The first method can only be applied if definitions of
concepts have been laid down in writing and can be subject to philosophical
investigation. The second method is good in all cases where oral communication prevails or is being inter-utilised with written communication. As the
latter was the case throughout the Middle Ages, the second method shall be
applied in this book.

Thus the conceptual history of medieval culture focuses on changes of
concepts and strives to put them into the context of action. These contexts
have been referred to ingeniously by Michel Foucault (1926–84) as 'spaces of

---

1 Edgar Morin, *Penser l'Europe* (Paris, 1987), p. 27.
2 Charles Kay Ogden, Ivor Armstrong Richards, *The Meaning of Meaning* (London, New
   York, 1923), pp. 1–23.

communication'.[3] By that phrase, Foucault meant reconstructed units of time, space and groups within which successful direct communication is possible. In other words, Foucault designed spatial, temporal or social units within which every person communicates his or her thoughts about a certain subject matter through standardised sequences of known words without intermitting translations or interpretations. A space of communication can be defined in three different ways: first, in spatial terms as the area within which such direct communication can be facilitated with success, for example, among the speakers of the same language; secondly, it can be defined in temporal terms as the period within which direct communication is possible, such as, the reading of texts in modern English; and finally, it can be defined in social terms as the group whose members avail themselves of certain formulae of oral expression, literary styles, jargons or sociolects which remain unintelligible to outsiders. These three ways of defining a space of communication do not have to overlap, because it is conceivable that, for example, a certain group uses a professional jargon which draws on a kind of language which is no longer spoken by members of other groups living in the same area at the same time. Likewise, it is possible that words from one language are borrowed by another language and continue to be used in that language long after having been discarded by the original. Finally, it is possible that, within a given area and at the same time, speakers of different languages interact with frequency and create interferences among the various languages involved.

Foucault's phrase, the space of communication, also applies to concepts. Since most concepts change, they are specific to certain spaces of communication, and it becomes difficult to communicate them across the boundaries of these spaces of communication. It may happen that a certain concept is expressed by a different word or is split up into various concepts which, each in turn, are expressed by new words. It may also happen that the same concept continues to be expressed by different words. And, finally, changes of concepts may occur simultaneously with changes of the subject matter, for which the concepts are abstractions, and of the words by means of which the concepts have to be expressed. Empirically, the latter case is by far the most frequent.

Consequently, the process of defining a concept is obviated by the three-fold difficulty: first, that no concept can be defined in isolation from the subject matter for which it stands as an abstraction and from the word or words through which the concept needs to be expressed; second, that most definitions of concepts are unlikely to attain a degree of validity that extends across the boundaries of spaces of communication; and, third, that the definitions of many concepts take place under the condition of lingual interferences

---

3 Michel Foucault, *L'archéologie du savoir* (Paris, 1969), pp. 216–31. There is some similarity between this concept and the more frequently used concept of mentality as reflected in patterns of individual and group actions. However, space of communication has the advantage of greater flexibility through the inclusion into it of the dimensions of space and time and through its applicability not only to actions, but also to perceptions.

and cultural contacts through which elements of contingency may be introduced into the processes of defining concepts. All in all, these factors add to the fuzziness and changeability of most definitions of concepts. For each semantic triangle within which a concept must be defined is likely to be part of a cluster made up from several other semantic triangles, and it is probable that each semantic triangle, together with the cluster itself, will be rearranged across the boundaries of spaces of communication.

Changes of semantic triangles are more or less well recorded. They may be easily recognisable in cases where new words appear or where the formation of new concepts requires their explanation. But they may go unrecorded in cases where there are gradual transformations of already existing concepts or equally gradual changes in the meaning of words. Specifically, the latter cases demand the critical attention of historians who have to read sources between the lines and compare statements contained in one source carefully with seemingly similar statements in other sources, be they contemporary, earlier or later. Likewise, changes of words and concepts may not always take place at the same time in all groups using one and the same language so that the possibility arises that different jargons or sociolects at the same time avail themselves of different concepts while using the same words for the expression of the concepts.

There are a large number of concepts within each space of communication to which these difficulties apply. Discussing and explaining all these concepts requires the knowledge of more than one author and exceeds the limitations of a monograph. Hence, the choice of concepts included in this book depends on the definition of the concepts behind the words 'Europe' and of 'culture'. However, as will be shown later in some detail, to both of these concepts the above-mentioned threefold difficulty of conceptualisation also applies, which means that the definitions of the concepts of 'Europe' and of 'culture' are inescapably vague and elusive. Thus the concepts discussed in this book do not claim to be representative of all aspects and facets of European culture. Instead, five practical objectives have guided their selection: first, to provide insight into the changeability of European culture across the boundaries of spaces of communication; secondly, to allow the differentiation of culture according to groups wherever applicable; thirdly, to describe the changing principal patterns of action; fourthly, to analyse the major changing normative frameworks for the maintenance of order within which actions take place; and, fifthly, to set the main changing norms for communication as a form of interaction. Changes of these concepts shall be studied within the successive spaces of communication of which medieval European culture appears to consist.

With regard to the concepts which can or must be selected to form the core of the conceptual history of medieval European culture, I take the view that the selection can and ought to be based on criteria which existed at the time. Since the later Middle Ages, one of the more persistent ordering devices has been derived from the *artes liberales*. This combined body of general theoretical and empirical knowledge has excluded the specialised knowledge which

has been transmitted within the three academic disciplines of theology, jurisprudence and medicine and has likewise been seen as separate from the technical expertise required for the several crafts. I shall focus on concepts which
have by convention been included among the *artes liberales* and shall concen-
trate on generally applicable concepts rather than on concepts whose applicability is confined to a particular discipline. That is to say that, while I shall
exclude matters related to theology, jurisprudence and medicine on the one
hand, and engineering on the other, I shall include matters related to religion,
law, health and technology to the extent that they are relevant to the conceptual history of European culture as a whole.[4]

Conceptualising culture historically is by no means self-evident. Instead,
many twentieth-century philosophers and social scientists, including social
and cultural anthropologists, tended to regard concepts, such as culture[5] and
society,[6] as static and held the view that some general validity could be
ascribed to these concepts, making them applicable beyond the limits of space
and time. However, this view is inconsistent with an historical investigation
due to a reason which has partly been expressed in the following statement by
Claude Lévi-Strauss (b. 1908):

> Both history and ethnography are concerned with societies other than the one
> in which we live. Whether this otherness is due to remoteness in time or to
> remoteness in space, or even to cultural heterogeneity, is of secondary impor-
> tance compared to the basic similarity of perspective. . . . In both cases we are
> dealing with systems of representation which differ from each member of the
> group and which, on the whole, differ from the representations of the investiga-
> tor.[7]

Lévi-Strauss reveals the difficulty of communicating across spaces of communication and rightly insists that the subject matter, the concepts and the words
about and through which we communicate may differ from society to society,
both in space and in time. However, profound as these observations certainly
are, they are not radical enough. For they also apply to the one concept which
Lévi-Strauss sets as a constant, and that is the concept of 'society'. As will be
shown in a later part of this book, the currently used social science concept of
'society' is an abstraction drawn on a specific type of social group which was
absent from the Middle Ages and did not appear before the end of the eighteenth century. Therefore it cannot be generalised to cover the previous
periods of European history together with the variety of non-European types
of groups. Hence, if we historicise Lévi-Strauss's concept of 'society', his
observations cease to be communicable because they hinge upon the general

---

4   I follow the precedent of Jacob Burckhardt, *Die Kultur der Renaissance in Italien*, ed.
    Walther Rehm (Herrsching, 1981), p. 27 (first published Basle, 1860).
5   Leslie A. White, *The Concept of Cultural Systems* (New York, London, 1975).
6   Talcott Parsons, *The Social System* (New York, 1966).
7   Claude Lévi-Strauss, *Structural Anthropology* (Garden City, 1967), pp. 16–17 (first pub-
    lished Paris, 1958).

applicability of that very concept and the comparability of the subject matter from which they are abstracted.

The difficulty raised here is a fundamental one in conceptual history because, in the last resort, all concepts have the potential to be subjected to changes in space, time and groups. Thus, in the last analysis, all concepts would have to be historicised depriving us of all possibility of communication. However, such an outcome cannot be the goal of an historical inquiry. For some concepts must remain generally applicable for purposes of facilitating the inquiry and allowing comparisons across spaces, periods and groups. Hence, a fair compromise has to be sought between, on the one hand, the principled demands of a critical conceptual history that historicises and thereby reduces the applicability of concepts, and, on the other, the pragmatic demands of communicability which rest on the general applicability of the concepts used in an historical inquiry. A compromise between both demands can be found when we remain aware of the necessity that we cannot at the same time both historicise a set of concepts or parts of them *and* regard them as constants. Instead, conceptual history can only remain communicable if and as long as we consciously exclude from the investigation all those concepts which we use for the purposes of the inquiry and for comparisons across spaces, periods and groups. Admittedly, this compromise is theoretically a nuisance. But it is a demand of practical reason and, moreover, not specific to seemingly idiosyncratic concerns of conceptual history. Instead, it is a compromise on which critical historical inquiries proceed at large, for all history deals with change, and change is not recognisable except against the background of continuities.

There are two criteria according to which the boundary between change and continuity can be set. One follows from the subjective interests of the retrospective historian; the other is, once again, a standard which pertains to the spaces of communication. The first criterion demands from the retrospective historian a consciousness of what he or she wishes to regard as continuous. Under this condition, the retrospective historian is legitimised, first, to define in his or her own concepts and words what he or she has chosen to regard as continuous, and, second, to superimpose these definitions upon whatever part of the past. The appropriateness of these definitions will then be judged solely on the grounds of their communicability in the historian's present and does not depend on the extent to which these definitions were accepted in the past.

The other criterion is more delicate. It emerges from the observation that there is no inherent necessity that the process of time must always be recognised as change.[8] For it may be that, in a given space of communication, manifestations of past or ongoing changes are abundant while contemporaries ignore these manifestations or downgrade them towards a status of

---

8   Martin Heidegger, *Sein und Zeit*, §§ 78–82, Heidegger, *Gesamtausgabe* I/2 (Frankfurt, 1977), pp. 534–75.

seemingly insignificant variations of manifestations of eternity.[9] Thus, change can be perceived as a process that takes place against overwhelming forces of continuity and can be ignored by contemporaries, or, vice versa, change can be perceived as a driving force in itself which easily overpowers the forces of continuity and induces contemporaries to adjust themselves to, or even try to control, change. In other words, cultures can be investigated as changing, although perceptions of change can be culturally specific. History can be recognised as the long story of the human incapability of maintaining stability in a divinely ordained or otherwise well-ordered world of things. Or, history can be recognised as the long story of human adaptability to a changing world. In any case, the retrospective historian needs to be aware of the preferences characteristic of the space of communication under review and, furthermore to account for changes in these preferences across the boundaries of spaces of communication. Therefore conceptual historians must respect attitudes towards change pertaining to a space of communication different from their own.[10]

As Edgar Morin has already remarked, 'Europe' as a concept defies precise definition in terms of space and time. One major reason for the fuzziness of the concept of 'Europe' is that the concept has its own history and, consequently, has had a variety of meanings in the course of the last 2000 years or so. This places the conceptual historian of European culture in the midst of the above sketched dilemma. Should the large number of sources be respected which contain evidence on the changeability of the concept of 'Europe'?[11] Then, the inquiry into the conceptual history of European culture would have to deal with a substantial variety of concepts of Europe, each specific to a given space of communication, and what was meant by Europe, say in the eighth century, would not be comparable with what was meant by Europe, say in the twelfth or the fifteenth century. Or should a fixed concept be defined and retrospectively superimposed upon the whole cultural history of Europe? Moreover, are we justified in superimposing a unifying concept upon a subject matter which appears to be, at least at times, heterogeneous and diverse? Finally, whenever the subject matter has been perceived as uniform, what concept of unity or, for that matter, uniformity, has been applied? These questions augur in favour of caution in the definition of Europe as an all-inclusive concept and encourage its tentative pragmatic restriction to Latin Christendom, even though this definition necessarily excludes parts of the subject matter which at times were considered to be integral.

The definition of Europe which shall be applied in this book is drawn on the fusion between the two ancient concepts of 'Europe' and of the 'Occident'.

9   John Comaroff, Jean Comaroff, *Ethnography and Historical Imagination* (Boulder, San Francisco, Oxford, 1992), pp. 24–5.

10 Comaroff (see note 9).

11 Jürgen Fischer, *Oriens, Occidens, Europa,* Veröffentlichungen des Instituts für Europäische Geschichte Mainz XV (Wiesbaden, 1957). Denys Hay, *Europe*, Edinburgh University Publications. History, Philosophy and Economics VII (Edinburgh, 1957).

Europe as the Occident can be understood to have come into existence after the formation of the post-Roman kingdoms (regna) which were formed within or on the fringes of the western hemisphere of the Roman Empire of Antiquity since the late fifth century, subsequently stood under the rule or fell within the area of influence of the Carolingian dynasty during the ninth century and was extended to include Scandinavia and east-central Europe as a consequence of the Catholic mission. This definition of Europe thus excludes Middle Eastern, Greek and Roman Antiquity, the Byzantine world in the Middle East and south-eastern Europe, the Ottoman Turkish Empire in south-eastern Europe and, finally, the Russian Empire in the East. However, the concept includes the Jewish, Greek, Roman, Byzantine, Muslim, Central Asian and African heritages as far as they impacted on the 'Occident'. In addition to the pragmatic reason stated above, there is a more substantive argument supporting this admittedly rigid definition. The reason is that, as Edward Said (b. 1935) has reminded us, much of humanistic thinking has, since the fifteenth century, been biased in claiming that the Occident was the major or even the sole inheritor of the various classical heritages.[12] It is only under the dominance of this claim that classical Antiquity and Europe can be fused into one single concept, the latter being regarded as the continuation of the former. There is no doubt that such a claim can be supported by Occidental beliefs in the continuity of some institutions during and beyond the Middle Ages, such as the papacy and the Roman Empire. But, already in their own times, these beliefs were partial and contested, being coeval with rival beliefs cherished among the various Oriental churches as well as with the Byzantine and the Russian Empires of the East. More importantly, these beliefs cannot obscure the fact that the ancient Middle Eastern, Greek and Roman heritages were not only taken over in the Occident, but also in the Orient, and that there much of these heritages was preserved, perhaps with greater diligence, respect and attention than in the Occident, by Armenians and Greeks in Byzantium, Jews and Arabs in the Mediterranean area and, last but not least, by Ethiopians in northern Africa. In short, separating the concept of 'Europe' in its temporal dimension from Antiquity is not meant to belittle the impact of the classical heritages on 'European' culture; yet it is designed to place the classical heritages in Europe on an equal footing with other sources of European culture and, at the same time, with the classical heritages in the various parts of the 'Orient'.

On the other side, the time span covered by this book shall be limited to 'European' culture as a whole up to the sixteenth century. The argument in support of this limitation is that, between 1600 and 1800, the idea became popular that national cultures should be organised and respected as the focal points of economic, political and cultural activities. The consequence of this change can easily be detected in the emerging linguistic diversity of post-1600 Europe when national languages were established and the unifying conscious-

---

12 Edward W. Said, *Orientalism*, new edn (New York, 1994; first published London, 1978).

ness of an all-European culture began to compete with the partialising consciousness of national cultures. At the same time, boundary rectifications, which had been a persistent phenomenon up to the eighteenth century and which had indirectly, but fundamentally, contributed to the formation of a unifying consciousness in Europe, became major causes of political conflicts. In these conflicts, it was commonly contended that national and other administrative boundaries should remain stable and should be devised so as to embrace the national cultures. The centralising powers of the governments which imposed themselves as ruling institutions above these national cultures accomplished both the repression of local diversities and the weakening of the consciousness of European unity.[13] Moreover, it may be so that, in consequence of the emergence of national cultures, the pattern of changes which occurred most frequently during the Middle Ages differed from that which occurred in the centuries thereafter. In this case, the descriptive and analytical instruments which are suitable to the study of the Middle Ages may be inadequate to the study of the subsequent centuries.

For the variety of intermediate temporal spaces of communication between the fifth and the sixteenth centuries, the conventional periodisation of 'medieval' or 'the Middle Ages' shall be applied. This shall be done although, evidently, this periodisation is, again, a retrospective construct which was alien to the contemporaries, and, more importantly, although it is fundamentally questionable in itself. It is so because much of the argument in this book shall seek to prove that the so-called 'Middle Ages' were anything but a uniform temporal space of communication. However, this conventional periodisation will be retained as a convenient and current label for the ease with which it facilitates communication.

A long tradition of functionalist anthropology has understood culture as a static concept which is defined in spatial or social terms and in which history is reduced to an insignificant variable or is even ignored as if it did not exist at all.[14] Initially, the early- and mid-twentieth-century functionalists who were the most vocal in supporting this view had taken a strong and justified stand against nineteenth-century evolutionistic beliefs in the development of culture. Functionalists denounced such beliefs as unempirical and unscientific and tried to narrow the general concept of 'culture' *per se* to the concept of 'culture' as a particular system within boundaries which could demarcate a certain culture against its environment.[15] In this respect, functionalist anthropologists were in agreement with the contemporary proponents of general

---

13 Robert Muchembled, *Popular Culture and Elite Culture in France 1400–1750* (Baton Rouge, London, 1985; first published Paris, 1978).
14 For a survey of definitions of 'culture' see Alfred Leslie Kroeber, Clyde Kluckhohn, *Culture* (Cambridge, Mass., London, 1952).
15 Bronislaw Malinowski, *A Scientific Theory of Culture and other Essays* (New York, London, 1960), pp. 3–35, 38.

systems theory who regarded systems as self-perpetuating units.[16] To functionalists, these units were made up of a multitude of functional and institutional manifestations which appeared to be part and parcel of the real world of tangible or otherwise objectifiable matters.

However, the functionalist ahistoricity of the concept of 'culture' as a smoothly operating system has subsequently been called into question. It has been challenged with the argument that 'cultures' cannot be regarded as parts of the real world of tangible or otherwise objectifiable matters, but that, instead, a 'culture' should *prima facie* be regarded 'as a shifting semantic field of symbolic production and material practice empowered in complex ways'.[17] This definition does not only liberate culture from a spatial or social substrate as the static, uniform and integrated framework for patterns of behaviour, but it also includes internal inconsistencies and conflicts and takes into consideration endogenous factors of change. Explicitly, it stands against the functionalist view that a culture is coherent[18] as a system and 'the integral whole consisting of implements and consumers' goods, of constitutional charters for the various social groupings, of human ideas and crafts, beliefs and customs', as Bronislaw Malinowski (1884–1942) put it. Moreover, more recently, theorists have warned that external or retrospective observers may objectify features of culture which had remained unrecognised or had been ignored by actors in the system and thereby contribute to culture change.[19]

This combination of the systemic analysis of cultures with due consideration for internal conflicts and factors of change is suitable to the work of conceptual historians. This is so for three reasons. First, it allows conceptual historians to analyse a culture as a changing system; secondly, it supports conceptual historians in their efforts to conceptualise a culture, not merely as a random collection, but also as a meaningfully interconnected arrangement of words, concepts and subject matter; thirdly, it promotes the conceptual historians' investigation into internal inconsistencies and conflicts among the several concepts harboured in a culture as well as into endogenous factors of change. In summary, conceptual history displays a culture as a system under the condition of change.

Because European culture as a whole shall be the focal point of the entire book, little attention will be paid to matters of local cultures and the diversity of regions within Europe. Conceptual history is not cultural history or, for that matter, an equivalent of history from below or the history of everyday

---

[16] E.g. Ludwig von Bertalanffy, 'An Outline of General Systems Theory', *British Journal for the Philosophy of Science* I (1950), pp. 155–7.

[17] Comaroff (see note 9), p. 30. Cf. Clifford Geertz, 'Thick Description', in Geertz, *The Interpretation of Cultures* (New York, 1973), pp. 3–32. Earlier contributions by archaeologists emphasise the same point. See David Leonard Clarke, *Analytical Archaeology* (London, 1968), pp. 48–51. Colin Renfrew, Kenneth L. Cooke, eds, *Transformations* (London, 1979), pp. 482–5, 492, 497–9.

[18] Malinoswki (see note 15), p. 38. The contrary view has been argued by Comaroff (see note 9), p. 27.

[19] Comaroff (see note 9).

life.[20] It takes into consideration local peculiarities if they are of significance for the whole of European culture, but it cannot present an all-inclusive picture of the varieties of local cultures. Moreover, because the emphasis of conceptual history is on culture change, the criterion for measuring significance is the degree by which a local event or feature contributes to the description, analysis and explanation of change.

From a functionalist point of view, it is difficult to accommodate the systems approach to cultures with culture change, because paramount attention is given to the stability of cultures as systems. As long as this attitude prevails, change within cultures as intra-systemic change is possible only as long as it does not effect core structures of the system. This must be so because, were change to affect core structures of the system, the system as such would collapse, and, in consequence, the change would no longer be intra-systemic, but a change of the system as a whole. In other words, functionalists admit only the dichotomy of intra-systemic change versus change of systems, whereby the latter type of change leads to the collapse of one system and its replacement by another one or its absorption into the environment. This is the position taken by what is perhaps the most penetrating functionalist 'theory of culture change' which was advocated around the middle of the twentieth century by Julian H. Steward (1902–72).[21] The focal point of Steward's theory was the explanation of the factors of instability which may contribute to the collapse of cultural systems. Viewing cultural systems 'in terms of socio-cultural integration', Steward credited these systems with a 'trend to perpetuate themselves', and he would only admit that changes occur 'over the millennia'.[22] He assumed that cultures accomplish stability through adjustments to their environments, but acknowledged that there is one factor of instability which can jeopardise the supposed perseverance of cultural systems, and that is to be found in the seemingly empirical evidence that 'no culture has achieved so perfect an adjustment to its environment that it is static'.[23] Hence, Steward denied the existence of any endogenous factors of change in cultural systems and took the factuality of change to be the outcome of some imperfection of the world as it happened to be.

Since the later 1960s, however, archaeologists and sociologists[24] have challenged this functionalist theory of culture change. They have used the then recent interactionistic offshoot of general systems theory advocated by René

20 As in Peter Dinzelbacher, ed., *Europäische Mentalitätsgeschichte* (Stuttgart, 1993). Heinrich Fichtenau, *Lebensordnungen im 10. Jahrhundert*, 2 vols, Monographien zur Geschichte des Mittelalters XXX (Stuttgart, 1984), and Reinhart Koselleck, *Vergangene Zukunft* (Frankfurt, 1985), have argued a position which is closer to conceptual history.
21 Collected under the title Julian Haynes Steward, *Theory of Culture Change* (Urbana, Chicago, 1955).
22 Ibid., pp. 47, 37.
23 Ibid., p. 5.
24 Clarke (see note 17). Renfrew and Cooke (see note 17). Anthony Giddens, *The Constitution of Society* (Cambridge, 1984), pp. 288–304.

Thom (b. 1923) and Ilya Prigogine (b. 1917),[25] among others, and have acknowledged that structural elements of systems are transient and that successive cultural and social systems are interrelated by morphogenesis and structuration. These concepts denote 'mechanisms that generate pattern and form'[26] and, in application to archaeology and sociology, were used to study processes of change through which the generation of cultural and social systems has been interconnected with intra-systemic changes in previously existing cultural and social systems. Put differently, morphogenesis narrows the gap between intra-systemic and systems change and conceptualises systems change as a period of transition with some durability of its own.

According to this interactionistic revision of general systems theory, change is never absolute and can be defined as the demarcation of temporal boundaries. This definition implies that such boundaries do not sever successive systems, but, as with all other boundaries, have the dual task of separation and interconnection. Consequently, it is difficult to perceive changes of cultural systems as abrupt collapses. Instead, the distinction between change of cultural systems and change within cultural systems is a gradual one which demands precise description and careful analysis.

This interactionistic revision of general systems theory appears to be helpful for purposes of the conceptual history of medieval culture. Medieval Europe can be perceived as one single system within the time frame between the fifth and the sixteenth centuries. It allows for some fuzziness of the temporal boundaries of the concept and promotes the awareness of internal contradictions and conflicts within a cultural system. It displays culture as in flux and helps to recognise change as an integral aspect of culture.

---

[25] René Thom, *Structural Stability and Morphogenesis* (Redwood City, Menlo Park, Reading, Mass., 1989; first published Paris, New York, 1972). Ilya Prigogine, Isabelle Stengers, *Order out of Chaos* (Toronto, 1984). Cf. Eric C. Zeeman, *Catastrophe Theory* (Reading, Mass., 1977).

[26] Robert Rosen, 'On a Theory of Transformations for Cultural Systems', in Colin Renfrew, Michael J. Rowlands, Barbara Abbott Segraves, eds, *Theory and Explanation in Archaeology* (New York, London, 1982), p. 301.

GENERALITIES

I

Experiences of Time

Mundus senescit*

– Fredegar

Introduction

What, then, is time?

Who can give a quick and easy answer, who can find the proper words to make clear what it is? Which word is more familiarly used or more easily recognised in our conversation than 'time'? We certainly understand what is meant by the word when we use it ourselves and when we hear it used by others.

What, then, is time?

I know well enough what it is, as long as nobody asks me; but, if I am asked what it is and try to explain, I do not know what to say. All the same I can confidently say that I know that, if nothing passed, there would be no past time; if nothing were going to happen, there would be no future time; and if nothing were, there would be no present time. Of these three divisions of time, then, how can two, the past and the future be, when the past no longer is and the future is not yet? As for the present, if it were always present and never moved on to become the past, it would not be time but eternity. If, therefore, the present is time only by reason of the fact that it moves on to become the past, how can we say that even the present is, when the reason only is that it is not to be. In other words, we cannot rightly say that time is, except by reason of its impending state of not being. Yet we speak of a 'long time' and a 'short time', though only when we mean the past or the future. For example, we say that a hundred years is a long time ago or a long time ahead. A short time ago or a short time ahead, we might put at ten days. But how can anything which does not exist be either long or short? For the past is no more and the future is not yet. Surely, then, instead of saying 'It is a long time', we ought to say of the past 'It was a long time' and of the future 'It will be a long time'. . . .

Let us see, then, whether at least the one year in which we are is present. If we are in the first month, the other eleven are future. If we are in the second month, the first has passed and the rest are still to come. So we cannot even say that the whole of the current year is present, and if the whole of it is not present, the year is not present. For a year is made up of twelve months. Any one of

---

* The world grows old.

them, the current one, is present, but the others are either past or future. It is
not even true that the current month is present, but only one of its days. If it is
the first day, the remainder are future. If it is the last day, the rest are past. If it is
any day in the middle of the month, it falls between past and future days.

Thus the present which, as we saw, was the only one of the three divisions of
time that could possibly be said to be long, had been reduced to the space of
scarcely one day. But here again we must look into the matter more closely,
because not even the whole of one day is present. It is made up of hours of
darkness and hours of daylight, twenty-four of them. In relation to the first
hour, the others are future; in relation to the last, the others are past; and any
intermediate hour comes between the hours which precede it and those which
follow it. Even that one hour consists of minutes which are continuously
passing. The minutes which have gone by are past, and any part of the hour
which remains is future. In fact the only time that can be called present is an
instant, if we can conceive of such that cannot be divided even into the most
minute fractions, and a point of time as small as this passes so rapidly from the
future into the past that its duration is without length. For if its duration were
prolonged, it could be divided into past and future. When it is present is does
not have an extension.[1]

St Augustine, the Bishop of Hippo in North Africa (354–430), took down
these reflections on time in AD 397 or 398 in a private record of his life. He
encapsulates the late-Roman urban civilisation and, therein, leads us into a
series of paradoxes about time and of contradictions in speaking about time.
If time exists, it is not present, because it has no duration; but if it has a duration, then it is either past or future, and, then, we cannot say that time is,
because the past is no longer, and the future is not yet. But, nevertheless, time
exists.

The paradoxes and contradictions arise because St Augustine thought of
and wrote about time as a universal astronomical entity and as an object of
scientific inquiry, about which he tried to make general statements purported
to be true, and whose quality and attributes he attempted to describe and
explain.

There is, however, another approach to time, and this approach ignores
questions about the objective quality of time and, instead, focuses on the
subjective experiences of time by human beings as persons and in groups.
When following this approach, we can try to find out about the various experiences of and reactions towards time. This approach leads to an inquiry
about the various concepts of time and its changes, and, *in fine*, to a conceptual history of experiences of time.

How, then, did St Augustine experience time?

The most general remark about St Augustine's experience of time is that he
perceived it as a remote process, far beyond the practical command and intellectual grasp of human beings, perplexingly created by the divinity, with an

---

1   Augustine, *Confessions*, cap. XI/14–15, ed. James J. O'Donnell (Oxford, 1992), pp.
    154–5.

absolute dominance over the human world, moving on autonomously from
the past into the future and preventing human beings from penetrating its
inner nature. Time appeared to St Augustine as a phenomenon of fundamental importance to, and yet totally aloof from, the human world. Whatever
human beings were capable of achieving was no more than to measure some
portions of time. Apart from the Biblical world chronology, the chronology
ab urbe condita and the Roman consular years as measurements of past time,
St Augustine knew centuries, years, months, days, hours and minutes as measurable time spans, and, although he did not refer explicitly to the week in his
deliberations on time, the week was known to him as an important element in
Christian liturgy.[2] He assumed that it was a necessity for time to be measured
with precision, and he credited human beings with the capability to make
testable statements about time, although he limited this capability to the past
dimension of time, because the future cannot be known to human beings and
the present has no duration. Thus, according to St Augustine, the human experience of time was indirect, transmitted through instruments for the measurement of time, on the one side, and, on the other, through the human mind
through which knowledge of the past could be recreated by the use of words.

From a present perspective, St Augustine's observations on time provide
few difficulties, because, during the twentieth century widely heralded experiences of time were basically similar. For example, in 1928, Edmund Husserl
(1859–1938) praised St Augustine for having made observations on time
which Husserl considered to be relevant, and Husserl's views have been shared
widely throughout the remaining part of the century.[3] But, in the European
Middle Ages, at least up to the thirteenth century, experiences of time were
totally different from those of St Augustine, although, during the entire
Middle Ages, the latter was perhaps the most frequently read, discussed and
quoted of authors. How can we account for such breaches of tradition in the
experiences of time?

Measurements of current time in the early Middle Ages

One striking difference was that, in the early Middle Ages, there was no longer
agreement about the necessity of measuring time in precise terms. By
contrast, time spans were estimated rather than measured: While the tradition of Roman periodisations of past time continued to be applied well into
the early Middle Ages, the century was dropped as a counter even though it
continued to be known as a concept. And although the Roman calendar

---

2   In *De Genesi contra Manichaeos* (*PL* 34, col. 190), Augustine likened the six ages of the
    world before the expected return of Christ to the six days of the creation week to which
    he added one day of rest. Similarly, Isidore, *Quaestiones in Vetus Testamentum* (*PL* 83,
    cols 213–16).
3   Edmund Husserl, *Vorlesungen zur Phänomenologie des inneren Zeitbewußtseins,* ed.
    Martin Heidegger (Halle, 1928), pp. 368–73. Kurt Flasch, *Was ist Zeit? Augustinus von
    Hippo: Das XI. Buch der Confessiones* (Frankfurt, 1993).

enforced under Julius Caesar continued to be employed, the years could have a variety of beginnings, ranging from 1 September (Byzantine style), through 25 December (Christian style), 1 January (Circumcision style) to 1 March (ancient Roman style, which was adhered to in Venice until 1797) and to the Easter style according to which each year had a different beginning. While months, as the intervals between two successive full moons, and days, as the intervals between two successive sunrises, were retained as portions of time, hours became the shortest measurable portions of the day.[4]

Moreover the length of the hours varied according to the seasonal distribution of daytime and nighttime. In accordance with the custom of antiquity, the fixed number of twelve hours each was assigned to day and to night, that is, the two periods from sunrise to sunset and from sunset to sunrise, so that each of the twelve nightly hours lasted longer during the winter than during the summer, and, vice versa, each of the twelve day hours were shorter during the winter than during the summer. This custom was convenient in a world in which the hours of the day were usually not counted from midnight as the beginning of the first hour but where usually dawn was used to determine the beginning of the first hour. Under this condition, the beginning of the day varied according to the seasons, and it made sense to have shorter hours for day time and longer hours for night during winter when dawn is late and, vice versa, to have longer hours for day time and shorter hours for night during summer when dawn is early. Finally, no precise concept of minutes existed, because, prior to the fourteenth century, there was no single instrument for the measurement of time that could relate minutes to hours. This implied that, whenever portions of time shorter than one hour were measured, they appeared as entities in themselves, without relation to the hour.

In summary, unlike the world of St Augustine, in the early Middle Ages and up to the thirteenth century, there were few general 'objective' standards regarding time and equally few instruments for the precise measurement of time. Instead, in the Middle Ages up to the thirteenth century, preference was given to natural rhythms like day and night, the seasons, the sequence of harvests, or the revolutions of the moon as indicators of the process of time, and local groups of settlers in villages were accustomed to control their own time rather than being controlled by it. The natural rhythms had the charac-

---

4   In his late-seventh-century work *De Temporum Ratione*, cap. III, Bede acknowledged the existence of 'minutissima temporum spatia', and in his subsequent treatise *De Temporum*, he had 'momenta' as the shortest time span (Charles William Jones, ed., *Bedae Opera de temporibus*, Mediaeval Academy of America Publication XLI [Cambridge, Mass., 1943], pp. 182, 295. Another ed. by Charles William Jones, *Bedae venerabilis opera*, vol. 6: *Opera didascalia*, part II, CCSL. CXXIII B [Turnhout, 1977], p. 276). However, in agreement with the heritage of antiquity, Bede insisted that the hour was the shortest measurable unit of time, and he defended this rule on etymological grounds, assuming that the Latin word *hora* had been derived from the (in fact, unrelated) Greek word *horos* ('boundary') and concluding that hour meant the border of time. Similarly, Raban Maur, *De universo libri XXII*, cap. XI/1–13 (*PL* 111, cols 285–302).

teristic of being directly experienced by human beings in the local groups and, consequently, promoted the variation in measurements of time in the medieval world. Some types of groups, such as kin groups, were thought by their members to outlast the process of time, as they comprised the living and the dead.[5]

The second point on which early medieval experiences of time departed fundamentally from those of St Augustine concerns the effects which the progress of time was held to have on human actions. For in the earlier Middle Ages and up to the thirteenth century, it was difficult to accept St Augustine's suggestion that time would pass inexorably, subjecting all of human activity to its own control. By contrast, in the early Middle Ages, it was maintained that time's progress varied and could, on occasion, be rapid, while, on other occasions, progress might be slow or might not occur at all. Likewise, time was experienced as proceeding only as long as its progress could be observed. Because time's progress cannot be observed by human beings when they are asleep, this qualification implied that time was not regarded as proceeding during the sleeping hours and, consequently, it could neither be lost nor wasted. There are an abundance of sources which inform us that, in several important aspects and walks of life in the early Middle Ages, there prevailed a conspicuous irreverence toward the progress of time. Such irreverence can be gleaned, among others, from the predilection for feasting, rituals and formalities of behaviour as well as for the slowness and time-consuming dignity of communication. Hence it was the performance of interactions in groups which mattered, not the amount of time required for the interaction. Likewise, in the rural world of agricultural producers, which was almost everyone's world in the early Middle Ages, adjustment to the natural rhythms mattered more than the rigid adjustment to the progress of time as an intangible astronomical entity. Evidently, what mattered more than time in such agricultural habitats were the groups within which a person could survive, outside of which a person was exposed to the hazards of a threatening environment. Or, put differently, the human being, wretched, wicked and, above all, temporary in its existence, counted little in itself, unless it was integrated in and devoted to the groups to which it belonged. It was only within the groups that the inescapable temporariness of human existence could be transcended and, hence, sustaining groups mattered more than adjusting oneself to time's progress.[6]

The third, and most fundamental, point of difference between St Augustine's and early medieval experiences of time concerns the impact of these

---

5 As will be shown in Chapter 4.
6 For example, Bishop Rather of Verona [*Praeloquiorum libri sex*, cap. I/13, ed. Peter L. D. Reid, Corpvs Christianorvm. Continuatio Medievalis (Turnhout, 1984), pp. 16–17], in the tenth century, wrote in a brief description of the activities of merchants that, instead of pursuing their own greed, they should have faith in God and should entertain Christ and his disciples at their homes with feasts. Remarkably, the author hid his request that merchants should support the church behind the metaphor of feasts and other entertainments of groups.

experiences on human perceptions. According to his view of the former, human beings could only hope to be able to make sense of the progress of time from the past to the future if they accepted that past time was gone and that past facts could only be recreated in human memories by the 'words based on our memory pictures of those facts'.[7] This view implied that, to St Augustine, the past could only be recollected in the form of images of past facts. By contrast, in the early Middle Ages, membership in groups and the cult of the dead constituted a permanent relationship between the present and the past. In churches the deceased venerated patron saint was present and could be the real recipient of donations; in monasteries the monks and nuns formed communities of the living and the dead; in the Christian lay kin groups the deceased ancestors continued to be present in rituals, primordial myths and prayers which, much as we know, had been believed already in pre-Christian times. These experiences implied that, contrary to St Augustine, groups were taken to be objective emanations from the past independent of time's progress. Hence, while St Augustine's late-Roman urban experiences of time focused on the person, the early medieval experiences of time focused on the group. Therefore, rituals, primordial myths and prayers had the essential task of turning the past into the present.[8]

To sum up, early medieval experiences of time differed fundamentally from the heritage of Roman antiquity as provided in the works by St Augustine. Contrary to St Augustine, in the early Middle Ages, there was little continuous need for the precise measurement of time. Likewise, in the rural worlds of agriculturalists, little respect was paid to the continuous movements of time. Finally, St Augustine's contention was rejected that the past owed its existence in any present solely to the memory images preserved in the human mind; instead, it was maintained that the mortal human being could transcend the temporal boundaries between the past and the future by joining in and remaining with groups. Hence, early medieval experiences of time exhibited a marked cultural gap in concepts between antiquity and medieval Europe. However, the overall framework for long-range periodisations enshrined some remarkable continuities.

---

7 Augustine, *Confessions* (see note 1), cap. XI/18, pp. 156–7.
8 Recorded in some works of early medieval historiography, namely Fredegar, *Chronicarum libri IV,* cap. III/9, ed. Bruno Krusch, *MGH SS rer. Merov.* 2, pp. 94–5; the *Origo gentis Langobardorum*, ed. Georg Waitz, *MGH SS rer. Lang.*, pp. 2–3, and in the *Libri memoriales* which were kept in several larger monasteries. The *Libri memoriales* contain lists of deceased benefactors, clerics, monks and noteworthy lay persons for whom the resident monks were expected to say mass. See: Johanne Autenrieth, Dieter Geuenich, Karl Schmid, eds, *Das Verbrüderungsbuch der Abtei Reichenau,* MGH Libri memoriales et necrologi. N. S. I (Hanover, 1979). Karl Schmid, ed., *Die Klostergemeinschaft von Fulda im früheren Mittelalter,* vol. 1, Münsterische Mittelalter-Schriften VIII (Munich. 1978). W. de Gray Birch, ed., *Liber Vitae: Register and Martyrology of New Minster, Winchester* (London, 1892). Eduard Hlawitschka, Karl Schmid, Gerd Tellenbach, eds, *Liber memorialis von Rémiremont,* MGH Libri memoriales I (Munich, 1970).

The periodisations of past time in the early Middle Ages

Throughout the Middle Ages, the heritage of Antiquity shaped the long range periodisation of past time. Past time was defined as the history of the world since its creation by divine will. Time itself was thus a finite temporal entity which was regarded as imperfect because of its changeability. Human-made periodisations divided the history of the world into various numbers of 'ages' through which the changeability of the world was made explicit and were manifest in the various world chronologies which in turn were gleaned from accounts in the Bible. Since the beginning of the fourth century, Christian authors had become used to associating a major epochal change with Christ, his birth, his Sermon on the Mount, or his crucifixion.[9] Among those who favoured the partition of world history into six 'ages' were Augustine, Isidore (c. 560–636) and Bede (c. 675–735) whose view was subsequently accepted by the majority of medieval authors. It became understood that, within this sequence of six 'ages', the fifth 'age' would end and the sixth 'age' would begin with Christ. The five 'ages' up to Christ were measured by various lengths expressed in different numbers of years, but in any case the extension of each of the five 'ages' was indicated in exact numbers. By contrast, the sixth 'age', covering the period between Christ and the believed end of the world was regarded as unmeasurable. Hence time was fixed only as past time, whereas the interval between any present and the then believed end of the world with the subsequent resumption of eternity was taken to be unknowable by the majority of thinkers on this matter.[10] But there was an undercurrent of attempts to predict the length of the interval between the present in the early Middle Ages and the expected future end of the world. Such attempts could be founded on the phrase in the Second Epistle of Peter 3: 8 which equated each day of the creation with one thousand years, and this reference could be combined with the statement in Revelations 20: 7 which announced that one thousand years would pass before signs of the near end of the world would emerge, among them the release of the devils and the breaking out of the mythical peoples Gog and Magog from their confinements in the east of Asia. The latter statement made it clear that changes in the sixth 'age' were seen as indications for increasing instability and a means for the prediction of the coming end of the world.[11]

---

9   Eusebius of Caesarea, *Chronicorum libri II* (*PG* 19, col. 383). Augustine, *De Genesi contra Manichaeos* (*PL* 40, cols 43–4). Isidore, *Etymologiarum sive originum libri XX*, cap. V/38, ed. W. M. Lindsay (Oxford, 1911). Isidore, 'Chronica', ed. Theodor Mommsen, *Chronica minora, MGH AA* 11, p. 454.

10 Augustine, *De Civitate Dei*, cap. XX/9, CCSL XLVIII (Turnhout, 1955), pp. 715–19.

11 Seventh- and eighth-century calculations of the age of the world arrived at periodisations which came close to 6000 years. For example, Victorinus, 'Chronicon', ed. Theodor Mommsen, *Chronica minora, MGH AA*, vol. 11. 1894, p. 492, equated AD 673 with the world age 5874. Similarly, Isidore of Seville paralleled AD 615 with the world age 5813 (ibid., pp. 479–80). The continuator of the chronicle of the so-called Fredegar juxtaposed AD 736 against the world age 5937 (see note 8), cap. 16, p. 76.

It appears that this undercurrent of speculative thought repeatedly gained steam at times of crisis in late antiquity and throughout the Middle Ages and was frequently turned into more or less radical and militant scepticism. Towards the turn of the third century, this was evident when scepticism provoked bitter complaints by Hippolytus (dec. 235) against the deterministic equation of the world's total age with 6000 years. Hippolytus sought to fend off such 'millenarian' determinism with the argument that only the divinity could know the exact age of the world and that human beings should not try to interfere with the divine plan. Later, in the early fifth century, St Augustine drew on the same arguments against similar undercurrents of 'millenarian' thought which had arisen after the sack of Rome in 410, adding that the Christian Catholic Church was a continuing insurance that the divinity had not yet willed the world to come to its end. By the beginning of the sixth century, the belief that the sixth 'age' of the world had begun with the birth of Christ became strong enough to lay the foundation for new calculations of the Easter cycle as the basis for the annual calendar of the church. This was done with the argument that the Easter cycle was an element of sacred chronology which should not remain connected with 'pagan' ways of time-reckoning. Hence Dionysius (dec. before 556), a scholar and chronologist working in Rome, suggested that the counting of the years of the ecclesiastical chronology should begin with the birth of Christ as the year of the Incarnation. The resulting Anno Domini (AD) chronology was propagated by Bede from around 700.[12] The Easter cycles were noted in tables wherein the Easter date for each year was indicated following Christ's crucifixion and resurrection, eventually according to the AD style. Since the eighth century, the AD style has been applied also in secular chronology.

That the reconstruction of chronology during the sixth century grew out of a sense of crisis and was connected with fears of the approaching end of the world is well attested in a letter by Pope Gregory I (c. 540–604) of AD 601. In this letter, Gregory warned that 'the end of the world is approaching' and that 'many things threaten which have never happened before. These are changes in the sky and terrors from heaven, unreasonable tempests, wars, famines, pestilence, and earthquakes in diverse places.' The letter was sent to another St Augustine (dec. c. 605), the papal emissary to Britain who had been given the task of introducing the Christian Catholic faith to the island.[13] However, Gregory added the proviso that, although signs of the near end of the world were there, the actual end was not imminent, and so he urged the missionary in Britain to act faithfully and to convert as many souls to the Catholic faith as he could. Thus Gregory agreed with the teachings of previous theologians that the Catholic Church was a comfort and a safeguard in times of crisis.

Controversies of a similar kind resurfaced during the tenth and early

---

12 Bede (see note 4), p. 265.
13 Recorded by Bede, *Historia ecclesiastica gentis Anglorum*, cap. I/32, ed. Bertram Colgrave, R. A. B. Mynors (Oxford, 1969), pp. 110–14.

eleventh centuries, predominantly in Ireland, England, Flanders and France.[14] In one Old English source, a late tenth-century homily, the end of the world appears to have been envisaged as impending. The homilist wrote:

> The world shall end with the age which is now current. For five of the ages have passed up to this age. Then shall this earth end [with the end of the current age], and most of this [current] age has passed until this year, which is the year [AD] 971. Not all of the world ages had the same length, but the sum of all of them was three thousand years, some were shorter, some were longer.[15]

Like Gregory, the homilist argued that one should be prepared for the end, although it was generally agreed that only the divinity would know precisely when the end would come. Nevertheless, the homilist urged believers to accept it as a well ascertained fact that the world would come to its end soon. On the European mainland, a mid-tenth-century source had already tentatively equated the coming of the Magyars with the apocalyptic prophecy of Gog and Magog breaking their walls and used the Magyar conquests as an indication supporting the belief of the near end of the world.[16] A number of further references at the turn of the millennium seem to confirm that 'millenarian' creeds loomed large in western Europe, that is the passing of the first one thousand years after the birth of Christ according to the AD chronology.[17] None of these expressions of fearfulness and anxiety was explicit in determining that the world would come to its end precisely in the course of the year 1000 AD; for such a statement would have raised suspicions of heresy and would then have entailed persecution. Compromises were offered, but they only betrayed the intensity of worries current at the turn of the millennium. For one, Byrhtferth (c. 960–1012), an eminent scholar of the time, drew on Revelations 20: 7 for his suggestion that even after one-thousand years had passed, such merely numerical terms might be meaningless in view of Christ's 'presence' (andweardnysse) in the world. For Christ's 'presence' in the world would not be countable in cycles of earthly years.[18] Byrhtferth's comment shows that reading the signs of foreshadowed disaster and preparing oneself for the worst could go together with a sense of hope. This was also the morale

---

14 The basic texts are in: Ernst Sackur, ed., *Sybillinische Texte und Forschungen* (Halle, 1891) (repr., ed. Raoul Manselli [Turin, 1976]). *Le Livre de Sibile de Philippe de Thâon*, ed. H. Shields (London, 1979). Adso of Montier-en-Der, *De ortu et tempore Antichristi*, ed. Daniel Verhelst, CCCM XLV (Turnhout, 1976).

15 *Blickling Homilies*, No. 11, ed. R. Morris, Early English Text Society. Original Series LVIII, LXIII, LXXIII (Oxford, 1874–80), pp. 117–19. The figure of 3000 years given in the text is normally regarded as an error for 6000.

16 Robert B. C. Huygens, 'Un témoin de la crainte de l'an 1000. La lettre sur les Hongrois', *Latomus* XV (1956), pp. 229–31.

17 Wulfstan, *Sermo Lupi ad Anglos*, ed. Dorothy Whitelock, 3rd edn (London, 1963), p. 47. Wulfstan, 'Homily Secundum Marcum', ed. Dorothy Bethurum, *The Homilies of Wulfstan* (Oxford, 1957), p. 136.

18 Byrhtferth, 'De sexta etate', in: Byrhtferth, *Manual*, ed. S. J. Crawford, Early English Text Society. Original Series CLXXVII (Oxford, 1929), pp. 238–40.

which was behind the early-eleventh-century visions of Ademar of Chabannes (c. 988–1034), who seems to have been the first to link 'millenarian' fears with events in Palestine. During one night, Ademar had seen a bleeding crucifix with a lamenting Christ. Many years after he had seen this vision, he sat down to write a chronicle of the world and he inserted a report on his vision into his chronicle. In retrospect, he interconnected the vision with events which had occurred in Palestine under the rule of Khalif al-Hakim who had authorised persecutions against Jews and Christians. As a consequence of these persecutions, the Church of the Holy Sepulchre had been destroyed. Apparently, Ademar had heard of these events through pilgrims' reports, and he understood the news as a sign of the approaching end of the world. And yet, writing several years after the event, Ademar drew comfort from the fact that al-Hakim had been removed from the Khalifate and that peace had been restored in Palestine.[19] The 'millenarian' fears may also have inspired the eleventh-century church-reform movement, providing in turn one incentive for the spreading crusading rhetoric in western Europe after the middle of the century.[20]

In summary, the world-age chronologies which were founded in the Old and the New Testament and became formalised through theological doctrine in late Antiquity provided a rich heritage of experience of past time throughout the early Middle Ages up to the eleventh century. Apart from the AD chronology, Antiquity bequeathed to the Middle Ages a framework of thought within which these experiences would oscillate between hope and fear towards the believed end of the world. Experiences of time were closely tied to a conception of the world according to which beliefs in continuity outweighed experiences of change. However, the prolonged crisis which was represented by the crusades of the late eleventh, twelfth and thirteenth centuries unleashed reformulations of experiences of time, even though, inside church institutions, mainly monasteries, novel experiences of time had already emerged early in the eleventh century.

Novel experiences of time in the high Middle Ages

In principle, the Christian mass service demanded the precise observation of specific hours for worship, namely prayers, and due respect had to be given by monks and nuns to these demands. Therefore, monk scholars were concerned about the development of instruments for the precise measurement of hours, irrespective of day and night. To that end, water clocks (clepsydras), sand dials and oil clocks were refined to the degree that they allowed the measurement of portions of time shorter than the hour and could continue to work

---

19 Ademar of Chabannes, *Chronique*, cap. III/46–7, ed. Jules Chavanon (Paris, 1897), pp. 168–71. Similarly: Abbo of Fleury, *Liber apologeticus* (*PL* 139, cols 471–2).

20 See Benzo of Alba, 'De Christo dixit regnum quoque stemata scripsit', Benzo, *Panegyricus*, cap. I/15, ed. Georg Heinrich Pertz, *MGH SS* 11, p. 605.

while the monks and nuns were asleep. However, these efforts were then limited to life within the walls of monasteries and, initially, had little impact on the outside world.

Much more important as factors bridging the gap between the heritage of Antiquity and medieval practice was the development of urban markets and 'bourgeois' long-distance trade since the later eleventh century. The people gathering in newly founded or rapidly growing towns and cities were heterogeneous in origin but united in their contempt for, or determination to cut, traditional kinship ties. These persons had to be risk-prone and achievement oriented as they could not expect to be backed or protected by the kin groups from which they had originated. Therefore, they had to create, accumulate and maintain their fortunes by themselves and for themselves. This was easiest if the fortune consisted of moneyed wealth. From the thirteenth century onwards, the urban clergy were confronted with a sin which had rarely been confessed before, namely the supposed misuse of time for the purpose of accumulating capital. More generally, problems began to emerge when business activities began to include the strict observation of contractually defined and mutually accepted time spans with the proviso that violations of such agreements would entail punishment. These practices reflected the increasingly common custom of banking and other forms of money lending within time spans which were defined through human will, set voluntarily and agreed upon contractually. Philosophers of this period did not remain confined to the ideas of St Augustine but took a step further back to the sources on which St Augustine's concept of time had been based, first and foremost Aristotle. Aristotle had defined time as the number from which the previous (*prius*) and the later (*posterius*) had to be derived. That meant that, according to Aristotle, time was a linear process and was to be experienced objectively as the sole arbiter of past and future and that the early medieval insistence on the subjectivity of the experience of time had to be relegated to the realms of superstition and erroneous beliefs. The Aristotelian concept of linear time overlapped with its counterpart, the practical experiences of time of the merchants. Both experiences of time shared the demand that its progress should be measured with precision and included the obligation that persons should adjust themselves to it.

The initial response by the clergy was one of storming protest: They drew on the exegesis of the Book of Genesis and argued that time had been God's prime creation, that God had created time as a prime mover and that time was not for sale in exchange for money. Early in the twelfth century, the monk Honorius of Autun denounced merchants as persons with virtually no chance of redemption, and subsequent preachers warned that Christian believers ought not try to influence the vicissitudes of nature and fortune and should not interfere in God's arrangements concerning time.[21] This argument by the

---

21 Honorius of Autun, *Elucidarium* (*PL* 172, col. 1148). Berthold of Ratisbon, *Vollständige Ausgabe seiner Predigten,* vol. 1, ed. Franz Pfeiffer (Vienna, 1862), pp. 437–40 (repr., ed. Kurt Ruh [Berlin, 1965]).

clergy was novel in that it contained a concept of time which had been alien to early medieval experiences, namely the concept of time as an astronomical entity principally outside the realm of human interference. But it meant driving out the devil with Beelzebub. For Aristotle's concept of time had been accepted, and the merchants and their intellectual supporters could insist that they should be allowed to employ time as a factor, even if they were unable to control it. Petrarch (1304–74) advised Emperor Charles IV to consider that 'time is the most precious matter which can hardly be overestimated'.[22] Already in the thirteenth century, bills of exchange came into frequent use, interest became customary, and money came to be used as capital. Giving up its initial reluctance, the Church eventually opted in favour of toleration.[23] A series of debates began about the questions whether, and, if so, why and under which circumstances time should be money. The change occurred simultaneously with the rise of 'bourgeois' trade and with the revival in the thirteenth and fourteenth centuries of the scholarly experiences of time preserved within the heritage of ancient Greek philosophy.[24]

The most obvious indicator for this process of the transformation of the early medieval experiences of time is the appearance of mechanical clocks in the late thirteenth century. Most astonishingly, the first recorded mechanical clocks were astronomical instruments of awe-inspiring size, designed to combine the continuous measurement, not only of hours, but also of weeks, months, years and longer astronomical cycles. Needless to say, they could only operate if the hours and other units of current time were measured as units of the same length throughout the day. But these early mechanical clocks were not merely instruments for the measurement of current time, instead they facilitated also the calculation of past and future Easter dates and, beyond that, they could provide periodisations of world history as past time. They were located in churches, and the earliest clock makers were monks, such as Robertus Anglicus (fl. 1272) and Richard of Wallingford (c. 1292–1336), who felt compelled to construct complex instruments for the measurement of all conceivable experiences of time.[25] Most conspicuously, mechanical clocks could measure time continuously and at equal intervals. Hence, the hours came to be measured at equal length throughout the year, irrespective of seasonal variations.

The new art of clockmaking spread rapidly. In Italy, a movement towards the installation of mechanical clocks in towns and cities became visible in the early fourteenth century, when public clocks appeared at Orvieto in 1307, at Modena in 1309, at Parma in 1318, at Milan in 1336, at Padua in 1344, and at

---

22 Quoted in Hans Rupprich, ed., *Die Frühzeit des Humanismus und der Renaissance in Deutschland* (Leipzig, 1938), p. 76.
23 See Pietro di Giovanni Olivi, *De usu paupere: The Questions and the Tractatus*, ed. D. Burr, Italian Medieval and Renaissance Studies IV (Florence, 1992).
24 William Ockham, *Philosophia naturalis*, cap. IV/3 (Rome, 1637), pp. 87–8.
25 *Gesta abbatum monasterii S. Albani*, vol. 2, ed. Henry T. Riley, Rerum Britannicarum medii aevi scriptores XXVIII (London, 1868), pp. 181–199 (repr. New York, 1964). John D. North, ed., *Richard of Wallingford: An Edition of his Writings*, vol. 1 (Oxford, 1976).

both Florence and Genoa in 1354. The city councils took great care to employ specialists for the maintenance of the clocks which were usually attached to high towers, sometimes church steeples, so as to be widely audible and visible (in Milan, at San Gottardo, in Genoa, at the Cathedral). But also town and other governments elsewhere in Europe had clocks installed at town halls or royal palaces, such as in Perpignan in 1356 and at Windsor Castle in 1352. In 1355, the council of the French town of Lyon commissioned a public clock to be erected in the town centre, stipulating that regular working hours were to be observed in accordance with the indications of the clock. Hence, since the middle of the fourteenth century, working hours have been regulated, subjecting the inhabitants of urban communities to ever-increasing supervision of their time. In the course of the fourteenth century, the new practice of measuring time continuously and controlling time publicly became widely accepted, as can be gleaned from the following passage of a statute of the Nuremberg Town Council of 1389, which subjected itself to the following rule:

> The committee of five city councillors shall meet for two hours each before and after lunch time. As soon as all five councillors have assembled, the acting chairman shall turn upside down a sand dial, and all councillors shall sit together for the period of two hours, regardless of whether they have work to do or not.[26]

In other words, the city council forced its committee members to assemble for two sets of two hours, regardless of the amount of work to be done, and to complete their work within the two sets of two hours, no matter how long the agenda was. Necessarily, that rule was perfunctory only under the condition that the meeting began on time. To that end, the city council further ruled that late-comers were to be fined. Similarly strict rules for the observation of time were imposed on church sermons as well as on university lectures during the fifteenth century. 'In monasteries, religious men and women follow the candle and the clepsydra and, in cities and towns, men and women follow the strikes of the mechanical clock,' comments an early fifteenth century English clergyman in a sermon on the creation myth in Genesis 1: 14–19.[27]

However, the introduction of newly regulated linear time was confined to daily life in urban communities and did not reach the population in the rural countryside, namely peasant farmers and the landed non-urban aristocracy, who continued to live according to conventional experiences of time.

---

26 Werner Schultheiss, ed., *Satzungsbücher und Satzungen der Stadt Nürnberg aus dem 14. Jahrhundert*, Nürnberger Rechtsquellen III (Nuremberg, 1965), p. 331. Cf. the chronicler Galvano Fiamma who observed for 1336 that the public clock at the church of San Gottardo measured the hours of equal length throughout a period of twenty-four hours, that it did so by indicating the first hour with one stroke and adding one further stroke at each of the following hours and that it was a most necessary instrument for all inhabitants of the city. See Fiamma, *Opusculum de rebus gestis ab Azone Luchino et Johanne vicecomitibus*, ed. C. Castiglioni (Bologna, 1938), p. 16.

27 *Dives and Pauper*, Commandment I, cap. XVIII, ed. Priscilla Heath Barnum, Early English Text Society. Original Series CCLXXV (London, 1976), p. 120.

Moreover, the topographical range of the new experience of time was limited, because the mechanical clocks were local and, initially, immobile and because there was no standardisation of the measurement of time in between the various places where clocks had been installed. Consequently, clocks were of little use for travellers, most noteworthy of which were the merchants. This deficit was remedied by the invention of the portable clock at the very end of the fifteenth century.

However, the sixteenth century witnessed continuing debates about and critical attitudes towards the regularisation of linear time. One of the clearest expressions of such criticism was provided by William Shakespeare (1564–1616) in his monologue of King Richard II after the king's arrest in Pomfret Castle:

> Music do I hear?
> Ha, ha! keep time. How sour sweet music is
> when time is broke and no proportion kept!
> So is it in the music of men's lives.
> And here have I the dauntiness of ear
> To check time broke in a disorder'd string;
> But, for the concord of my state and time,
> Had not an ear to bear my true time broke.
> I wasted time, and now time wastes me;
> For now hath time made me his numbring clock;
> My thoughts are minutes; and with sighs they jar
> Their watches on unto mine eyes, the outward watch,
> Whereto my finger like a dial's point,
> Is pointing still, in cleansing them from tears.
> Now, sir, the sounds that tell what hour it is
> Are clamorous groans which strike up on my heart,
> Which is the bell. So sighs, and tears, and groans,
> Show minutes, times and hours.[28]

Shakespeare directs Richard II from the listening of music through the complaint over the brokenness of time to the measurement of time as the expression of Richard's inability to adapt himself to and to act in accordance with time's progress. Thus Shakespeare lets Richard realise and acknowledge

---

28 William Shakespeare, *Richard II* V/5, 41–63 [various editions]. An earlier case from the world of aristocratic courts is recorded in the note book of Emperor Frederick III under the year 1437. In this entry, Frederick deplores the necessity to adjust oneself to the course of time and quotes from *Ecclesiastes* III/1. See Joseph Chmel, *Geschichte Kaiser Friedrichs IV. und seines Sohnes Maximilian I.*, vol. 1 (Hamburg, 1840), Beylage XXX, No. 89, p. 578. Still in the eighteenth century, Goethe noted in the diary which he kept on his Italian journey that the townspeople of Verona measured units of the day in accordance with the natural variations of the seasons rather than in accordance with astronomical clocks. See Johann Wolfgang von Goethe, 'Aus der "Italienischen Reise", 17 September 1786,' Goethe, *Vermischte Schriften*, ed. Emil Staiger (Frankfurt, 1965), p. 65.

the necessity that the individual should act in conformity with time's progress in the Aristotelian–Augustinian sense. But, in the same context, Shakespeare has Richard express grief about that very necessity. Given the fact that Shakespeare's dramatic works were warmly received by the London urban audience at the end of the sixteenth century, it can be concluded that resistance against attempts at the coercive installation of continuous and public measurements of time as an objective astronomical entity was still formidable at the end of the sixteenth century. That resistance allowed Shakespeare to anticipate that the critical distance of one of his protagonists against the regularisation of linear time and the subjection of human life to it would be understood and welcomed.

The dynamisation of past time

Criticism against the novel experiences of time continued to be informed by an undercurrent of the experiences of time which continued from the old Biblical experience of past time as the divinely ordained movement from the creation to the end of the world.[29] This experience of time continued to be linked to the world as the divinely created space where human life existed. Corresponding to the belief in the finiteness of time, the world was believed to be an essentially static, though ageing entity on which changes could not have more than marginal effects even if they could be categorised as adding to the stability of the world. Still, in the seventeenth century, theologians, such as Thomas Burnet (c. 1632–c. 1715) adhered to a Eurocentric world picture in terms of the three continents making up the 'Old World', namely Africa, Asia and Europe, and as the theatre in which the movement of time towards the ultimate end of the world would proceed.[30] Yet at the same time, Martino Martini (1614–61), a Jesuit historian of China, raised the problem of the settlement of China. Martini believed that people had come to China from western Asia after the debacle of the Babylonian Tower. He searched for references to the Flood in Chinese sources and convinced himself that many such references existed. He further argued that the earliest of these references were to be found at the time of the legendary Emperor Fu Xi (Fohius) whose reign he dated around 2952 BC. This date allowed only a few years for the settlement of China.[31]

---

29 See Hartmann Schedel, *Das Buoch der Cronicken vnd Gedechtnus wirdigern Geschichten von Anbegyn der Werlt bis auf dise vnßere Zeit* (Nuremberg, 1493), applied the world age chronology (ending in the year 6691) together with the AD chronology (ending in the year 1492) and added a brief chapter on the seventh and eighth ages of the world about the antichrist and Judgment Day, fols CCLIXverso–CCLXIIverso. Cf.: Jean Bodin, *Methodus ad facilem historiarum cognitionem* (Paris, 1566), pp. 346–61; newly edited (New York, 1966, pp. 291–302), on the tradition of the world empires.
30 Thomas Burnet, *Sacred Theory of the Earth*, repr. ed. Basil Willey (Carbondale, Ill., 1965; first published London, 1681), p. 273.
31 Martino Martini, *Sinicae historiae decas prima* (Munich, 1658), pp. 3, 11.

But the so-called 'discovery' of America around 1500 had already fuelled
doubts about the biblical chronology. Not only did difficulty arise in how
America was to be integrated into the Biblical world picture, but also in how
America could have been settled by human beings. Some solved the question
in the sixteenth century by flatly denying to native Americans the status of
human beings.[32] But this was soon rejected as an illegitimate position which
ignored the doctrine that the divinity had created all human beings as
equals.[33] Under this condition the only possible answer was drawn on the
assumption of an Asian–American land bridge across which native Americans might have migrated. This assumption was possible because, up to the
beginning of the eighteenth century, European geographers had no means of
ascertaining the continental identity of America. In a more fundamental
sense, therefore, the further question arose how life at large could have come
to America after the Flood, if America was a continent in itself. The difficulty
was that even the staunch traditionalists who refuted the continental identity
of America could not convincingly argue that all living species had migrated
from Noah's Ark to the remotest parts of the world and that they had done so
within a short time after the Flood.

Moreover, sixteenth-century naturalists had already discovered many
species which were peculiar to America and not known elsewhere. How
would one account for the geographical variety of the distribution of species
the origins of which, according to the Biblical traditions, would have to be
traced to one single spot on earth? In 1667, this problem was discussed by Sir
Matthew Hale (1609–1676), a scientist of renown who investigated the 'primitive origination of mankind' on the basis of research on other living species.
Hale attributed the post-diluvial diversity of species to migration in the first
place, to 'an anomalous mixture of species' in the second place, and, in the
third, to 'some accidental variations in the process of time'.[34] These three
factors, namely post-diluvial migration out of Noah's Ark, mutation in consequence of genetic irregularities and gradual adaptation, together served to
support his conclusion that the unequal distribution of living species across
the continents did not refute the truth of the Old Testament mythology of the
Flood. But the three factors stood against the postulate that, on principle, all
species had been preserved in the forms which they had had as they had
walked out of Noah's Ark.

But the mythology of the Flood contained further pitfalls. During the
second half of the seventeenth century, interest began to spread in the study
of a peculiar kind of stone whose shapes were strikingly similar to those of
living organisms. Immediately, the question arose as to whether these objects,
called fossils then as now, were real stones or in fact petrified organisms of the
antediluvian ages. The question was a difficult one because some fossils repre-

---

32 John Major, *In secundum librum sententiarum* (Paris, 1519), fol. CLXXXVII recto.
33 Pope Paul III, 'Veritas ipsa [2 June 1537]', ed. Josef Metzler, *America pontificia primi
     saecvli evangelizationis 1493–1592*, vol. 1 (Vatican City, 1991), pp. 364–66.
34 Matthew Hale, *The Primitive Origination of Mankind* (London, 1677), p. 201.

sented shapes which could not be linked with any living species. As some of these stones had been found outside the Old World and on the top of high mountains their distribution had to be explained. If these fossils were indeed petrified organisms of extinct species, the implication was that not all the species still existed that had once descended from Noah's Ark. In short, the fossils placed the problem of the historicity of nature on the agenda. As yet, few were ready to accept the imminent conclusion that the Bible was wrong. Instead, most scholars argued that fossils were a special kind of stone which had by accident taken the shape of organisms, and could be dismissed as jokes of nature. Other scholars focused on the Flood. Thomas Burnet, for one, insisted that the Flood had changed the surface of the earth, and believed that, before the Flood, the earth had had an even, plane surface, an axis vertical to the surface and, consequently, no variations in climate. During the Flood, Burnet thought, subterranean water masses and exuberant rainfall had flooded everything except Noah's Ark, and had destabilised and weakened the earth, leaving its surviving inhabitants to confront a hostile fallen nature, a 'broken globe'[35] with valley rifts, mountain peaks, a declining axis and resulting diversity in climatic conditions. Burnet recognised fossils as petrified organisms, but he used his reconstruction of the effects of the Flood as an explanation for the existence of fossils at odd locations and for changes in and of species. Hence fossils became a source of knowledge of antediluvian life and, in that capacity, did then neither call into question the truth of the Biblical creation myth nor effectively challenge the belief in the Biblical world chronology. Instead, like his senior contemporary Robert Hooke (1635–1703)[36] and his junior Giambattista Vico (1668–1744),[37] Burnet condensed the ante- and post-diluvian world into the Biblical time frame of the six world ages and gave the world 'no more than fifteen hundred years to go till the end'.[38] If the world's age was no more than 6000 years altogether, the Flood must have occurred in relatively recent times.

However, little more than thirty years after the third edition of Vico's work appeared in 1744, Buffon's Les époques de la nature were published in 1778.[39] In this work, Buffon (1707–88) took a radically different view and argued that the current age of the world was about 75,000 years, that the world had undergone many changes during these many years and that it had about 45,000 years to go. In unpublished manuscripts written after 1749 on the same matter, Buffon went even further, postulating an age of the world of roughly three-million years. But he hesitated to argue this view in a published book. In any case, in the second half of the eighteenth century, the Biblical

---

35 Burnet (see note 30), p. 81.
36 Robert Hooke, The Posthumous Works, ed. Richard Waller (London, 1705), pp. 299, 333 (repr. London, 1971).
37 Giovanni Battista Vico, Principij di una Scienza Nuova, 3rd edn (Naples, 1744), table facing p. 37 (repr. Tokyo, 1989).
38 Burnet (see note 30), p. 83.
39 Georges Louis Le Clerc, Comte de Buffon, Les époques de la nature, Buffon, Œuvres complètes, vols 9, 10 (Paris, 1778).

world chronology ceased to inform scholarly thoughts about the earth and what then came to be perceived as the many changes in its history. Summing up these thoughts in the four volumes of *Ideas on the Philosophy of the History of Mankind*, Johann Gottfried Herder (1744–1803) attempted in 1784 to show that 'our earth has undergone many revolutions before it became what it is now'[40] and that the earth was a 'laboratory'[41] from which successive sets of living species had emerged. But the rejection of the Biblical world chronology, coupled with the injection of dynamic views of the earth as an ever-changing entity, unleashed fears of instability and warnings that chaos and confusion are not to be introduced into the order of nature.[42] According to this view, human beings were given the task of providing for the stability of the earth as the physical environment. Along these lines, a sceptical Kant (1724–1804) already in 1784 tried to limit the range of change provoking human action by insisting that there was a pre-determined 'plan of nature' according to which the changes from the past to the future would proceed.[43] Kant's was a conservative position which sought to counterpoise the fears of instability with the argument that nature would not allow its own destruction. But he could not prevent the dynamisation of the experience of time and the widening use of the concept of biological evolution.[44]

The open-ended dynamism of biological evolution demanded the wholesale and unrestricted acceptance of the Aristotelian concept of time. Therefore, this concept has become dominant again from the beginning of the nineteenth century and also, to the extent that he himself had used Aristotelian formulae, St Augustine's observations on time once again received the general approval which they had enjoyed in late-Roman Antiquity.

40 Johann Gottfried Herder, *Ideen zur Philosophie der Geschichte der Menschheit* [1784–91], ed. Bernhard Suphan, Herder, *Sämmtliche Werke*, vol. 13 (Berlin, 1887), title of Book One, Chapter Three, p. 21.

41 Herder (see note 40), title of Book Two, Chapter One, p. 47.

42 James Hutton, *Theory of the Earth*, repr. ed. Victor A. Eyles, George W. White (Darien, 1970), pp. 125, 128 (first published in *Transactions of the Royal Society of Edinburgh*, vol. 1, pt 2 [1788], pp. 209–304).

43 Immanuel Kant, 'Idee zu einer allgemeinen Geschichte in weltbürgerlicher Absicht', *Berlinische Monatsschrift* (Nov. 1784), pp. 385–411. New edn in Kant, *Werke in zwölf Bänden*, ed. Wilhelm Weischedel, vol. 11 (Frankfurt, 1968), pp. 33–50.

44 In the twelfth edition of his work *Systema naturae*, published in 1766, Carl von Linné admitted for the first time the possibility that the human species is interconnected with other living species through evolution.

II

Conceptions of Space

natura lapsa*
– Thomas Burnet

Introduction

Not only space itself is multidimensional, but also the concept of space. Its dimensions branch out into mathematics as well as physics,[1] phenomenology[2] and politics.[3] Today, the most general concept of space finds its roots in the views of mathematicians and physicists and includes the perception of space as a homogeneous, continuous and universal entity without visibly conceived boundaries. This concept of space is a theoretical construct originating in seventeenth-century physics and it has never gained general currency in the sense of penetrating daily experiences and perceptions of terrestrial space. Instead, previous concepts of space, such as the one argued by Aristotle,[4] covered varieties of heterogeneous and qualitatively different places and was perceived as an entity of limited extension. Likewise, phenomenologists among philosophers and psychologists have repeatedly emphasised the coexistence of several, partly overlapping, concepts of terrestrial space which can be perceived or experienced by persons and groups.[5] Finally, social scientists and historians have debated the figurative use of the concept of space in politics and society as an ordering principle through which hierarchies of men and women are established and maintained.[6]

---

* Nature has fallen.
1 See Alexander Goszonty, *Der Raum*, 2 vols (Darmstadt, 1976).
2 See Otto Friedrich Bollnow, *Mensch und Raum*, 5th edn (Stuttgart, Berlin, Cologne, Mainz, 1985; first published Stuttgart, 1963).
3 See Jürgen Habermas, *Strukturwandel der Öffentlichkeit*, new edn (Frankfurt, 1990; first published Neuwied, 1962). English version s. t.: *The Structural Transformation of the Public Sphere* (Cambridge, Mass., 1989).
4 Aristotle, *Physics*, 233a22–233b15, 237b23–238b22.
5 Sigfried Giedion, *Space, Time and Architecture*, 4th edn (Cambridge, Mass., London, 1962; first published Cambridge, Mass., 1944). Elisabeth Ströker, *Philosophische Untersuchungen zum Raum*, Philosophische Abhandlungen XXV (Frankfurt, 1965).
6 Andreas Gestrich, *Absolutismus und Öffentlichkeit*, Kritische Studien zur Geschichtswis-

However, as these distinctions have emerged within the recent concept of space, it is difficult to apply them in the broader context of conceptual history. Instead, the concept of space will be discussed according to the perceptions and experiences which persons may have of or may gather in space. In this context and with these criteria, the three categories that emerge are the space of daily experience, the space of regular communication, and the world.[7]

The difference between the first and the second category can, but does not necessarily have to be equated with the dichotomy of the private versus the public. In this sense, the space of daily experience can, but again does not necessarily have to, be perceived as the property of a person or a group (for example, a kin group), the space wherein one is accustomed to organise one's daily activities, the retreat into which one retires when one seeks privacy, the place where one sleeps. More generally speaking, the space of daily experience represents the inner side of a person's life and the inner circle of activities of persons in groups, the estate, the 'house', or the 'room'. The space of daily experience is private space in the sense that one regards it as the inside and believes that one is its sole master. It can be represented by a private household, kin-group owned plots of land or a settlement. It is many times demarcated by recognisable boundaries, the unlicensed trespassing of which has frequently been equated with breaches of peace.[8]

Beyond that space of daily experience is the outside, categorised as either the space of daily experience of another person or group or of the space of regular communication, where one meets others, outsiders, friends, aliens, or enemies. The space of regular communication is public in the sense that it is not solely owned by one person or group, but is ready for use by anyone (although not necessarily everyone). Since the eighteenth century, ownership of public space as space of regular communication has been vested into institutions, such as the state, which represent or incorporate a defined number of persons and groups. However, previously, public space may also have fallen under the jurisdiction of the legitimate ruler, or the community, over of a defined number of persons and groups. Public space as space of regular communication is commonly regarded as the space designed for unrestricted, though not uncontrolled, use, and its boundaries are normally imagined lines of separation and are frequently defined in administrative terms or as the

---

senschaft CIII (Göttingen, 1994). Maure L. Goldschmidt, 'Publicity, Privacy and Secrecy', *Western Political Quarterly* VII (1954), pp. 401–16. Alfred Haverkamp, ' "... an die große Glocke hängen". Über Öffentlichkeit im Mittelalter', *Jahrbuch des Historischen Kollegs 1995* (1996), pp. 71–112. August Nitschke, 'Raumerfahrungen und Selbsterfahrungen', in Nitschke, Jochen Martin, eds, *Zur Sozialgeschichte der Kindheit*, Historische Anthropologie II (Freiburg, Munich, 1986), pp. 591–607. Hans-Jürgen Teuteberg, ed., *Homo habitans* (Munster, 1985). Andreas Würgler, *Unruhen und Öffentlichkeit*, Frühneuzeit-Forschungen I (Tübingen, 1995).

7   They are to be found already in Augustine, *De civitate Dei*, cap. XIX/5, CCSL XLVIII (Turnhout, 1955), pp. 669–70.

8   Already in the (probably) sixth-century laws of King Aethelbehrt of Kent, cap. 17, ed. Felix Liebermann, *Die Gesetze der Angelsachsen*, vol. 1 (Halle, 1903), p. 4, and in the late seventh-century laws of King Ine of Wessex, cap. 6, ed. Liebermann, *Gesetze*, pp. 90, 92.

customary boundaries within which regular communication among a defined number of persons and groups takes place most frequently. However, physical features, such as woodlands, have also served as markers of space of regular communication; moreover, there have been many cases, in which administratively defined boundaries and the customary boundaries of regular communication have not overlapped, and, without exception, such discrepancies have constituted grave administrative, political and social problems.

The distinction between inside and outside is applicable not only in the space of daily experience but also in the space of regular communication. With regard to the latter, the inside constitutes what political scientist Karl Wolfgang Deutsch (1912–92) has termed the 'we-feeling', a sense of belonging together beyond the factors of cohesion pertaining to kin groups and neighbourhoods. Hence the space of regular communication can be related to the interactions among members of various types of groups which, nevertheless, share some communicative codes (such as a common written or spoken language or codes of non-verbal communication), cultural traits (such as a common cultural heritage, common past experiences, common religious practices and beliefs, patterns of thinking and modes of behaviour) or loyalty to institutions or other manifestations of customary authority (such as those following from membership in associations and organisations).

Moreover, space of daily experience and space of regular communication share the pragmatic feature that they are related to action by persons and groups. Hence persons and groups can know the space of daily experience and the space of regular communication through their own manifest action, namely by way of movement and communication. By contrast, the world as a category of terrestrial space cannot be experienced pragmatically as long as one stays on it, because the world can neither be conceived exclusively as someone's partial inner space of activities nor can it be set as the partial space of regular communication of a defined type of group. Instead, the world must be perceived inclusively as the universal terrestrial space, though not necessarily as the globe, and the general property of everyone. As a theoretical concept of terrestrial space, the world can be known by persons and groups on earth solely by theoretical consideration and not through any action other than thinking. In fact, the association of the world with the globe as a category of terrestrial space is relatively young and must not be taken for granted in the context of historical inquiries. Up to the eighteenth century, the most widely used European concept of the world as terrestrial space covered only parts of the globe, which means that such perceptions of the world were universal and could include the three-dimensional depiction of the world, but were not global in the sense that they covered the entire globe. In other words, they were all-inclusive but competed with other universal perceptions of the world and coexisted without being interrelated. In consequence, the global acceptance of a single perception of the world as the globe is the result of the globalisation of one particular perception of the world and, as such, demands explanation.

All three categories of the concept of space include the common feature that they vary from space to space and they change through time. Hence they are the properties of culture and have a history of their own. For example, the space of daily experience may vary and change in consequence of different and changing meanings of the concept of the private. So too does the space of regular communication in consequence of different and changing meanings of such concepts as state, nation and society. Likewise, perceptions of the world in relation to the globe may vary and change; for example, the world may be featured as a smaller or larger portion of the globe. Finally, variations and changes may also affect perceptions of the boundaries between and the interrelations among several spaces. For example, the boundaries separating various spaces of daily experience may vary from demarcations of portions in rooms to spacious gardens or parks comprising several separate dwelling places; variations may also serve as an indicator of rank or status. Changes in the concept of boundaries of spaces of daily experience may occur in the sense that the preferred or most frequently applied sizes of such spaces can expand or contract. In the case of boundaries between spaces of regular communication, variations may affect the perception of these boundaries as, for example, stretches of no man's land or as artificial lines demarcating separations in an otherwise continuous landscape. Likewise, boundaries may be perceived primarily as lines or zones of demarcation the purpose of which is the prohibition or restriction of trespass, or they may be conceived as links in communicative networks.

Concepts of space in the early Middle Ages

With regard to the space of daily experience, priority was given to group organisation over territorial organisation in the early Middle Ages. This means that social organisation was based on the relations among persons in groups as well as among groups and not a homogeneous space of limited extension, to which we may refer as territory. In other words, groups constituted space more frequently than space constituted groups.

In Figure 1 we see an arrangement of persons in groups around a centre. The centre could be filled with a person or object of overwhelming significance, in this case Christ, or, alternatively, a ruler or a church building. In any case, the outward boundaries of space displayed in pictures are represented by the group which frames the centre. Surely there have survived from the early Middle Ages other pictorial sources in which the boundaries of space are depicted in the form of walls or fences, and there is no scarcity of sources in which boundaries are demarcated by physical phenomena, such as rivers, man-made geographical phenomena such as roads, or artificial lines drawn between two remarkable spots in the landscape. Nevertheless, such markers of boundaries of privately, or kin-group, owned households or plots of land were usually not ends in themselves, but instruments to recognise a territorial base which could be identified as the living space of the groups settled on it. Consequently, such boundaries could shift when the groups settling within

Fig. 1 Christ and his followers. Codex Egberti, Reichenau Island, c. 980. Stadtbibliothek Trier, Cod. 24, fol. 22r. The central figure of Christ stands in the middle between two groups. Groups determine space in the picture.

them reconstituted themselves, when they migrated or when the property passed into someone else's possession. Theoretically speaking, one might say that space was perceived as the aggregate sum of qualitatively different places occupied by persons, groups or objects and not as the space in between persons, groups and objects.

That this was so becomes evident when one considers that migrations constituted a major daily experience throughout the early Middle Ages up to the seventh century. They engulfed major parts of the western Eurasian continent, namely the part west of the Volga river. They extended over several generations and across wide areas, and they could only be accomplished if the social organisation of the migrating groups provided a cohesion beyond *ad hoc* places of settlement or traditionally occupied territories. Hence we have a plethora of place names recorded from the early Middle Ages which were derived from the names of groups or persons. If, according to this name-giving custom, groups or persons could become name-givers to places of post-migration settlements, this shows that groups, with an autonomous organisation or as the followers of a person as a locator, preserved their identities beyond the migration processes, as settlers in a new physical environment, or as continuing or return migrants.[9]

9 Alternatively, migration by groups into demarcated and settled areas occurred and was reflected in place names. For one, the place name Canterbury is to be understood as the

For example, the English place name Meeching, Sussex (named Newhaven since 1586), is derived from the name of a group which referred to itself or was referred to by others as 'Meacingas' or people of Meaca. This group name can be connected with a continental personal name Meaca, mentioned in a poem of the seventh or eighth century as the ruler of the Myrgings in southern Jutland.[10] The poem preserves the record of a presumably late fourth-century Anglian defeat of the Myrgings. The Myrgings are reported in the poem to have left their settlements. Apparently, as the people of Meaca, they migrated to the British Isles. They appeared there in Meeching and various places in East Anglia where one finds place names with the same root as Meeching. Meeching is located in the eastern part of the area which later became the county of Sussex, in proximity to fifth-century cemeteries for settlers from the continent, which confirms the chronology. But the land in this area which later came to be called Sussex was not uninhabited, and the local residents, namely Romano-British settlers, began to campaign militarily against the continental immigrants and, towards the turn of the sixth century, inflicted certainly one, and perhaps several, sweeping defeats on them. Apparently, some of Meaca's people who had moved to Meeching returned to the continent, where, under the authority of the Frankish kings, they were allocated lands in an area called 'Mecingun' in the Low Countries.[11]

The Meeching case shows the persistence of group cohesion during and beyond the migrations and highlights the necessity of ranking group membership higher in priority than territorial conceptions of social organisation. If migrating groups continued to exist beyond a generation, membership in these groups was a means to transcend the bounds of space and time. Usually, outside the confines of the Roman Empire of Antiquity, the post-migration group settlements were small and separated from neighbouring settlements by more or less extensive marshes and woodlands. The settlements were predominantly agricultural and could be regarded as spaces of daily experience if they were occupied by a more or less homogeneous group. Alternatively, they could be regarded as spaces of regular communication if they were inhabited by various groups with different customs and traditions of origin. In any case, the marshes and woodlands, into which the settlements had been cleared, served as the spacious boundaries, stretches of no man's lands, and represented a physical environment which was perceived as hostile towards human life. Thus trespassing the woodland barriers was regarded as a hazard, demanding particularly tight group cohesion among those whose

settlement of migrants into Kent. Kent is the name of the area which had already been in use among the population settling in the area before the coming of the migrants. But again, the group of migrants acted as the name-giver for the space of the settlement.

10 See *Widsith*, vv. 23, 41–9, ed. Kamp Malone (Copenhagen, 1962), pp. 23, 24.
11 Allen Mawer, Frank Merry Stenton, J. E. B. Gower, *The Place-Names of Sussex*, English Place-Name Society IV (Cambridge, 1929; repr. Cambridge, 1986), pp. 323–4. Peter von Polenz, *Landschafts- und Bezirksnamen im frühmittelalterlichen Deutschland*, vol. 1 (Marburg, 1961), pp. 176, 178.

profession or specific purpose it was to migrate or to travel. That these groups, if they were kin groups, transcended the boundary between life and death, is shown by the fact that there is archaeological evidence of cemeteries and individual graves located in proximity to a farmstead on land which may have belonged to the inherited property of the kin group. This means that the dead were believed to have a continuing impact on the living; the living and the dead forming a local community as long as the settlement continued to exist. We have surprising records which show that even long-distance migrants made substantive efforts to keep in touch with their relatives who had stayed at home.[12] Hence, the group defined the space of daily experience and the space of regular communication.[13]

By the seventh century at the latest, Catholicism had sufficiently penetrated daily life in these settlements in order to support the beginning of a fundamental transformation of the structure of kin groups in western and west-central Europe. The transformation becomes visible in the beginning of the relocation of the cemeteries to the churchyards, facing the churches.[14] That churchyards became graveyards had two lasting consequences. First, the cult of the dead was subjected to the control of the Church and, second, the ties between the living and the dead as members of kin groups were cut. In consequence, the living had to rely on the intermediation of the Church in order to secure a good life after death, while they did no longer have to integrate themselves into the time-transcending continuity of their kin groups. From the point of view of a person, this meant that he or she could severe the ties to his or her kin group if and when he or she was certain that assistance from the Church would be granted. The clergy supported this attitude and encouraged newly or recently converted Christian believers to separate themselves from their kin groups and to devote their lives to the Church.[15] Rules

---

[12] Procopius, *Bellum Gothicum* cap. II/15 (various editions). He describes at length the efforts made by the Heruli at Singedon (in the vicinity of modern Belgrade) to keep up relations with their people in the traditional homelands in what is today southern Sweden.

[13] The early ninth-century Old Saxon epic poem *Heliand*, v. 5139, ed. Otto Behaghel, 10th edn by Burkhard Taeger, Altdeutsche Textbibliothek IV (Tübingen, 1996), p. 182, made this verbally explicit. It defined Jews as a 'thiod', that is a politically active group, and referred to non-Jewish warriors arriving in Palestine under the command of Pilatus as 'elilandige man', that is outlanders (whereby the prefix *eli-* is a derivative of Latin *alienus*). The terminology shows that there was no native Saxon word for persons originally from another land.

[14] Already in the course of his conquest of Saxony, Charlemagne prohibited burials on pagan cemeteries in the area: Alfred Boretius, ed., *MGH Capit.* 1, No. 26, p. 69 (*Capitulatio de partibus Saxoniae*, 775–90, cap. 29).

[15] Separation from the kin group was recommended at the close of the fifth century by Bishop Avitus of Vienne to King Clovis of the Franks in the course of the preparation for the king's baptism (*Opera quae supersunt*, ed. Rudolf Peiper, *MGH AA* 6, 2, pp. 75–6). St Boniface devoted his life to the Church after separating from his parents whom he never saw again after becoming a monk. See Wilhelm Levison, ed., *Vitae sancti Bonifatii archiepiscopi Moguntini*, cap. 1, *MGH SS rer. Germ.* (57), pp. 5–6.

for monks and nuns demanded that, upon entry into a monastery, novices should give away all their property in order to live their lives in poverty and in dependence upon the Church. The Church expected that the monasteries which the novices joined would become the recipients of the donations from their new members. This expectation was frequently but not always fulfilled.[16]

For the topographical organisation of the settlements, the change implied that cemeteries were moved from the hereditary lands of the kin groups to the proximity of, or, in case of particularly elevated persons, inside the church buildings themselves in order to be nearer to the saint(s) for whose cult the Church had been erected. Initially, the kin groups responded to this novel burial custom by establishing church buildings on their own hereditary lands and seeking to promote the cults of one of their dead as the saints venerated in these churches. Kin groups also founded their own monasteries for the commemoration of deceased kin members and for the cult of kin saints. In this way, a multitude of local cults of saints appeared from the seventh century onwards, many of whom were venerated in proprietary churches belonging to the kin groups.[17] But another development was ultimately more successful, namely the evolution of the cemetery as the centre of communication in the settlements.

This development was enhanced by the translocation of the churches into the centres of rural settlements. From the seventh century onwards,[18] church buildings came to be built more frequently than before in the centres of rural settlements, specifically in newly cleared woodlands. The centricity of the church building constituted an interface where various and potentially conflicting group interests could enter into discourse under the direction of the Church. One consequence was that church buildings were transformed into centres of communal life; this implied that, in order to participate in communal life, one had to be present in and around the church. Another consequence was that the cemeteries in the churchyards became the preferred areas of public communication; this implied that the cult of the dead became intertwined with the communicative interaction among the living. While the church encouraged the first implication, it tried to prevent the second. In the early eleventh century, Bishop Burchard of Worms (c. 965–1025) betrayed his keen interest in suppressing what seemed to him to be indecent behaviour in the churchyards, whereby he explicitly referred to such communicative interaction as the singing of nightly songs and the performance of dances on or in the proximity of the graves.[19]

16　Caesarius of Arles, *Regula ad virgines*, cap. 6, 21 (*PL* 67, cols 1108, 1110).

17　A good case is the foundation of a monastery by Friduric, a local aristocrat, at Breedon-on-the-Hill (Leicestershire) in the seventh century. See Walter de Gray Birch, ed., *Cartularium Saxonicum*, No. 841, 842, vol. 2 (London, 1887; repr. New York, 1964). Cf. Peter Hayes Sawyer, *Anglo-Saxon Charters* (London, 1968), No. 1803, 1805.

18　See Günther Peter Fehring, 'Missions- und Kirchenwesen in archäologischer Sicht', in Herbert Jankuhn, Reinhard Wenskus, eds, *Geschichtswissenschaft und Archäologie*, VuF XXII (Sigmaringen, 1979), pp. 547–91.

19　Burchard of Worms, *Decretorum libri XX*, liber XX, Interrogatio 54, 86 (*PL* 140, cols

The Church also insisted that principles of Roman property law should be applied with regard to land tenure. According to Roman law, land tenure was identical with the legitimate exercise of *dominium,* that is the absolute holding of all rights over a plot of land by a single person, and was normally recorded in documents which were signed in the presence of public notaries. This legal practice stood against the principle of communal ownership of land by members of a kin group. This principle made it difficult to alienate kin land and transfer it into the *dominium* of a person. But the Church claimed that its own holdings should be regarded as land tenure by *dominium* and that they should be recorded in written charters.

The emergence of church buildings as the centrepieces of settlements and the introduction of personal land tenure marked the beginning of the territorialisation of the previously group-defined spaces of daily experience and regular communication in these settlements. Initially, territoriality provided for nothing more than a spatial framework for interaction across the various groups in a settlement. The church and the churchyard did not constitute a distinct space of regular communication in their own right. For kin members could continue to perceive the graves of their ancestors as their property and thus as parts of their own space of daily experience, even though this perception militated against the position which was taken by the church authorities. Consequently, controversies arose concerning whether the space of regular communication (as dominated by the church) was and ought to be distinguishable from the space of daily experience (as dominated by the kin groups). Likewise, up to the late ninth century, secular spaces of regular communication were not integrated into a legal category of their own, but continued to be aggregate sums of qualitatively different places. A privilege which granted London port customs dues to the Bishop of Worcester in the name of King Alfred of Wessex ruled that merchants should pay customs dues to the owner of the market in London on which they traded their goods. Hence there was neither a general tax nor a single market in London at the time.[20]

Thus the distinction between the space of daily experience and the space of regular communication was vague and shifting in the early Middle Ages and allowed frequent overlaps. This was the case not only inside settlements, but also in larger administrative units. Thus it was possible that the space of daily experience of a given kin group could be extended to cover the space of regular communication of specifiable groups of persons. For example, between the fifth and the ninth centuries, the Frankish kings ruled their kingdom as if it were their own household. But, at the same time, they

577, 579). See for earlier prohibitions by the Council of Toledo (589), canon XXIII, the statutes of St Boniface (745), canon XXI, the homily of Pope Leo IV (847–855), cap. XL, and the Council of Mainz (813), canon XLVIII: Johann Dominicus Mansi, ed., *Sacrorum Conciliorum nova et amplissima collectio,* vol. 9, col. 999, vol. 12, col. 385, vol. 14, cols. 74, 895 (Paris, 1901; repr. Graz 1960)

[20] Birch (see note 17), vol. 1, No. 561. Sawyer (see note 17), No. 346.

respected the privileges of aristocrats in their entourage and of the churches. This means that administrative units, such as kingdoms, were not merely territorial units, but also associations of freemen and aristocrats. In summary, space of daily experience and space of regular communication were not mutually exclusive, but could overlap in spatial terms as well as with regard to political organisation because they were group-centred. The construct of public space as accessible by everyone did not feature in the early Middle Ages.

The best illustration, although perhaps a late one, for the group centredness of the early medieval space of regular communication comes from the Old English epic of *Beowulf*. The poem was laid down in writing around AD 1000, but may have been compiled during the ninth century. In the poem, the gathering place of a king and his retainers is described as a huge, magnificent hall erected by the command of the king after a victory in battle.[21] The hall in *Beowulf* was not a permanent residence in the sense of a royal 'palace', where the king lived. In this sense, it did not pertain to the space of daily experience of the king. Instead, the kingdom in *Beowulf* as well the real-world kingdoms in early medieval Europe usually had no residential capitals as paramount centres, but the king used several places among which he would itinerate, as he could also stay in monasteries or even the households of aristocratic kin groups. In the *Beowulf* poem, the hall had ceremonial tasks in that it housed the king's companions for feasting and drinking for several successive days and nights. Although magnificent and unusual in size, the hall was not 'royal' in itself in that it had peculiar structural features pertaining to royalty; instead, it became 'royal' through its use by the king and his retainers. In this task, the hall was elevated above the average buildings, but it did not constitute a space of its own, as the distinction between the private and the public would invoke. Hence the hall in *Beowulf* was conspicuous as the ceremonial feasting place of the king, but it did not manifest space of regular communication as a distinctly public space. Instead, it made visible space as a category of value which was to be determined by the groups that occupied it legitimately. Consequently, various types of groups could create different qualities of space, and these different qualities could coexist or compete with each other as long as the groups occupying them continued.

Likewise, during the early Middle Ages and even up to the fourteenth century, landscapes as representations of the space of regular communication were not featured in pictorial representations of space, and literary descriptions of landscapes, as in that which follows, were rare, sketchy and viewed the physical environment as hostile. The physical environment was seen to be in opposition to the human-made environments, displaying little more than a constraining framework for human action:

> He who has the bliss of life, who, proud and flushed with wine, suffers few hardships in the city, little believes how I often in weariness had to dwell on the

---

21 *Beowulf*, ed. Frederick Klaeber, 3rd edn (Lexington, Mass., 1950), vv. 64–85, pp. 3–4. *Heliand* (see note 13), vv. 2728–84, pp. 101–2.

ocean path. The shadow of the night grew dark, snow came from the north, frost bound the earth, hail fell on the ground, coldest of grain.[22]

What was outside the confines of human settlements was thus not only perceived as unpleasant but also as unorganised and, therefore, insecure. It was difficult to conceive of space of regular communication as a concept which overarched the settlements or even engulfed sizeable waterways. The lack of distinctiveness in the space of regular communication rendered the governance of large areas and numerous heterogeneous population groups difficult, hazardous and, therefore, exceptional. Moreover, it posed a barrier against the reception of the public law of the Roman Empire of Antiquity. The reception in the early Middle Ages of Roman public law was difficult because, in Roman Antiquity, public law as the imperial law governing the space of regular communication was conceivable only in so far as it stood in opposition to civil law as the law governing the space of the daily experience of persons and groups. By contrast, the vagueness of early medieval concepts of the space of regular communication discouraged the build-up of lasting and centralised administrative bureaucracies and usually confined the range of rulers' activities to areas within which, by early medieval standards of the speed of communication, the maintenance of regular communication was possible.[23] These were usually small. Ninth-century Frankish literary descriptions of the Occident joined in with high medieval Scandinavian sagas which recorded perceptions of the world as an assembly of small village settlements inhabited by mainly small politically active groups. This was so despite the fact that woodlands came to be afforested under Frankish rule in continental Europe during the ninth century and were thereby subjected to some degree of territorial legislative authority of the Frankish kings. However, this legislative competence was used mainly for the purpose of granting privileges for the establishment of new settlements on isolated woodland clearings.[24]

Whereas, during the early Middle Ages, the space of daily experience and the space of regular communication remained largely untouched by the legacy of Roman imperial administration, the early medieval concept of the world inherited much from classical Antiquity. The world picture that had been schematised at the time of Augustus and which formed the basis for the standard concept of the world throughout the Middle Ages, described it as a

---

[22] Seafarer, vv. 27–33, in *The Exeter Book*, ed. George Philip Krapp, Elliott van Kirk Dobbie, Anglo-Saxon Poetic Records III (New York, London, 1936), p. 144. The translation is R. K. Gordon's, *Anglo-Saxon Poetry*. (London, New York, 1964), p. 76.

[23] King Edgar of England enforced a monetary reform in 975, according to which his subjects were obliged to return current coins at regular intervals to a mint in their neighbourhood. Edgar saw to it that mints were established countrywide so that they could be reached within one day. See *Flores historiarum*, ed. Henry Richards Luard, vol. 1, Rerum Britannicarum medii aevi scriptores XCV (London, 1890; repr. New York, 1965), p. 514.

[24] See Engelbert Mühlbacher, ed., *MGH DD Karol.* I, No. 213 [1.12.811], No. 218 [9.5.813]. Raban Maur, *De universo*, cap. XVI, 1–3 (*PL* 111, cols. 435–51).

single, coherent unit of land encircled by a strip of water referred to as *okeanos*. The land was called *orbis, terra, mundus* or *ecumene*, and included the three major continents into which the land was divided, namely Asia, Africa, Europe; and the division was standardised in such a way that Asia occupied half of the land and Africa and Europe together covered the other half.[25]

The picture of the world shown in Figure 2 locates paradise in the east of Asia and the city of Jerusalem in the centre of the *ecumene*, and it does so in accordance with Ezekiel 5: 5. Biblical phrases also inspired the ascription to the *ecumene* of the largest portion of the surface of the earth. This view, which implies that land outweighs water, was informed by the apocryphal Book of Esdras (4: 6, 42) which assigned to land six-sevenths of the size of the earth. Another implication of this world picture was that it rendered permeable the world as a whole. This world picture was perfunctory in the early Middle Ages, because it boosted the extensive migrations which were being conducted during the fourth, fifth and sixth centuries and, during the eighth, ninth and tenth centuries, it stimulated seafaring activities along the coastlines of the North and Baltic Seas.[26] To these ends the world picture of Antiquity was suitable because it made it possible to transcend the factual localism of the space of regular communication.[27] However, the world beyond the confines of local settlements was perceived to be full of hazards which faced those who set out to migrate, travel or otherwise penetrate the physical environment. The hazards of long-distance migration and travel became explicit in some of the Old English elegies in which the sorrows and dangers of travel by land and sea form the poetic themes:

> I, sundered from my native land, far from noble kinsmen, often sad at heart, had to fetter my mind, when in years gone by the darkness of the earth covered my gold-friend, and I went thence in wretchedness with wintry care upon me over the frozen waves, gloomily sought the hall of a treasure-giver wherever I

25 For early medieval descriptions of the world which were consciously drawn on the world picture of Antiquity see: Augustine, *De Civitate Dei*, cap. XVI/17, CCSL XLVIII (Turnhout, 1955), p. 521. Dicuil, *Liber de Mensura Orbis Terrae*, cap. I/2, ed. J. J. Tierney, Ludwig Bieler, Scriptores Latini Hiberniae VI (Dublin, 1967), p. 44. *Die Kosmographie des Aethicus*, ed. Otto Prinz, MGH Quellen zur Geistesgeschichte des Mittelalters XIV (Munich, 1993), pp. 89–90, 92–93. Isidore of Seville, *Etymologiarum sive originum libri XX*, cap. XIV/2, ed. W. M. Lindsay (Oxford, 1911). Orosius, *Historiarvm adversvm paganos libri VIII*, cap. I/2, ed. Carl Zangemeister, CSEL V (Vienna, 1882; repr. New York, 1966), pp. 9–40.

26 *The Old English Orosius*, cap. I/1, ed. Janet M. Bately, Early English Text Society, Supplementary Series VI (London, New York, Toronto, 1980), pp. 13–18. On the location of paradise see Vincent of Beauvais, 'De Asia et eius capite quod est paradisus', Vincent, *Speculum naturale*, cap. XXX/2 (Douai, 1624), col. 2400. Cf.: Bartholomaeus Anglicus, *De rerum proprietate* (Frankfurt, 1601), pp. 680–682 (repr. Frankfurt, 1964).

27 Early in the fifteenth century, Pierre d'Ailly insisted that the world could be perambulated in 1570 days. See Pierre d'Ailly, *Imago mundi*, cap. V, ed. Edmond Buron (Paris, 1930), p. 189.

Fig. 2 Map of the world (mappamundi) contained in a psalter manuscript, thirteenth century. London, British Library, Add. Ms. 28681, fol. 9 recto. Reprinted by permission of The British Library. The world is displayed beneath Christ. The orientation is eastward, that is, east is at the top. It shows paradise in its upper part, that is, in Asia, and features Jerusalem in the centre. The Straits of Gibraltar are located at the very bottom of the map. Europe forms the lower left, and Africa the lower right side. Two dragons in the bottom part of the picture represent the underworld ruled by the devil. Because the dividing lines between the continents have the shape of a T and fall within the depiction of the world as a circle, this type of world picture is known as the T-O map.

could find him far or near, who might know me in the mead hall or comfort me, left without friends, treat me with kindness.[28]

Nevertheless, the risks of long distance travel might be worth taking. As the tenth-century legend of St Brendan displays, God's Own Country, the believed island of eternal happiness, could be imagined as located just about one hour's voyage west of Ireland, even if it might take seven years to penetrate the mist that shrouded the ocean and to arrive in the land of promise.[29]

Like the anonymous author of the legend of St Brendan, many medieval cartographers believed that the land of promise was to be found on earth, sometimes in the midst of the ocean or otherwise in a remote part and, in any case, difficult to access. Indeed, terrestrial paradise was depicted frequently in medieval world maps, commonly in eastern Asia. This world picture enjoyed a remarkable continuity well beyond the early Middle Ages. In its basic structure, the world picture remained that of classical Antiquity throughout the fifteenth century. With missionary and merchant activities extending into eastern Asia during the thirteenth century and to the eastern coasts of Africa in the fourteenth century, this world picture became even the basis of practical travel guides. The wonders of the East replaced the previously ubiquitous monsters populating the outward fringes of the earth and began to attract traders, as news of the fictitious Prester John encouraged clergymen and missionaries to travel to Asia, using world maps as instruments for their orientation in the world.[30] For example, the mid-fourteenth-century travel book of Sir John Mandeville employed a conventional world map as the geographical basis for its fictitious descriptions of Asiatic lands and seas.[31]

Concepts of space in the high and late Middle Ages

In the meantime, however, important changes in the relationship between space and groups had begun to take place, and they affected first and foremost the definition of the space of daily experience. Beginning at the end of the tenth century, and advancing greatly throughout the eleventh and twelfth centuries, a new type of church building appeared which outstripped all previous structures in sheer size. Such huge church buildings were designed to bring together groups and persons from various walks of life for the purpose

---

28 Wanderer, vv. 19–29, ed. Krapp, Dobbie (see note 22), p. 134. The translation is R. K. Gordon's (see note 22), p. 73.

29 *Navigatio Sancti Brendani abbatis,* cap. 1, ed. Carl Selmer (Notre Dame, Ind., 1959), pp. 4–8.

30 Otto of Freising, *Chronica sive historia de duabis civitatibus,* cap. VII/33, ed. Adolf Hofmeister, *MGH SS rer. Germ.* (45), pp. 365–7. Letter of Prester John, Cod. hist. 61, Göttingen University Library [fifteenth century]. A printed version has been edited by Vsevolod Slessarev, *Prester John. The Letter and the Legend* (Minneapolis, 1959).

31 *Mandeville's Travels . . . from Ms. Cotton Tiberius C XVI,* ed. P. Hamelius, 2 vols, Early English Text Society, Original Series CLIII–CLIV (New York, London, 1919–23; repr. New York, 1973; London, 1961).

of participating in mass services, among them the clergy, monks, the secular clergy, the secular rulers and their kin, the ordinary parishioners, and, where applicable, pilgrims who would travel from afar in order to venerate a local saint. An early case of such a comprehensive church building was the cathedral of Old Minster, Winchester, dedicated in 983. Churches such as the cathedral at Winchester were built as multifaceted structures, wherein the variety of participating groups were assigned specific, segregated places. For example, the west works were usually reserved for the rulers and their kin, whereas the use of the eastern part, in proximity to the altar, was mainly confined to the monks and the clergy.

The partitioning of the internal space of the church generated the impression of diversity and impenetrability, so that, according to a contemporary description of Winchester cathedral, a guide was necessary to lead an inexperienced visitor through the church from the entry in the west to the apse in the east.[32] Thus, these churches were designed as structures, whose monumentality was expressed by their size and the length of time required to erect them. In the Winchester case, the construction process lasted for more than a generation's time and thus extended far beyond the usual term of a person's office. Correspondingly, the building must have been planned as a durable structure, for, when it was torn down in 1093, it was still in perfect condition. Such building habits support the conclusion that these churches were considered to be of value as monuments in their own right. As monuments, these churches were designed to represent a higher, divinely willed spatial order into which the groups of church-goers were incorporated upon entering the building. Hence, in the case of the cathedral at Winchester and other contemporary cathedrals, the space manifested by these buildings was primary, and the groups were secondary. Whereas, late in the ninth century, the groups of retainers to a king meeting in the ceremonial halls constituted the space of these halls as royal, in the course of the tenth century, the large-size cathedral churches began to appear as manifestations of space as a value in its own right. In terms of theory, scientists began in the thirteenth century to conceptualise space as the space in between persons, groups and objects, that is, as a continuum in which objects can exist and living beings can move.[33]

Ranking space over groups became the leading principle for the organisation of the space of daily experience and can be observed from changes of patterns of aristocratic settlement. By the end of the tenth century, a process of social stratification began in consequence of which inhabitants of settlements became subject to rigorous distinctions of rank between ordinary peasant farmers and those who were wealthy enough to be able to equip themselves with horses and heavy martial arms and to engage in warfare. The

32 Wulfstan Cantor, 'Narratio de sancto Swithuno', vv. 41–56, in *Frithegodi monachi Breuiloquium Vitae Beati Wilfredi et Wulfstani Cantoris Narratio de sancto Swithuno*, ed. Alistair Campbell (Zurich, 1950), pp. 66–7.

33 Albertus Magnus, *De caelo et mundo*, cap. III/1, III/2, ed. Paul Hossfeld (Munster, 1971), pp. 55–9 (Alberti Magni Opera omnia. 5,1.)

ability to ride on horseback and to bear heavy martial arms as well as military professionalism emerged as the distinctive criteria for the aristocracy as the holders of power (*potentes*) over powerless and frequently impoverished peasant farmers (*pauperes*) who were in turn dependent upon the *potentes* for protection. By the eleventh century, aristocratic kin groups separated themselves from the main group of peasant farmers and established their residences in nearby stone-built hilltop castles overlooking the settlements of the peasant farmers under their rule. Sometimes, when the landscape was unfavourable, such castles would even be erected on artificial mounds, such as in the case of the Anglo-Norman mottes. One important consequence was that the aristocratic kin groups as residents in and owners of hilltop castles became confined to the limited space of these human-made environments, and that meant that, among the aristocrats, the kin group was to consist of no more than the cohabitative three-generation family, whose space of daily experience was the hilltop castle. Thus the hilltop castle emerged as the conspicuous manifestation of the aristocratic way of life and of the domination by the inhabitant aristocrats over the peasant farmers in their lowland settlements. The castle dungeon was identified as the centrepiece of an aristocratic settlement and at the same time the symbol of aristocratic rule over land and people. Aristocratic kin groups began to name themselves after the place of their residence and dropped the ancient custom of considering themselves as descent groups derived from respected ancestors. Again, the space of the hilltop castle constituted the group living there and determined the space of daily experience within permanent and architecturally manifest boundaries which isolated the inhabitants of hilltop castles from their social and physical environments. Likewise, places of administration, such as rulers' palaces emerged as centres of urban settlements which were transformed into residential capitals, such as Paris and the City of Westminster, west of London. Hence, in the eleventh century, the centralisation of space followed its territorialisation.

Second, a similar process of spatial diversification and centralisation occurred with regard to the space of regular communication, and was visible in changes of settlements of groups of certain specialist professionals, also during the eleventh century. Specialist artisans and merchant traders began to form contractual groups endeavouring to create their own segregated settlements and self-rule. To this end, they tried to obtain privileges from kings or aristocratic rulers in the vicinity or from the emperors, if the latter were in control of the land in question. If these bids by merchants and artisans were successful, their segregated settlements as towns or cities were established under special legislation in the proximity of hilltop castles, on hills, at major crossroads or by rivers. Like hilltop castles, most of these settlements were demarcated against the surrounding landscape by walls, which visualised the segregation of urban life. Although not every resident in a town or city had equal access to privileges and legal rights in the participation of the affairs of the community, all permanent residents (*manentes, habitantes*) could be perceived as members of a comprehensive community of intramural settlers.

The residents in the urban communities of towns and cities adopted the custom of using surnames, some of which were derived from the lanes or the houses where they lived; the surnames characterised them as town or city dwellers. Within the towns or cities, the space of daily experience was the household or residence of the three-generation family and their servants. The generic term for this new concept of the space of daily experience was the 'house'. The 'house' was both an organisation and a building. Beginning in the eleventh century, private houses began to be built from stone, so as to outlast the lifetime of a person and form the architectural and legal substrate on which the house as an organisation could persist. In consequence, in the urban communities of towns and cities, space also began to constitute the group; no longer did the group determine space.

One consequence of the diversification of the settlements was that the concepts of space as the space of daily experience and as the space of regular communication came to be diversified between town and castle, on the one side, and the country, on the other. In the towns and cities as well as in the hilltop castles, the space of daily experience was territorialised, drawn on well-demarcated plots of land as the property of households. By contrast, kin-group based concepts of the space of daily experience continued in the countryside beyond the remaining part of the Middle Ages. The other consequence was that, in the world of towns and cities as well as among the aristocrats in their hilltop castles, the concept of the space of daily experience came to be sharply demarcated against the concept of the space of regular experience. In its confinement to the plot of land, the space of daily experience in the castles as well as in the towns and cities became identified as the space of the 'private house', whereas the space of regular communication became the 'public' space, architecturally explicit in the geometrically patterned open squares and the streets in late medieval towns and cities and the territories under the control of aristocratic rulers.

In the twelfth century, aristocratic lords in the Empire as well as kings elsewhere began to establish themselves as supreme rulers of territories by public law.[34] These territories denoted the public space of regular communication and comprised forests, fields, rural settlements and towns. Inside the Empire, rule over a given territory came to be regarded as exclusive in the sense that the rights and titles of one lord ultimately excluded rights and titles of all other lords or other members of a kin group when related to the same territory. The obverse of the coin was that rule over a territory came to be regarded as inclusive in the sense that it included the *dominium secundum*

---

[34] A controversial term for the period under discussion here. However, it can be justified by the juristical distinction between the 'dominium secundum proprietatem' (ownership by private law) and the 'dominium secundum imperium' (rule by public law) which was current among thirteenth-century jurists, such as Bulgarus. Already in 1192, Duke Leopold V of Austria may have been the first to claim for himself the title 'dominus terrae'. See *Urkundenbuch zur Geschichte der Babenberger in Österreich* ed. Oskar von Mitis, Heinrich Fichtenau, Erich Zöllner, vol. 1, Publikationen des Instituts für Österreichische Geschichtsforschung Series III, vol. 1 (Vienna, 1950), No. 86.

imperium over all rights and titles over the resident population in the territory and merged them into a single, interdependent, coordinated and centralised territorial administration, regardless of their traditional status or inherited privileges. The formation of territories still allowed for some continuity of group-based administrative organisation, specifically in the countryside, where it continued well into the eighteenth century. Moreover, the goal of rounding off territories as exclusive *dominia* under the government of one and the same aristocratic ruler was not immediately accomplished everywhere. The territorialisation of rule advanced farthest in England and the least in southern and central Europe, and the simultaneous emergence of urban communities of towns and cities with their own tendency to territorialisation posed an obstacle to the rounding-off of territories under aristocratic rule. Nevertheless, the new concept of the space of regular communication under the *dominium secundum imperium* of a ruler over the population group of residents in a given territory promoted the formulation of the concept of 'public' space as the space which was accessible by everyone and was under the *dominium* of the territorial ruler. In this sense, 'public' space was set off against the 'private' space which remained under the *dominium secundum proprietatem* of private persons and kin groups. The public sphere (*districtum, territorium*) has from then on been definable as the space of regular communication and has been sharply distinguished from the 'house' as the 'private' sphere of persons and kin groups.

By the twelfth century, the new concept of the space of regular communication as the space of 'public' rule was sufficiently institutionalised to allow the reintroduction of Roman public law. The doctrine that every king is emperor in his own kingdom appeared in twelfth-century theories of canon law and subsequently established the principle of the sovereignty of the temporal ruler over the people and the land of his kingdom. With the help of Roman law and the jurists trained in it, territorial rulers gradually managed to superimpose 'their' territorial law upon the residents under their rule and installed themselves as the supreme arbiters in legal procedures. In consequence, a process of centralisation of rule began, lasting up to the early sixteenth century, through which the residents in a territory became the subjects of the territorial ruler.[35] This type of the organisation and conceptu-

---

35 See the remark by the Italian annalist Tolomeo of Lucca (1236–1326/7) about Rudolf of Habsburg after his election as German king. Tolomeo describes Rudolf as a poor aristocrat while insisting that he had had considerable experience in fighting wars with the dukes of Savoy about territorial boundaries. Tolomeo de Lucca, *Die Annalen des Tholomeus von Lucca in doppelter Fassung*, s. a. 1274, ed. Bernhard Schmeidler, *MGH SS. Rer. Germ.* N. S. 8 (1930), pp. 173–4. For a late record of the continuing difficulties faced by territorial rulers who insisted on their rights to rule over the resident population, see the register of papers by Bishop Sixtus of Freising of the late fifteenth century. The bishop's rule was plagued by some insurgent dissatisfied peasant farmers who were unwilling to pay taxes to the bishop and who openly revolted. The bishop's rule was also limited due to attempts by the Bavarian dukes to assert their territorial rule in the bishop's lands and to jurisdictional privileges which the emperor held. See Franz

Fig. 3a *Sachsenspiegel,* illumination of the Heidelberg manuscript (description under Fig. 3b). The picture illustrates Book II, Art 49, §§ 1 and 2 of the *Landrecht.* The paragraphs rule that gutters have to be arranged in such a way that the rain flows into the owner's plot.

Fig. 3b *Sachsenspiegel,* illumination of the Heidelberg manuscript, early thirteenth century. Heidelberg University Library, Cod. Pal. Germ. 164, fol. 8r, 26v. The picture illustrates Book II, Art 52, §§ 1 and 2 of the Landrecht. The paragraphs contain a rule for the case that trees have grown in such a way that their branches extend over the neighbour's plot. If it happens, these branches shall be cut by their owner. If the owner fails to do so, the neighbour is entitled to pull the branches and keep what falls onto his plot.

alisation of the space of regular communication then continued up to the end of the eighteenth century.

Moreover, rulers tried to demarcate their territories in precise ways by means of border stones which they had placed along the agreed boundaries, and they enacted laws according to which crossing the boundaries between two territories became subject to strict regulations. For example, laws were enacted which prohibited the pursuit of deer across lines of demarcation which divided the woodlands of two adjacent territories. Hence afforested woodlands ceased to be impenetrable no man's lands and were subjected to extensive forestry legislation. Roads became privileged trajectories of public communication, the king's or the emperor's roads being under the special protection of kings and the emperor and everyone being allowed to use them.

Martin Mayer, 'Über die Correspondenzbücher des Bischofs Sixtus von Freising', *Archiv für österreichische Geschichte* LXVIII (1886), pp. 474–500.

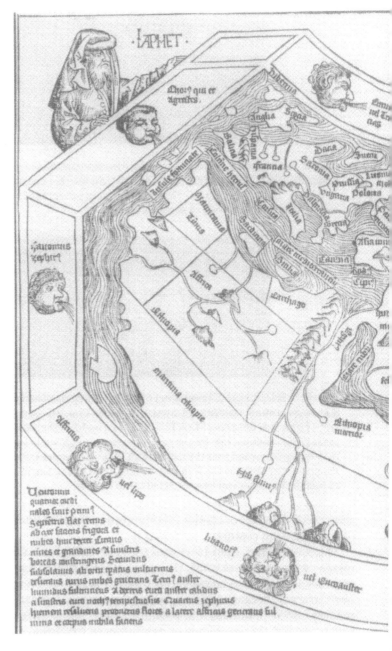

Fig. 4 World map from Hartmann Schedel, *Das Buoch der Cronicken vnd Gedechtnus wirdigern Geschichten von Anbegyn der Werlt bis auf dise vnßere Zeit* (Nuremberg, 1493), fols XII verso–XIII recto. A Ptolemaic projection is used which omits longitudes and latitudes but places the north at the top. Note that the Indian Ocean ('Mare Indicum') is characterised as an inland sea because some hypothetical land bridge is displayed to link Africa with the north-east of Asia. The map thus implies that Africa is not circumnavigable.

ties of towns and cities. Merchants' companies were founded and towns and cities formed unions among themselves, such as the Hanseatic League, whose goal it was to maintain permanent trade relations among cities in northern and north-western Europe. Likewise, the woodlands came to be perceived as attributes of villages, towns and cities, supplying certain raw materials for urban manufacturing and rural agricultural production, such as timber, coal and mineral resources. To some extent, these newly supplied raw materials facilitated the expansion of urban as well as rural settlements and contributed to the generation of moneyed wealth.

Living in the woods demanded the existence of a market. For only if the people in the woods could receive an income in terms of money from their work, could they afford to purchase the necessary victuals and technical instruments which alone enabled them to live in the woods. Otherwise, woodlands would either continue to lay waste and be impenetrable no man's lands as border areas, or they would have to give way to clearing efforts for the purpose of establishing new regular settlements. The intensity of the use of woodlands by specialised producers of goods for sale in a market differed from the early medieval Frankish afforestation which had established no more than a nominal and not immediately economically relevant overlordship over woodlands. By the fourteenth century, the frequency of interrelations between towns, cities and villages on the one side and woodlands on the other became manifest also in initial efforts towards the preservation of woods as such. These efforts reflected the consciousness that woods were neither a source of evil nor an unlimited reservoir of raw materials, but demanded care, circumspection and measures for preservation in their own right. Thus efforts towards woodland preservation made it clear that, despite the continuing segregation of spaces of daily experience into a plethora of small plots of land, the space of regular communication became conceived as a continuous entity which could overarch administrative and other boundaries. As in the case of time, space could be viewed as a neutral device for the ordering of objects and living beings in the world, so to speak, as the space in between these objects and living beings, and as a category of its own, separable from the concept of groups.

The formation of territories still allowed for some continuity of group-based administrative organisation, specifically in the countryside, well into the eighteenth century. Although among the peasant farmers the traditional kin groups persisted well beyond the Middle Ages, the rural settlements also became territorialised from the thirteenth century. They were made up of fenced plots which were neatly partitioned and under the governance of strict laws, as the *Sachsenspiegel* shows.

Newly established farming settlements came to be arranged according to preconceived layouts in geometrical forms with a common, the church and the cemetery in the centre, and a degree of communal self-administration was established, which was akin to the practices in the towns and cities, although the villages were never able to shake off the rule of their territorial lords, as some of the towns and cities could.

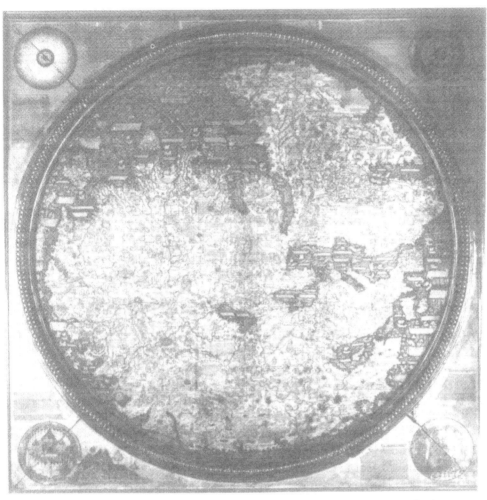

Fig. 5 Contemporary copy of a map of the world drawn by Fra Mauro in Venice in 1459 at the request of the King of Portugal. Venice, Biblioteca Nazionale Marciana. The map follows the Arab convention of placing the south at the top and describes Africa as circumnavigable. It does so by using the conventions of a T-O *mappamundi* of having the ocean encircling the *ecumene*. As in the T-O *mappaemundi*, Fra Mauro depicts many islands in the ocean, among them the island of Zipangu ('Giava') which Marco Polo had mentioned but adds a vision of the Indian Ocean for which, perhaps, he drew on high medieval Arab nautical experience and earlier fifteenth-century Italian cartographical practice. Note that paradise has been removed from the *ecumene* and has come to be placed outside the ocean in the lower left corner of the picture.

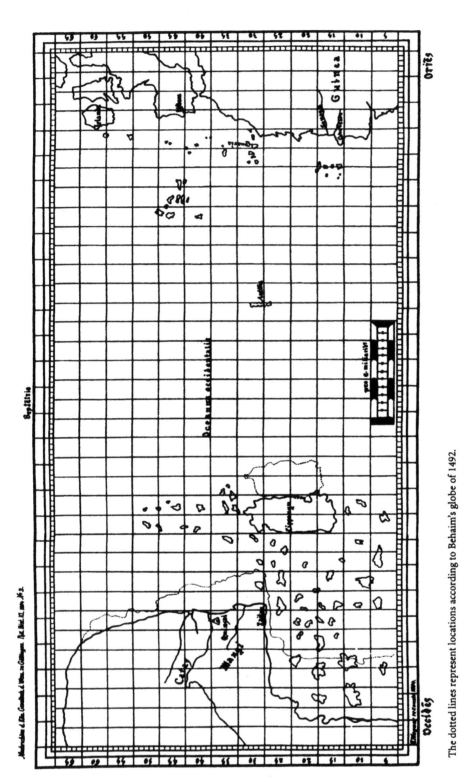

The dotted lines represent locations according to Behaim's globe of 1492.

Fig. 6 Reconstruction by Hermann Wagner (1894) of a map made by Paolo dal Pozzo Toscanelli in Florence, 1474. The map joins together the western side of Europe and Africa and the eastern side of Asia. It has the north at the top. It shows many islands in the double strip of the ocean which extends between Asia and Europe, among them the island of Zipangu as mentioned by Marco Polo. Reprinted from: *Nachrichten von der Akademie der Wissenschaften in Göttingen. Philol.-Hist. Klasse* (1894).

the villages were never able to shake off the rule of their territorial lords, as some of the towns and cities could.

Throughout the time when these transformations occurred, the world as a concept of space remained largely unchanged. Much long-distance travel took place along the beaten tracks, although the crusades re-emphasised the Mediterranean Sea as a major trading route. But the catastrophic failure of the crusades during the thirteenth century and, eventually, the Ottoman Turkish conquest of Byzantium in 1453, stimulated the search for further trajectories for missionary and merchant activities, first to the south and then to the west of Europe. During the fifteenth century, the search was mainly focused on Africa and resulted in a number of expeditions organised and stipulated by the Portuguese royal court. Already by the late 1450s, these expeditions entailed one fundamental revision of the world picture inherited from Antiquity. This revision concerned the circumnavigability of Africa. In some world maps, the African continent was linked with Asia through a land bridge that turned the Indian Ocean into an inland sea.

Turning the Indian Ocean into an inland sea caused problems to all attempts to circumnavigate Africa. But before the end of the 1450s, a new theory was proposed which used a pictorial feature of the medieval T-O maps, namely the depiction of the ocean as a strip of water encircling the *ecumene* as a whole. According to this cartographic type, the ocean strip surrounded Africa and made the continent circumnavigable towards Asia. Ascertaining the circumnavigability of Africa and establishing the seaway to Asia became an attractive goal after the Muslim occupation of the eastern shores of the Mediterranean Sea. The circumnavigability hypothesis was pictorially manifest in the world map completed by the Camaldulese monk Fra Mauro (dec. 1460) in Venice in 1459, anticipating later Portuguese expeditions up to Vasco da Gama's (1469–1524) voyage to India from 1497 to 1499.

But there was also a minority position which, contrariwise, argued that the nearest seaway to Asia was the route west from Europe. This hypothesis seems to have been argued first by a Florentine mathematician and astronomer, Paolo dal Pozzo Toscanelli (1397–1482). In 1474, Toscanelli drew a map, so to speak, of the back side of a medieval [T-O] world map, depicting Europe and Africa on the right, Asia on the left side and a number of islands, among them St Brendan's island, the Antilia of Portuguese geography and Marco Polo's (1254–1324) Zipangu in the middle of the ocean between Europe and Asia.

Toscanelli's map appears to have been known to Christopher Columbus who also studied a printed version of Marco Polo's report when he prepared for his transoceanic voyage. Columbus took Toscanelli's map at face value and was certain that he was in the proximity of Zipangu during his first voyage in 1492. He staunchly defended the conventional world picture, into which an inhabited continent separating Europe and Africa from Asia would not fit.[36]

36 See N. Sumien, ed., *La correspondence du savant florentin Paolo dal Pozzo Toscanelli avec Christophe Colomb* (Paris, 1927). Christopher Columbus, *Diario de abordo*, ed. Luis Arranz (Madrid, 1985), pp. 86, 105, 166, where the text reports that the admiral

However, the subsequent 'discovery' and conquest of 'America', initially regarded as a large island and rightly referred to as the 'New World' from the point of view of the medieval world map, quickly destroyed the world picture which the Middle Ages had inherited from Antiquity. Within less than twenty years of Columbus's first voyage, the medieval world maps disappeared. Geographers recognised that the largest portion of the surface of the earth was covered by water which could be depicted as interspersed with land, they gave up imagining the world as a concentric circle with Jerusalem in or close by the middle and they designed a world view in which there was no longer room for paradise or any other land of promise.

But, it was not before the beginning of the eighteenth century that European cartographers generally accepted the full extension of the 'New World' and its continental identity. It took until the end of the eighteenth century to remove the mythical Southern Continent from the world maps which was believed to cover the southern hemisphere and reach close to the southernmost tips of America and Africa. Only then were discoverers persuaded that attempts to search for the Southern Continent were vain. Still the no-more-than-gradual recognition of the continental separation of America did permit the recasting of the European world picture. Since Antiquity, the concept of the universality of the world had been based on a theoretical construct which had been confined to the space depicted in the medieval maps. During a lengthy process between the sixteenth and the eighteenth centuries, the concept of the universality of the world became inseparable from the factual globality of the world as it exists.

The politicisation of the space of regular communication and the emotionalisation of the space of daily experience

The globalisation of the space of the world left untouched the multifarious divisions of the many spaces of regular communication which had emerged during the later Middle Ages, even though cross-boundary communication through travel and the exchange of goods became increasingly common. However, the gap between the spaces of regular communication and the spaces of daily experience widened further. One dividing factor was legal in kind. Towards the end of the sixteenth century, theorists of politics and administration cast into legal terms the distinction between *dominium secundum proprietatem* and *dominium secundum imperium*. According to the new doctrine, the *dominium* was confined to private ownership in land, against which the control that rulers exercised by public law became classed as *imperium*. *Imperium* was taken to be that form of control over land which

believed himself to be in the vicinity of Zipangu. Columbus, Letter to Pope Alexander VI, 1502, in Columbus, *Lettere e scritti (1495–1506)*, ed. Paolo Emilio Taviani, Consuelo Varela, vol. 2 (Rome, 1993), pp. 274–9, where Columbus claims to have found more then 1400 islands.

Fig. 7 David Rötlin, Rottweil town map, 1564. Stadtmuseum Rottweil.

consisted in the competence of law-making and law-enforcing over the population settling in a territory.[37]

On the one side, the identification of the space of daily experience as the *dominium* land under private ownership was recognised in increasing concerns which theorists awarded to the definition, and even more so, the protection of private ownership in land. For example, Justus Lipsius (1547–1606) assigned to rulers of territories the task of defining and protecting private ownership in land.[38] It is also noteworthy that, since the sixteenth century, settlements were displayed cartographically as assemblies of private plots of land into which public places such as roads and squares, rulers' offices and church buildings were interspersed. The sixteenth-century map shown in Figure 7 may stand as one example of many.

On the other side, the identification of the space of regular communication as the public *imperium* under the control of one and the same territorial ruler was confirmed by the large number of manifest boundaries. These linear boundaries demarcated two or more coexisting territories which stood under different *imperia*. Trespassing from one territory as a space of regular communication into another required, with increasing frequency, passports. These passports were legal documents which were authenticated by officials of the territorial ruler during the sixteenth, seventeenth and eighteenth centuries. They needed to be presented to inspectors at border checkpoints and allowed a person to leave the territory with the legal permission of the ruler under whose *imperium* a person stood. Such minutely demarcated territories were controlled by bureaucracies which were manned in the central palaces of the territorial rulers. Not infrequently, these palaces and their vicinity were built and arranged according to geometrical patterns which displayed the palace as the centre of radial axes linking up the inside of the palace with the outside territorial lands.

The politicisation of the space of regular communication had its counterpart in the emotionalisation of the space of daily experience which had already begun in the fifteenth century. Private houses in towns and cities as well as the aristocratic castles became the sanctuaries for the maintenance of benevolent parent–child relationships against an outside world which was frequently perceived as governed by the stern rules of market competition among manufactures as well as between traders and by the equally strict rules of status competition among the several ranks of aristocratic kin groups. Parents were given the task of devoting themselves to the education of their children,[39] and school teachers faced the demand that they should treat the schoolchildren with affection, patience and didactic skill.[40]

---

37 Andreas Knichen, *De iure territorii* (Hanover, 1613), pp. 11–12.

38 Justus Lipsius, 'De constancia libri duo', Lipsius, *Two Bookes of Constancie*, ed. John Stradling (London, 1584). Repr. ed. R. Kirk, C. M. Hall (New Brunswick, 1939), pp. 95–6. Cf.: John Locke, *Two Treatises of Government* (London, 1698), Book II, Chapter VII: 'Of Political and Civil Society', ed. Peter Laslett (Cambridge, 1970), pp. 336–48.

39 Leon Battista Alberti, *I Libri della famiglia*, ed. Renée Neu Watkins, *The Family in Renaissance Florence* (Columbia, S.C., 1969). Johann Michael Moscherosch, *Insomnis:*

Footnote 40 on following page.

Both processes further widened the gap between the spaces of daily experience and the spaces of regular communication. Towards the end of the eighteenth century, both spaces were not merely placed in opposition to each other, but ranked at different levels in a hierarchy of legal significance. Political theorists supported this hierarchy in that they assumed that *dominium* could not exist without *imperium* and that, consequently, the politicised space of regular communication had to obtain priority over the emotionalised space of daily experience.[41] Therefore, the elevation of the public over the private as representatives of the space of regular communication and of the space of daily experience was the end product of a long process of the diversification of these two concepts of space which began in the eleventh century and was not concluded before the end of the eighteenth century.

Conclusion

This overview of the conceptual history of space in European culture has led to the recognition of six fundamental changes which affected the three categories of space unevenly and at different times. The early medieval group-centred space was transformed into territorial space during the period between the twelfth and the fifteenth centuries. Moreover, during the same period, the perception of space as an aggregate sum of qualitatively different places gave way to the perception of space as a homogeneous continuity and an ordering device for persons, groups and objects. Likewise, during the same period, the space of regular communication was identified as the public sphere, whereas the space of daily experience became associated with the private house. Around 1500, the medieval universal world picture gave way to a category of space that comprised the world as a globe. During the fifteenth, sixteenth and seventeenth centuries, the space of regular communication as the public sphere was politicised, whereas the space of daily experience as the private space was emotionalised. Finally, towards the end of the eighteenth century, a hierarchy emerged according to which the space of regular communication was given priority over the space of daily experience under the proviso that the exercise of control over the space of regular communication was in accordance with the metaphysical category of law.

Cura parentum: Christliches Vermächtnuss. Oder Schuldige Vorsorg eines Trewen Vatters bey jetzigen hochbetrübtsten gefährlichsten Zeiten den seinigen zur letzten Nachricht hin derlassen (Strasbourg, 1643).

40 Jan Amos Comenius, 'Didactica magna', Comenius, *Opera didactica omnia*, cap. 16–18 (Amsterdam, 1657), cols 70–9.

41 Immanuel Kant, 'Metaphysische Anfangsgründe der Rechtslehre [Königsberg 1797]', *Werke in zwölf Bänden*, ed. Wilhelm Weischedel, vol. 8 (Frankfurt, 1968), pp. 336–41.

III

The Body – Modes of Behaviour

> For by Art is created that great Leviathan . . .
> which is but an Artificiall Man
>
> – Thomas Hobbes

Introduction

Writing the history of the human body may appear to be a contradiction in terms. For, if we define the *conditio humana* in biological terms, the human body has to be set as a constant and, consequently, does not tolerate any of the changes that constitute history. In fact, during the Middle Ages, no physical transformations of human bodies of any structural significance seem to have occurred. But these continuities do not and have not excluded changes in perceptions of the human body, because, even if it has not changed, the human body has been perceived in different ways.

Changes of such perceptions can be of significance because they may correlate with changes in the modes of behaviour which shape a person's actions and the interactions between person, groups and the physical environment. Hence modes of behaviour, at a given time and in a given group, can impact upon the psychology of a person as a group member. Irrespective of sex and group membership,[1] modes of behaviour provide for a grammar for the measurement of the success and failure of human action. They can vary across spaces of communication in the sense that the willingness to act or the initiative for interactions may be considered to be due to different factors. On the one side, persons can assume that their bodies are an autodynamic instrument which they can and ought to use in accordance with their own will,

---

[1] Recent studies by social historians have shown that, in Europe, sex differences have been described in predominantly biological categories only since the second half of the eighteenth century, until when it was believed that there were no physical differences between the sexes except for the sexual organs. See Claudia Honegger, *Die Ordnung der Geschlechter: Die Wissenschaften vom Menschen und das Weib 1750–1850* (Frankfurt, New York, 1991). Ruth Hubbard, *Women Look at Biology Looking at Women* (Rochester, N.Y., 1979). Evelyn Fox Keller, *Reflections on Gender and Science*, 2nd edn (London, 1995; first published London, 1985). Londa Schiebinger, *The Mind Has no Sex? Women in the Origins of Modern Science* (London, 1989). Cf. chapters IV and V.

where they depend mainly on themselves and where the decision upon the success or the failure of an action or an interaction depends mainly on the intensity by which persons can act without the support of others. On the other side, the human body can also be perceived heterodynamically, namely in such a way that the willingness to act among persons and the initiative for interactions among persons, groups and the physical environment are believed to originate in an external source outside a person's body and where the decision upon success and failure of an action or interaction depends mainly on the degree by which a person can avail him- or herself of the assistance of other human or non-human agents. In groups in which autodynamic modes of behaviour are standard, it will be common to appreciate persons who act on their own as much as possible and do so in accordance with their own wishes and desires, whereas it will be uncommon to praise them for their determination to seek advice from others and to wait for help in order to succeed. The reverse is the case in groups in which heterodynamic modes of behaviour prevail. The change between these two modes of behaviour constitutes the conceptual history of the body. In the case of Europe, a change occurred from heterodynamic to autodynamic modes of behaviour.

Heterodynamic modes of behaviour in the early Middle Ages

In the early Middle Ages, long-distance migrations loomed large, the physical environment was often regarded as hostile and dangerous, and weather, plants and animals posed numerous threats against the human individual. Under such circumstances, it was hardly surprising that persons were convinced that their lives depended on the reception of energies from the outside, be it from other living group members, deceased ancestors, rulers, a divine agency or other superhuman forces in the physical environment. The human body was thus regarded as the recipient of various external influences and pressures, negative as well as positive in kind. Hence, in the same way as the group determined space in the early Middle Ages, the group, together with a divine agency or other superhuman forces in the physical environment, also shaped the identity of its members and awarded its members their rank and legal status. Group members conducted their lives under the impression that, whatever they could or ought to accomplish, was possible only insofar as each member acted in agreement with the behavioural and legal norms accepted by the group and with the stipulations which were taken to have been released by the divine agency or superhuman forces in the physical environment.

Adherence to heterodynamic modes of behaviour becomes evident from a large variety of early medieval records, among them the following incident reported by Procopius of Caesarea (c. 500–c. 562) in the sixth century. Procopius tells the story of the end of the Heruli of Singedon as a political group. Some of the Heruli had migrated from Scandinavia, and a branch of them, under the rule of a king, had settled in the vicinity of the Roman town of Singedon in the Balkans. After the death of one of their kings, the Singedon

Heruli had to search for a successor, says Procopius, and they decided to dispatch an embassy to their homelands in what is southern Sweden today in order to select their new king. The reason for this procedure was that the Heruli, as did many late Migration Age political groups, believed that they could select their rulers only from among the members of a specifically royal kin group within which the signs and symbols of royalty were exclusively inherited. The royal kin group of the Heruli had continued to live in their homelands. According to Procopius, the embassy was expected to be on its way for a long time because it had to cover the distance of some 2000 km each way. But the journey lasted even longer than anticipated because the first chosen candidate died on the way back. The embassy had to return to Scandinavia to choose another candidate. In the meantime, the Singedon Heruli had given up the embassy, believing that too much time had passed since their departure. Instead of continuing to wait, they decided to approach the Roman Emperor in Byzantium, Justinian, and asked him to send a new candidate whom they could elect as king. Indeed, Justinian found a Herulian hostage living in Byzantium and sent this person to Singedon, where he was accepted and chosen as king. However, soon after the election, the embassy returned from Scandinavia with the candidate from the royal kin group. As soon as the news of the arrival of the new candidate spread, the Heruli defected from the king who had been sent by Justinian and elected the newly arrived candidate. The defection led to serious, though unspecified difficulties between the Heruli and the Emperor, after which the Singedon Heruli vanished from the records.[2]

The incident shows two characteristics of heterodynamic behaviour. First, following decades and even centuries of migration, the kinship ties between the migrant and the resident members of a political group remained virtually undisturbed. Such continuity was necessary, because it secured the persistence of the migrating group and, through that, the safeguard of its members. Specifically, institutions, such as kingship, could persist only under the condition that a royal kin group with the legitimacy of a recorded and accepted long hereditary tradition existed from among which kings could be chosen. Considerable efforts were deemed necessary in order to maintain traditions of kingship across long distances. Second, in the case that such continuity was in jeopardy, the group was also in danger. An alternative solution, namely the choice of a king from a non-traditional and non-royal kin group, provoked dissent rather than smoothing away the difficulties; in the end, the Singedon Heruli met with a fate which strikingly resembled that of most of the Migration Age groups, few of which continued beyond the eighth century.

From the early Middle Ages, we have a great variety of archaeological finds, mainly tombstones and pieces of decorative art, as well as textual sources which appear to demonstrate that not only groups but also persons were exposed to hazards of and threats from the environment. The incised stone in

---

2 Procopius, *War of the Goths*, cap. II/14–15 (various editions).

Fig. 8 A stone from Niederdollendorf (Rhine), c. 700. The stone shows a solitary warrior and two animal heads above his head. The animal heads are made to approach the arms of the warrior as if to bite them.

Figure 8 shows the picture of a solitary warrior who defends himself against a worm arching above his head. The worm has two heads on either side of its body and appears to attack the warrior with its open mouths. With his right hand, the warrior holds a shield against the worm while, with his left hand, he grabs the blade of his sword. His right arm is bent upwards to hold the shield and his left arm is bent downwards so as to reach towards the sword. Both arms together are depicted in the form of a swastika. It remains unclear from the picture whether the warrior wins the struggle, but the stone does convey the impression that the warrior has the willingness and the capability to fight.

It is well known from early medieval textual sources that willingness and capability to fight evil worms threatening the human world were the hallmark of outstanding persons. From the pre-Christian time, there is abundant evidence of dragon fights, mainly, but not exclusively in texts of English and Scandinavian origin. Among these texts, the Old English epic *Beowulf* contains accounts of an aged ruler who wants to fight the dragon alone using his shield, succeeds in killing the dragon, frees his people from the evil, but loses his own life in the fight.[3] In the twelfth-century account of Danish history written by Saxo Grammaticus (c. 1150–c. 1220), King Frotho fights the dragon for his own pride, kills the creature and lives on.[4] Legends of solitary dragon fighters also featured in the Bible[5] as they were prominent in stories about approximately 55 angels, such as Archangel Michael, and saints, such as St George. Psalm 90: 13 assured a believer that he or she would be enabled by the divinity to tread on a lion and a dragon. Early in the fifth century, St Augustine commented that the dragon stood for the underworld controlled by the devil and that it was the message of the psalm to support the belief that devout Christians could win over the world of evil. He also argued that the psalm was the means with which the devil tried to tempt Christ on the grounds that, according to Matthew 4: 6, the devil, tempting Christ, quoted this psalm.[6] Still in the early ninth century, Christ was described as a victorious war leader and depicted as the winner in struggles against a lion and a dragon, receiving support from God the Father.[7] (Figure 9)

Likewise, when persons were depicted as winners over environmental and other threats, they were shown to be assisted by swastika-shaped special victory helpers, such as the one which appears on the helmet illustrated in Figure 10. The presence of a victory helper seems to indicate that the javelin to be hurled by the mounted warrior will reach its target because the warrior can avail himself of the assistance of the victory helper. The message of the display on the helmet thus seems to be that even warriors can succeed in a hostile environment only with the help of superhuman forces.

Obviously, warriors of all ages can only win if they are willing and as long as they remain able to use their technical skills and physical strength. But they seem to have perceived themselves as being in need of more than technical skills and physical strength in the early Middle Ages. Although, in warfare, the contest was primarily one between human capabilities, there were perceived to be occasions where success and failure depended upon the availability or the lack of availability of supportive superhuman forces. Hence the solitary dragon fighters were different from common warriors in two respects, first, that they fought against non-human threats to the human world, and, second, that they acted on their own. Such solitary fighters, who were not in need of

3   *Beowulf*, vv. 884–97, 2200–323, 2337–41, 2345–54, 2522–4, 2529–537, ed. Frederick Klaeber, 3rd edn (Lexington, Mass., 1950), pp. 33–4, 82–9, 95.

4   Saxo Grammaticus, *Gesta Danorum*, cap. II/1–3, ed. J. Olrik, H. Raeder, vol. 1 (Copenhagen, 1931), pp. 36–7.

5   For example, Job 2: 7; Psalm 90: 13.

6   Augustine, *Enarrationes in psalmos LI–C*, ed. Eligius Dekkers, Jean Fraipont, CCSL 39 (Turnhout, 1990), p. 1254, 1275–6. Cf. Cassiodore, *Expositio psalmorum LXXI–CL*, ed. Marcus Adriaen, CCSL 98 (Turnhout, 1958), pp. 829, 834.

7   *Heliand*, vv. 1211b–78, 4198–293, ed. Otto Behaghel. 10th edn by Burkhard Taeger, Altdeutsche Textbibliothek IV (Tübingen, 1996), pp. 49–51, 150–3. Cf. Widukind of Corvey, *Rerum gestarum Saxonicarum libri tres*, cap. I/11, ed. H.-E. Lohmann, Paul Hirsch, MGH SS rer. Germ. (60), p. 18, mentions an aged warrior named Hathagat who when encouraging his fellow Saxons to continue battle grabbed a standard with a 'lion and a dragon' as proof of his own daringness. Widukind's phrase recalls psalm 90.

Fig. 9 Christ as victor over the lion and the dragon, ninth century. Stuttgart, Württembergische Landesbibliothek, Ms. Bibl. Fol. 23, fol. 107 verso, illustrating Psalm 90: 13. Note that the hand of God extends down from heaven in the upper part of the picture, symbolising divine support for the dragon fighter.

Fig. 10 Side of a helmet from Vendel (Sweden), seventh century. The ornament shows a mounted warrior hurling a javelin. A swastika-shaped victory helper is attached to the back side of the javelin.

Fig. 11 Crucifixus, ninth century. Stuttgart, Württembergische
Landesbibliothek, Ms. Bibl. Fol. 23, fol. 27 recto, illustrating Psalm 21: 19–22.
Christ is displayed with open eyes and the bodily features of a living person.

support from anyone else and could still accomplish their goals, were the
most extraordinary people, predestined to become rulers or other persons of
influence. Heterodynamic modes of behaviour thus stimulated body perceptions through which persons became recipients of support or pressures from
external sources, whereby the givers of support or pressure were the rulers,
divine agencies or superhuman forces, and the recipients were the common
people as the ruled.

Heterodynamic modes of behaviour were not only characteristic of the
pre-Christian world of the Migration Period and the early Middle Ages but
continued after the conversion to Christianity. Although the Catholic Church
was hostile towards the kin-group networks and tried to limit their influence
on believers, and although beliefs in support or pressures, conveyed upon the
common people from rulers, divine agents or superhuman forces in the
physical environment, were soon denounced as superstition, the heterodynamic mode of behaviour was retained in substance. This can be gleaned
from the following sources.

First, the Catholic church seems to have skilfully employed the pre-

Christian belief in the victory helper by combining with it the Christian legend of Constantine, who was recorded to have won a battle in 312 after he had seen the holy cross and had pledged to convert to Christianity in the case of his victory.[8] Following this legendary tradition, Christ came to be displayed on early medieval crucifixes as a winner who could convey safety and power to his followers (see Figure 11). In these as in other crucifixes, Christ is not represented as a human sufferer in great pain, but as the immortal divine triumphant victor of earthly struggles. Christ's extraordinariness is displayed through his ability to accomplish deeds which ordinary human beings could not without fear of death.

Second, the continuing belief that energy flows from the physical environment to the human individual is shown in early medieval book illuminations of Pentecost (See Figure 12). Here, the delivery of the Holy Spirit is depicted in the form of beams flowing outward from heaven; heaven symbolises the realm of the divinity, the beams, which in other illuminations may be replaced by a dove, manifest the belief that the human being is the recipient of energies of divine origin.

Third, there was the Carolingian custom of admonition among rulers and lay persons, by the clergy towards lay persons as well as among monks and nuns who, like St Boniface, would exchange advice, comfort and admonitions among themselves in their letters.[9] Again, this custom shows that the person was considered to be weak and frail and in need of support through the activities of others, be they persons of rank, divine agency or other superhuman forces.

By contrast, leading representatives of the Catholic church seem to have acted in accordance with an ideal through which they were represented as energetic men and women, outstanding in their Christ-like capabilities of resisting and fearlessly overcoming the dangers and restrictions imposed by the physical environment. A good case was the late seventh-century abbot and bishop St Wilfrid (c. 634–709) of Hexham in Northumbria who devoted his life to the establishment of a second archbishopric for Britain at York. To accomplish his grand goal, he travelled to Rome three times, using all journeys for missionary efforts. On one occasion, wrong winds drove his boat across the North Sea to the Frisian coast, where Wilfrid was shipwrecked. Using the time which he had to spend ashore before being able to continue his voyage, Wilfrid began the Christian mission among the Frisians and laid the foundations for a bishopric at Utrecht. On another occasion, he was expelled from Northumbria due to the enmity of the Northumbrian ruling kin group. Wilfrid left in order to present his case to the Pope in Rome and first went

---

8   Eusebius of Caesarea, *Vita Constantini*, cap. I/28 (*PG* 20, col. 943).
9   For the lay persons see Dhuoda, *Manuel pour mon fils*, cap. IV/1 [841–3], ed. Pierre Riché, Sources chrétiennes CCXXV (Paris, 1975), pp. 198–204. Charlemagne's *Admonitio generalis* of 789, ed. Alfred Boretius, *MGH Capit.* 1, No. 22, pp. 52–62, also falls into this category of text. See, for the clergy, Michael Tangl, ed., *Die Briefe des Heiligen Bonifatius und Lullus*, No. 9, 23, 27, 61, 64, 73–5. *MGH Epp. sel.* 1, pp. 4–7, 38–41, 47–9, 125–7, 146–58.

Fig. 12 Pentecost, Reichenau lectionary, eleventh century. Universitätsbibliothek Würzburg, M.p.th.q.5, fol. 32 recto. The human world receives energy from the physical environment.

south into the kingdom of Wessex, where he immediately began to preach, but did not stay long. Continuing his journey into Sussex, he found that this 'kingdom' was under the rule of a 'pagan' king whom he converted to Christianity and persuaded to agree to the foundation of a bishopric, which later came to be located at Selsey. Wilfrid died in 709 and, thus, did not live to see his grand goal of founding the archbishopric of York accomplished, but no one could or would deny that, when the archbishopric eventually came into existence in 735, this had been mainly the result of Wilfrid's incessant efforts.

This image of incessant missionary activity and indefatigable pursuit of his own goals was conveyed in the early eighth-century biography of Wilfrid, written by one of his followers[10] for the purpose of spreading his cult as a saint. Wilfrid's image was not uncommon as that of a saint. Indeed, seventh- and eighth-century saints, men and women alike, were venerated, even while alive, on the grounds of the strength of their influence upon others, and, consequently, sainthood was to be granted to those persons who could be credited with exceptional accomplishments for their actions. Consequently, it is not surprising to observe that members of some royal kin groups, specifically in the British Isles, were eager to seek affiliations with the Church and to acquire the paraphernalia of sainthood. They did so because sainthood carried with it the impression that the royal saints, like all other saints were sources of support and, for that matter, could be holders of political power.

Not only saints, but also rulers could employ Christianity for the purpose of continuing to act as the conveyors of support or to exert pressure upon the ruled. A good case, albeit a controversial one, was Charlemagne. Through a war that altogether lasted thirty years, he defeated the Saxons, among whom Christians had been in the minority early in the ninth century. Eventually succeeding in this show of strength, and forcing Saxons to adopt Catholicism as their religion, Charlemagne received ample praise in the ninth century for having acted as the apostle of the Saxons. He was also credited with the merit of having been able to use the language of weapons for the purpose of converting Saxons to Catholicism.[11] Likewise, in the ninth century, King Ramiro of Asturias (dec. 850) authorised an inscription in which he was given the title *famulus Christi* (servant of Christ), a title otherwise used by monks.[12] At the turn of the millennium, Emperor Otto III employed the preposterous title *servus Iesu Christi* (servant of Jesus Christ) in charters which were issued in his name while he was about to establish an archbishopric in the Polish town of Gniezno and a system of bishoprics in Hungary for missionary purposes. The title was controversial because it had been reserved for the

---

10 Eddius Stephanus, *The Life of Bishop Wilfrid*, cap. XIII, XXVI, XL, XLI, ed. Bertram Colgrave (Cambridge, 1927; repr. Cambridge, 1985), pp. 26–8, 52, 80–4.

11 *Translatio S. Liborii*, cap. 5, *MGH SS* 4, p. 151.

12 See Albrecht Haupt, 'Die spanisch-westgotische Halle zu Naranco und die nordischen Königshallen', *Monatshefte für Kunstwissenschaft* IX (1916), p. 245. Bede, *Historia ecclesiastica gentis Anglorum*, preface, ed. Bertram Colgrave, R. A. B. Mynors (Oxford, 1969), p. 2.

Apostles in the New Testament and its use for the emperor could be under-stood as the claim that the emperor's position was higher than that of the Pope of Rome.[13] Consequently, Christianity, as promoted by the Catholic Church, appealed to rulers and groups of higher rank more than to ordinary persons. Among the common people, the perception of the human body as poor, frail, weak and subject to pressures and restrictions from the physical environment shaped their heterodynamic mode of behaviour. Even under the impact of Christianity, this mode of behaviour continued to suggest that the pressures and restrictions imposed by the physical environment could only be resisted or overcome through the association of persons into groups under the leadership of an extraordinary person with outstanding capabilities.

Such fears were by no means unfounded. Palaeopathological research has disclosed skeletal finds which exhibit a wide variety of diseases inflicting con-siderable and incessant pain upon human beings, first and foremost of which were bone and tooth aches. In the late sixth century, Bishop Gregory of Tours (538/9–after 593) wrote an account of the history and activities of the Frankish kings. On many occasions, he described violent injuries which the persons inflicted upon each other, and he has one account of King Sigibert the Lame (dec. c. 508) who had one of his knees destroyed in battle, but con-tinued to act as a military leader.[14] It is difficult to believe that Sigibert could have done so without extensive pain or other serious handicaps. There are also skulls that show major fractures resulting from physical violence, probably in the context of military action, from which the sufferers survived for a while. It is equally difficult to imagine that such victims of physical violence could ever have recovered to lead a normal life.

On the other side, there are also early medieval archaeological finds which show that weapons and agricultural tools did demand a great deal of physical strength for their handling. Hence, we must assume that the ordinary person had in fact a considerable amount of physical strength available. Nevertheless, such manifest physical strength may have mattered little in view of the hard-ships conditioned by the physical environment, the persistence of pain, muti-lations and incurable diseases. Rather, we have to imagine that, at the time, physical strength was measured, not with regard to the ordinary life and the labours or toils of daily work, but in connection with political and military leadership. The implication was that, through its own legendary tradition of conveying victories and success, the spreading of Christianity was greatly eased among those of high rank whose task it was to display and radiate the physical strength which appeared as essential as a conveyor of energy for the ordinary people in their own daily struggles.

13 Theodor Sickel, ed., *MGH DD Otto III*, No. 344–61, 366, 375, all AD 1000. The use of the apostolic title may have been influenced by a phrase in the *Life of Constantine*, cap. I/6, (*PG* 20, col. 917) by Eusebius of Caesarea who described the emperor as the 'ser-vant of the highest lord'.

14 Gregory of Tours, *Historiarum Francorum Libri X*, cap. II/37, ed. Bruno Krusch, Wilhelm Levison, *MGH SS rer. Merov.* 1, pp. 87–8.

The devictorisation of leaders

However, the victory-conveying capabilities of Christianity entailed the fundamental difficulty that the leading representatives of the universal Catholic Church had to cope with self-reliant, intrusive and power-acquiring particularistic local lay ruling élites who were themselves determined to take possession of and control church institutions. Consequently, immediately after the conversion of the ruling élites, the Church had to make a difficult choice between its own acceptance of the superiority of the ruling élites and the delay of the conversion process. Initially, the Church opted for the first choice, but it later made extensive efforts towards regaining control of its own institutions and enforcing abidance by the universalistic beliefs which the Church took to be its major task to promote. These efforts included the revision of the bodily image of Christ and of the saints as the major ecclesiogene symbols for modes of behaviour. Since the tenth century, the image of physical strength of the bodies of Christ and the saints gradually waned. The process first touched upon the representation of the bodies of royal saints, that is those saints whose kin group was royal or who had been kings themselves. Conspicuously, St Edmund, King of East Anglia, who had been murdered by Danish Vikings, perhaps in 870, came soon to be venerated as a local saint, and his cult was not then directly controlled by central church institutions. But at the end of the tenth century, the Church began to supervise the cult and centralised the veneration of St Edmund in an abbey church which was to be erected in East Anglia at a place that was to bear the saint's name (Bury St Edmunds). A well-known hagiographer was invited from the continent, Abbot Abbo of Fleury (c. 940–1004), to write the biography of the saint, and the Church took great care to disseminate the cult by way of sending out copies of Abbo's *Life of Saint Edmund*. The image which was created by Abbo about St Edmund differed fundamentally from the description of St Wilfrid's deeds in the early eighth century. Abbo described St Edmund as a frail sufferer, who gained martyrdom by wilfully exposing himself to cruel and painful tortures, before he was eventually put to death.[15] Hence late tenth-century hagiography emphasised physical suffering and reinstalled the ancient image of the saint as the victim rather than the victor. This image was much more befitting to the monks and clergymen who ruled the Church than to rulers and lay kin groups. Consequently, the number of royal saints has plummeted since the tenth century. But the new image was ultimately also applied to rulers. Early in the eleventh century, Emperor Henry II and his wife received praise for their asceticism, especially for what was supposed to be their virgin marriage life, and in the twelfth century, King

---

[15] Abbo of Fleury, *Passio Sancti Eadmundi regis ac martyris*, ed. Thomas Arnold, *Memorials of St. Edmund's Abbey*, vol. 1, Rerum Britannicarum medii aevi scriptores XCVI (London, 1890; repr. New York, 1965), pp. 15–16.

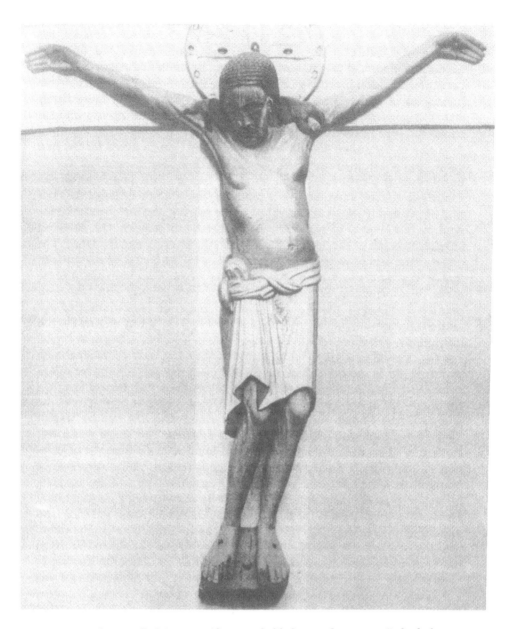

Fig. 13 The so-called Gero crucifixus, probably late tenth century. Cathedral Church in Cologne. Christ is displayed as a dead person, with his eyes closed.

Henry I of England could be depicted as dreaming about dangerously rioting peasant farmers and knightly aristocrats trying to murder him in the future.[16] In the same century, historiographers, such as William of Newbury (1125/38–1198), included a plethora of ghost stories in their narratives and conveyed the impression that there was little possibility for human beings to resist the activities of these evil-doers.[17]

The same process of devictorisation and the increasing sense of bodily frailty also became explicit in changes in the image of Christ at the same time. Early in the eleventh century, the chronicler Ademar of Chabannes recorded a vision of his own which he retrospectively dated in the year 1010. He claimed to have seen a suffering Christ on the bleeding crucifix, which he took to be an indication of the coming end of the world.[18] Already by the end of tenth century, crucifixes were made which portrayed Christ as a mortal sufferer (see Figure 13); one of them even decorated the crown worn by the emperors since the turn of the eleventh century at the latest. Through these images the painfulness of crucifixion was dramatically implanted in believers' minds.

The new image was that of a Christ who was the pale, cadaverous bearer of earthly sins with profusely bleeding wounds. It entailed a perception of the human body as not only frail, but also as the sinful prison of the soul, and led to a sense of asceticism among believers who sought to castigate their bodies in a Christ-like image with the ultimate goal of achieving a mystical union between themselves and Christ.

This combination of mysticism and asceticism peaked in the twelfth, thirteenth and fourteenth centuries, when wandering mendicant friars, beguines and beghards, as well as an astonishingly large number of children opted for a life of poverty, refused to eat and keep their bodies clean, sought to become infected with diseases, and castigated themselves in private. They did so because they were convinced that such was necessary in order to achieve a life in Christ and to acquire the paraphernalia of sainthood. At the same time, literary descriptions of the human body as rotting, worthless and no more than the temporary earthen residence of the eternal spirit loomed large. In the fourteenth century, these descriptions peaked in the disgusting though controversial classification of the human body as a 'night soil pail with nine holes'.[19] The heterodynamic expression of bodily weakness and imperfection could hardly be more dramatic.

---

[16] Ms. Corpus Christi College Oxford 157, fol. 382 verso.

[17] William of Newbury, *Historia rerum Anglicarum*, cap. V/24, ed. Richard Howlett, *Chronicles of the Reigns of Stephen, Henry II and Richard I*, vol. 2, Rerum Britannicarum medii aevi scriptores LXXXVIII (London, 1885; repr. New York, 1965), pp. 474–82.

[18] Ademar of Chabannes, *Chronique*, cap. III/46–7, ed. Jules Chavanon (Paris, 1897), pp. 168–71.

[19] Johann von Tepl [John of Saaz], *Ackerman*, cap. XXIV, ed. Willy Krogmann. 4th edn, Deutsche Klassiker des Mittelalters, N. F. I (Wiesbaden, 1978), pp. 125–6. The text is a fictitious dialogue between Death and a farmer whose beloved wife had died. The phrase occurred in a statement by Death and is being refuted by the farmer in his reply which is contained in cap. XXV, pp. 126–8.

The emergence of autodynamic modes of behaviour

It is difficult to specify the groups which were affected by these radically heterodynamic modes of behaviour beyond the ordained clergy and lay clerics. Virtually no records exist with regard to peasant farmers before the fourteenth century. However, the appearance of the above quotation in a literary text about peasant farmers may indicate that heterodynamic modes of behaviour were widespread in the countryside.[20] Nevertheless, during the high and late Middle Ages, there were two groups which were only marginally affected by the otherwise increasing mysticism and asceticism; they were the emerging military aristocracy of the knights and the urban patriciate of merchant traders. To be sure, asceticism and mysticism also occurred among members of these groups; most noteworthy was the career of St Francis of Assisi who gave up his status as a member of the urban patriciate to become a mendicant friar. But St Francis was noteworthy because, among his group, he was exceptional. Unlike St Francis, merchant traders opted for an image of their bodies characterised by self-reliance, the search for independence and competitiveness. They appreciated their temporal existence within the human world and optimistically believed that the human will and human efforts could improve the conditions of their lives.[21] The crucial means to accomplish this goal was the exchange of goods so as to allow a more variegated, cultivated and enjoyable way of life. As the organisers and performers of trade, these merchants soon developed into monetary professionals and, by the end of the eleventh century, established themselves as indispensable to the organisation of local and long-distance trade. Equipped with special privileges, they, together with specialised artisans and craftsmen, settled in specific communities, encircled by walls and marked out as market towns and cities under a special jurisdiction. These towns and cities were separated from the surrounding countryside and soon developed into autonomous entities in southern and central Europe.

During and after the eleventh century, town dwellers developed a habit of building magnificent houses of stone,[22] loved market entertainment and lavish festivals,[23] launched daring business enterprises and trading guilds, had their sons trained in urban professional schools for law and medicine, such as

---

20 See also the Nackenheim *weistum* of 1510 in Jacob Grimm, ed., *Weisthümer*, vol. 4 (Göttingen, 1863; repr. Darmstadt, 1957), pp. 594–6.
21 Geoffrey Chaucer, 'Canterbury Tales: The Shipman's Tale', Chaucer, *The Works*, ed. F. N. Robinson (Oxford, New York, 1985), pp. 156–60 (first published Boston, 1933).
22 In the early Middle Ages, stone structures had been built mainly for ecclesiastical purposes and occasionally for rulers at royal vills. See, for the Carolingian royal vill of Annapes (c. 810), Alfred Boretius, ed., *MGH Capit.* 1, No. 128, p. 254. For monasteries built of stone, see the ideal plan of a monastery preserved in St Gall. Cf. Konrad Hecht, *Der St. Galler Klosterplan* (Sigmaringen, 1983), pp. 221–45.
23 Willian FitzStephen, 'Descriptio nobilissimae civitatis Londoniae', ed. Susan Reynolds, Wiebe de Boer, Gearoid Mac Niocall, *Elenchus fontium historiae urbanae* (Leiden, New York, Copenhagen, Cologne, 1988), p. 76–85.

in the newly established urban universities of Salamanca, Salerno, Padua or Bologna, and gave names to their daughters which expressed concerns for beauty and virtue. In other words, contrary to the otherwise widespread belief in the inescapable weakness and sinfulness of human existence, the towns-people appreciated bodily beauty and demanded the willingness to make use competitively of whatever physical energies as well as intellectual and technical skills were contained in their bodies, for the ultimate goal of doing whatever could be done to improve the conditions of life. For example, when a strong earthquake hit the Alpine regions in January 1348 damaging mainly the stone structures in the towns and cities, the inhabitants took the initiative, gathered what remained of their wealth and began to reconstruct their dwelling places. Hence, much as the physical environment continued to be seen as a threat to human activity, the urban traders, artisans and scholars, as the three major groups of inhabitants of urban communities, adopted an autodynamic mode of behaviour and accepted it as their task to use their own bodily energies and financial capabilities to overcome the disaster.[24]

Hence it was in the urban communities of towns and cities where the demand first arose that difficulties and restrictions which appeared to be raised against the perfectibility of human life ought to be overcome by human initiative and self-controlled efforts rather than by trust in or awe towards the support or pressures issued by members of ruling kin groups, divine agents and supernatural forces in the physical environment. Such demands required a new perception of the human body, for which the twelfth-century correspondence between Abelard and Héloïse contains some early indications. Abelard was made to say that everything can be used to meet the demands of the body while whatever is used should be consumed with consideration and temperance.[25] Thus it was in the towns and cities that the intellectual and technical means were developed during the twelfth, thirteenth and fourteenth centuries which supported the optimism that this demand for the use of human initiative and physical energies contained in the body was just and that the common people could act in accordance with it. Even if they otherwise had little in common, the traders, craftsmen and scholars joined in efforts to meet these demands.

In the case of the knights, it was self-evident that the acquisition and preservation of physical strength was a goal to be accomplished, especially because techniques of cavalry warfare, spreading since the eleventh century, demanded the building of heavy armouries which, in turn, required substantive energies for their handling. Moreover, fighting on foot with the sword

---

24 *Annales Frisacenses*, ed. Ludwig Weiland, *MHG SS* 24, p. 67. Hermann Wiessner, ed., *Die Kärntner Geschichtsquellen 1335–1414*, No. 340, 867, Monumenta historica ducatus Carinthiae X (Klagenfurt, 1968), pp. 121, 270–1. Remarkably, much to the dismay of the lord of the town, the inhabitants of the badly hit town of Villach in Carinthia rebuilt their own houses first before turning to the rebuilding of the town walls.
25 J. T. Muckle, ed., 'The Letter of Heloise on Religious Life and Abelard's First Reply', *Mediaeval Studies* 17 (1955), pp. 256–7.

also came to demand even greater physical strength than during the early Middle Ages, because, since the thirteenth century, the length and weight of the swords increased. Such changes necessitated the training of the body for physical fitness together with flexibility and moveability for fights on foot and on horseback. Hence, it is no surprise that the period witnessed the widening reception of the fourth-century Roman military-drill manual by Flavius Vegetius Renatus who had written extensively on the necessity of training soldiers for physical strength as a condition for military success.[26] However, contrary to the early Middle Ages, during the thirteenth, fourteenth and fifteenth centuries physical strength no longer legitimised political power, but was then a condition for recognition as a member of the knightly aristocracy. This aristocracy formed a social group of military professionals who were employed for military service by the rulers, who could themselves claim to be, but by no means always were, military professionals. Next to the merchant traders, it is within this social group of aristocratic military professionals that the autodynamic demand for the physical strength of the body, coupled with a sense of self-reliance, independence and competitiveness, was upheld against the ascetic image of bodily frailty.

The aristocratic fighting habit became most explicit in the highly stylised and ceremonial, though risky, jousts. The jousts were sequences of engagements between two mounted competitors. There were breaks in between the sequences when hits could be counted and listed. There were also foot tournaments with two competitors trying to strike at each other with swords. In both cases, the preferred aristocratic way of fighting was the straightforward, unilinear strike against the opponent, and the rules for the tournaments strictly prohibited bodily twists, turns, bents and feints. The tournaments thus displayed the dominant aristocratic mode of fighting, namely the use of a person's bodily energies in order to hit an opponent as directly and as soon as possible in dual combats. To that end, military strategy consisted in the choice and preparation of the battlefield so that it was best suited to stand against the primal shock of the opponent, to force the opponent to open his ranks and to allow the continuation of the battle in dual combats. Even non-aristocratic fighting forces, such as the armies of peasant and urban Swiss infantrymen, followed this strategy well into the sixteenth century.

Although aristocrats had settled in urban communities of towns and cities in northern Italy since the early eleventh century, it was not before the fourteenth century that the worlds of the knights and of the urban merchant traders which had originally separated between town and country, began to merge as more knights became residents in towns and cities. One indicator is the spreading of aristocratic fighting techniques as the martial arts of the towns and cities where the profession of fencing masters began to flourish in

---

26 For one, see Geoffrey Lester, ed., *The Earliest English Translation of Vegetius 'De Re Militari',* ed. *from Oxford MS Bodl. Douce 291,* cap. I/6–19, Middle English Texts XXI (Heidelberg, 1988), pp. 53–66. Cf. Walter de Milemete, *De nobilitatibus sapientus et prudentiis regum,* ed. Montague Rhodes James (London, 1913), pp. 124–6.

Fig. 14 From Hans Talhoffer's fencing manual, Ambraser Codex, c. 1430. Ms. Vienna, Kunsthistorisches Museum, Waffensammlung, KK 5079, plate 89.

the late fourteenth century.[27] The fencing masters trained the inhabitants of towns and cities in variants of the martial arts of the aristocrats, including sword fencing and duelling, and composed measured sequences of guards and bouts (Latin *mensurae*) which their customers were to learn. The modes of behaviour underlying urban fencing resembled those of aristocratic warriors. Early fifteenth-century pictorial manuals displayed fencers in positions from out of which they could strike against an opponent with a sword or a lance in sequences which were modelled upon the tournament (see Figure 14).

The two fencers shown in Figure 14 thrust straight at each other. Their bodies lean towards each other and they direct their energies against each other. A leg stretched out to the back and the upper part of the body form almost a straight line. Hence both fencers adopt positions in which, while they use their energies against each other, they trust that the opponent will continue to push straight without twists or turns. The townspeople also imitated the aristocratic tournament in their own way. If there was a river near the town, they placed rowers in two boats together with a man in each boat who held a stick similar to the lance of an aristocrat. The rowers steered the boats towards each other as fast as possible until each of the two sticks crashed against the man in the opposite boat, either broke or sent one or both of them

---

[27] See Fiore dei Liberi, *Flos duellarum in armis, sine armis, equester, pedester*, ed. Francesco Novati (Bergamo, 1902). Hans Talhoffer, *Fechtbuch (Ambraser Codex)*, ed. Gustav Hergsell (Prague, 1889).

Fig. 15 Dance at the court of Yon of Gascoigne, c. 1489. Ms. Paris, Bibliothèque de l'Arsenal, Ms. franç. 5073, fol. 117 verso, Cliché Bibliothèque nationale de France, Paris.

into the water.[28] These contests were less hazardous than aristocratic tournaments, but still there was the risk of drowning for those joining the contests without being able to swim.

While it was recognised that fencing and duelling was a serious martial art with potentially lethal consequences, similar rules were applied for such leisure-time activities as dancing. In the course of the fourteenth century, dancing masters began to compose choreographies with precisely measured paces and sequences (French *mesures,* from Latin *mensurae*) and to train their aristocratic lords and urban customers in the art of enacting them. The preferred dances were slow and straightforward ceremonial step dances, as Figure 15 shows. These dances were processions in the course of which the dancers were expected to observe meticulously the prescribed steps to the front or backwards or some little hops as they moved on.

Hence, the knights' and merchant traders' worlds began to impact upon one another, and created an atmosphere where knightly efforts towards the

28 An early report is in FitzStephen's description of London (see note 23).

Fig. 16 Antonio del Pollaiuolo, Men fighting, c. 1475. Berlin, Staatliche Museen
Preußischer Kulturbesitz, Kupferstichkabinett. The picture shows men with lavish muscles
who use their own bodies as a source of physical energy. Photo: Bildarchiv Preußischer
Kulturbesitz. Photographer: Jörg P. Anders (1999).

training of the body for fitness, flexibility and moveability were introduced
into the urban communities of towns and cities, while the knights began to
dispatch some of their kin to the towns for study at the urban universities. By
the fifteenth century, this autodynamic cultural amalgam of quests for bodily
strength, intellectual skills and professional achievement created a sentiment
which was powerful enough to replace the previous heterodynamic image of
bodily frailty as the dominant modes of behaviour.[29] While much of the traditional modes of behaviour continued among peasant farmers and the
growing underprivileged groups of poor residents in the towns and cities well
into the eighteenth century, the new demands became accepted by political,
military, ecclesiastical, trading élites and intellectual opinion leaders. From
the beginning of the fifteenth century in southern Europe and elsewhere,
eventually, around 1500, the majority of them underwrote the demand that
everyone should use his or her own energies for the purpose of acquiring
physical strength, intellectual skills and professional achievements.

A new perception of the human body thus emerged, the essentials of which

---

[29] See Leon Battista Alberti, *I libri della famiglia*, ed. Renée Neu Watkins, *The Family in Renaissance Florence* (Columbia, S.C., 1969), p. 63.

are displayed in the drawing shown in Figure 16, which is from the second half of the fifteenth century. The human body came to be depicted and described as energetic, enduring and as a source of original, not divinely ordained, creative activity. The fighting men bend, turn and twist their bodies freely, they thrust and strike from many different positions and in many different directions, and they avail themselves of their own physical energies. Unlike their early fifteenth-century predecessors, they were no longer willing to stick to rules which limited the choice of their movements.[30]

The change can best be seen in the examples of the two prints in Figures 17 and 18. The first is a woodcut depicting the balance of power at the time of Emperor Frederick III, father of Maximilian I. The woodcut shows the pope and the emperor holding each other on top of the mast of a ship which, according to an inscription on its planks, symbolises the dukes of Austria. The mast is held upright by ropes representing the King of Hungary, the King of Poland, and the Duke of Bavaria. The emperor places his right foot on the back of a *lion couchant,* being the Duke of Burgundy, and stretches his left foot out towards a spindle representing Bohemia. He holds the broken upper part of the spindle in his left hand. In this position, the emperor gains stability because the pope, with his left foot on the mast and his right foot close to the spindle, holds the emperor's upper body with this left arm. The pope has a pair of scales in his right hand, which signifies *roma* and is placed above the spindle. Immediately above the scales, in the upper left part of the woodcut, a fleur-de-lis is shown to be the representation of the King of France, and, further above that, we find an eagle standing for the Empire. In the lower right part, we see a truncated tree, bearing the inscription *Jherusalem,* from which another fleur-de-lis hangs. In the upper right, there is a comet, which is identified as the origin of the sibyllinic prophecies related to the approaching end of the world. The beams of the comet touch the head of the *lion couchant,* somehow attached to the mast of the ship, and the bodies of the emperor and the pope.

The bodies of the emperor and of the pope are depicted naked, in a style following the conventions of fifteenth-century painting, as frail beings, devoid of physical strength, with thin arms and legs, without muscle. The emperor and the pope appear with few features indicating their individuality; instead, they are shown as anthropomorphic representations of their respective roles and as temporary incumbents of the traditions of their respective offices. The bodies seem to be weightless, receiving their energy from the outside through the beams of the comet, and, as it were, hovering in space, for the artist leaves it open as to whether the emperor has his foot on the spindle or not. What keeps them in balance is not their own physical strength, but an external force.

This woodcut, apparently a piece of papal propaganda, was reissued in Italy in the early sixteenth century, with significant stylistic differences. In the

---

30 Hans Lecküchner, *Der altenn Fechter anfengliche Kunst* (Frankfurt, 1531) (repr. *Flugschriften-Sammlung Gustav Freytag.* Mikrofiche ed. No. X/1422).

Fig. 17 Emperor and Pope on the mast of a ship, c. 1470. Washington, National Gallery of Art, Rosenwald Collection. Inv.-No. 1943.3.9128 (B-11196)/PR.

later woodcut (Figure 18), the beams of the comet no longer touch the bodies of the protagonists, because the comet remains detached, with only one beam touching the *lion couchant*. It appears as a source of light rather than as a source of energy for the acting protagonists. Their actions are depicted as resulting from the energies incorporated in their own bodies. Consequently, the sixteenth century artist shows the muscle which the pope uses for the purpose of holding the emperor, and which the emperor uses for the purpose of grasping the broken spindle. Thus the balance emerges from the use of energies which are contained in the bodies of the protagonists themselves. Moreover, the sixteenth-century artist made an effort to depict the protagonists as having some weight; for example, they are shown to rest firmly on the mast of the ship, the *lion couchant* or the spindle.

The difference in both representations of the balance of power reflects the change from heterodynamic to autodynamic modes of behaviour. Whereas in the fifteenth-century woodcut, both representatives of universalistic powers do not act according to their own impetus, but upon divine will or some supernatural force for which the comet stands as a representation, in the sixteenth-century woodcut, the protagonists act on their own behalves and use the energies contained in their bodies in order to achieve their respective goals.

The concept of the autodynamic mode of behaviour must not be confused with the concept of individualism, for, even though both concepts have been fused in Europe since the later fifteenth century, they can be traced to different origins. While the concept of the autodynamic mode of behaviour focuses on specific interactions between the human body and the social or physical environment, the concept of individualism refers to a tendency of the individual to emphasise his or her own significance, wishes and desires *vis-à-vis* those of other group members. The more radical individualists of the twelfth and thirteenth centuries, such as Emperor Frederick II or the mendicant St Francis of Assisi, unequivocally subscribed to the heterodynamic modes of behaviour current in their times. Vice versa, such early radical proponents of autodynamic modes of behaviour as the fourteenth-century philosopher William Ockham (1285/90–1348) or the fourteenth-century merchant trader Francesco Datini of Prato (c. 1335–1410), or, during the fifteenth century, Pope Pius II or King George of Podiebrad, the Hussite ruler of Bohemia, can hardly be associated with tendencies of claiming for their own lives and personalities a particular (and, for that matter, higher) importance or respect which they were unwilling to grant to others in their own group.

One important source for the rise of individualism is the spread of autobiography from the fourteenth century, which indicated that persons developed concerns for their own identity and ranked it above their group affiliations. Around 1500, the fusion of individualism with autodynamic modes of behaviour was best illustrated and propagated by Emperor Maximilian I, who tirelessly compelled himself and his aides and servants, warriors and artists, not only to assert themselves as individuals, but also to make use of the physical

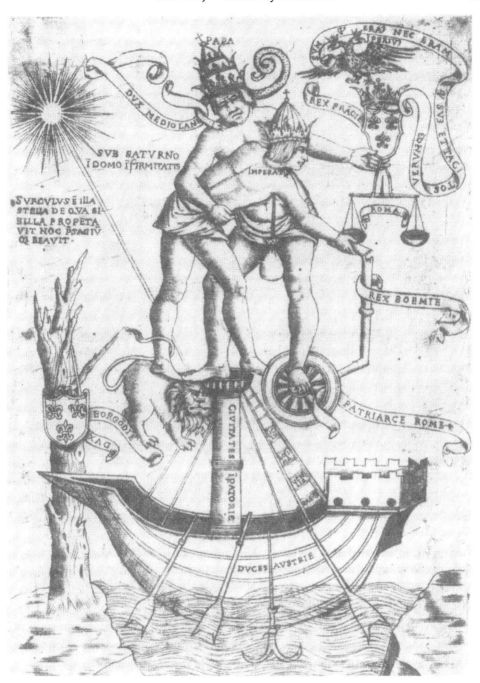

Fig. 18 Emperor and pope on the mast of a ship, early sixteenth century. © Copyright The British Museum.

Fig. 19 Emperor Maximilian I fighting a foot tournament with Leonhard
Rueshaimer, early sixteenth century. Vienna, Kunsthistorisches Museum,
Waffensammlung, Ms. KK 5073, fol. 3 recto.

energies, intellectual and technical skills contained in their bodies[31] and to
engage in manifold and not necessarily serious activities for their own benefit.
He encouraged the lansquenets, his own fighting force of infantrymen, to
practice a training formation that differed fundamentally from the tournaments with their straightforward movements. It consisted of a circular movement in the course of which the members of a band of pikemen would array
themselves into ranks and files, move in a circular fashion while drifting
slowly to the outside, stop upon the command of their leader and charge their

---

31 Maximilian, *Weisskunig* (Vienna, 1775; repr. Weinheim, 1985), pp. 76–101. Likewise,
Giovanni Pico della Mirandola, 'Oratio de hominis dignitate', Pico, *Opera omnia*, vol. 1
(Basle, 1557; repr. Hildesheim, New York, 1969), pp. 314–15. Alberti (see note 29), pp.
167–9.

Fig. 20 Urban dance, sixteenth century. From the Nuremberg Schembart book, Stadtbibliothek Nürnberg, Ms. Nor. K. 444, fol. 1 recto. Dancers enact a row dance with musicians accompanying them. They turn and twist their bodies in many different ways, some jump, while others stretch their legs to make a huge step ahead.

pikes into the direction which the band leader commanded.[32] In this way, the lansquenets, like the fencers late in the fifteenth century, were accustomed to turn and to strike into many different directions. Performances of martial arts and of exuberant festivals attracted many participants who were ready to join in such activities. Likewise, dancers were taught to enact circular movements in addition to the steps to the front and to the back.[33]

Participants of many walks of life thus joined in displays of their bodily energies. In doing so they adopted equilibrium positions which allowed twists and turns into many different directions as well as jumps and other extravagant and energetic movements. Legs stretched out to the back did not any more form a straight line with the upper parts of the bodies, which were kept upright and flexible. Dancers were trained not only to move forwards or backwards, but also to enact circular movements. Fencers and dancers tried to

---

[32] First recorded for the year 1488 by Jean Molinet, *Chroniques*, ed. Jean-Alexandre Buchon, vol. 2 (Paris, 1828), pp. 207–8. Another edn by Georges Doutrepont, vol. 1 (Brussels, 1935), pp. 587–8.

[33] One of these dances was the *Verçeppe* referred to as *scaramuccio* (skirmish) by Antonio Cornazzano, a dancing master who was also well versed in military strategy. Antonio Cornazzano, 'Libro dell' arte del danzare [1455]', ed. C. Mazzi, *La Bibliofilia* XVII (1916), pp. 18–20 (English edn s. t. *The Book of the Art of Dancing* [London, 1981]).

act independently and to keep as much space around themselves as possible so as to be able to move freely.

Maximilian himself had claimed to possess the capabilities of a daring warrior as well as a spectacular fencer and dancer, an efficient organiser and a prolific planner, a skilful merchant and shrewd negotiator, a successful administrator, a learned scholar and a lover of the arts. Not surprisingly, Maximilian took part in or attempted to dominate various preferred fields of innovative activities around 1500, such as extensive warfare, competitive sports, overseas trade and conquest, the advancement of scholarly knowledge and the reform of administrative institutions.[34]

Conclusion

The conceptual history of the body in European culture thus exhibits two overlapping processes. The first process led to the transformation of autodynamic into heterodynamic modes of behaviour. This process took place between the eleventh and the fourteenth centuries. It appears to have been the result of changes of kin-group structures which were in turn conditioned by the introduction of Christianity. The reduction of the kin groups proffered the reliance of persons on their own bodily energies and their own skills which they particularly sought to employ efficiently when they became settlers in urban communities of towns and cities. The second process concerned the emergence of individualism during the same period. Its proponents insisted that the wishes and desires of the individual should be awarded a higher importance than those pertaining to groups and institutions. The fusion of heterodynamic modes of behaviour and individualistic perceptions of the human body and its needs occurred around 1500.

34 For parallels, see Baldassare Castiglione, *The Book of the Courtier* (Venice, 1528). English version (London, 1561; repr., Tudor Translations I, 23 [New York, 1967]), pp. 54–5. Michel de Montaigne, *Œuvres complètes*, ed. Albert Thibaudet, Maurice Rat, vol. 1 (Paris, 1962), pp. 151–3. 'Here begynneth the note and trewth of the moost goodly behavior in the receyt of the Ladie Kateryne . . . yowen in mariage goinet to Prince Arthur, son and heir unto o[u]r noble Soferynge of Englond King Henry the VIIth, in the XVII yeare of his reign [1501]', ed. Francis Grose, F. G. Th. Astle, *The Antiquarian Repertory* II, 1 (1808), pp. 249–331. For criticisms specifically of extravagant dances, see Florian Daul, *Der Tantzteuffel* (Frankfurt, 1569; repr. ed. Kurt Petermann, Documenta choreologica VIII [Leipzig, 1978]), fols 6–23. Johann Münster, *Ein gotseliger Tractat von dem ungotseligen Tantz* (Frankfurt, 1594).

IV

Groups

Introduction

It has been a core assumption of nineteenth- and twentieth-century social theorists that societies are territorialised and ordered social systems under the government of norms and rules[1] and represent the paramount type of groups into which persons can enter, far outweighing the importance of other types of groups, such as kin, age groups, totem groups, neighbourhood, contractual, political and social groups. It has further been assumed that, although societies are not a primordial form of human social organisation, they represent the standard into which human social organisation has evolved or will evolve with some historical inevitability.[2]

These evolutionist assumptions can only be accepted on the basis of the nineteenth- and twentieth-century idea that societies resemble 'organic bodies' which engulf their members, are something more than the sum of their constitutive parts and require specific efforts for their formation and preservation. The model on which such a concept of 'society' is drawn is the living body. Because this model is biological, it has been consistent that theorists who have worked with it have usually felt justified in employing the metaphorical language of life and death in their analyses of societies. It cannot be denied that such evolutionist as well as biologistic theories of society have been helpful instruments to analyse and explain nineteenth- and twentieth-century European societies because, first and foremost, members of these societies in general, and not only social theorists, seem to have perceived

---

* The *gens* has received its name from the successions of kin groups, that is from being generated, in the same way as the *natio* has received its name from being born.

1 For an early reference, see Lorenz von Stein, *Geschichte der socialen Bewegung*, vol. 1 (Leipzig, 1850), p. 32.

2 See, among many, Albert Schäffle, *Bau und Leben des socialen Körpers*, vol. 4, 2 (Tübingen, 1881).

societies in evolutionist and biologistic terms. Nevertheless, the question arises whether such biologistic evolutionism is equally helpful for the study of groups which were in existence during the Middle Ages.

Doubts that an affirmative answer can be offered to this question were articulated already in the nineteenth century. Biologistic evolutionism was accused of being an overly simplistic theory of society based on no more than unverifiable analogues.[3] Even Johann Caspar Bluntschli (1808–81), a then leading social and political theorist, accepted the criticism that the concept of 'society' as engulfing all social relationships was partial, owed its origin to the bourgeoisie and was incompatible with the concept of the 'nation' as an all-inclusive political group: 'The entire concept of society in its social and political meaning has its natural basis in the customs and attitudes of the Third Estate. It is not an inclusive term for a nation, but always only a term characteristic of the Third Estate.'[4] The concept of 'society' has thus been recognised as a historical one, which means that society has been credited with a conceptual history of its own and must not be taken for granted. Instead of assuming a metaphysical or at least seemingly autonomous process of the 'integration' of various types of group into 'societies', the conceptual historian must specify the factors which contributed to this result.

Such an analysis can avail itself of the work of social anthropologists[5] and social historians[6] who suggest that persons were given a limited but crucial choice among various types of coevally existing groups, which have been identified as kin groups, totem groups, age groups, residential groups of neighbours, groups established by legally binding contractual agreements for a specific purpose, social groups subjected to certain common laws, and groups tied together by politically relevant religious beliefs or traditions of common origin. It has also been observed that all of these various types of group were governed by different sets of values, norms and rules and enforced various modes of behaviour. It can be shown that these types of group were of significance in medieval Europe, although, contrary to many other parts of the world, totem and age groups do not seem to have played any significant role there. The coexistence of vertically coordinated types of group can be ascertained from the fact that, up to the high Middle Ages, there was no generally applicable word whose meaning covered the full variety of existing types of group. The word 'group' itself, which is common to most European languages, was derived from an unknown origin and came into use only by

---

3   Albert Theodor van Krieken, *Ueber die sogenannte organische Staatstheorie* (Leipzig, 1873).

4   Johann Caspar Bluntschli, 'Gesellschaft', in Bluntschli, K. Bräter, eds, *Deutsches Staatswörterbuch*, vol. 4 (Stuttgart, Leipzig, 1859), p. 247.

5   George Caspar Homans, *The Human Group* (New York, 1950).

6   Otto Gerhard Oexle, 'Soziale Gruppen in der Ständegesellschaft', in Oexle, Andrea von Hülsen-Esch, eds, *Die Repräsentation von Gruppen*, VMPIG CXLI (Göttingen, 1998), pp. 9–44.

about the eleventh and twelfth centuries, although the ninth-century Old English word *geferscipe* came close to it in meaning.[7]

The pluralism of types of group was also inherent in the meaning of the Latin word *gens* which early medieval administrators, historians and social theorists used. Students of classical and early medieval ethnography and historiography as well as of legal records have long recognised that the word *gens* and its Greek counterpart γένος were used and sometimes interutilised with the words *natio, genus* and *genealogia,* as well as their Greek counterparts, in frequent references to a considerable variety of types of group which could range from small bands of men and women to specific representations of human character or even mankind as a whole. Among these various usages, the frequent oscillation between the use of the word *gens* for the concept of a group constituted by and maintained through beliefs in common descent, on the one hand[8] and, on the other, for the concept of groups with a distinct political tradition of its own is most interesting.[9] For example, at the time of the Roman Empire of Antiquity, talk about kin groups such as the *gens Iulia* or the *gens Claudia* was as frequent as there were descriptions of various politically active groups as *gentes* outside the Roman Empire, such as the 'Germanorum gentes'.[10] Likewise, in early medieval historiographic works, law codes and administrative records, we find notes about kin groups such as the 'gens nobilis Ayglolfinga' or the Bavarian 'genealogiae' as we come across references to political groups such as the 'gens Saxonum' or the 'gens

---

7   *The Old English Version of Boethius De Consolatione Philosophiae,* ed. Walter John Sedgefield (Oxford, 1899), p. 40. Similar meanings lurk behind the medieval use of such words as *fraternitas, societas* and *communitas* which could gloss *geferscipe* and were subsequently employed, among others, by Thomas Aquinas, *Contra Impugnantes Dei Cultum,* cap. 3, ed. Roberto Busa, *Sancti Thomae Aquinatis Opera omnia,* vol. 3 (Stuttgart, 1980), pp. 532–7. The word *societas* was also used as a technical term for armies or units of armed forces. See *Vita Edwardi secundi,* ed. William Stubbs, *Chronicles of the Reigns of Edward I and Edward II,* vol. 2, Rerum Britannicarum medii aevi scriptores LXXVI (London, 1883; repr. New York, 1965), p. 201.

8   For reviews, see Alfred Dove, *Studien zur Vorgeschichte des deutschen Volksnamens,* ed. Friedrich Meinecke, Sitzungsberichte der Heidelberger Akademie der Wissenschaften, Philos.-Hist. Kl. 1916, 8 (Heidelberg, 1916), pp. 34–5. Eugen Ewig, 'Volkstum und Volksbewußtsein im Frankenreich des 7. Jahrhunderts' in *Caratteri del secolo VII in occidente,* Settimane di studio del Centro Italiano di studi sull' alto medioevo V (Spoleto, 1958), pp. 626–8 (repr. Ewig, *Spätantikes und frühmittelalterliches Gallien,* vol. 1, Beihefte der Francia III [Munich, 1976], pp. 271–3). Patrick Geary, 'Ethnic Identity and Situational Construct in the Early Middle Ages', *Mitteilungen der Anthropologischen Gesellschaft Wien* CXIII (1983), pp. 22–5. Walter Pohl, 'Tradition, Ethnogenese und literarische Gestaltung', in Karl Brunner, Brigitte Merta, eds, *Ethnogenese und Überlieferung* (Vienna, 1994), pp. 10–11. Reinhard Wenskus, *Stammesbildung und Verfassung,* 2nd edn (Cologne, Vienna, 1977), pp. 38–9, 319–20 (first published Cologne, Graz, 1961). Herwig Wolfram, 'Gothic History and Historical Ethnography', *Journal of Medieval History* VII (1981), pp. 309–19.

9   See Wilhelm Emil Mühlmann, 'Ethnogonie und Ethnogenese', *Studien zur Ethnogenese,* Abhandlungen der Rheinisch-Westfälischen Akademie der Wissenschaften LXXII (Opladen, 1985), pp. 9–27.

10 Tacitus, *Germania,* cap. 44 (various editions).

Francorum'.[11] Similarly, a curious late seventh-century Mercian name list which seems to have been drawn up for administrative purposes,[12] contains side by side the names of groups whose members appear to be tied together by kin relations, groups whose members may have settled together in a local neighbourhood without kin relations, groups whose members will have been affiliated to each other through some voluntary contract, and groups which may have been constituted by common political traditions and experiences.

Consequently, the following analysis shall focus on the problem of the processes that led to the disappearance of the variety of types of group to which a person could choose to belong. Because age groups do not appear to have played a significant role in medieval European culture, they will therefore be omitted in this context.[13]

Kin groups

Kin groups are groups constituted by accepted beliefs about parent–child relationships. Kin groups can embrace the direct descendants of a couple together with collateral and affinal relatives; if they do, they tend to be large in size and unite persons from various places of residence into a social network with a potential for economic and political significance. The most general statement that can be made with regard to the history of European kin groups is that, during the Middle Ages, their shrinking size corresponded with the decline of their economic and political significance.

Before the acceptance of Christianity, the most widespread rule of inheritance in the kin groups was double descent, which allowed the tracing of descent through the maternal and the paternal lines; even if the paternal side was frequently preferred, the possibility of tracing one's descent through the maternal side gave ample influence to matrilateral kin. These double-descent kin groups were vertically arrayed, and each represented a social unit in itself. The rights, privileges, personal achievements, affluence and influence of a person depended on his or her kin group rather than on his or her own

11 Fredegar, *Chronicarum libri IV,* cap. IV/52, ed. Bruno Krusch, *MGH SS rer. Merov.* 2, p. 146. *Lex Baiwariorum,* cap. 3, 1, ed. Ernst von Schwind, *MGH LL nat. Germ.* 5, 2, pp. 312–13. Bede, *Historia ecclesiastica gentis Anglorum,* cap. V/11, ed. Bertram Colgrave, R. A. B. Mynors (Oxford, 1969), p. 486. Gregory of Tours, *Historiarum libri X,* cap. II/12, V/prol., VI/2, ed. Bruno Krusch, Wilhelm Levison, *MGH SS rer. Merov.* 1, pp. 61, 193, 266.

12 See Wendy Davies, Hayo Vierck, 'The Contexts of Tribal Hidage', *Frühmittelalterliche Studien* VIII (1974), pp. 223–93.

13 There are scraps of evidence on groups of young men in sources of Antiquity on western and northern Europe beyond the boundaries of the Roman Empire. But the significance of these groups was necessarily confined to a person's young age and, consequently, not a permanent feature of life. See Heinrich Härke, ' "Warrior Graves"? The Background of the Anglo-Saxon Weapon Burial Rite', *Past and Present* CXXVI (1990), pp. 22–43. Otto Höfler, *Kultische Geheimbünde der Germanen,* vol. 1 (Frankfurt, 1934), pp. 323–41. Lily Weiser, *Altgermanische Jünglingsweihen und Männerbünde,* Bausteine zur Volkskunde und Religionswissenschaft I (Bühl, 1927).

achievements and personal capabilities. That descent shaped the identity of kin members became explicit in the name-giving habits. In early medieval kin groups names were thus not chosen randomly or through some personal taste but in accordance with the traditions of the kin group. It was a common understanding in the early Middle Ages that names ought to allow the identification of the kin membership of a person.[14] Genealogical records have been preserved which show that kin members were given names which were taken over from other kin groups.[15] For example, the West Saxon royal kin group began to use names at the turn of the eighth century which had been common before in the Northumbrian royal kin group of Bernicia.[16] The reception of the Bernician names in Wessex can only be understood as the result of a marriage alliance between both kin groups through which the Bernician names migrated to Wessex. In this case, then, women could act as the inheritors of traditions of name giving, and this implies that women had the power to determine the identity of kin members. Likewise, there were memorial records which show that collateral kin groups included living and dead members and thereby provided an institutional framework which normally exceeded the lifetime of their members.[17]

In some kin groups, totems may have been used for the visual expression of this continuity. Eighth-century Lombard historiography recorded the tradition that the Lombards had had the group name Vinnili which they had changed in connection with a battle before beginning their migrations to northern Italy. At the time before the change of names, some Vinnili, perhaps high-ranking people who were related by kinship, had appeared on ritual occasions with totems in the form of dog heads,[18] and this report can be confirmed from hero lore which referred to Lombards as Hundings (hounds people).[19] Similar names are also on record for other groups, such as for the Myrgings, the horse people, probably of Saxon origin, or the Wuffingas or Wylfings, the wolf people of Scandinavian stock.[20] It so appears that the totems to which reference was made in some of these names served as visible

---

[14] See: Reinhard Wenskus, *Sächsischer Stammesadel und fränkischer Reichsadel*, AAWG XCIII (Göttingen, 1976).

[15] An eighth-century collection of genealogies of English kings has been edited by David N. Dumville, 'The Anglian Collection of Royal Genealogies', *Anglo-Saxon England* V (1976), pp. 23–50 (repr. in Dumville, *Histories and Pseudo-histories of the Insular Middle Ages*, Collected Studies Series CCCXVI (Aldershot, 1990), No. V).

[16] Dumville (see note 15), p. 34a.

[17] Mainly the so-called *libri memoriales*. See, for example, Eduard Hlawitschka, Karl Schmid, Gerd Tellenbach, eds, *Liber memorialis von Rémiremont*, MGH Libri memoriales I (Munich, 1970). Johanne Autenrieth, Dieter Geuenich, Karl Schmid, eds, *Das Verbrüderungsbuch der Abtei Reichenau*, MGH Libri memoriales et necrologia N. S. I (Hanover, 1979). Cf. Chapter I.

[18] *Origo gentis Langobardorum*, ed. Georg Waitz, *MGH SS. rer. Lang.*, pp. 2–3.

[19] *Widsith*, v. 23, 81, ed. Kamp Malone (Copenhagen, 1962), pp. 23, 25. See also Karl Hauck, 'Lebensnormen und Kultmythen in germanischen Stammes- und Herrschergenealogien', *Saeculum* VI (1955), pp. 186–223.

[20] *Widsith* (note 19), vv. 4, 23, 42, 84, 96, pp. 23–5 [on the Myrgings]. Bede (note 11), cap. II/15, p. 190 [on the Wuffingas].

signs indicating that it was a major task of kin groups to provide and transmit internal rules and conventions which were handed down from generation to generation and subjected the members to strict behavioural codes. It seems possible to suppose that these norms and rules concerned hereditary succession and name-giving in the main. In return for their subjection to these norms and rules, group members were entitled to receive support from and protection by their kin, specifically at times of illness, economic difficulties, legal and political conflicts. Hence the double-descent kin groups provided a network of interpersonal relations which subjected their members to their own constraining norms and traditional collective values, but provided the degree of protection that was considered necessary in a hostile and frequently insecure environment. This does not mean that kin groups were always and by necessity uniform blocks from which dissent and controversy were absent. For example, at the time of their conversion to Catholicism in the later eighth and early ninth centuries, several of the Saxon aristocratic kin groups seem to have been divided for some time into Christian and non-Christian branches. Moreover, because kin groups represented only one type of group and competed with other types of group, contending obligations could exist which caused stress and uneasiness. Likewise, kin groups seem to have had the right to expel their members in cases of grave offence against the kin group. Last but not least, in kin groups whose members were eligible for high offices, such as royal kin groups, rivalries among equally privileged contenders were frequent and led to serious conflicts which could result in war.[21]

With the beginning of the Catholic mission, however, the earliest attempts were launched towards imposing stricter kin delineations than those that had been common among the pre-Christian kin groups. Already, sixth- and seventh-century church synods began to enforce a change of exogamy rules according to which marriages between persons of closely related kin were prohibited. Throughout the early Middle Ages, the Catholic Church followed these rules, promoted its own way of counting degrees of kinship and repeatedly ruled that persons of the same kin could neither be married legitimately nor have legitimate offspring if they were more closely related to each other than the fifth, sixth or seventh ecclesiastical kinship degree.[22] According to these ecclesiastical principles of counting kinship degrees, the first generation, that of *ego*, was omitted,[23] and, further up, only generations of direct ascent up to the seventh degree were counted, so that orally transmitted genealogies could be discarded as mythical.[24] In this way, higher representatives of the Church strove to acquire a position where they could authoritatively decide

---

21 For a case, see *The Anglo-Saxon Chronicle: A Collaborative Edition*, vol. 3, Ms A, s. a. 755, ed. Janet M. Bately (Cambridge, 1986), pp. 36–8. The entry records a conflict within the West Saxon royal-kin group.

22 Regino of Prüm, *Liber de synodalibus causis et disciplinis Ecclesiasticis*, ed. Friedrich Wilhelm Hermann Wasserschleben (Leipzig, 1840), pp. 286–7. Ludwig Weiland, ed., *MGH Const.* 1, p. 629 (synod of 922, cap. 1).

23 Peter Damian, *De parentelae gradibus*, cap. X (*PL* 145, cols 200–1).

24 Explicitly stated by Burchard of Worms, *Decretorum libri XX* (*PL* 140, col. 781).

on the legitimacy of successors to rule.[25] But, initially, this policy militated against the intention of kin-group elders who, up to the ninth century, tried to remain in control of their own kin-group succession rules.

There were three main long-term goals which guided the attitudes of the Church towards the kin groups. The first was to limit the number of kin members who were entitled to inherit kin rights and property, mainly in order to exclude hereditary succession through matrilineal descent. The second goal was to intercept the ties between the living and the dead in order to establish church control over the cult of the dead. And the third goal was to reduce the norm-preserving, rule-enforcing and legitimacy-conveying capabilities of the kin groups in order to be able to subject them to the universal norms and rules which the Church sought to install in the long run.

The first goal greatly eased the conversion process because it met with support from those kin groups whose members were incumbents of high office, such as royal kin groups. It was in the interest of these kin groups to limit the number of rival contenders for succession and to enhance the continuity of the royal office by excluding collateral kin and promoting succession rules in which patrilinear descent featured as the sole principle of hereditary succession.[26] At the end of the seventh century, attempts were first made in Kent and Wessex to change succession rules so that collateral branches of royal kin groups could be excluded from hereditary succession. In Wessex, a change of name-giving custom was promoted under 'King' Coenred who affiliated his sons with the Bernician royal kin group in Northumbria and made efforts to elevate his own descendants to a higher rank than other members of the royal kin group.[27] In Kent, King Wihtred established himself as the sole ruler in the kingdom during the 690s after years of shared and polyarchic rulership during the second half of the seventh century. It was Wihtred's policy to downgrade his predecessors to the status of illegitimate usurpers in order to reserve legitimate succession for his own descendants.[28] In both cases, rulers were advised by holders of high offices in the Catholic Church, the Bishop of Winchester and the Archbishop of Canterbury. The cooperation between the Church and the rulers in Wessex and Kent was of advantage to both sides. It brought the Church into a position where it could act as a legitimacy-conveying agent in competition with the kin groups and

---

25　The best recorded case of church intervention in kinship policies of rulers is the controversy over his divorce between King Lothair II of the Franks and Archbishop Hinkmar of Rheims who preserved the files of the case. See Hinkmar, *De divortio Lotharii regis et Theutbergae reginae*, ed. Letha Böhringer, MGH Concilia 4, Supp. 1 (Hanover, 1992).

26　See the provision in the *Divisio Regnorum* of 806, cap. 6–20, ed. Alfred Boretius, *MGH Capit.* 1, No. 45, pp. 128–30. This is a text which was devised to establish a succession to royal (not imperial) rule after Charlemagne, and it stipulated legal procedures for the non-violent settlement of conflicts within the ruling kin group. This provision reflected the willingness of the Carolingians as a ruling kin group to maintain their own legislative competence even though they employed legal procedures suggested by the Church.

27　See Bruce Dickins, ed., *The Genealogical Preface to the Anglo-Saxon Chronicle* (Cambridge, 1952), p. 4.

28　Bede (see note 11), cap. IV/26 [24], p. 430.

could exert its own influence on royal succession, and it allowed each ruler to expect a smooth transition to the person chosen as heir among his descendants. Nevertheless, both strategies towards the introduction of new succession rules failed in their own time. In Wessex, in the entire eighth century, no king was elected who was a descendant of Coenred, and in Kent Wihtred's successors returned to the practice of shared rule which Wihtred had tried to abolish. Therefore, some impact of ecclesiastical norms and rules existed on secular institutions of rulership but this impact was limited at the turn of the eighth century and continued to be so throughout the century. Indeed, up to the ninth century, collateral kin groups were able to defend their positions. Nevertheless, although these early attempts failed in their own time, they did provide the precedents through which later generations could repeatedly try to attain the same goal, for example the Carolingians and their successors in the Frankish Kingdom, as well as King Alfred and his successors in England.

However, the second goal, namely the interception of ties between the living and the dead was more difficult to accomplish. Conversion to Catholicism made it necessary that the rulers should renounce their belief that kin groups included both living and deceased. Charlemagne prohibited the continuing use of pre-Christian burial sites for Christian funerals. He insisted that deceased kin members be moved into the custody of the Church and that the change of religion was to become visible in the relocation of cemeteries.[29] This demand implied that rulers could no longer derive the legitimacy of their rule through their descent, but had to search for novel grounds, which could only be successful if they were accepted by the ruled. But there are indications which show that it was difficult to find such acceptance. In the case of the late sixth-century conversion of Aethelberht of Kent, for example, an apostate reaction occurred under this king's son Eadbald. This reaction implies that opponents of Aethelberht's decision rallied behind his son so as to stop the progress of the conversion.[30] That the Kentish opponents against the conversion to Christianity would not directly stand up against the reigning king, but seek the support of his son and expected successor, may have been enforced by the desire of these opponents to strengthen the powers of the kin group. So opponents of the Catholic mission must have believed that the strengthening of the royal kin groups could be accomplished only if the ruler was not a Christian. In another case, from the late fifth century, the Frankish king, Clovis, was advised by Bishop Avitus of Vienne (c. 460–518) to give up the cult of his deceased ancestors and instead rely on the church as the conveyor of legitimacy.[31] After initially accepting Avitus's plea and acting forcefully against other members of his kin, Clovis later complained that he had to live a

---

29 *Capitulatio de partibus Saxoniae* [775/790], cap. 22, ed. Alfred Boretius, *MGH Capit.* 1, No. 26, p. 69

30 Bede (see note 11), cap. II/5, p. 150. Cf. Günther Peter Fehring, 'Missions- und Kirchenwesen in archäologischer Sicht', in Herbert Jankuhn, Reinhard Wenskus, eds, *Geschichtswissenschaft und Archäologie*, VuF XXII (Sigmaringen, 1979), pp. 556–67.

31 Avitus of Vienne, *Opera quae supersunt*, ed. Rudolf Peiper, *MGH AA* 6,2, pp. 75–6.

solitary life after having been forced to remove many of his kin in order to consolidate his position.[32]

The third goal, namely the reduction of the norm-preserving, rule-enforcing and legitimacy-conveying competence of the kin groups was even more difficult to accomplish. Although there is a scarcity of evidence on the precise nature of the norms and rules which the kin groups controlled, it can be inferred from aspects of the name-giving practice that such particularist norms and rules must have existed. For it was common for at least the more important Germanic aristocratic kin groups to identify their members through the common use of certain well-known names or well-defined parts of the usual dithematic personal names common in the Germanic languages. In consequence of this rule, the bearer of a certain name or part of a name could be identified as the member of a certain kin group, and, as the ninth century *Hildebrandslied* confirms, these particularist name-giving rules were generally known across the continent.[33] A certain name-giving rule could only be characteristic of a certain kin group, if it had been practised for a long time, which implies that it must have been transmitted across several generations within the kin group applying it.

The fact that this name-giving practice, with variations, was still widely followed in the ninth century, shows the stubbornness with which the kin groups defended their privileges of preserving and enforcing their own particularist norms and rules against the universal principles informing the laws which were enacted by or under the authority of the Church and the secular rulers. By the ninth century, some higher aristocratic kin groups may have been willing to follow suit to the royal kin groups in narrowing down the scope of their kinship under the advice of clergymen.[34] Still, if they wished, they could retain their position as a ruling élite in the entourage of kings and emperors, even if much of the practical administrative work in writing was done by clergymen. They also continued to be influential as organisers of and donators to local church institutions, notably proprietary churches on their own hereditary lands and monasteries which had been endowed with funds from the aristocracy.[35] Finally, the preservation of particularist aristocratic

---

[32] Gregory of Tours (see note 11), cap. II/42, p. 93.

[33] *Das Hildebrandslied*, Hartmut Broszinski, ed., *Das Hildebrandslied*, vv. 7–19, 2nd ed. (Kassel, 1985).

[34] The mid-ninth-century *Liber manualis* of Dhuoda, who was a woman of high aristocratic status in the Frankish Kingdom and wrote the book to advise her son on morality, displayed the ambiguity of adherence to the universalist norms and values promoted by the Church and the particularist norms and values transmitted within kin groups. She advised her son to lead his life in accordance with Christian norms and values but to respect his father as the head of the kin group at the same time. She made no reference to her own position inside the kin group. See Dhuoda, *Manuel pour mon fils* [841–43], cap. III/1, IV/1, ed. Pierre Riché, Sources chrétiennes CCXXV (Paris, 1975), pp. 134–40, 198–204. Similar demands were articulated at the same time by the clergy. See Raban Maur, *Epistola ad Ludowicum imperatorem* [834], ed. Ernst Dümmler, *MGH Epp. Karol.* 3, No. 15, pp. 404–6.

[35] The foundation of monasteries through the private initiative of aristocratic kin groups

kin traditions was facilitated through oral communication which continued to contribute towards their potential to exert political influence. This is attributable to the fact that the secular rulers were tied together with the aristocratic kin groups through purposefully established marriage bonds and because the kin groups still then continued to stay in control of their own proprietary ecclesiastical institutions.[36]

But in the course of the tenth century, the higher aristocratic kin groups lost important positions in the church organisation, first, after the aristocratic lay clerics, who had resided in monasteries and other ecclesiastical institutions, were forced out, and were replaced by ordained monks and nuns; and, second, after more aristocratic proprietary church institutions and the saints venerated therein were placed under the supervision of the central episcopal administration. It is difficult to determine what led to the beginning of the decline of the kin groups at that time. But it is evident that the decline began with the reduction of the matrilineal element in the double-descent kin groups. This process strengthened the position of the male household chief at the expense of women, the elderly and the young. The male household chiefs began to perceive as salient the fragmentation of the larger non-residential kin groups into smaller communities of kin-related residents at a given place and considered less relevant the collateral relations with kin-group members residing elsewhere.

This process began in the ruling kin groups and was supported by bishops and abbots, because it was congruent with the long-term church goals of reducing the importance of the kin groups. It brought together into a fragile coalition secular rulers on the one side and bishops as well as ordained abbots on the other. It was a coalition of mutual benefit. The ordained clergy could free themselves from domination by the aristocratic kin groups, and the secular rulers could raise their position above that of the aristocracy with approval by the Church. And although agreements to similar ends had been achieved already on various occasions since the early eighth century, they had then been no more than temporary but were successfully opposed in many

---

is frequently attested to in saints' lives, traditions of monastic foundations and charter evidence. See, for example, *Vita S. Geretrudis*, cap. 2, ed. Bruno Krusch, *MGH SS rer. Merov.* 2, pp. 455–6. *Chronicon Monasterii de Abingdon*, ed. Joseph Stevenson, vol.1, Rerum Britannicarum medii aevi scriptores II (London, 1858; repr. New York, 1968), p. 8. The aristocratic practice of keeping proprietary churches was described by Archbishop Hinkmar of Rheims in the ninth century in his tract *Collectio de ecclesiis et capellis*, ed. Martina Stratmann. MGH Fontes iuris Germ. ant. XIV (Hanover, 1990). As early as in the seventh century, wooden church buildings on the margins of cemeteries outside settlements seem to confirm the existence of such proprietary churches. See Fehring (see note 30), pp. 556–9.

36 A ninth-century case is recorded in Asser's *Life of King Alfred*, cap. 2, ed. William Henry Stevenson (Oxford, 1904), p. 4 (repr. ed. Dorothy Whitelock [Oxford, 1959]), who mentions that Alfred's mother Osburh preserved vernacular traditions in a 'book', the contents of which Alfred was made to learn by heart. Although nothing is known about what Alfred learned, it is safe to conclude that at least some of the traditions belonged to the kin group.

instances by aristocrats in the royal entourage. Still in the tenth century, rulers attempting to elevate themselves above their aristocratic retainers faced opposition by disgruntled aristocrats. A dramatic case of such opposition occurred at the end of the tenth century, when Emperor Otto III was harshly criticised for having introduced a new seating order for imperial feasts. According to the new seating order, which was styled after Byzantine models, Otto was to take a seat at his own table, separate from and elevated above the table at which his aristocratic retainers were to sit.[37] Otto tried to revise what appears to have been the traditional seating order according to which the lord, the lady and their retainers sat at one and the same table.[38] The symbolism of the novel arrangement implied that the emperor, as an ecclesiastically legitimised ruler, was demonstrating that he no longer owed his position to the faithfulness of his retainers, but to the support of the Church and that, consequently, his own position as a secular, though religiously sanctioned ruler was fundamentally different from that of his lay aristocratic entourage. Despite vocal criticism, however, the aristocratic traditions eventually could not be retained.

Instead, the higher aristocracy quickly followed suit in the precedent set by the secular rulers and abandoned their independent kin traditions. Already in 948, a church council advised all Christian believers to lay down their genealogies in writing in order to avoid incestuous marriages.[39] This meant that, at this time, the clergymen gathering at the council believed that not every person had the knowledge which was necessary to identify all members of a kin group with whom exogamy rules had to be observed according to canon law. These clergymen were also convinced that oral tradition was insufficient as a means of preserving genealogical knowledge, so they recommended that such knowledge be entrusted to written texts. Evidently, there was thus a declining willingness and capability among kin groups to preserve genealogical knowledge so that it was difficult for a person to identify his or her cognates if they were related through more remote ancestors. This observation can be confirmed from changes of the name-giving practices. In the ninth century, learned genealogists began to fill up name lists of royal kin groups with material of biblical origin and from the history of the Roman Empire of antiquity. In this way, the genealogies grew in length but lost their distinctive features.[40] From the eleventh century, aristocrats began to name themselves after the hilltop castles which they had begun to erect for their households overlooking the settlements of peasant farmers. The new name-

---

[37] Thietmar, *Chronicon*, cap. IV/47, ed. Robert Holtzmann, *MGH SS rer. Germ.* N. S. 9, pp. 185–6.

[38] The seventh-century *Laws of Hlothere and Eadric of Kent*, cap. 12, 13, ed. Felix Liebermann, *Die Gesetze der Angelsachsen*, vol. 1 (Halle, 1903), p. 11, prohibited the display of weapons during feasts and prescribed a fixed drinking order. A similar record is contained in *Beowulf*, vv. 64–85, 611–28, 2633, ed. Frederick Klaeber, 3rd edn (Lexington, Mass., 1950), pp. 3–4, 21–2, 99.

[39] Synod of Ingelheim (7.6.948), ed. Ernst-Dieter Hehl, *MGH Concilia* 6, p. 162.

[40] For an example, see Erna Hackenberg, 'Die Stammtafeln der angelsächsischen Königreiche' (unpublished Ph.D. thesis, University of Berlin 1918), pp. 12–15.

giving practice replaced the previous name-giving practice in almost all aristocratic kin groups. Moreover, a new type of aristocracy began to rise in military services, in many cases from humble origins. These knightly retainers, sometimes called *ministeriales*, began to replace the traditional aristocracy during the Crusades and opened their new positions to the war-proneness and the administrative skills of their male heads. As newcomers in the aristocratic world, they displayed their own consciousness of status by creating a highly distinct atmosphere of courtly life, which they could only maintain if they were successful in keeping together their own heritage and in limiting access to the aristocracy by establishing the right of noble birth. Hence these new aristocratic kin groups were the promoters of small patri-linear residential households. The aristocracy began to define itself as a social group in legal terms and obstructed access into its ranks through various legal and moral barriers. Within itself, however, this aristocracy became highly stratified according to the titles and privileges which its members could claim and over which intensive competition took place. Kinship ties across the various residential kin groups no longer entailed the giving of rights to collateral kin even though matrilinear descent continued to be respected in cases where, for lack of offspring, the search for heirs required compromises.

This new kinship structure gradually permeated all European kin groups, although with marked differences in time. In the urban communities of towns and cities, the settlers were drawn from many different areas and kin groups and had cut or severed their traditional ties when or before moving into their new settlements. Therefore the bonds of kinship, the moral and legal norms and the traditions associated with them were less significant to these settlers than their efforts to acquire a professional distinction and political power in their new settlements. Consequently, the lack of traditional kinship ties helped these settlers to constitute themselves as the social group of the 'bourgeoisie' as the core group of inhabitants in the urban communities of towns and cities during and after the twelfth century. The urban patriciate recruited itself largely from the basis of these new kin groups between the eleventh and the eighteenth centuries, although with a sharply declining frequency. By contrast, peasant farmers retained collateral kinship well into the eighteenth century.

In summary, the history of kin groups in Europe includes fundamental changes in the kinship structure and the legal competence of the kin groups during the high Middle Ages. By the thirteenth century, these changes were accomplished in the aristocracy and the 'bourgeois' communities of towns and cities, whence they became universalised throughout Europe. For the kin groups, the changes implied a fundamental decline of their legal and political significance *vis-à-vis* other types of groups. In the early Middle Ages, the double-descent kin groups represented a vertical array of particularistic organisations which were difficult to subject to the control of overarching institutions of rule. With their decline, the kin groups gave way to competing types of group.

Neighbourhood groups

During the same period, neighbourhood groups as local clusters of kin groups and their dependants living together in residential communities faced a similar, though less dramatic, decline. This can be said even though neighbourhoods continued to have certain obligations throughout the Middle Ages, namely poor relief and care for innocent vagrants.[41] It is often difficult to discern neighbourhood groups as a distinct type of group, because they have tended to appear only on specific occasions, while, when they accomplished some degree of perseverance, they tended to merge with social groups (which will be discussed later). Nevertheless, there were two major types of occasion on which neighbourhood groups appear in the sources, namely migration and violent forms of protest.

Neighbourhood groups were recognisable in times of large-scale migration, mainly from the fifth to the seventh as well as during the twelfth and thirteenth centuries. The effects of the activities of neighbourhood groups can be ascertained mainly in place names. During the earlier period, there are some place-name correlates between the Continent and the British Isles which may have resulted from the migration of neighbourhood groups. Possible correlates are Beverungen (Westphalia) and the deserted village Beverington (Sussex). In this case, the name Beverington may have been formed by the addition of the suffix -*tun* (farmstead) to the previously existing place name Beverungen. Hence the original meaning of Beverington may have been 'farmstead of [the people of] Beverungen'. This derivation implies the migration of a group of people from Beverungen and their collective resettlement in the British Isles. This name-giving practice seems to indicate that the group of migrants identified itself or was identified by others as a group constituted by the commonalities, first, of the settlement from which their migration had begun, second, of the joint experience of the migration and, third, of the place of their resettlement. Thus the constitutive factor of the group of migrants from Beverungen may have been their neighbourhood.

Similar cases of correlates resulting from early post-migration inland colonisation in the British Isles confirm this practice. In Sussex, there are name pairs such as Goring/Goringlee and Hastings/Hastingford, where the longer place names were formed by adding a suffix to place names which had already existed in the area. In these cases it can be shown that the original names are related to places located in the Sussex coastal zone, whereas the derived place names were applied to places which were subsequently occupied in the uplands of Sussex. It thus can be concluded that the migration was carried out by neighbourhood groups of settlers on the coast who established new and planned settlements in the hinterland.[42]

---

[41] For an early record, see *Admonitio generalis* (23.2.789), ed. Alfred Boretius, *MGH Capit.* 1, No. 22, p. 60.

[42] The process of planning new settlements is reflected in a provision of the late seventh-century laws of King Ine, cap. 40, ed. Liebermann (see note 38), p. 106. The provision

During the twelfth and thirteenth centuries, migrations towards the north-east of Europe led to the formation of several place names by adding on the prefix 'new', such as in the case of Neubrandenburg, and the duplication of place names, such as Osterode in the Harz and Osterode in East Prussia. Again, such a name-giving convention confirms the existence of neighbourhood groups at the core of the migrants.

The activities of neighbourhood groups, however, did not necessarily have to be peaceful under all conditions. Instead, neighbourhood groups could also become instruments to articulate discontent through the submission of grievances and the organisation of violent protest. In fact, many protest movements up to the eighteenth century occurred in the form of neighbourhood groups whose grievances were articulated against a perceived intrusive and/or unjust authority. The greater urban revolutions, such as the ones in Rome 1149, Erfurt 1283, Cologne 1288 and 1396, Nuremberg from June 1348 to October 1349, Ulm 1397, in Flanders in the fourteenth and fifteenth centuries, and in Prague in 1419, were acts of violence which were organised by townspeople against their lords or, inside the towns and cities, by guilds or other groups of manufacturing artisans as well as residents of town quarters against the urban patriciates.[43] Likewise, peasant farmers would unite against their lords or they would join in other protests in clusters of adjacent villages, usually without much coordination in wider areas.[44] If, however, against the rule, wider coordination did occur and sent the inhabitants of larger territories into revolt, such as during the so-called English peasant rising of 1381, the fifteenth century Bohemian Hussite movement or the German Peasants' War of 1524–25, and, as late as in the early eighteenth century, the rising of Baltic peasant farmers against Swedish rule, these acts of violence were of profound severity and a fundamental threat to the established ruling authorities.

Therefore, although usually confined to local interests and activities, discontent emerging from neighbourhood groups did have the potential of spreading and articulating demands on behalf of the joint interests of the inhabitants of larger areas.

In summary, it can be said that, during the Middle Ages, neighbourhood groups were manifest as groups by common experiences or with joint interests, if and as long as these experiences and interests were related to specific

stipulated that landowners must build and keep in order fences around their plots in order to prevent their neighbours' cattle from roving in their own plots.

43 For sources see, among others, 'Verbundbrief [Cologne, 13.9.1396]', ed. Walther Stein, *Akten zur Geschichte der Verfassung und Verwaltung der Stadt Köln im 14. und 15. Jahrhundert*, Publikationen der Gesellschaft für Rheinische Geschichtskunde X (Bonn, 1893; repr. Bonn, 1993), pp. 187–98. Dorothea Reuter, ed., 'Der Große Schwörbrief: Verfassung und Verfassungswirklichkeit in der Reichsstadt des Spätmittelalters', in Hans Eugen Specker, ed., *Die Ulmer Bürgerschaft auf dem Weg zur Demokratie* (Stuttgart, 1997), pp. 508–14.

44 For a fifteenth-century Bavarian case, see Franz Martin Mayer, ed., 'Über die Correspondenzbücher des Bischofs Sixtus von Freising, 1474–1495', *Archiv für österreichische Geschichte* LXVIII (1886), pp. 496–500.

places of residence. Neighbourhood groups could overlap with kin groups in cases where, as in aristocratic hilltop castles, local settlements were confined to members of a single kin group or, as in an agricultural settlement, they could overarch a limited number of kin groups. Under such conditions, the goals set by neighbourhood groups could conflict with the norms and rules set by the kin groups, but both types of groups could also support each other. The latter seems to have occurred in cases where discontent was articulated and protests were organised. By contrast, in the urban communities of towns and cities, where traditional kinship ties among double-descent kin groups played no role, the settlement as a whole became the primary focal point of social organisation and, hence, could absorb many of the tasks which the extended double-descent kin groups had been in charge of before and left to the neighbourhood groups the task of articulating discontent.

Contractual groups

Next to the two previously discussed types of group into which access was normally accorded by birth, there was another type of group into which persons could enter at their own discretion and wherein the ties among the members were not maintained through some pre-existing authority, but were voluntarily agreed upon through contracts. As with the kin groups and the neighbourhood groups, the contractual groups faced a significant decline of their social and political importance during the Middle Ages.

The contracts created mutual obligations of loyalty and protection which might – and frequently did – contradict the norms and values existing within kin and neighbourhood groups. Moreover, whereas a person would normally belong to a kin and a neighbourhood group, membership in a contractual group was optional and voluntary. The voluntariness of membership implied that the contractual groups needed to offer specific gains in order to attract members. Usually, these gains were offered through the initiative of a person who took the position of a leader inviting others to join in a specific enterprise with clearly defined goals. These goals were frequently related to military actions, either for the purpose of settling in new lands or of foraging for prey.[45] Contractual groups could also result from agreements of friendship and mutual support which were, as a rule, concluded as alliances among

---

[45] Gregory of Tours (see note 11), cap. III/3, p. 99. *Beowulf* (see note 38), vv. 1201–14, pp. 45–6. The *Anglo-Saxon Chronicle*, Ms. E, s. a. 793, ed. Charles Plummer, *Two of the Saxon Chronicles Parallel*, vol. 1, repr. (Oxford, 1952), p. 55 (first published Oxford, 1892), and the *Annales qui dicuntur Einhardi*, s. a. 800, ed. Friedrich Kurze, *MGH SS rer. Germ.* (6), p. 111, mention Vikings and the latter source refers to them as 'pirati Nordmannici'. Reference to the same type of group is also contained in the late Old English poem *The Battle of Maldon*, v. 26, ed. D. G. Scragg (Manchester, 1981), p. 57. Paul the Deacon, *Historia Langobardorum*, cap. I/11, ed. Georg Waitz, *MGH SS rer. Germ.* (48), pp. 59–60, referred to similar types of group, as did Saxo Grammaticus, *Gesta Danorum*, Book VII, cap. X/11, vol. 1, ed. J. Olrik, H. Raeder (Copenhagen, 1930), p. 209.

equals, even though similar forms of contract seem to have been reached also among persons of different rank and status in the ninth and tenth centuries.[46] Further contractual groups focused their activities on religious goals, mainly mission in service to the Catholic Church and the foundation and maintenance of monasteries.[47] Finally, there were guilds established for mixed purposes.[48]

Most contractual groups were composed of retainers who had entered into contracts under the leadership of locators, warlords, abbots or other persons of elevated rank. These leaders voluntarily departed from their kin groups or may have been forced to form their contractual groups after having been disinherited by or expelled from their own kin groups. The contractual groups would then provide leadership and a share of the gains to their retainers in return for service and loyalty. Hence they had a hierarchical order despite the mutuality of the contracts on the basis of which their existence was derived.

The groups directing their activities towards military goals and the friendship groups were most frequent in the early Middle Ages, when narrative sources abound with references to them. However, the disruptive effects of the actions by members of militarily active contractual groups may, on occasion, have been overdramatised.[49] Beyond their military activity, the contractual groups, under the leadership of aristocratic locators, featured prominently during the period of wide-ranging internal colonisation between the seventh and the thirteenth centuries. Nevertheless, the autonomous, militarily organised contractual groups were by necessity a burden and a source of worry for existing administrative institutions. Between the eighth and the eleventh centuries, rulers undertook repeated efforts, often in vain, to defend the land and people under their control against contractual groups, to subdue them to some central institutional control and to channel their activities into regularised defence efforts.[50] These goals were difficult to accomplish, mainly because the rulers had to rely on the military service paid to them by the aris-

---

46 A case for the latter is recorded in the Treaty of Coulaines concluded between Charles the Bald and his West Frankish retainers in 843, ed. Alfred Boretius, Viktor Krause, *MGH Capit.* 2, No. 254, pp. 253–5.

47 Michael Tangl, ed., *Die Briefe des Heiligen Bonifatius und Lullus*, No. 29, 31, 38 etc., *MGH Epp. sel.* 1, pp. 52–3, 54–5, 63.

48 Bedwyn guilds, ed. Benjamin Thorpe, *Diplomatarium Anglicum aevi Saxonici* (London, 1865), pp. 605–14. Pope Gregory I, Ep. No. IX, *MGH Epp.* 2, ed. Paul Ewald, Ludo Moritz Hartmann, pp. 118–19, mentioned a late sixth-century guild of soap makers in Naples.

49 E. g. *Anglo-Saxon Chronicle* (see note 21), s. a. 1001, pp. 79–80.

50 The *Annales regni Francorum*, s. a. 798, ed. Friedrich Kurze (see note 45), pp. 102–4. Einhard, *Vita Karoli Magni*, cap. 7, ed. Oswald Holger-Egger, *MGH SS rer. Germ.* (25), p. 9, complained about the lack of defensive frontiers between the kingdom of the Franks and the Saxon areas and argued that this was the major reason for Charlemagne's wars against the Saxons. An early written source for a planned system of defensive earthworks is the so-called *Burghal Hidage*, probably of the early tenth century. The text contains a list of places at which the local residents were ordered to erect defences, keep them in good repair and guard them in cases of invasions. See Agnes J. Robertson, ed., *Anglo-Saxon Charters* (Cambridge, 1939), pp. 246–9. 2nd edn (Cambridge, 1957).

tocracy. As warriors, some of the higher aristocrats were able to retain their positions as leaders of contractual groups well into the fifteenth century, and even continued to conduct their feuds with the help of contractual warrior groups against prohibitions by the Church and the rulers who, between the eleventh and the fifteenth centuries, tried to enforce peace regulations for the territories under their control.[51] Thus, the contractual groups led by the aristocracy resisted the centralising effects of rule until the time when the rulers became vested with the largest single share of rights on landed property in a given area. This was accomplished in England at the end of the thirteenth century, in France towards the end of the fourteenth century and elsewhere during the fifteenth century.[52]

The second type of contractual groups rose with the spread of Catholicism from the sixth and seventh centuries. Initially, monasteries were fiercely independent church institutions which ruled themselves through abbots or abbesses chosen by the monks and nuns.[53] They were not subjected to the control of bishops, except in those cases where abbots were bishops themselves. The combination of the two offices was frequent practice in the early medieval Irish church. But in the course of the seventh and eighth centuries, the Pope of Rome obtained suzerainty over the monasteries and made efforts to subject the monasteries to the control of the local bishops, even though some prominent monasteries, such as the Abbey of Fulda, remained exempt from episcopal legislation. Moreover, many Catholic monasteries in areas outside the Roman Empire of Antiquity had been inhabited by lay persons belonging to certain particular kin groups, whereas elsewhere, communities of monks and nuns had been established on the basis of contractual rules. But the monastic revival of the tenth and eleventh centuries reduced the influence of lay monks and nuns who were replaced by ordained clergymen, at least in

---

51 Most vocally in the eleventh century, Bishop Gerard of Cambrai. See *Gesta episcoporum Cameracensium*, cap. III/27, III/52, *MGH SS* 7, p. 474, 486. For territorial peace regulations, see *Constitutio pacis* (Mainz, 15.3.1235), ed. Ludwig Weiland, *MGH Const.* 2, pp. 241–7.

52 A good example for the autonomy of contractual warrior groups in the late Middle Ages is the well-recorded controversy between the Free Imperial City of Frankfurt and the neighbouring Lords of Kronberg in 1389. The Lords had for a while been in paid service as the mercenaries of the city before they left in disgruntlement and declared a feud against the city. This feud was initiated by a letter signed by 46 neighbouring and supporting lords before it was dispatched to the city on 8 January 1389. The lords were later joined by two rulers of larger territories. King Wenzel, in his capacity as the ruler of Germany and superior lord of the city of Frankfurt, ordered the city to intervene against fortifications which the lords had erected for their defence. The city began a military campaign against the lords, but its troops were badly defeated on 5 June 1389. The defeat obliged the city to pay 73,000 guilders of ransom for its prisoners of war before peace was concluded on 28 August 1389. See Heinrich Reimer, ed., *Hessisches Urkundenbuch*, vol. II, 4 (Leipzig, 1897; repr. Osnabrück, 1965), pp. 418–23, 428–9, 440–6. Benedict Jacob Römer-Büchner, *Die Entwicklung der Stadtverfassung und der Bürgervereine der Stadt Frankfurt* (Frankfurt, 1855), pp. 84–5.

53 Already Caesarius of Arles, *Regula ad virgines* (*PL* 67, cols. 1103–16) emphasised the autonomy of monasteries.

the higher ranks of the church administration. With their ascendance, the contractual organisation of ordained clergy under the central authority of the church became the dominant principle of monasticism.[54] The ordained clergy not only executed religious services, but were also the main bearers of the literary traditions of learning, and offered academic education in monasteries as well as in association with cathedral churches. Even though monasteries formed the basis for religious contractual groups until the Reformation of the sixteenth century, their overall importance declined in the course of the Middle Ages due to the secluded character of the monastic lifestyle. That monastic communities were the principal models for religious contractual groups during the Middle Ages is amply shown by the fact that lay associations, for example bridge-building guilds, borrowed their own organisational principles from those of the monastic communities.

By contrast, guilds, as the third type of contractual group, rose in significance with the spread of trading activities and the formation of urban communities in towns and cities. Although they had originated already in the early Middle Ages and had then been frequently associated with much the same antagonistic sentiment as the military contractual groups,[55] since the twelfth century, the guilds as conjurations were used to establish artisans' and merchants' organisations. They pursued three main purposes: to limit competition among guild members through price controls, to enforce quality standards for production, and to provide for rules for training future generations of craftsmen. They also formed an almost perfect instrument for those merchant companies engaged in long-distance and overseas trade. In these contexts, lay contractual groups could equitably distribute the risks involved in trade. They flourished from the twelfth century and, sometimes, overlapped with kin groups, as in the cases of the Fugger, Welser, Tucher and Behaim families. Because these artisans' guilds and merchant companies operated in many places and cooperated among themselves, they formed a highly flexible and mobile social element which could claim to be autonomous in the sense that it needed little or no financial and organisational support from the administrative institutions of rule and, consequently, owed little or no allegiance to anyone. Consequently, the free or autonomous, self-governing city was the appropriate political organisation for these artisans' guilds and merchant companies. Although, within their towns and cities, the artisans' guilds and merchant companies were subjected to the local urban legislation enacted by the town and city councils, the legitimacy by which the councils could govern was in itself not always derived from a superior authority (secular territorial or religious), but was frequently based contrac-

---

54 For a defence of this type of monastic organisation see Abbo of Fleury, *Liber apologeticus* (*PL* 139, cols 461–72) .

55 *Capitulary of Heristal* (779), cap. 16, *Capitulary of Aquitaine* (789), cap. 16, *Capitulary of Diedenhofen* (805), cap. 9, ed. Alfred Boretius, *MGH Capit.* 1, No. 20, p. 51, No. 24, p. 66, No. 44, p. 124.

tually on the consent of the governed.[56] And although, well into the sixteenth century, travelling merchants on the continent were in need of protection against hostile actions by the landed aristocracy[57] and demanded their protection through professional warriors from the town councils, they pursued their own commercial interests with little external interference and could thereby create the impression that autonomous marketing rules existed which were subject only to the stern logic of economic gains and losses and immune from interventions by rulers.

However, with the exception of the artisans' guilds and merchant companies, other lay contractual groups, namely the autonomous militarily organised groups, were integrated into the emerging framework of territorial administrative control through a long process between the end of the eleventh and the late fifteenth centuries.[58] The outward expressions of the waning of these contractual groups were the widening demands which were initially articulated in the western European peace movement in the eleventh century, which became manifest in territorial peace legislation during the thirteenth and fourteenth centuries, and which peaked in the call for a general and perpetual peace. This was finally agreed upon, within the Holy Roman Empire, during the Diet of Worms of 1495.[59] As a consequence of the establishment of a perpetual universal peace within the Empire as well as in other parts of Europe, the autonomous lay contractual groups had to subordinate themselves to general laws applicable throughout the territories under the control of one and the same ruler, and they had to subject themselves to arbitration and adjudication through regularised judicial processes of conflict resolution.

Summary on kin groups, neighbourhood groups and contractual groups

The three types of groups discussed so far displayed the common feature that they did not claim exclusive membership. That is to say that one person could be a member of a kin group, a neighbourhood group and a contractual group at the same time. Likewise, the coexistence and competition among these types of group gave a person some possibilities for choice. For example, someone dissatisfied with his or her kin group could opt out of this type of

56 See the early twelfth-century Freiburg town privilege, ed. Friedrich Keutgen, *Urkunden zur städtischen Verfassungsgeschichte* (Berlin, 1902; repr. Aalen, 1965), No. 133.
57 On the animosities between landed aristocrats outside the towns and cities and urban merchants, see Ulrich von Hutten, 'Praedones', in Hutten, *Schriften*, vol. 4, ed. Eduard Böcking (Leipzig, 1860), pp. 366–74.
58 An early case is the Peace of God in the Archbishopric of Cologne, recorded for 1093, ed. Lorenz Weinreich, *Quellen zur deutschen Verfassungs-, Wirtschafts- und Sozialgeschichte bis 1250*, Freiherr-vom-Stein-Gedächtnisausgabe XXXII (Darmstadt, 1977), p. 140.
59 The rules of the Diet of Worms of 1495 are to be found in Arno Buschmann, ed., *Kaiser und Reich* (Munich, 1984), pp. 157–64.

group and join a contractual group.[60] Cases were also recorded in early medieval sources where persons purposefully renounced kin membership in order to join a religiously active contractual group and where persons were expelled from a kin or neighbourhood group and sought affiliation with a contractual group.[61] Finally, switching membership between contractual groups did occur.[62] With the declining importance of these three types of groups from the tenth and eleventh centuries, these choices were greatly reduced, and the reduction of choices supported the increase in importance of the two types of groups which remain to be discussed.

Political groups as groups by tradition

Groups are political when they convey upon their members a common identity through the acceptance of and adherence to institutions of rule, forms of production, area of settlement, legal norms, rules, values, conventions and certain patterns of communication which, each by itself or all together, demarcate one such group against all others. Such groups are termed political because it is understood among their members that the maintenance of these groups demands the joint activity and efforts of all or at least a particularly active core of their members. Political groups are thus not primordial; they emerge under various conditions. First, it is possible that heterogeneous groups agglomerate around a core kin, neighbourhood or contractual group. This has frequently been observed during the later Migration Age when a variety of different types of groups successively joined a core group and established themselves as 'migration avalanches'[63] which appeared in close contemporary sources, among others, as political groups bearing such names as 'Goths' or 'Vandals'. In this case, the formative factor of the political groups is the commonality of the experiences of their members in the course of their migrations. Second, it may happen that a core group imposes itself as a group of rulers over other groups as the ruled, whereby both gradually establish a common identity and emerge as a political group. In this case, the formative factor for the political group is the acceptance of institutions of rule. Such processes were, among others, behind the formation of the early Germanic kingdoms in Britain.[64] Third, a group may claim for itself an area of settlement and it may be understood that the location of a person's birthplace

---

60 *Hildebrandslied* (see note 33).
61 *Vitae Bonifatii archiepiscopi Moguntini*, cap. 1, ed. Wilhelm Levison, *MGH SS rer. Germ.* (57), pp. 5–6. *Wulf and Eadwacer, The Wife's Lament, The Exeter Book*, ed. George Krapp, Elliot van Kirk Dobbie, Anglo-Saxon Poetic Records III (New York, London, 1936), pp. 170–80, 210–11.
62 *Anglo-Saxon Chronicle* (see note 21), s. a. 755, pp. 36–7.
63 This term was coined by Wenskus (see note 8), pp. 75–6, to describe the cases of migrating groups which could grow considerably in size during their migrations if they were regarded as successful.
64 For a study of these processes, see Harald Kleinschmidt, 'The Geuissae, the West

identifies him or her as the member of a certain political group. In this case, interconnectedness with a given area achieves primacy over other formative factors for political groups. One such case is recorded in the seventh century *Liber historiae Francorum* in which a person was defined as a Burgundian when he or she came from the area of Burgundy, regardless of his or her descent.[65] Subsequently, the mid-seventh-century edict of the Lombard King Rothari (dec. 652) and the eighth-century Frankish laws of the Ribuarians were explicit in stating the principle of the personality of law which meant that, wherever lawsuits were to take place, that law should be applied which was valid at the place where the defendant had been born.[66] Fourth, political groups might establish themselves newly as offshoots from an already-existing political group and claim an identity and an area of settlement of their own. The formation from the ninth century of the political group of the Germans, initially within the confines of the Frankish kingdom, and the gradual establishment from the end of the tenth century of the political group of the Austrians within the Duchy of Bavaria are cases in point.[67] In all cases, these political groups were identifiable only if they existed for some time on some at least vaguely demarcated territory and under the control of a ruler or group of rulers. In this sense, political groups were groups whose traditions were associated with institutions of rule over land and people.

For the early Middle Ages, it needs to be taken into consideration that, from the time before the eighth century, there are no unequivocal contemporary sources which prove that political groups were conceptualised as a generic type of their own. Instead, their identity-conveying task seems to have been absorbed by other types of groups, mainly the kin, neighbourhood and contractual groups. Hence, whenever certain 'ethnic' names appeared in sources up to the seventh century, such as 'Angli', 'Franci', 'Burgundiones', 'Saxones', 'Gothi', these names stood for kin, neighbourhood or contractual groups and must not be misread as names denoting political groups. In the early eighth century, however, evidence appeared for the use of some of the previously recorded names together with the Latin appellatives *gens* and *natio* to denote political groups as groups by tradition and a distinct type of groups.[68] Although some of these names, such as 'Angli' and 'Franci', had been used before, the new and widening gentile terminology of the eighth century suggests the formation of political groups as a distinct type of group at that time.

Since the eighth century, the gentile terminology has continued to be used

Saxons, the Angles and the English: The Widening Horizon of Bede's Gentile Terminology', *NOWELE* XXX (1997), pp. 51–91.

65 *Liber historiae Francorum*, cap. 36, 40, ed. Bruno Krusch, *MGH SS rer. Merov.* 2, pp. 305, 310.

66 *Lex Ribuaria*, cap. 35, 5, ed. Franz Beyerle, Rudolf Buchner, *MGH LL nat. Germ.* 3, 2, p. 87. *Edictus Rothari*, cap. 26–8, ed. Friedrich Bluhme, Alfred Boretius, *MGH LL* 4, p. 17.

67 For descriptions, see Herwig Wolfram, *Die Geburt Mitteleuropas: Geschichte Österreichs vor seiner Entstehung* (Berlin, 1987).

68 Bede (see note 11), cap. III/7, p. 232.

in Europe in different successive contexts. First, between the tenth and the thirteenth centuries, the political groups became substrates of the exclusive domination of territorial rulers, except when they succeeded in establishing themselves as autonomous entities, which were then mainly organised on contractual principles, for instance the Swiss Confederation. However, the territorialisation of rule did not always, and not even in many cases, take place in the way that the traditional loyalties of the political groups were respected by the territorial rulers. Instead, in the larger number of cases, these traditional loyalties were altered in accordance with the goals and the rationality of the rulers' policies which divided the previously existing political groups onto numerous territories. Consequently, the late early medieval gentile terminology for political groups referred to a stratum of group tradition which has frequently predated the formation of the institutions of territorial rule. This principle applies to a large number of cases of the continental gentile terminology, where such gentile names as Frisians, Swabians, Franconians, Burgundians or Flemish have lost association with a specific single territory under the control of a secular ruler or were fragmented into various such territories. Examples of continuing usage are rare, such as those of the Danes, the English and the French, whose names and traditions date back to the early medieval period of the formation of political groups.

Second, while secular territorial rule continued between the thirteenth and the eighteenth centuries, attempts were made to establish new political groups. Inside the Empire, the territorial rulers were technically known as 'estates' (*Stände*).[69] Not infrequently, rulers inside the Empire strove to convert groups of ruled with heterogeneous political traditions into novel political groups, and they did so by way of enforcing territory-wide oaths of allegiance which the ruled had to swear to the rulers. But only in rare cases is it arguable that such strategies were successful in accomplishing the intended results. Among the successful cases can, perhaps, be counted the Bavarians and the Saxons as political groups inside the Empire. But in many other cases, such as those of the Hessians, similar attempts failed because of the lack of continuity of institutions of territorial rule. In consequence of this practice, a pluralism of competing political groups existed inside the Empire. Other attempts arose among contractual communities such as the Swiss Confederates in the fifteenth and sixteenth centuries and the Dutch revolutionaries in the sixteenth and seventeenth centuries, or from movements which were formed by neighbourhood groups such as the Hussites in Bohemia during the fifteenth century. The fusion of geographical and social criteria for the naming of these areas was emphasised through the interutilisation of the

---

69 For a definition, see Johann Jakob Moser, *Von der teutschen Reichs-Stände Landen, deren Landständen, Unterthanen, Landes-Freyheiten, Beschwerden, Schulden und Zusammenkünfften*, Moser, Neues teutsches Staatsrecht, vol. 13, 1 (Frankfurt, Leipzig, 1769; repr. Osnabrück, 1967), p. 322. Moser, *Von der Landeshoheit derer teutschen Reichsstände überhaupt*, Moser, Neues teutsches Staatsrecht, vol. 14 (Frankfurt, Leipzig, 1773; repr. Osnabrück, 1968), p. 13.

appellatives 'land' and 'nation'. Already in the fourteenth century, the whole world could be described as an array of territories and political groups.[70]

The early sixteenth-century allegory of Europe shown in Figure 21 visualises these attempts in a crowned female ruler whose body consists of the territories some of which, rightly or wrongly, bear traditional gentile names of political groups (e.g. 'Dania', 'Anglia', 'Francia', 'Bohemia', 'Vandalia'), while others are derived from the geographical knowledge of Antiquity (e.g. 'Italia', 'Hispania', 'Gallia', 'Germania', 'Scythia') or from late medieval geographical terminology (for example, 'Moscovia'). Nevertheless, the allegory suggests that Europe was viewed by the artist as being composed of relatively stable sizeable territories, each under the control of a single ruler and inhabited by political groups. The artist imagined that categories of space mattered more than traditional group cohesion in the definition of political groups. The artist also displayed Europe as an integrated space of regular communication.

Social groups as groups distinguished by the law

It was possible that a person regarded membership in all four previously discussed types of groups in terms of rights as well as obligations, benefits as well as sacrifices. But the fifth and last type of group to be discussed here represents one distinct from the four types previously mentioned. This type of group organised large numbers of persons in many different areas and places of settlement and subjected its members to obligations rather than rights. Social groups arrayed their members in accordance with economic, social or legal criteria, such as wealth, professional identity or availability of the use of the means of production, but irrespective of contractual obligations, political traditions, kin affiliations or place of residence. They became manifest through sets of distinct legal rules, moral norms and esthetic values all of which were specific to members of one social group only. Social groups could be defined horizontally in terms of ranks which could be regarded as obtainable by birth. This was the case first and foremost for the aristocracy and the peasantry in the Middle Ages. The aristocracy took the view that access to its group had been limited to the right of birth by divine will. The clergy also emerged as a horizontally stratified social group but one to which access was based on merit, education and willingness to serve the Church. But social groups could also be defined vertically in terms of professional organisations pulling together persons in the same professions. Access to these social groups could be determined by birth, but was more frequently voluntary. Some professional social groups overlapped with contractual artisans' guilds

---

[70] For one, Ludwig von Eyb, *Denkwürdigkeiten*, ed. Constantin Höfler (Bayreuth, 1849), p. 144, used the fomula 'in the Roman Empire of the German Lands' where the standard usage was 'Holy Roman Empire of the German Nation'. For descriptions of the world as the sum of territories see Domenico Bandino de Actis, *Liber de mundo*. 1391. Ms. Gaddi 126, Florence, Biblioteca Nazionale Laurentiana. *Libro del conoscimiento*, ed. Márcos Jiménez de la Espada (Madrid, 1877), pp. 1–116.

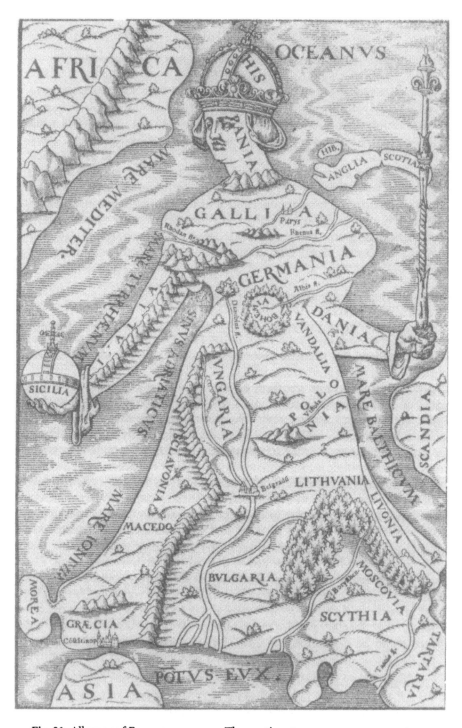

Fig. 21 Allegory of Europe as a queen. The continent appears as an aggregate of territories rather than of population groups. From Sebastian Münster, *Cosmographia* (Basle, 1628), p. 54 (first published Basle, 1544). Münster borrowed the picture from Johannes Pucius who first printed it in 1537.

and merchant companies. Social groups were in existence already in the early Middle Ages, but they rose gradually in importance during the high Middle Ages and went through few changes up until the eighteenth century.

However, both kinds of social group were referred to with the same generic expressions and one, at that, which was also applied to the rulers of some territorialised political groups. The expressions were either the Latin word *ordo* or the French word *état* and its correlates, such as English *estate* and German *Stand*. Next to the political connotation which these words had inside the Empire, their most common meaning referred to three characteristics of social groups: first, that the social groups were conceived as permanent; second, that they carried with them a rigid order which was to be enforced through legal rules, moral norms and esthetic values; third, that the applicability of these codes for each social group was taken to be universal and not confined to specific places and periods.[71] In other words, the aristocrat was to be an aristocrat everywhere in the world, and so was the clergyman, the peasant farmer, the merchant or the member of any social group of professionals. It was thus taken for granted that the rules, norms and values which were assigned to each social group could be enforced upon members even against their will. This was the most important distinguishing criterion between contractual and social groups. Because membership in social groups was involuntary and regarded mainly as the source of obligations, the necessity of justifying social groups arose whereas the existence of other types of groups could have been taken for granted.

The simplest form of justification was the theoretical claim that the legal act establishing this type of group had been commissioned by the divinity because of human sinfulness and that, in consequence, each individual member had to accept membership in one of these groups as an inalterable fact, whether assigned by birth or acquired during a later period of life. The three social groups of the clergy as the *oratores*, the aristocracy as the *bellatores*, and the peasant farming population as the *laboratores* were justified in this way already in the earlier Middle Ages.[72] Likewise, slavery was considered to be justifiable as a part of the divine creation of the world and, therefore, as 'natural' and as an inevitable fate.[73] After the tenth century, the social groups

---

[71] The universalist approach to social groups is best demonstrated in the early fifteenth-century south-German verse novel by Heinrich Wittenwiler, *Der Ring*, ed. Horst Brunner (Stuttgart, 1991).

[72] In the late tenth and early eleventh centuries, Adalbero of Laon, *Carmen ad Robertum regem*, vv. 296–9, ed. Claude Carozzi, *Adalbéron de Laon, Poème au Roi Robert*, Les classiques de l'histoire de France au Moyen Age XXXII (Paris, 1979), p. 22. Aelfric of Eynsham, *Die Hirtenbriefe Aelfrics in altenglischer und lateinischer Fassung*, ed. Bernhard Fehr, Bibliothek der angelsächsischen Prosa IX (Hamburg, 1914; repr. Darmstadt, 1966), pp. 225–6. Aelfric, *Lives of Saints*, vol. 2, ed. Walter William Skeat, Early English Text Society, Original Series CXIV (Oxford, 1890; repr. London, New York, Toronto, 1966), pp. 120–2. Aelfric, *Treatise on the Old and the New Testament*, ed. Samuel John Crawford, Early English Text Society. Original Series CLX (London, 1922), pp. 71–2 (repr., ed. Neil Ripley Ker [London, New York, Toronto, 1969]).

[73] Isidore of Seville, *Sententiarum libri tres*, cap. III/47 (*PL* 83, col. 77). Gregory I, *Moralia*

of the clergy, the aristocracy and the peasantry were regarded in this way as sanctioned by divine ordination, and their members were subjected to rigorous constraints that, in the case of the peasantry, could include a prohibition against spatial and social mobility. However, the negative impact of these constraints was limited throughout the Middle Ages, because peasants still retained some, though not always sufficient opportunities to transfer to another type of group or even to another social group and to choose new places of residence if they so desired. In fact, the coming into existence of many of the medieval towns and cities was a result of the fact that peasant farmers as rural *laboratores* escaped the constraints of their rural existence and joined one of the lay contractual groups in the towns and cities. Subsequently, the early medieval ternary classification scheme was formalised into that of the Church, aristocracy and the commons, who, in the fifteenth century, came to be classed as the Third Estate in France. The Third Estate comprised the rural peasantry and the inhabitants of urban communities of towns and cities, but the latter were also conceptualised as a separate estate in the sixteenth and seventeenth centuries elsewhere in Europe.[74] With the declining significance of the kin, neighbourhood and contractual groups, and as a consequence of the territorialisation of political groups during the fourteenth and fifteenth centuries, the relative impact of social groups on their members increased, and left them an ever-decreasing number of options against the social group into which they had been born. Hence, since the fourteenth century, social groups have gradually risen to a position of dominance over other types of groups, and it became possible to enforce the legal principle that members of parliamentary representative bodies should be selected on the basis of membership in these groups.[75]

The clergy had acquired a fair degree of homogeneity in the tenth and eleventh centuries[76] when monastic reforms restricted access to the monasteries to ordained monks and nuns and enforced a strict separation of the ordained clergy from the lay church members. The clergy was able to main-

---

in *Job*, cap. 21, 15, 22, ed. Marcus Adriaen, CCSL CXLIIIA (Turnhout, 1985), pp. 1082–3.

74 For elaborate descriptions of one of these social groups, see Charles Loyseau, *Traité des ordres et simples dignitez* (Paris, 1613), p. 96. Paul Negelein, *Vom Bürgerlichen Standt* (Amberg, 1600), p. 5.

75 *Modus de tenendi parliamentum*, ed. William Stubbs, *Select Charters and other Illustrations of English Constitutional History*, 5th edn (Oxford, 1884), pp. 503–5. According to the text, the king presided over the meetings of Parliament and called its members in accordance with minutely established criteria of selection which were based on membership in social groups.

76 Beyond the ternary schemes of social groups into which persons were born, further schemes existed which presented more diversified professional groups whose number could be considerable. See K. A. Barack, ed., *Des Teufels Netz. Satirisch-didaktisches Gedicht der ersten Hälfte des 15. Jahrhunderts*, Bibliothek des Literarischen Vereins in Stuttgart LXX (Stuttgart, 1863). Jost Ammann, *Eygentliche Beschreibung aller Stände* (1565), republished under the title *Das Ständebuch von 1565* (Leipzig, 1934). Other editions are (Wiesbaden, 1960), (Nuremberg, 1962), (Frankfurt, 1976).

tain its homogeneity as a social group throughout the Middle Ages and well into the eighteenth century.

The aristocracy which had begun to separate itself from the peasant farmers in the tenth century at the latest, constituted a social group in its own right to which access was possible principally, though not exclusively, by birth[77] and it defended this secular rule for the acquisition of membership in its ranks with the argument that the social groups had been established through the divine act of creation as inalterable elements of the order of the world.[78] These privileges facilitated the emergence of the aristocracy as a comparatively homogeneous social group, whose members continued to adhere to common legal rules, moral norms and esthetic values despite a variety of distinctions of rank among them. But, in the long run, they were more a curse than a favour; for they forced aristocrats to justify their position in the conventional early medieval way, namely as one ordained by the divinity even when such aristocratic self-esteem became despised and ridiculed as a conceit by members of the other social groups. Moreover, aristocratic insistence that its privileges were divinely willed was convincing only if the aristocracy maintained that the other social groups were also justifiable as the result of divine intervention. Yet, except for the clergy, members of most other social groups objected to this perception. Consequently, the aristocracy took a view of social groups which militated against perceptions shared by other social groups. Finally, such conventional attitudes could only be expected to be acceptable if the aristocracy retained its conventional extravagant way of life, namely that of rural landowners, independent military professionals and as the proprietors of rights in land tenure.

That is not to deny that aristocrats could appreciate the value of money; sooner or later, some aristocrats did well as military entrepreneurs between the fourteenth and seventeenth centuries, displayed their commercial ambitions by moving into the towns and cities from the eleventh century, became heads of governments there in the late Middle Ages, and many aristocrats were accustomed to the display of monetary wealth on the occasion of knightly tournaments mainly in the fifteenth and sixteenth centuries.[79] And yet, those who used money did so less for the purpose of accumulating capital than for the display of aristocratic lifestyle. In any case, up until the end of the Middle Ages, those who became accustomed to urban lifestyles represented no more than a small minority in most parts of Europe compared with the majority who chose to stay aloof from or were even opposed to the urban communities. One exceptional area was northern Italy where a system of

---

77 An early reference is in the tenth-century *Gesta Caroli Magni Imperatoris*, by Notker of St Gall, cap. I/1, ed. Hans Frieder Haefele, *MGH SS rer. Germ.* N. S. 12, p. 2.

78 See Etienne de Fougères, *Livre des manières*, vv. 581–676, ed. Josef Kremer, Ausgaben und Abhandlungen aus dem Gebiete der Romanischen Philologie XXIX (Marburg, 1887), pp. 129–31.

79 Georg Rüxner, *Von Anfängen, Ursachen, Ursprung und Herkommen der Thurnier im heyligen Römischen Reich Teutscher Nation* [1530], ed. Sigmund Feyerabend (Frankfurt, 1566).

city-states emerged during the Middle Ages in which many aristocrats joined
the urban patriciates. Moreover, aristocrats who were seriously involved in
manufacturing, trade and business, such as Earl Heinrich Rantzau (1526–98)
in sixteenth century Schleswig-Holstein, or some aristocrats in Brandenburg[80]
and elsewhere during the seventeenth century, adhered to conventional ways
of life and continued to choose reactionary strategies for the preservation and
justification of their social group. Such conservatism barred many of them
from participating significantly in the new, capitalist forms of production and
trade, which emerged in the urban communities of towns and cities.

By contrast, the heterogeneous group which was sometimes classed as part
of the Third Estate comprised the diverse populations of the towns and cities.
It is therefore hard to define as a specific social group in its earlier history. For
its classification as 'bourgeois' owes its origin to the late eighteenth and the
nineteenth centuries and has little bearing on the medieval self-image of the
groups so denoted. However, it is possible to show that, by the twelfth century,
written legal frameworks were set up as constitutions in certain towns and
cities by their governments, according to which the settlers were considered to
form sworn-in contractual communities under the rule of law. In turn, these
constitutions legitimised rules which the urban governments enforced and
according to which the inhabitants of towns and cities, namely merchant
traders, artisans, clergy, scholars and land-holding aristocrats or their urban
representatives, were stratified. Such constitutions could be transferred from
one place to another, and this process occurred with regularity when new
towns were founded by neighbourhood groups migrating from their established place of residence to new settlements, mainly established in the north-
east of Europe during the twelfth and thirteenth centuries. Consequently, it is
possible to say that, by the twelfth century, the groups of settlers in urban
communities began to identify themselves as a distinct social group, even
though it did not necessarily comprise all inhabitants of a town or city, nor
did it uniformly include the inhabitants of all towns and cities. With their
emergence as a distinct social group, the retrospectively so-called 'bourgeoisie' felt the need to justify its existence. But its justification deviated fundamentally from the conventional religious means of justification used by the
aristocracy. The differences were, first, that the 'bourgeois' means of justification were secular in that they were not based on an exegesis of Biblical tradition and, second, that the 'bourgeoisie' employed for its justification the
dominant feature characterising the activities of its paramount contractual

---

[80] Rantzau developed a remarkable skill in monetary business and, on one occasion, lent
out 375,000 thalers to the city of Antwerp. Even if, in consequence of the war of the
Netherlands against the King of Spain, Rantzau was unable to retrieve the money from
the city, he remained a wealthy landowner to his death. See *Inventare hansischer Archive
des sechzehnten Jahrhunderts: Kölner Archive*, No. 230, ed. Konstantin Höhlbaum, vol. 2
(Leipzig, 1903), pp. 882–3 (a letter by Dr Heinrich Sudermann, Cologne citizen and
Hansa syndic who informed Rantzau about the financial difficulties of the Antwerp city
government in spring 1586). For the Brandenburg aristocracy, see *Kurmärkische Stän-
deakten*, ed. Walter Friedensburg, vol. 1 (Munich, 1913–16), pp. 37–9, 57, 82–3.

groups, namely the contracts establishing the guilds and companies of merchant traders. Through their rejection of divine ordination as the justifying ground for their own social group and through the acceptance of contractualism as the leading justifying principle, the 'bourgeoisie' became the most dynamic of all social groups in the later Middle Ages and was capable of employing the then newly evolving experiences of time, concepts of space and modes of behaviour for its own benefit. In consequence, the towns and cities became the centres of innovation, and their leading patriciates powerfully articulated demands for change.

Moreover, the use of contractualism as a justification of the 'bourgeois' social group was already manifest in the thirteenth century, when town councils began to codify rules for the town government, which was perceived as rule by consent,[81] and when the urban patriciates began to establish contractual unions among themselves, originally designed for the management of joint defence and to minimise the risks involved in long-distance trade.[82] These unions could also develop into territorial alliances, of which the most successful and lasting was the union of towns and local aristocratic landowners in the Netherlands.[83] This union was formally established only in 1579, but it originated in the early fourteenth-century contractual arrangements between urban communities of towns and cities and aristocrats on their joint resistance against the King of France as the territorial ruler in the area. The initial key goal of this and other unions was the preservation of the freedom of the market against intrusion or intervention from outside governments. Finally, early in the fourteenth century, contractualism emerged as the dominant means of justifying existing administrative institutions.[84]

Throughout the high and late Middle Ages, the rural peasantry continued as a social group from the *laboratores* of the early Middle Ages. For different reasons, the clergy, the aristocracy and the 'bourgeoisie' looked down upon them. The clergy did so because, in its own hierarchical world view, the peasants formed the 'feet' of the 'body politic', its lowest and least significant part.[85] The aristocracy looked at the peasants as their servants and sources of revenue. Moreover, because the peasants were excluded from participating in the life of the courts with their peculiar moral norms and esthetic values, the aristocracy maintained that the peasants had rude manners,[86] were 'unreaso-

---

81 Joseph Baader, ed., *Nürnberger Polizeiordnungen aus dem XIII. bis XV. Jahrhundert*, Bibliothek des Litterarischen Vereins in Stuttgart LXIII (Tübingen, 1861; repr. Amsterdam, Atlanta, 1966), pp. 25–6.

82 Keutgen (see note 56), No. 251.

83 Ernst Heinrich Kossmann, A. F. Mellink, eds, *Texts Concerning the Revolt of the Netherlands* (Cambridge, 1974).

84 Engelbert of Admont, 'De ortu imperii Romani', cap. 2, ed. Melchior Goldast, *Politica Imperialia* (Frankfurt, 1614), pp. 754–5.

85 John of Salisbury, *Policraticus*, cap. VI/20, ed. C. J. Webb (London, 1909; repr. New York, 1979), pp. 618c–19c.

86 See, for example, *Neidharts Lieder*, Winterlied 24/III, 31/VII, ed. Moriz Haupt, 2nd edn by Edmund Wiessner (Leipzig, 1923; repr. Stuttgart, 1986), pp. 74, 90.

nable men and did not know how to behave'.[87] The 'bourgeoisie' was contemptuous of the peasants because the peasants preferred to adhere to conventional agricultural practices and did not participate in the urban life in towns and cities where children would go to school and adolescents would be trained as apprentices or could study in universities, where merchants would know how to trade in precious goods of remote origin, to deal with money and to handle a wide difference of currencies and where artisans would excel in the best and most recent techniques of production. Hence, from the point of view of the 'bourgeoisie', the peasants were uneducated and simple folk.[88]

However, for much of the entire Middle Ages, the disproportionate number of sources written by the clergy, aristocrats and townspeople prevent us from having a great deal of insight into the norms and rules, images and self-esteem which the peasants may have developed as a social group at the time. Nevertheless, the peasantry was in itself stratified. At a time when land-holding aristocrats and other free persons still had their residences in agricultural settlements, archaeological and some written sources do seem to suggest that a dependent peasantry already existed in western Europe in late Roman times and that it greatly increased in number during the early Middle Ages. During the fourteenth, fifteenth and sixteenth centuries when some legal documents were created which reflected the world of the peasantry, we can observe that this social group was, in fact, capable of articulating its own demands *vis-à-vis* the landed aristocracy and the territorial rulers and of establishing communal organisations on the basis of neighbourhood groups.[89] Therefore it has been erroneous to assume that peasant farmers as a dependent social group lived a solely passive life. Instead, peasant farmers who were ready to enter into critical discourse, were not without success at local levels and were thus able to ferment change throughout the Middle Ages.

Conclusion

The overview of the conceptual history of the five types of groups shows that the importance of three of them, kin groups, neighbourhood groups and contractual groups declined during the high Middle Ages. In the case of the kin groups, the decline was a consequence of their shrinking size and the loss of their norm-preserving, rule-enforcing and legitimacy-conveying capabilities. The importance of the neighbourhood groups waned mainly because migrations occurred less frequently after the seventh century and left less

---

87 *Anonimalle Chronicle*, s. a. 1381, ed. Vivian Hunter Galbraith, Publications of the University of Manchester. History Series XLV (Manchester, 1927), p. 139.

88 Sebastian Brant, *Narrenspiegel* [first edn (Basle, 1494)], No. 72, ed. Elvira Pradt (Frankfurt, 1980), pp. 205–7.

89 See, for one, Jakob Grimm, ed., *Weisthümer*, vol. 4 (Göttingen, 1863; repr. Darmstadt, 1957), pp. 594–6.

room for their autonomous organisation. However, neighbourhood groups remained active throughout the Middle Ages as instruments for the articulation of protest and for violent resistance. Among the contractual groups, the militarily active groups were gradually subjected to the control and peace legislation of territorial rulers from the eleventh century, and the religiously active contractual groups of monks and nuns were already coming under closer supervision of bishops by the tenth century. Artisans' guilds and merchant companies, however, remained in existence and constituted the 'bourgeoisie' as the most innovative types of groups after the eleventh century.

The shrinking size, reduced competence and declining autonomy of kin, neighbourhood and contractual groups paved the way for the rising administrative and legal importance of political and social groups. The territorial rulers of the high and late Middle Ages faced waning resistance from kin groups against their bid for the accumulation of rights to rule over land and people, placed themselves in control of the mainly rural neighbourhoods either directly or through mediatised lesser aristocrats, and could thus constrain the activities of the militarily active contractual groups. They could finally emerge at the top of a hierarchy of social groups which they could portray as static and divinely willed. Moreover, the territorial rulers became the most effective promoters of political groups, although few of them actually succeeded in constituting new political groups. At the same time, the rules and norms governing social groups could be applied more rigorously, because members of social groups had at their disposal a declining number of options among the groups into which they had been born or had otherwise been integrated.

V

Men and Women

The most general statement that is possible about the history of the relations
between the sexes in Europe is that, throughout several periods in its history,
Christianity, as represented by the Roman Catholic and the Protestant
Churches, has thoroughly impacted on the relationship between men and
women. These impacts have been twofold: first, Christian moral doctrine has
denounced sexuality as evil; second, Christian ontology has depreciated
women by supporting the classification of the female sex as secondary and
weak and has enforced as well as amplified the androcratic conventions which
were inherited from Roman law and which had also been enshrined in
Germanic traditions. Taken together, these impacts have fundamentally transformed the triad of relations between persons of either sex, namely institutionality, emotionality and sexuality.

This statement is not intended to repeat the assertion, from a proposal by
Tacitus that was developed in the late eighteenth and the nineteenth centuries,
that women in Germanic Antiquity and the early Middle Ages enjoyed a
happy status of freedom and equality and that they lost this status in the
course of the Middle Ages.[1] Evidently, Tacitus as well as his romanticist
followers overlooked the fact that the Germanic and early medieval world was
male dominated and hierarchically structured. Yet it is equally inappropriate
to overlook the lack of manifest anti-feminism and explicit misogynistic
rhetoric in the substantive early medieval corpus of saints' lives and the preva-
lence, at the time, of double-descent kin groups wherein women did enjoy

---

* To my grief you have torn the shining summer flower of my pleasure from the treasure
   of my heart; you have treacherously disrupted my happiness, my chosen turtle dove;
   you have robbed me irredeemably.
[1] Tacitus, *Germania*, cap. 7, 18, 19 [various editions]. William Alexander, *The History of
   Women from the Earliest Antiquity to the Present Time* (London, 1779). John Mitchell
   Kemble, *The Saxons in England*, vol. 1 (London, 1849), p. 233.

equal opportunities as inheritors of rights-and traditions.[2] The statement is also valid despite the existence, since the Middle Ages, of authoritative opinions and even laws against the depreciation of women.[3] Finally, the statement is not invalidated by the fact that there have been, throughout European history, individual women who have successfully asserted their abilities and capabilities in a male-dominated world, and that, since the eighteenth century, organised women's liberation movements have had considerable success in reducing the depreciation of women.

There is then a marked contrast between the female–male relationships in the early Middle Ages on the one hand and, on the other, in the high and late Middle Ages when a massive corpus of explicitly misogynistic rhetoric and, more importantly, manifest acts of discrimination against and suppression of women are on record. The origins of misogynistic rhetoric and of discriminatory and suppressive androcratic practices need to be explained.

Double descent in early medieval kin groups

Early medieval kinship was based on double descent. Double descent did not rule out androcracy but it did award equal significance to both women and men in the formation and maintenance of their kin groups as lineages in which descent was the single most important status-conveying factor.[4] Hence the history of the relationship between the sexes in high and late medieval European culture is the history of the waning of double descent and of the intensification of androcratic rules, attitudes and practices within kin groups. An important, if indirect, piece of evidence for the practical aspects of the relationship between the sexes is contained in extant king-lists and genealogies. Collections of such lists of names have been preserved in English manuscripts that are probably late eighth century. They array names either according to parent–child sequence (genealogy or pedigree) or by the succession of incumbents to the royal office (king-lists). In the present context, genealogies are more important than king-lists because they may also list names of ancestors who were not incumbents to a royal office. Moreover, Old English genealogies are particularly interesting because, up to the eighth

---

2   For studies of these matters, see Cordula Nolte, *Conversio und Christianitas: Frauen in der Christianisierung vom 5. bis 8. Jahrhundert*, Monographien zur Geschichte des Mittelalters XLI (Stuttgart, 1995), pp. 296–7. Friedrich Prinz, 'Der Heilige und seine Lebenswelt', *Santi e demoni nell' alto medioevo occidentale*, Settimane di studio del Centro Italiano di studi sull' alto medioevo XXXVI (Spoleto, 1989), p. 302.

3   Among others, St Thomas Aquinas argued that the Biblical account of the creation did not license an exegesis to the disadvantage of women. However, the principle has remained uncontested in Christian doctrine that the male sex is and ought to be dominant. See Thomas Aquinas, *In quattuor libros sententiarum*, II dist. 18, qu. q, art. 1, ed. Roberto Busa, *Sancti Thomae Aquinatis Opera omnia*, vol. 1 (Stuttgart, 1980), p. 175.

4   For an early reference to this notion of descent group see Cassiodore, *Variarvm libri XII*, cap. XI/1, ed. Åke J. Fridh, CCSL XCVI (Turnhout, 1973), p. 424.

century, several independent kingdoms coexisted, whose royal kin groups
were closely related by kinship ties. These royal kin groups were not always
united and their members did not always share common interests, but they
seem to have agreed upon a ranking scheme according to which the rank of a
kin group was determined by the length of the kin tradition which was
recorded orally in genealogies. The difference in rank among these kin groups
was expressed after marriage arrangements through the practice of transfer-
ring names from the kin group with a higher rank to that of a lower rank. The
implication of this practice was that women acted as important agents of the
transfer of genealogical tradition within the relations among the various royal
kin groups and, at the same time, as authoritative transmitters of genealogical
knowledge.[5] This position was not unique to the British Isles but can be found
in various parts of early medieval continental Europe as well. It displays
double descent as the standard early medieval succession rule. For example,
when Charlemagne prohibited the transmission of lay 'songs', he did so in a
capitulary concerning nunneries. This must be read as an indication that the
women living in nunneries at the turn of the ninth century were involved in
the transmission of oral material among which genealogical knowledge was
usually featured.[6] Therefore, the genealogies cannot have been straightforward concoctions as long as they were transmitted orally, even though they
may have been adapted to the changing interests of the kin groups within
which they were passed on. Likewise, the influence which women could exert
in monasteries did not result from a particular care which the Church applied
to women but flew from the positions of respect which women could hold in
the extended double-descent kin groups. That this was so becomes evident
from the fact that a large number of early monastic foundations were proprietary institutions maintained by the kin groups whose members acted as
founders while they did not immediately come under the sway of the Church.
Moreover, most female saints up to the ninth century were women from royal
or high aristocratic kin groups.

The ability of women to transfer genealogical tradition and to transmit
genealogical knowledge from one royal kin group to another and from
generation to generation, was a factor of political power, even if, as a rule,
women were not admitted to the royal office itself. They played integral parts
in the royal ceremonial,[7] supported military action[8] and shaped political

---

5   Asser, *Life of King Alfred*, cap. 2, ed. William Henry Stevenson (Oxford, 1904), p. 4
    (repr., ed. Dorothy Whitelock [Oxford, 1959]).
6   Alfred Boretius, ed., *MGH Capit.* 1, No. 19, p. 63. That genealogical knowledge was con-
    tained in oral narratives emerges from *Beowulf*, vv. 1063–159, ed. Frederick Klaeber, 3rd
    edn (Lexington, Mass., 1950), pp. 40–4.
7   For a vernacular narrative source, see *Beowulf* (see note 6), vv. 612–30, 1192–1231, pp.
    23–4, 45–7. For a normative source, see the so-called Edgar *ordo* of the late tenth
    century, ed. Percy Ernst Schramm, *Kaiser, Könige und Päpste*, vol. 2 (Stuttgart, 1968),
    pp. 239–40.
8   *Tain Bo Culaigne*, ed. Thomas Kinzella (Philadelphia, 1970), p. 208. Fictional reports on
    female warriors commonly referred to as Amazons featured in medieval literature, for
    example in the fourteenth-century *Book of the City of the Ladies* by Christine de Pizan,

decisions.[9] Likewise, they could hold, dispose of and inherit landed property in their own right as the large number of private charters which name women as land donors confirm.[10] Hence they had a share in the long-term rise and fall of royal kin groups and, for that matter, in the formation and decline of kingdoms as a whole.

Early medieval legal sources differentiated between the position of women as kin members (*ingenuae*) and ordinary women. Specific efforts were made to protect the bodily integrity of *ingenuae* by means of strict prohibitions of purposeful touching of the woman's body. Four different kinds of purposeful touching were prohibited and anyone infringing these prohibitions had to pay the following compensations, according to the eighth century Frankish Salic Law: If an *ingenuus*, a man of kin, touched the finger or the head of an *ingenua*, he had to pay fifteen shillings or half of the fine for the forced abduction of a woman. If an *ingenuus* touched an arm of an *ingenua*, thirty shillings were due, the exact equivalent of the fine for the same crime. If an *ingenuus* placed his hand on an elbow of an *ingenua*, the compensation fee was thirty-five shillings or the equivalent of the fine for the intended mutilation of a finger used for shooting arrows. Finally, if an *ingenuus* dared to touch an *ingenua*'s breast, he was forced to give forty-five shillings, equivalent of what had to be paid for illegal sexual intercourse with a married *ingenua*.[11] The severity of these punishments suggests that, in the eighth century, the specified acts of illegal purposeful touching of parts of a woman's body were categorised as attempted attacks on the woman through abduction, injury or sexual abuse. Because these punishments were specifically applied to attacks on women of kin, they can thus be understood as efforts to prevent potential or manifest acts of aggression against women as protected members of kin groups.[12] Evidently, men regarded women not merely as sex objects in the early Middle Ages.

At first sight, however, it may appear that the laws could also fundamentally reduce the position of women in the kin groups because women could be

Le Livre de la cité des dames, ed. Maureen Cheney Curnow, vol. 1. PhD dissertation (Vanderbilt University, 1975), part I, cap. XVI–XVII.

9 A good case is reported in the seventh-century *Vita Columbani Abbatis discipulorum-que*, cap. 19, ed. Bruno Krusch, *MGH SS rer. Merov.*, vol. 4, pp. 87–8. The saint had made an effort to convert sons of Frankish kings to a religious life, but encountered the staunch resistance of the elderly Queen Brunichildis who insisted that the members of the royal kin group ought to remain committed to their traditional activity as rulers. The story was inserted in the Chronicle by the so-called Fredegar, *Chronicarum libri IV*, cap. IV/ 36, ed. Bruno Krusch, *MGH SS rer. Merov.* 2, pp. 135–6. Likewise, according to the *Life of St Gertrud*, this seventh-century Frankish saint, could refer to her mother as the 'mater familias'. *Vita S. Geretrudis A*, cap. 2, ed. Bruno Krusch, *MGH SS rer. Merov.* 2, pp. 455–6.

10 See, for example, *Urkundenbuch der Abtei Sanct Gallen*, ed. Hermann Wartmann, 4 parts (Zurich, St Gall, 1863–99).

11 *Lex Salica. 100-Titel Text*, cap. 26, 1–4, ed. Karl August Eckhardt (Weimar, 1953), p. 142.

12 *Lex Salica* (see note 11), cap. 93, pp. 232–4. For an empirical case, see *Vita S. Geretrudis A* (see note 9), cap. 2, pp. 455–6.

subjected to the jurisdiction of a male kin group elder who dominated the living members of the kin group under his charge. It was also possible to have specific forms of marriage concluded as contracts between male kin-group elders who would not inquire about the will of the marriage partners (*munt*). The male kin-group elders could occupy such positions because they were credited with the task of representing all living kin-group members *vis-à-vis* the dead. Thus the belief that the kin groups comprised living as well as dead members awarded to the male kin-group elders a position of unrivalled respect. But, in contrast with Roman law, the dominant position of male kin-group elders did not exclude the rule of double descent for hereditary succession and thereby women retained their own distinct role as the bearers of genealogical tradition within and across the boundaries of their kin groups.

From the very beginning of the Christian mission in areas north of the Alps, the Church intervention in marriage rules had the effect of weakening the position of women in the kin groups. One important instrument was sexual discrimination. For example, seventh-, eighth-and ninth-century ecclesiastical canons prevented menstruating women from attending mass service, thereby temporarily segregating women from the community of believers, and subjected sexual intercourse and childbirth to a number of taboos.[13] The Church applied the theory of concupiscence took the position that painful birth was a divine punishment for human sinfulness, and made pragmatic efforts to limit sexual intercourse to what was held to be the divinely ordained necessity of human reproduction.[14] The combination of both attitudes had three consequences: first, a ban on extra-marital sexual intercourse, second, the downgrading of marital sexual intercourse to a licensed evil act, excusable only if conducted with the explicit goal of producing legitimate children, and, third, the praise of celibacy and service to the Church as a means to obtain eternal rewards in the afterlife.

The church intervention in pre-Christian marriage rules then depreciated women in a variety of different ways. First, the Church accepted as legitimate only marriages which were concluded by the free will and mutual consent of the partners.[15] Even though the Church did so explicitly in an attempt to achieve the equality of marital status for both men and women, throughout the early Middle Ages, the only noteworthy results of this attempt were that the status of women who had not been married in accordance with the canonical rules was reduced to that of concubines and that the number of illegitimate children increased. This was so because male kin-group elders main-

---

13 *Das Theodor'sche Rechtsbuch*, cap. XI, ed. Hermann Josef Schmitz, *Die Bußbücher und das kanonische Bußverfahren*, vol. 2, *Die Bußbücher und die Bußdisciplin der Kirche* (Düsseldorf, 1898), pp. 575–9.

14 Augustine, *De Genesi ad Manichaeos*, cap. II/19 (*PL* 34, cols 210–11). Implicit in 'The Old English Genesis', vv. 740–62, ed. George Philip Krapp, *The Junius Manuscript*, Anglo-Saxon Poetic Records I, (New York, London, 1953), pp. 25–6. Jonas of Orléans, *De institutione laicali*, cap. II/10 (*PL* 106, cols. 186–7).

15 An early reference to consensus marriage is in a letter by Pope Nicholas I of 13 June 866, ed. Ernst Perels, *MGH Epp. Karol.* 4, p. 315.

tained their prerogative of arranging marriages for junior kin members. Moreover, pre-Christian kin groups had known a variety of different forms of legitimate marriage. Next to the *munt*, these forms included, among others, the levirate[16] as the marriage with a female widowed kin member. Variegated forms of legitimate marriage served to interconnect the kin groups and to provide support for widows. A compromise between the kin-group conventions and canon law was possible if the *munt* marriage was agreed upon as the sole type of legitimate marriage. This was acceptable for the kin-group elders who retained their positions of respect and also for the Church which could ban rival forms of marriage.[17] But the compromise subjected women in wedlock to the rule of men. Moreover, attempts were made to enforce the Roman principle of the indissolubility of legitimate marriages. Because the Church strove to enforce this principle at the same time when it effectively supported the *munt* marriage, women were deprived of important legal means for the termination of marriage arrangements which they found unsatisfactory, even though men also lost their freedom to terminate marriages.[18] Finally, the Church tried to change the exogamy rules by extending the kin grades within which legitimate marriages were forbidden. As a result, the Church came to adopt a position according to which a marriage could only be terminated if it had been concluded illegally, namely incestuously, that is in violation of the new exogamy rules, or without mutual consent of the marriage partners.

The process of enforcing these rules was incremental. At about AD 600, Pope Gregory I had been aware that some of the principles governing the kin groups outside the Roman Empire of Antiquity were difficult to reconcile with Christian canon law, but he advised his missionaries to refrain from attempting to enforce canon law in the communities of newly converted believers.[19] During the remaining part of the first millennium, however, the

---

16 Bede, *Historia ecclesiastica gentis Anglorum*, cap. I/27, ed. Bertram Colgrave, R. A. B. Mynors (Oxford, 1969), p. 84. The church ban on leviratic marriages had been approved by the Nicene Council of 325.

17 Marriages 'against the law and the stipulations of the king and the bishops' were banned in the *Laws of King Wihtred of Kent*, cap. 5, ed. Felix Liebermann, *Die Gesetze der Angelsachsen*, vol. 1 (Halle, 1903), p. 12. These late seventh-century laws reflect the practice of marriage contracts which were concluded against the will of the Church and the rules which the king tried to enforce upon recommendation by the Church. The logic of the rule can only have been to put an end to a widespread custom.

18 A particularly controversial case occurred in the second half of the ninth century when Emperor Lothair II wished to divorce from his wife Theutberga and was resisted by Pope Nicholas I who argued for the indissolubility of marriage. See Regino of Prüm, *Chronica*, s. a. 864, ed. Friedrich Kurze, *MGH SS rer. Germ.* (50), pp. 80–2. Hinkmar of Rheims, *De divortio Lotharii regis et Theutbergae reginae*, ed. Letha Böhringer, MGH Concilia. Supplementum I (Hanover, 1992).

19 Pope Gregroy I, *Libellus*, containing replies to questions on liturgy and canon law asked by Archbishop Augustine of Canterbury, the Catholic missionary to England. The *libellus* has been preserved in Bede (see note 16), ibid. Still in the eighth century, questions regarding canonical marriage law were vital, and Pope Gregory's *libellus* was considered

clergy made its own effort towards subjecting the particularist kin groups to the universalist principles governing canon law, and secular rulers began to sever kinship ties through the introduction of novel legislation, which affected the legal status and the traditional privileges of women more than those of men.[20] The changes of marriage rules had the long-term consequence that the kin groups declined, their capability of providing security and support for its individual members waned, and the original rights of women were reduced, as they found it increasingly difficult to act as the transmitters of a genealogical tradition of their own inside and beyond the kin groups.

Moreover, the Church used its authority to construct an opposition between the kin groups and the emerging religious communities of monks and nuns. For example, the church propagated the ideal that female and male believers seeking entry into religious communities had to agree to lifelong separation from their own kin groups. A hagiographic topos appeared in monastic communities according to which the venerated saint had purposefully separated him- or herself from the kin group of his or her origin and entrusted his or her life totally to the Church. This hagiographic topos implied that the Church began to act as a competitor with the kin groups in the provision of security and support in life and, even more importantly, in eternity. It did so despite the fact that a number of cases were recorded where mothers continued to live together with their children even after the children had devoted themselves to the Church.[21] Because, initially, this hagiographic topos was applied to men and women alike, entry into monastic communities was attractive to both sexes. But the Church did not restrict its activities to the establishment of institutions which were understood as antitypes to the kin groups. Instead, the Church also tried to intervene directly in the affairs of the kin groups themselves, specifically the royal and high aristocratic kin groups. It did so by supporting succession rules according to which candidates of only one branch of a royal kin group could be eligible for succession, while collateral branches were to be excluded. The best-known early case is the conversion of the Frankish King Clovis to Catholicism at the end of the fifth century. The king had expressed his anxieties that he might suffer from a reduction of his power in the case of separating himself from his ancestors of the Frankish royal kin group, but he was advised by Bishop Avitus of Vienne that the Church was an equally powerful legitimising institution.[22] However, neither

a major guideline. See *Die Briefe des Heiligen Bonifatius und Lullus*, No. 33, ed. Michael Tangl, *MGH Epp. sel.* 1, pp. 56–8 (a letter of St Boniface in which he asked Archbishop Nothhelm of Canterbury to provide him with a copy of Pope Gregory's *libellus*).

20 See Jonas of Orléans (see note 14), cap. II/8, cols 183–4. *Lex Visigothorum*, cap. III/5,2, ed. Karl Zeumer, *MGH LL nat. Germ.* 1, pp. 159–60. *Laws of Liutprand* (723), cap. 32, 76, ed. Georg Heinrich Pertz, *MGH LL [in folio]*, 4, pp. 123, 138. See also note 16 above.

21 Willibald, *Vita Bonifatii*, cap. 1, ed. Wilhelm Levison, *MGH SS rer. Germ.* (57), pp. 5–6. *Vita S. Sadlabergae abbatissae*, cap. 11, ed. Bruno Krusch, *MGH SS rer. Merov.* 5, p. 55.

22 Avitus of Vienne, *Opera omnia quae supersunt*, ed. Rudolf Peiper, *MGH AA* 6, 2, pp. 75–6.

Clovis himself nor his immediate successors renounced their ancestry. The earliest recorded attempts to manifestly exclude collateral lines from succession to kingship date from around AD 700 and were controversial.[23]

Nevertheless, the kin groups did not give in easily. The struggle between the Church and the kin groups lasted throughout the conversion phase, and the latter could maintain their position well into the tenth century, although with declining success. During this long period of transition, some, mainly royal and high aristocratic kin groups were faster than others in trying to narrow down the scope of their kinship ties to partilinear descent. This tendency was most notable in the royal kin groups. Others may have been more resilient. Thus the early eleventh-century Worms *hofrecht* recorded the continuing existence of kin groups as support organisations in the rural settlements under the control of the Bishop of Worms.[24] In either case, the maintenance of the rights and privileges of kin group members of either sex crucially hinged upon the continuing particularism of the norms and values transmitted within the kin groups and upon the maintenance of their legitimacy-conveying, norm-preserving and law-enforcing capabilities.

For the most part, the temporary success of the kin groups in maintaining their positions was due to their ability, first, to obtain high positions in ecclesiastical institutions, such as the offices of abbots and abbesses in monasteries, and bishops' offices, and second, to create cults of saints around some of their deceased members. The strategy was successful in many cases where kin groups of high rank and sufficient wealth were involved who could endow and maintain churches and monasteries from their own funds. For example, in Britain, the royal kin groups of East Anglia, Mercia, Kent and Wessex were conspicuous in establishing a large number of cults of saints for deceased members of their kin in the seventh, eighth and ninth centuries. Examples of similar activities were recorded about aristocratic kin groups in Mercia and Wessex. In both cases, men and women were roughly equally represented among the venerated saints.[25] That is to say that, although aristocratic kin groups supported the conversion process they did so by way of founding their own proprietary churches and establishing monastic communities at their own costs and under their own leadership.[26] Whereas the ban by canon law against women priests prevented women from becoming bishops, no such discrimination existed in connection with the monastic communities and the cult of the saints. Under the protection of the kin groups women could hold

---

[23] Associated with King Ine of Wessex and his contemporary King Wihtred of Kent. Bede (see note 16), cap. III/7, p. 242, referred to controversies about West Saxon succession in passing, and Abbess Eangyth and her daughter Heaburg, called Bugga, hinted at similar difficulties in Kent in their letter to Boniface (see note 19), no 14, p. 23.

[24] Burchard of Worms, *Lex familiae Wormatiensis ecclesiae*, cap. 30, ed. Heinrich Boos, *Urkundenbuch der Stadt Worms*, vol. 1 (Worms, 1886), pp. 43–4.

[25] See the (probably) late tenth-century list of English royal and aristocratic saints in Felix Liebermann, ed., *Die Heiligen Englands* (Hanover, 1889), pp. 10–20.

[26] Hinkmar of Rheims, *Collectio de ecclesiis et capellis*, ed. Martina Stratmann MGH Fontes iuris. Germ. ant. XIV (Hanover, 1990).

high offices in monasteries; most notably, some of the double monasteries had abbesses as their heads. Women were also active as lay founders of monastic institutions, as missionaries, as learned correspondents and as patrons of the clergy.[27]

Within the overarching structure of the double-descent kin groups, the emotional features of the relationship between women and men remains vague and unclear for the early Middle Ages. This is partly due to the fact that most of the extant written sources from the period describe the interactions between men and women from the point of view of the Catholic clergy who, as a rule, showed little interest in describing emotional matters. In the few sources containing references to emotionality, the dominant issue was extramarital sexual intercourse, with the male side taking an active part.[28] Also, there are penitential canons which denounced as 'fornicatio' extramarital sexual intercourse in which females initiated the encounter.[29] But the evidential value of such sources concerning the personal features of the relationship between women and men is restricted: first, because these sources focus on the physical side of sexuality, second, because a reference to extramarital sexual intercourse may represent an accusation maliciously targeted at the protagonist who is mentioned in the source, and, third, because canons are normative sources and, therefore, are not representative of the variety of features that may actually have existed. Hence, one cannot glean from such sources the impression that there might have been a general lack of affectionate emotionality among the sexes in the early Middle Ages. Such a hypothesis is further weakened by the counter-evidence that, among the earliest extant personal letters written by early medieval missionaries, pieces exist which show a substantive emotionality of relations between men and women, although, in these cases, these relations stood outside the confines of marital life and, much as we know, excluded sexual intercourse.[30]

Consequently, it appears to be more appropriate to suggest that affectionate emotionality did not feature prominently in the extant sources because what mattered under the conditions of life in double-descent kin groups was not the fulfilment of the personal wishes and desires of the members, but rather the maintenance of variegated networks of relations as represented by the kin groups as a whole. Under these conditions, affectionate emotionality had to be, as it were, distributed among various kin members,

---

27 Boniface, Letters (see note 19), No. 27, 29, 30, 35, 65, 66, 67, 94, 97, pp. 47–9, 52–4, 137–40, 214–15, 217–18.
28 *The Anglo-Saxon Chronicle: A Collaborative Edition*, vol. 3: Ms A, s. a. 755, ed. Janet M. Bately (Cambridge 1986), pp. 36–8. In this entry, the reigning King Cynewulf of Wessex is subjected to harsh criticisms for inapt behaviour in office to the disadvantage of his retainers.
29 *Poenitentiale Bedae*, ed. Friedrich Wilhelm Hermann Wasserschleben, *Die Bußordnungen der abendländischen Kirche* (Halle, 1851), p. 223 (a penitential rule against Lesbian relations).
30 Boniface, Letters (see note 19).

whereas its focus on two individuals of either sex required separation for the most part from the kin groups to which they respectively belonged. Such a separation required extraordinary circumstances, such as those conditioned by church-stipulated activities, namely missionary travel or pilgrimages. Hence, the appearance in the early medieval missionary correspondence of examples of affectionate emotionality in the relations between men and women, evinces both that affectionate emotionality did occur in the early Middle Ages and that it was an exceptional occurrence if two individuals focused their affectionate emotionality exclusively on each other.

In summary, the double-descent kin groups which had emerged as the paramount social and political institutions during the early Middle Ages, could accomplish the tasks of distributing or dispersing three initially separate aspects of the relations between men and women, namely institutionality, sexuality and emotionality. The various types of relations, which were possible within and across these kin groups, made it possible for persons of either sex to interconnect these different aspects of the female–male relationship with different individuals at the same time. Thus the institutionalisation of marriage did not require the focus of the other two aspects coevally on identical individuals, neither from the female nor from the male side. Instead, it offered varieties of choice for the distribution or dispersal of those relationships among various persons of either sex, both for the purpose of personal satisfaction and for the maintenance of kin networks.

The waning of the double-descent kin groups

Even if, throughout most of the conversion process, the kin groups managed to stay in control of the lives and fates of their members up until the eighth and ninth centuries, the Church eventually, though gradually succeeded in absorbing the major tasks of the kin groups, namely the care of the dead, the protection of the unmarried and the maintenance of the existing traditions of double descent. Eventually, by the tenth century, the Church became powerful enough to force lay kin members out of the monasteries, where they had been represented as lay clerics, and, moreover, out of the larger proprietary religious institutions, where the Church began to insist upon the principle of non-intervention from the side of secular lords and rulers. Moreover, the Church succeeded in subjecting the local cults of saints to its own central administrative control, concentrated saints' relics in central places and began to establish a formal procedure for the canonisation of future saints under its own exclusive control and the effective supervision of the pope.

The reduction of the influence of the kin groups ushered in an increase of personal competition among men for secular achievements in war as well as rule over land and people. This was so because the kin groups were no longer capable of assuring their members the rights and privileges they had formerly enjoyed and left it to their individual members to assert their own status, accumulate their own wealth and protect themselves against rivals. This competition became visible first in the Church itself, where individuals could be forced to compete for offices on the basis of merit rather than through their kin affiliations, and also in the lay bureaucratic institutions, which were created by rulers of the larger territories. Because church offices related to priesthood were reserved for men, and were on principle open to everyone upon whom the orders of the Church had been conveyed, the more men had to subject themselves to rigorous church discipline, the more the influence of the kin groups in the Church declined. A further consequence was that men's interest in the maintenance of their own traditional collateral kinship ties waned.[31]

Moreover, the Church downgraded the position of women as holders of offices in the Church. This became evident from the fact that, even if nunneries continued and even rose to prominence in areas such as Saxony during the tenth century, double monasteries were dissolved during the ninth century.[32] Although a few double monasteries reappeared in the twelfth century, some even under the rule of abbesses (such as Fontevrault), the decline of these institutions meant that, inside the Church, women could hardly occupy positions of command over men. Moreover, fewer women were canonised as saints after the ninth century than before. Deprived of many of their positions of command in the Church, women, although they continued to be able to own and inherit property, now found it difficult to assert themselves inside the kin groups. Instead, the rights, privileges, affluence and influence of women came to be defined primarily through the personal achievements of male heads of households. The new households embraced kin members and resident servants but excluded collateral kin and came to be referred to as *familiae* in the eleventh century. This Latin word had not been a kinship term in the early Middle Ages but had denoted groups of residents of a subordinate or otherwise inferior status. Under these circumstances, women were what they were through the achievements of the male heads of their households rather than through their own contributions. Consequently, women were able to offer little resistance against church pressure which confined their roles to child-bearing and child-raising, except if they chose a life of celibacy devoted to the Church. With sexuality being legitimised only in wedlock and morally admitted only for the purpose of human reproduction, womanhood could only be identified as motherhood.

In other words, the traditional double-descent extended kin groups shrank in size and were reduced in their capacity to offer protection and support as well as transmitting authoritatively kin-group related genealogical traditions. This diminished capability of kin groups made them less attractive to their

---

31 Thietmar of Merseburg, *Chronicon*, cap. II/29, IV/38, IV/42, VI/43, ed. Robert Holtz-mann, *MGH SS rer. Germ.* N. S. IX, pp. 74, 174–6, 180, 326–8. Thietmar referred to his paternal as well as maternal ancestry with pride.

32 Second Nicene Council, 787.

male members who had to face personal competition with other men in church and lay institutions and, eventually, the extended kin groups gave way to residential households headed by a senior male member. While those changes did not in principle abolish matrilineal succession at the same time, they did confine the female household members to tasks the execution of which did not necessitate maintaining their own contacts with the outside world. Thus the androcratic tendencies which had been balanced by double descent in the early medieval kin groups were intensified into an under-standing of descent according to which kinship was mainly, though, up to the fifteenth century, not exclusively defined unilaterally in patrilinear terms. This was the case mainly in the higher aristocracy while many lesser and impover-ished aristocrats were mediatised and sought closer connections with the inhabitants of towns and cities.

Finally, the transformation of the double-descent kin groups into mainly patrilinear residential households necessitated the recasting of the three aspects of the female–male relationships, namely sexuality, emotionality and institutionality. The previous coeval distribution of these three aspects to different persons of either sex was no longer possible, because only one type of marriage remained in existence and because, in the new households, the descent-based autonomy of women disappeared. Hence the institutional aspect of the relationship between men and women had to be combined with sexuality and with emotionality or with both. It is from the latter type of fusion that, since the eleventh and twelfth centuries, the standard type of European 'family' evolved in the castles of the higher aristocracy and the urban communities of towns and cities, comprising, as a rule, a residential household of three generations of kin plus resident servants.

The amplification of misogyny

A whole range of misogynistic phrases and perceptions which were found in Aristotle's philosophy[33] appeared during and after the twelfth century. St Thomas Aquinas, who was by no means a gynaecophobe, insisted that women were in the state of 'economic and civil subjection'[34] to men, and assigned to men the role of governing women as their wives, daughters or unmarried female dependants. Thomas's view was amplified by further derogatory state-ments, such as that women – in accordance with a phrase in the Apostle Peter's First Epistle[35] – ought to be classed as the 'weaker vessels', because their

---

33 Aristotle, *Generation of Animals*, 728a8.
34 Thomas Aquinas, *Summa contra gentiles*, cap. III/123, ed. Roberto Busa, *Sancti Thomae Aquinatis Opera omnia*, vol. 2 (Stuttgart, 1980), p. 101. Thomas, *Summa theologiae*, I, qu. 92, ar. 3, ibid., p. 321. In the fourteenth century, similar arguments were articulated by Francesco Barbaro, 'De re uxoria liber', ed. Attilio Gnesotto, in *Atti e memorie della Reale Accademia di Scienze, Lettere ed Arti di Padova* CCCLXXV (1915–16), p. 87.
35 I Peter 3: 7.

child-bearing role depended on the provision of male sperm. Thomas followed his learned teacher Albert the Great (c. 1200–80) in elaborating on the Boethian definition of the woman as the 'imperfect or contingent man'. This statement reflected a crude biological theory of the time, according to which women would bear daughters after the act of the generation of sons had been intercepted by some organic difficulty in the mother or by obverse influences from the outside, such as excessive air moisture or other unfavourable weather conditions.[36] It was elaborated in another theory, according to which women as 'imperfect men' were considered to be weaker than men in physical strength and by nature defective because they were unable to process blood into sperm. Therefore, St Thomas concluded philosophically, women were to be governed by men, confined to the house and sheltered in the household against the evil influences of the outside for the alleged purpose of protecting their own security, virtue and dignity.[37] Needless to say that, in daily practice, such 'government' was likely to turn into the application of physical violence against women, as Christine de Pizan (c. 1365–1429/30) pointed out in the early fifteenth century.[38]

On the other hand, lords claimed for themselves the privilege of having sexual relations at their own discretion with their female servants and the female part of the dependent peasant farming population. While extramarital sexual intercourse was to considered to be a disgrace for women, men were given license to carry out what was justified as their natural sexual appetites: 'One should allow it for men, but not for women,'[39] was the dominant attitude towards extramarital sex, although it stood in opposition to the patristic rule that 'the husband is not allowed to do what the wife is not allowed to do'.[40]

Christine de Pizan described some of the effects which such ecclesiogene misogynistic doctrines and sentences were having on women. By chance, she told her readers, she pulled a book from the shelves which, upon closer inspection, turned out to be a *florilegium* of negative male images of women compiled, so she thought, from the works of illustrious authors. Initially, she became angry at herself for being a woman because she tended to believe what authorities had written. But after continuing to read for a while she changed her mind, began to denounce such misogyny as heretic on the

36 Albert, *Questiones super de animalibus*, lib. III, qu. 22, lib. V, qu. 4, ed. Ephraim Filthaut Thomas, Albertus Magnus, *Opera*, vol. 12 (Munster, 1955), pp. 135–6, 156. Aquinas, *Summa theologiae*, I, qu. 92, ar. 1 (see note 34), p. 320. Cf. Anicius Manlius Boethius, *Philosophiae consolatio*, cap. III/2, IV/7, ed. Ludwig Bieler, CCSL XCIV (Turnhout, 1984), pp. 38–9, 87.

37 Thomas Aquinas, *Summa contra gentiles* (see note 34), p. 101.

38 Christine de Pizan (see note 8), part I, cap. I–XI.

39 Albrecht von Johansdorf, 'Lieder', No. 4, in *Des Minnesangs Frühling*, ed. Karl Lachmann, Moriz Haupt, re-edited by Friedrich Vogt, Carl von Kraus, 36th edn by Hugo Moser, Helmut Tervooren (Stuttgart, 1977), p. 184.

40 Ambrose, *De Abraham* (PL 14, col. 452).

grounds that the divinity had created men and women equal, and asked critical questions about the truth of what she had read in the book. Relying on her own judgement, she started to destroy the misogynistic images. She accused men of resorting to misogynistic rhetoric because of their own vices and set out to construct a fictitious city of the ladies to which only reasonable and virtuous women were to be given access. These reasonable and virtuous women were to act as protective shields against continuing unfounded evil male allegations against women and would thus demand the equality of treatment of persons of either sex. However, the criteria of reason and virtue which Christine established portrayed her as an aristocratic woman who was in full agreement with the canon of norms and rules governing aristocratic residential households as they had developed since the eleventh century. Rather than calling into question the rule over women by men, Christine did no more than criticise exaggerations. Thus she demanded equality of education for men and women as a core condition for reasonableness and virtuousness. Only under this condition could women, in her view, become capable of acting loyally, wisely and intelligently, honourably, reliably and faithfully as well as in charity and with justice.[41] Thus Christine produced probably the earliest feminist critique of male domination over women without, however, fundamentally challenging the rules governing the female–male relationship.

The residential household from the eleventh and twelfth centuries

The transformation process, which established the residential households, did not take place uniformly across all types of kin groups, nor did it occur at the same time all across Europe. Specifically, in the larger number of kin groups, making up the rural farming population, residuals of extended kin groups lingered on throughout the Middle Ages. Among the features characterising rural kin groups was some continuity of double descent, so that, for example, even in the fifteenth century, Joan of Arc could trace her descent through her father and her mother alike.[42] Moreover, the impoverishment of the peasant farming population, increasing throughout the high and late Middle Ages, obstructed the division of labour between men and women within the family. This meant that, on the one side, female as well as male peasants shared their status as a dependent labour force, while, on the other side, women, in addition to the labours of child-bearing, were subjected to the same austere conditions of life as men. The severity of these conditions was recognised by contemporaries in the fifteenth century, when Sir John Fortescue (c. 1394–1476/79), a theorist of politics and government, advised the English king to grant to the peasant farming population that degree of decency and

---

[41] Christine de Pizan (see note 8).
[42] *Procès de condamnation de Jeanne d'Arc*, ed. P. Champion, vol. 2, Bibliothèque du XVe siècle XXIII (Paris, 1920), p. 355.

respectability of life which enabled them to produce the yields of agricultural harvests that they were expected to turn out.[43] Finally, the servitude of peasant farmers in late medieval and early modern Europe outside Scandinavia had the consequence that intermarriage among village communities pertaining to different seigneurial lords was possible only under the condition that intermarriage contracts were approved by the lords. This condition was necessary because the resettlement of women from a village community under the control of one lord into a village community ruled by a different lord implied the reallocation of the woman's labour force; thus such transfers had to be mutual in order to be acceptable to the lords. In consequence, the peasant farming population tended to intermarry within narrowly confined numbers of settlements, a practice which ushered in the establishment of closely knit kin networks,[44] frequently ignoring the exogamy rules set by the Church. These kin networks promoted the principle of double descent and allowed the distribution of the three aspects of the female–male relationship among a variety of different persons, similar to the early medieval practice.

By contrast, in most parts of Europe, from the eleventh century, the aristocracy developed its own conventions of sexuality, values of emotionality and norms of institutionality with regard to the female–male relationship. This was a consequence of the social and spatial seclusion of the higher aristocracy into hilltop castles overlooking the peasant farming village communities under their rule. In social terms, already in the eleventh century, patrilinear three-generation families abandoned their previous custom of identifying themselves with groups of descendants from a prominent ancestor and began to constitute themselves as residential households in hilltop castles. The names of the places at which these hilltop castles were constructed, also served as the names of the families residing in them. These castles were also the visual manifestation of the aristocratic claims to rule over the land and people in the surrounding areas. Usually, the castles had high central towers, the word for which, in western Europe, was derived from the vulgar Latin *dominationem* and appeared in Old French and Middle English as *donjon* (whence Modern English dungeon). These higher aristocratic households stood under the command of the male head of the family residing in them. As members of the aristocracy, the male heads of households established close, though competitive, ties among themselves and could also enter into regional unions of knights, such as the south German Sankt Jörgenschild of the later Middle Ages. Women were excluded from these unions.

Not all aristocratic kin groups could afford the lifestyle of the knights. Many of the lesser aristocrats established themselves as residents in towns and cities where they adopted 'bourgeois' ways of life. But these syncretisms did not affect the ideal of the aristocrat as the knightly lord residing in a hilltop

---

43 John Fortescue, *The Governance of England*, ed. Charles Plummer (Oxford, 1885), pp. 116–56.

44 For a case, see Michael Mitterauer, *Ahnen und Heilige* (Munich, 1993), p. 13.

castle. This ideal prevailed throughout the Middle Ages. The castle-based patrilinear residential three-generation families had to practice exogamy as a marriage rule. Upon marriage, women were thus transferred to their husband's kin through the marriage contract, and because all male children were, to some extent, entitled to share the heritage, the male heads of the households had to make sure that the offspring were of their kin. Hence, in the higher aristocracy, husbands began to strictly control the sexual behaviour of their wives, although in the lesser aristocracy and among the inhabitants of towns and cities women were more outgoing. One consequence was the enactment of a rigorous prohibition of extramarital sexual intercourse on the part of married women. When convicted of adultery, married women could be decapitated, a fate that, for example, Mary Duchess of Brabant, wife of Duke Louis II of Bavaria (in office 1253–94), met in 1256. Likewise, a man arrested *in flagranti* while having sexual intercourse with a married woman, could be killed by her husband or severely punished, usually by castration.[45]

Such supervision had two major consequences: first, that, through the marriage contract, women became subjected to their husbands' wills. Hence, the higher aristocracy accepted a type of relationship between men and women according to which the legal norms attached to marriage as an institution came to dominate the conventions of sexuality. This meant that, within these aristocratic households, sexuality was expected to be confined to the lifelong relations in the 'societies' established between the husbands and their wives, as St Thomas Aquinas put it in the thirteenth century.[46] Even if St Thomas Aquinas argued that, since Eve had been created from Adam's rib but not from his head and not from his feet, women were neither to be regarded as the rulers nor as the slaves of men;[47] moreover, even if women retained positions of respect as king's wives, as did Eleanor of Aquitaine (c. 1127–1204), if they managed to maintain their own relations with the outside world and if they came into positions of command, the enforcement of the legal and moral equality of men and women in a marriage 'society' did not and could not prevent the sharp decline of the social and political position of women in aristocratic households,[48] because whatever rights and privileges they might have, they could, as a rule, receive them only through the positions of the male heads of the households. The second consequence was that, within the confines of the narrow world of the hilltop castles, the

---

45 Matthew Paris, *Chronica Majora*, ed. Henry Richards Luard, vol. 5, Rerum Britannicarum medii aevi scriptores LVII (London, 1880; repr. New York, 1965), p. 34.

46 Thomas Aquinas, *Summa theologiae*, III, qu. 105, ar. 4 (see note 34), p. 506.

47 Thomas Aquinas, *Summa theologiae*, II/1, qu. 92, ar. 3 (see note 34), p. 321.

48 Asser (see note 5), cap. 13, p. 11, observed that, in the ninth century, there was a sharp distinction in rank between the king and the king's wife. But this account reflected an exceptional situation which changed by the tenth century. Even in the ninth century, it was exceptional in Wessex as can be seen from the fate of Judith, daughter of Charles the Bald, successively wife to King Aethelwulf and King Aethelbald of Wessex and the first king's wife in Wessex to be consecrated as a queen.

rights, privileges, wealth and personal tastes and capabilities of each household member attained an ever-increasing degree of importance, both for the married couple as well as for their children. For the children, their parents and some grandparents, as long as they were alive, became focal points of personal relationships and were, therefore, the pivotal factors in shaping their own personalities, by far outweighing the impact of the non-residential collateral kin. Likewise, to adult men and women, the personal characteristics of their marriage partners increasingly impinged on their own lives and created a sense of individuality whereby what constituted the individual as a person came to be regarded as more powerful than the multifarious roles and tasks which persons would have or could have carried out as members of the early medieval extended double-descent kin groups.

However, it was characteristic of the small world of the aristocratic households that emotionality was not necessarily a constitutive part of regular married life, even though emotionality was the subject of much courtly literature during the twelfth and thirteenth centuries. Within this literature, several specific literary genres flourished, namely love lyrics, epics, as well as theoretical tracts on the 'ars amandi', the art of loving. In the texts consisting of this love literature, the emotionality in the relations between men and women was treated as a case of 'curialitas', implying sets of social norms which were attached to and constitutive of life in the residential hilltop castles, referred to as the 'courts' of the higher aristocracy. Hence, although emotionality was perceived as principally conditioned by the vicissitudes of the personal likes and dislikes of the loving individuals, it was, nevertheless, subject to certain normative principles.

One of these literarily styled normative principles was the obligation of a man to serve a woman as the *domina* (the lady) for his own moral improvement and in return for the woman's 'love'. This obligation formed the background motif for a great many 'adventures' of which the courtly love literature consisted. It has always been understood that the obligation of knightly courteous men serving a lady for her love was a poetic fiction with little bearing on and relation to actual daily life. But it has frequently been overlooked that the individualism inherent in these emotional female–male relationships matched neatly the norms governing aristocratic married life, in that these relationships focused the totality of female–male relations exclusively on two individuals of the opposite sex. Hence the courtly love literature with its moral demands for total devotion reflected the institutional norms and sexual conventions of aristocratic married life, even if, what was described as an obligation by men towards women in the literature, was, in the daily life in the hilltop castles, an obligation by women towards men.

That courtly love was the counter-model of married life can further be ascertained from the *artes amandi*. The late twelfth-century, probably French, author of the Latin tract *De amore*, who gives his name as Andreas Capellanus, made it explicit that courtly love and marriage were mutually incompatible. Andreas described marriage as being governed by the rule of laws of obedience, although he conceded that it may also result in some affection; but he praised love as ruled by free emotions and controlled only by the equality of mutual attraction. Characteristically, this description took the form of a presumably fictitious judgement, passed by some Countess of Champagne and ostensibly dated 1 May 1174. In this judgement, the Countess is reported to have ruled that 'love cannot unfold its power between a married couple, because their relations are guided by laws and can neither enhance the moral improvement of the husband nor of the wife. In a similar, presumably also fictitious judgement, the Viscountess of Narbonne went even further in declaring that 'a newly concluded marriage does not end a previous love relationship'. Andreas added his own conclusion that 'marriage is not a sufficient reason to renounce love'.[49] Probably, the literary style of these fictitious judgements grew out of courtly games in which mock trials were staged, usually with women as judges.

Courtly love could, but did not necessarily include sexual relations. If sexual relations were included, and if one of the loving partners was married, courtly love was clearly and admittedly adulterous;[50] otherwise, the combination of sexuality with emotionality was considered to be possible only between non-married couples as loving friends. Pictures showing private love scenes displayed a man touching a woman's breast as a sign of intimacy and affection. Literary descriptions of love scenes featured kissing as an expression of emotionality.[51] In a different textual genre and a different social group, the theories of the aristocratic *ars amandi* were ably confirmed in the perhaps fictitious correspondence between Abelard (1079–1142) and Héloïse (1100–64). Héloïse is made to write to Abelard in her first letter: 'Even if the name of the wife appears to be more holy and gratifying, the name of the friend has always been sweeter to me – or, if you don't take it to be too unbecoming, the name of the concubine or prostitute.' In his own *Historia calamitatum*, Abelard reconfirmed that Héloïse, after having given birth to his child, refused to get married, because she did not want to be tied to him by the contractual restrictions of marriage.[52] The contrariness of institutionality and emotionality in the female–male relationship cannot be expressed in a more dramatic way. In summary the courtly love literature did not contradict – and

49 Andreas Capellanus, *De amore libri tres*, Book I, cap. VI/F (Epistola remissa a comitissa Campaniae), Book II, cap. VII/8, ed. E. Trojel, 2nd edn (Copenhagen, 1892; repr., ed. Walther Bulst [Munich, 1972], pp. 153–4, 280.

50 Adultery is not prominently featured in the medieval love literature. But see the satirical poem by Der Stricker, 'Der Minnesänger', in *Die Kleindichtung des Strickers*, vol. 5, ed. Ulrich Müller, Fritz Hundsnurscher, Cornelius Sommer, Göppinger Arbeiten zur Germanistik CVII, 5 (Göppingen, 1978), No. 146, pp. 83–97.

51 Master E. S., A loving couple. c. 1460. Vienna, Graphische Sammlung Albertina. *Sir Gawain and the Green Knight*, vv. 1758, 1794–96, ed. Israel Gollancz, Early English Text Society, Original Series CCX (London, 1940; repr. London, New York, Toronto, 1966), pp. 65, 67.

52 J. T. Muckle, ed., 'Abelard's Letter of Consolation to a Friend (*Historia Calamitatum*)', in *Mediaeval Studies* XII (1950), p. 189. Muckle, ed., 'Litterae Heloisae', in *Mediaeval Studies* XV (1953), Letter One, p. 71.

was not supposed to do so – the general decline of the position of aristocratic women *vis-à-vis* men from the eleventh and twelfth centuries. Instead, it confirms that, in the aristocracy, the relations between men and women had come to be perceived as sets of relations between two unequal individuals of the opposite sex.

'Bourgeois' families in the towns and cities followed suit in some but not all of the principles of aristocratic family structure. There were three significant differences. First, while both types of families shared the common characteristic that they fused the aspects of sexuality and institutionality of the female–male relationship, and while both focused these relations on the ties between partners of the opposite sex in residential households, the 'bourgeois' type of family also integrated the aspect of emotionality. In the fourteenth century, it became customary among merchants to write private letters. Through these letters, merchants would communicate with their wives while they were on business journeys. It was not uncommon to include declarations of love and expressions of care into these letters. The presence in these letters of a tone of affection shows that, contrary to the aristocracy, the 'bourgeois' families took it for granted that the married couple should be united in love.[53] The integration of emotionality into 'bourgeois' married life may have been due to the fact that the residents of the urban communities of towns and cities usually arrived as uprooted persons who had cut the ties to or were disinherited by their extended kin groups in the rural countryside. Hence these newly immigrating settlers were induced to develop novel families from scratch which could be based on new principles of household organisation. The heads of the more wealthy of these households could also execute political power inside the towns and cities through their monetary affluence, the holding of high offices or military expertise. However, these powers could only be held within the established institutional frameworks of the towns and cities.

Second, dwelling within the narrow confines of densely populated walled towns and cities, the 'bourgeois' family lent itself more readily to cross-family social networking than the aristocratic family; the latter feature becomes evident from the merchant and artisan guilds into which the male heads of the households were united. The 'bourgeois' companies and guilds restricted, but did not abolish, the competition among rival merchants and artisans. Because 'bourgeois' families could only thrive if they succeeded in competing with rival merchants and artisans within the same and among different towns and cities, the mutual cooperativeness of the family members was essential to the continuing existence of the family. Hence the positions and roles of women were more important in the 'bourgeois' families than in their aristocratic counterparts.

53 See, for example, Alfred Hartmann, ed., *Die Amerbachkorrespondenz*, No. 214, 234, vol. 1 (Basle, 1942), pp. 201–2, 220–1. For further references, see Mathias Beer, *Eltern und Kinder des späten Mittelalters in ihren Briefen*, Nürnberger Werkstücke zur Stadt- und Landesgeschichte XLIV (Neustadt/Aisch, 1990).

Third, it was understood that, in a 'bourgeois' family, husband and wife had to contribute jointly to the family's income. This practice led to a sense of cooperation between husband and wife which allowed women a wide scope of autonomous business activities and to maintain autonomous social interactions within the towns and cities. The greater financial independence and social autonomy of 'bourgeois' women, compared to aristocratic families, restricted, but did not abolish the androcratic structure which permeated families everywhere under the sanctions of the Church. But, even if husbands were usually the heads of families in the towns and cities, they depended more on the willingness of their wives to cooperate than male members of the landed aristocracy.

While these observations must remain conjectural for most of the eleventh and twelfth centuries, much supportive evidence exists for the fourteenth and fifteenth centuries in moral and educational tracts.[54] This evidence shows that the 'bourgeois' integration of the three aspects of the female–male relationship had by then become accepted as the basis upon which the normative principles could be formulated that the married couple should be united in love and that both parents should devote themselves to the education of their children. However, daily practice could and frequently did oppose these principles. Like aristocratic women, 'bourgeois' women continued to suffer from misogynistic invectives. Giovanni Boccaccio's fourteenth-century imaginary portrait of the Florentine urban world is populated with sexually demanding and politically active women.[55] Hence, at this time, it was possible to portray 'bourgeois' women – even if only in literary fiction – as active inside and outside their households. But, already late in the same century, and even more so in the following centuries, Boccaccio's *Novellae* served as the proverbial source for never-ending references to cases of women's allegedly insatiable and decadent sexual lust, along with the seeming necessity to subject them to the control and rule of men.[56]

Conclusion

The conceptual history of the relations between men and women displays a continuous decline of the position of women *vis-à-vis* men during the Middle Ages from the eighth century. As long as the extended kin groups remained capable of sustaining their positions of power as tradition-transmitting, norm-preserving and rule-enforcing groups, the position of women was shaped through the position that the kin group to which they belonged could

54 Leon Battista Alberti, *I libri della famiglia*, ed. Renée Neu Watkins, *The Family in Renaissance Florence* (Columbia, S.C., 1969).
55 Giovanni Boccaccio, *Decamerone*, editio princeps (Venice, 1492).
56 See, among many, *Le menagier de Paris: Traité de morale et d'œonomie domestique composé vers 1393 par un bourgeois Parisien*, vol. 1 (Paris, 1847; repr. Geneva, 1982), pp. 125–8. Baldassare Castiglione, *Book of the Courtier* (Venice, 1528), English version (London, 1561), p. 66 (repr., Tudor Translations, I, 23 [New York, 1967]).

claim in its relations with other kin groups. Within their kin groups, women could act as transmitters of their own traditions and had full rights to land tenure and inheritance. Women appeared as rulers and influential policy makers. In the Church, women held positions equal to those of men in monasteries and were venerated as saints no less frequently than men. The three aspects of the female–male relationship, namely sexuality, emotionality and institutionality could, but did not have to be focused on the same persons who could be integrated into wider networks of interpersonal relations within and across their kin groups.

In the later seventh century, the Catholic Church began to enforce its own rules for marriage and for the determination of the legitimacy of descent in Europe beyond the confines of the Roman Empire of Antiquity. The gradual enforcement of these rules subjected women to more rigorous surveillance by church institutions than men and provided a potential for misogynistic rhetoric. Accompanying factors, such as the decline of the kin groups and the waning position of women in church institutions other than nunneries entailed the consequence that, by the tenth century, more women became subjected to the rule of men than in the early Middle Ages and had to define their own status and identity through their husbands and fathers. This process was fastest in the aristocracy where men sought to control the activities and behaviour of their wives and daughters most rigidly. In the aristocracy, institutionality and sexuality as aspects of the female-male relationship were combined and focused on the same married couple. Henceforth, aristocratic wives had to confine their activities to the private sphere of the residential household and were expected to be faithful to their husbands in sexual respects, caring for their husbands in emotional respects and supportive of their husbands in social and economic respects. Conversely, men maintained the relations of the residential household with the outside world and had a degree of sexual freedom, emotional and social as well as economic independence which they frequently denied to their wives.

The process was slowest in the peasantry where suffering was common to both sexes. Only in 'bourgeois' families, a middle path was chosen which made it possible to integrate emotionality and allowed women to develop some degree of independence, mainly in economic respects.

ACTION

General Introduction

Since the writings of the eighteenth-century moralists,[1] European theoretical considerations about the concept of action have been embedded in Aristotelian thinking about causality. The main supportive reason for this type of conceptualisation has been that, in accordance with the dominant concept of rationality, action has been understood as a means towards an end rather than as a process. The conclusion, argued by Max Weber (1864–1920), has been that only end-rational action can be identified as rational action *per se*.[2] However, although Weber's equation of the rationality of action with the instrumentality of action has been accepted by subsequent theorists,[3] its acceptability is the consequence of certain changes in the conceptual history of action in Europe, which shall be traced in three steps: First, action shall be described in its interconnecting impact on the world of tangible realities, for which production and distribution stand; here, change of production and distribution will be analysed under the aspects the emergence of the end-rationality of action and the delocalisation of markets. Second, action shall be described in its disruptive impact with regard to the world of tangible realities, for which war stands; here, change in the definition of war aims will be analysed as a process from stability-orientation to the focus on the promotion of change through war. Third, action shall be described in its ordering impact on the world of intangible realities, for which the world of thought stands; here, change will be analysed as the transformation of thinking from a process of interconnecting synthetic concepts into a process of isolating concepts from their contexts.

These descriptions and analyses will proceed from the following questions: in the case of production and distribution, I will consider action as a process by which we may inquire as to how actions were conducted; in the case of war, I shall examine action within the context of goal orientation for the purpose of inquiring to what ends actions were conducted; in the case of thinking, I shall investigate the definability of action in order to try to find out what was conceived as action. In this way, I shall historicise concepts which are commonly held to pertain to economics, military science and epistemology.

---

1 Christian Wolff, *Psychologia empirica* (Frankfurt, Leipzig, 1738), pp. 716–19 (repr., ed. Jean Ecole, Wolff, Gesammelte Werke, part II, vol. 5 [Hildesheim, New York, 1968]).
2 Max Weber, *Wirtschaft und Gesellschaft*, 5th edn, 14th–18th printing (Tübingen, 1980), p. 331 (first published 1922).
3 Talcott Parsons, *The Structure of Social Action* (Glencoe, 1949), pp. 44–5. Jürgen Habermas, *Theorie des kommunikativen Handelns*, vol. 1, 4th edn (Frankfurt, 1987), pp. 126–8 (first published Frankfurt, 1981).

VI

Action I: Production and Distribution

> Entrez dans la bourse de Londres, cette place plus respectable que bien des cours; vous y voyez rassemblés les deputés de toutes les nations pour l'utilité des hommes. Là, le juif, le mahométan et le chrétien traitent l'un avec l'autre comme s'ils étaient de la même religion, et ne donne le nom d'infidèles qu'a ceux qui font banqueroute.*

> – Voltaire

Weberian conceptualisations of action have informed much of contemporary theorising about trade as action and traders as actors. However, regarding trade as a case of end-rational action becomes problematic if non-European or early European forms of trade come under review. The scholar for whose work this is first and foremost the case is Karl Polanyi (1886–1964).

Introduction: Polanyi's forms of trade and his theory of the 'ports of trade'

Despite a wealth of suggested taxonomic categories which can be used to describe and analyse processes of change in economic history, Polanyi's work on historical forms of trade represents the retrospective superimposition upon the past of the Weberian focus on the instrumentality of end-rational action as the sole form of rational action. On the basis of this view, Polanyi reduced the interpretative significance of his descriptive and analytical categories for the observation of changes in the more distant past. For example, Polanyi narrowed the focus of his theories to long-distance trade in luxury products, which he took to represent the most elaborate kind of trade as an end-rational action.[4] But this focus is too narrow, for two reasons: first, the retrospective distinction between domestic and long-distance trade is far from obvious, specifically under the condition that, as in early medieval

---

* Enter the London Stock Exchange, the place which is more respectable than most of the courts; there you will see the deputies of all nations assembled for the common benefit of men. There, the Jew, the Muslim and the Christian deal with each other as if they were of the same religion, and they do not give the name of Infidel to anyone except those who go bankrupt.

4 Karl Polanyi, 'The Economy as Instituted Process', Polanyi, M. Arensberg, H. W. Pearson, eds, *Trade and Market in the Early Empires* (New York, 1957), pp. 243–70.

Europe, groups demarcated the areas of their settlements with no more than vague and equivocal boundaries; second, Polanyi's focus on long-distance trade isolates trade as the action of the distribution of goods from the action of the specialised production of goods, even though both types of action may have corresponded closely.

These principal observations are necessary for a critical assessment of the applicability to history of the taxonomy which Polanyi suggested. He distinguished three 'forms' of long-distance trade – reciprocity, redistribution and exchange – all of which he understood as ideal types in the Weberian fashion. This meant that Polanyi did not array his forms of trade in a temporal sequence, as a history of trade, but rather as a typology, the parts of which, to him, did not always have to appear in separation from one another (although Polanyi also used these forms of trade as markers of time).

According to Polanyi, reciprocity is gift-giving or bartering of goods which are considered to be equal in value. Hence reciprocity does not require regulating institutions or any more elaborate normative codes than what can be enshrined into the *do-ut-des* principle. By contrast, Polanyi regarded redistribution as a form of trade which involved architecturally manifest political centres into which luxury goods were absorbed for the purpose of supporting the clientele of rulers. Here, a framework of institutions was required which was based on taxation through which payment for luxury goods could be effected which, in turn, were required to buy services from the rulers' clientele. However, Polanyi believed that in neither of these 'forms' of trade, did there exist the full range of 'market elements', namely place, goods, supply crowds, demand crowds, custom and law as well as equivalences, which, to him, were constitutive of the third 'form' of trade, namely exchange. He argued that the combination of these 'market elements' into exchange developed only relatively late and absorbed into itself the core tasks of reciprocity and redistribution without replacing them completely.

Polanyi's taxonomy of the 'forms' of trade rested on his definition of trade as the peaceful exchange and transportation of goods by traders on the basis of bilateral deals. Under this condition, accomplishing the goals of trade required the existence of certain places, where the goods could be exchanged, as if in a market. But the existence of market places was denied by Polanyi for reciprocity and redistribution. Instead, he concluded that the places where the trading goods were to be exchanged under the auspices of reciprocity and redistribution, were uninhabited, politically amorphous and remotely located 'ports of trade', or neutral spots where local buyers and sellers would meet the long-distance traders on more or less regular occasions and without interfering much into the affairs of each other.[5]

It is precisely at this point that Polanyi's views become irreconcilable with empirical evidence from early medieval Europe. For, unlike Polanyi's 'ports of

5   Karl Polanyi, 'Ports of Trade in Early Societies', *Journal of Economic History* XXIII (1963), pp. 30–45.

trade', most of the trading spots, which were newly founded in western Europe towards the end of the seventh century, were populated with agriculturalists, manufacturers of goods for local consumption, as well as with traders. These trading spots, such as Quentovic and Dorestad in the Kingdom of the Franks, Duisburg on the lower Rhine in an area possibly under Frisian control, Haithabu in the Kingdom of the Danes, Lundenwic (west of the walls of Roman London) in the Kingdom of Essex or Hamwih/Southampton in Wessex, were manifestations of the active territorial administration under a nearby ruler, and they were administratively and economically interconnected with their respective hinterlands.[6]

Apparently, in these trading spots, Polanyi's three forms of trade not only coexisted already side by side, but, more importantly, production and distribution formed a closely intertwined network of interactions, with the implication that it was difficult to disentangle local and long-distance trade from production. Likewise, not all actions performed at these trading sports were end-rational in kind, because at some of these places, trading activities, including the use of money for transactions, took place side by side with practices of hoarding money and with religious cults. These observations seem to confirm that, contrary to Polanyi's expectations, the actions performed in these trading spots were not primarily instruments for the accomplishment of pre-conceived goals but processes with a value of their own.

For the purpose of describing the transformation of the trading action, the focus will be on the successive emergence in Europe, first, of trade as a networking form of the distribution of goods in relation to production, and, second, of regular markets as organised places for managed exchange.

The emergence of trade as a networking action

It seems easiest to describe the dominant types of economic action among the late Migration Age groups of settlers in the terms used by Marshall D. Sahlins (b. 1930)[7] for what he referred to as the affluence of self-sufficient forms of production. Although there is an insurmountable scarcity of sources for the fifth and the immediately following centuries, sufficient archaeological evidence exists apt to show that late Migration Age 'settlement areas' (*Siedlungskammern*) were largely self-sufficient with regard to basic commodities where they continued through the vicissitudes of the times.[8]

These settlements can be described as 'naturally' affluent and, therefore, not requiring trade in daily commodities. We may assume that this was so because the action of producing goods was in agreement with the yearly

---

6   Richard Hodges, Brian Hobley, eds, *The Rebirth of Towns in the West. A. D. 700–1050*, Council for British Archaeology, Research Report LXVIII (London, 1988).

7   Marshall D. Sahlins, *Stone Age Economics* (Chicago, 1972).

8   For a description of such settlement areas, see Wendy Davies, Hayo Vierck, 'The Contexts of Tribal Hidage', *Frühmittelalterliche Studien* VIII (1974), map following p. 288.

cycles and was aimed at the provision of commodities for local consumption among their producers. We can support these assumptions mainly from the plethora of local styles for such commodities as pottery, specifically cremation urns, until the end of the sixth century,[9] and from the existence of certain local-dress provinces within which definable garment styles prevailed among the autochthonous population.[10] A final, indirect indicator is the fact that, at least in a number of cases, Roman roads which had been the major traffic trajectories up until the fourth century, fell out of use in areas north of the Alps and in Britain from the fifth century,[11] even if some Roman cities continued to operate there as centres of production and trade well into the early Middle Ages. The latter change can only be understood if it is assumed that there was a reduction of communication by land, including a decline of trade among settlements at a distance.

However, this picture of essentially self-sufficient late Migration Age settlements is fundamentally incomplete. This is so because, first, there is no necessity to assume that all settlements were always self-sufficient with regard to all daily commodities; and, moreover, it is impossible to believe that, within each settlement, all households were also self-sufficient. The latter is impossible because there is positive evidence for the existence of specialist craftsmen, the most prominent among them being metal workers. Evidently, the households of these specialist craftsmen must have been provided for with victuals and other necessary commodities by other members of the settlement, and they must have been able to avail themselves of such services through sales of their own products. Hence we must assume that, at the time, production was sufficiently specialised and diversified so as to enforce the action of distribution together with the action of production, even if there may have been cases where the networking among these actions was confined to the settlements themselves. In any case, this implies that, contrary to long-cherished views by economic historians like Henri Pirenne (1862–1935) and economic anthropologists like Karl Polanyi, agrarian economies have not necessarily done without trade. Instead, it must be assumed that various patterns of trade have been integral parts of agrarian economies.

Second, there appears to be evidence for the existence of specialist metal workers who, for want of a better word, might be referred to as migrant

---

9 Cf. Christopher J. Arnold, 'Territories and Leadership', in S. T. Driscoll, M. R. Nieke, eds, *Power and Politics in Early Medieval Britain and Ireland* (Edinburgh, 1988), pp. 111–27. Audrey L. Meaney, Sonia Chadwick Hawkes, *Two Anglo-Saxon Cemeteries at Winnall* (London, 1970), p. 45.

10 Cf. Hayo Vierck, 'Trachtenkunde und Trachtengeschichte in der Sachsen-Forschung', in Claus Ahrens, ed., *Sachsen und Angelsachsen*, (Hamburg, 1978), pp. 231–70.

11 This can be inferred from earthworks constructed on Roman roads and from the decline in the distribution of common commodities, such as pottery. Cf. Desmond Bonney, 'Early Boundaries in Wessex', *Archaeology and the Landscape: Essays for Leslie Valentine Grinsell*, ed. Peter Jon Fowler (London, 1972), pp. 168–86. B. H. St. J. O'Neil, 'Grim's Bank, Padworth, Berkshire', *Antiquity* XXVII (1943), pp. 188–95. William I. Roberts IV, *Romano-Saxon Pottery*, British Archaeological Reports, British Series CVI (Oxford, 1982), pp. 1–11.

producers. One type of a precious-metal commodity, a certain type of brooches, seems to have spread from northern to western Europe during the late Migration Age with the help of specialist craftsmen who were themselves migrants, for instance from the central part of Scandinavia to the British Isles and perhaps elsewhere in Europe.[12]

Hence there seems to have been a pattern of distribution by which, not the produced goods, but the producers, or a specialised production technique and a style, moved. Again, it is inconceivable that such migrant producers could have existed without support from their neighbours in the settlements where they worked. Hence, in the case of the distribution of commodities for daily use, self-sufficient production did not exclude the necessity for trade within a settlement or beyond its confines.

Third, that patterns of the distribution of goods existed beyond the boundaries of settlements is further proven by the presence among grave finds of high value luxury goods of remote provenance, specifically oriental metal ware.[13] Some of these luxury goods may have been used as heirlooms before there were deposited as grave goods; but they may also have been specifically acquired by wealthy persons as pieces of private property and have followed their owners into the graves. It so appears that, up until the seventh century, these luxury goods were mainly delivered by Roman or Syrian professional traders through the Mediterranean Sea, whence the preference of luxury goods from the eastern Mediterranean area at this time. But there were also professional traders who operated on their own or with support from Frankish Kings in areas east of the Frankish Kingdom where they may have been involved in the slave trade.[14] Moreover, there are also written sources that show that even less durable luxury goods such as spices from central and southern Asia were present in the Occident in the tenth century. These may have been taken there along different trade routes and by different kinds of traders.[15]

The existence of luxury goods of remote provenance in the property of a

---

12 For a study of these forms of production, see Egil Bakka, 'On the Beginning of Salin's Style I in England', *Universitetet i Bergen Årbok*, Historisk Antikvarisk Rekke III (1958), pp. 1–83.

13 Cf. Christopher J. Arnold, 'Wealth and Social Structure: A Matter of Life and Death', in Philip Rahtz, Tania M. Dickinson, Lorna Watts, eds, *Anglo-Saxon Cemeteries 1979*, British Archaeological Reports, British Series LXXXII (Oxford, 1980), pp. 81–142.

14 The seventh-century chronicles which were attributed in the sixteenth century to a Fredegar contain a report of a merchant named Samo who became a ruler among Slavs and died around AD 600. The report makes it clear that while Samo acted on his own, the Frankish King demanded compensation for murdered merchants during wars between himself and Slavs. This would imply that some merchants operating in this area did in fact receive protection from rulers. See *Chronicarum libri IV*, cap. IV/48, IV/68, ed. Bruno Krusch, *MGH SS rer. Merov.* 2, pp. 144–5, 154–5. The implication can be confirmed by Charlemagne's Diedenhofen capitulary of 805, cap. 7, wherein merchants trading in eastern Europe are prohibited from bearing arms (*MGH Capit.*, vol. 1, ed. Alfred Boretius, p. 123).

15 See Georg Jacob, *Arabische Berichte von Gesandten an germanische Fürstenhöfe aus dem 9. und 10. Jahrhundert*, Quellen zur Volkskunde I (Berlin, 1927).

person in, say, the southern British Isles during the fifth century, would char-
acterise the wealth of its owner, and it would indicate a degree of social differentiation within the settlements that sufficed to allow or to necessitate
markers of wealth. In other words, even if, within the settlements whose residents subscribed to subsistence production, 'natural' affluence existed, this
did not preclude the unequal distribution of wealth. In some cases, wealth
may have been used for the acquisition of luxury goods; in other cases, such as
the one provided in the epic of *Beowulf,* it may have been used for the purpose
of redistributing benefits to clients or other dependants in return for services.[16] In any case, luxury goods served the purpose of converting markers of
wealth into markers of rights and privileges.

These forms of distribution of goods within dominant, self-sufficient
agrarian production presuppose the existence of settlements as established
habitats without more than the necessary interaction with their environments. They did not, therefore, build up a network of interconnections on
which several settlements had to depend in order to be able to continue to
exist. In other words, the late Migration Age forms of distribution were in
flux, subject to local conditions of demand and supply and could be inter-
rupted or cancelled at any time.

Moreover, there was at least one case where, despite all changes, the
unstable interconnectedness of production and distribution continued from
late Roman times until well into the twelfth century. This was the case of the
gynaecaea, or women's work houses. Already in existence in the *latifundia* of
late Antiquity, they were well recorded in eighth- and ninth-century capitu-
laries as well as in narrative sources of the twelfth century and in archaeological records of the tenth century.[17] The *gynaecaea* were places for the
manufacture of garments and other apparel where mainly young women were
employed. They were located within or near aristocratic residences and royal
vills and produced primarily for local consumption. However, at least in the
eleventh and twelfth centuries, surplus products were distributed by peddlers
or merchants in the services of rulers or the landed aristocratic lords. The
profits from the trade were added to the wealth of the rulers and aristocratic
lords who paid no more than minimal wages to the working women.
However, it fell within the logic under which these manufactures operated
that the products which they turned out would be sold on the market only if
and when surplus production was possible. Hence no permanent supply of

---

16 Scenes showing the redistribution of luxury goods were literarily described in the poem
Beowulf, vv. 1193–205, 2172–6, ed. Frederick Klaeber. 3rd edn (Lexington, Mass., 1950),
pp. 45–6, 81.

17 *MGH Capit.* 1, No. 32, cap. 43, ed. Alfred Boretius, p. 87 (*capitulare de villis*). Hartmann
von Aue, *Iwein,* vv. 6156–206, ed. Ernst Schwarz, Hartmann von Aue, *Erec, Iwein: Text,
Nacherzählung, Worterklärungen* (Darmstadt, 1967), pp. 510–12. Paul Grimm, 'Zwei
bemerkenswerte Gebäude in der Pfalz Tilleda. Eine zweite Tuchmacherei', *Prähistorische
Zeitschrift* XLI (1963), p. 74. Grimm, 'Neue Hausfunde in der Vorburg der Pfalz Tilleda',
Prähistorische Zeitschrift XL (1962), pp. 220–51. A. Geijer, *Die Textilfunde,* Birka III
(Stockholm, 1938), pp. 19, 41–5.

these trading goods was envisaged although sectors of the economy could, at times, be organised on the basic supply orientation.

Outside the core areas of the Roman Empire of Antiquity, some transformation of these fluid patterns of distribution into networking trade seems to have occurred from the turn of the eighth century in connection with the inception of territorial forms of political organisation, the beginning of the hierarchisation of horizontally stratified groups, and the superimposition of a centralised ecclesiastical administration. Although all of these processes were then just in their nascent stages, they benefited from the simultaneous emergence of networking forms of distribution through which local settlements became interconnected into larger compounds of ethnically defined groups referred to as *gentes*.[18] At the same time, the rulers of the *gentes* placed themselves in control of the newly emerging patterns of distribution in order to provide regimes for the conduct of these patterns of distribution. Hence the emergence of long-distance trade in early medieval Europe was at the same time a condition for and a result of the transformation of the political, social and religious organisation from the turn of the eighth century.

The architectural manifestation of the emergence of long-distance trade as a networking action was in the new trading spots which were constructed as permanent settlements where agricultural and other producers, as well as local traders, would interact with long-distance traders under the authority of a ruler. It so appears that some of these trading spots were fortified as, for instance, was Hamwih/Southampton in Wessex around 900, or had fortifications in their proximity as did Birka in Sweden. Moreover, they were subject to the legislation and jurisdiction of the rulers by whose will and by whose means they had been established, and, finally, they were systematically interconnected by alien long-distance traders who also defined themselves as members of *gentes*. These trading *gentes* placed themselves in control of the long-distance trade and interacted with local traders at the trading spots, where the supply of trading goods, so far as they were available, determined the terms of trade. One of the rules of local trade in the trading spots was that alien long-distance traders were to be strictly controlled when doing business in the area in and around the trading spot.[19] Such strict control was thought

---

[18] An indirect indication of this process is the increasing care which was awarded by Mercian and Frankish rulers to the building and maintenance of bridges during the eighth century. See *MGH Capit.* 1, No. 91 (late eighth century), No. 93, cap. 7 (c. 787), No. 94, cap. 9 (787), No. 140, cap. 8 (818/19), No. 141, cap. 7 (819), No. 148, cap. 11 (823/5), ed. Alfred Boretius, pp. 192, 197, 199, 288, 290, 301. Charter of King Aethelbald of Mercia to Evesham Abbey, dated AD 716, ed. Walter de Gray Birch, *Cartularium Saxonicum*, No. 134, vol. 1 (London, 1885; repr. New York, 1964). Cf. Peter Hayes Sawyer, *Anglo-Saxon Charters* (London, 1968), No. 83.

[19] *Laws of Ine*, cap. 25; 25, 1, ed. Felix Liebermann, *Die Gesetze der Angelsachsen*, vol. 1 (Halle, 1903), p. 100. The same laws, cap. 23, 1, Liebermann, p. 98, also ruled that half of the wergild for an alien who had been killed was to be paid to the king and the other half to a political group, presumably the group to which the alien had belonged as a

to be required in order to distinguish the legal business of trade from robbery. Consequently, these trading spots were the meeting places between local producers and distributors on the one hand, and alien traders on the other. Because the alien long-distance traders usually operated without the protection of established rulers, they had to provide for their own safety and therefore acted also as military professionals. As a rule (and, in this respect, Polanyi was right), these specialised groups of alien traders were defined as political groups with a distinct gentile tradition of their own, among them Frisians, Danes, Norwegians, Slavs and Sembs.[20] Their preferred areas of operation were the coastlines of the North Sea and the Baltic Sea through which connections were established to central and western Asia.

Interest in these seaways was put on record in the ninth-century Old English version of the early fifth-century world history of Orosius (380/85–after 416). The translators inserted two reports which seafaring merchants had communicated to King Alfred of Wessex at the end of the ninth century. Both reports concerned seafaring on what was regarded as the northern portion of the ocean (*okeanos*). One merchant, whose name is given as Ohthere, provided details on the route from the northern fringes of the *ecumene* at what is probably northern Norway today to the British Isles in the west, whereas the other report, by someone named Wulfstan, described the seaway west to north to a trading spot named Truso near Elbing on the southern coast of the Baltic Sea. Both reports converge in presenting an alternative to the Mediterranean Sea as a trading route to areas further east in the *ecumene*.[21] These experiences were later made visible in an early eleventh-century world map which originated in the British Isles and displays in great detail the routes that had been described by Ohthere and Wulfstan. The map betrays its insular origin by allocating much more space to the British Isles than to other parts of the *ecumene*, and it is unusual in giving much space to the ocean seaway from the British Isles to Asia via the northern seas and the central Eurasian river systems.[22]

Against the alien 'gentile' traders, the particular social group of professional merchant traders of Roman origin appears to have faced severe competition during this time, which meant that the trade connections with the

trader. The rule confirmed that these aliens were regarded primarily as members of political groups and not as kin members. Evidence for the control of production and distribution emerges also from the mainly ninth-century Carolingian polyptyques. See Dieter Hägermann, Konrad Elmshäuser, Andreas Hedwig, eds, *Das Polyptychon von Saint-Germain-des-Près. Studienausgabe*, cap. V/110 (Cologne, Weimar, Vienna, 1993), p. 38, where a *mercator* is mentioned as a settler in the village of Verrières belonging to the Abbey of Saint-Germain-des-Près.

20 Adam of Bremen, *Gesta Hammaburgensis ecclesiae pontificum*, cap. I/60, ed. Bernhard Schmeidler, MGH SS rer. Germ. (2), p. 58. Rimbert, *Vita Anskarii*, cap. 19, 20, ed. Georg Waitz, MGH SS rer. Germ. (55), pp. 39–46.

21 *The Old English Orosius*, cap. I/1, ed. Janet M. Bately, Early English Text Society, Supplementary Series VI (London, 1980), pp. 13–18.

22 London, British Library, Ms Cotton Tiberius B V, fol. 65 verso.

Mediterranean Sea were reduced in significance without, however, collapsing entirely.[23]

In summary, during the period between the fifth and the seventh centuries, at the end of which trade as a networking distribution of goods appeared, most distribution was innately interconnected with production. The extant sources do not permit us to specify the ends and means associated with the actions of the production and distribution of goods at this time. Yet it is hard to dissociate this type of action from the chthonic practices and beliefs of agriculturalists current in early medieval Europe, when the process of an action was given at least the same importance, if not priority, over the ends in pursuit. The 'gentile' traders who began to establish trading networks towards the end of the seventh century seem to have shared these practices and beliefs because their careers as traders did not have to be lifelong and they seem to have conceived their trade as a supply-oriented action. Instead, they could revert to farming life when they so desired. However, as these 'gentile' traders operated on principles of oral communication the details of their conduct of business remain unknown. Nevertheless it is possible to conclude that, even in the predominantly agricultural world of early medieval Europe, trade was a normal activity which did not differ fundamentally from the concept of action shared by the farming population. But it was the specific task of the alien 'gentile' traders to interconnect the various trading spots through their activities and to create and maintain a network of trade relations which interconnected a substantive number of settlements and spanned from the remotest parts of western Europe across the northern seas into central and western Asia.

The emergence of regular markets and the formation of contractual groups of professional merchants

Remarkably, the trading spots founded from the end of the seventh century gradually petered out between the ninth and the twelfth centuries; some of them were even destroyed or deserted. Hamwih/Southampton had a declining population from the middle of the ninth century and petered out in the tenth century; Lundenwic gave way to nearby Lundenburh (inside the Roman walls) towards the end of the ninth century; Dorestad ceased to exist as a trading place and was deserted at the same time; Duisburg was replaced by the nearby centre of royal administration at Kaiserswerth during the tenth century; and Haithabu also became an administrative centre which was trans-

---

[23] The early tenth-century *Vita Sancti Gerardi Aurillacensis* by Odo of Cluny, cap. I/7–8, 17–18 (*PL* 133, cols 646–7, 653–4) recorded the presence of professional traders in Rome and Pavia at the turn of the tenth century. These merchants traded in imports from the Orient and Byzantium.

located to nearby Sleswig.[24] New places where fairs were held were founded further inland and inherited the tasks of the previous trading spots, such as Montreuil which succeeded Quentovic. Other trading spots, mainly along the Baltic Sea, may have continued into the high Middle Ages although irregular coastal markets appear to have become prominent, for example, in Gotland, during the eleventh century.[25] Evidently, some change in the supply-oriented trading pattern rendered the early medieval trading spots less perfunctory and led to their decline from the ninth century.

This process is difficult to disentangle from the concurrent process of the agricultural revolution during the ninth, tenth and eleventh centuries which led to an invigorated agricultural work ethic, stimulated by the rulers, and, eventually, to an increase in yield ratios, the intensification of agricultural administration and of the use of new technologies, the improvement of traffic, and also to an extension of arable lands at the expense of woodlands.

The agricultural revolution of the ninth, tenth, and eleventh centuries entailed a surplus of certain agricultural products, such as rye, which demanded an outlet. It also increased the demand for the long-distance trade in rare goods, such as salt or metals. Two types of outlet were established, one in the provision of specialised foodstuffs for entertainment at the ruler's curia,[26] the other in the enhancement of the marketing of agricultural products. The latter became recognisable in the variegated ninth-, tenth- and eleventh-century legislation on the establishment and maintenance of market places which came to be subjected to the specific fiscal regulations under the authority either of the kings (mainly in western Europe) or the emperor and seigneurial lords as territorial rulers (mainly inside the Empire).[27] These markets were in operation mainly for domestic trade and were regularised or permanent institutions. Their locations frequently developed into central places, most noteworthily in England and the lower Rhine area, where many of the ninth- and tenth-century market places became the urban administrative centres of shires from about AD 1000 onwards. The traders, who exchanged their goods at regular market places, were different from the people gathering at the previous trading spots. While the latter had been the meeting places where local producers and distributors would meet alien traders, the former were the gathering places where artisans and local producers and local customers would meet, even though alien traders may also have been present there on occasions. Some of these local markets soon

---

24 For surveys see Hodges and Hobley (see note 6). Max Ebert, *Truso* (Berlin, 1926). Alan Vince, *Saxon London* (London, 1990), pp. 13–25.

25 See Björn Ambrosiani, 'The Prehistory of Towns in Sweden', in Hodges and Hobley (see note 6), p. 64.

26 *Capitulare de villis* (see note 17), cap. 70.

27 For example, charter by King Alfred of Wessex and Aethelred, under-king of the Mercians, to Bishop Waerfrith of Worcester, AD 889, in *Cartularium Saxonicum*, No. 561 (see note 18), vol. 2. Sawyer (see note 18), No. 346. Charter of Emperor Otto II, dated, 26 June 975 on Magdeburg traders. *MGH DD Otto II*, no. 112, p. 126. Charter of Emperor Otto III to Quedlinburg, dated 23 November 994, *MGH DD Otto III*, no. 94, pp. 566–7.

developed into centres for specialised production and distribution of products designed for consumption at any place. The demand side of trade
increased in importance.

In western Europe, the territorial rulers, such as the kings of England and
France who supervised the establishment of these regular markets, simultaneously created legislation on monetary affairs, the goal of which seems to have
been the enactment of measures against unauthorised devaluations of circulating coins; in England, the monetary reform of 975 under King Edgar
enforced the provision of exchange standards and the obligation to return
circulating coins in exchange for new issues at authorised minting places
within regular intervals.[28] These measures were unfavourable for the autonomous
'gentile' groups of alien traders because these groups were neither capable nor
willing to regularise their trade and anticipate demands of customers.

This process of the regularisation of local markets was misunderstood by
Henri Pirenne in 1925 as the rebirth of towns and cities in medieval Europe
after the collapse of the Roman imperial administration and urban civilisation in late Antiquity. The misunderstanding was due to Pirenne's failure to
recognise that the alien traders, as the 'gentile' groups interacting in the earlier
trading spots and across the North Sea and the Baltic Sea, had already established a novel network of trade in western and northern Europe. This trading
network prevailed beyond the demise of the early medieval trading spots and
helped maintain trade relations beyond the time when the meeting places of
the 'gentile' traders petered out.

The eventual failure of the 'gentile' traders and of their trading spots was
due to the formation of a new group of traders who were not tied together by
bonds of political tradition and no longer subjected to particularist 'gentile'
norms and rules. Instead, what constituted this new type of group of professional traders as merchants was the contractualism which they employed to
create the norms and rules guiding them. Hence, these new merchants were a
contractual group, which, initially, was open for anyone who subscribed to
their norms and rules, did not adhere to any specific tradition, and did not
restrict the range of his activity to one particular place. Instead, these
merchants appeared as merchants wherever they went, and they tried to
organise the supply of trading goods in accordance with the anticipated or
ascertained demands of their customers.

Instead of particularist political traditions as well as 'gentile' norms and
rules these professional merchants availed themselves of a rational choice of
general principles on which everyone had to agree who wanted to join their
groups, and insisted on the general applicability of these principles without
confinement to certain places or periods and for the purpose of the maximi-
sation of profits. Hence these traders were not merely a new type of professional, but mainly a novel type of contractual group whose goals were
directed towards the organisation of trade along with two new principles of
action. These principles were the autonomy of the trading action and the use

---

28 Cf. Hans Bertil Alfons Petersson, *Anglo-Saxon Currency* (Lund, 1969).

of action for the purpose of capital gain on the side of the traders.[29] Both principles were closely intertwined. For the merchants as a contractual group could only devise their trade for the purpose of accumulating capital gain under the condition that they were exempted from the intervention of external administrative agencies, such as the territorial rulers outside towns and cities. Merchants insisted that they were not in need of protection from these agencies and could not be obliged to compensate these agencies with a substantial share of the profits from their trade. In short, the previous supply orientation gave way to demand-oriented trade.

Consequently, in order to be able to conduct their trade in accordance with their own norms and values, the contractual groups of merchants and artisans ventured to obtain special privileges from territorial rulers allowing them some degree of self-government and budgetary autonomy under the condition that they conducted the trade at their own risk. There were three ways of accomplishing such 'freedom': first, by a general charter granting to the town dwellers the right of self-government and the freedom from intervention in return for the payment of certain dues to a nearby territorial ruler;[30] second, by an incremental enforcement of communal rights and freedoms through current practice with or without the eventual recognition by a ruler; third, by the granting of several specific privileges which, in their sum, amounted to the equivalent of a general charter. The first possibility occurred in the Empire north of the Alps where, from the twelfth century, a number of urban communities were founded on the basis of a freedom charter and sometimes documented their privilege by choosing the programmatic name 'free town' – 'Freiburg'. The second case was used more often, specifically in the emerging 'urban landscapes' of northern Italy (Venice, Florence, Milan etc.) and Flanders (Bruges, Gent, Antwerp, etc.), but the same practice was followed in many of the so-called 'Imperial' cities inside the Empire whose governments obtained a freedom from intervention by local territorial rulers by placing themselves under the direct authority of the emperor. The third choice was limited mainly to France and England where, legally, no 'free' towns and cities existed, although many urban communities of artisans and merchant traders developed fully fledged self-government. In any case, the towns and cities established themselves as sworn-in communities of residents.

On the basis of such privileges, urban communities of towns and cities were encircled with walls as architectural manifestations of their separateness in legal terms which could isolate them from the surrounding countryside. Not infrequently, such communities were built on elevated grounds so that they were visible from afar. Thus, from the eleventh century, some towns and

---

29 Francesco Balducci Pegalotti, *La pratica della mercatura*, ed. Allan Evans, Mediaeval Academy of America Publication XXIV (Cambridge, Mass., 1936; repr. New York, 1970).
30 See the foundation charter of 1120 for the town of Freiburg, ed. Friedrich Keutgen, *Urkunden zur städtischen Verfassungsgeschichte*, No. 133 (Berlin, 1901; repr. Aalen, 1965).

cities were transformed into places where regular trade fairs, mainly for cloth and apparel, were held and merchants gathered for the purpose of exchanging their trading goods. Towns and cities were also centres of production where artisans produced specialised goods for sale everywhere, and where the heads of trading households could enter into merchant companies for the purposes of maintaining offices and staplehouses in other towns and cities and of reducing the trading risks. Through these companies, interrelations among towns and cities could be established which, ultimately in the thirteenth century, resulted in a Europe-wide trading network. In turn, this trading network was interconnected with other trading networks in the Middle East, south Asia, east Asia and Africa, so as to constitute a world-system of trade. Likewise, artisans could establish guilds among themselves for the purposes of excluding bothersome competitors, providing professional training for the young and maintaining quality standards as well as price levels.

Finally, the towns and cities were also local markets, attracting peasant farmers from the surrounding villages who could sell their agricultural surplus products to the town dwellers. Hence these urban communities had close economic ties with the outside world despite the fact that most of them were manifestly separated from their rural environment by the walls and a distinct legal status resulting from the privilege of self-government.

Under these conditions, the conduct of the actions of production and distribution could be regarded as an autonomous business, subject only to the stern logic of mathematical calculations and the invisible regulating forces of the 'market'. The concept of the calculability of action had two facets: first, calculability of action implied the measuring of the weights and sizes of the goods to be produced and traded, the fixing of the distances in space and the length of time necessary to be bridged by the transportation of the goods, as well as the determination of the sale prices of the goods on the market; second, calculability of action was understood to emerge from the availability of sufficient repetitive experiences on the basis of which rational assumptions about future events were conceivable.

In both its facets, calculability of action was difficult to accomplish, whenever trade was to interconnect various areas. First, in the absence of general standards for the measures of weights and sizes, comparisons of the plethora of local styles required detailed knowledge and expertise. Second, in the absence of ubiquitously available standard maps and of translocal measurements of astronomical time, the precise calculation of distances and time spans was impossible. This deficit was partly overcome by the making of portulan maps into which, since the fourteenth century and at least for the purposes of sea-borne traffic, precise distances were noted from which at least rough calculations of duration could be gleaned. Third, merchants were required to devise elaborate computational tables fixing the exchange rates among the multifarious local currencies in central and southern Europe which differed from market place to market place and initially defied general standards. Since the thirteenth century and first of all in northern Italy, a specialist contractual group of urban bankers placed themselves in charge of financial transactions, money lending and savings. Between 1311 and 1361, the city of Lübeck kept an official register of debits and credits agreed upon by contracting parties in the city.[31] The register was open for the use of all citizens and served the purpose of recording the sums agreed upon and often also the terms of the agreement. The official register may have been a necessity in Lübeck early in the fourteenth century because, at that time, not every private creditor was in the habit of keeping books. However, merchants were required to be able to know their own gains and losses at all times so as to facilitate exact calculations of the trading risks. In order to meet this need, even under the condition of intensified trade, consistent double-entry bookkeeping spread in the fourteenth century.[32] Thus, the Lübeck official register was used by fewer contracting parties, and in the years before it was eventually closed, it had become redundant. Fourth, the calculability of the conditions of trade required the verification of contractual agreements over the trading goods, the time required for transportation and the sale price due upon the delivery of the goods. These contractual agreements on the terms of trade could be verified only under the condition that they were made in writing, and, consequently, literal communication became the hallmark of the merchant traders. Fifth, in order to facilitate the uninterrupted delivery of trading goods, the physical environment had to be kept stable so that raw materials, such as wood, and energy reserves, such as those drawn from hydro-energy, could be made available whenever there was a demand for them. However, in view of seasonal changes and natural disasters, this requirement was difficult to accomplish. The town dwellers reacted by devising schemes for the efficient use and the preservation of the physical environment as far as it was required for purposes of production. From the thirteenth century, governments of urban communities bought agricultural lands in the vicinity (as in the cases of Ulm and Nuremberg), expanded the construction of hydraulic instalments, such as water mills, in the vicinity of towns and cities (as in the Netherlands), developed schemes for the preservation and regeneration of woodlands (as in the case of Nuremberg), constructed elaborate irrigation systems in areas with a seasonally uneven distribution of rainfall (as in Spain and northern Italy where Arab models came to be employed), drained marshlands so as to increase the size of arable lands (mainly in the Netherlands) and tried to place themselves in direct control of major resources of non-agricultural raw materials, such as silver- and goldmines. Sixth, the stability of the social and political environments was required, but equally difficult to maintain. In many urban communities, merchants established themselves as the patriciate ranked above the less-privileged groups of artisans. But the merchants failed to dominate the governments of the urban communities, because they had to rely on production by the local artisans, and, therefore, had to compromise in cases of dom-

---

[31] Archiv der Hansestadt Lübeck, Niederstadtbuch.
[32] Luca Pacioli, *Exposition of Double Entry Bookkeeping* (Venice, 1494), ed. Basil Yamey (Venice, 1994).

estic strife and unrest which was frequently organised by artisanal neighbourhood groups. Moreover, merchants were not the only persons who engaged in trade, as they faced competition from artisans and other persons acting in the urban communities, such as itinerant peddlers. Hence, it was unusual for the urban patriciates to succeed in retaining an unshaken position throughout the Middle Ages; instead, they might be forced into emigration or to share power.[33] A rare exception was the city of Nuremberg, where the patriciate managed to maintain its power without artisanal guilds. Externally, the merchant traders were confronted with an environment that was frequently hostile to their own ends. Land transportation was jeopardised by the activities of disquieted members of the lesser nobility as well as by bands of ordinary robbers, who tried to extract their share from the merchant profits. In defence against such pressures, merchants had to provide for their security by hiring their own mercenaries as military professionals who guarded outgoing and incoming merchants within an area of a day's journey and protected the major roads to and from their town or city;[34] likewise, from the second half of the fourteenth century, urban governments launched efforts for the defence of their towns and cities by deploying the newly developed firearms through which the larger cities gradually gained a tactical superiority over the aristocrats in their vicinity.

In summary, the professional merchant traders' attitudes toward production and distribution as end-rational action was highly specific and limited in reach to contractual groups in the urban communities of towns and cities. The rationalisation of production and distribution implied that attempts were made towards the separation of these kinds of action from the natural seasonal growth rhythms in order to facilitate the continuous supply of trading goods. Likewise, production and distribution became disentangled from each other and less coordinated with regard to local needs; instead, distribution began to be concentrated on the supply of trading goods even if these goods were also available from local production. This shift in emphasis from the mutual dependence between production and distribution at given locations to product-centred distribution patterns entailed competition between products from local production and imported products of the same or similar kind, whereby these products were no longer by necessity differentiated generically, but according to quality and price. Consequently, the locality of production mattered only in so far as it was supportive of the

---

33 Cf. chapter IV, note 43.

34 For example, the treaty concluded between the Frankfurt City Council and the Electorate of Mainz in 1389. In this treaty, the city agreed to protect the roads and waterways leading to its territory within a distance of five miles from the city's gates. The treaty was concluded for four years. Stadtarchiv Frankfurt, RS Urkunden 88. It replaced a previous agreement of a similar kind which had been in force between 1377 and 1380. Ibid., Kb 6, fol. 15 verso.

generation of high-quality products which could yield higher sales prices as trading goods. Hence the rationalisation of the trading action implied the delocalisation of production and distribution and their subjection to the general logic of product-centred markets.

Initially, the end rationalisation of the trading action was not easily employed elsewhere. Attempts at the transfer of this concept of action upon other groups and into non-urban communities were made occasionally, such as by the papal curia which, during the fourteenth century, tried to avail itself of the techniques of Cahors merchants so as to increase its revenues. Nevertheless, such attempts were short-lived and without long-term results during the Middle Ages.

The expansion of European trade

Although long-distance trade had been common throughout the early Middle Ages, it is fair to say that, as a consequence of the Crusades, its extent, its political significance and its economic importance greatly increased. Much of the increase of trade was accomplished on routes on or along the Mediterranean Sea. Hence, while the Baltic Sea had served as the major trade trajectory between the eighth and the twelfth centuries, the Mediterranean Sea again took the largest share of the long-distance trade during the later Middle Ages. From the point of view of the history of action, long-distance trade became by far the most significant economic activity after the fifteenth century. Therefore, production and local trade will not be discussed in the remainder of this chapter.

There are some indicators suggesting that the reallocation of the major trading routes was accompanied by an increase in the trading activity and the sizes of the cargo loads. First, the amount of empirical geographical knowledge about central, south and east Asia and its markets increased in consequence of planned expeditions of reconnaissance during the thirteenth and early fourteenth centuries, which, among others, traders such as the Venetian Polo family, papal emissaries such as the Franciscan John of Plano Carpini (c. 1198–c. 1242) and missionaries such as John of Marignola (dec. 1358/59) undertook. The contemporary popularity of travel reports and the willingness of mainly urban reading publics to absorb handy information on trading issues is underlined by the success of the mid-fourteenth-century travel log of the legendary Sir John Mandeville that included much information about distant markets and exotic goods which had been gleaned from the reports of actual travels.[35]

---

35 *Marco Polo and the Description of the World*, ed. Arthur Christopher Moule, Paul Pelliot, vol. 2 (London, 1938). John of Marignola, 'Chronicon', ed. Josef Emler, *Prameny dejin ceskych vydávané z nadání Palackého péci 'Spolku Historického v Praze'*, Fontes rerum

Second, two major trading cities on the shores of the Mediterranean Sea, namely Venice and Genoa, became directly involved in the political and military struggles of the Fourth and Fifth Crusades, and betrayed their immediate interests in the eastern Mediterranean and the 'Syrian' territories of the Middle East. It is difficult to understand Venice and Genoa's involvement in these struggles in any other way than as a consequence of manifest trading interests in pursuit of which these cities were conduced to invest in the crusading campaigns.

Third, and most importantly, there is direct evidence of the availability in Europe of goods, techniques of production and practical knowledge of 'Oriental' origin. This indicator applies first and foremost to paper. The earliest evidence in the Occident for the existence of paper mills on the outskirts of urban communities dates from the thirteenth century. Likewise, there is a conspicuous growth of written records on high cuisine, namely cookery books, which, since the fourteenth century, display the widespread desire for 'Oriental' spices and dishes of 'Oriental' origin.[36] Moreover, new technologies of metalwork, such as the manufacturing of firearms and printing by moveable type may have been inspired by Chinese models in the fourteenth and fifteenth centuries. Last but not least, from the thirteenth century there was a growth in the general appreciation of Arabic culture. This was not only reflected in the interests of knowledgeable individuals, such as Emperor Frederick II, who was fluent in Arabic, but also in the widening general interest in Arabic science and technology.

The spread of these and other goods and techniques of 'Oriental' origin indicates the networking accomplishment of long-distance trade. Within these trading networks, specific market places soon developed into centres for the marketing of special products, such as London for wool, Bruges for textiles, Augsburg and Milan for jewellery and precious metals, Venice for glassware, Genoa for armoury and crossbows. These market places combined local production with the purposes of distribution through long-distance trade. These networks of product-centred long-distance trade remained remarkably stable, even if occasional shifts did occur, such as the transfer of the textile trade from Bruges to Antwerp around 1500.

Far beyond the Middle Ages, much long-distance, even inter-continental, trade continued to be undertaken mainly by merchant companies. They operated at their own risk and were established by private law, even if the larger of them received charters of privilege from territorial rulers. As a rule, however,

Bohemicarum III (Prague, 1882), pp. 494–518. *Mandeville's Travels: Edited . . . from Ms Cotton Titus C XVI*, ed. P. Hamelius, vol. 1, Early English Text Society, Original Series CLIII (London, 1919). John of Plano Carpini, 'Ystoria Mongolorum [1246–7]', ed. Anastasius Wyngaert, *Sinica Franciscana*, vol. 1 (Quaracchi, 1929), pp. 3–130.

36 *Le Menagier de Paris: Traité de morale et d'economie domestique composé vers 1393 par un bourgeois Parisien*, 2 vols (Paris, Geneva, 1829; repr. Geneva, 1982).

territorial governments did not intervene in trade, with the noteworthy exception of the Portuguese-American and Spanish-American economic relations that were maintained under control of the kings of Portugal and Spain respectively. The private trading companies also acted as connecting trading agencies and thereby emerged as international actors in their own right, not unlike the 'gentile' traders of the early Middle Ages.

Conclusion

The major changes in production and distribution as actions can be summed up as follows.

With regard to the goals of trading action, the heterodynamic, status-maintaining, subsistence orientation of the Middle Ages gave way to an auto-dynamic, income-generating surplus orientation during the sixteenth century. Subsequently, the range of the trading action was enlarged to cover the distribution not only of goods, but also of capital and services. With regard to the type of actor, the accidental or alien 'gentile' traders were replaced by professional merchant traders as members of autonomous contractual groups during the eleventh and twelfth centuries. These contractual groups of merchants retained their privileges up to and beyond the sixteenth century. With regard to the spatial dimension of the trading action, it had been the overall purpose of trade in the early Middle Ages to supply goods at places where they were not produced. By contrast, in the twelfth century, a steadily growing, ultimately global network of trade relations came into existence which still facilitated the consumption of goods at places where they were not produced, but, more importantly, provided for the competitive selection of various goods of the same or a similar kind, but with differences in quality and price. During this period, trade could supplement, and also occur in competition with, local production. With regard to the temporal dimension of trade, prior to the twelfth century production and trade took place in accordance with the natural rhythms of the growth of raw materials. From the twelfth century the temporal dimension was of significance with regard to the time required for transportation as well as the time in which financial transactions could occur or were required to be conducted. With regard to the effects of the trading action, the scope was widened after the eleventh century from the manifest or anticipated demands of known individual recipients or recipient communities to anonymous product-centred market structures and translocal profit-accumulating marketing strategies, for which the localities of production were not of primary concern, but mattered only as a pricing instrument. With regard to the practical organisation and implementation of trading action, after the twelfth century contractual groups were used in order to overcome the hostilities of the physical environment and to minimise the risks of long-distance trade. The classification of production and distribution as a category of end-rational action was in itself the product of change during the eleventh and twelfth centuries. In consequence of this change, production and distribution as 'economic' activities became dissociated from local needs as well as from the rhythms of natural growth and they were subjected to the general logic of market regulations. These market regulations were conceived as transcending space and time and were expected to be autonomous from external 'political' interference. Their acceptance coincided with the formation of self-governing urban communities and replaced the previous custom of subjecting production and distribution to the particularism of local and group needs and demands.

The conceptual history of production and distribution thus does not support an economic determinism which suggests the general autonomy of market regulations. Instead, the belief in the autonomy of market regulations has been shown to stem from a specific political will in its favour.

VII

Action II: War

> They beget of a just war the best child, peace.
> – Philip Sidney

Introduction

During the twentieth century, war has mainly been equated with a violent contest over rights to rule over land and access to natural and human resources by martial arms and involving, as the contending parties, armed forces as parts of unified 'societies'. This socialisation of war was first conceptualised in the early nineteenth century, and found its most powerful expression in the general theory of war which was devised by Carl von Clausewitz (1780–1831) and of which fragments were published posthumously in 1832.[1] It appears to have materialised in a dramatic 60 per cent war-related increase in the numbers of refugees since the beginning of the twentieth century, and, even more strikingly, in the correlated increase in the numbers of civilian non-combatant war casualties, from approximately 5 per cent of the total number of war-dead during World War I, to 50 per cent during World War II, to approximately 80 per cent during the Lebanese Civil War of 1982, and to more than 90 per cent during the war in Bosnia-Hercegovina.

Several subsequent theories of war have been conceived under the impact of Clausewitz's thought. Early in the twentieth century, the social philosopher Georg Simmel (1858–1918) argued that warfare is an appropriate instrument for the accomplishment of national cohesion. Like many other German intellectuals of his time, Simmel welcomed the launching of the 'Great War' in August 1914 as a valuable contribution to the formation of a genuine 'national sentiment' and as a suitable instrument for 'nation-building'.[2] Remarkably, Simmel's arguments were not abandoned with the catastrophic

---

[1] Carl von Clausewitz, *Vom Kriege* (Berlin, 1832; 16th edn by Werner Hahlweg [Bonn, 1952]).

[2] Georg Simmel, *Der Krieg und die geistigen Entscheidungen* (Munich, Leipzig, 1917), pp. 7–29. He applied to warfare the concept of social integration which was widely applied in nineteenth-century theoretical sociology in ideologies of state-making.

ending of the war, but lingered on and continued to be applied throughout the 1920s and 1930s.[3]

Another set of theories has been culled from a number of other sources in addition to Clausewitz's thought. They rest on the conventional assumption, ultimately rooted in medieval ideas about just wars, that the legitimate conduct of domestic as well as of 'international' war is considered to be the privilege of the institutions that comprise states and that it requires a regularised process as well as morally justifiable goals. The legitimists among these theorists have taken the view that the legitimate conduct of war requires the existence of legitimate institutions of government and that, consequently, military violence by non-government actors represents acts of banditry and not war;[4] and they have concluded that war, when legitimate, can be subjected to general, legally binding rules of conduct. They have also sought to determine general 'correlates of war' as the factors which conduce legitimate governments to opt for war by some purported rationality.[5] Critics have argued that, in the capacity ascribed to them by the legitimists, states become the prime legitimisers of violent action as well as the major provoking agents for the infliction of mass violence, both legitimate and illegitimate in kind, and that the formation of states has commonly taken place, at least in Europe, through warfare.[6]

These and other nineteenth- and twentieth-century theorists of war have not, however, only defined war as a socialised type of violent action, but they also rested their work on a concept of action according to which action is end-rational and, moreover, committed to the competitive attainment of goals capable of changing the physical and socio-political environments. Such changes are taken to emerge from a dynamism which, in turn, is seen as resulting from a certain 'friction', 'tensions'[7] or 'contradictions'[8] among conflicting forces in the physical and socio-political environment. Specifically, proponents of this dynamic perception of war have attributed to the

---

3 Max Scheler, *Der Genius des Krieges und der deutsche Krieg* (Leipzig, 1915; 3rd edn [Leipzig, 1917]), pp. 370–3, new ed. in Scheler, *Gesammelte Werke*, vol. 4, Politisch-pädagogische Schriften, ed. Manfred S. Frings (Bern, Munich, 1982), pp. 149–53. Paul Schmitthenner, *Krieg und Kriegführung im Wandel der Weltgeschichte* (Potsdam, 1929). Schmitthenner, *Krieg und Staat in der Weltgeschichte* (Leipzig, 1936). A post-World War II applicant of Simmel's theories was Lewis A. Coser, *The Functions of Social Conflict* (Glencoe, 1956).

4 Ultimately, this is one core aspect of the medieval theory of just wars as expressed by St Thomas Aquinas, *Summa theologiae*, II/2, qu. 40, ar. 1–4, ed. Roberto Busa, *Sancti Thomae Aquinatis opera omnia*, vol. 2 (Stuttgart, 1980), pp. 579–80.

5 Cf. Bruce Bueno de Mesquita, *The War Trap* (New Haven, London, 1981). This idea was expanded to include 'civilizations' as long-lasting entities, by Samuel Huntington, *The Clash of Civilizations* (Boston, New York, 1996).

6 Cf. Charles Tilly, *Coercion, Capital and European States A. D. 990–1992* (Oxford, 1992).

7 Clausewitz (see note 1), Book I. Heinrich Gottlieb Tzschirner, *Ueber den Krieg* (Leipzig, 1815), pp. 103–5.

8 Friedrich Engels, *Herrn Eugen Dührings Umwälzung der Wissenschaft* (first published Leipzig, 1877), new edn in Karl Marx, Friedrich Engels, *Gesamtausgabe* (MEGA), Part I, vol. 27 (Berlin, 1988), pp. 368–70.

conflicting parties the desire to employ war for the implementation of strategies through which friction, tensions and contradictions can be resolved. In short, what is implied in the current theories of war is that wars and other forms of violent struggles are and ought to be instruments to promote change through the resolution of existing friction, tensions and contradictions.

A perceived friction, some recognised tensions and some observed contradictions have consequently been held to determine the motivations leading contending parties to enter into war, be it, that friction and tensions have been regarded as a necessary initial, though not sufficient, step towards war,[9] or that they have been believed to shape all conceivable categories of war aims.[10] Conversely, wars which neither result from friction, tensions or contradictions nor contribute to their resolution, make no sense within the descriptive and analytical frameworks of these theories.

In the context of conceptual history, however, the question is whether these characteristics of current nineteenth- and twentieth-century theories of war can be generally applied to wars conducted within European history during the Middle Ages. Already one initial observation casts doubt on the generalisability of these theories; it emerges from the fact that much nineteenth-and twentieth-century military historiography abounds with the criticism that, in Europe prior to the nineteenth century, wars were fought without much recognisable change resulting from them.[11] This criticism rests on the principal expectation that war belongs to the category of end-rational action which must usher in change.

By contrast, it is arguable, and there is an abundance of evidence to support this cardinal point, that war can also result from categories of action which are associated with the goal of preserving a stable physical and socio-political environment. Specifically, this was the case inside Europe during the Middle Ages, when the majority of wars were fought for such goals as the maintenance of a certain status by the contending parties and the prevention of attempted status alterations by an actor or group of actors or the preservation of the 'power' of one contending party against the perceived threats of one or more others. Consequently, if the concept of war has to include violent action which can, but does not have to promote change, it must be defined more broadly. Hence, in this context, war shall be understood as any kind of violent action that is regarded by contemporaries as the legitimate use of

---

9 Lewis Fry Richardson, *Statistics of Deadly Quarrels* (London, 1960).
10 Friedrich von Bernhardi, *Deutschland und der nächste Krieg* (Stuttgart, 1912). For a recent restatement see Francis Fukuyama, *The End of History and the Last Man* (New York, Toronto, 1992), pp. 254–7. Criticism of these views was already argued by Hans Delbrück, *Die Strategie des Perikles erläutert durch die Strategie Friedrichs des Grossen* (Berlin, 1890). Delbrück, *Geschichte der Kriegskunst im Rahmen der politischen Geschichte*, vol. 4 (Berlin, 1920; repr. Berlin, 1962).
11 Bernhardi (see note 10). For a recent restatement see Paul W. Schroeder, *The Transformation of European Politics 1763–1848* (Oxford, 1994), pp. 5–11.

martial arms and follows some recognisable regularised process.[12] This definition takes into account various conceptualisations of war, relative to the space
of communication within which they appear.

Fighting for Status I: The quest for control of people and the absence of expectations of war-proneness

Despite an abundance of descriptive and analytical writing on many issues
and aspects of warfare, and despite a substantial corpus of legal and moral
rules guiding the conduct of war in Europe from the time of St Augustine, at
no time prior to the early nineteenth century was any single attempt made to
compose or even publish a comprehensive theory of war. Instead, up to the
nineteenth century, war was continuously treated matter-of-factly as an evil,
which had been placed in the world by the divinity through the act of creation. Specifically, even though there were scattered disquisitions about fundamental issues related to warfare, such as whether participation in war is
permissible for Christians, such disquisitions, together with writings on such
practical matters of war as tactics and military technology, were never tied
together into a coherent, complex and general theory of war. The heuristic
implication is that there cannot be certainty in comprehensive statements
about the various European concepts of war before the nineteenth century,
because such statements cannot be based upon explicit evidence. Instead,
indirect approaches have to be used, which enforce constraints on the validity
of interpretations.

Nonetheless, a number of safe observations can be made. One is that early
medieval sources commonly referred to fighting forces in 'gentile' terms,
which meant that fighting forces were described as being seemingly political
groups by tradition and not professional warrior bands. This 'gentile' terminology for fighting forces originated as a heterostereotype which was initially
applied by Roman authors to groups of origin outside the confines of the
Empire. When these authors used the 'gentile' terminology as a heterostereotype, they pursued specific and easily comprehensible goals. For example,
when Velleius Paterculus (c. 20 BC; year of death unknown)[13] described some
Langobardi whom a Roman army had defeated as 'surpassing even the
Teutons in savagery', or when Bishop Sidonius Appolinaris (c. 430–479/86)[14]
rated successfully embattled Saxons 'an enemy fiercer than any other', they
created the impression that formidable, namely cohesive and war-prone,

---

12 The definition excludes piracy and privateering, because they were not considered to be
legitimate and did not follow recognisable regular actions. See Thomas Aquinas (see
note 4). Hence, piracy and privateering have nothing to contribute to a conceptual
history of war.

13 Velleius Paterculus, *Res gestae Divi Augusti*, cap. II/106 (various editions).

14 Sidonius Apollinaris, [Letter to Namatius], cap. 6, in *Gai Solii Apollinaris Sidonii Episto-
lae et Carmina*, ed. Christian Luetjohann, *MGH AA*, vol. 8, p. 132.

fighting forces had been encountered and, at least temporarily, overcome. The use of the 'gentile' terminology together with explicit ascriptions of war-proneness thus had the effect of aggrandising the Roman victories by exaggerating the fighting power and the ferocity of their alien adversaries. But the terminology as it was applied upon these alien fighting forces and the ascriptions of war-proneness with which their fighting habits were labelled reflected a Roman perspective which did not necessarily have to match the actual conditions under which the supposedly 'barbarian' invaders organised themselves in war. Hence, in all probability, references using the nomenclature of political groups by tradition, such as the *Langobardi* and the Saxons, must neither be misunderstood as implying that these fighting forces were actually political groups rather than professional, presumably contractual warrior bands, nor is it *prima facie* acceptable that the ascriptions of war-proneness always encapsulated their actual fighting habits.

However, the 'gentile' terminology with its associated values was perfunctory as long as they were applied as a heterostereotype in service to a Roman audience. It only became problematic when it was transformed into an autostereotype in consequence of its reception by early medieval authors who were no longer committed to serving the interests and expectations of Roman readers. For example, when Gregory, the sixth-century Bishop of Tours, reported that, in the late fifth century, there was a battle 'between Saxons and Romans', it is evident that Gregory used a 'gentile' terminology without wishing to imply that the warring parties were political groups; instead, he can only have meant that there was a battle between some Saxons and a part of the Roman army.[15] The same can be surmised with regard to a well-known passage in Bede's early eighth-century *Historia ecclesiastica gentis Anglorum*, where he mentions that some migrants came to Britain from 'three very powerful groups, namely Saxons, Angles, and *Iutae*'.[16] In both cases, the 'gentile' terminology does not cogently support the conclusion that the groups referred to were political groups; instead, it allows the assumption that they could have been contractual or neighbourhood groups. Thus the continuity into the early Middle Ages of the use of 'gentile' terms for fighting forces according to Roman usage did not imply a continuity of meaning, even though varieties of group-specific tactics and modes of fighting continued to distinguish fighting forces with different cultural backgrounds.[17]

There seems to be good reason to believe that the standard non-Roman fighting force in early medieval Europe was not the political group but the autonomous warrior band as a contractual group organised by a warlord. It seems to have been the goal of these warlords to attain or maintain a certain

[15] Gregory, *Libri Historiarum X*, cap. II/19, ed. Bruno Krusch, Wilhelm Levison, *MGH SS rer. Merov.*, vol. 1, p. 65.

[16] Bede, *Historia ecclesiastica gentis Anglorum*, cap. I/15, ed. Bertram Colgrave, R. A. B. Mynors (Oxford, 1969), p. 50.

[17] As described, among others, for the Huns by Jordanes, *Getica*, cap. 261, ed. Theodor Mommsen, *MGH AA* 5, 1, p. 125.

status through successful fighting experiences, in order to be able to attract large numbers of retainers joining them in their bands. In a number of cases, these warlords may have been attractive as band leaders for the reason that they were credited with a divine ancestry. Two cases of such warlords with divine ancestries seem to have been recorded as the leaders of the Myrgings in southern Jutland, some of whom may have migrated to Britain, and their enemies, the leaders of the Angles, who are recorded to have migrated to Britain from Angeln, also located in southern Jutland.[18] But in more numerous cases, the divine ancestry of these warlords appears to have been established in retrospect through intermarriages between their own male descendants and daughters of rulers who had already been credited with a divine ancestry and passed them on through marriage affiliation and matrilateral succession. Such seems to have occurred in the cases of some of the purportedly Saxon immigrants to Britain.[19] One can conclude that the warlords either had already divine ancestry which allowed them to occupy powerful positions as band leaders, or they acquired it as a consequence of marriage alliances which had no direct relation to warfare.

For the warlords themselves, then, few indicators of status were available. Display and distribution of battle prey was obviously one; it is frequently on record in written sources,[20] and also grave finds seem to suggest that wealth was a marker of status.[21] However, looting for booty was a hazardous business and not always successful. Moreover, even successful warlords had to compete with other wealthy persons in a given settlement, for example with those who had inherited their wealth from previous generations. Hence, the capability of

18 The divine ancestry of the Anglian war leader can be established on the grounds of Bede's report about this group which he calls Wuffingas and traces back to the war-god Woden. For the Myrgings, divine ancestry can only be postulated under the assumption that the Myrgings were a Saxon royal kin group with a divine ancestor, perhaps Seaxnot. See Bede (see note 16), cap. I/15, II/15, pp. 50, 190. *Widsith*, vv. 41–4, ed. Kemp Malone (Copenhagen, 1962), p. 24. Reinhard Wenskus, 'Sachsen–Angelsachsen–Thüringer', Wenskus, *Ausgewählte Aufsätze zum frühen und preußischen Mittelalter* (Sigmaringen, 1986), p. 195.

19 The (probably) late ninth-century *Anglo-Saxon Chronicle* mentions the names of Cerdic and Cissa as allegedly late fifth-century Saxon conquerors, although the names betray Celtic origin. In these cases, the Celtic background of the names given to these persons may indicate that they had been born in Britain and of Celtic mothers even though the later record claimed that they were immigrants themselves. *The Anglo-Saxon Chronicle: A Collaborative Edition*, vol. 3: Ms A, s. a. 477, 495, ed. Janet M. Bately (Cambridge, 1986), p. 19.

20 Gregory (see note 15), cap. III/3, p. 99, records the looting expedition of the Danish king Chlochilaicus to Gall and says that the king stayed on the seashore for a while after the main warrior band had already boarded their ships loaded with prisoners and prey. The king had thus distributed wealth among the members of his band before returning home. According to Gregory, this custom was fatal for the Danish king, because the Frankish King Theoderic was given time enough to approach Chlochilaicus, defeat and kill him and even rescue the prey in a sea battle from those who had already embarked on their ships.

21 For a survey, see Christopher J. Arnold, *An Archaeology of the Early Anglo-Saxon Kingdoms* (London, New York, 1988), pp. 142–62.

displaying and distributing wealth was insufficient as a marker of the special status of a successful warlord.

What was left then to them as a lasting indicator of status was the recognition of, or continuous support for, a warlord as the ruler over people. This meant that warlords could acquire a stable status as leaders of their retainers if they were not only successful in battle, but could convert their military success into a lasting rule over various groups, thereby establishing themselves as ruling kin groups or receiving recognition as legitimate successors to rule.[22] Likewise, although kin relations or friendship contracts did not always prevent dissent and war, they could be used as the bases for agreements that, with the restoration of good relations and the termination of war, former lack of loyalty and previously committed acts of military violence should be 'nullified', that is, deleted from memory.[23] Thus competition for rule over people as an indicator of status seems to have been a major, if not the predominant war aim which outweighed, in the early Middle Ages, the ancient Roman quest for rule over land. The same war aim was explicitly adduced by contemporary authors in relation to warfare among already established rulers. Perhaps the most successful rulers following this pattern were the kings of the Franks themselves. Indeed, Charlemagne was noteworthy[24] for his ability to force a great variety of groups residing in a vast area under the sphere of influence of the Frankish kings. But, up to the ninth century, the Frankish kings did not pursue a rigorous policy of colonising the conquered groups by subjecting them to Frankish norms and values. Instead, in cases where the local population was not deported or resettled, it was allowed or even encouraged to retain its own distinct legal status and political traditions. The consequence was that the rule of the warlords usually extended over motley groups of people and reflected a practice which accounted for both the rapid expansion of such rule and its transience.

The goal of subjecting further groups to the rule of a warlord as the dominant war aim in the early Middle Ages appears to have induced such warlords to confine their activities to what was deemed necessary for the accomplishment of this goal. Although warfare was incessant, and although critical contemporaries,[25] such as Gregory of Tours, were vocal in denouncing as evil

---

22 For example, *Anglo-Saxon Chronicle* (see note 19), s. a. 449, p. 17. The entry follows Bede. Bede (note 16), cap. IV/15, p. 380, also has a report on Caedwalla, who is said to have invaded Sussex and 'wasted it by depopulation', at the time when, as a pretender, he had been expelled from the kingdom of Wessex.

23 For sources on the *adnullatio* see *Vita S. Sturmi*, ed. Georg Heinrich Pertz, *MGH SS* 2, p. 374 [an eighth-century life of the first abbot of the monastery of Fulda]. *MGH Formulae*, ed. Karl Zeumer (Hanover, 1886), p. 412, Nr. 27 [a ninth-century formulary for a letter on the conclusion of a peace between two kings].

24 His biographer Einhard explicitly praised him for that. See Einhard, *Vita Karoli Magni*, cap. 15, ed. Oswald Holder-Egger, *MGH SS rer. Germ.* (25), pp. 17–18.

25 In the Gothic version of the Bible translated by the Visigothic bishop Ulfilas in the fourth century, the Book of Kings is omitted. The omission provoked the early fifth-century Cappadocian church historian Philostorgius to surmise that Ulfilas had refrained from translating this book because it contains numerous battle reports and

their rulers' inclination towards violence, early medieval sources provide little explicit evidence for war-proneness or outright delight in atrocities on the side of those engaged in war.[26] A spotlight on one incident may serve as an illustration. The case shows that the rule of the warlords was exposed to much jeopardy, which could be fatal. In the entry under the year 755, the *Anglo Saxon Chronicle* records an incident which must have taken place in 784[27] and in which Cynewulf, the then ruling King of the West Saxons, was killed by a pretender named Cyneheard who was also killed. In the well-composed entry under the year 755, King Cynewulf is rebuked for having provoked the incident by enjoying the company of a woman instead of executing his duties as the lord of his warriors. The retreat of the king is adduced as the context which provides an opportunity for Cyneheard to attack the king's retainers in an attempt to oust Cynewulf from rulership. Caught by surprise, Cynewulf rushes to the battle scene and begins to fight, but is again rebuked for having left a tactically favourable position in the doorway of a hall because of his war-proneness. The consequences are described as grave; not only does the king pay with his life for his bellicosity, but also many of his retainers find it impossible to defend themselves adequately, once their lord is gone. Although they ultimately succeed in killing Cyneheard in revenge, the entry ends tragically. Thus the annalist left no doubt in his argument that Cynewulf's war-proneness in combination with his departure from the retainers was not heroic at all, but distinctly unwise, a fatal nuisance for some of his retainers and, ultimately, an act of negligence regarding his duties as a ruler. Hence, even though warfare was ubiquitous, exuberance in military pride and lack of caution and restraint were considered to be unfavourable when they occurred.

Despite the sometimes critical or even cynical close contemporary reports of acts of brutality and vandalism said to have been committed by war leaders, the lack of esteem for war-proneness in the early Middle Ages interconnects well with the then dominant heterodynamic perceptions of the body, according to which an individual was held to receive energies from the group in which the individual was a member or from some non-human source in the physical environment. Concretely speaking, status could be attained or maintained by a warlord if he succeeded in dispersing his energies upon or

because Ulfilas had not wanted to raise what Philostorgius believed to be the customary readiness of northern peoples to go to war. However, there is no way of ascertaining what Ulfilas's actual motives had been. See Wilhelm Streitberg, ed., *Die gotische Bibel*, 6th edn (Heidelberg, 1971; first published Heidelberg, 1908), pp. XIX–XX.

26 Perhaps, Charlemagne's reported massacre of 4500 Saxons at Verden (Aller) received notoriety because of the rare occurrence of such events. *Annales qui dicuntur Einhardi*, s. a. 782, ed. Friedrich Kurze, *MGH SS rer. Germ.* (6), p. 65. See also Abbo of Saint Germain, 'De bellis Parisiacae urbis', ed. Paul von Winterfeld, *MGH Poetae Lat.* 4,1, pp. 77–122.

27 *Anglo-Saxon Chronicle* (see note 19), s. a. 755, pp. 36–8, 39. The entry appears to have been misplaced by the chronicle compilers. It records events referred to again in the same work under the year 784.

distributing his spoils of war among the members of the war band rather than by absorbing or misusing the energies of the latter.

In summary, early medieval military campaigns were limited in their disastrous consequences, although such acts of violence were numerous and did entail suffering for persons and groups, of which our sources tirelessly remind us. But these remarks express the contempt of those acting in excess of the proper limits rather than displaying the regularity of conduct. Instead, in the early Middle Ages, war and peace were no opposites in the sense of being mutually exclusive; rather, they were coexistent and difficult to disentangle. For wars, frequent as they were, were hardly ever long and would normally not have lethal consequences for many non-combatants. As Isidore of Seville insisted, peace-making was identical with the conclusion of contractual agreements between the contending parties.[28] That supports the conclusion that wars were then neither fought in conditions of tension nor for the purpose of promoting change. Charlemagne's Saxon wars, which lasted for thirty three years with significant interruptions, were recognised as exceptional in the ninth and tenth centuries by historians and the scribe of a St Gall charter who referred to them in a dating clause.[29] Yet decisive victories, when they occurred, could promote considerable stability, as is shown, as late as in the tenth century, when King Otto I defeated the Magyars in 955 in what is today southern Germany and forced them into acquiescence for more than two generations until they could resume battle in 1030.

Fighting for Status II: Cavalry versus infantry and the quest for rule over land and people

Occidental warfare in the high Middle Ages has frequently been criticised for its rudeness and lack of sophistication. Specifically, when compared to late-Roman and Byzantine practices, occidental armies have been blamed for the lack of sophistication of their tactics and logistics, a lack of discipline, and an inclination towards the infliction of massacres upon prisoners of war and non-combatants. Military institutions and the concept of martial law appeared to be in a nascent stage at best. Last, but not least, the weaponry preferred during the high Middle Ages seemed to suggest that the most frequently applied tactics were those of dual combat, on foot and on horseback, and that such tactics were far inferior against the elaborate schemes used by the Roman armies of Antiquity, the Byzantine, Magyar and Arab armies of the Middle Ages, or the occidental armies after the twelfth century.

But such verdicts are hardly fair. First, the standards against which the occi-

---

[28] Isidore of Seville, *Etymologiarum sive originum libri XX*, cap. XVIII/1, 11, ed. W. M. Lindsay (Oxford, 1911).

[29] Einhard (see note 24), cap. 8–9, pp. 11–13. Widukind of Corvey, *Rerum gestarum Saxonicarum libri III*, cap. I/12–13, ed. Paul Hirsch, Hans-Eberhard Lohmann, *MGH SS rer. Germ.* (60), pp. 20–3. Hans Wartmann, ed., *Urkundenbuch der Abtei Sanct Gallen*, Nr. 163 (802), vol. 1 (Zurich, 1863), p. 154.

dental armies of the high Middle Ages have mainly been measured have been external ones, not derived from the habits, needs and demands of the contemporary fighting forces themselves. Second, the verdicts do not account for the fact that, in some core aspects of the military, the 'barbarian' occidental warriors displayed skills with which they superseded the Roman military organisation, notably with regard to horse-riding and smithery.[30] The development of mastery over these particular skills suggests a type of military organisation which gave preference to small, highly mobile units and to dual combat over the massive deployment of regularised, drilled and disciplined armed forces. Third, these verdicts do not do justice to the fact that the overall war aim had not necessarily been the establishment of some bureaucratic type of long-lasting administration, but, as has been argued above, the subjection of various groups to the status-maintaining or status-enlarging rule of a warlord. This goal enforced a preference given to minimal military organisation as a means to prepare for battle, and, as a rule, of small fighting forces composed of warriors who were united in contractual groups and who could handle their weapons both as cavalrymen and as infantrymen.

By the tenth century, however, in the core parts of the Occident after their inclusion into the Carolingian Empire, it had become difficult to maintain these mobile types of fighting force composed of unspecialised warriors. There are several reasons for this. First, within the several kingdoms and the Empire, the significance of horizontally stratified social groups as groups by law had begun to rise, which widened the gulf between the majority peasant farmers and the minority aristocrats. The latter began to establish themselves as a military élite. Second, a process of the territorialisation of the space of regular communication had been launched in consequence of which the concept of rule over people was to be expanded to include control over land and thus could no longer be limited to the control by a warlord type of ruler. But, in the long run, control had to emerge from a regularised ruling bureaucracy. This factor became visible in a series of defensive measures which were launched in England perhaps late in the ninth century and on the Continent early in the tenth century. These measures consisted in the erection of defensive earthworks against invading enemy forces. The earthworks were ordered to be built against armies of Scandinavian and Magyar origin at places of believed strategic importance for the purpose of protecting areas of settlement. The fortifications were guarded continuously, and the tasks of building, maintaining and guarding them were laid upon the resident population in the vicinity. In return for the accomplishment of these tasks, the resident population was entitled to use their fortification as a refuge at times of danger. As these fortifications were grouped together into defence systems, they made manifest the idea that wars could no longer be fought only for control of

---

30 Already noted by Richard Joseph Edouard Charles Lefèbvre des Noëttes, *L'attelage: Le cheval de selle à travers les âges* (Paris, 1931).

people but must also be fought for land.[31] The first factor led to a social strati-fication in consequence of which the aristocratic élite could restrict access to certain types of weaponry for its own members. Aristocrats could eventually reserve for themselves the use of cavalry arms, thereby placing themselves above the 'agrarii milites' who may have served as infantrymen in the ruler's service during the tenth century.[32] The second factor unleashed a fusion of the military and the administrative élites with the implication that the aristo-cratic warriors were also expected to be capable of leading a bureaucratic ad-ministration of land and people under the control of territorial rulers, mainly the kings and the emperor.

In combination, both factors sparked a gradual division of the armed forces into cavalry and infantry. Initially, already in Carolingian times, both types of fighting force appear to have been ranked hierarchically, with the cavalry being the preferred fighting force of the aristocracy, whereas their tactical differentiation in battle seems to have begun only in the tenth century. Such can be inferred from the explicitness with which contemporary sources referred to the deployment of heavy cavalry by Otto I in the battle against the Magyars in 955, when he used eight units of *legiones* of cavalry in a sweeping frontal attack.[33]

Because the horse and the equipment had to be provided by the caval-rymen themselves, affluence became a precondition for membership in the cavalry. Therefore, the process of institutionalising the cavalry as a regular armed force was slow and uneven. On the one hand, in 991 a fighting band of 'Vikings' crossed the North Sea to the British Isles and landed in the Black-water estuary near Maldon in Essex with the recognised intention of taking booty and extracting tolls in currency. A local fighting force was hastily convened to defend the area against the incoming 'Vikings'. After the 'Vikings' had left their boats, they began to fight on foot, and their opponents, including their aristocratic commander, were also infantrymen. The 'Vikings' held sway over the defenders, who appear to have been ill organised under a commander who was censured for his excessive war-proneness.[34] The scene shows that, around AD 1000, the conventional type of unspecialised warrior still existed in Scandinavia and was not uncommon in Britain. But, on the other hand, already at the end of the ninth century, the tripartite scheme of social groups appeared which classed warriors (*fyrdmen, bellatores*) as a social group of its own and associated it with a higher status than that of ordinary farmers (*laboratores*).[35] Likewise, the tenth-century term 'agrarii milites' may

---

31 Widukind (see note 29), cap. I/35, pp. 48–9. 'Burghal Hidage', ed. Agnes J. Robertson, *Anglo-Saxon Charters* (Cambridge, 1939), pp. 246–9 (2nd edn [Cambridge, 1957]).

32 Widukind (see note 29), cap. I/35, pp. 48–9.

33 Widukind (see note 29), III/44, III/48, pp. 123–9. Gerhard, *Vita Udalrici*, ed. Georg Waitz, *MGH SS* 6, pp. 401–2.

34 *The Battle of Maldon*, vv. 89–95, ed. D. G. Scragg (Manchester, 1981), p. 60.

35 *King Alfred's Old English Version of Boethius, De Consolatione Philosophiae*, ed. Walter John Sedgefield (Oxford, 1899; repr. Darmstadt, 1968), p. 40. *Miracula S. Bertini, MGH SS* 15, 1, p. 513. Aelfric, 'Passio Machabeorum', Aelfric, *Lives of Saints*, cap. XXV, vol. 2,

have come into use for the purpose of designating a group of farmers (*agrarii*) who were more closely related to military service (*milites*) than ordinary farmers. Eventually, by the end of the eleventh century, the cavalry composed of knights or aristocratic military specialists known as *milites* had established itself as the paramount fighting force in wars which were then conducted for the purpose of establishing or maintaining rule over land and people.[36]

The peace of God: peace movements and territorialisation

The fusing of the distinctly aristocratic social status with the quest for seigneurial lordship and rule over land and people became the hallmark of the knights. They displayed the distinctness of their knightly dignity from the eleventh century by cultivating the specific literary image of chivalry, setting segregated moral codes for themselves as courtiers and erecting hilltop castles as architectural manifestations of their quest for domination over peasant farmers. The moral codes included the obligation that the knights should follow rigorous rules of honour and constrain their war-proneness. It has frequently been asserted in recent studies on knighthood and chivalry that these demonstrations and manifestations of knightly dignity reflected a set of ideals rather than ubiquitously current practice. The demand is thus justified that the literary images and moral ideals ought not to be misunderstood as a faithful depiction of actual conduct; however, it also needs to be recognised that, by virtue of being transmitted at the 'courts' in the hilltop castles before and by an aristocratic audience, these ideals were accepted as such and were therefore more than mere speculations flowing from the fanciful minds of creative poets. Likewise, the moral codes represented in the twelfth-century statutes of the religious orders of knighthood or the preaching of St Bernard of Clairvaux (1090–1153) among others, did contain evidence that the knights were obliged to fuse the demands arising from their military status with the demands enshrined in the monks' traditions of the spiritual fight against the temptations of the devil.[37] Yet, again, while it must be admitted

---

ed. Walter William Skeat, Early English Text Society, Original Series CXIV (London, 1890; repr. London, 1969), pp. 120–2. Aelfric, *Die Hirtenbriefe Aelfrics in altenglischer und lateinischer Fassung*, ed. Bernhard Fehr (Hamburg, 1914), pp. 225–6 (repr., ed. Peter Clemoes, Bibliothek der angelsächsischen Prosa IX [Darmstadt, 1966]). Aelfric, *The Old English Version of the Heptateuch, Aelfric's Treatise on the Old and the New Testament and his Preface to Genesis*, ed. Samuel John Crawford, Early English Text Society, Original Series CLX (London, 1922; repr. London, 1969), pp. 71–2. Wulfstan, *Die 'Institutes of Polity, Civil and Ecclesiastical': Ein Werk Erzbischof Wulfstans von York*, cap. IV, ed. Karl Jost, Schweizer Anglistische Arbeiten XLVII (Bern, 1959), pp. 52–7.

36 *Ruodlieb*, ed. Benedikt K. Vollmann (Wiesbaden, 1985).

37 Bernard of Clairvaux, 'Liber ad Milites Templi De laude novae militiae', ed. Jean Leclercq, H. M. Rochais, *Sancti Bernhardi Opera*, vol. 3 (Rome, 1963), pp. 205–39, was of the opinion that the knights in one person combine the combat of flesh and the combat of spirit. See also Anselm of Havelberg, *Dialogues*, vol. 1, Renouveau de l'Eglise, ed. Gaston Salet (Paris, 1966), pp. 98–100.

that perhaps only a few of the knights actually followed these demands, the orders of knighthood were manifest institutions which attracted numerous followers, not only in Palestine at the time of the Crusades, but also in the Occident itself.[38] Hence, the fact that not all aristocrats lived up to the literary ideal of chivalry, and the argument that not all aristocrats acted in accordance with the preaching of St Bernard of Clairvaux or the statutes of the orders of knighthood, do not refute the principal observation that the ideal and moral codes of courtly chivalry sanctioned rigorous rules of conduct in battle, imposed constraints against belligerence and still served as visible markers of aristocratic status.

Nevertheless, new war aims emerged during the eleventh century. On the Continent, conflicts arose mainly about proprietary rights over towns and cities, and because the aristocracy was neither homogeneous nor unified but composed of increasingly antagonistic three-generation residential households. Their inter-competitiveness and their separation from the communities of peasant farmers became visible in the hilltop castles as centres of territorial administration whose boundaries had to be established through disputes among neighbouring aristocrats. Due to the absence of overarching arbitrary institutions, these conflicts had to be settled in feuds with martial arms. The right to feud, together with its variant the duel, took the form of a judicial trial with the divinity as the judge.

Already early in the eleventh century, high representatives of church institutions, notably bishops in Western Europe, began to stand up against such status-related violent action. They argued in favour of arbitration and sought to impose themselves as arbiters in lieu of the divinity. Specifically, these bishops took action against clergymen who acted as military men or did otherwise practice military values.[39] However, although territorial rulers as well as town councils made the same efforts with increasing frequency between the twelfth and the fifteenth centuries, neither feuds nor duels could be suppressed during the Middle Ages, which fact reveals the tenacity of this type of status-related violent action.

Hence, while it is true that few battles were actually fought over hilltop castles during the Middle Ages, it needs to be taken into consideration that these castles were the focal points of warfare in the indirect, deictic sense of representing the power centres of seigneurial lordship and rule over land and people in the grip of kings and aristocrats. Not infrequently, belligerent seigneurial lords and territorial rulers would pitch their castles on opposite hills within eyesight, so as to make their competitiveness visible across the intervening territorial boundaries that separated them.

Nevertheless, this competition had the character of protracted knock-out matches which lasted from the eleventh until the fifteenth century and led to a

---

38 *Die Statuten des Deutschen Ordens nach den ältesten Handschriften*, ed. Max Perlbach (Halle, 1890).
39 Most vocally, Bishop Gerard of Cambrai. See Gesta episcoporum Cameracensium, cap. III/27, III/52, *MGH SS* 7, pp. 474, 485.

selection of only some seigneurial lords and rulers over land and people whereas the majority of others either perished or became mediatised under the suzerainty of their more successful competitors. In most parts of continental Europe, it was the winners of the competition who, by the fifteenth century, rose to the status of all-embracing paramount rulers. These rulers managed to combine their several privileges into the exclusive right to rule over land and people. Although, in this process, various factors, such as the availability of actual financial and human resources, of organisational skills and of progeny in sufficient numbers, were frequently crucial in decisions about success or failure, also fitness for combat and the ability to organise and command a fighting force were essential. The main theatre of war, where these campaigns were conducted most frequently, was in the local neighbourhoods, although large-scale campaigns, such as the warfare accompanying the Investiture Controversy or Frederick Barbarossa's Italian wars, also occurred.

However, at the same time, wars were also fought for the purpose of annihilating the opponent. This goal was explicitly associated with the specific type of wars which were conducted as Crusades between the late eleventh and the fifteenth centuries. Crusades were wars fought for the purpose of annihilating non-Christians (mainly Muslims) and heretics (mainly Hussites and Albigensians) or subjecting them to Christian religious authority. Ideologies were composed according to which Crusades were to be fought as a means to promote Christianity and as a manifest indication of secular change.[40] They required authorisation by the pope and needed to be carried out by the emperor or some high-ranking Christian ruler or aristocrat. In all Crusades, fighting involved an amount and an intensity of violence which was purposefully inflicted upon those at whom the Crusades were targeted and which far exceeded what was common in the feuds. These campaigns united a multitude of aristocratic warriors for fights against non-Christians or heretics, and, in some instances, brought the aristocratic warriors together with masses of non-combatant pilgrims to Palestine. The emergence of the crusading ideal was closely intertwined with the emergence, during the eleventh century, of the custom of commuting punishments for religious sins into specific kinds of penitential actions, including the payment of indentures for fighting the enemies of the Catholic Church.[41] Contrary to the previously discussed type of warfare, the Crusades were religious wars insofar as they were conducted under the overall goal of extending by military force the world of Christendom at the expense of other religions.

Nevertheless, that such religious fervour did not rule out the existence of other war aims is well recorded, even during the Crusades, by conflicts over strategies and goals among the crusaders in Palestine themselves as well as between the crusaders and the non-combatant pilgrims and the representa-

---

40 Gregory VII (Proclamation for the defence of Byzantium, 1 March 1074), in Gregory, *Registrum*, No. I/49, ed. Erich Caspar, *MGH Epp sel.* 2, 1, pp. 75–6.

41 Lampert of Hersfeld, *Opera*, s. a. 1065, ed. Oswald Holder-Egger, *MGH SS rer. Germ.* (38), pp. 93–8.

tives of church institutions under whose aegis the pilgrimages took place. While the pilgrims and members of the higher clergy argued for the priority of the religious goal of establishing Christian control over Palestine, the aristocratic crusaders were ready for a multitude of specific agreements through which their own interests could be accommodated with those of local Muslim rulers. The difference in goals displayed the coexistence, even under crusading conditions, of religious fervour with the kinds of secular war aims for which aristocrats would go to war in their Occidental homes, namely to erect hilltop castles, establish themselves as territorial rulers over land and people, and promote or maintain their own status as warlords. The predominance of secular war aims over religious fervour also holds true for other Crusades under aristocratic leadership, notably for the wars conducted by the Teutonic Order in Prussia during the thirteenth century.

In summary, despite their horrors of violence,[42] and despite the clichés of anti-Muslim sentiment cultivated in the Occident,[43] the Crusades do not support the contention that medieval European warfare as a whole between the eleventh and the thirteenth centuries was generally characterised by an excessive war-proneness which could generate a lust to kill. Instead, the contests for status among the members of a competitive aristocracy took place under significant constraints and were further constrained during the period by regulations for the preservation of peace which the Church and secular rulers over land and people began to enact in the twelfth century.[44]

New weapons, new strategies, new forms of military organisation

Whereas the Crusades in Palestine were fought mainly with conventional tactics, the later thirteenth, the fourteenth and the fifteenth centuries witnessed changes in consequence of which the tactical significance of the mounted aristocracy declined. These changes concerned weapons technology. From the fourteenth century, new types of weapon were devised, mainly in two contexts: first, the deployment of larger numbers of infantry forces, and, second, siege warfare. The increase in numbers and tactical significance of infantry forces began in the early fourteenth century, when infantry forces of protesting neighbourhood groups in Flanders and Switzerland won a series of battles against heavily armed cavalry. The first of these engagements was the

---

42 Fulcher of Chartres, *Historia Hierosolymitana ab anno 1095 ad annum usque 1127*, cap. 16 (*PL* 155, cols 849–50), also ed. Frances R. Ryan (New York, 1973), p. 112, reports acts of cannibalism on the side of the crusaders.

43 Taking the form of outright hatred. See *Richard Coeur de Lion*, vv. 3214–21, 3532–62, ed. Karl Brunner, *Der mittelenglische Versroman über König Löwenherz*, Wiener Beitrage zur Englischen Philologie XLII (Vienna, Leipzig, 1913), pp. 256, 271–2.

44 See, for example, Tolomeo de Lucca, *Die Annalen des Tholomeus von Lucca in doppelter Fassung*, s. a. 1274, ed. Bernhard Schmeidler, *MGH SS rer. Germ.* N. S. 8 (1930), pp. 173–4 who characterised Count Rudolf of Habsburg as experienced in defensive warfare with the dukes of Savoy over the maintenance of territorial boundaries. *Constitutio pacis* [Mainz, 15 August 1235], ed. Ludwig Weiland, *MGH Const.* 2, pp. 241–7.

Fig. 22 Drawing of a fourteenth-century firearm, c. 1400. From Conrad
Kyeser, *Bellifortis*. Niedersächsische Staats- und Universitätsbibliothek
Göttingen, Cod. fol. Ms. philos. 63 Cim, fol. 104 verso.

battle of Kortrijk in Flanders which was fought in 1302 between revolting
Flemish urban guilds and the French king as the then suzerain of the Count of
Flanders. The use of siege warfare represented the partial reception, from the
thirteenth century onwards, of ancient Roman military practice, as laid down
in the military manual by Flavius Vegetius Renatus. Vegetius's fourth-century
manual had been known throughout the Middle Ages, although little had
been made of it in terms of its practical application.[45] But, in the course of
Frederick Barbarossa's Italian wars, machines for siege warfare were extensively employed, and, from the thirteenth century onwards, Vegetius became a
frequently read and copied author, with an emphasis on the sections of technology. Up till the fifteenth century, Vegetius provided to engineers, miners
and sappers a reservoir of ideas for the construction of war machines, tunnels
and ditches.

However, siege warfare concentrated upon the fortified towns and cities,
which were the targets of attacks by seigneurial lords and rulers over land and
people, the latter of whom tried to absorb the economically affluent towns
and cities into their own territories. Because sieges could be lengthy, siege
warfare had a retarding and an expanding effect, on the one hand reducing

---

[45] Flavius Vegetius Renatus, *De re militari*, ed. Alf Önnerfors (Stuttgart, Leipzig, 1995).

Fig. 23 Siege warfare against a castle, c. 1400. From Conrad Kyeser, *Bellifortis*. Niedersächsische Staats- und Universitätsbibliothek Göttingen, Cod. Fol. Ms philos. 63 Cim, fol. 50 recto.

Fig. 24 Siege warfare against a fortified town, fifteenth century. From *Das Feuerwerksbuch von 1420*. First printed 1529.

the mobility of the fighting forces, on the other increasing the costs of maintaining them and of providing the machines to be deployed during the siege.

Another new type of weapon unleashed a reconceptualisation of military action as such. This was represented by projectiles which were developed during the fourteenth and fifteenth centuries from the arrow. In the Occident, the arrow came into use against cavalry forces in two different ways: first, by means of the longbow as a weapon of the light infantry of peasant farmers and, second, by means of the crossbow as a weapon which was initially reserved for the use of specialised forces, but was soon applied by the cavalry and the infantry. For technical reasons, longbowmen had to be able to move their bodies more extensively than was possible for mounted cavalry. Likewise, longbowmen needed both their arms for the handling of the weapon and, therefore, could not carry their own shields or swords. This meant that longbowmen were defenceless unless they were protected against enemy action by cavalry forces. Consequently, longbowmen could only be deployed successfully in battle if coordinated tactical formations brought together various contingents of specialists from different social groups. Hence, first and foremost, the successful use of longbowmen required the readiness of the knighted mounted aristocrats to abandon parts of their privileges and join tactical formations for the purpose, among others, of protecting peasant farmers as longbowmen. These tactical formations emerged from a concept of battle action as a sequence of preconceived and strategically designed acts. These planned choreographic sequences appeared because it was then considered to be useful that strategic designs should be made for the purpose of coordinating the successive single acts of military violence by one warrior with those of other warriors. Since the second half of the fourteenth century, English longbowmen were requested by the government to train themselves regularly in the use of their arms and to do so in peace time.[46] Hence, battle action would no longer consist of dual combats exclusively, but warriors would be asked to take over specific tasks as members of a military unit which was to preserve its coherence and integrity during the battle as much as possible. Moreover, the entire army would consist of several of such units each being composed for the purpose of taking over predesigned tasks and being equipped with only a small variety of weapons. The purpose of organising armies into tactical formations was that, through coordinated battle action, goals could be accomplished which were otherwise out of reach of warriors who were only committed to dual combat. Thus military action had become end-rational in the sense that goal attainment began to dominate the choice of tactics and weapons. In summary, while wars continued to be fought for the maintenance or restoration of the *status quo*, they came to be conceptualised in terms of a new concept of action according to which means were not ends in themselves, but instruments towards the accomplishment of set goals.

Yet the practical requirements to accomplish these goals stood in oppo-

---

[46] Proclamation by King Edward III [1 June 1363], ed. Thomas Rymer, *Foedera*, vol. 3, 3 (The Hague, 1740), p. 79.

Fig. 25 Arranged units of cavalry and infantry in the late fifteenth-century *Hausbuch*, fols 51 verso–52 recto, an illuminated manuscript in possession of Fürst Waldburg-Wolfegg. Reprinted by permission.

sition to the general tendency of the aristocracy to dissociate themselves socially as knights from the peasant farmers, so that the use of longbowmen in battle was a rare asset of armed forces. Moreover, longbowmen had to be deployed in large numbers so as to have a greater effect. For example, in the Battle of Falkirk in 1298, Edward I may have led an army of some 25,000 men, predominantly longbowmen, together with a cavalry force of some 3000 men.[47] Such large armies did not only demand elaborate logistics and appropriate forage, but also tactical designs for the ordering of the warriors and the conduct of battles. It was in this context that Vegetius's manual provided valuable advice.

In England, longbowmen were employed in the Scottish and Welsh wars under Edward I around AD 1300, and they formed a regular set of contingents in the English armies up to the sixteenth century. In France, regular contingents of longbowmen were formed in response to the English victories during the early phase of the Hundred Years War. English longbowmen were also employed as mercenaries in the Italian wars of the fourteenth and fifteenth centuries, and at the end of the fifteenth century Charles the Bold, the Duke of Burgundy, relied heavily upon the use of longbowmen. However, the French longbowmen failed to compete successfully with their English model, the English mercenaries in Italy remained an alien fighting force, and Charles the Bold's campaigns ended in a catastrophic failure. The conclusion is that the application of longbowmen outside the British Isles was hardly successful.

Crossbows were a different matter. Technologically more sophisticated than the longbows, crossbows had been in use since Antiquity. During the Middle Ages, their tactical disadvantage was that they were too expensive to allow their deployment in numbers tantamount to those of the longbows. They were usually handled by specialists, some of whom were mounted. Nevertheless, by the fifteenth century, preparations were made for combat units of more than 1000 crossbowmen, as we can judge from the storage figures recorded for crossbow stocks in the armouries of continental armies[48] and from flourishing specialised crossbow-manufacturing centres such as Genoa with their large outputs.

Because both the longbow and the crossbow were targeted at cavalry, their use sparked a hasty process of the improvement of knightly armours. While, during the twelfth century, attempts had been made to prohibit the legal use specifically of the crossbow as an excessively lethal weapon,[49] the aristocracy

---

[47] Walter of Hemingburh, *Chronicon*, ed. Reinhold Pauli, Wilhelm Levison, *MGH SS* 28, p. 641.

[48] *Das Grosse Ämterbuch des Deutschen Ordens*, ed. Walther Ziesemer (Danzig, 1921), s. v.: Elbing 1384, 1396, 1402, 1404, 1412, 1416, 1428, 1432, 1440, 1446, 1451; Königsberg 1414, 1415, 1422, 1424, 1431, 1436, 1437, 1438, 1440; Osterode 1397, 1407, 1410, 1411, 1413, 1437, 1438, 1446, 1449, 1477; Ragnit, 1396, 1400, 1407, 1412, 1414, 1416, 1418, 1425.

[49] In 1139, at the Second Ecumenical Lateran Council, the use of the crossbow was anathematised: *Conciliorum oecumenicorum decreta* (Basle, 1962), p. 179.

began to demand more sophisticated mail shirts and armours which could accomplish the twofold task of protecting the horsemen and their horses against the deadly arrows and, at the same time, allow both warrior and horse the necessary degree of mobility. The resulting brasses became the standard equipment for mounted aristocrats well into the sixteenth century. Because their manufacturing process was lengthy and complicated, the costs for these defensive arms were high and could be provided for only by the upper stratum of wealthy aristocrats, mainly the rulers of larger territories. In consequence, the size of the cavalry forces declined in favour of increasing numbers of infantrymen, each of them specialising in the use of only one weapon.

A third type of new weapon was the pike. An infantry weapon, the pike grew out of the horsemen's lance. Like bows, pikes were targeted against cavalry, but they could also be, and frequently were, used in infantry battles during and after the fifteenth century. Their spread, however, was gradual, if not slow, in comparison with the inflationary increase of the bows. During the second half of the fifteenth century, Charles the Bold, a major military innovator, used little more than 1000 pikemen, compared with the more than 3000 longbowmen serving in his army. However, at the same time, the Confederate Swiss, Charles's main enemy, had at their disposal armies of more than 3000 pikemen, who were then regarded as élite forces. The Swiss pikes were more than five metres long and were used in tactical formations for primal shocks against approaching cavalry. Since the Swiss held sway over Charles the Bold's forces in 1476 and 1477, the superiority of pikes over longbows was recognised as an established fact in continental warfare from the end of the fifteenth century. This led to the expansion of forces of infantry pikemen forces throughout the sixteenth century, by the end of which single-battle units of 70,000 infantrymen could be contemplated.[50] Numbers of infantrymen approaching that size could be provided for only by protesting neighbourhood groups, such as the revolutionary Hussites and Confederate Swiss of the fifteenth century, the revolting peasants of the early sixteenth century, or otherwise only by the rulers of large territories who were in a position to draft substantial numbers from the peasant farming population into military service.

A fourth type of new weapon was the firearm, of which the earliest Occidental versions became known around the middle of the fourteenth century. Again, as in the case of the pikes, the evolution of the firearm was slow, and only gradually did iron-forged and iron-cast firearms become typologically isolated from other uses of fire as a weapon, such as burning arrows. The spread of firearms was retarded by several factors. In economic respects, they could only be employed under the condition that sufficient capital was available for their manufacture and the peace-time preparations for their deployment and handling. In terms of professional organisation, they required highly qualified manufacturers, and the artillerymen using them had to be

---

50 Zacharias Lochner, *Zwey Büchlein der gerechneten Schlachtordnung*, Ms Munich, Bavarian State Library, cgm 6029. Published Ingolstadt, 1557.

professional specialists. Hence firearms developed into a special category of weapon, which were not integrated into the general army organisation during the Middle Ages. Instead, artillerymen were regarded as combatant artisan specialists and not as regular members of the fighting force. In technical respects, firearms needed elaborate logistics, particularly of stones and bullets of a suitable calibre, which had to be prepared well ahead of the combat, stored in arsenals and transported to the battle field. Their use thus demanded an organisational infrastructure which extended far beyond the actual conduct of battles. Likewise, firearms were difficult to reload, because, prior to each shot, the ammunition had to be fitted neatly into the guns, which was time consuming and often not successful. Finally, early firearms could not target precisely, so they were of little tactical effect in the battlefields, although, in siege warfare, they could help destroy the walls of besieged towns and cities. Consequently, there was a remarkable development, during the fifteenth century, of large and heavy cannon, whereas portable firearms were not widely used before the very end of the century. Because it was capital intensive and required the planning competence of civil institutions, the development of firearms was promoted mainly in the urban communities of towns and cities.

All of these new types of weapon brought about numerous changes in tactics and strategy. First and foremost, the new weapons ushered in a dramatic increase in the funds required for the conduct of war. Already by the fourteenth century, the funds demanded for a year's campaign would be in excess of what an aristocratic castle-owner could afford, specifically regarding the numbers of combatants and the provision of military technology. By the fifteenth century the gap had widened further, for the aristocracy, as a rule, was incapable of acquiring or using firearms. In other words, the major innovations in military technology passed by the aristocracy whose members were then frequently unable to provide the financial means to compete successfully in the arms race and were usually unwilling to integrate themselves into the tactical formations required for the efficient use of bows and pikes, with the notable exception of the English aristocracy during the Hundred Years War. In consequence, the aristocracy-led cavalry gradually declined in number relative to the increasing size of infantry and in its tactical importance as the paramount fighting force which it had enjoyed during the eleventh, twelfth and thirteenth centuries. Hence the new weapons promoted profound tactical changes. By and large, those armies succeeded in battle action which could integrate themselves throughout the battle as lasting tactical formations of specialised contingents.

The major innovators in weapons technology and military tactics were thus dissenting neighbourhood groups and the councils of towns and cities. In the long run, the aristocracy had little to offer against the capital with which the councils of towns and cities advanced the development and use of heavy firearms and against the forces of social cohesion which characterised the dissenting neighbourhood groups of the Confederated Swiss and the Hussite revolutionaries. Moreover, since the early Middle Ages, the aristocracy

had preferred dual combat as their specific combat style, because it implied
the necessity of fighting the enemy face to face. But while the development of
the new weapons widened the distance to be kept between the fighters on
either side, aristocrats regarded it as a matter of honour to uphold the tradition of dual combat and rejected the long-distance weapons for their own use.
In their place, they cultivated the dual combat in the form of the knightly
tournament.

However, the emerging territorial rulers benefited from the changes in
tactics and military technology. This was so because some of these rulers were
in charge of territories large enough to draft the necessary number of infantrymen into military service, and because they headed nascent bureaucracies.
These bureaucracies could be entrusted with the tasks of military planning
and the provision of a regular flow of tax revenue and of the logistical and
organisational infrastructure necessary for the deployment and use of the new
weapons. For example, the Teutonic Order, as a ruler over land and people in
Prussia, was a major non-urban protagonist of the new military organisation,
but, also during the fourteenth and fifteenth centuries, the dukes of Burgundy
as well as the kings of England and France acted as military innovators.

In consequence, war could no longer be conceived as the peripheral business of status-loving aristocratic horsemen-warriors. Instead, long wars
became increasingly frequent. What had been a rare occurrence at the time of
Charlemagne became a standard feature of warfare during the fourteenth and
fifteenth centuries, namely campaigns that would last many years. Thus war
began to impress itself upon the lives of everyone, both, in the direct sense
that greater numbers of men were recruited for service, and in the indirect
sense that the non-combatant population was charged with the payment of
additional taxes together with the serious toll of human suffering which was
inflicted upon them in consequence of battle action as well as during sieges.
War also became the topic of an increasing number of scholarly writings
devoted to military affairs, such as artillery manuals,[51] military ethnogra-
phies,[52] treatises on the law of war,[53] and didactic treatises on the 'Art of
War'.[54] Likewise, war began to feature as the subject of legislation at the hands
of rulers. Although already known since the time of Frederick Barbarossa,

---

51 *Das Feuerwercksbuch von 1420.* Reprint of the first edition of 1529, ed. Wilhelm Has-
   senstein (Munich, 1941). Conrad Kyeser, *Bellifortis*, ed. Götz Quarg (Düsseldorf, 1967).
52 Berry Herald, *Le livre de la description des pays*, ed. E.-T. Ham (Paris, 1908).
53 Honoré Bonet [Bouvet], *L'arbre des batailles*, Ms. Paris, Bibliothèque Nationale, Fonds
   franc. 1274. First printed Paris, 1493; new edn (Brussels, London, Leipzig, New York,
   1883). Another edn by George W. Coopland (Liverpool, 1949).
54 Alain Chartier, *Le quadrilogue invectif*, ed. E. Droz (Paris, 1923). Giovanni de Legnano,
   Tractatus de bello, de repressaliis et de duello, ed. Thomas Erskine Holland, The Classics
   of International Law VIII (Oxford, 1917). Jean de Meun, *Li abregemenz noble honme
   Vegesce Flavie Rene des establissemenz apartenenz a chevalerie*, ed. Leena Löfstedt,
   Annales Academiae Scientiarum Fennicae Series B, vol. CC (Helsinki, 1977). Christine
   de Pizan, *The Book of Fayttes of Armes and of Chyvalrye, Translated and Printed by
   William Caxton*, ed. A. T. P. Byles, Early English Text Society, Original Series CLXXXIX
   (London, 1932).

statutes and articles of war became the standard legal instruments to preserve order and discipline among the fighting forces.[55] It was against this background that St Thomas Aquinas could elaborate his theory of the just war and argue that wars could only be just if they were fought under the leadership of a legitimate ruler, for morally defendable goals and after an explicit public declaration of war.[56]

The negative impacts of these changes were manifest and already lamented by contemporaries. Around 1387, Honoré Bouvet (1340/45–1405/10) explained the title of his book on the law of war, *L'Arbre des batailles* [The Tree of Battles], by saying that he meant the 'tree of battles' to signify a growing 'tree of mourning'.[57] Supplementing the high medieval peace legislation, proposals for sustained peace surged from the beginning of the fourteenth century and peaked in 1464 with the grand proposal for perpetual peace by the Hussite King of Bohemia, George of Podiebrad.[58]

In summary, by the fifteenth century, war had become a ubiquitous feature without being yet socialised. For, although war could involve everyone directly or indirectly, it did not militarise everyone's lives. The best evidence for the still-constrained character of warfare is provided in the fifteenth century by the area under control of Duke Charles the Bold of Burgundy. It included the urban landscape of centres of production and distribution in the Low Countries, then one of the most prosperous parts of Europe. The financial capacities of these towns and cities allowed Charles the Bold to establish his formidable fighting force, while the cities themselves were hardly affected by the wars which the Duke fought and lost. Instead, the towns and cities in the Low Countries continued to thrive without interruption after Charles's defeat and violent death in 1477. Notwithstanding the limitations of war at the time, it cannot, however, be denied that the amount of human suffering caused by the wars substantially increased, with its increase being felt and lamented. It was in response to this obvious suffering that, from the fourteenth century, war came to be conceptualised as separate from and as the alternative to peace.

Fighting for Power: the Rise of War-proneness

From the end of the fifteenth century, both the European theatre of war and the intensity of warfare, were continuously expanded. During the sixteenth century, the goal of annihilating the opponent also contributed to genocide conducted together with, and in consequence of, the European conquest of

[55] Charter of Emperor Frederick I, 1158, ed. Heinrich Appelt, *MGH DD F I* 10, 2, No. 222. Wilhelm Beck, ed., *Die aeltesten Artikelsbriefe für das deutsche Fußvolk* (Munich, 1908), pp. 56–8.

[56] Thomas Aquinas (see note 4).

[57] Bouvet (see note 53), frontispiece. Printed in Michael Prestwich, *Armies and Warfare in the Middle Ages* (New Haven, London, 1996), p. 241.

[58] George of Podiebrad, *Tractatus pacis toti Christianitati fiendae*, ed. Jiří Kejř (Prague, 1972).

Fig. 26 Swiss pikemen in battle, c. 1500. The pikemen march into battle in close array with the upper parts of their bodies slightly leaned to the front. In battle, they thrust their pikes in only one direction and try to maintain the array as long as possible after the initial attack. From: Diebold Schilling, the Elder, *Berner Chronik*, Burgerbibliothek Bern, Mss. h.h. I 3, p. 635.

America. The purposeful butchery, at the hands of European conquerors, of native American warriors as well as non-combatants, specifically women and children,[59] falsifies the contention that violence, purposefully inflicted upon civilians, has been a peculiar feature of twentieth-century European-style warfare.

[59] Bartolomé de Las Casas, *Historia de las Indias*, 3 vols, ed. Agustin Millares Carlo, Lewis Hanke (Buenos Aires, Mexico City, 1951). A sixteenth-century English version appeared under the title Las Casas, *The Spanish Colonies, or Briefe Chronicle of the Acts and Gestes of the Spaniards in the West Indies*, The English Experience DCCCLIX (London, 1583; repr. Amsterdam, Norwood, N.J., 1977). Estimates of the demographic change brought about among the native American and Siberian population in consequence of the European conquests suggest that the native American population in Central America and the Caribbean had, by the end of the sixteenth century, declined to about 20 per cent of the size it had been at the time of the arrival of Columbus. A similar, though less drastic decline has been estimated for the Siberian native population during the eighteenth century.

The sixteenth century marked the most dramatic phase of the expansion of military activity. It was enhanced by the promotion of autodynamic modes of behaviour from the turn of the sixteenth century. This meant that every warrior was expected to make self-reliant use of the energies contained in his own body for his own benefit. In consequence, such actions were rewarded, through which a warrior could display his personal willingness and capability to use his own bodily energies for the purpose of overcoming his opponent. Under the ensuing condition that many persons accepted the challenges of the autodynamic mode of behaviour, competition for the successful assertion of personal capabilities increased. It increased the inclination to engage in risky military operations, entailed the spreading of war-prone attitudes and the readiness for violent actions. Not infrequently, such actions had an unconcealed sadistic touch and were pursued for the plain purpose of inflicting pain and deadly wounds upon non-combatants and already defeated opponents.[60] Such readiness was amply confirmed by the fact that, from the time of Columbus, successful military entrepreneurs, such as Cortés, were demonstrably rewarded for their daringness.[61]

The distinctions that have been made can be visualised by comparing the drawings in Figures 26 and 27, one late fifteenth century and one early sixteenth century, which depict a similar theme. The dates of both pictures are only a generation apart. In the late fifteenth-century illumination, the artist displayed warriors in a densely packed array, namely the tactical formation in which Swiss armies were accustomed to march into battle and to fight in its course. By contrast, the artist of the early sixteenth-century drawing showed a series of individual warriors engaged in dual combat with much space around themselves. A comparative view of both drawings confirms that the display of individual bodily strength was the goal of the early sixteenth-century artist. In his drawing, the individual warriors act from a position in which they could autodynamically strike or thrust in many different directions. By contrast, in the fifteenth-century illumination, the fighters are characterised by their mutual dependence on the strength which they accumulate as constitutive parts of their joint tactical formation. Hence, in the fifteenth-century picture, the tactical formation as a whole conveyed the strength, not the individual warrior, whereas, in its sixteenth-century counterpart, the relationship was reversed, with the individual warriors, not the tactical formation, forming the centre-pieces of the battle action.

These examples are not unique. Indeed, a multitude of drawings and paintings on military topics exists from the early sixteenth century; they visualise autodynamic modes of behaviour. Many of these pictures were commis-

---

60 There are many records detailing such excesses. See, as examples, the accounts by Hans Jakob Christoffel von Grimmelshausen, *Der abenteuerliche Simplicissimus* [1668] (Stuttgart, 1985). Hans Wilhelm Kirchhof, *Wendunmuth*, ed. Hermann Österley, 4 vols, Bibliothek des Litterarischen Vereins in Stuttgart XCV–XCIX (Stuttgart, 1869).
61 Instruction by Emperor Charles V to Hernán Cortés, dated 26 June 1523, in Hernán Cortés, *Cartas y documentos*, ed. Mario Hernández Sanchez-Barba, Biblioteca Porrúa II (Mexico City, 1963), pp. 585–92.

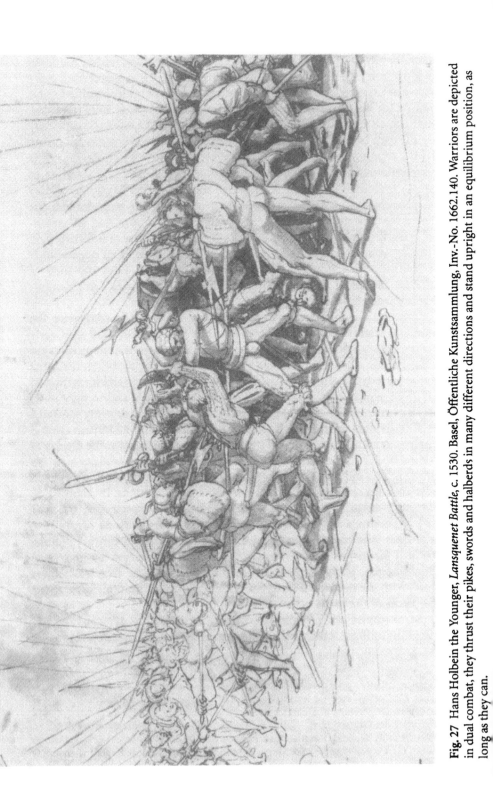

Fig. 27 Hans Holbein the Younger, *Lansquenet Battle*, c. 1530. Basel, Öffentliche Kunstsammlung, Inv.-No. 1662.140. Warriors are depicted in dual combat, they thrust their pikes, swords and halberds in many different directions and stand upright in an equilibrium position, as long as they can.

sioned by Maximilian I as Roman King, Emperor Elect and Roman Emperor, who employed the most well-known German artists of his time for the production of encomiastic pieces of art.[62] In all these pictures, Maximilian's paramount fighting force, the lansquenets, who were otherwise well-known for their war-proneness, were represented.[63] But the expression of war-proneness was not confined to pieces of imperial propaganda. In practice, it led to the popularisation of martial arts, specifically fencing and wrestling, whose practitioners rose in social status and moral appreciation and became a ubiquitous feature in sixteenth-century towns and cities.

Conclusion

Warfare in the Middle Ages demonstrates a fundamental transformation of war aims, an equally fundamental change of arms technology, and the rise of war-proneness. In the early Middle Ages, the fighting forces consisted of unspecialised warriors under the leadership of mainly aristocratic warlords, who fought their wars mainly for the control of various types of groups, and most hostilities ceased when one party regarded this goal as accomplished. At the time, few attempts were made to subject conquered areas to continuous bureaucratic rule, as warlords, unlike Roman emperors, were concerned with maintaining their status or increasing it rather than with converting military successes into bureaucratic control. A phase of transition in the tenth and the eleventh centuries witnessed the rise of specialist warriors who fought on horseback and therefore had to have a social status which allowed them to equip and maintain war horses. It made little sense for these warriors to fight only for control over people, for they could only maintain their status if they could also convert military success into rule over land. Consequently, from the eleventh century, wars were increasingly often fought for control over land and people upon whom a ruler strove to enforce his own legislation. Wars occurred frequently when people called into question a ruler's right to enforce legislation or when rival rulers subjected their conflicting claims to the divine ordeal that wars were taken to be. A stable hierarchy was established which placed rulers over land and people at its top, aristocratic horsemen as seigneurial lords below the rulers and above peasant farmers who were at the bottom of the hierarchy and might serve as subsidiary infantrymen. While the aristocratic right to feud as a means of settling disputes became subject to the tightening control of territorial rulers, the number of wars fought for control over

---

62 Maximilian I, *Weisskunig* (Vienna, 1775; repr. Weinheim, 1985). Maximilian, *Ehrenpforte*, ed. Eduard Chmelarz, *Jahrbuch der Kunsthistorischen Sammlungen des Allerhöchsten Kaiserhauses*, supplement to vol. IV (Vienna, 1885–86; repr. Graz, 1972). Maximilian, *Theuerdank, Jahrbuch* . . . VI (1888; repr. Plochingen, 1968). Maximilian, *Freydal*, ed. Quirin von Leitner, 3 vols (Vienna, 1880–82).

63 A description of the lansquenets' war-prone, though disciplined, fighting style is contained in Willibald Pirckheimer, *Bellum Suitense sive Helveticum*, cap. II/4 (Zurich, 1737), p. 11 (new edn by Fritz Wille [Baden-Baden, 1998]).

land and people increased, and wars became more costly in consequence of
the late medieval technological revolution which brought to the fore more
sophisticated types of weapons. The core aspect of this revolution was the
deployment of projectiles which were released either from longbows and
crossbows or from various kinds of firearm. Only a few territorial rulers could
provide the capital which was required for the acquisition and the deployment of firearms, the logistics and the training of specialists for handling
them. Hence, the technological revolution of late medieval weaponry gave a
tactical advantage to the urban communities of towns and cities which
became the forerunners in the use of firearms during the fourteenth and
fifteenth centuries. The technological changes were amplified by changes of
tactics and strategy in consequence of which, from the fourteenth century,
formations of infantrymen increased in numbers and were given higher significance. More sophisticated weapons, requiring logistics, strategic planning
and tactical preparations for battle, and the use of advanced, specialised
fighting forces which had to be integrated into tactical formations, all
promoted the conceptualisation of war as a choreography of action for the
accomplishment of preconceived goals. Armies could be expected to succeed
in battle under the conditions that the actions of individual warriors were
prepared, coordinated in every formation, and focused on set targets. Hence
warfare was converted into an end-rational action. Towards the end of the
fifteenth century, infantrymen began to develop a new fighting habit which
relied more on autodynamic modes of behaviour. These autodynamic modes
of behaviour in turn gave rise to the war-proneness which became constitutive of sixteenth-century warfare. The fusion of the new military technology
with autodynamic modes of behaviour provided the basis on which, subsequently, warriors could want to enjoy the experience of tensions, and it
provoked the optimism which supported the conceptualisation of war as an
instrument for the promotion of change. Conducting such expensive wars
and taking substantive risks could only appear to make sense under the
premise that the expected rewards were high. In the case of land wars and
even of naval wars, the rewards were ever more often conceived in terms of
the control of the natural and human resources to be found on land in Europe
as well as on islands within and across the oceans. Hence warfare came to be
defined as a struggle *pro aris et focis* where decisions were made about control
over territory.

VIII

Action III: Thinking

Le philosophe est l'amateur de la sagesse et de la verité: être sage,
c'est éviter les fous et les méchants. Le philosophe ne doit donc
vivre qu'avec des philosophes.*

– Voltaire

Introduction: thinking and history

Taking thinking to be a kind of action means to postulate that the activity of
thinking can be interrelated with the previous categories of action. This
postulate entails the further assumption that thinking is neither an art in itself
nor, as it were, autonomous in its patterns and processes, but a social activity
in a given cultural setting. In other words, if thinking is regarded as an action
or a series of acts, the historicity and the cultural specificity of thinking must
be claimed. However, both, the assumption that thinking is an action and the
postulate that there is a history of thinking, have met with serious objections.
With regard to the first postulate, David Hume (1711–76), in his refutation of
arguments by René Descartes (1596–1650), took the view that thinking is
neither an action in itself nor even a condition for action.[1] Instead, Hume
maintained that thinking is merely the configuration of ideas whose transformation into manifest actions requires passion as the stimulus of the individual's will. But Hume's moral philosophy of thinking rests on the partial claim
that only what is empirically recognisable by others can be acknowledged as a
person's action. This claim is tenable only within a concept of action which
manifests itself in recognisable bodily movements and excludes all activities
which do not lead to bodily movements. By that count, dreaming, for
example, cannot be an action, because it does not necessarily translate into

---

* The philosopher is the lover of wisdom and truth: being a sage means avoiding the
  fools and the villains. The philosopher can only live with philosophers.
[1] The position which Hume attacked can be found in René Descartes, *Discours sur la
  méthode*, cap. III/14 (first edn Paris, 1637; new edn Paris, 1973), pp. 249–364. David
  Hume, *A Treatise of Human Nature* (first edn London, 1739–40), ed. Thomas Hill
  Green, Thomas Hodge Grose, vol. 1 (London, 1886; repr. Aalen, 1964), pp. 385–94.
  Hume's position was taken up by Jürgen Habermas, *Theorie des kommunikativen Handelns*, vol. 1, 4th edn (Frankfurt, 1987), pp. 146–7 (first published Frankfurt, 1981).

movements, and, likewise, such forms of believed interaction as magical influence which transgresses space and time, cannot be accepted as action. Hence, while Hume's concept of action is acceptable as a partial concept derived from a specific cultural background, it does not have universal validity. However, the conceptual history of thinking must rest on a concept of action which is flexible enough to allow interconnections and comparisons between various periods, areas and types of groups within which persons can act. Such a concept of action has to include activities which do not translate into bodily movements. Under this condition, thinking can be regarded as action in this wider sense of the term.

An objection against the second assumption was raised by Kant and has, in recent times, been articulated again most vocally by Peter F. Strawson (b. 1919).[2] Strawson maintained that the basic patterns of thinking have no history at all because they are common to all humankind. The argument is sound, and no one nowadays wants to deny the capability of thinking to any human being, no matter whether past or present. However, Strawson's claim that, so to speak, the principal patterns of thinking as action are the property of all humankind and, consequently, are a constant feature, can be subjected to powerful counter-arguments. First, there is no reason to accept Strawson's premise, drawn on the work of previous theorists, that such principal patterns of thinking, if they existed and were indeed shared by all humankind, are specifically human in that they are not shared by other living beings. If thinking is an action that is characteristic of certain species of living beings, it belongs to biological evolution and, for that matter, is in itself a historical phenomenon. Second, Strawson rightly observed that those aspects of thinking, which he believes to be the property of humankind *per se*, cannot be discovered empirically and through inductive approaches, but they must be reconstructed through metaphysical reasoning. However, Strawson fails to draw the appropriate conclusion from this observation. For, if metaphysical reasoning is supposed to conclude in rational statements about what purports to apply to or be valid for humankind as a whole, it excludes history on simple definitional grounds and not because of any reason which is related to thinking itself. But, as metaphysical reasoning is in itself historical, it cannot be used for the purpose of denying the historicity of thinking.

Hence the contention that ahistorical features exist is true insofar as it applies to what has been set by definition as a constant feature of humankind. But this contention does not rule out investigations into principal changes of thinking within the history of humankind or any given part of it. Thus we can easily accept the hermeneutical definition of thinking according to which all human beings practice, among other common features, thinking as a set of soliloquial acts through which perceptions of objects are related to concepts. But this definition is flexible enough to allow the tracing of spatial, temporal

---

2   Immanuel Kant, *Kritik der reinen Vernunft* (first edn Riga, 1781), ed. Wilhelm Weische-
    del, Kant, *Werke in zwölf Bänden*, vol. 3 (Frankfurt, 1968), pp. 100–102. Peter Frederick
    Strawson, *The Bounds of Sense* (London 1966), pp. 33–42.

and social variants in the interconnections between perception and conception. The tracing of such variants even appears to be a necessity, because hermeneutics tells us that objects can hardly be perceived unless already existing concepts of the perceived objects are available in a given culture.[3] Consequently, if objects can only be perceived by means of already existing, culturally specific concepts, it is difficult to disentangle thinking as an action from specific cultural backgrounds. Moreover, under regular conditions, thinking as the action of transforming perceptions into concepts can hardly be dissociated from communication through language, because concepts need to be expressed through words as the properties of specific spaces of communication. Hence, we can specify the definition of thinking as an action by means of which persons successively perceive objects on the basis of already available concepts, relate these perceptions to concepts, and then communicate them through words.[4] And we can simultaneously assume that these particular acts are controlled by the cultural conventions within which persons act and in consequence of which perceptions of objects, relations of these perceptions to concepts, and communication of the concepts through words may differ across the boundaries of spaces of communication.[5]

The Historicity of the semiotic triangle

It is easy to understand that the formation, communication and expected retrieval by others of the semiotic triangle among objects, concepts and words can follow from different procedures, depending on the specific cultural background against which these triangular interrelationships exist. For instance, we can suppose that the Japanese phrase 'Kore wa hon desu' relates a single specified object (in this case a paper codex) to the concept 'book' and expresses this concept with the word 'hon' in such a way that the specified object is subsumed under an undetermined (generic) concept. Then a literal English rendering of the Japanese phrase might be: 'As this specified object is concerned, it belongs to the concept of book.' The phrase implies that the

---

3 Hans-Georg Gadamer, *Wahrheit und Methode* (first edn Tübingen, 1960), new edn in Gadamer, *Gesammelte Werke*, vol. 1. (Tübingen, 1986), pp. 298–300.
4 Charles Kay Ogden, Ivor Armstrong Richards, *The Meaning of Meaning* (London, New York, 1923), pp. 1–23. Of course, *in nuce*, the concept of the semiotic triangle was already expressed by Gottfried Wilhelm Leibniz, *Unvorgreifliche Gedanken betreffend die Ausübung und Verbesserung der deutschen Sprache* (written c. 1697; first printed 1717), ed. Uwe Pörksen (Stuttgart, 1983), p. 6; and John Locke, *An Essay Concerning Human Understanding* (first edn London, 1690), ed. Alexander Campbell Fraser, vol. 2 (New York, 1959), pp. 16–17. However, as a nominalist, Locke treated the formation of concepts as a part of the speculative history of the human mind and sought to establish the conditions under which general concepts had once come into existence.
5 This appears to be one common denominator in the otherwise opposing views by the two leading anthropologists who have studied the history of thinking. See Claude Lévi-Strauss, *La pensée sauvage* (Paris, 1962); Jack Goody, *The Domestication of the Savage Mind* (Cambridge, 1977), pp. 36–51.

specified object is not identified (in Heidegger's sense) with the concept of 'book', but the specified object as a concrete thing becomes associated with the generic concept as an abstract category to which reference is made with the noun 'book'. By contrast, the English phrase 'This is a book' is the result of a different process in the formation of the semiotic triangle. The 'is' in the English phrase identifies the specified object as a concrete single case of the generic concept of 'book' which is made explicit by a noun with an indefinite article. Consequently, the phrase allows the communication of the concept 'book' only under the condition that the word expressing the generic concept is coupled with an article which has the task of restricting, in this particular case, the semantic range of the concept to the one specified object. Other potential ways of expressing the identification of an object are not feasible, for a phrase like 'This is book' is not communicable, and a phrase such as 'This is *the* book' carries a different meaning in that it expresses an extraordinary esteem for or importance of a certain book.

Likewise, the formation, communication and expected retrieval of the semiotic triangle may depend on the speaker's intentions. For example, the phrases 'It is good to observe principles derived from the categorical imperative' and 'It is good to observe the principles derived from the categorical imperative' differ with regard to the determinedness of the number of principles involved. In this case, both phrases are grammatically possible and semantically meaningful, so that the choice of phrases is not restricted by the availability or unavailability of grammatical structures, but depends solely on the relative degree of determinedness that the speaker intends to express.

Moreover, at the level of conceptual analysis, the problem of the formation, communication and retrieval of the semiotic triangle is not only how to cope with series of culturally specific acts of thinking, but also how to describe and explain what happens when, intra-culturally, such series of acts of thinking undergo change. This latter problem cannot be solved at the level of the conventional history of thought, which has long been practised as a field of inquiry, because answers to the question of what has been thought do not provide clues to the further question of how a series of acts of thinking has been practised and how such practice has changed.[6] Thus the history of thinking needs to be concerned with the changing conceptual frameworks within which the formation, communication and retrieval of the semiotic triangle can occur, and the Middle Ages have their own place in the history of thinking.[7]

That such changes occurred can be shown from the conceptual history of the word 'word'. Within medieval theology, the prologue of the Gospel of

---

6   Robin George Collingwood, *The Idea of History* (written in 1936, first published post-humously Oxford, 1946), ed. T. M. Knox (London, Oxford, New York, 1956; repr. 1969), p. 215, coined the phrase '[a]ll history is the history of thought', but ignored the fact that thinking has its own history.

7   This has not always been duly recognised. For example, C. von Bormann, R. Kuhlen, L. Oeing-Hankoff ignore the Middle Ages entirely in their article 'Denken', *Historisches Wörterbuch der Philosophie*, vol. 2, ed. Joachim Ritter (Basle, 1972), cols 60–102.

John provided an important text in connection with which the changing practices of the formation of the semiotic triangle can be studied. The exegetical problems focused on the association in this text of the word 'word' with the divine:

> In the beginning was the word,
> and the word was with God,
> and God was the word.

Throughout the early Middle Ages, the exegesis given to this phrase by St Augustine of Hippo was dominant. In his exegesis, St Augustine followed the teachings of Roman grammarians and distinguished the word 'word' from the concept 'word', assigning to the former the external sound (*sonus*) and to the latter an internal, 'spiritual' character (*verbum quod vere spiritualiter dicitur*).[8] The word, then, has a dual character; in one respect, it serves as the medium of oral communication as used in the real world; and, in the other respect, it is both eternal and divine *per se*. St Augustine made no effort to explain his equation of the conceptual part of the word with the divine; instead, he proceeded with a simile which likened the character of a word to that of a plan for a building (*consilium*): St Augustine argued that, when humans make a plan before constructing a building, the plan remains unaltered with the planners even after the building has been completed. In a like manner, St Augustine observed, the word as a concept remains in its original association with the uncreated and thereby unchangeable divinity even after the word as a sound has been pronounced to the world as the divine message. Then St Augustine used another simile, likening the word to Christ: Like the word, Christ has the dual character of an abstract and a concrete existence; and, like the word, Christ communicates in the world and, at the same time, remains divine as an unchangeable plan.

What becomes clear from this argument is that St Augustine used an all-embracing concept of 'word' which, through a twofold simile, allowed its equation with the divine. He could accomplish this equation with such ease because, to him, the pronunciation of a word meant much more than the utterance of an ordered sequence of sounds in that it was part of an integrated process of communicative action. Thus communicative action was understood as involving communicating persons totally, and this understanding of communicative action helped St Augustine in his direct equation of the concept of 'word' with the most comprehensive of all thinkable concepts, namely the divine itself. Moreover, it is important to note that St Augustine did not associate the concept of 'word' with the divinity in a symbolic way – as if the word was a kind of representative for or abbreviation of the divine or a feature upon which the divinity could confer some of its characteristics. Instead, following the Gospel text closely, St Augustine insisted that the word

---

8 St Augustine, *Tractatus in Joannis Evangelium* (*PL* 35, cols 1379–84). Cf. Heinrich Keil, ed., *Grammatici Latini*, vol. 4 (Leipzig, 1864; repr. Hildesheim, 1961), pp. 47 (Probus), 367 (Donatus).

is not only divine, but it is itself the divinity. Put differently, in St Augustine's use of the semiotic triangle, concept and matter melted into a single entity with regard to the sphere of the divine and were separated only for the limited purpose of communicating the exegesis of the Gospel. Taken comprehensively, the concept of 'word' defied determinedness and, for that matter, stood in itself as a metaphysical totality.

Up to the twelfth century, St Augustine's views continued to be accepted as the standard exegesis of the prologue to the Gospel of John. After the twelfth century, however, a different approach to the formation of the semiotic triangle took precedence. It was most powerfully represented in the work of St Thomas Aquinas. Rejecting as too schematic St Augustine's differentiation of the external word (the sound) and the internal word (the divine plan), St Thomas made a substantive effort towards distinguishing the divine word from the human word. To the divine word, he ascribed the characteristics, first, of being 'semper in actu' (the word always has a real existence), second, of existing 'unicum verbum in actu' (the divinity expresses everything in a single word at the same time), and, third, of being 'eiusdem nature' (the divinity itself is the word). By contrast, St Thomas ascribed the following characteristics to the human word: First, the human word exists 'in potentia et in actu' (humans need to form a concept before they can pronounce a word); second, the word exists 'divisim' (humans require series of words used in succession for the expression of the conceptualised matter); third, the human word does not exist 'eiusdem nature' (humans use the word, but they are not words; instead, the relationship between humans and the word is equivalent to the relationship between communicating persons and the communicated matter).[9]

In ascribing to the divine word characteristics in opposition to those of the human word, St Thomas retained the Augustinian conviction that the comprehensive divine word is a totality and, in this capacity, uniquely divine. But, at the same time, St Thomas denied the validity of this Augustinian conviction for the human word. The consequences for the exegesis of the prologue to the Gospel of John were grave. Because of the elaborateness of the differences between the divine and the human word, the christological exegesis of the prologue became exceedingly difficult. Where St Augustine needed no more than a twofold simile, St Thomas had to delve into logical and philological niceties. Where St Augustine had been able to claim the identity of the word with Christ, St Thomas assumed a parallelism according to which the relationship between God and Christ ought to be seen as equivalent to the relationship between the divine and the word. Where St Augustine could argue that Christ remained divine as the divine plan even after he had begun to communicate in the human world, St Thomas had, on the one hand, to identify Christ as the personified integration of the otherwise separated spheres of the divine and the human word, while, on the other, having to

9   Thomas Aquinas, *Super Evangelium S. Joannis Lectura*, ed. Roberto Busa, *Sancti Thomae Aquinatis Opera omnia*, vol. 6 (Stuttgart, 1980), pp. 229–31.

retain the belief that Christ was coeternal with God. St Thomas was aware of the possibility that his exegesis might trigger debates over the question whether God and Christ were one and the same essence. He was worried about the inherent possibility that – Christ being partly human – the God–Christ relationship could be seen as personified in the form of the material generation of the son through the father. In order to protect himself against such a potentially heretic misunderstanding, he concluded his exegesis with the argument that, in the prologue, Christ had not been named because the evangelist had wished to refer to the God–Christ relationship in the terms of an immaterial 'intelligibilis processus'.

However, even that elaborate and painstakingly symbolic analysis of the God–Christ–human relationship as expressed through the concept 'word' and the word 'word' did not satisfy St Thomas. For he had compared the Greek and the Latin versions of the Gospel and found that, in the Greek version, an article precedes the word, 'ὁ λόγος' (*ho logos*), whereas, in the Latin version, no article appears in connection with 'verbum'. St Thomas concluded that, in the Latin version, the article must have been dropped. Why did that happen? Following the conventions set by ancient Greek and Latin grammarians, he argued that the article would have determined or specified the meaning of the concept so expressed, and concluded that such usage would have restricted the 'supereminentia verbi Dei', the complexity or totality of the divine word. Because this consequence was not desirable, St Thomas declared that the Latin version was preferable over the Greek usage. But that only meant that St Thomas understood that words can represent their concepts more or less adequately and that the concepts can no longer be identical with the matter they denote. In short, to St Thomas the semiotic triangle was composed of the three separate categories – words, concepts and matter – which did not overlap in human language.

To sum up the impact of these matters on the history of thinking, a change occurred, from a preference given to synthetic thinking in categories of comprehensiveness in the early Middle Ages, towards analytical thinking in categories of particularity from the twelfth century onwards. As a consequence of this change, it was perceived as becoming increasingly difficult to embrace totalities conceptually. It will be shown in what follows how this change of thinking affected the formation of concepts and the use of words.

Changes in thinking and their impact on the use of words

One possibility in approaching the effects of changes in thinking on the use of words is to trace changing forms of determinedness in the expression of concepts through words. Determinedness of words is a means of expressing totalities or particularities of conceptualised matter. It can be regarded as a universal element of language[10] and can be expressed through a variety of

10 Jiří Krámský, *The Article and the Concept of Definiteness in Language*, Janua Linguarum, Series Minor CXXV (The Hague, Paris, 1972), pp. 30–44.

different grammatical and morphological structures. Hence, the expression of conceptualised totalities versus particularities of matter can undergo changes which are traceable in given preferences for certain grammatical or morphological structures. Within the corpus of Germanic and Romance languages, historically considered, such changes occurred prior to the twelfth century, and they led to the establishment of the articles as a word category which was then novel to these languages. Two categories of articles have been distinguished: the so-called definite articles, which determine particularities in a finite number; the so-called indefinite articles, which make reference to one single particularity as a part of the same category of matter.

Admittedly, as St Thomas Aquinas had observed, articles were not new *per se*, for they had been in use already in Ancient Greek as an indicator of cases. But articles neither belonged to the stock grammatical features of Latin and its derivative languages nor to the vernacular idioms of the Germanic and the Slavonic languages. Remarkably, articles have never been introduced into Slavonic languages. This observation raises the question: under which conditions were articles formed in some European languages during the Middle Ages? So far the most convincing answer to this question was suggested by the Austrian philologist Adolf Lichtenheld (1843–1915) in 1873. Lichtenheld maintained that 'the definite article is put before a noun to show that the idea expressed by the noun has already been stated, and to refer back to that statement'.[11] With his view Lichtenheld placed the so-called definite article in proximity to the demonstrative pronoun and, indeed, was able to show that, in terms of word history, the article as a word category in the Germanic as well as the Romance languages had its roots in demonstrative pronouns. Lichtenheld's view can easily be confirmed by adducing the derivation of Middle Italian *il* and Middle French *le* from Latin *ille* and of similar derivations in the Germanic languages.[12] By a similar reduction, the so-called indefinite article, such as the English *a*, emerged as the reduced form of the numeral *one*.

Difficulties, however, arose once the question of the date came up at which the demonstrative pronouns became reduced to the so-called definite articles and at which the numeral one was shortened to the so-called indefinite article. On the one hand, as far as the definite article in French is concerned, St Thomas Aquinas testifies that the process had not completely ended by about 1200, because to him, the article *le* was still a novelty which demanded an explanation. On the other hand, the existence already in Ancient Greek of articles and the authority of Greek as a model language in which authoritative texts had been transmitted had stimulated repeated attempts to create articles in other languages as well. For example, as early as the first century BC, the Latin scholar Marcus Terentius Varro (116 BC–27 BC) had postulated the

11 Henry Sweet, *A New English Grammar, Logical and Historical*, vol. 2, *Syntax* (Oxford, 1898), p. 55. Adolf Lichtenheld, 'Das schwache Adjektiv im Altenglischen', *Zeitschrift für deutsches Altertum und deutsche Literatur* XVI (1873), p. 338.
12 Lichtenheld (see note 11), pp. 350–1.

existence of a 'pronomen articulae' as a category into which he subsumed demonstrative pronouns such as *hic, haec, hoc,* if they were directly connected with a noun.[13] Hence, through the influence of the Greek language and Latin grammatical theory, and because early medieval grammarians tended to follow the Roman models, there must have been some pressure on the transformation of the demonstrative pronouns into articles in the vernacular languages. Thus Lichtenheld may well have been justified in his claim that, in certain contexts, the Germanic demonstrative pronouns had already acquired some tasks of the so-called definite article before 1000, while retaining their demonstrative tasks in other contexts. Because there is no unequivocal evidence to suggest that the inception of this new usage began already in the early Middle Ages,[14] we may conclude that, by the eleventh century at the latest, the so-called definite article had come into use, but was still recognisable as a demonstrative pronoun rather than as the case-forming part of a sentence by which the article in Ancient Greek had been defined.[15]

What does this change imply for the expression of concepts through determined or undetermined words? The first point to make here is that neither the Latin translators of the Greek text of the Bible, the early medieval translators of parts of the Bible into vernacular languages, St Augustine, nor his early medieval commentators sensed any necessity to adopt the Greek usage of articles in Latin. Hence the grammar and syntax of Latin was then considered to be sufficient in order to express degrees of determinedness. Thus, whenever, in the early Middle Ages, the necessity arose to give expression to a particular concept, the then existing grammar and syntax of Latin and the vernacular Romance and Germanic languages sufficed. A specific need to express concepts through determined words did not arise. The implication is that, among the users of these languages without demonstrative pronouns as articles, a way of thinking prevailed by which a specified object was related to rather than identified with a generic concept. This was so because demonstrative pronouns were in use in Latin, as well as in the vernacular Romance and Germanic languages during their early periods, for the purpose of specifying an object retrospectively rather than identifying it as a specific case of a generic concept. This can be discerned from the following phrase which is taken from the text of the epic of *Beowulf,* written down at about AD 1000, containing a praise for the deceased King Scyld Scefing, the mythical founder of a purportedly Danish royal kin group. The praise reads: 'þæt wæs god cyning'.[16] By means of a demonstrative pronoun, the phrase specifies the object of the praise, namely the deceased king who had been mentioned in the

13 Marcus Terentius Varro, *De lingua Latina,* cap. VIII/45, VIII/52, VIII/63, X/18–20 (various editions). Isidore of Seville, *Etymologiarum sive originum libri XX,* cap. I/8, ed. W. M. Lindsay (Oxford, 1911), took up Varro's definition of the article.
14 Ashley Crandell Amos, *Linguistic Means of Determining the Dates of Old English Literary Texts,* Mediaeval Academy Books XC (Cambridge, Mass., 1980), pp. 110–24.
15 Dionysius Thrax, *Ars Grammatica,* ed Gustav Uhlig (Leipzig, 1883), pp. 61–2.
16 *Beowulf,* v. 11b, ed. Frederick Klaeber, 3rd edn (Lexington, Mass., 1950), p. 1.

previous lines. The demonstrative pronoun, a neuter, relates the specified object to the generic concept 'king', which is qualified by means of the generic attribute 'good'. Yet the phrase does not identify the dead king as a special case of the generic concept 'good king'.

By contrast, in Geoffrey Chaucer's late fourteenth-century *Canterbury Tales*, there is the following passage in praise of Theseus, the mythical founder of Athens:

> Ther was a duc that highte Theseus;
> Of Atthenes he was lord and governour,
> And in his tyme swich a conquerour,
> That gretter was there noon under the sonne.[17]

The praise is formulated with two so-called indefinite articles in connection with pronouns. In the first occurrence, the article is used, together with a de- monstrative pronoun, in order to identify 'a' ruler of the name Theseus who was in control of Athens. In the second occurrence, the article is used, together with a personal pronoun, in order to identify Theseus as a special case of 'a' conqueror, whereby this generic concept is qualified by the attribu- tive phrase that Theseus was a more successful conqueror than anyone else in the world. The only occurrence in this passage, where no article is used in connection with the naming of Theseus is the phrase where he is specified as the ruler in charge of Athens; but here, Theseus becomes identified, not as a special case of a generic concept, but as the holder of a specific office. This negative instance confirms the usage of articles as reduced demonstrative pronouns, and not, as in Ancient Greek, as case-forming parts of a sentence; it required and promoted a way of thinking by which a specified object was identified as one representative of a generic concept.

Thus it can be argued that a change took place between the eleventh and the thirteenth centuries in the course of which thinking was transformed from sets of relational acts to sets of identity-establishing acts. The first kind of action implied the coordination of a specified object with a generic concept, whereas the second kind of action resulted in the subordination of the former under the latter. Hence relational thinking supported the prefer- ence of words which were grammatically undetermined and whose determin- edness, when required, had to be achieved by syntactical means, for example by demonstrative pronouns or by the frequent use of such attributes as *supra- dictus* or 'aforesaid'. By contrast, identity-establishing thinking supported the preference of words which were grammatically determined through articles. These articles were derived from demonstrative pronouns which were replaced for syntactical means of expressing determinedness.

---

17 Geoffrey Chaucer, *The Canterbury Tales*, The Knight's Tale, vv. 360–3, ed. Fred Norris Robinson, *The Complete Works of Geoffrey Chaucer*, reissue (Oxford, 1985; first pub- lished Boston, 1933), p. 24.

Changes in thinking and their impact on the use of concepts

With regard to concepts, similar changes can be observed, and they become visible, among others, from changes in the concept of person. It has long been recognised that verbal, pictorial and sculptural descriptions of individuals as persons were stereotyped in the early Middle Ages. The early medieval technique of describing persons as bearers of roles rather than as individuals coincided with a concept of the person that differed markedly from later usages. The changes from the early medieval to the high and later medieval concept of the person can easily be gleaned from contemporary exegetical views on the Holy Trinity. Enforced by the fixing of trinitarian theological doctrine through the Nicene Council in 325, that is, since acceptance of the formula 'tres personae – una substantia', the concept of person retained much of the schematicism which had adhered to the Latin word *persona* and its Greek relative πϱόσωπον (*prosopon*), for the original meaning of both words belonged to the world of the stage and denoted theatrical masks as the bearers of the stereotyped schematic totality of a moveable image.

The latter meaning was a requirement for ancient and early medieval Christianity, because, as St Augustine's exegesis of the prologue to the Gospel of John (as well as other writings on trinitarian doctrine) shows, without the schematic totality adhering to the concept of person, it was difficult to reconcile the Nicene creed with the logos christology of the Gospel.[18] For it is only the stereotype schematicism attached to the concept of person that allows the conceptualisation of the inner trinitarian relations in terms of an immaterial relationship and, beyond that, the simultaneous association of Christ with the divine and the human world.

Against St Augustine's doctrine, the temptation to perceive the inner trinitarian relationship between God and Christ in terms of a physical father–son relationship was strong. Gregory of Tours mentioned the case of King Chilperic I of the Franks (reigned 561–84) who apparently wrote a theological tract condemning the application of the word *persona*. According to Gregory, Chilperic argued that *deus* ought to be the appropriate word for the trinity because the word *persona* carried with it the connotation of humanness and that, consequently, it was blasphemous to refer to the divine trinity as 'tres personae'.[19] Chilperic seems to have made efforts to enforce his view in his kingdom by decree, being convinced of its appropriateness. Apparently, the king turned to a usage of the word *persona* which is recorded elsewhere from the fifth and sixth centuries, first and foremost in the work of Boethius who had defined the *persona* as a human being and 'nature's rational individual substance', and, in the second place, in Isidore who had argued that nouns

---

18 Gregory of Nyssa, *Quod non sint tres Dii* (*PG* 45, cols 124, 126). Augustine, *De trinitate libri XV*, cap. VII/6 (*PL* 42, col. 943).

19 Gregory of Tours, *Libri historiarum X*, cap. V/44, ed. Bruno Krusch, Wilhelm Levison, *MGH SS rer. Merov.* 1, pp. 252–4.

Fig. 28 Display of *personae* as theatrical masks used in dramas by Terence, ninth century. Vatican City, Bibliotheca Apostolica Vaticana, Cod. Vat. lat. 3868, fol. 3 recto © Biblioteca Apostolica Vaticana.

denoted the *persona* as a human actor and the verb a person's action.[20] However, Gregory claimed to have convinced the king of his errors so that the king gave up his views.

Despite Boethius's and Isidore's statements and despite the difficulties of communicating St Augustine's trinitarian doctrine to the believers, the concept of 'person' as a schematic totality prevailed throughout the early Middle Ages and was used to encapsulate what is typical of humankind and of the world at large in an individual, both in physical and in spiritual respects. At the end of the eighth century, when Alcuin, abbot of St Martin in Tours (c. 732–804), discussed false testimony, he categorised three *personae* who could be victimised by this vice: the divinity whose omnipresence had been despised, the judges who had been made to believe in a lie, and the innocent suspect who had been hurt. Likewise, in a praise letter written for Charlemagne in June 799, he identified the three highest *personae* of the human world not as individuals but as roles, namely the apostolic highness (*apostolica sublimitas*), the imperial dignity *(imperialis dignitas)* and the royal dignity *(regalis dignitas)*.[21] The concept of 'person' was thus applicable to the divine and the human world alike and could denote offices as well as their holders. Another instance emerges from the early eighth-century *Life of St Wilfrid*, Bishop of Hexham and York, which described the saint in the following way:

> During his boyhood he was obedient to his parents and beloved of all men, fair in appearance, of good parts, gentle, modest and firm, with none of the vain desires that are customary in boyhood; but 'swift to hear, slow to speak', as the Apostle James says: he always ministered skilfully and humbly to all who came to his father's house, whether they were the king's companions or their slaves, even as the prophet says, 'all shall be taught by the Lord'. At last, however, when fourteen years of age, he meditated in his heart leaving his father's fields to seek the Kingdom of Heaven. For his step-mother (his own mother being dead) was harsh and cruel.[22]

Several features in the characterisation of young Wilfrid stand out as remarkable: first, that, in accordance with the usage of the time, standard biblical phrases, such as a reference to quickmindedness, can be used to describe the specific habits of the individual; second, that generalising attributes, such as Latin *pulcher, mitis, modestus, stabilis*, can express the physical and intellectual characteristics of the individual; third, that accounts of common practices, such as treating guests with hospitality can represent special abilities of the

---

20 Anicius Manlius Severinus Boethius, *Liber de persona et duabus naturis*; persona quod sit (*PL* 64, cols 1342–3). See also Isidore (see note 13), cap. I/6.

21 Alcuin, *Liber de virtutibus et vitiis* (*PL* 101, cols 629–30). Alcuin, 'Epistola', Nr. 174, ed. Ernst Dümmler, *MGH Epp.* 4, p. 288.

22 Eddius Stephanus, *The Life of Bishop Wilfrid*, cap. 2, ed. Bertram Colgrave (Cambridge, 1927; repr. Cambridge, 1985), pp. 4–7. I use Colgrave's translation because of its currency although it could be improved. See also 'Old-Irish Table of Communication', No. 1, ed. Ludwig Bieler, Donald A. Binchy, *The Irish Penitentials* (Dublin, 1963), p. 278.

individual; fourth, that stereotypical motivations, such as escaping an allegedly cruel stepmother, can account for the personal motives for concrete action by the individual; fifth, that topical patterns of events, characteristic of early medieval hagiography as a literary genre, such as abruptly leaving the parents' home, can be adduced as the formative events in the individual's own life; sixth, and finally, that a saint is conceived and born as a saint, the sainthood of an individual can be announced miraculously before his birth and becomes recognisable through manifest actions immediately after birth. Thus, during the early Middle Ages, the sainted individual did not convert to a saint, but, as his life advanced, adopted his divinely ordained role as actors in a play adopt their *dramatis personae*. It is difficult to explain these features in the early medieval descriptions of individuals except under the assumption that the underlying concept of 'person', up to and throughout the tenth century, retained core elements of the schematism which had belonged to the concept in Antiquity.

However, during a period between the eleventh and the fourteenth centuries, the concept of 'person' became dissociated from the schematicism of the theatrical mask and coincided with the concept of the individual as the *creatura racionalis*,[23] the natural person as an individual actor. Life-size sculptures, which had appeared during the later tenth century, began in the early thirteenth century to express individual bodily features and specific emotions.

Compare the account of the early life of St Francis of Assisi by his first, thirteenth-century hagiographer, Thomas of Celano (c. 1190–c. 1260). He reports how young Francis, born of a family of the urban patriciate, enjoyed the youthful pleasures of life in the company of his comrades. Then, a divine intervention caused him to change his attitudes and convert to a religious life.[24] Thus, in thirteenth-century and later hagiography, the sainted person became a saint through a conspicuous change which alters the fundamental conditions and patterns of his or her life. The person was no longer superimposed upon the individual as the role it had to play, but the person became synonymous with the individual.

Only in the jargon of jurists was the previous schematism retained and, at the same time, enlarged to express the *persona juridica*, the legal person. This applied to a group of individuals or an institution as the legal equivalent of the individual and as a collective actor. But this jargon could not stem the individualisation of the concept of 'person' and, beyond that, the rising tide of an entire body of political thought which, since the twelfth century,[25] had centred on the perception of political groups as a body politic as a metaphorical representation of the *persona naturalis*. In consequence, St Thomas Aquinas had to employ an elaborate apparatus of logical, philological and

23 Conrad of Megenberg, *Yconomica*, cap. I/2, ed. Sabine Krüger, MGH Staatsschriften des
    späten Mittelalters III, 5 (Stuttgart, 1973), p. 25.

24 Thomas of Celano, 'Traité des miracles de S. François d'Assise', ed. A. van Ortois,
    Analecta Bollandiana XVIII (1899), pp. 81–176.

25 John of Salisbury, *Policraticus*, cap. V/6, VI/1–21, ed. Clement C. I. Webb (Oxford, 1909;
    repr. New York, 1979), pp. 548d–54a, 587d–620a.

metaphoric arguments in order to provide an exegesis for the mystical union of persons and substance of Christian trinitarian doctrine.

In conclusion, the history of thinking underwent a process of change between the eleventh and the thirteenth centuries. Thinking as an action involving the interrelation of totalities was replaced by a preference for thinking as an action involving the identification of particularities, and the latter has continued since the thirteenth century. As will be demonstrated in the following chapter, the early medieval concept of thinking was suitable in a culture which was based on oral communication as the norm even if writing was practised by certain groups.

The introduction of autodynamic modes of behaviour into thinking

Nevertheless, there were elements of continuity in the medieval history of thinking, and these elements concerned assumptions about the effects which thinking could have on conceptualised and verbally expressed objects. 'All our knowledge has its beginning in sense,' St Thomas Aquinas wrote[26] when he set out to explain why the Bible makes frequent use of similes of corporeal things for the expression of spiritual matters. Indeed, the polysemic dimension of medieval culture has been emphasised many times. It stimulated multi-tiered interpretations of identical matters, proceeded from the concrete to the abstract and expressed abstract matters through similes of concrete matter. Correspondingly, the medieval art of memory drew on the use of images for the purpose of training the memory and allowing persons to memorise abstract matters. Although St Thomas was well aware of the dangers implied in such mnemonic techniques he recommended their use in the form which had been transmitted from late Antiquity into the Middle Ages.[27] St Thomas did so with the argument that 'man cannot understand without images; the image is a similitude of a corporeal thing, but understanding is of universals which are to be abstracted from particulars'.[28] In other words, thinking uncovered the order of matter, made this order explicit and helped persons to re-create the order in their memories. If the order of things was to be uncovered and recalled through thinking, it had to be considered to be pre-existent as an element of the divine creation. Thus, even up until the sixteenth century, the belief in the divinely ordained order of things prevailed. As late as 1533, a

---

26 Thomas Aquinas, *Summa theologiae*, I, qu. 1, ar. 9, ed. Roberto Busa, *Sancti Thomae Aquinatis Opera omnia*, vol. 2 (Stuttgart, 1980), p. 186.

27 Harry Caplan, ed., *Rhetorica ad Herennium* (Cambridge, Mass., London, 1978), pp. 205–25. Hugh of St Victor, 'De tribus maximis circumstantiis gestorum', ed. William M. Green, *Speculum* XVIII (1943), pp. 484–93. Thomas Bradwardine, 'De memoria artificiale adquirenda', ed. Mary J. Carruthers, *Journal of Medieval Latin* II (1992), pp. 35–41.

28 Thomas Aquinas, *In Aristotelis libros De sensu et sensatu, De memoria et reminiscentia commentarium* , ed. Roberto Busa, *Sancti Thomae Aquinatis Opera omnia*, vol. 4 (Stuttgart, 1980), p. 371.

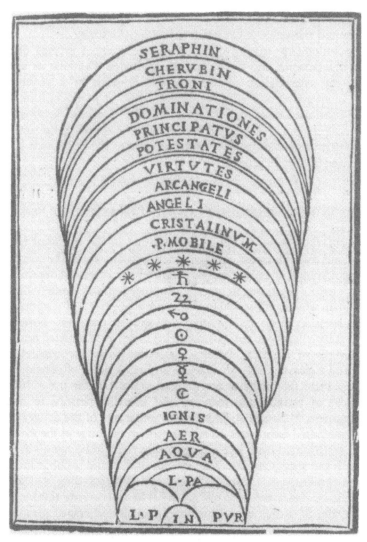

Fig. 29 Scheme of the spheres of the universe as a mnemotechnic device. From Johannes Romberch, *Congestorium artificiose memorie* (Venice, 1533), fol. 32 recto.

printed version of a fifteenth-century theoretical tract on memory appeared which had been written by the Dominican friar Johannes Romberch (c. 1485–1532).

In the tract, a spherical scheme of the universe (see Figure 29) was used as a mnemotechnic device for the recollection of matters related to sacred history and recorded in the Bible. Here we find in an artful array from bottom to top the elements, the planets, the fixed stars, the celestial spheres and the orders of angels. The semicircle forming the bottom is filled with letters standing for heavenly paradise, earthly paradise, purgatory and hell. According to this scheme, Romberch suggested, the names and facts from sacred history could be remembered in accordance with the true order of the world. Concrete images were adduced and were ordered in accordance with the spherical ordering scheme so that the person trying to memorise something could wander through it in his or her mind and connect with the images of abstract Biblical names and facts. Retrieving these names and facts from memory would then be done with the help of these images following the order of the spherical scheme. In summary, processes of the formation, communication and retrieval of semiotic triangles were regarded as possible on the basis of beliefs in the divinely willed order of the world. Because, throughout the Middle Ages, this accomplishment in thinking was an integral part of the belief in the divine creation as recorded in the Bible, the formation, communication and retrieval of semiotic triangles was considered to belong not to logic but to ethics and metaphysics by the majority of thinkers in the tradition represented by St Thomas Aquinas. The subsumption of considerations about thinking into ethics necessarily included the categorisation of thinking as an action in its own right.

However, in the thirteenth century a minority of thinkers began to take a different point of view. Foremost among them was the Franciscan scholar Roger Bacon (c. 1219–92) who insisted that thinking as an action had to take into account empirical observations of the physical and socio-political environments. This empiricism led Bacon to call into question the otherwise accepted theological doctrine that observations of the physical and socio-political environments had the sole task of verifying *a priori* metaphysical statements about the divinely created world.[29] Although Bacon's attack was subsequently taken up by such fourteenth-century encyclopaedic empiricists as Conrad of Megenberg (1309–74),[30] it was refuted at the time on the grounds, first, that it implied the claim that thinking included the action of synthesising an order among disparate matters in the physical and socio-political environments, and, second, that actively synthesising such totalities lay beyond the reach of the human mind. Nevertheless, the late medieval empiricists argued more forcefully than mainstream thinkers that thinking should be regarded as a human action which made it possible to construct totalities on an empirical basis within the confines of what was compatible with the Biblical record. This minority view received some support from moderate fourteenth-century epistemological nominalists, particularly William Ockham. Ockham argued that, although the human mind was incapable of penetrating the mystery of the divine creation, it was capable of conceptualising empirical observations autodynamically. Like the view of the empiricists, the moderate nominalist stand argued in favour of the acceptance of a division between, on the one hand, what was empirically recognisable by

---

[29] Roger Bacon, *Opus maius* (London, 1733), pp. 445–65. Another edn by John Henry Bridges, vol. 2 (Oxford, 1897), pp. 167–222.

[30] Conrad of Megenberg (note 23), cap. I/1, pp. 23–4.

the human mind and, on the other, what had to remain behind the divinely willed veil of ignorance.

Conclusion

In summary, the history of thinking exhibits two fundamental changes. The first, occurring between the eleventh and the thirteenth centuries, materially transformed thinking as a series of acts of relating totalities towards thinking as a series of acts of identifying particularities. The second, beginning in the thirteenth century, was concomitant with the introduction of autodynamic modes of behaviour and led to the conceptualisation of thinking as an action establishing a human-made order of the world.

These changes occurred simultaneously with other changes of action and thereby confirm that thinking is an action and that, in this capacity, its changes have taken place in a wider cultural and social setting.

INTERACTION

General Introduction

In the next three chapters, I shall discuss three major areas in which the concept of interaction changed, first, in communication among persons and groups in a given period, second, in communication across time, and third, in communication across space. First, changes of concepts underlying communication among persons and groups will be described in terms of the means or instruments which dominated the communication process; second, changes of concepts informing communication across time will be described through the example of world historiography; and finally, changes of the concepts shaping communication across space will be described through the movement of persons. In the first chapter, I will analyse the change from the spoken to the written word as the dominant means of communication. In the following chapter, I will trace the transformation from static to dynamic attitudes towards the past. And in the final chapter, I will present a survey of the processes by which concepts of the movement of persons were reoriented from migration in groups into migration into well defined territories. I shall historicise concepts which are usually taken to pertain to linguistics, history and the sociology of migration.

IX

Communication I:
Communication in a Given Present

Veir dites, jol sai bien*
– Chanson de Roland
(Oxford Manuscript)

Introduction

When we communicate with our relatives, friends, neighbours or with guests, strangers and even enemies, we transmit certain types of message through various types of meaningful sign without being free to choose whatever signs we may want to send out. Our limitations are twofold: first, we can communicate only under the condition that we transmit our messages through such types of sign which the imagined or real receivers of our messages can pick up; second, the types of sign which we use for the communication of our messages must abide by rules and norms accepted in a given group and must be suitable to the situational, social and lingual contexts within which the communication takes place. Thus, direct meaningful communication is a complex process of interaction from person to person in which the senders and the receivers of messages interact within certain contexts that are definable in terms of time, space, group and the actual situation. Moreover, communication occurs through various types of sign, namely words and other audible signals we express, gestures, rituals or other visible signals we give out, as well as the bodily bearing and movements we adopt or enact. But communication may also take place through the employment of technical devices. At present, there does not seem to be any state in existence in the world whose inhabitants do not avail themselves of at least three types of means of communication, namely: first, the more or less standardised sequences of sound which flow out of the mouth, that is oral communication; second, the more or less standardised hand-written or mechanically reproduced sequences of graphemes or pictures, that is literal communication; and

---

* Well said, I know it well.

third, electro-technical means by which sounds, graphemes or pictures may be transmitted in various ways, that is telecommunication.

However, whereas the types of meaningful communicative sign mentioned above appear to be constitutive of humankind as a whole, in the sense that all human beings, in various contexts, can use them, not all of humankind has used all the means available for the transmission of meaningful communicative signs at all times. This is self-evident for the electro-technical devices, but it also applies to the various ways of communicating through written texts. This discrepancy between, on the one hand, the ubiquity of types of meaningful communicative signs as the property of humankind and, on the other, the variety of uses of technical devices for the communication of meaningful signs, constitutes the history of communication. From this discrepancy, a number of variations have arisen concerning the interrelationship between, on the one hand, the several types of sign which can be selected for meaningful communication, and, on the other, the means of communication which may or may not be employed for the transmission of these signs.

At present, literacy, as the use of the written word, is more highly valued than orality, as the communication by means of the spoken word. Although, perhaps, no longer advancing, literacy has, since the beginning of the twentieth century, been elevated to the dominant type of communication with the implication that, among others, standards of authenticity in terms of historical criticism and the validity in legal terms of communicated signs have come to depend heavily on their being laid down in writing. Likewise, literacy has become the hallmark of what has been referred to as 'progress' or 'development' in cultural politics. However, from the point of view of the history of communication, the direct and unequivocal association between literacy and 'progress' or 'development' is not self-evident and, therefore, has to be called into question. For it may well have been that orality was recognised by the groups using it as a means of communication equal in effectiveness or even superior to literacy. If such a conviction prevailed the transition from orality to literacy can hardly have been experienced in terms of progress or development.

It is easy to understand why this was so. If the premise is accepted that communication is not random, but has to follow certain standard rules and norms current in and accepted by the group within which the communication takes place, it follows by necessity that communication constitutes a relatively stable, tradition-bound social element which characterises the group within which it occurs. In the case of orality, this means that orality shapes the habits of communication not only among the living members of a given group at a certain point of time, but also implies the communication of oral traditions containing memories of previous generations and recording rules and norms received from previous generations. Therefore, changes of the means of communication may have grave effects on the group structure, and these effects may not be of a kind that is appreciated by those individual group members who are affected by it.

Such effects can be practical in nature. From the point of view of an individual group member, the first and foremost condition under which oral communication can be successful is the physical presence at the same place of both the sender and the receiver of a message. The implication is that the transmission of sounds cannot be separated from the conveyance of other types of sign which living beings exchange while they communicate. Hence, orality tends to evolve into an integrated process of communicative action wherein speaking occurs together with the enactment of gestures and other visible signals as well as with the bodily bearing and movements we adopt and certain rituals we may perform. Under these circumstances, communication is successful if and as along as it transmits a properly understood message as well as if and as long as the integrated process of communicative action remains perfunctory. Thus orality demands an integrated process of communicative action and implies that the recipient of a message can meaningfully interconnect the spoken words, the gestures, the performances of rituals, bodily bearings and movements of the sender. By contrast, if the process of communicative action remains unintegrated, such as, if the spoken words do not correspond with the sender's gestures, bodily bearing and movements, the message may be difficult to receive or it may be rejected by the recipient. Alternatively, under the auspices of orality, if a sender wishes to lie, the sender has to fake the entire integrated process of communicative action and not only the words as one of its constitutive parts. Therefore, orality emerges from and re-enforces a closely knit network of social bonds and ties among the members of the group within which it is practised.[1] Orality is a powerful means of constraining and controlling social action, and mastery in integrated processes of communicative action creates social power. Social power can be converted into political power exercised through specific offices to which the preservation of group-related oral traditions may be assigned as a task.

Integrated processes of communicative action can, and frequently do take place in groups within which literacy is accepted as the standard type of communication. However, the noting down of messages into written texts may interrupt these processes, because the use of writing as a means of communication does not confine interaction to the direct communication between the sender and the recipient of a message, as both do not have to be present at one and the same place. Consequently, literacy can fragment the

---

[1] A good case for the integration of processes of communicative action in the early Middle Ages was recorded by Bede, *Historia ecclesiastica gentis Anglorum*, cap. IV/22, ed. Peter Clemoes, R. A. B. Mynors (Oxford, 1969), pp. 400–4. He tells the story of Imma who was successively kinsman of Queen Aethelthryth, wife of King Ecgfrith of Northumbria, and of Aelfwine, his brother. He was captured after a battle between Ecgfrith and King Aethelred of Mercia. Imma tried to save his own life by pretending to be a peasant farmer, but was recognised as an aristocrat by one of Aethelred's retainers through the combination of his appearance (*uultus*), his bodily bearing (*habitus*) and his speech (*sermones*). Imma was bound and then sold as a slave to a Frisian trader in London. However, his fetters would always break and he was eventually released against the payment of a ransom.

integrated process of communicative action and, further to this, it severs the bonds and ties which interconnect the recipients and senders of messages within a given group. It allows for the ubiquity of written texts as originals and copies, but also increases the potential for falsification. In other words, under certain conditions, a written message may have a higher probability than an orally communicated message of remaining in its original shape, but it has an even higher probability of being faked because it cannot be checked against the context of the other elements constitutive of an integrated process of communicative action. Therefore, historians of communication must take into account the practical experiences and theoretical orientations current in groups among which a transformation from orality to literacy occurred.

Early medieval integrated processes of communicative action

There have been many instances of groups within which orality and literacy have merged. Early medieval groups reflected a type of merger within which elements of literacy were injected into groups which mainly communicated through the spoken word. Nevertheless, contemporary ninth-century written narrative sources record the practice of maintaining an integrated process of communicative action even across distances. This was made possible by means of sending out personal envoys who were entrusted with communicating to the recipient the message which their lord intended to convey. The wording of such sources is interesting. For example, Nithard (dec. c. 845), who was himself an envoy to Charles the Bald (823–77) in 840–1, began his description of a commission by which he was dispatched to Charles's brother Lothair (795–855): 'Nithardum et Adelgarium . . . ad Lotharium direxit mandans ac deprecavit ut. . . .' Charles dispatched Nithard together with a companion to his brother Lothair, requested and demanded that. . . .[2] Charles himself dispatched the envoys, he addressed his brother himself as if he were physically present at the spot where his envoys met Lothair. The envoys were no more than the mouthpieces of their lords. Probably, they carried with them a formal letter of authentication which, however, did not refer to the contents of the message which they had been dispatched to convey. After having been addressed by Charles's envoys, Lothair flatly refused to use them for returning his own message, but dispatched his own envoys instead. Maintaining the integrated process of communicative action even across long distances was thus a goal which ranked higher than speed and efficiency. There seem to have been many such envoys, as monasteries were obliged in the ninth century to host messengers as the 'bringers of words' to rulers in whose territories the monasteries were located.[3]

2   Nithard, *Historiarum libri IIII*, cap. II/2, ed. Ernst Müller, *MGH SS rer. Germ.* (44), p. 14.
3   Charter of King Berhtwulf of Mercia to the monastery of Bredon, Worcestershire (AD 848), in *Cartularium Saxonicum*, ed. Walter de Gray Birch, vol. 2 (London, 1887; repr.

Fig. 30 Dedication picture, ninth century. Vivian Bible, Paris, Bibliothèque nationale de France, Ms. fonds lat. 1, fol. 423 recto. Cliché Bibliothèque nationale de France, Paris.

A further case for the injection of elements of literacy into groups which principally communicated through the spoken word can be seen in the mid-ninth-century book illumination shown in Figure 30. In 845 or 846, Count Vivian, lay abbot of the monastery of St Martin at Tours (in office 844–51), donated a Bible to emperor Charles the Bald. The book opens with a dedicatory frontispiece which shows how the Bible is being given to the emperor. The crowned emperor is seated on a throne and is dressed in a ceremonial tunic. In his left hand, he holds a staff and with the index finger of his right hand he points toward a group of three monks on his lower right. One of these monks holds the book. The three monks are part of a circle of thirteen other persons, eight of whom are also displayed as clergymen whereas five others appear to be warriors or lay courtiers. The circle begins on either side of the imperial throne, moves downwards along the right and left sides of the picture and extends to its lower three-quarters. It is arranged in such a way that the person forming the bottom part of the circle stands directly opposite the emperor. At the same time, this figure occupies a central position in the circle which is expressed through gestures by which the person, like the conductor of an orchestra, points to the right with his raised right hand and to the left with his raised left hand. These gestures are taken up by most of the other persons in the circle, whereby their gestures are pointed at the emperor, at the group of monks around the Bible or at the central person at the bottom of the circle. In most cases, the eyes of the persons forming the circle are shown to follow the directions in which their fingers point. The remaining upper part of the picture shows a curtain-like veil above the imperial throne. Above the veil, the hand of God extends downwards from heaven and beams of light stream from the tips of its fingers onto the emperor's head through the veil. The entire scene is framed with an arcade in two columns which is guarded by wolf-like animals and from out of which two persons, on the upper left and right sides of the picture, are shown to hold scales in the space above the veil.

There are two remarkable features about this dedication picture. First, the scene does not show how the Bible comes into the emperor's hands; instead, it remains unmoved, with the monks holding it. The interconnection between the group around the Bible and the emperor is depicted solely through the deictic gestures which are performed by the persons in the circle and to which the emperor responds. Specifically, the emperor's right hand points towards the group around the Bible and takes up the gestures of the latter. The same kind of gesture is repeated by the courtier standing on the right side of the imperial throne. With his right hand, this person points towards the group around the Bible while, with his left hand, he touches the throne while he looks at the emperor's face. The courtier's gestures thus emphasise the interconnectedness of the emperor with the Bible. Likewise, a group in the lower right side of the circle have their hands pointed at the Bible and, in this case,

New York, 1964), No. 454. The charter contains a wrong date and some spurious formulae. Cf. Peter Hayes Sawyer, *Anglo-Saxon Charters* (London, 1968), No. 197.

their eyes also follow the direction in which the hands point. Hence the donors of the Bible are displayed as part and parcel of the group which joins the emperor as his retainers, and the interconnections between the Bible, the monks around it, the emperor and the other persons forming the circle are established through movements resulting in deictic gestures. The persons in the circle communicate among themselves about the book, but the book is not the medium of the communication. Instead, communication about the book is carried out solely through an integrated process of communication.

Second, because the Bible is kept in the hands of the monks around it, these movements do not usher in interactions through space. Instead, the movements become frozen in the deictic gestures. Through these gestures, the persons forming the circle become intertwined with one another, with the Bible and the emperor. No markers of time allow a prediction for how long the group will stay together in the way in which it has been assembled in the picture. Likewise, no markers of space define the location where the gathering takes place and the precise distances in between the various persons making up the group. Hence, in the picture, the deictic movements lead to the formation of an imperial entourage which is timeless and not limited in its actions by certain spatial boundaries and which is made up of monks and other clergymen as well as warriors and lay courtiers, with the monks dominating numerically.[4] By contrast, the space which is established by the arcade on the two columns neither defines the group nor does it determine its communicative actions. For the space created by the arcade is open in the sense that it remains unspecified whether or not the space within the arcade and the columns is to be viewed as the space inside a building. Hence the arcade and the columns are predominantly decorative and are not correlated in a substantive way with the communicative action that established the group as shown in the picture. In summary, in the picture, the integrated process of communicative action has constituted and maintained this group. Although evidently a written document, the book carried with it in the ninth century basic features of oral communication.

The peculiar features of this ninth-century dedication picture become clear when they are compared with similar pictures of later periods. For example, in the early eleventh-century dedication picture of the book of gospels authorised by St Bernward (c. 960–1022), Bishop of Hildesheim, the saint holds the book of which the picture is a part, and is about to place it on the altar of his church (see Figure 31). The book forms the centre-piece of the picture. There is no group of persons displayed in the picture. Instead the book, as a material object, together with its invisible written record of Biblical traditions, is shown as the transmitter of communicative signals.

Pictures such as those shown in Figures 30 and 31 served as a permanent record of the donations they depicted. In both cases, when opening them

---

4   The Treaty of Coulaines of 843, *MGH Capit.* 2, ed. Alfred Boretius, Viktor Krause, No. 254, pp. 253–5, cast this ideology in legal terms and extended the ruler's entourage to the group of subjects of Charles the Bald.

Fig. 31 Dedication picture, eleventh century. Gospel book of St Bernward of Hildesheim, Hildesheim Cathedral Museum, Ms. 18, fol. 26 verso.

readers of the books were reminded of the history of the book. The Vivian Bible dedication picture established the situational context in which the donation had taken place as an integrated process of communicative action whereas the Bernward Gospels displayed no more than the donor, the donated book and the Church as the receiver. In the first case the group witnessing the donation appears in the permanent record contained in the book; by contrast, in the second case, the communicative process is reduced to the interaction between the saint and the Church. Consequently, while the group had been the focal point of the integrated process of communicative action in the Vivian Bible dedication picture, the Bernward Gospels dedication picture displayed the book itself as the centre-piece of the communicative action. In other words, what mattered for the artist of the Vivian Bible dedication picture was the group and the traditions communicated therein, whereas the artist of the Bernward Gospels dedication picture was solely concerned with the traditions written down in the book and paid no attention to the group concerned with their communication. In either case, the book and the letters it contained[5] were conveyors of an energy in their own right and warranted great care. Such care reflected the belief that manuscripts of the Bible and books written by saints counted as relics and this was ably confirmed by the practice of swearing oaths on manuscripts of the Bible.[6]

Hence these two dedication pictures – like the plethora of other dedicatory frontispieces from the early Middle Ages – displayed the ambivalence of the injection of literacy into mainly orally communicating groups. On the one hand, sacred traditions could be preserved authoritatively in writing, and access was limited to those who could read. On the other hand, entrusting traditions to the memory of written texts deprived the kin groups and other traditional élites of one of their essential tasks, namely that of commemorating traditions and communicating them orally from generation to generation. Moreover, using written texts as justificatory pieces of evidence meant that the standards of legal validity were changing, favouring those who could produce a written text over those who could adduce personal witnesses.

The first consequence can be confirmed from changes in the transmission of early medieval genealogies. Genealogies are lists of names which are arrayed in a meaningful way. The meaning results from the usually implicit claim that the sequence of names listed in a genealogy reproduces parent–child relationships. The names contained in genealogies were meaningful to the groups within which they were transmitted because they carried with them elements of orally preserved tradition. As long as these traditions continued to circulate within groups, the sequences of names continued to be meaningful.[7] Once the traditions were lost, the names ceased to be mean-

---

5 Bede (see note 1), cap. IV/22, p. 402, referred to the belief that letters can have the power of loosening fetters (*litterae solutariae*).

6 For example, Fulda, Hessische Landesbibliothek, Ms. Bonifatius 1, a manuscript believed to have been written by St Boniface. The *Vita antiqua* of Bishop Eusebius of Vercelli (dec. 371) reported that the saint had written a gospel book with his own hand and warned that whoever spoke a false oath on this book would immediately be inflicted with a series disease. See 'Passio vel Vita Sancti Eusebii Vercellensis Episcopi', ed. Ferdinando Ughelli, *Italia sacra sive De episcopis Italiae et insularum adjecentium*, vol. 4 (Venice, 1719; repr. Nendeln, 1970), col. 761. The Vercelli Cathedral Library holds a gospel book which may date from the late fourth century and thus may be the manuscript to which reference was made in the Life of Eusebius.

7 In the Old English poem *Beowulf*, queen Wealhtheow is introduced as a woman with a

ingful, and the genealogies could be rearranged. Hence, it can be assumed that certain traditions were attached to these names and that the members of the group in which the genealogies were communicated knew these traditions even though they were usually not mentioned explicitly in the genealogies. In early medieval manuscripts, a variety of genealogical records have been preserved in which names of rulers are listed as the successors of sons to fathers. They commonly took the shape of the following Kentish name list:

Aethelbriht	Wihtreding
Wihtred	Ecgberhting
Ecgberht	Erconberhting
Erconberht	Eadbalding
Eadbald	Aethelberhting
Aethelberht	Eormenricing
Eormenric	Oesing
Oese	Ocging
Ocga	Hengesting
Hengest	Witting
Witta	Wihtgisling
Wihtgisl	Wægdæging
Wægdæg	Wodning
Woden	Frealafing.[8]

Note: The suffix -*ing* added to the names in
the right column indicates that these persons
were fathers of the persons named on the left.

Because Aethelbriht, the first name in the list, is recorded without a successor, it can be assumed that the genealogy contains material which was compiled during the lifetime of this person. Aethelbriht is well-known from narrative sources as a king of Kent who ruled from 725 to 762. The genealogy thus lists Aethelbriht's ancestry and claims that all of his predecessors were his ancestors. The names display certain regularities, in that most of them alliterate vocalically. Names following this alliterative style are those of Ocga's descendants and Aethelbriht with the exception of Wihtred. That the name-giving practice appears to have changed with Ocga is of significance because, in earlier written records, Hengest, as Ocga's father, was named as the first ancestor of the Kentish royal kin group in Britain and the leader of fifth-century continental immigrants.[9] The genealogy thus claimed the existence of

reputation for being 'cynna gemyndig', that is capable of memorising traditions. Since the poet gave ample record of names, but made no effort to provide information about these traditions, it must be been taken for granted that the contemporary audience of *Beowulf* knew them from the names only. *Beowulf*, vv. 612–18, ed. Frederick Klaeber, 3rd edn (Lexington, Mass., 1950), pp. 21–2.

8 Printed by: David Dumville, *Histories and Pseudohistories of the Insular Middle Ages* (Aldershot, 1990), No. V, p. 34.

9 Bede (see note 1), cap. I/15, p. 50.

Aethelbriht's ancestry beyond Hengest and, instead, named Woden, son of Frealaf, as his first ancestor. Woden is known to have been an ancient Germanic war god. Thus the genealogy can be understood as claiming divine origin for that part of the Kentish royal kin group to which Aethelbriht belonged.

It is difficult to surmise that this genealogy could have been composed without Aethelbriht's knowledge and approval; it is more probable that Aethelbriht himself either authored the genealogy or authorised it. In any case, it is likely that the genealogy was compiled in close connection with parts of the Kentish royal kin group and that it contained intentional data which reflected the partial claims held by at least some members of this kin group at the time when Aethelbriht was king. During the early eighth century, King Aethelbriht and his aristocratic entourage were probably not used to reading and writing, but communicated in accordance with the integrated process of communicative action. Therefore, the original genealogy must have been made up of oral traditions under the control of and possibly by the Kentish royal kin group itself.

Perhaps at the end of the eighth century, Aethelbriht's genealogy changed its means of transmission, for it was written down at about this time, presumably for the first time. Through this change of recording, the genealogy passed out of the control of the Kentish royal kin group into that of a learned, probably Anglian monastic scribe who added a brief statement to the genealogy. In this statement, the learned genealogist recorded that Saxons had been accepted in Britain by some 'Wyrtgeornus' [Vortigern] in the year 349. The date was imperfectly derived from Bede's account of the Anglo-Saxon settlement which dated it as AD 449.[10] This means that the learned genealogist felt free to place Aethelbriht's genealogy in a literarily transmitted historiographical context of which it was not originally a part.

The conclusion is that, by around AD 800, the integrated process of communicative action by which the Kentish royal kin group previously abided, had been fragmented, with a literate genealogist taking over the task of writing down former oral traditions. That such traditions were also preserved in writing elsewhere is confirmed by Asser, a Welshman who became Bishop of Sherborne around 892 and wrote a biography of King Alfred of Wessex. Asser reported that Osburh, the King's mother, had a book of traditions in her possession and taught her children to memorise them.[11] These techniques of memorisation seem to have been experienced by contemporaries as specific and deviating from the principles which were contained in the rhetorical *ars memorativa* of Antiquity. Late in the eighth century, Alcuin, head of a monastic school in Tours and adviser to Charlemagne, explicitly

---

10 Dumville (see note 8), p. 34a. Cf. Bede (see note 1), cap. I/15, p. 50.
11 Asser, *Life of King Alfred*, cap. 2, ed. William Henry Stevenson (Oxford, 1904), p. 4 (repr., ed. Dorothy Whitelock [Oxford, 1959]).

rejected as vain and superfluous the *ars memorativa* as it was known to him.[12] Therefore, the literal mnemotechnic tradition of Antiquity was recognised also among the ordained clergy as deviating from the norms of communication which informed the integrated process of communicative action of the time. But still, the Bible remained *vitae fons*, the source of life, for Alcuin.[13]

The second consequence is reflected in an episode recorded in the later sixth century by Gregory, Bishop of Tours, a town under the rule of the Frankish kings. A certain Andarchius was about to marry a woman, but he was accepted as the bridegroom only by the woman's mother, whereas her father Ursus hesitated to agree. Andarchius did not want to give up marrying the woman and, in order to succeed, he conceived the following strategy. He deposited armour in a chest and brought it to his fiancée's home. Meeting the mother there, he explained to her that he had put 16,000 gold coins into the chest as his pledge of faithfulness. The mother accepted the chest without opening it. Then Andarchius looked out for someone whose name was also Ursus and, after he had found such a person, bribed him to sign a written document. In this document, the second Ursus swore that he would return 16,000 gold coins to Andarchius in the case that Ursus should refuse to agree to the marriage of his daughter to Andarchius. The second Ursus found no problem with signing this document, for he had neither refused to marry his daughter to Andarchius nor had he ever received 16,000 gold coins from Andarchius. Andarchius then took the document to court and began to sue the first Ursus on either agreeing to the marriage between his daughter and Andarchius or returning the 16,000 gold coins. But the first Ursus did neither. The court ruled that, because the first Ursus was unwilling to repay the 16,000 gold coins, he had to forfeit his property to Andarchius. Soon after Andarchius had moved into the first Ursus's house, a fire destroyed the building, put Andarchius to death and allowed the first Ursus to return to his property.[14]

As Gregory of Tours tells it, the episode is a story of a crime committed with the employment of a written document with the explicit goal of deception. The written document intercepted the regular integrated process of communicative action to the disadvantage of an honest and faithful person. Thus the story displays several remarkable features about the injection of written texts into a group within which oral communication is the standard practice. The first of these features is that, in the post-Roman, sixth-century city of Tours, the declining population could no longer, as under Roman rule, avail itself of institutions for the purpose of authenticating or testing the authenticity of written documents. Had such institutions been in existence in Gregory's time, the unlucky Ursus would not have been victimised by the

---

[12] See Wilbur S. Howell, ed., *The Rhetoric of Charlemagne and Alcuin* (Princeton, Oxford, 1941), pp. 136–9.

[13] Alcuin, 'In sacrum bibliorum codicem', v. 21, in *MGH Poetae Lat.*, vol. 1, ed. Ernst Dümmler, p. 287.

[14] Gregory of Tours, *Libri historiarum X*, cap. IV/46, ed. Bruno Krusch, Wilhelm Levison, *MGH SS rer. Merov.* 1, pp. 180–3.

fraud, and the tricky Andarchius would have had to conceive a different technique by which to cheat. Moreover, institutional constraints would have been able to prevent the execution of the fraud, for the first Ursus could have been in a position to prove that he had not signed the document. Still, however, written documents carried with them the weight of legal validity, against which oral protestations were evidently worthless.

The second feature is that, within groups in which orality was predominant, it is difficult to punish abuses and frauds where they occur. The first Ursus was saved, not by secular adjudicatory institutions, but by the divine intervention to which Gregory adduced the coming of the fire and the ensuing death of Andarchius. Hence, it was the divinity who ultimately saved and vindicated the first Ursus. Thus, whenever a written document was employed in a group in which oral communication was the rule, the genuine and honourable goals of communication were difficult to accomplish without resorting to religious or metaphysical means. The extant early medieval charters themselves provide ample evidence for the fact that, what Gregory described in the episode, was part of a wider and more irksome problem. For many charters included a specific formulaic element, namely *sanctiones*, through which infringements of the charter could be banned and persons infringing upon charters were threatened with heavy punishments frequently touching upon the life of their souls after death. The *sanctiones* developed from the formulary of the late Roman charters, but underwent significant changes. Whereas, in late Antiquity, the *sanctiones* had contained the threat of punishment for persons infringing upon a charter and stipulated the terms by which government agencies were authorised to punish violations, the early medieval *sanctiones* abound with religious punishments to be inflicted by the divinity against forgers of charters. Hence, in the early Middle Ages, the book charter as a legal document had come to stand by and for itself, not protected in its authenticity and validity by the secular institutions of government, but sanctioned only by the fear of divine intervention.

The third feature in the Andarchius episode illustrates the link between the spread of literacy and the Christian, specifically the Catholic, mission. The actual reason why Gregory told this story was to provide a further example of the salience of confidence in divine protection as mediated by the Catholic Church, then the sole operating translocal agency in the early medieval Occident. The point which Gregory was trying to make was that whoever was in trouble ought to have faith in God whose omniscience and omnipotence would ultimately be victorious over those who committed mischievous actions. But it is extraordinary to have such a message conveyed in the context of a case where a written document was abused for immoral purposes. For the Church was the promoter of the use of written charters and sought to obtain as many as possible of its own legal titles through the writing of such documents. Thus the fact that Gregory recorded the incident against the prevalent attitudes of the literarily communicating clergy displays the strength of oral communication practised elsewhere at the time.

The fourth feature of the episode exhibits the communicative habits dominant in the group of inhabitants of sixth-century Tours. The woman's mother saw no reason to look into the chest in order to make sure that the 16,000 gold coins were actually contained therein. Moreover, Andarchius must have been able to calculate that the woman would not look into the chest, for otherwise, his trick would have been disclosed early on. The implication is that in sixth-century Tours the spoken word carried with it a high degree of acceptance and credibility on which, even if for different purposes, both parties relied. Further to this, Andarchius made an effort to search for a man who also had the name Ursus; this means that, despite his immorality and criminal intelligence, Andarchius must have been convinced that it would have been improper to approach just anyone and use a faked name. Likewise, Andarchius took great pains not to forge the charter himself, but, at his own risk, involved a third party in order to make sure that the charter was formally genuine and that the second Ursus did not have to make out a charter containing something that was manifestly wrong as far as he was concerned. All these are indications that in sixth-century Tours oral communication was accepted as the standard. However, the involvement of a written document rendered vain one core element of oral communication, namely the simultaneous presence of those communicating. Had this been the rule, the first Ursus would have been allowed to swear that he had neither received the gold coins from Andarchius nor ever signed the document in question. Finally, in a place like Tours with a relatively small population, the two men named Ursus would have ultimately been confronted with each other. Again, Andarchius's trick could only have worked because he could have been certain that that would not happen. Thus the episode portrays the difficulties resulting from the use of written legal documents in a group in which orality was the standard.

The names of the two protagonists in the episode are of Romance origin and thus indicate that their bearers were of Roman origin in the town of Tours. As is known from contemporary legal sources, people of Roman origin as inhabitants of the Frankish kingdom lived under a kinship rule according to which the kin group did not exercise any rights or privileges over the members of individual households as the descendants of a married couple or other dependants. This rule implied that, among people of Roman origin, the kin group as such had no principal legal titles in landed property, but that these rights rested with the heads of the households. Hence, the absence of kin-group-based rights in landed property was the final factor which made the Andarchius–Ursus episode possible. For Andarchius's strategy could only have been successful if he could have addressed his faked charges to Ursus alone. Had his kin group had any rights in the real estate, Ursus would not have been forced to forfeit it to Andarchius. Instead, members of Ursus's kin group would have stepped in to protect their rights. Therefore, the Andarchius–Ursus episode was possible only within a population which lived inside the Frankish kingdom according to the conventions of written Roman law while the institutions enforcing the law had vanished or been replaced by other institutions. That this argument is not entirely speculative emerges from a rule preserved in the eighth-century *Lex Alamannorum*, according to which witnesses to a donation of landed property to a church had to testify in the case that the children of the donor should challenge the authenticity of the transaction. The rule makes it clear that, at the time, kin members frequently intervened in transactions of landed property through chartered privileges on the grounds that such transactions alienated kin-group property and involved the consent of the kin group.[15]

Thus the Andarchius–Ursus episode confirms that communication is not primarily a matter of cognition, but essentially a matter of social organisation. The shrewd employment by Andarchius of the advantages inherent in a written document put at a disadvantage those who in sixth-century Tours had to rely on law-enforcing institutions for the preservation of their legal titles. Yet in the Frankish kingdom, the kings themselves had neither the willingness nor the means to act as heads of bureaucracies in the tradition of the Roman Empire of Antiquity.[16] They could take this attitude because, among Franks, kin groups had the power to act as guaranteeing institutions. But among the population of Roman origin living under Frankish rule, kin groups had no such power. Hence for them, Frankish kings also had to act as the donors of solemn charters and, at least on principle, as the ultimate agents for the authentication of such legal instruments, even if this principle was not often translated into practice. Therefore, in the special case of Tours, difficulties of communication arose from, on the one hand, the continued principled reliance on administrative institutions to authenticate statements, and, on the other, the manifest absence of such institutions. Also elsewhere in the non-Roman world, similar conflicts seem to have occurred. For the Ostrogothic kingdom in Italy, Cassiodore (c. 485–c. 580) recorded the legal norm that, in cases of legal strife between a Goth and a person of Roman origin, the court of the Goths would decide the matter after consulting a learned specialist in Roman law.[17] Although it cannot be determined to what extent this rule was actually followed, its very existence points towards the group-specific awareness of legally valid differences in norms informing communicative action. By contrast, in Europe beyond the confines of the Roman Empire of Antiquity, where there was no tradition of written Roman law, kin groups had wide-ranging control over their members and were in themselves the guardians of

15 *Lex Alamannorum*, cap. II/1, ed. Karl August Eckhardt, *MGH LL nat. Germ.* 5, 1, pp. 66–7.
16 Even though solemn charters were made in the names of and with the approval of Merovingian Frankish kings, none of them signed these legal instruments personally. Nevertheless, some of them took a personal interest in writing. Gregory of Tours (see note 14), cap. V/44, p. 254, noted that King Chilperic of the Franks ordered young boys to be taught a new alphabet with four additional letters which the king claimed to have invented on the basis of the Runic alphabet. The passage shows that Chilperic wished to increase the spread of literacy. However, Gregory's own comments declare Chilperic a fool and make it clear that the activities of this king were considered to be eccentric.
17 Cassiodore, *Variarvm libri XII*, cap. III/7, III/43, VII/3–4, IX/14, ed. Åke J. Fridh, CCSL XCVI (Turnhout, 1973), pp. 103, 126, 262–3, 360–2.

the norms and rules underlying communication. Because these rules and norms appear to have been handed down from generation to generation within these groups in association with genealogies or other mnemotechnic devices, the means of transmitting them were oral in kind. Under such conditions, the Andarchius–Ursus episode could hardly have happened as recorded by Gregory of Tours.

If orality was the type of communication dominant among groups within which kin groups were the major tradition-transmitting, norm-preserving and legitimacy-conveying institutions, the injection of literacy could only develop into fully fledged literalisation under the condition that the kinship structures were significantly transformed so that the kin groups could no longer act as guardians of the law. In early medieval Europe, outside the confines of the Roman Empire of Antiquity, the combined processes of literalisation and the transformation of the kin groups took more than four-hundred years, despite continuous efforts by the Church towards enforcing and standardising literacy. During the entire period before the end of the tenth century, the *literatus* was a person knowledgeable in reading and writing Latin, and uses of literacy remained confined mainly to a few regnal chancelleries, monastic scriptoria, as well as episcopal churches, and hardly penetrated into the communicative practices of the rulers, the lay aristocracy and the average farming population, as long as its communicating persons lived outside church murals. Even inside monasteries, the transmission of oral traditions through professional singers was customary up to the ninth century. Aldhelm (c. 640–709), successively Abbot of Malmesbury and Bishop of Sherborne, was well known as a professional singer of Biblical and, perhaps, other tales; and at the end of the eighth century, Alcuin complained bitterly about the singing of non-Christian lay songs in monasteries.[18] In a capitulary, Charlemagne banned the recording of such songs, conspicuously in a passage related to nunneries.[19] Finally, liturgical sources confirm that, among the lay people of Roman origin in Gaul, Spain and Italy, passages from canonical Christian texts were read to the community of believers. This custom seems to suggest the partial reoralisation of these groups and to support the charter evidence from Tours. Instead, the meticulous observation of liturgical rules in the way they were recorded in books was mandatory for the literarily trained clergy.[20] The perseverance of orality throughout much of early medieval Europe and instances of the reoralisation of literarily communicating groups in southern Europe support the claim that orality was not understood as defective literacy, but as a type of communication in its own right, and which its practitioners found difficult and awkward to give up.

---

18 For Aldhelm, see William of Malmesbury, *De gestis pontificum Anglorum*, cap. 190, ed. N. E. S. A. Hamilton, Rerum Britannicarum medii aevi scriptores LII (London, 1870; repr. New York, 1964), p. 336. For Alcuin, see his letter No. 124, in *MGH Epp.* 4, ed. Ernst Dümmler, p. 183.

19 Capitulary of 789, cap. 19, ed. Alfred Boretius, *MGH Capit.* 1, No. 23, p. 63.

20 Alcuin (see note 13), vv. 178–83, p. 292.

Admitting that orality was a type of communication in its own right during the early Middle Ages does not, of course, imply that the production of written texts during the period was neglected or depreciated. On the contrary, a respectable number of solemn charters, mainly books recording transactions of landed property, and privileges along with other contents, are extant from the early Middle Ages in originals and copies and many more are known to have been lost. Likewise, the corpus of original writing on theology, science, history, administrative matters and fictional literature, as well as of texts copied from Antiquity, was substantial, even if the largest European libraries, such as that of the monastery of St Gall, hardly contained more than 2000 volumes. But mere numbers did not matter, for the material value of many of these volumes was to be measured in the quality of the material used for writing and the length of time invested in it. For example, the Codex Amiatinus, a manuscript of the Bible written for St Peter in Rome, was written on vellum, that is precious parchment, for which about 500 calves had to be slaughtered, and the time used for drawing up a solemn charter on a single sheet could well exceed one year's time. These figures give ample evidence of the appreciation of writing in the early Middle Ages, and they confirm the above observation that the book was accepted as a means of communication in its own right.

The fragmentation of the integrated process of communicative action

Given the complexity of the integrated process of communicative action, it is safe to say that the gradual spread of literacy was not primarily due to changes in cognition, but to the waning impact of the law-enforcing, norm-preserving and legitimacy-conveying capabilities of the kin groups. Moreover, the truly consequential push towards the literalisation of Europe did not derive from the legacy of Antiquity as inherited by the Christian Churches, but it came from a novel factor, namely the new social groups emerging from the decline of the kin groups in the urban communities of towns and cities during and after the eleventh century. The use of literacy by these groups was originally innately pragmatic, as the bulk of existing records show, namely invoices, records of business transactions, private contracts, commercial and other notebooks as well as statistics, although at least during the formative phase of these communities the transmission of technical knowledge, such as techniques of production, was oral in kind. One common characteristic which was shared by almost all members of the urban social groups was their separation from the bonds of kin-group tradition and the legal constraints of kin-group-based rule. Instead, the urban communities were places where, within the bounds of chartered privileges, the inhabitants were their own lords, free to enter into contractual agreements among themselves when they wished to establish themselves as merchant companies or artisans' guilds. Because these agreements were no longer fed by the conventions inherited from and enforced by kin-group-based traditions, their existence and their terms were no longer self-evident or supported by customary practice, but had to be formulated in such a way that they could be preserved, checked and counterchecked by all contracting parties without limitations of time. This demand greatly favoured the use of writing and the deposition also of private contracts as regular written documents in such a way that manipulation or mutilation could be prevented. Another factor emerged from the necessity of having knowledge available about business transactions when these transactions, such as trade, covered large spaces, took place over some time and involved a variety of different interacting parties. Under these conditions, it was necessary to know the numbers and the kinds of trading goods as well as the terms of trade under which the goods were to be exchanged on the market, and the practice of bookkeeping was the result. In summary, the freedom of engaging in contracts, together with the professionalisation of production and distribution, as the hallmarks of the population in the urban communities of towns and cities, brought about the acceptance of literacy and promoted its use as the dominant means of legally binding communication.

The pragmatic process by which literacy expanded began in the mainly autonomous urban communities of northern Italy, where extant written records have been preserved since the eleventh century in places such as Lucca, Prato and Venice. Already by the twelfth century, the practice of establishing local communities wherein persons could autonomously enter into contracts had gained currency all over Europe. Not only business records were laid down in writing, but also legal matters came to be recorded in formal ways. A formulary began to replace the solemn charter for which the scribes drew on models of late Roman Antiquity. These were the private letters. The advance of the *litterae* superseding the solemn charter as the standard form of legal instrument began in England late in the tenth century and spread in the urban communities of towns and cities. In these communities, the new formulary was used because it allowed the swift recording of the multifarious business and legal activities and also the private matters of the non-traditional and non-kin-group affiliated trades people and artisans living there.

This meant, first and foremost, a spectacular increase in the use of writing. In the towns and cities, writing became everyone's art and practice and, thus, writing could be used as a means of communicating a wide range of subject matters which included the transmission of knowledge, legal matters as well as private affairs. The increased frequency of the use of reading and writing can be inferred from the ubiquity, since the fourteenth century, of private letters in which matters of everyday life were communicated. The Latin word *littera* has been retained for this specific type of writing until today in many European languages.[21] Likewise, the personal signature was added to the

---

21 English *letter*, French *lettre*, German *Brief* which is derived from Latin *breve* as another word for *littera*.

means of authentication of legal documents. The preference given to literal communication can also be detected in the invention and increasing use of spectacles in the thirteenth century as a means to remedy defective eyesight.[22]

The shrinking size and loss of legitimacy-conveying, norm-preserving and law-enforcing competence of the aristocratic kin groups and their transformation into residential three-generation households also eased the spread of literacy in the aristocracy after the eleventh century. Some aristocratic hilltop castles emerged as 'courts' in which a specific lifestyle was practised which differed fundamentally from those preserved in the countryside and those newly developed ways of production and trade in the urban communities of towns and cities. One aspect of the new aristocratic lifestyle was represented by the appearance in these 'courts' of specialist lay poets who communicated a new kind of poetic story to their audience. These stories were no longer drawn on Biblical or particularist kin-group-bound traditions. Instead, poets recited stories which could stem from pools of traditions that, like tales about King Arthur, were filled up with knowledge from written sources, or, like traditions about the Nibelungs, had been dissociated from specific kin groups and could thus travel freely across Europe. Alternatively, gifted poets could take pride in modifying or even inventing such stories by themselves. The universalisation of oral traditions as such was not confined to the aristocracy, for eleventh-century annals record the recital among peasant farmers of oral traditions which were not confined to specific settlements or kin groups.[23] Eventually, during the twelfth century, poets who served the aristocracy began to lay down their fiction in writing, and a 'literature' in the proper sense of the term emerged. This 'literature' began to be recorded in written collections and specific lay codices in the twelfth century. This practice implied that, although much of this 'literature' might be produced for initial oral transmission, the form in which it was communicated from one generation to the next changed to writing, and by the thirteenth century there were lay poets who wrote their works solely for literal communication and not for any kind of oral performance.

Finally, the Church began to spread its writing activities beyond the murals of monasteries and episcopal churches. Whereas many cities with a foundation in ancient Roman times had housed episcopal churches throughout the early Middle Ages, from the thirteenth century onwards, the newly founded urban communities of towns and cities also attracted scholars. The Church quickly availed itself of this centripetal process which soon developed a

---

22 For early medieval treatments of diseases of the eye without spectacles, see Peter Köpp, ed., *Vademecum eines frühmittelalterlichen Arztes. Die gefaltete lateinische Handschrift medizinischen Inhalts im Codex 217 und der Fragmentensammlung 1396 der Stiftsbibliothek in St. Gallen*, Veröffentlichungen der Schweizerischen Gesellschaft für Geschichte der Medizin und der Naturwissenschaften XXXIV (Aarau, Frankfurt, Salzburg, 1980), p. 33.

23 *Annales Quedlinburgenses*, ed. Georg Heinrich Pertz, *MGH SS* 3, p. 31. According to the report, traditions about Theoderic of Bern were communicated among peasant farmers in central Germany.

dynamic of its own. The Church did so essentially in two ways: first by developing a position from which it could privilege urban centres of learning, and, second, by eliminating oral communication from scholarly discourse.

With regard to the first measure, the task was to keep control over scholarly curiosity and to prevent the rise of independent, secularised and self-contracting academic corporations, equivalent to the merchant companies and artisans' guilds. The danger that such corporations could be established was not purely theoretical. In Toledo, for example, a centre of learning had long existed within the chapters of the archiepiscopal church. During the twelfth century, a school of translators was established there which devoted itself to the transmission of Arab texts into Latin. An important consequence of these translations was that they made available knowledge of ancient Greek philosophy and sciences, especially Aristotle, through the translations of what had been rendered from Greek originals into Arabic in the schools of Baghdad and elsewhere during the ninth and tenth centuries. The dissemination of ancient Greek philosophical classics through the medium of the Arabic language eventually constituted entirely new disciplines of empirical, mainly scientific, academic inquiry which seemed to warrant the formal organisation of secularised teaching and research. In the Toledo case, academic inquiries were conducted under church supervision and, consequently, posed no serious problem there. If, however, the Church was to retain its dominant position over educational matters outside the kin groups and, beyond that, in social relations at large, it was bound to stay in control of the newly developing sciences also outside its own existing institutional framework. The Church accomplished this goal through privileging specific novel institutions of learning and research devoted to general studies and named *universitates magistrorum et scholarum*. They claimed to be in charge of the entirety of knowledge as it was laid down in the ancient Greek classics. Again, the practice of privileging 'universities' began in southern Europe. Institutions of that kind were privileged at Salerno at about 1000, at Parma in 1065, at Bologna in 1119, at Modena in 1175, at Salamanca in 1218, at Padua in 1222 and at Naples in 1224. They rapidly spread to western Europe where a 'university' existed at Paris in the twelfth century and others were privileged at Oxford in 1163 and at Cambridge as well as at Toulouse in 1229. Elsewhere on the Continent, the process of privileging universities was somewhat slower, but, by the thirteenth century, urban centres of learning, though not yet acknowledged as 'universities', had been established under church control at Erfurt and Cologne, and new 'universities' were founded at Prague in 1348, at Vienna in 1365, at Krakow in 1364 and at Heidelberg in 1368.

The ubiquity of literacy meant that learning took place essentially by means of the book as a container of wisdom laid down in writing. Book production greatly increased during the thirteenth, fourteenth and fifteenth centuries, with professionals for the writing and copying of books, the *stationarii*, establishing themselves in the towns and cities, and with public collections of books becoming accessible to scholars and students there. The book, which had previously had a sacred character and had been an instrument of

Fig. 32 Rogier van der Weyden, Dedication picture. In Jacques de Guise, *Chroniques du Hainault*, c. 1448. Brussels, Bibliothèque Royale de Belgique, Ms. 9242, fol. 1 recto.

communication in its own right, turned into a medium to preserve and communicate knowledge as well as a medium for scholarly controversy. As the book became the standard medium of communication among the learned at all places, a reading public began to demand equal access to identical copies of written texts. Whereas previously, the art of writing a book had been practised by professional scribes whose task it was to provide an individual piece of art, the new type of copies had to be mass produced, and the value of the copy was not to be measured in its artistic quality, but in the degree of reliability with which it faithfully reproduced the original. Thus the fewer features of originality it contained, the higher was the value of a copy.

The mid-fifteenth century book illuminations in Figures 32 and 33 shed light on the change. The first example of a late medieval dedication picture is contained in the frontispiece which Rogier van der Weyden (1399/1400–1464) contributed to the *Chroniques du Hainault* by Jacques de Guise (c. 1334–c. 1399). In the picture, the author of the book is shown as he presents his work to Duke Philip the Good of Burgundy and his son, Charles the Bold. The author kneels before a group of standing persons, the Duke in the centre, Charles the Bold on his left, and an entourage of altogether eleven persons. The scene is set in the audience chamber of the ducal palace which is clearly marked as an interior space and, among others, features the ceremonial ducal chair under a baldachin. The Duke's entourage falls into two groups, a minor group of three persons standing on the Duke's right side and a major group of eight persons assembled, without any clear pattern, behind and at the left side of Charles the Bold. There are no deictic gestures; instead, the scene is frozen like a photograph in which the interacting persons seem to stand still for a moment. The Duke and the author are connected through eye contact, and young Charles is made to look at the author. Some members of the entourage are depicted as casting looks at the author and his work while others direct their eyes on the Duke or elsewhere.

Rogier's work displays some characteristic features which differ from the Vivian Bible dedication picture. First, the groups making up the Duke's entourage stand in no particular order; instead, they appear to be distributed where the space of the audience chamber permits them to stand. In this way, the artist makes the viewers aware of the fact that the dedication scene occurs at a given place which is identifiable through specific architectural features. Hence space, not the group, is the framework within which the depicted communicative action takes place. Second, the only persons connected through pictorial displays of action are the Duke and the author. The bystanding entourage communicate only through their eyes and not with deictic gestures; hence they appear as attending and witnessing observers of the scene in the ducal palace and not as integral parts of a permanent group. Specifically, the author appears alone and in isolation from the group of bystanding witnesses. Hence the book is not dedicated to the Duke by the ducal entourage, but rather by an individual author in the presence of the witnessing group of bystanders. The book is recognisable, not as the embodiment of sacred and age-old tradition, but as the container of this author's original creation, and the author acts as the donator. What unites these three kinds of actors is the space of the ducal palace and the scene taking place within it. Consequently, there are no visualised movements in the picture and no deictic gestures constituting those present as a single coherent group.

This style of depicting a dedication scene has a grave impact on the message contained in the picture, although in one respect Rogier followed the conventional early medieval style of dedication pictures: this is the convention of leaving the dedicated book in the hands of its donor.[24] But Rogier used this convention in a different way. Jacques de Guise is shown as extending his arms toward the Duke for the purpose of handing over the book. But neither the Duke nor any member of the bystanding entourage make any corresponding gesture nor do they commit themselves to any action at the end of which the book might have passed into the Duke's hands or the hands of any member of the entourage. Instead, the photographic freezing of the scene demands that the viewer imagine that, at some time in the near future, one of the persons will receive the book from its author. The viewers are able to imagine such future actions because actions are depicted as being performed

---

[24] Late fifteenth-century dedication pictures departed from this convention in that they placed the dedicated book in the hands of both the author and the recipient. See, for example Honoré Bonet [Bouvet], *L'arbre des batailles* (Paris, 1493), frontispiece.

Fig. 33 Frontispiece to Jean le Tavernier, *Croniques et Conquestes de Charlemaine*, by David Aubert. 1458. Brussels, Bibliothèque Royale de Belgique, Ms. 9066, fol. 11 recto. The text has been edited by Robert Guiette, 3 vols (Brussels, 1940–51).

within the pictorially fixed spatial configurations of an ordered and proportionately designed room. These spatial configurations inform the viewer
about the distances between the various persons and the relative size of the
room. The picture thus sets up an implicit time span and allows the viewer to
assume that the persons united in the room will not stay there indefinitely, but
only for the purpose of attending to or witnessing the dedication of the book.
Thus, in the fifteenth century, communication no longer took place primarily
within groups, but at identifiable places and within estimable time periods.

The second picture (Figure 33) confirms these observations. It displays a
walled city as a market spot, a place of leisure and a centre of administration
and learning. Trade is occurring in the foreground outside the walls, whereas
within the walls the townsfolk are enjoying demonstrations of a falconer's art.
Curiously, the main scene of the illumination, namely the dedication of the
book where it is contained, features only in its upper right-hand corner. None
of the townspeople takes any notice of the dedication. In what may represent
the palace of the dukes of Burgundy, to one of whom, Philip the Good, the
book is dedicated, the mid-fifteenth-century artist, Jean le Tavernier (dec.
after 1477), made the author submit the book to the attention of the duke,
with a number of courtiers standing by. In contrast to the dedication picture
in Bernward's book of Gospels, the book is no longer in the centre of the
picture; instead, the dedication scene is represented as taking place inside a
building located at an identifiable place. Like the *Chroniques du Hainault*, the
book contains a secular text, namely a version of David Aubert's mid-
fifteenth-century *Croniques et Conquestes de Charlemaine*; hence, again, the
book is shown as the transmitter of secular knowledge to be harboured in the
ducal library. The book thus became an instrument of communication
among the literate whose gathering places were the towns and cities. The
communication process was no longer an integrated process of communicative action; instead, it became fragmented, with oral communication, gestures
and bodily bearing being no longer necessarily linked to the transmission of
the material contents of the information noted down in books or other pieces
of writing. In summary, what mattered was the communication of contents at
or from given places, not the establishment or maintenance of groups.

The reverse side of this spread of literacy consisted in the devaluation of
and eventual discrimination against the practices of those who were unwilling
or unable to give up orality. This can be seen from one conspicuous development, which is characteristic of the later Middle Ages, namely the social
degradation of peasant farmers. With regard to this process, the court literature of the later Middle Ages[25] as well as much early-modern administrative
writing[26] contain numerous examples of derogatory descriptions of the

---

25 Neidhart von Reuenthal, *Die Lieder Neidharts*, Winterlieder 3/V, 24/III, 31/VII, ed.
Moriz Haupt, Edmund Wiessner (Leipzig, 1923; repr. Stuttgart, 1986), pp. 39, 74, 90.
26 Johann Khevenhueller-Metsch, *Theater, Feste und Feiern zur Zeit Maria Theresias
1742–1776*, Sitzungsberichte der Österreichischen Akademie der Wissenschaften,
Philos.-Hist. Kl. CDLXXVI (Vienna 1987), pp. 62–3 (20 August 1747), 156–7 (30 July

peasant farming population as dirty, dumb, stupid, uneducated, uncivilised and ignorant, together with further negative attributes. Such labels appeared at the very time when the courtly aristocracy took to book-based learning and literacy, transforming their residential castles into centres of music and poetic art and establishing themselves also as residents in towns and cities. Next to the widening social distinction between the hereditary aristocracy and the peasant farming population, an educational distinction emerged between the literate inhabitants of castles, towns and cities on the one hand and, on the other, the various *illiterati*[27] who were not only ignorant of Latin but who were also regarded as willingly excluding themselves from literacy and book learning, then understood to be learning *in toto*. Lack of willingness and ability to communicate through literacy became a stigma and equated the *illiterati* with uneducated (*indoctus vulgus*) as well as plain folk (*simplices*)[28] and placed them on a par with the poor and criminals. In English, this stigmatisation became explicit in the new connotation which the word *villanus* obtained during the later Middle Ages. Whereas this word had previously been used to signify countrymen in general, its new meaning was restricted to criminals.

Printing

Within this gradual fragmentation of the early medieval integrated process of communicative action, taking place between the eleventh and the fifteenth centuries, the invention of printing by moveable type appears to be much less significant or revolutionary than it has sometimes been assumed. Although it is true that, eventually, printing promoted the dissemination and amplification of literacy, it rather appears as the *end result* of the fragmentation of the integrated process of communicative action than as its *cause*. Hence, with regard to the introduction of printing by moveable type, one must not mistake ultimate results for initial goals. Up till the sixteenth century, rewriting manuscripts as identical copies remained the profession of the *stationarii*, and printing with woodblocks was already not uncommon early in the fifteenth century. Compared with these techniques, the method of

---

1755). Gerhard Ulrich Anton Vieth, *Versuch einer Encyklopädie der Leibesübungen* (Leipzig 1795; repr., Studientexte zur Leibesübung VIII [Frankfurt 1970]), p. 443.

27 On the one hand, Ulrich von Lichtenstein, the mid-thirteenth-century aristocrat who spent his life perfecting knightly virtues, was unable to read a letter which a woman had sent him; see Ulrich von Lichtenstein, *Der vrouwen buoch*, ed. Karl Lachmann (Berlin, 1841), p. 60; on the other hand, Conrad of Würzburg, around 1270, listed reading and writing as the arts which aristocrats ought to excel in; see Conrad of Würzburg, *Engelhard*, vv. 747–57, 2nd edn, ed. Paul Gerecke, Ingo Reiffenstein, Altdeutsche Textbibliothek XVII (Tübingen, 1963), p. 33.

28 Report by an anonymous Eichstätt clergyman on a peasant protest movement in the Franconian village of Niklashausen in 1476, printed in Klaus Arnold, *Niklashausen 1476*, Saecvla Spiritalia III (Baden-Baden, 1980), p. 214.

printing with moveable type which Johannes Gutenberg of Mainz (c. 1400–68) introduced to Europe was initially slower, and more costly at that. Moreover, Gutenberg's technology did not attempt to achieve a new goal. For, like the *stationarii* and the woodblock printers, Gutenberg set out to provide near identical copies of already existing texts. That this was his initial goal can be inferred from the fact that his career as a printer began with work on the Bible. In other words, copying manuscripts by whatever means made sense only under the condition that a market was in existence for large numbers of near identical copies of the same original. This market had gradually evolved from the twelfth century, mainly in the urban centres of literacy and learning. It was these customers whom the *stationarii*, the woodblock printers and eventually Gutenberg, all members of urban guilds, tried to satisfy. Hence, it is correct to say that book production increased during the fifteenth and the sixteenth centuries, but it is erroneous to assume that this process would have taken a different direction without Gutenberg's technology.

Conclusion

There is no *prima facie* reason to regard the fragmentation of the early medieval integrated process of communicative action as an improvement. For the balance sheet of literalisation is negative. It was accompanied by severe changes in the structure of communicating groups, and there are no unequivocal signs that these changes were approved of or promoted by the many whom they affected. Literalisation meant the impoverishment of communication to those who, unlike traders, bureaucrats and intellectuals, did not immediately and directly benefit from them. The push towards literalisation, which was a factor of the fragmentation of the integrated process of communicative action and was promoted by the Church, was long resisted by the peasant farming population and initially also by traditional aristocracy whose members had to rely on oral traditions for the purpose of maintaining their prerogatives. But eventually, after the social coherence of their kin groups had been undermined, they lost out against rival types of group rising in the urban communities of towns and cities. While the aristocracy quickly adapted itself to literacy in the high Middle Ages, the peasant farming population continued to adhere to orality at the price of social degradation and stigmatisation.

X

Communication II:
Commemorating the Past – World Historiography

> Wer Ime in seinem leben kain gedaechtnus macht der hat nach
> seinem todt kain gedaechtnus vnd desselben menschen wirdt mit
> dem glockendon vergessen.*
>
> – Emperor Maximilian I

Introduction

Lévi-Strauss's distinction between 'cold' and 'hot' groups (which he describes as 'societies') focuses on the respective ways in which members of 'societies' commemorate the past. According to Lévi-Strauss, in 'cold societies', little attention is paid to factors of change, whereas, in 'hot societies', perceptions and attitudes are demanded which precipitate and help to adjust persons to change. Thus, according to Lévi-Strauss, 'societies' can either be hot or cold, but they cannot be both. It follows that Lévi-Strauss takes for granted that 'hot societies' stay 'hot' and 'cold societies' stay 'cold' without changing from 'hot' into 'cold' or vice versa.[1]

Lévi-Strauss's distinction partly overlaps with the late eighteenth-and nineteenth-century dichotomy of tradition versus history. According to this dichotomy, on the one side, history was described as an *epídosis eis háuto*, a constant process of dynamic self-amplification through which retrospective and politically relevant attitudes towards the past remain under continuous modification.[2] On the other side, within this dichotomy, tradition has been

---

* Whoever does not establish himself in collective memory during his own lifetime will not be commemorated after his death and this person will be forgotten at the moment when the bell tolls.

1 Claude Lévi-Strauss, *Structural Anthropology*, vol. 2 (London, 1977), pp. 29–30 (first published Paris, 1958).

2 See, among others, August Ludwig von Schlözer, 'Vorstellung seiner Universalhistorie' [first edn Göttingen, Gotha, 1772], ed. Horst Walter Blanke, Dirk Fleischer, *Theoretiker der deutschen Aufklärungshistorie*, vol. 1, Fundamenta historica I (Stuttgart, 1990), pp. 664–9. Johann Gustav Droysen, *Historik: Rekonstruktion der ersten vollständigen Fassung der Vorlesungen (1857), Grundriss der Historik in der ersten handschriftlichen*

regarded as the assembly of conserved or even fossilised, politically relevant attitudes and perceptions which are characterised not by their change-provoking but by their continuity-enhancing capabilities. Thus the dichotomy of history versus tradition, like the distinction between 'hot' and 'cold' societies, encapsulates the variability of types of commemorating the past that may occur in political groups, corresponding with either static or dynamic attitudes and perceptions among those who commemorate the past. However, both Lévi-Strauss's distinction and the dichotomy of tradition versus history differ in that the latter is held to be subject to change, whereas the former is believed to be stable. In the following chapter, changes in the conceptualisation of the interrelationship between history and tradition will be described as processes through which the 'cold' type of commemorating the past became a 'hot' one in the context of European history.

The present between past and future: group-bound traditions in early medieval Europe

The earliest political groups which we encounter in early medieval Europe emphasised the aspect of tradition in their commemoration of the past. In many of these political groups, rulers were involved in the process of passing on to future generations the inherited traditions which contained norms of behaviour as well as conventional group-related attitudes and perceptions. The task of passing these traditions on was associated with and had to be executed through specific public, transient, and therefore regularly repeated, rituals which facilitated the recognition of the commemoration of the past by group members.[3] One element of these rituals was represented in genealogies and regnal lists, most of which were recorded as peaking in a primary divine ancestor, mainly the ancient Germanic war god Woden.[4] Through these gene-alogies, each ruler became integrated into a continuous line of successors which was believed to be of divine origin and to continue endlessly.[5] The following early eighth century genealogy makes this clear:

Ine	Cenreding
Cenred	Ceolwalding
Ceolwald	Cuþwining
Cuþwine	Celing
Celin	Cynricing

Fassung (1857/1858) und in der letzten gedruckten Fassung (1882), ed. Peter Leyh (Stutt-gart, 1977), p. 421 (after Aristotle, De anima II/5,7).

3　*Origo gentis Langobardorum*, ed. Georg Waitz, *MGH SS rer. Lang.*, pp. 2–3. Fredegar, *Chronicarum libri IV*, cap. III/9, ed. Bruno Krusch, *MGH SS rer. Merov.* 2, pp. 94–5.

4　Aelfric, 'De falsis deis', vv. 139–43, ed. John Collins Pope, *Homilies of Aelfric*, vol. 2, Early English Text Society, Original Series XXLX (London, New York, Toronto, 1968), p. 684.

5　I have borrowed this phrase from the definition of sacral kingship by Horst Nachtigall, *Völkerkunde* (Frankfurt, 1974), p. 129.

Cynric	Creoding
Creoda	Cerdicing
Cerdic	Alucing
Aluca	Giwising
Giwis	Branding
Brand	Bældæging
Bældæg	Wodning
Woden	Frealafing[6]

Note: The suffix *-ing* appended to the names
in the right column identifies these persons
as fathers of the corresponding person in the
left column.

The genealogy portrays the West Saxon King Ine as the reigning monarch whose ancestors are lined up from top to bottom until the line reaches Woden as their divine originator. It contains exclusively names of males who are described as belonging to one and the same kin group descending from each other in a father–son relationship. The connecting element is the patronymic *-ing* added to the names of the fathers. The female side is omitted, but this does not exclude the political significance of matrilinear descent, for some names in the genealogy betray affiliation with a Northumbrian genealogy of about the same age. Because the West Saxon genealogy emphasises the father–son succession, the import of Northumbrian names can only have resulted from marital affiliations between the Northumbrian and the West Saxon royal kin groups. Thus names could have been transmitted through matrilinear descent, despite the emphasis on father–son succession in the genealogical records themselves; the imported names could serve as a permanent record of kinship affiliations as a part of the politically relevant traditions as long as the political group continued, the genealogy was preserved and the group was considered to be of political significance.[7] The political significance of these traditions resulted from the fact that they provided for the legitimacy of the incumbent rulers of the political groups within which they were transmitted.

Evidently, these traditions did not only consist of simple names, but were made up of orally transmitted narratives. Some elements of these narratives have been preserved even in retrospective historiographical writing, namely by Jordanes (dec. c. 552) on the Ostrogoths, Isidore of Seville for the Visigoths, Gregory of Tours, the seventh- and eighth-century chronicles by the

---

6 Printed in David Dumville, 'The Anglian Collection of Royal Genealogies and Regnal Lists', in Dumville, *Histories and Pseudo-Histories of the Insular Middle Ages* (Aldershot, 1990), No. V, p. 34a.

7 See Cassiodore, *Variarvm libri XII*, cap. XI/1, ed. Åke J. Fridh, CCSL XLVI (Turnhout, 1973), p. 424.

so-called 'Fredegarius Scholasticus', and the *Liber Historiae Francorum* on the Franks, Paul the Deacon (720/30–c. 799) on the Lombards, Bede (673/4–735) on the Anglo-Saxons, and Widukind of Corvey (dec. after 973) on the Saxons.[8] In all of these cases, these elements contained traditions of origin and reflected a type of commemorating the past which was seen as peculiar to the groups within which the traditions were transmitted. Thus the traditions were drawn on a particularistic chronology relevant only to the group in which these traditions were transmitted and did not include a reference to universal experiences of time and concepts of space. Hence, the time-reckoning employed in these traditions was based on the sequence of the rulers as recorded in the genealogies, and the concepts of space upon which these traditions were held to focus was limited to the space of regular communication of the group members. Some of these orally transmitted traditions appear to have been rather tenacious. Around AD 900, Asser, the biographer of the West Saxon King Alfred, reported that Alfred's mother Osburh had narrated such traditions to her children and that Alfred had commemorated them eagerly.[9] Although none of Osburh's traditions have been preserved, it is safe to conclude, first, that these oral narratives were similar to the kinds of record preserved by previous historiographers, and second, that women were active and instrumental in this type of commemoration of the past. It is important to note that these oral narratives were believed to contain true records of the past, whose reliability and authenticity was to be confirmed by the social status of the person narrating them. Therefore these traditions could transmit sanctioned rules, norms and values which, in turn, authoritatively shaped the attitudes and perceptions of the group members; the oral traditions were the instruments of the preservation and the legitimation of the unchangeable and, in this capacity, the good old law. The interconnectedness of oral tradition and law became manifest in the early Middle Ages through the fact that many genealogical records were noted down in manuscripts which also contained legal records.[10] This is not to say that changes were not noticed. But it does imply that those commemorating the past made little effort to emphasise factuality and the effects of changes.

8   Jordanes, *Getica*, ed. Theodor Mommsen, *MGH AA* 5,1. Isidore of Seville, *Historia Gothorum, Wandalorum, Sueborum ad a. DCXXIV*, ed. Theodor Mommsen, *MGH AA* 11, pp. 242–303. Gregory of Tours, *Libri historiarum X*, ed. Bruno Krusch, Wilhelm Levison, *MGH SS rer. Merov.* 1. Fredegar (see note 3), pp. 215–328. Bede, *Historia ecclesiastica gentis Anglorum*, ed. Bertram Colgrave, R. A. B. Mynors (Oxford, 1969). Paul the Deacon, *Historia Langobardorum*, ed. Georg Waitz, *MGH SS rer. Lang.*, pp. 12–187 (also ed. separately in *MGH SS rer. Germ.* 48). Widukind of Corvey, *Rerum gestarum Saxonicarum Libri tres*, ed. Paul Hirsch, Hans-Eberhard Lohmann, *MGH SS rer. Germ.* (60).
9   Asser, *Life of King Alfred*, cap. 2, ed. William Henry Stevenson (Oxford, 1904), p. 4 (repr. ed. Dorothy Whitelock [Oxford, 1959]).
10 For example, King Alfred's law book was entered into the same manuscript as one version of the so-called *Anglo-Saxon Chronicle* (Ms CCCC 173). Conversely, Widukind of Corvey (see note 8), cap. I/14, p. 24, presented an account of Saxon traditions and explicitly noted the fact that a law book to which he referred as *Lex Saxonum* had been written down in separation from the accounts of these traditions.

The past as the future: associating group particularisms with universalism

The acceptance of Catholicism entailed a major breach with these particularist law-enforcing and legitimacy-conveying traditions. For one core element of Christianity has been its character of being a universal religion which did little service to the particularist rules, norms and values of specific groups. First and foremost, the belief in the divine origin of the rulers militated against fundamental principles of Christian theological doctrine. Because the Christian divinity was believed to be the sole creator of everything and because the act of creation could not be represented as a material generative act, no human being could claim his or her origin to be in the Christian trinity. Instead, rulers' genealogies as everyone else's recorded ancestry had to be linked to the divinity indirectly through Adam as the first man in accordance with the sacred genealogical traditions recorded in the Bible. Likewise, in Christianity, the past was constituted by the narratives which were written down in the holy scriptures, and assigned no value to the particularist traditions which were transmitted within political groups. Also, the Christian Churches enforced the rule that believers in the Christian faith had to respect the holy scriptures as the ultimate source of both tradition as well as justice. Consequently, the various processes of the Christianisation of early medieval political groups required the weaving of the several particularist, group-bound traditions into the universal tradition laid down in the holy scriptures. Thus, for a while, the particularist traditions coexisted with Church administered means for the legitimation of incumbent rulers, such as installation rites performed in churches and the use of titles which associated the legitimacy of rulers with divine right.

One way of accomplishing this goal of combining particularist and universal traditions was chosen after the middle of the ninth century, when the existing rulers' genealogies were extended backwards beyond the divine ancestor by means of agglutinating Old Testament names and linking them with Adam who was to take the role of the new ultimate ancestor. The following genealogy of the West Saxon King Aethelwulf, father of King Alfred, was recorded late in the ninth or early in the tenth century and can illustrate this procedure:[11]

Ethelwulf	Ecgbrehting
Ecgbryht	Ealhmunding
Ealhmund	Eafing
Eafa	Eopping
Eoppa	Ingilding

---

11 Printed in *The Anglo-Saxon Chronicle: A Collaborative Edition*, vol. 3, *MS A*, s. a. 855, ed. Janet M. Bately (Cambridge, 1986), pp. 45–6.

Ingild wæs Ines broþur Westseaxna cyninges [. . .] *and* hie waeron Cenredes suna[12]

Cenred	Ceolwalding
Ceolwald	Cuþaing
Cuþa	Cuþwining
Cuþwine	Ceaulining
Caewlin	Cynricing
Cynric	Cerdicing
Cerdic	Elesing
Elesa	Esling
Esla	Giwising
Giwis	Wiging
Wig	Freawining
Freawine	Friþogaring
Friþogar	Bronding
Brond	Beldæging
Beldæg	Wodening
Woden	Friþowalding
Friþuwald	Frealafing
Frealaf	Friþuwulfing
Friþuwulf	Finning
Fin	Godwulfing
Godwulf	Geating
Geat	Tetwaing
Tetwa	Beawing
Beaw	Sceldwaing
Sceldwea	Heremoding
Heremod	Itermoning
Itermon	Hraþaing

se wæs geboren in þære earce;[13]

Noe, Lamach, Matusalem, Enoh, Iaered, Maleel, Camon, Enos, Sed, Adam primus homo; et pater noster est Christus, amen.[14]

The genealogy incorporated the previous one with significant changes. It echoed the stability of tradition by preserving the existing ancestry. But, in addition, it contains names of insular Celtic and Germanic, of Scandinavian and of Biblical origin. It thus served various purposes: first, to humanise the previous divine ancestor, namely Woden; second, to display Woden himself as a part of the divine creation; third, to retain the tradition-bound principle of the legitimation of incumbent rulers even within Christianised political groups; fourth, to aggrandise the ruling king's ancestry by amplifying the

---

12 Translation: Ingild was the brother of Ine, King of the West Saxons . . ., and they were sons of Cenred.
13 Translation: he was born in the Ark.
14 Translation of text from the name Adam: Adam [was] the first man; and our father is Christ, Amen. Note that these Latin phrases occur in an otherwise Old English vernacular text.

number of names of his ancestry; and fifth, to furnish the genealogy with variegated traditions of diverse origins, thereby fusing into a single ideological amalgam the previously segregated traditions of various insular, Scandinavian and Biblical origins. In its dual character of employing pre-Christian and Biblical textual forms for the legitimation of incumbent rulers, this type of genealogy stands out as a brave attempt to rescue the conventional particularistic group-bound traditions into a church-controlled, centralised and universal commemoration of the past as the all-embracing sacred history.

However, the chances of long-lasting success for this type of genealogy, as the continuing embodiment of tradition and as the provider of legitimacy for rulers, were minimal. Already by the middle of the tenth century, a church council recommended the use of written genealogies for the purpose of tracing kin relations correctly. This recommendation implied that oral traditions were no longer considered reliable transmitters of legal norms or authoritative conveyors of legitimacy, and thereby reflected the waning faith in orally transmitted genealogical knowledge. While descent continued to be an important factor of the legitimacy of succession to high office and while controversies about descent continued to be at the heart of much political strife and warfare, the appropriateness of claims for the priority drawn on descent rested no longer on orally transmitted kin traditions but on genealogical knowledge which was laid down in writing.[15] Up to the turn of the twelfth century, rulers eventually lost direct control over their genealogies which passed into the custody of learned scholars. In these new contexts, genealogies continued to provide an ordering principle to authors who, like William of Malmesbury (c. 1095–1143) or the authors of the *Grandes Chroniques de France*,[16] wished to display the history of a kingdom as the succession of rulers who were purportedly or actually related by kin. These authors displayed hereditary succession to the royal office not as a privilege which belonged to the heritage of the kin group but as a right which the divinity had conferred upon the first-born son. In this sense, the high and late medieval written genealogies and genealogically arrayed histories were not in themselves legal instruments for the legitimation of royal succession but literary means to support ideologies of rule. The obsolescence of genealogies as a mode of preserving traditions was essentially due to three successive factors: first, the introduction of a novel, non-group-centred way of historical time reckoning from the early eighth century; second, the amplification of the range of the conventional world picture of Antiquity to include the northern seas; third, a new attitude towards the conceptualisation of change which connected with the resurgence to paramountcy, at the time of the Crusades, of ideologies of universal rule.

15 Synod of Ingelheim [7 June 948], cap. XII, ed. Ernst-Dieter Hehl, *MGH Concilia* 6, 1, p. 1662.
16 William of Malmesbury, *De gestis regum Anglorum*, ed. William Stubbs, Rerum Britannicarum medii aevi scriptores XC (London, 1887–89; repr. New York, 1965). *Grandes Chroniques de France*, ed. Jules Marie Edouard Viard, 10 vols (Paris, 1920–53).

Problems with the future: coping with a universal and an eschatological chronology

The novel reckoning of historical time drew on the Bible and was promoted by the scholarly work of the Venerable Bede. The monk of Jarrow had already established himself as an expert in chronology and the universal scriptural traditions when he set out to produce his own synthesis from his computistical works, his chronicles and the insular group-related traditions made known to him from a variety of written and contemporary oral sources. The first synthesis of this kind ever to have been undertaken in Europe was a masterpiece and set the standard for thinking and writing about the past. Remarkably, Bede, who had used the word *chronica* as the title for his previous writings on the Biblical traditions, in 731 chose the conventional word *historia* in order to denote his synthetic way of commemorating the past. By convention, the Latin word *historia*, in sources known to Bede, had meant a secular account of the past compiled from a variety of sources and describing events of the human world set apart from the divine world. However, Bede limited the range of the meaning of *historia* by adding two qualifying attributes.[17] First, his *historia* was to be an 'ecclesiastical' one. This attribute was derived from the precedence of the work of Eusebius of Caesarea (260/64–339/40), who had written an ecclesiastical history, and it gave expression to Bede's insistence that the commemoration of the past was to be placed in the context of the universal advancement of Christianity, as Orosius had already suggested in the fifth century.[18] Bede added the further specification that his *Historia ecclesiastica* was to be partial in dealing only with matters related to the *gens Anglorum*, understood to comprise the group of Germanic settlers in the British Isles as a former part of the Roman Empire. Again, the choice of words reflected a well-considered programmatic intention, namely to display all these immigrant settlers as members of a single overarching political group called 'the English'. Thus, on the one hand Bede integrated his account of the history of the Church into the universalism represented in the Biblical traditions, while on the other he separated his account from the universal background into which this history had been placed by authors such as Eusebius and Orosius.

Bede also departed in methodology from the group-centred oral narratives and their representations in the genealogies, although he used them as sources. Where the latter had been affirmative in authoritatively stating beliefs about the past, Bede's approach was critical in the sense that, with the exception of the holy scriptures, he made conscious efforts to relate the evidence which one source preserved to what could be ascertained from other sources,

---

17 Bede (see note 8), preface, V/24, pp. 3–6, 566. Bede provided a definition which was similar to that given by Isidore, *Etymologiae*, cap. I/41, ed. W. M. Lindsay (Oxford, 1911).

18 Eusebius, *Chronicon* (*PG* 19, col. 383). Orosius, *Historiae adversus paganos*, cap. I/1, ed. Carl Zangemeister, CSEL V (Vienna, 1868; repr. New York, 1966), pp. 3–8.

as he also tried to weigh the relative evidential value of the several sources available to him. Moreover, whereas the orally transmitted traditions had retained their validity and authenticity without fundamental change by virtue of being handed down from generation to generation in particularist groups, Bede, like the historians of late Antiquity, committed himself to the writing and publication of a text which he expected to be communicated through reading and copying and whose reception, by virtue of these communicative techniques, was no longer confined to one particularist group. Likewise, where the oral narratives had been preserved in vernacular languages, Bede used Latin as a *lingua franca* through which matters could be communicated beyond the confines of particularist groups. Thus Bede imagined a learned general reader who could, on principle, live anywhere. Finally, where the group-bound traditions had contained particularist norms and values, Bede's work represented the universal norms and values which were inherent in the doctrines of the Catholic Church and with which the 'English' were shown to have become acquainted through the Roman missionary efforts.

Therefore, Bede's main problem in describing the 'church history of the English' seems to have been one that had been alien to his predecessors during the fourth, fifth and sixth centuries. The problem concerned the Roman Empire as the most important administrative entity to be described in an historiographic context. Eusebius and Orosius had been able to take for granted the existence of institutions making up the Roman Empire and these institutions could then arguably be described as universal. Others, namely, Isidore of Seville, Jordanes, and Gregory of Tours could take the view that the theatre of their histories was the territory of the Roman Empire. But Bede had to cope with the fact that, as far as Britain was concerned, the immigrants, who were to become Bede's 'English' had destroyed these very institutions. Consequently, universalism, at Bede's own time, could no longer be anchored in manifest institutions of secular rule. Hence Bede could have confined his *historia* to the particularism of what happened among the 'English'; but then his *historia* would not have been more than a translation of the particularist oral narratives into the communicative medium of a Latin written text. Moreover, the coming of Catholicism would then have appeared as what the local kin and neighbourhood groups in all probability perceived it to have been, namely the intrusion of an outside and alien framework of norms and values, attitudes and perceptions. Therefore, Bede had to trace the process of the coming to Britain of the Catholic Church as the representative of universalism, outside of, but historically interconnected with the institutions of the Roman Empire. In this way, Bede could describe the Catholic mission as the process of the interaction of the universal Catholic Church with local rulers at a time when institutions of Roman imperial rule were no longer extant in Britain.

But this synthesis had to pay a high price. This was because Bede's *historia* had to include descriptions of institutional changes which annihilated the universal character of the institutions of the Roman Empire. Bede had to cope with the establishment in Britain of local institutions, the representatives of which did not regard themselves as affiliated with or subjected to the Roman Empire. Thus Bede's *historia* came to include accounts of institutional changes which differed fundamentally from the paradigms which were allowed for in the scriptural traditions of the four world empires, of which the Roman Empire was considered to be the last. In accordance with these traditions, one universal institution would give way to a successor of the same kind, and a universal institution would always exist. But Bede's problem, once again, was to describe the transition from a universal institution to the set of local particularist institutions in existence in Britain at his own time. Hence he could neither rely exclusively on the paradigms provided by the Bible and its exegesis nor on the particularist group-related oral traditions. Bede refused to classify this process as the destruction of the Roman Empire; he could not do so because that would have meant to argue against the belief that the Roman Empire was the last world empire before doomsday. Instead, he admitted that institutions of Roman rule had been annihilated in Britain and then insisted that, as far as Britain was concerned, universalism had been vested in the institutions of the Catholic Church. In this way, however, Bede allowed change to intrude in the commemoration of the past.

Because the local rulers in Britain reckoned the historical time of their own group-related traditions in particularist ways which were neither compatible with Roman time-reckoning nor with a Biblical chronology, Bede could only succeed in describing the process of the transfer of power from the institution of the Roman Empire to local institutions in Britain if he applied a chronometric framework which allowed the counting of years without regard to the vicissitudes of the administrative institutions making up the Roman Empire. Such a framework had been developed, among others, by the Roman monk Dionysius Exiguus (on whom see Chapter I), who in the early sixth century had proposed to begin a new era with the birth of Christ as the Annus Domini (AD) and to count the years from then. However, not much had been made of this proposal during the sixth and seventh centuries. For Bede, however, Dionysius's proposal was ideal because it allowed him to date the change from Roman universal rule over Britain to the establishment of local rulers in Britain by means of a chronology that was not tied to the Roman administrative institutions but focused on Christ. Therefore, Bede became the first historian to use the AD chronology consistently, and his doing so has set the standard for historiographic time-reckoning in Europe.[19]

Bede's success in describing the transition from Roman universal rule to local rule in Britain was also due to the continuity into his own time of the Mediterranean world picture which had been associated with Roman imperial rule from its establishment at the time of Augustus and which continued to serve as the vehicle for the expression of the universality of rule. In other

---

[19] In England, the manuscripts of the *Anglo-Saxon Chronicle*, of which the oldest appears to have been written in the early tenth century, employ the AD chronology together with the BC formula ('ÆR Cristes geflaescnesse'), *Anglo-Saxon Chronicle* (see note 11), p. 2.

words, universalism, be it associated with the Roman Empire or with the Christian Churches, was bound to be defined in the terms which were set by the world picture that had been transmitted in the Roman Empire from the establishment of the Principate. In this world picture, the *ecumene* had to be depicted as permeable so as to let Roman universal rule appear as land-borne, and it had to display the Mediterranean Sea as the main trajectory of domestic interactions, not as a boundary.

The consistency of this world picture was first called into question after the Mediterranean Sea had ceased to be the main trajectory for trade and other types of exchange. Already during Bede's lifetime, this change was becoming contagious. For, from the later seventh century, the Mediterranean Sea began to face competition with the other major trade route which used the northern seas and the central Eurasian river systems. Within the confines of the conventional world picture, the routes along the northern seas were represented as a part of the stretch of water which encircled the *ecumene*, was technically known as the ocean, and connected the northern part of the *ecumene* with its centre through various river systems.

The knowledge available to the seafarers about the northern seas confirmed what appeared to be the case in the conventional world map. In the standard medieval world map, the ocean was displayed as circumnavigable from Europe to Asia, and one would locate Scandinavia as an island in the northern part of the ocean. Consequently, in such a world map, the Baltic Sea was not encircled by land, but was part of the ocean strip. Although it is impossible to experience the Baltic Sea as a part of the ocean, because there is no sea connection between the Baltic and the Barents Seas, it was possible to use the connecting northern and central Eurasian river systems for the dual purpose of travelling mainly by ship to western Asia, thereby confirming one essential claim of the conventional world map, namely that the centre of the *ecumene* is accessible through waterways from the northern parts of the ocean. In the late ninth century a remarkable book was produced which joined the geographical knowledge of late Roman Antiquity together with the newly acquired knowledge which was drawn on mariners' observations. Like Bede's main work, the book circulated under the title *historia*, as it was based on one of the sources which Bede himself had used, namely Orosius's text.[20]

Unlike Bede, the anonymous ninth-century authors retained Orosius's historiographic framework and translated much of the contents of the work into English. But, into the first part, where Orosius had provided a description of the world, the ninth-century authors inserted two lengthy vernacular reports on seafaring in the northern parts of the ocean. Both reports were based on oral interviews given to King Alfred of Wessex by traders, one of Scandinavian origin, the other ostensibly English (on whom see Chapter V).

---

20 *The Old English Orosius*, cap. I/1, ed. Janet M. Bately, Early English Text Society, Supplementary Series VI (London, New York, Toronto, 1980), p. 16–18. Cf. Dicuil, *Liber de mensura orbis terrae*, cap. VII/11, VII/13, ed. J. J. Tierney, Ludwig Bieler, Scriptores Latini Hiberniae VI (Dublin, 1967), p. 74.

This insertion adapted the description of the world as known to Orosius to the area where much trade was ongoing during the ninth century. It also displayed the consciousness of the ninth-century authors that the description of the world provided by Orosius was imperfect and needed to be supplemented by the new evidence that had come to light. Hence, while Orosius's account of the past continued to be accepted as an account of the history of the Roman Empire, his description of the world was confronted with current knowledge. Although the geographical framework represented in a conventional world map was not abandoned, its adaptation to the current state of knowledge was informed by the necessity to adjust the conventional world picture to the new knowledge circulating in the ninth century. The ninth-century translators of Orosius's book were neither more nor less rational, nor were they more nor less empirical, than the author of the original. They were merely exposed to the necessity of having to move the focus of the world picture from the Mediterranean to the northern seas. Hence, by the ninth century, changes of world pictures and of the world maps representing them had become thinkable.

Nevertheless, the way towards the recognition of history as a feasible way of commemorating the past was long. The difficulty was that, where tradition identified the present as part and parcel of the past, history linked the present with the past through the medium of change. During the entire Middle Ages this implication of the concept of history was never theoretically accepted. The reason was as simple as it was hard to overcome: from the point of view of the kin and political groups which were constituted by the adherence to their own traditions, change was not neutral; instead, because change could reduce the validity of the good old law, it connoted negative values such as decay, instability and volatility. In this respect, pre-Christian group-related norms and values agreed with Christian doctrine. However, the factuality of change was undeniable. Even in the Bible the coming and going of three world empires had been described, and, since St Augustine, no one would deny the changes that had occurred or were going to occur in consequence of the advent of Christianity. Also, St Augustine had offered a cogent explanation for change. He had argued that only God had perfect ever-lasting stability, whereas changeability was the consequence of the imperfection of human existence.[21] Therefore, Augustine had allocated change to the time-bound world of the 'earthly city' which he had juxtaposed with the permanent, timeless and thus unchangeable 'City of God'. However, not only Orosius, but many other subsequent historiographers, such as Bishop Frechulph of Lisieux (dec. c. 864), failed to take up Augustine's vision of history even though they continued to postulate the continuity of the Roman Empire.[22] Only from the tenth century did concerns about the near end of the world as the most

---

21 Augustine, *De civitate Dei*, cap. XXII/30, CCSL XLVIII (Turnhout, 1955), pp. 862–6.
22 Frechulph, *Chronica* (*PL* 106, cols 917–1258). This work consisted originally of two chronicles, one from Adam to the birth of Christ, the other from the birth of Christ to

fundamental of all theoretically conceivable changes raise awareness of and anxieties about past and ongoing changes. The Roman Empire, the last of the four universal empires of Christian eschatology, was considered to be in disarray and in need of some reinvigoration in order to be able to continue.[23] It was understood that, in order to continue, the Roman Empire needed a strong head which could execute the demands of universal rule. But there was mounting dissent about the fundamental principles according to which universal rule should be organised between the various secular rulers and the highest representative of the Catholic Church. And there was the increasing military pressure against the empire from the Muslim rulers in Palestine, north Africa and the Iberian peninsula. They opposed those who theoretically claimed the universality of rule for the Roman Empire against the empirical world of real politics.

It was this clash between eschatological hopes and the manifest conditions of the real world which induced Bishop Otto of Freising (c. 1112–58), half-brother to the then reigning King Conrad III, to present a rather gloomy narrative of human history from the expulsion from paradise up to his own times. The 'History of the Two Cities', sometimes also referred to as *Chronica*, provided an account of history in seven books, to which Otto added a speculative eighth book on the future of the 'City of God' when there would be no history. Otto completed his work in 1146, the year in which the abortive Second Crusade began and in which he, his nephew and the future Emperor Frederick, as well as King Conrad, took part. Otto's narrative abounded with laments about the volatility of empires which he felt to be increasing during his own time. This feeling led Otto to believe that he and his contemporaries were living 'at the end of times', with the end of the world as the most fundamental of all changes approaching.[24] Contrary to previous historiographers, Otto thus made full use of Augustine's model and compared the human world with the 'changing sea which at one moment swells with rain water and at another sinks through natural decline'.[25] He also followed Orosius from whose work he took over the division of his narrative of the past into seven books, even though Otto had to cover 700 years of history more than Orosius. But he differed from both Augustine and Orosius in that he associated an epochal change with the birth of Christ, whom Otto described anachronistically as a 'citizen of Rome':

Pope Gregory I. In the course of the manuscript transmission, the two works were combined into one manuscript. See also Ado of Vienne, *Chronicon* (*PL* 123, cols 23–138).

23 Ademar of Chabannes, *Chronique*, cap. III/46–7, ed. Jules Chavanon (Paris, 1879), pp. 168–71. Abbo of Fleury, *Liber apologeticus* (*PL* 139, cols 471–2). Letter by Gauzlin, Abbot of Fleury, to King Robert of France (c. 1027), printed in André de Fleury, *Vie de Gauzlin*, ed. Robert-Henri Bautier, Gillette Labory (Paris, 1969), pp. 160–1. Fulbert of Chartres (Letter to King Robert of France, c. 1027), Fulbert, *Letters and Poems*, No. 125, ed. Frederick Behrends (Oxford, 1976), pp. 224–6.

24 Otto of Freising, *Historia de duabus civitatibus*, Prologus ad Isingrim, ed. Adolf Hofmeister, *MGH SS rer. Germ.* (45), p. 7.

25 Ibid., cap. II/51, pp. 128–9.

I must add that God's incarnate son wanted to be registered as a Roman subject. For what reason can the *Princeps* and the Initiator of the Divine City have wanted to be born as a citizen of Rome (which was without doubt an earthly city) other than to demonstrate that he had come in order to turn this earthly city in a miraculous and inexplicable way into his own city. To be precise: Born among Jews he became a citizen of that pagan realm so as to make manifest that the grace [of God] had been transferred from the Jews to the pagan peoples. After the new man had been born in this way to replace the old, we shall end the chronology which we have used from Nimur to the foundation of the city and from then on to his time, and we shall begin to count the years from his birth.[26]

Otto's problem then was how to adapt to his own time the various chronological frameworks which he found in his sources. From the Bible, he took the chronology of the world ages for the early parts of his work; from Orosius he borrowed the chronology of the foundation of Rome (AUC) and the arguments through which the coming into existence, spreading and continuity of the Christian religion could be linked with the Roman Empire. But it was from Bede that Otto received the idea of counting the years after the birth of Christ, so that he could continue his narrative beyond the fifth-century institutional crisis of the Roman Empire. The Orosian chronology had been institutional in that it tied the counting of the years of the 'earthly city' to the institutions making up the Roman Empire; therefore, Christianity could exist in association with the existence of the administrative framework of the Roman Empire; consequently, although Orosius ended his sixth book with the birth of Christ, he continued to count the years according to the AUC chronology. By contrast, the Bedan chronology was eschatological in kind, because it could transcend the temporal boundaries which were set by the changes of the institutional framework of the Roman Empire. Otto combined both chronologies and added the Biblical world-age chronology in his efforts to 'write history for the purpose of demonstrating the changes of things' and in order to give support to his conviction that 'through this change of the empires, we shall be directed towards the immutability of the heavenly empire'.[27] In this way, chronology itself became a means of demonstrating the changeability of the past and the conditions of life in the present before the coming of the 'City of God'. Thus Otto reversed the early medieval kin-group-based perception of the human world as essentially stable and replaced it by his view of the human world as innately unstable. And although he credited human actors with some degree of freedom of promoting or resisting change, he insisted that transitoriness had been divinely ordained and was therefore an unalterable quality of human existence. Moreover, Otto observed an increase in the thoroughness and the frequency of changes. While, contrary to Orosius, Otto concluded all but one of the first seven books of the *Historia* with a lament about the changeability of times, in his fifth book, he complained more bitterly than elsewhere that the Frankish kings, as the

---

[26] Ibid., cap. III/6, pp. 141–3.
[27] Ibid., cap. V/36, pp. 260–1.

bearers of the Roman imperial title, and their successors had been incapable of providing a safe haven for the Empire 'after its flight from the Orient',[28] and he spent this and the following sixth and seventh books on descriptions of what he took to have been the continuous wilful weakening of the Empire. He did so explicitly for the purpose of demonstrating that 'only God is immobile and remains unchangeable'.[29]

The loss of the future: the separation of history from eschatology

In Otto's world view change dominated human affairs and demanded its recognition by the historiographer, whereas he left to the theologian the task of showing that the changes recorded by historiographers occurred for the eventual goal of achieving stability in eternity. While, during the early Middle Ages, stability had been a real-world experience of commemorating the past, in the course of the twelfth century it was explicitly transferred into the realm of religious speculation about the future. Religious speculation thus set a stable framework of totality within which world history as a whole was to take place between the fall of humankind as its ascertainable beginning and Judgement Day as its presumed definitive end. In Otto's work, world history came to be viewed as a computable, finite, yet unstable entity under the control of change. But soon after its lavish explication by Otto, this view of world history came under stress. Two factors caused the stress: first, there was the manifestly continuous existence of the world despite the eschatological belief that the predicted end of the world was close; and second, there was the reception in the Occident, during the twelfth and thirteenth centuries, of the Aristotelian concept of time as an endless process.

The first factor was enhanced by the AD chronology itself which had helped to deal historiographically with the institutional discontinuities of the Roman Empire. Because the AD chronology provided an absolute standard for the reckoning of time, every new year could be added to the previous AD, irrespective of the place where the time-reckoning took place and without any relation whatsoever to existing institutions. Hence the AD chronology was ultimately in conflict with the eschatological belief in the finiteness of the existence of the world as an 'earthly city'. The consequences of the break-up of Otto's grand synthesis were already to be seen by the thirteenth century. While in the thirteenth, fourteenth and fifteenth centuries, world histories continued to be written as narratives along the lines which had been set in late Antiquity and the early Middle Ages, and they continued to begin with the sacred history as recorded in the Bible, they became open-ended. Thus history retained its beginning, but lost its end, and the past became associated with a

---

28 Ibid. He was much less pessimistic in his accounts of the previous transfers of the empires and thereby indicated his worries that the weakening of the Roman Empire as the last of the four world empires would bring about the end of the world.

29 Ibid.

process of endless change. Likewise, world historiography became intermingled with local or regional historiography, once the accounts of historiographers reached their own times. A good example is the *Chronica majora* written by Matthew Paris (c. 1200–59), Benedictine monk of St Albans, in the 1240s and continued up to 1259. Until 1234, Matthew compiled his material from the Bible and previous historiographic works, whence the scope of his narrative was universal in kind. But, although he kept an eye on continental European affairs and events in Palestine, for the thirteenth century his primary attention was concentrated on England where he obtained the sources for his work.[30] The narrowing down of the focus of world historiography to secular local affairs in a given area helped to promote the indefiniteness of historical time, and relieved the universal historical narrative from the task of speculating about the end of the world at large. This did not imply that the narrative fusion of accounts on the past with speculation about the future of human existence was no longer practised after Otto of Freising, but it did mean that such speculations were no longer necessarily connected with comprehensive accounts of world history. The fourteenth-century Northumbrian *Cursor mundi*, for example, is a text providing a poetic account of the sacred history of the world during its six ages together with a speculation about the 'seventh age' following the antichrist.[31] But, contrary to Otto of Freising, the work does not contain accounts of the events following the birth of Christ in the sixth age; instead, it proceeds directly from the birth of Christ to eschatology without a lament about the changeability of times.

The second factor which caused stress on Otto of Freising's historico-eschatological framework of description was more theoretical in kind. Otto had still applied the then conventional concept of time according to which time was regarded as a process which the divinity had willed to be limited to the 'earthly city', so that the eternity of the 'City of God' was not under the government of time. According to this understanding, time was cosmological as well as historical and, in itself, finite. But this concept of time militated against the Aristotelian definition of time, which was reintroduced in the Occident through the Arab translations of Aristotle's original works from the twelfth and thirteenth centuries. According to the Aristotelian concept, time was regarded as the mover of all things, elevated above all other divine creations. Time had an abstract quality which elevated it above everything else. In consequence of the spread of this concept of time, it became difficult to conceive existence without time, even beyond Judgement Day. In other words, if time was prior to everything else, existence became inconceivable outside of or beyond time and thinking about a world without change became subject to fairy tales and mere speculation. In the fourteenth century the Aristotelian concept of infinite time as the primary factor of change was posited against

---

historical time.[32] Although concepts of historical time continued to be influenced by Biblical traditions during and beyond the Middle Ages, its end
became more remote. For example, Cardinal Nicholas of Cusa (1401–64)
assumed that the world would come to its end early in the eighteenth century,
whereas Giovanni Pico della Mirandola (1463–94) believed that the world
would continue until 1994. In any case, the distinction between the infinite
time of the universe and the finite time of history resulting from the eschatological check against the recognition and acknowledgement of the ubiquity
and perpetuity of change gave way to the opposing scientific analysis. The
consequence was that commemorating the past as a whole lost its tradition-
ality and became equated with the recognition and acknowledgement of its
ever-changing character as history.

Globalising the past: the problem of correlating different world chronologies

In the course of the fifteenth century, commemorating the past as the
changing history of the world became more directly intertwined with the
geographical, specifically maritime, exploration of the world in the quest for
the seaway to India or the hypothetical southern continent which was thought
to connect Africa with Asia. The extending recognition by Europeans of the
pluralism of continents on the surface of the earth made an oddity of the
conventional medieval world picture and the medieval way of counting years
and commemorating the past.

The largest and the latest, although no longer successful effort to rescue the
medieval ways of time reckoning and of commemorating the past and to
extend them to the then-known world was laid down in the printed book of
world history published by Hartmann Schedel (1440–1514) of Nuremberg in
1493. The layout of the work followed its high medieval predecessors in that it
displayed world history in the sequence of six ages and gave a universal
account with regard to the first four ages. With regard to the fifth and sixth
ages, it followed Otto of Freising and the later world historiography, paral-
leling world-age chronology with the AD chronology, and weaving in descriptive reports on current affairs. Unlike Otto, Schedel was parsimonious with
his descriptions of the coming of the antichrist in the seventh age and of
Judgement Day in the 'last age'. In the manner of Matthew Paris's *Chronica
majora*, Schedel's book acquired a local touch once the narrative approached
the fifteenth century. But unlike Matthew, Schedel presented a comparative
survey of the local histories of several of the territorial administrative units
existing in his own time, among which Palestine featured with Jerusalem as
the capital, no longer as the city in or near the centre of the world.[33] What
mattered to Schedel was no longer its place in sacred history and in or near

---

32 William Ockham, *Philosophia naturalis*, cap. IV/3 (Rome, 1637), pp. 87–8.
33 Hartmann Schedel, *Das Buoch der Cronicken und Gedechtnus wirdigern Geschichten von*

the centre of the world, but its location in Palestine as the purported centre of a territorial administrative unit. Thus Schedel made an effort to represent the world known to him as the sum of its constitutive administrative parts. The entry on Portugal displays Schedel's intentions directly:

> In the year of the Lord 1483, King John of Portugal, a man of noble mind, equipped several galleys with all necessities for life and sent them beyond Hercules's Columns southwards for the purpose of exploring Ethiopia. And he appointed two commanders for these ships or galleys. They were Jacobus Canus, a Portuguese, and Martin Behaim, a German, born from a noble family in Nuremberg, well versed in knowledge about geographical matters and experienced in navigation. He knew quite well from experience and a long career as a navigator the longitudes and latitudes in the Occident, and after the successful end of their expedition, they returned to Portugal after fifteen months, although they lost many of their company who died because of the overheated air.[34]

Schedel praised the Portuguese kings for their explorations along the west African coasts. He proudly recorded the labours and successes of his fellow Nuremberg citizen Martin Behaim (1459–1507) who had been a navigator in the service of the Portuguese kings. Thus Schedel combined a universal approach to history with accounts of the activities of heads of state as well as of local matters in his home town of Nuremberg. He availed himself of current knowledge which had been traded among the Portuguese seafarers and which Behaim may have reported when he returned to Nuremberg. Schedel's method of the acquisition of topical news was conventional; Bede, for instance, had used it. But the actual content of the reports was novel, namely the very idea was new that new lands could and ought to be discovered and that, consequently, the geographical range of history might be enlarged beyond confines of what had been depicted in a conventional medieval world map.

Hence, without knowing about Columbus's voyage, Schedel, the humanist whose work abounds with reference to the classics, was anything but hostile towards innovation and 'news' in the literal sense of the word. Instead, he joined in with the widespread sentiment that many humanists of the time shared, which can be described as a bias towards the new. Soon after Schedel, some humanists even went so far as to compare the European 'discoveries' of America and other parts of the world with the accomplishments of the ancients, and they found that their own time witnessed the greater accomplishments.[35] The consequences of this judgement were far reaching. First, the fifteenth century explorations and the 'discovery' expeditions around the year

---

Anbegyn der Werlt bis auf dise vnßere Zeit (Nuremberg, 1493), fols XVIIrecto, CCLIXverso–CCLXIIverso.

34 Schedel (see note 33), fol. CCLXXXVverso. Hercules's Columns is a reference to the Strait of Gibraltar; Ethiopia, a generic term for Africa.

35 Sebastian Brant, *Das Narrenschiff* [first edn Basle, 1494], cap. 66, ed. Elvira Pradel (Frankfurt, 1980), pp. 187–90.

Fig. 34 Miniature of the 'people of Calicut' (*Kalkutische leut*) representing the 'Far East' in Emperor Maximilian I's *Triumphzug*, planned from 1507. Vienna, Graphische Sammlung Albertina, Inv. No. A. CK. P. 1 n. 34. The picture displays early sixteenth-century European images of native Americans, but also includes one female figure in African dress (the woman in the centre who holds a child in her arms and looks back to other members of the group).

Fig. 35 Banner with the inscription 'XVc Inseln' (1500 islands), representing the 'Far West' in Emperor Maximilian I's *Triumphzug*, planned from 1507. Madrid, Biblioteca Nacional, Res. 254. A similar banner with the same inscription is contained in Emperor Maximilian I's *Ehrenpforte* in the right column of the central tower. London, British Museum.

1500 quickly destroyed through empirical evidence the conventional theoretical world picture, the essentials of which had been enshrined in the ecumenical world maps throughout the Middle Ages. Second, the emphasis on the novelty of these empirical explorations, that is, the insistence that nothing comparable had occurred in world history before the contemporary 'discoveries', enhanced the readiness for accepting change as the underlying nature of history at large.

The practical implications of the fragmentation of the medieval theoretical world picture were soon realised by politicians and statesmen. Necessarily, this process met with the keenest attention of the head of that foremost institution of universal rule, namely the Roman emperor. At the time, the office-holder was Maximilian I, the German king who, since his coronation in 1508, bore the title 'Elected Roman Emperor'. Maximilian saw it as his personal task to preserve and, if possible strengthen the foundations of the Roman Empire, and he believed that the aggrandisement of his own power would be beneficial to the accomplishment of this goal. From 1492 onwards, Maximilian was interested in panegyric and autobiographical writings and, in 1507, he launched preparations for the production of the *Weisskunig*, a major panegyric work about himself to be written, printed and published in German.[36] Simultaneously, Maximilian launched other major works of printed art, partly genealogical and autobiographical in content, partly pieces of imperial propaganda. He also began to give instructions about the building of his tomb. Among the pieces of imperial propaganda were the designs for a triumphal arch (*Ehrenpforte*)[37] and a monumental triumphal procession (*Triumphzug*).[38] The *Ehrenpforte* and the *Triumphzug* were vehicles for the depiction of Maximilian as a universal ruler, whereby universal rule was already understood as encompassing the entire globe as comprehended by European geographers and cartographers at the time.[39] Hence Maximilian broke with the theoretical concept of universality as depicted in the ecumenical world maps and availed himself of the most recent geographical knowledge current at his time. Maximilian articulated his claims of universal rule by carefully presenting himself as the kin elder over the kings of Portugal and the rulers of the Spanish kingdoms. Indeed, he was related to the Portuguese kings through his mother Eleanor (1434–67, daughter of King Edward of Portugal) and to the Spanish rulers through the double marriages of his son Philip and his daughter Margaret to the heirs of the Spanish kingdoms. Because, in the early

---

36 Maximilian I, *Weisskunig* (Vienna, 1775; repr. Weinheim, 1985).

37 Ed. Eduard Chmelarz, *Jahrbuch der Kunsthistorischen Samlungen des Allerhöchsten Kaiserhauses*, supplement to vol. 4 (Vienna, 1885–86; repr. Graz, 1972).

38 Ed. Franz Winzinger, *Die Miniaturen zum Triumphzug Kaiser Maximilians I.*, Veröffentlichungen der Albertina V (Graz, 1973). Franz Schestag, 'Kaiser Maximilian I. Triumph', *Jahrbuch der Kunsthistorischen Sammlungen des Allerhöchsten Kaiserhauses* I (1883), pp. 154–81.

39 The work by Matthias Ringmann and Martin Waldseemüller, *Cosmographiae introductio* (Strasbourg, 1507) (repr., ed. Franz Ritter von Wieser, Drucke und Holzschnitte des 15. und 16. Jahrhunderts XII [Strasbourg, 1907]) was dedicated to Maximilian.

sixteenth century, the kings of Portugal claimed to be rulers over Africa and large parts of southern Asia, and the rulers of the Spanish kingdoms were in the process of extending their rule over parts of the Caribbean and continental America, Maximilian could in fact display himself as the overlord of the world in the sense of the entire globe.

Thus Maximilian immediately and skilfully used the ongoing globalisation of the world picture for this transformation of the conception of imperial rule. In short, whereas most of the medieval Roman Emperors had confined themselves to theoretical claims towards universal rule in the sense which informed the medieval ecumenical world maps, Maximilian turned the establishment of world overlordship into an issue of practical politics.

However, Maximilian also tried to preserve and invigorate traditions which has been attached to the imperial office already in the Middle Ages and which had been transmitted in his own dynasty of the Habsburgs from the later thirteenth century. He had inserted a chapter in the *Weisskunig* under the title 'How the Young White King [i.e. Maximilian himself] greatly loved the old memories'.[40] In this chapter, he lamented his contemporaries' craving for novelty and the disregard for traditions, while he praised himself for what was described as his exceptional capability and willingness to know and preserve the traditions of his own kin group and those of the imperial office as well as traditions related to other ruling institutions.[41] The *Weisskunig* reports that Maximilian had sent out researchers with the order of investigating ancient records. Indeed, it can be confirmed that one scholar, Jacob Mennel (c. 1460–before 1526), was sent out at the emperor's request to consult archival sources as well as other records, such as tombstones, in order to trace the history of the Habsburg dynasty.[42] Another scholar, Johannes Stabius (c. 1450–1522), worked himself through historiographical records for the purpose of providing the stuff for the imperial propaganda laid down in the *Ehrenpforte*.[43] As a result of these historical researches, the Habsburg dynasty was established as the group of descendants from Noah to whom Maximilian came to be linked through the medieval genealogies. Hence Maximilian still availed himself of the belief that the presumed or concocted length of genealogical tradition of rulers would translate into the stability of the institution of which these rulers were in control. This seems to have been the reason why

---

[40] Maximilian I, *Weisskunig* (see note 36), pp. 68–9.

[41] Such thinking in the sixteenth century was not peculiar to Maximilian. Instead, the desirability of keeping memories of the past was also articulated by philosophers of history, among them Francesco Patrizi, *Della historia diece dialoghi* (Venice, 1560), pp. 18–19. However, Maximilian articulated his beliefs relatively early in the century.

[42] Mennel's researches have been preserved in a rare print and a number of manuscripts. See Jacob Mennel, *Chronica Habsburgensis nuper rigmatice edita* (Constance, 1507). Vienna, Austrian National Library 38.R.2. One manuscript has been edited by Wolfgang Irtenkauf, *Der 'Habsburger Kalender' des Jakob Mennel (Urfassung)*, Litterae LXVI (Göppingen, 1979). Others have been preserved in the Austrian National Library, Cod. Vind. Palat. 3072x, 3073, 3074, 3075, 3076, 3077, 3305, 7892.

[43] Stabius was also the author of a global map of the world which was first printed in 1512.

Maximilian criticised the disregard for traditions of rulership and emphasised the importance of preserving these traditions as 'memories'.[44] Nonetheless, the medium for the preservation of these traditions was unequivocally the written text to which pictures could be appended.

Maximilian applied these convictions practically in the grandiose designs for his tomb, which was to serve as a permanent memory of his own accomplishments. For about a decade before his death Maximilian was busy pressing for the implementation of his designs, for which he requested the services of the leading artists of his time, among them Albrecht Dürer (1471–1528) and Peter Vischer (c. 1460–1529). Forty statues of prominent factual and purported ancestors were to encircle the tomb, a genealogy, as it were, cast in bronze.

Maximilian's archaic *faible* for genealogical manifestations of institutional continuity may appear as an odd companion to his recognisable openness towards the changing conditions of rule at his own time. However, in Maximilian's own perception, change and continuity as the two complimentary aspects of history were perfectly compatible because the biblical framework of time-reckoning in world history was still intact and no one dared to call it into question. However, Maximilian's grand designs failed. His bid for recognition as the world's overlord was thwarted by the King of France in his very neighbourhood. Maximilian's demand for respect in, and manifest control of, the Empire was ignored by many territorial rulers inside the Empire, and the Swiss even forced Maximilian to acknowledge their autonomy. The fate of his planned works of art was correspondingly disappointing, for none of them were fully executed. His tomb remained a cenotaph, the *Weisskunig* remained a torso, and the *Ehrenpforte* and the *Triumphzug* remained designs on paper, which were never actually fulfilled. Thus Maximilian's grand designs for the fusion of conventional and non-conventional types of commemorating the past in the ongoing political process of the globalisation of universal rule were not implemented. Instead, world historiography became difficult to conceive and, for that matter, to write. As the world picture changed dramatically in the early years of the sixteenth century, historians sensed the twin difficulties of reconciling universalism with the new global world picture and of interconnecting the imperial institutions of the sixteenth century with the Roman Empire of Antiquity. The only feasible answer was the recognition of change and the acceptance of the possibility that change could also affect institutions of universal rule.[45]

---

44 Maximilian I, *Weisskunig* (see note 36), p. 69.

45 For authors who struggled with the legacy of the Roman Empire in the sixteenth and early in the seventeenth centuries, see Jean Bodin, *Methodus ad facilem historiarum cognitionem* (Paris, 1566), pp. 346–61 (new edn [New York, 1966], pp. 291–302). Johannes Kepler, 'De stella nova' [first edn Frankfurt, Prague, 1606], new edn Kepler, *Gesammelte Werke*, vol. 1 (Munich, 1938), p. 329. Aegidius Tschudi, *Die uralt wahrhafftig Alpisch Rhetia* (Basle, 1538), fol. B IV recto. Joachim Vadianus, 'In farraginem antiquitatum', ed. Melchior Goldast, *Rerum Alamannicarum scriptores*, vol. 3 (Frankfurt, 1661), p. 12.

Conclusion

The transformation of the 'cold' into the 'hot' type of commemorating the past has been described here in the context of world historiography. This has been done because the long-term perspective and wide geographic range of world historiography most easily displays the gradual process of 'heating up' the European type of commemoration of the past. It began with the absorption of particularist group traditions into the universal framework of sacred history recorded in the Bible and the promotion of awareness of the possibility of change inside the otherwise continuous framework of Biblical traditions and chronologies in the eighth century. It intensified with the juxtaposition of infinite astronomical time and the open-ended AD chronology with finite historical time during the thirteenth century. Together, both factors provided the platform from which the separation of world historiography from eschatological beliefs could proceed. During the fifteenth and sixteenth centuries, this separation became mandatory as the spatial theatre of world history extended beyond the tri-continental world picture in which the hitherto accepted concept of universality had been enshrined. The fifteenth and sixteenth century 'discoveries' did not merely prompt the establishment of a new picture of the world in its spatial dimension, but also added to the pressures upon trust in the finiteness of historical time. They did so by forcing questions about the possibilities of integrating the New World and the hypothetical Southern Continent into the Biblical framework of time-reckoning. In the sixteenth century, the 'cold' type of commemorating the past discovered its potential for being 'heated up' following the collapse of the conventional medieval world picture.

XI

Communication III:
The Movements of Persons and Groups

eac beþarf seo sawel on domes dæg rihtes weges and clænes and
staðolfæstre brycge ofer þone glideran weg hellewites brogan*
– Wulfstan, Archbishop of York

Introduction

Communication through the movement of people may take either of two
forms: a unidirectional movement from one place to another without an
intention of returning, or movement with an intended return. In the first case,
the movement is commonly referred to as migration if the moving people
transgress boundaries of recognised significance; we even refer to this movement as migration when moving persons are led to return to their place of
origin against their initial intentions. By contrast, in the second case, the
movements are commonly known as travel, even though travel becomes
migration when, against their initial intention, travellers do not return to
their place of origin. Therefore, although migration and travel overlap significantly with regard to the moving action, both types of movement display
fundamental differences with regard to the factors leading to their inception
and, likewise, with regard to their impacts on the moving people, the groups
from which they depart as well as the groups at whose places of settlement
they arrive and into which they may wish to become integrated. Hence it is
not suitable to subsume both types of movements into a single concept, such
as 'mobility'. Instead, both forms of communication through the movement
of persons and groups shall be discussed separately. Likewise, it is not advisable to fuse solitary movements of persons with movements of groups,
because intentions and attitudes of those who move and the reactions of
those who are affected by the movements may differ depending on the
number of migrants.

---

* Moreover, on Domesday, the soul needs a well prepared path and a steadfast bridge
across that slippery way of the terror of punishments in hell.

Migration

The various successive migration patterns shall be dealt with here in the light of two questions: first, what was the social organisation of the migrants? and second, who controlled the migrants?

The Migration Age was characterised by the long-distance migration of mainly autonomously organised smaller or larger groups who frequently looked out for target areas for their migrations within the space of the Roman Empire of Antiquity. During the fourth, fifth and earlier sixth centuries, the dominant groups of migrants were mainly kin groups, neighbourhood groups and contractual groups; these could unite into migration avalanches in the course of the migration process. Although many of these migration avalanches were accommodated and were eventually integrated into pre-existing resident population groups, their appearance could also cause or aggravate economic, political and cultural problems among the latter. Not infrequently, therefore, disputes occurred between the resident population and the immigrants, and the latter, specifically in the remoter parts of the Roman Empire of Antiquity, established themselves as rulers in the area of their new settlement and over the resident population.[1] One reason for such disputes may have been continuing immigration, which would imply that the Migration Age did not end abruptly during the sixth century. Hence, the Migration Age rather petered out gradually into the migrations of small groups and solitary persons, into remigration on a lesser scale and into domestic colonisation, all of which continued well beyond the seventh century.

For example, linguistic and place-name evidence seems to indicate that migration across the English Channel was still a fairly common phenomenon in the seventh century. In a number of cases, the migrants were still identifiable as members of a political group, such as those Frisians and Angles who, as perhaps others were coming from the British Isles, settled in the eastern part of the Frankish kingdom in the sixth century, after the Thuringian kingdom had been destroyed.[2] Likewise, a group calling itself the Mece or Meaca people must have been settled under the authority of the Frankish king in the northern Netherlands where an area name Mecingun is on record.[3] Such small groups, much as those of the migration avalanches of the previous centuries, organised themselves autonomously and determined the time and

---

1 These consequences were made explicit in a sixth-century source on the appearance of continental migrants in Britain. Gildas, *De excidio et conquestu Britanniae*, cap. 22–4, ed. Michael Winterbottom, Gildas, *The Ruin of Britain and Other Works* (Chichester, 1978), pp. 96–8.

2 Procopius, *Wars of the Goths*, IV/19 (various editions), mentions these groups as migrants to Britain. For place-name evidence on their remigration see Reinhard Wenskus, 'Zur fränkischen Siedlungspolitik im Saalegebiet', Wenskus, *Ausgewählte Aufsätze zum frühen und preußischen Mittelalter*, ed. Hans Patze (Sigmaringen, 1986), pp. 208–9.

3 See Peter von Polenz, *Landschafts- und Bezirksnamen im frühmittelalterlichen Deutschland*, vol. 1 (Marburg, 1961), pp. 176, 178.

the conditions of their migrations by themselves, even if their decision to migrate may have occurred in response to events which were not under their control and which they may have regarded as unfavourable to their purposes. However, the smaller groups differed from the migration avalanches of the previous centuries in having less freedom of choice of the target areas of their migration and of their establishment as settlers in these areas. Instead, their migrations more frequently than in the centuries before were directed into target areas to which the migrants were directed under some degree of administrative control by rulers over land and people.

Perhaps the most important stimulus for group migration in the early Middle Ages resulted from the pluralism of competing types of group which offered a variety of membership options to a person. The availability of such choices had the consequence that a person could well become an outcast in relation to a certain group or type of group but could hardly become an outcast *per se*. For example, a person could voluntarily leave his or her kin or neighbourhood group[4] or a kin group could expel one of its members after he or she had committed a crime.[5] In such a case, the person or group of persons had the option of joining another type of group, such as a contractual group. Likewise, resettlement in a new neighbourhood group was relatively easy. The later recension of the Frankish *Lex Salica* ruled that anyone can move into a settlement if no one objects and that the immigrant shall be safe and regarded as an ordinary neighbour if none of the settlers testifies against the immigrant within one year.[6] Likewise, late eighth-century legislation enforced poor-relief and care for innocent vagrants as regular tasks of members of neighbourhood groups.[7] The Church was more restrictive. As early as the sixth century, Bishop Aurelianus of Arles (523–51), who wrote a rule for nuns, insisted that fugitive slaves and other unfree persons must not be permitted to enter a monastery.[8]

Remarkably, cases of the expulsion or banning of persons were rarely put on record in normative sources.[9] Instead, in the early Middle Ages, reports on expulsions were often contained in narrative sources.[10] Likewise, rules concerning expulsions were conspicuously absent from early medieval written legal records. Probably, the reason was that the rulers who enforced statutory laws did not have at their disposal sophisticated bureaucracies

---

4   Hartmut Broszinski, ed., *Das Hildebrandslied*, vv. 18–19. 2nd edn (Kassel, 1985).
5   *Wulf and Eadwacer*, v. 12, ed. George Philip Krapp, Elliott van Kirk Dobbie, *The Exeter Book*, Anglo-Saxon Poetic Records III (New York, London, 1936), p. 180. The Old English word *utlah* (outlaw) appeared first in the eleventh-century laws of Cnut, cap. II/31, 2, ed. Felix Liebermann, *Die Gesetze der Angelsachsen*, vol. 1 (Halle, 1903), p. 336.
6   *Lex Salica, 100 Titel-Text*, cap. 80, ed. Karl August Eckhardt (Weimar, 1953), pp. 203–5.
7   *Admonitio generalis* [23.3.789], ed. Alfred Boretius, *MGH Capit.* 1, No. 22, p. 60.
8   *S. Aureliani Arelatensis Regula ad virgines* (*PL* 68, col. 401).
9   The pre-Alfredian English laws knew of expulsion only in cases of aliens with deviant behaviour. See *Laws of Wihtred*, cap. 4, 28. Liebermann (see note 5), pp. 12, 14.
10 For an example, see Gregory of Tours, *Libri historiarum X*, cap. VII/21, VII/39, VIII/18, ed. Bruno Krusch, Wilhelm Levison, *MGH SS rer. Merov.*, vol. 1, pp. 339–40, 362–3, 384–5.

which could carry out expulsion orders. It is therefore more likely that the expulsions of which we know from narrative sources fell within the competence of kin groups and were relatively rare even then at the time.[11] With regard to the British Isles, this assumption can be confirmed by the use of the two most frequent Old English words for peace, namely *frith* and *sib*. Both words denoted the protection provided by kin groups, and the word *sib* is itself a term for the kin group. Peace was thus understood as a condition under which a person could enjoy the protection and friendship of his or her kin. In Old English, a person from whom groups had withdrawn their protection was referred to as *wineleas* (without friends) and was described as someone whose friends were wolves and who could be torn to pieces by them.[12] Expulsion could thus result in the withdrawal of support and protection from a person, mainly by kin groups, and it was therefore a severe punishment, often the equivalent of a death sentence. The severity of expulsion as a penalty sheds light on the constraints against which migration took place in the early Middle Ages. Migration is displayed as a movement in the course of which people could transform their group membership while they were exposed to threatening hazards in the physical environment. The only means available to ordinary people to resist these constraints was to seek affiliation with powerful people as leaders of migrating groups. Moreover, migrants needed a strong incentive in order to overcome the hazards posed by extensive overseas voyages as well as journeys into unknown lands. Impressions of these hazards were elegantly described in two (possibly) tenth-century Old English elegies, as well as in the Latin *Navigatio Sancti Brendani* which may have been written at about the same time.[13]

The settlements which were newly established under royal patronage during and after the eighth century exhibited a novel migratory pattern which was to become common during subsequent centuries, up to the end of the Middle Ages. This new pattern of migration extended across shorter distances into unsettled land, mainly by way of the clearing of woodlands.[14] At least since the seventh century, the clearing of woodland seems to have occurred under some degree of supervision by rulers who had afforested the woods. Through such acts of afforestation, rulers such as the kings of the Franks or the various rulers in the southern British Isles, claimed regalia over uninhabited woodland. This novel pattern, however, says as little about the motives which drove migrants into such lands as it tells about the conditions under which the migrants lived at the time of the launching of their migrations. But it is possible to surmise that this type of migration was no longer undertaken

---

[11] Gregory of Tours (see note 10), cap. II/42, p. 93, referred to people without kin as wandering 'peregrini inter extraneus', that is people without a home.

[12] *Maxims*, vv. 146–7, 173, ed. Krapp/Dobbie (see note 5), pp. 161, 162.

[13] *Wanderer*, vv. 19–25, ed. Krapp (see note 5), p. 134. *Seafarer*, vv. 27–33, ed. Krapp (see note 5), p. 144. *Navigatio Sancti Brendani abbatis*, cap. 1, ed. Carl Selmer (Notre Dame, Ind., 1959), pp. 4–8.

[14] Felix Liebermann, *Über Pseudo-Cnuts Constitutiones de foresta* (Halle, 1894), pp. 49–55.

for the purpose of establishing separate, so to speak, 'independent' settlements in no man's lands within forests.

Place names confirm the supposition that, as a rule local separatism was no longer the paramount motive which made migrants move. In the southern British Isles, where this migratory patterns seems to have occurred as early as the seventh century, place names betray a tendency towards the use of name elements which were taken from names of older settlements in coastal zones. In Sussex name pairs such as Goring/Goringlee, Hastings/Hastingford, the derivative place name ends in a suffix which indicates a woodland clearing or other settlement in the woodlands, whereas, in the case of the name-pair Poling/Peeling, an umlaut betrays the derivation of the latter from the former. In each of these cases, the derivative place names denote settlements which are in the upland woodland regions whereas the stem names refer to places located along the Channel coast or other nearby locations. Hence, these place names contain records of a colonisation process which led migrants from the coastal zones in the southern British Isles to extend their fields of activity into the woodland zones of the hinterland. Place names also show that the migrants continued to operate in groups, mainly contractual groups which had been established for the specific purpose of founding new settlements by the command of a locator, but also in neighbourhood groups and possibly in kin groups.

Where such colonisation processes became recorded on the Continent (outside Scandinavia and the Iberian peninsula) from the end of the eighth century, they seem to have occurred under the authority of the rulers over land and people, such as the Frankish kings. Charlemagne, for example, authorised the clearing of woodland under the condition that the Frankish king retained some degree of overlordship over the clearers of the woodland.[15] Hence the migrants appear to have left their former settlements in search of further privileges (*libertates*) in addition to the tenurial rights which they could have held in traditional settlements. They may have acquired these additional privileges as a reward for woodland clearing and life in an environment that many perceived as hostile and dangerous and tried to avoid. But the settlers did not accomplish fully fledged freedom in the sense that they obtained the privilege of ruling themselves. One of these additional tenurial rights seems to have been the privilege of inheritance of the cleared woodland within the group of descendants of the original immigrants. In a few much later cases, a further motive was recorded, namely religious dissent. From the thirteenth and fourteenth centuries, cases are known where clearings of woodland were undertaken by sectarian groups, such as the Waldensians in Alpine valleys of Savoy in northern Italy. As a whole, however, this migratory pattern consisted of peaceful migrations and thereby differed fundamentally from the migrations of the Migration Age which had frequently involved hostilities. Instead, the woodland clearers reduced the migration effort to the

---

15 Engelbert Mühlbacher, ed., *MGH DD Karol. I*, No. 213 (811), No. 218 (813).

minimum of what was necessary to establish themselves as privileged settlers in the initially hostile environment of the woods.

There were two exceptional, large-scale migrations during the high and late Middle Ages: first the so-called Viking migration processes, and, second, the migration of Germans to the Baltic areas. The series of 'Viking' movements took place between the eighth and the twelfth centuries, along the Baltic Sea coast, across the northern Atlantic to Iceland, Greenland and 'Vinland' in North America, as well as along the western European coastline into the northern part of the Frankish kingdom, the British Isles and into the Mediterranean Sea. These movements were commonly organised by contractual groups and frequently accompanied by acts of violence.[16] Nevertheless, settlement in previously unoccupied areas may only have been one motive among a number of others, specifically the collection of tribute and booty as well as trading. Some 'Viking' foundations, such as Dublin, became trading spots, which shows that the establishment of settlements and the conduct of trade could appear together as migratory motives. The other exception, the migration of contractual groups from German speaking areas, was into Poland, Prussia, Lithuania, Latvia and Estonia during the twelfth and thirteenth centuries. The German migration into Prussia was accompanied by extensive military violence, less so the penetration into Poland and areas on the eastern part of the Baltic Sea.

The high and late Middle Ages witnessed a slow but steady decline of the ease with which the status change from alien to resident could be accomplished. One reason was the gradual territorialisation of rule which increasingly defined the population of an area as subjects of territorial rule. Hence after moving into new settlements immigrants arrived as outsiders and had to be admitted as residents in the new settlements before being considered as insiders. Specifically, when territorial rulers and councils of urban communities began to keep administrative records, the procedure for switching the status of immigrants from aliens as outsiders to residents as insiders became bureaucratised and, consequently, ever more difficult and burdensome. The keeping of administrative records made it possible to differentiate consistently and in legal terms between three categories of aliens: the traveller who was passing through a territory, the alien settler who lived in a territory but continued to be an outsider, and a resident of whatever origin who had settled in a territory as an insider. The thirteenth-century Saxon law book *Sachsenspiegel* confirmed that the middle category of the resident alien was then current as a legal category. The law book ruled that no alien was obliged to accept the law of the settlement where he or she lived but could claim to be judged according to the law of his or her place of origin.[17] This principle of the personality of law was widespread during the high and late Middle Ages

---

[16] For a close contemporary description, see *The Battle of Maldon*, ed. D. G. Scragg (Manchester, 1981), pp. 57–67.

[17] *Sachsenspiegel*, Landrecht, cap. 79, 2, ed. Karl August Eckhardt, *MGH Fontes iuris Germ. ant.* N. S. 1, 2, p. 262.

Fig. 36 The legal status of a resident alien in the thirteenth century. From the Heidelberg manuscript of the of Eike von Repgow, *Sachsenspiegel*, Landrecht, Art. III, cap. 79, 2. Heidelberg, University Library, Ms. cpg 164, fol. 26 verso.

and implied that, wherever a person lived, he or she, so to speak, carried the law with him or her and could demand to be exempted from the law that was valid at the place of his or her residence.[18]

A miniature in the Heidelberg manuscript of the *Sachsenspiegel* (see Figure 36) visualised the middle position of a resident alien in the fo'' wing way: On its left, the picture shows a man with clothes that differ from those of the other figures in the picture. Moreover, the man has his arms folded so as to demonstrate that he is not connected with the event taking place on the right. On this side, the master of the village reads the chartered privileges and obligations to the peasant farmers in the settlement. The picture thus shows that a resident alien lived in this village and that the chartered privileges and obligations were not valid for him. The man is dressed according to Wendic fashion, a political group of Slav settlers in Lower Saxony. Wendic style may have been chosen for the simple reason that the Middle Low German word for the resident alien was *uzwendic man*. In this phrase the homophone *wendic* could either be read as the ethnic name for the Wends or could be associated with a resident alien as a man from areas beyond the walls. The inter-utilisation of an ethnic name and a generic word for a resident alien indicated that, even in the thirteenth century, it was difficult to conceptualise alienness as a generic term. This was not only the case in the German-speaking areas. For example, the English word 'foreign' became common only in the fifteenth century as a French loan word which, in turn, was based on medieval Latin *foranus*. In short, the *Sachsenspiegel*, like many other late medieval laws and statutes,

---

[18] First recorded in the *Lex Ribuaria*, cap. 35, 3, ed. Franz Beyerle, Rudolf Buchner, *MGH LL nat. Germ.* 3, 2, pp. 228–9. Also in Pippin's *Capitulare Aquitanium* [768], cap. 10, ed. Alfred Boretius, *MGH Capit.* 1, No. 18, p. 43.

determined the status of permanent resident aliens on the premise that such aliens should not be considered as insiders.

Likewise, territorial rulers, such as the Kings of France, took great care to keep records which allowed them to trace the origin of immigrants many generations after the immigration had taken place. This practice was considered to be required for the purposes of allowing the enforcement of administrative measures against resident aliens and of controlling privileges which had been granted to immigrants at the time of their immigration. But these records could also be used to determine who would have to leave a settlement in the case that a territorial ruler ordered the expulsion of a certain group of resident aliens. For example, the King of France revoked the right of residence of Italians in 1320 and the revocation was confirmed in 1324 forcing persons of Italian origin into exile. Similarly, Florentines were expelled from France in 1346, and English students were told to leave the city of Toulouse on the charge that they conspired to treason.[19] These expulsions could only have been carried out if the victims of these orders were recognisable as resident aliens. Similarly, the councils of late medieval towns and cities kept files of new residents and thereby documented across the centuries when and from where people had arrived in the town or city.[20] A thin but persistent line existed between alien residents as resident outsiders and the resident population as insiders.

However, migration in groups towards novel settlements was not the only migratory pattern during the Middle Ages, for solitary migration also occurred. In early medieval times, the most conspicuous solitary migrants or migrants in very small groups were monk missionaries who circumvented the prescription of the Benedictine rule of the *stabilitas loci,* the obligation to confine oneself to a single place,[21] and used the religious request for missionary activities, stipulated by the New Testament, in order to justify their separation from their local home communities and to wander into remote lands. Among them St Gall (dec. c. 650), St Wilfrid, St Willibrord (657/58–739) and St Boniface (672/75–754) were prominent in the seventh and eighth centuries.[22] Many of them were later venerated as saints and were commemorated as personages with outstanding physical energies and intellectual capabilities. The proof of these qualities was generally taken from the fact that they had undertaken long-distance solitary migrations. Thus the

---

19 Quoted from Claudine Billot, 'L'assimiliation des étrangers dans le royaume de France aux XIVe et XVe siècle', *Revue Historique* CVII (1983), p. 280.

20 For example, at Ratisbon in Germany. See also A.-L. van Bruaene, *De Gentse memorieboeken als spiegel van stedelike historisch bewustzijn* (Gent, 1998).

21 *Regula Sancti Benedicti,* cap. 4, 78; 58, 9, ed. Rudolph Hanslik, CSEL LXX (Vienna, 1960), pp. 37, 147.

22 *Vitae S. Galli,* ed. Bruno Krusch, *MGH SS rer. Merov.* 4, pp. 251–337. Eddius Stephanus, *Vita Wilfridi,* ed. Bertram Colgrave, *The Life of Bishop Wilfrid by Eddius Stephanus* (Cambridge, 1927; repr. Cambridge, 1985). *Vitae sancti Bonifatii archiepiscopi Moguntini,* ed. Wilhelm Levison, *MGH SS rer. Germ* (57). *Vita S. Willibrordi,* ed. Wilhelm Levison, *MGH SS rer. Merov.* 7, pp. 81–141.

freedom which was associated with solitary migration was available only to those who had at their personal disposal extraordinary physical energies and intellectual capabilities.

Beyond the missionaries there are dim records of migrating professionals, such as physicians,[23] or specialists who, for want of a better word, might be called 'migrating producers' (on whom see Chapter VI).[24] Oral traditions about migrating smiths, prevalent in Scandinavia, are also witness to the existence of migrant producers. Likewise, in Scandinavian as well as in Old English literature, there are references to migrant singers of oral traditions, to whom, again, unusual physical characteristics were ascribed, such as the exceptional size of their bodies or the ability to execute their professional duties at an extremely old age.[25] Thus, the ability and willingness to transgress the boundaries of space and, at least, to live up to the limits of one's lifetime, were fundamental values identified with solitary migrants, and, thereby, betray solitary migration as an activity which, in its medieval perceptions, did not bear the hallmarks of normality.

However, at the time of Charlemagne the recorded prohibitions against the harbouring of slaves who had escaped from agricultural settlements[26] seem to indicate that solitary migration did occur. It has to be assumed that fugitives would try to reach faraway places for purposes which will not necessarily always have been honourable and that they may have migrated across long distances in order to remain undiscovered in their new places of settlement. Such intentions, again, disclose migration as something equivalent to a last resort in order to escape from an otherwise intolerable or undesirable condition of life.

In the twelfth century, the Old English words for peace, *frith, sib* and other terms, fell out of use and were replaced by the Anglo-Norman word *pees* which in turn was derived from the Latin *pax* and is the root of the Modern English 'peace'. This word no longer implied the maintenance of peace through the protection of a person by groups. Instead, it referred to the peace which was taken to be divinely willed and to be guaranteed by a territorial ruler through the enforcement of statutory and common law.[27] Likewise, in

---

23 Peter Köpp, ed., *Vademecum eines frühmittelalterlichen Arztes. Die gefaltete lateinische Handschrift medizinischen Inhalts im Codex 217 und der Fragmentensammlung 1396 der Stiftsbibliothek in St. Gallen*, Veröffentlichungen der Schweizerischen Gesellschaft für Geschichte der Medizin und der Naturwissenschaften XXXIV (Aarau, Frankfurt, Salzburg, 1980).

24 Cf. Egil Bakka, 'On the Beginning of Salin's Style I in England', *Universitetet i Bergen Årbok*, Historisk Antikvarisk Rekke III (1958), pp. 1–83.

25 *Olafs Saga hins Helga*, in *Flateyjárbok*, vol. 2, ed. Guthbrandr Vigfusson, C. R. Unger, Norske historiske kildeskriftfondsskrifter IV (Oslo, 1868), pp. 134–5. *Widsith*, ed. Kemp Malone (Copenhagen, 1962).

26 Alfred Boretius, ed., *MGH Capit.* 1, No. 62, cap. 5 (809), p. 150, No. 63, cap. 4 (809), p. 152, No. 71, cap. 4 (811), p. 161. *Laws of Ine*, cap. 39, ed. Liebermann (see note 5), p. 106.

27 *Two of the Saxon Chronicles Parallel*, s. a. 1135, ed. Charles Plummer, vol. 1 (Oxford,

the rural countryside, the change of group structure was one factor affecting the increase of migrations. A curious set of mid-eleventh-century texts illustrates the change. As the record goes, a group of persons in the East Saxon village of Kölbigk was struck by a fatal passion to sing songs and to dance in the local churchyard on Christmas Eve 1020. The dancing continued without interruption for exactly one year until the dancers were relieved from their passion by divine intervention, some of them with lasting pains. It goes without saying that, as it stands, the report does not reveal the actual story. But it contains elements which seem to reflect conditions of real life at this time. For one, it can be accepted that it was understood by other members of the village community that the dancers had violated laws and customs and had been disregardful of their religious obligations. This can be assumed because singing and dancing in the churchyard was a breach of ecclesiastical canons.[28] Doing so on Christmas Eve at the time when services were to be held in the church was also an offence against the churchgoers. Likewise, if the reports encapsulate some truth, the Kölbigk singers and dancers were turned into outcasts after having been relieved from their passion, were expelled from their kin groups and began to wander as solitary migrants through western Europe perhaps reaching such distant places as the monastery of St Edith at Wilton in southern England.[29] News of the Kölbigk incident appeared even in Scandinavian sources.[30]

Some of the migrants seem to have been equipped with letters which contained the license for collecting alms from believers and church institutions. Such a collectant status placed the expellees under the protection of the Church and allowed them to survive as vagrants. As vagrants, they were not only outcasts and bereft of the friends and protectors of their kin groups, but, in the eleventh century, they could no longer join contractual groups. Moreover, the licences of their collectant status identified them so that their place of origin was recognisable wherever they appeared, and they may have faced difficulties settling in a new neighbourhood group. Probably this difficulty accounted for the continuation of their migration. Hence the surviving Kölbigk vagrants seem to have been confined to a solitary life. Moreover, the fact that at least some of the licences granting collectant status appear to have been forged shows that other vagrants who could not claim to have anything to do with the Kölbigk incident bandwagoned and used the incident as a good opportunity to obtain some relief. The experiences of the Kölbigk singers and

---

1892; repr. Oxford, 1952), p. 263. *Vices and Virtues*, vol. 1, ed. Ferdinand Holthausen, Early English Text Society, Original Series LXXXIX (London, 1888; repr. London, 1967), p. 59, 89, 95, 97, 99.

28 Raban Maur, *De magicis artibus* (*PL* 110, cols 1102–3). Burchard of Worms, *Libri decretorum XX*, lib II, int. 54, 56 (*PL* 140, cols 577, 579).

29 This report has been edited by Edward Schröder, 'Die Tänzer von Kölbigk', *Zeitschrift für Kirchengeschichte* XVII (1896/7), pp. 126–30.

30 'Kölbigk och Hagra', ed. Dag Strömbäck, *Arv* XVII (1961), pp. 1–48, XXIV (1968), pp. 91–132.

dancers put on record that in the eleventh-century poor-relief no longer existed as a duty of neighbourhood groups as it had in the eighth century. Instead, poor-relief passed into the competence of the Church.

The Kölbigk incident also demonstrates that peace came to be considered enforceable upon everyone in a given territorial administrative unit or a given urban community regardless of group membership. The maintenance of peace, law and order became an obligation which counted for more than the obligations resulting from membership in certain types of group. Those infringing the peace faced expulsion in the Kölbigk case, capital punishment or imprisonment in others. The wolves who had previously been regarded as the 'friends' of expellees were now associated with capital punishment as the wolf's head became a synonym for the gallows.[31] The most visible signs of the new conceptualisation of peace were the dungeons which emerged at the administrative centres in the hilltop castles of territorial rulers. Prisoners of the territorial rulers were held in custody in these dungeons or, in many of the smaller residences in a carcereal which was located under the ruler's or lord's private chambers. This practice reduced the status of prisoners to the equivalent of the private property of their rulers or lords.[32] Expulsion became more frequently a political instrument at the hands of rulers who wished to declare entire population groups as *personae ingratae*.

With the emergence of urban settlements in towns and cities from the eleventh century, the attitude towards solitary migration changed fundamentally. Much of the population of the rapidly growing urban communities must have been made up from country people who decided to leave their homes in search of better opportunities and conditions of life. The councils of many privileged continental towns and cities responded positively to this motive and applied the legal principle *Stadtluft macht frei* (the air of the town frees a person from his or her previous bonds). This principle implied that councils of towns and cities reserved for themselves the right to accept into the peace of their communities anyone who had arrived on their territory, regardless of previous bonds and ties, provided that he or she had been able to stay within the walls of the town or city for the period of one year and one day. Moreover, during the high and late Middle Ages, rules and customs emerged in the towns and cities which stipulated solitary migration of townspeople. It thus became customary for apprentices of urban artisans, students, technical and medical specialists, as well as musicians and other artists to migrate within the whole of the continent of Europe. Remarkably, the migrants were usually solitary or were members of very small groups, even if they migrated in fulfilment of requirements enforced upon them by their profession. The new attitude towards migration soon spread into the aristocracy, the Church and the peasant farming population. Aristocratic knights established the ideal of moving from court to court in attempts to fight for

---

[31] *Old English Riddle*, No. 55, v. 12, ed. Krapp/Dobbie (see note 5), p. 208.

[32] See Bronislaw Geremek, *Inutiles du monde. Truands et misérables dans l'Europe moderne (1350–1600)* (Paris, 1980), pp. 29–32.

honour and treasures at distant places; or they would join large scale migration movements which, like the Crusades to Palestine or the conquest of areas on the south-eastern shores of the Baltic Sea, combined migration with the execution of military assignments. As late as at the very end of the fifteenth century, the Swabian knight George of Ehingen (1428–1508), a friend of Emperor Maximilian, still adhered to this ideal, combining his willingness to migrate across long distances with a fighting spirit, and sought employment by the King of Portugal in a campaign against Muslims in Africa.[33] In the Catholic Church, special monastic orders were established in the thirteenth century for mendicant friars and migrating preachers, such as the Franciscans. Among the peasant farming population, the fourteenth and fifteenth centuries witnessed a high incidence of solitary migration and migration in small groups which may have involved up to 20 per cent of the residential population in a given area and usually concerned the poor who had to give up their residences in a given settlement.[34] The image of the population of the Middle Ages as immobile, confined to the soil and prone to residentialism is a myth; migration loomed large, although migrants had to make substantial efforts in order to succeed.

In summary, by the fifteenth century, solitary migration was turned into a common and ubiquitous phenomenon. It far outweighed migration in larger groups. Its increase coincided with a general increase in traffic and trade subsequent to the emergence of towns and cities as major trading places. Principally, solitary migration remained a core feature in Europe beyond the end of the Middle Ages, when estimates say that about 10 per cent of populations continued to be migrants.[35] The several migration patterns thus reveal the European population as pretty much on the move and in flux. These patterns varied according to the relative degree of autonomy of the migrants, an autonomy which has been found to have declined among group migrants during the eleventh and twelfth centuries. From that time migrations ceased to be autonomous movements of persons and groups. Other changes were equally significant, namely the rise during the Middle Ages of solitary migration and migrations of very small groups and the decline of migrations of

---

[33] See for an immigration regulation in the Netherlands for Nieuwpoort, 1282: *Oorkondenboek van Holland en Zeeland tot 1299*, vol. 4 (The Hague, Assen, 1997), pp. 333–4. See reports on aristocratic migration: Leo of Rozmital, *Ritter-, Hof- und Pilgerreise 1465–1467*, ed. Johann Andreas Schmeller, Bibliothek des Litterarischen Vereins in Stuttgart VII (Stuttgart, 1844). Georg von Ehingen, *[Itinerarium] Reisen nach der Ritterschaft*, Bibliothek des Litterarischen Vereins in Stuttgart I (Stuttgart, 1842). New edn by Gabriele Ehrmann, vol. 1, Göppinger Arbeiten zur Germanistik CCLXII (Göppingen, 1979), pp. 8–70. English version, *The Diary of Jörg von Ehingen*, ed. Malcom Letts (London, 1929).

[34] Recorded for mid-fifteenth-century Normandy. For demographic inventories, see M. Nortier, *Contribution à l' étude de la population de la Normandie au bas Moyen Age (XIVe–XVIe siècle)*, 4 vols, Cahiers Léopold Delisle XIX, XX, XXII, XXV (Paris, 1970–76).

[35] Cf. Carsten Küther, *Menschen auf der Straße*, Kritische Studien zur Geschichtswissenschaft LVI (Göttingen, 1983).

larger groups within Europe. In consequence of this change, migration became an element of regular business transactions through which communication was established and maintained all across Europe.

Travel

Travel will be discussed here by considering four questions: first, who controlled the travellers? second, how did the travellers organise themselves? third, were travels requested? and fourth, were travels conducted in pursuit of well-defined ends?

Travel, like migration, also displayed the hallmarks of the unusual and the exceptional in the early Middle Ages. The dominant condition under which early post-Migration Age local settlements existed seems to have been the self-sufficiency of the settlement. That is to say that, as a rule, little regular movement of persons across the boundaries of these settlements was necessary. However, it must be assumed that, during the phase of the conversion in the sixth and seventh centuries, not all settlements had churches and not all churches had permanent residential priests, and, consequently, many converts would have been obliged to travel from one settlement to another in order to be able to attend religious services.[36] But, at the time and during the following centuries, the church made considerable efforts to establish a territory-wide network of religious institutions at its own initiative or through the initiatives of wealthy private kin groups. These institutions, mainly religious communities of various kinds and parish churches, were set up for the purpose of providing religious services in as many settlements as possible. By the seventh century, this goal seems to have been accomplished in the core parts of southern Europe, by the eighth century in the core parts of western Europe, by the ninth and tenth centuries in the core parts of central Europe, and, by the eleventh and twelfth centuries in most of the then periphery to the north and east. Despite the length of this process with regard to Europe as a whole, the efforts which were made towards the establishment of parishes and to the building of parish churches show that the church missionary organisers wanted to bring the church to the people so as not to force them to travel across the boundaries of settlements.

Characteristically, on the other hand, the solitary travel of bishops and priests was initially frequent and ubiquitous. In England, for example, the rule that priests had to confine their work to a given diocese was not established

---

36 See the report by the twelfth-century historian William of Malmesbury on Aldhelm, who was successively abbot of Malmesbury and bishop of Sherborne. According to William, Aldhelm used to sing songs on bridges in order to remind newly converted Christian believers of their duty to attend church service when there was no church yet in their own settlement. William of Malmesbury, *De gestis pontificum Anglorum*, cap. 190, ed. N. E. S. A. Hamilton, Rerum Britannicarum medii aevi scriptores LII (London, 1870; repr. New York, 1964), p. 336.

until the tenth century, from which it can be concluded that earlier priests must have travelled extensively. Likewise, some of the early bishoprics were not founded with a diocesan see, but were allocated to political groups, such as the West Saxons, the South Saxons or the East Anglians. Again, this practice implies that the bishop would have to be constantly on the move within and beyond the confines of his diocese. Moreover, bishops tried their best to resist attempts by local rulers to reduce the size of their dioceses. On the many early medieval occasions when rulers tried to intervene in the internal organisation of the dioceses in areas under their control, such as in the case of the establishments of bishoprics at Sherborne, Bath and Wells, Ramsbury, Magdeburg, Gniezno or Bamberg, incumbent bishops made lasting efforts to resist the alienation of their rights and the curbing of their activities. Hence, the clergy were conscious, among others, of the extraordinariness of their capability of travelling and of the privilege of being able to do so. Not surprisingly, in early medieval saints' lives, travelling bishops, first and foremost among them St Wilfrid and St Boniface, were highly praised as persons of outstanding capabilities.[37] This implies that travel was regarded as an autonomous activity in its own right, not merely a means of getting somewhere.

There are also indirect references to the existence of migrant workers already in the time of Charlemagne.[38] But such kinds of travel will have occurred only rarely. Instead, a further case where regular travel was the distinctive hallmark of professional activity was the itinerant ruler. None of the early medieval kingdoms north of the Alps had permanent residential capitals for their rulers, although it was common that rulers had certain preferences in their selection of places to visit.[39] During the fifth and sixth centuries, attempts were made to establish central burial places of royal kin groups, such as the Frankish kings at Saint-Denis or the Ostrogothic kings in Ravenna. But these burial places did not emerge as permanent residential capitals. Although Gregory of Tours reported in the sixth century that Clovis, King of the Franks, had established his capital in Paris in 508, the subsequent partitions of the kingdom prevented Paris from emerging as a permanent residential capital of the Frankish kings during the early Middle Ages.[40] A few rulers of the eighth and ninth centuries tried to establish residential and administrative centres for their courts, first and foremost among them Charlemagne, who tried to develop Aix-la-Chapelle into an imperial centre after the model of the 'Roman' emperors of Byzantium. But Aix-la-Chapelle did not continue long as a 'capital' after Charlemagne's death. Similarly, when King Alfred and his son Edward of Wessex emulated Charlemagne and tried to develop the city of Winchester into a royal residential capital, this effort did

---

37 See above note 22 for Wilfrid and Boniface and cf. Adamnan, *De locis sanctis*, ed. Denis Meehan, Scriptores Latini Hiberniae III (Dublin, 1958).

38 *Capitulare de villis*, cap 67, ed. Alfred Boretius, *MGH Capit.* 1, No. 32, p. 89.

39 Brian Hope-Taylor, *Yeavering*, Department of the Environment. Archaeological Reports VII (London, 1977).

40 Gregory of Tours (see note 10), cap. III/38, pp. 88–9.

not last beyond the tenth century. Thus, in these cases, travelling was a ruler's principal task and it outweighed the competing practical tasks of organising and maintaining a regularised administration. This can only have been the case if it was taken for granted that travel was a major instrument for marking the difference between rulers and common people. Hence it may not have been by chance that in Old Norse poetic tradition, even gods were referred to by names denoting travellers, such as Gangleri, Gangrathr, Vafuthr, Vegtamr or Gestr.[41] Under this condition, decentralised structures of administration existed, mainly in the early Middle Ages but were rare after the eleventh century.

Moreover, it has to be assumed that, unlike migration, regularised travel by itinerant rulers was a well-organised, if not ceremonial, activity with a deictic significance of its own. For the Merovingian Frankish kings, the ritual of travelling around their kingdom was part of the inauguration,[42] and, throughout the Middle Ages, rulers' itineraries were carefully arranged, first, in order to interconnect stopovers at certain places with dates of significance, such as the high Christian festivals, second, in order to meet various and possibly competing demands or expectations from local populations.

Likewise, a particular journey undertaken by a ruler beyond regularised travel could have outstanding effects. The most conspicuous example was the journey undertaken by Emperor Henry IV, who, in the winter of 1076/7, travelled across the Alps to the castle of Canossa in order to seek relief from an excommunication which Pope Gregory VII had inflicted upon him. Because the emperor succeeded in accomplishing the journey, reaching the castle despite difficult weather conditions in the wintry Alps and approached the pope barefooted in a penitential robe, the pope eventually had to receive the emperor and, at least temporarily, settle the dispute. The contemporary descriptions of Henry IV abound with the astonishment that the emperor had been able to resist the hazards of nature and thereby confirm that successful particular journeys were then instruments of politics.[43] Other sources disclose the care with which particular journeys were prepared, as they describe the majestic grace with which the advance took place and show that, on such occasions, speed did not matter.[44]

Remarkably, group travel was rare. As a rule, pilgrimages in groups did not take place, mainly because, up to the tenth century, most cults of saints were

---

[41] The first elements of the dithematic names are derived from appellatives 'gang' and 'va' or 'veg' which mean to walk and the road. The monothematic name is derived from an appellative which means guest. Some of these names are mentioned in the *Nornageststhâttr*, ed. Ernst Wilken, *Die prosaische Edda im Auszuge nebst Völsungasaga und Nornageststhâttr*, vol. 1 (Paderborn, 1887), pp. 240–1.

[42] Einhard, *Vita Karoli Magni*, cap. 1, ed. Oswald Holder-Egger, *MGH SS rer. Germ.* (25), p. 3.

[43] See Lampert of Hersfeld, *Opera*, ed. Oswald Holder-Egger, *MGH SS rer. Germ.* (38), pp. 288–98.

[44] For example, Emperor Otto III's well-prepared journey to Gniezno for the purpose of founding a missionary archbishopric there. See Thietmar, *Chronicon*, cap. IV/45, ed. Robert Holtzmann, *MGH SS rer. Germ.* N. S. 9, pp. 182–4.

Fig. 37 A fourteenth-century horse cart, with three horses, tandem harnessing, horse-collars, traces, cart-saddle, double-shafted vehicle and horseshoes. Luttrell Psalter, London, British Library, Add. Ms. 42130, fol. 162 recto. Reprinted by permission of The British Library.

local and kin-group-related and, therefore, did not warrant long distance travel. Some solitary pilgrimages did occur in the early Middle Ages, but again, the most widely known cases were those of the clergy and rulers who, like Caedwalla and Ine of Wessex, went on pilgrimages after they had abdicated.[45] These cases confirm that travel was an end in itself, not merely an instrumental activity of moving from one place to another.

The late eleventh and particularly the twelfth and thirteenth centuries witnessed an increase in autonomous, instrumental and solitary travel related to trade, which followed the emergence of towns and cities. The increase is demonstrated by the expanding numbers and the increasing frequency of regular markets in towns and cities, by the emergence of the new social group of professional merchants, part of whose business it was to travel, and by guild regulations which stipulated the travel of apprentices as a requirement for their recognition as masters. It occurred jointly with a transport revolution in consequence of which it became possible to use horses more frequently than oxen as hauling animals. Because horses could haul faster than oxen the transport revolution enhanced and sped up trade and, together with it, the communication of persons and groups. Road networks were improved.[46]

Pilgrimages to the major ecclesiastical centres, which could be requested by church institutions as penance for previously committed sins began to multiply during the twelfth and thirteenth centuries and continued to do so throughout the later Middle Ages. Next to a plethora of ecclesiastical centres

---

45 Bede, *Historia ecclesiastica gentis Anglorum*, cap. V/7, ed. Bertram Colgrave, R. A. B. Mynors (Oxford, 1969), pp. 468–72.

46 At the end of the tenth century, Richer of Rheims, *Histoire*, cap. IV/50, ed. Robert Latrouche, vol. 2 (Paris, 1937), pp. 224–30, could still complain about the deplorable condition of a bridge on a road near the town of Meaux. But Emperor Otto II, in 975, threatened to place a ban on anyone who would dare to wilfully destroy bridges or obstruct passage on imperial roads. *MGH DD Otto II*, Nr. 112, p. 126.

and local places, Rome emerged as the overall destination for pilgrimages together with Santiago de Compostela in northern Spain. Specific maps were drawn directing pilgrims to these places. The map in Figure 38, printed in 1502, is one such example.

Residential capitals emerged from the eleventh century in Capetian France, at Paris, and in Norman England, at Westminster and London, for Bohemia in Prague, for Hungary in Buda and Pest, for Portugal in Lisbon, for Sweden in Stockholm, for Denmark in Copenhagen and for Poland in Krakow. Inside the Empire, where the emperors continued the practice of regularised travel, residences of territorial principalities emerged, among others, at Munich for Bavaria, at Dresden for Saxony, at Brunswick for the Welfs, at Brussels for Burgundy, while Mainz, Trier and Cologne developed into administrative centres of the ecclesiastical electorates. In northern Italy, the larger cities established themselves as the centres of territorial rule, mainly Venice, Florence and Milan, but also Genoa, Modena, Ferrara and Siena. These places necessarily attracted professional traders and peasant farmers as travellers to within their walls with the implication that solitary travel began to increase dramatically. An early, though rare, case of ruler-stipulated travel is recorded in late tenth-century England where, in 975, a monetary reform was inaugurated according to which residents in an area of about thirty miles around a mint were requested to travel to the mint once in a period of three years in order to exchange old coins for new.[47] However, solitary travel at the request of rulers remained uncommon during the Middle Ages. That this was so can be inferred from the astonishment which, in the early fourteenth century, met Marco Polo's report of the existence in China of a regular postal service through mounted messengers. According to Marco Polo, these messengers were equipped with bells which helped clear the way for the speedy travel of the messengers. In the fourteenth century popular fictitious travel report about Sir John Mandeville, Marco Polo's description was briefly repeated.[48]

Nevertheless, increasing traffic is indirectly recorded by the rise of commercial inns along major roads, the maintenance of hospitals at conspicuous or potentially dangerous places such as mountain passes as well as the organisation of bridge building and bridge maintenance work.[49] Moreover, in the twelfth century, travellers began to extend the geographical scope of their activities, and in the fourteenth century, the literary genres of descriptive travel reports and fictitious travel literature rose to popularity and prominence. Moreover, Boccaccio's *Novellae* and Geoffrey Chaucer's *Canterbury Tales* show that poets liked to posit fiction in scenes of travel. This litera-

---

[47] See Henry Richards Luard, ed., *Flores Historiarum*, vol. 1, Rerum Britannicarum medii aevi scriptores XCV (London, 1890; repr. New York, 1965), p. 514.

[48] Marco Polo, *The Description of the World*, cap. 98, ed. Arthur Christopher Moule, Paul Pelliot (London, 1938), pp. 242–7. *Mandeville's Travels . . . Edited from Ms Cotton Tiberius C XVI* ed. P. Hamelin, vol. 1, Early English Text Society. Original Series CLIII (London, 1919; repr. London,1960), p. 160.

[49] Evidence for the latter is in the Mainz peace of 1235, cap. 7, in Ludwig Weiland, ed., *MGH Const.* 2, No. 196, p. 243.

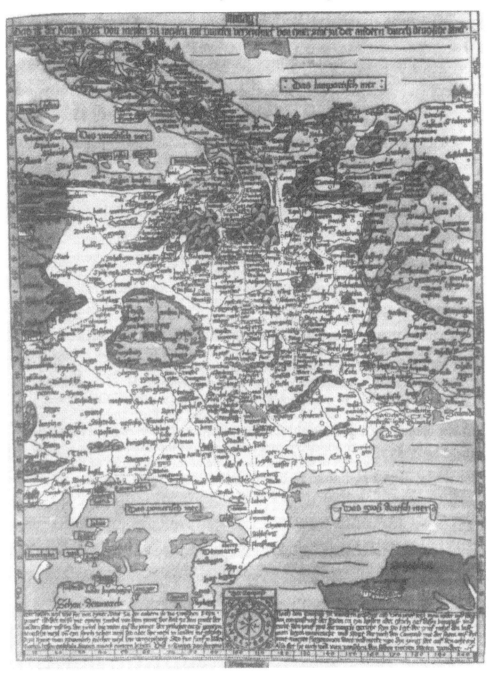

Fig. 38 Harald Etzlaub, map of roads leading to Rome, printed broadsheet, Nuremberg 1502. The map has Rome in the south at the top and Jutland at the bottom. It emphasises the major Alpine mountain passes as convenient roads leading to Rome.

ture contains evidence that travellers still took the activity of travelling to be of importance for its own sake, while they began to experience a certain joy or feeling of relief on their trips. A kind of tourist industry began to flourish which provided written tour guides, *devotionalia*, commemorative coins and medals and local food specialities. Nevertheless, travel in larger groups was extremely rare and, consequently, of high political significance when it occurred. One conspicuous case was the journey which was undertaken by King Edward III of England who travelled together with his court on the Continent from 1338 to 1340 for the purpose of seeking allies in his campaigns against the French king during the early phase of the Hundred Years War.

Solitary and group travel has been described here not only in terms of autonomy and organisation as a group or solitary enterprise, but also in terms of instrumentality and regularity. This has been done because, contrary to migration, travel may be and frequently was a recurrent phenomenon. Up to the end of the Middle Ages and beyond, travel appeared to have been undertaken autonomously by solitary travellers who could be priests, bishops, rulers or producers and other professional specialists who regarded travelling as an end in itself. Not withstanding the quantitative increase in travel from the eleventh and twelfth centuries, its qualitative continuity is remarkable because, for three centuries or so after the end of the Middle Ages, territorial rulers did little to curb or reduce such manifestations of personal autonomy. While the autonomy of travellers remained a constant feature, its instrumentality obtained a different quality with the emergence of professional merchant trading. In this context, travel became a purposeful and goal-oriented action which served to move people back and forth among the urban communities of towns and cities. Non-instrumental travel came to be associated with leisurely conducted movements[50] such as those described in the late medieval travel literature and which was similar to the tourism of the twentieth century. By contrast, requested travel did not loom large during the entire Middle Ages although it did occur on occasions.

---

[50] Early records on leisure journeys date from the fifteenth century. Gian Francesco Poggio di Guccio Bracciolini (1380–1459), secretary to the papal *nuntius* at the Council of Constance (1414–18) wrote to a friend in Florence about an excursion which had taken him to the spa at Baden (Aargau, Switzerland) in 1417, and he gave an impression of the pleasures which one could experience on leisure journeys. See Bracciolini, *Die Bäder zu Baden in der Schweiz* (s.l., 1780). Cf. Lothar Schmidt, ed., *Die Renaissance in Briefen von Dichtern, Künstlern, Staatsmännern, Gelehrten und Frauen*, vol. 1 (Leipzig, 1909), pp. 104–18. Likewise, the late medieval *Volksbuch Till Eulenspiegel* contained a scene where the hero goes on a journey to visit public baths. See *Eyn kurtzweilig lesen von Dyl Ulenspiegel*, reprint of the first printed edn (Strasbourg, 1515), ed. Hermann Knust, Neudrucke deutscher Literaturwerke des XVI. und XVII. Jahrhunderts LVI (Halle, 1884), fol. XCVIII.

Conclusion

Migration and travel as models of the movement of persons and groups display certain similarities. Movements in groups sharply declined after the sixth century and have been a rare phenomenon inside Europe since then. By contrast, solitary migration as well as all forms of travel dramatically and continuously increased from the eleventh and twelfth centuries. These changes occurred simultaneously with the changes in communicative habits discussed in the previous two chapters: namely the reduction of orality to the benefit of literacy as types of practical communication from person to person, and the acceptance of universalist principles informing the 'hot' type of commemorating the past. The literalisation of communication between persons, the universalisation of the commemoration of the past and the expansion of solitary migration and travel jointly extended the space of communication beyond the confines of divinely ordained time periods, local settlements and particularist kin groups.

IMAGES OF ORDER

General Introduction

In the following two chapters, I intend to describe two types of change: first, the change from a group-centered to a person-centered education of the young; second, the change from a group-centered to a space-centered concept of the socio-political environment. I intend to describe these changes by way of asking the following types of question: first, how was order perceived as being maintained in the succession of the generations as an aspect of time? second, to what end was order considered as having to be maintained in group relations? Hence, changes of the images of order shall be described and analysed in connection with the categories of time and group. These descriptions will historicise concepts which are commonly regarded as pertaining to the sociology of education and to political science.

Next to the categories of time and group, major changes of the experiences and attitudes towards the physical environment have been described already in previous chapters. Hence, they need be recapitulated here only in brief. In the early Middle Ages, attitudes towards the physical environment were shaped by the experience that the physical environment was hostile to humankind, divinely ordained, and that human beings had no power of changing it. In order to overcome resistance by and obstacles in the physical environment, people believed in the need to unite themselves in groups under the leadership of an outstanding person with extraordinary powers and energy. Hence large-scale migrations, long-distance travel, specifically across the seas, and the clearing of woodlands were undertaken in the context of a wide-spread sentiment that one's local settlement, the kin groups and the neighbourhood groups therein and in other settlements, were and ought to be the stable configurations in which a person's life was to take place. Consequently, up to the tenth century, long-distance travel was rare, and long-distance trade was in the hands of specialists who sought to organise themselves as political groups with their own traditions. Likewise, the woodlands into which a large number of the settlements on the Continent north of the Alps were carved were left uncultivated as no man's lands and were used mainly for pasture and for the gathering of fruits and wood for fuel. Although a phase of the afforestation of woodland and the subsequent clearing of parts of it swept across the Continent from the eighth to the eleventh century and the number as well as the size of settlements increased, there was still much upland or otherwise less favourable land left in reserve, and the remaining woods themselves were no more than rarely inhabited. The physical environment was thus perceived as static and subject to no other ordering power than divine will.

During the eleventh and twelfth centuries, this attitude towards the physical environment underwent a fundamental change. The newly founded hilltop castles, on the one hand, and the urban communities of towns and cities, on the other, were visual demonstration of the willingness of their residents to create their own human-made environment which was architecturally separated from the surrounding physical environment. Likewise, woodlands developed into economic units and became grounds for hunting and gathering as well as areas of specialised, non-agricultural production. Among the products were game, minerals, charcoal and the variety of products which required hydraulic energy. Because the producers were not agriculturalists themselves, they had to live on foodstuffs which they obtained from villages or towns in the vicinity. Thus, markets emerged where professionals in the woodlands, such as charcoal burners or miners, could sell their products in return for victuals and other necessities of life. In consequence, the woodlands became subjected to the administrative control of territorial rulers or the councils of towns and cities in their vicinity. Boundaries within the woodlands needed to be demarcated with precision, which implied that the woodlands became part of administratively organised space. During the thirteenth century, farmers in southern Europe, specifically on the Iberian peninsula, began to develop extensive irrigation systems under Arabic influence for the purpose of expanding arable lands and agricultural production.[1] During the same century, farmers in Italy added to this the further goal of extending water-bound traffic through the building of canal systems in Lombardy which were fed by the Alpine rivers. During the fourteenth century, efforts were begun to measure distances across the seas so as to make navigation predictable. Nautical charts or portolan charts were made which listed the distances in direct line between two ports so as to allow calculations about the time which a voyage between two ports could be expected to take. In this capacity, the physical environment, represented by the woodlands and the seas, lost its aura of hostility and impenetrability. In lieu of the *tremendum* with which the physical environment had been approached during the early Middle Ages, an attitude emerged according to which the physical environment could and ought to be subjected to human control in order to be exploited for human needs. The attitude towards the physical environment ceased to be group-centred and, instead, became space-centred.

During the fifteenth century, the new attitude was widened into the quest for the subjection of the human-made as well as the physical environments to certain geometrical shapes. The previously strict separation of the human-made and the physical environments was given up. Designs emerged according to which the architecture of towns could respond to certain features of the surrounding landscape.

A good case is the Italian town of Pienza which was rebuilt during the second half of the fifteenth century according to the design of Pope Pius II

---

[1] Yaha Ibn Muhammad, called Ibn al-Awwam, *Le livre de l'agriculture*, vol. 1 (Paris, 1866), pp. 117–34, 510–36.

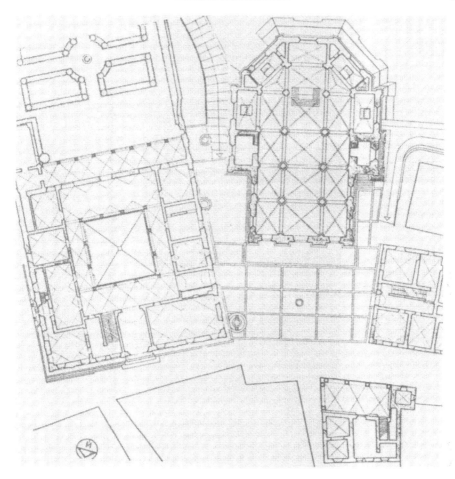

Fig. 39 Ground plan of the town centre of Pienza, in accordance with the designs made by Pope Pius II around 1460 for the rebuilding of his birthplace. From Luciano Finelli, Sara Rossi, *Pienza. Tra ideologia e realtà* (Bari, 1979), Fig. 91. Reprinted by permission.

(who was born there in 1405 and derived the new name of the town from the name which he had chosen for himself when ascending to the papal throne). The design was in accord with mid- and late fifteenth-century urban planning, as it resembled the prospect of an ideal city drawn by Piero della Francesca (c. 1415–92) around 1470. The town centre was arranged geometrically around a square which was open to one side, facing the landscape.

Among the grandest schemes of the age for the ordering of settlements and landscapes were the design for the fortification of Florence by Filippo Brunelleschi (1377–1446) and the proposal suggested by Leonardo da Vinci (1452–1519) to make Florence accessible to ship from the Mediterranean Sea. Leonardo proposed to the city council of Florence around 1500 AD the building of a canal from Florence that would pass through the Serra Valle

Fig. 40 Plan of an ideal city, attributed to Piero della Francesca. c. 1470. Urbino, Galleria Nazionale delle Marche, Palazzo Ducale.

mountains via a tunnel and rejoin the Arno valley immediately east of Pisa.[2] In order permanently to feed the canal with water, Leonardo made the further suggestion of tapping the upper Tiber, letting a part of its water run through a tunnel into Lake Trasimeno, extending this lake into a large reservoir in the Val di Chiara and connecting the reservoir by another canal to the Arno.[3] Although Leonardo modelled his proposal on the late medieval Lombard canal system, the confidence in his own newly acquired competence in hydraulics induced him to devise a scheme which was far more extensive than his model and would have subjected large parts of the central Italian landscape to a human-made order, had it been carried out.

Geometrical patterns and large-scale ordering schemes made visible human control over the physical environment and, at the same time, conveyed the visual impression of evenness, equilibrium and lack of changeability. As in the early Middle Ages, the physical environment was still considered to be essentially static. However, in contrast to the early Middle Ages, in the fifteenth and the immediately following centuries, the static order was regarded as having been imposed by human will.

---

2   Paris, Bibliothèque Nationale, Codex Atlanticus, fol. 46 recto–verso. Formerly Milan, Biblioteca Ambrosiana.
3   Windsor Castle, Ms. 12682.

XII

Images of Order I:
The Old and the Young

dat sagetun mi usere liuti . . . dat Hiltibrant haetti min fater: ih
heittu Hadubrant. forn her ostar giweit, floh her Otachres nid, hina
miti Theotrihhe enti sinerodegano filu.*

– Hildebrandslied

Introduction

The temporal aspect of order manifests itself through generation change.
Everybody's life span provides the experience of ageing and, in consequence
of that, a power transition from parents to children within kin groups and
from seniors to juniors in other types of groups. These power transitions are
steered by a conceptual framework of norms and rules which is not in itself
stable. Its changes render temporary the norms and rules through which
power passes from the old to the young.

Late nineteenth- and twentieth-century attitudes towards the old and the
young are characterised by the expectation that, under normal conditions,
death occurs most frequently in old age whereas sudden deaths of adolescents
or even adults through illness, warfare, criminal homicide or accidents are
taken to be an unusual and grave tragedy. Substantive and successful efforts
have been made to reduce mortality before old age. Because the occurrence of
death is primarily associated with old age the elderly are usually perceived as
frail, idle and ill, and this perception implies that the power transition from
the old to the young is expected to take place at the time of death. However,
prior to the nineteenth century, death was a ubiquitous event which was of
concern for everyone. Not only infant mortality was high; members of all
other age groups faced a high risk of death. Since there was no age-specific
mortality risk, there was also no particularly close association of death with
old age and different means for enacting the power transition from the old to
the young were employed.

---

* This I was told by our people . . . that my father was called Hildebrand: I am called
Hadubrand. Long ago he went to the east, he fled Otacher's hatred, away with Dietrich
and many of his warriors.

Age-grade Schemes

Sensitivity to the ubiquity of death could be more or less explicit. In the later Middle Ages and during the sixteenth century, such sensitivity was high and was recorded in *memento mori* sermons and the art and literature on death dance. These sermons, works of poetic literature and pieces of pictorial art were conceived, not as a comfort about untimely death, but as a warning that, since death could occur at any time, everyone should be prepared and conduct his or her life with the expectation of its impending end. They were also an implicit reminder that the world without death was the world of fairy tales.

Age was defined by a variety of different systems. The most popular schematic division of age grades during the Middle Ages was informed by the work of the Elder Seneca (c. 55 BC–AD 40) and consisted of five grades. Seneca's original scheme of 'infancy, boyhood, adolescence, young age and old age' was amplified in the late fourth century by St Augustine who distinguished two grades of old age, namely the age of the advanced years and senility. Presumably, St Augustine opted for six age grades because he wanted to equate the six age grades with the six world ages and the six creation days of the Biblical tradition.[1] In any case, St Augustine's age grades became canonised in the seventh century by Isidore who inserted them in his encyclopaedia.[2] These schematic age grades were conspicuous for their absence of a distinct concept of adult age as the intermediary between young and old age. Among the many later references to the Augustinian–Isidorian age-grade scheme were the fourteenth-century exegesis of the Bible by the Parisian theologian Jean Hesdin (dec. after 1378).[3] This age-grade scheme informed the perception that the power transition from the old to the young occurred directly without any intermediating age. However, by the turn of the sixteenth century, the three-generation residential family of grandparents, parents and children had become the most common type of kin group in the aristocracy as well as the inhabitants of towns and cities. It had grown powerful enough to inform the new perception that the generation change no longer occurred

1   Augustine, *De vera religione*, cap. I/26 (*PL* 34, col. 145): 'infantia, pueritia, adolescentia, iuventus, aetas senioris, deterior aetas'. The same identification of the six age grades with the six world ages occurred in a late medieval stained-glass window of Christ Church Cathedral, Canterbury. The window depicts the miracle of the wedding of Cana during which, according to the legend in the Gospel of John, six barrels of water were converted into wine. The Canterbury picture displays the barrels as the six human ages and the six world ages.

2   Isidore, *Etymologiarum sive originum libri XX*, cap. XI/2, ed. W. M. Lindsay (Oxford, 1911); he added cycles of seven years to each age grade: infantia, 0–7; pueritia, 7–14; adolescentia, 14–28; iuventus, 28–49, aetas senioris, 49–70; senectus, 70–. Cf. Raban Maur, *De universo libri XXII*, cap. VII/1 (*PL* 111, col. 179): 'infantia, pueritia, adolescentia, juventus, gravitas, senectus'.

3   Ed. Rolf Sprandel, *Altersschicksal und Altersmoral. Die Geschichte der Einstellungen zum Altern nach der Pariser Bibelexegese*, Monographien zur Geschichte des Mittelalters XXII (Stuttgart, 1981), pp. 164–86.

Fig. 41 The six ages of life. Book illumination for Psalm 89, c. 1300. From a psalter gloss, Paris, Bibliothèque nationale de France, Ms. fonds lat. 8846, fol. 161 recto. Cliché Bibliothèque nationale de France, Paris.

Fig. 42 Cornelis Visscher, The nine ages of life, seventeenth century. Single sheet, Rotterdam, Atlas Van Stolk, Historical Museum Rotterdam.

directly from the old to the young but indirectly from the old to some intermediate group of family members who were no longer young but not yet old. The new extension of the scheme became possible after the Augustinian–Isidorian age-grade scheme had lost its association with the world ages and allowed its extension beyond the number of six grades. The resulting scheme of seven age grades was used, among others, by Shakespeare and it was featured frequently in other verbal and pictorial sources during the sixteenth and seventeenth centuries.[4] Other schemes were developed which divided adulthood into several distinct age grades and therefore contained even higher numbers.[5] The conceptualisation of adulthood as a distinct age grade or set of age grades had the important consequences that the adults acted as the intermediaries between the old and the young, that the young and the old mutually no longer depended on each other, but that both depended on the adults. The new schemes also informed the perception that the power transi-

---

4 William Shakespeare, *As You Like It*, II/7 (various editions).
5 For example, ten age grades: Abraham a Sancta Clara, *Hui und Pfui in der Welt* (Passau, 1836), p. 473.

tion occurred from the ageing to adults and was of no concern for the young. Instead, adult age could be described and depicted as the peak of a person's life, as the picture in Figure 42 suggests.

Moreover, the various age grades had a legal significance in the respect that they determined the beginning of legal accountability which was variously fixed at the ages of 12, 15, 18 or 20 years, depending on the period and the social group in which they were applied.[6] However, determining the precise age of a person was difficult because birth dates were rarely recorded before the nineteenth century and because baptism was usually dated in terms of the day and the month, but not of the year in which it had occurred. Hence the assessment of a person's age depended on certain physical features and patterns of behaviour. Among them were the weaning from the mother's breast as a sign for the end of infancy, and the growing of a beard as well as the end of formal schooling as signs of the end of adolescence. Therefore, relatively rough age grades appeared preferable over precisely counted life years.

Controlling the Kin: the old and the young in the early Middle Ages

Medieval laments about the labours of old age are legion and occurred frequently in the context of the exegesis of the Bible, particularly of Psalm 89.[7] There were also explicitly misogerontic norms which restricted the rights of the old.[8] But such statements should not be misunderstood as implying that the old were principally approached with disrespect and purposeful neglect. For the laments about old age stood against the practice of kin groups which cherished their own traditions of descent. This was so because such kin groups were in need of old members who could know and transmit traditions to the subsequent generations. Moreover, to the extent that these traditions were the carriers of legal and moral norms, persons in charge of transmitting and interpreting these traditions authentically must have been invested with power. From the early Middle Ages, there are concrete cases which display the difficulties which could threaten the existence of kin groups without old members. Although such evidence is extant only from a number of royal kin groups, the principal difficulty must have been the same in all tradition-transmitting and legitimacy-conveying kin groups. The difficult condition of the Ostrogothic royal kin group of the Amali after the death of Theoderic in 526 is, at least in part, due to the absence of any influential senior descendant

6 For example, *Lex Visigothorum*, cap. X/1, 17 (12 years), ed. Karl Zeumer, *MGH LL nat. Germ.* 1, p. 389. *Golden Bulla of 1356*, cap. VII/4 (18 years), ed. Wolfgang D. Fritz, *Die Goldene Bulle Kaiser Karls IV. vom Jahre 1356*, MGH Fontes iuris Germ. ant. 11, p. 62. *Sachsenspiegel*, Landrecht, Book I, cap. 42, 1 (20 years), ed. Karl August Eckhardt, *MGH Fontes iuris Germ. Ant.* N. S. 1, 1, p. 105.

7 For the tenth century, see Remigius, MS Paris, Bibliothèque Nationale, Fonds Lat. 546. For the thirteenth century, see John of La Rochelle, *Commentary on Psalms*, Paris, Bibliothèque Nationale, Fonds Lat. 15602/15603. Ed. Sprandel (see note 3), pp. 86, 87.

8 *Sachsenspiegel* (see note 6), cap. Book I, cap. 52, 2, pp. 109–10.

of Theoderic who would be capable of preventing domestic strife among the Ostrogoths before their eventual defeat by Byzantine armies. Later evidence comes from the British Isles, where, from the beginning of the ninth century, the Mercian kingdom was shaken by several succession crises which, eventually, led to the extinction of the Mercian royal kin group in conjunction with the destruction of the kingdom itself.[9] Hence the absence of old persons as the authoritative transmitters of traditions must have proffered domestic strife. Consequently, it is difficult to believe that, in the early Middle Ages, the old were subjected to deliberately harsh treatment on the part of the younger generations, if the continuity of the kin group should depend on the power and longevity of its senior members.

There is further, although indirect, evidence for the active role of senior kin-group members of either sex in the transmission of group-bound traditions. A well-known case is the late ninth-century biography of the West Saxon King Alfred by Bishop Asser, who wrote that Alfred's mother Osburh made him commemorate 'Carmina Saxonica', that is vernacular oral traditions which had been entrusted to Osburh for transmission.[10] Asser thus provided the information that Alfred's mother had wanted to make sure that her son would himself be invested with the power to transmit these traditions, and Asser went on to remark that Alfred picked them up eagerly and memorised them with care. The point of the remark, however, is that Asser says that this happened during Alfred's youth, at a time when his mother could not possibly have foreseen that Alfred, her youngest son, would eventually succeed to the throne. It can thus be assumed that Osburh will have made the same efforts towards her other sons, even though Asser did not record these efforts. Presumably, Asser did not do so because, to him, what was important was solely the fact that Alfred, as the eventual ruler of Wessex, had been equipped with the capability of acting as the transmitter of kin-group-bound oral traditions. This allows the further assumption that, still at the turn of the tenth century, senior members of a kin group acted as the authoritative transmitters of oral traditions and that knowledge of these traditions was regarded as one condition for succession to rule.

The same principle was also applied to other royal kin groups and, in these cases, the evidence is even earlier. For example, in the eighth-century *Life of St Guthlac*, the saint, a descendant from an Anglian royal kin group, is described in his youth as having become acquainted with what the hagiographer termed the 'vain talk of old women, the empty fables of uneducated folk or of boorish

---

9 The Mercian kings Beornwulf (823–5), Ludeca (825–7), Wiglaf (827–9, 830–40), Beorhtwulf (840–52), Burgred (852–c. 874) and Ceolwulf II (874–before 883) are of unknown origin. Wiglaf fled the kingdom after losing a war against King Ecgbehrt of Wessex in 829, but recovered the kingdom in 830. Beorhtwulf was driven out in 852, Burgred fled, probably in 874, and Ceolfwulf II died under unknown circumstances at an unknown date.

10 Asser, *Life of King Alfred*, cap. 2, ed. William Henry Stevenson (Oxford, 1904), p. 4 (repr., ed. Dorothy Whitelock [Oxford, 1959]).

songs'.[11] *Prima facie*, the hagiographer displayed his contempt for the practice which he described, but it is evident that such contempt was conditioned by the literary conventions informing hagiographical writing. Within these conventions, only the literary traditions associated with the Bible could be approved, which means that, what Guthlac (c. 674–714) had been told was made up from traditions of non-Christian origin. Hence we can assume that vernacular oral traditions were transmitted in Guthlac's kin group. Remarkably, in both cases, transmitters of these traditions were identified as senior women.

Norse sagas of the high Middle Ages display some of the conditions under which the old could be treated as important. One such condition must have been that old age be combined with the ability of moving around and leading an active life. Characteristically, the old transmitters of oral traditions were highly esteemed as travellers at a time when travelling required strong physical energies. That is to say that aged travellers were not primarily highly esteemed for being old, but that they were regarded as important because, under the condition of their old age, they retained a full capacity to act so that they could travel long distances. This is a view which also prevailed in scholastic theological perceptions of the old as respectable when, and as long as, they were able and willing to work.[12] Obviously, not everyone was as potent as Jacob who, according to Genesis 49: 33, gave his last orders to his children, rested his feet on his bed and died. Nevertheless, early medieval reports of high-ranking, respected and powerful aged persons awaiting their death abound with praises of their continuing activity right to the end. Bede, for one, was hailed for having fulfilled his duties as a teacher right up to his death,[13] and Abbot Eigil of Fulda (c. 750–822) was revered for having begun to dig his own grave immediately before he became incapacitated and passed away.[14] William the Conqueror (1027/28–87) was renowned for having been completely capable of speaking and using his senses fully during the six weeks of his illness before his death.[15] Thus the old as members of kin and contractual groups and as holders of high offices seem to be have been respected when and as long as they could perform their duties. By contrast, the frequent laments about old age seem to have focused on frailty because it was prohibitive of the active life which was requested from the young as well as the old.

Another condition was that a kin group existed in which traditions were considered as group-preserving instruments that, in other words, there were young kin-group members who wanted or were required to continue the kin

---

11 Felix, *Life of Saint Guthlac*, cap XII–XIII, ed. Bertram Colgrave (Cambridge, 1956; repr. Cambridge, 1985), p. 78

12 Remigius (see note 7), p. 86.

13 Cuthbert's Letter on the Death of Bede, in Bede, *Historia ecclesiastica gentis Anglorum*, ed. Bertram Colgrave, R. A. B. Mynors (Oxford, 1969), pp. 579–87.

14 *Vita Eigilis*, cap. 25, ed. Georg Waitz, *MGH SS* 15, pp. 221–33.

15 Orderic Vitalis, *Ecclesiastical History*, cap. VII/14–15, vol. 4, ed. Marjorie Chibnall (Oxford, 1973), pp. 98–107.

group, care for the old and to receive the kin-group traditions from the old. This condition will have been self-evident for most kin groups throughout much of the early Middle Ages, but it became problematic in connection with church-stipulated attempts towards the reduction of the influence of the kin groups and the numbers of their members. Early medieval hagiography, for example, abounded with reports about the separation of the saint from the traditions and the entourage of his or her kin group at an early age. Best known is the report on Wynfrith, who later called himself Boniface. Wynfrith's eighth-century hagiographer made him quarrel with his parents as an adolescent. While his parents were described as determined not to allow their son to enter church service, Boniface was made to ignore all their arguments and to overcome all their threats, pressures and cries for sympathy. He eventually left home for good in order to lead a monastic life.[16] Although much of that may have been topically over-dramatised in this particular case, the topos itself is characteristic because it suggests that separation from the kin group at a young age was regarded as an important early indicator in the life of a saint for his or her determination to devote his or her life to the Church and to act against the interests of the kin group.

In another case, the departure of young kin members for church service was explicitly interconnected with the conversion to Christianity and eventual dissolution of a group. In the ninth-century *Life of St Liudger*, a Frisian born missionary who became Bishop of Munster (c. 742–809), a report is included about the birth of Liudger's mother Liafburh. Liafburh's paternal grandmother, a pagan woman, had wanted to have a grandson, and when she learned that her daughter-in-law had given birth to a daughter, namely Liafburh, she dispatched a number of warriors, whom she had told to murder the infant Liafburh, to the home of her daughter-in-law. Indeed, the warriors were about to drown the infant in a bucket when, with miraculous powers, the infant began to cling to the rim of the bucket and was saved by a woman in the neighbourhood who heard young Liafburh's screams. Thus Liafburh survived to give birth later to two future saints, Liudger and Hildigrim, Bishop of Châlons-sur-Marne and the rector of Halberstadt (dec. 827).[17] The old pagan woman was described as making an effort for the preservation of the kin group, and this effort was associated by the hagiographer with her preference for a grandson over a granddaughter. Remarkably, nothing is reported about the religion of the second generation, namely Liafburh's father and mother; but from similar cases, it may be inferred that Liafburh's mother

---

[16] Wilhelm Levison, ed., *Vitae Sancti Bonifatii archiepiscopi Moguntini*, cap. 1, *MGH SS rer. Germ.* (57), pp. 5–6. Apparently, one of the arguments of the parents was that, if Boniface left, they would have to live in misery when growing old. Similarly, *Vita S. Rusticulae sive Marciae*, cap. 5, ed. Bruno Krusch, *MGH SS rer. Merov.* 4, p. 342. In this case, the saint's mother complained that she had no one to rely on in her old age.

[17] Altfrid, *Life of St Liudger*, ed. Georg Heinrich Pertz, *MGH SS* 2, p. 406.

was a Christian, while her father was not.[18] That Liafburh was a Christian cannot be doubted because she allowed her two sons to enter church service; after this happened, the kin group became extinct. The only kind of respect that Liafburh could earn derived from her role as the mother of saints, for she no longer had any opportunity to act or be revered as the transmitter of vernacular oral traditions. In this case, the extirpation of a pre-Christian traditional kin group is described across four generations.

Both reports thus confirm that devoting one's life to church service at a young age could interrupt the usual power transition from the old to the young in tradition-bound kin groups. In these cases, the kin groups, specifically their old members, became subject to the care and the mercy of the Church. But opting for church service against the biblical Fifth Commandment was rare in the early Middle Ages because it occurred with frequency only in connection with the making of future saints. There are even a number of seventh-century saints' lives which confirm the perseverance of parent–child relations also in a monastic environment. For one, St Sadlaberga (fl. 640), abbess of the monastery of Laon, devoted her children to the Church but took great care that her daughter Anstrudis succeeded her in office. Likewise, St Gertrud of Nivelle (c. 626–59), daughter of Itta or Iduberga (dec. 652) and the Frankish *Majordomus* Pippin I (dec. 639/40), received much support from her mother who actually donated substantive funds from her own property to the newly established monastery.[19] Hence the reports of runaway youths turned into saints confirm the otherwise prevailing custom of revering the old when and as long as they could act as transmitters of kin-group-bound oral traditions during the early Middle Ages. In cases where royal and aristocratic kin groups established themselves as owners of proprietary monasteries, the pre-Christian process of power transition from the old to the young remained in force as long as the kin groups stayed in control of their institutions. But as soon as the old were deprived of their role as transmitters of tradition because the kin groups declined, the power of the old over the young declined proportionately.

Thus, during the centuries of the conversion to Catholicism the Church strove to attract the young rather than on the old. For the old were regarded as sources of traditionalism and potential or actual opponents against the new religion. With increasing frequency from the eighth century,[20] conversion to Catholicism and entrance into church service were interconnected with the transfer of property rights from the kin groups to church institutions, so that

---

18 A similar case was reported by Bede (see note 13), cap. II/5, p. 150, regarding the conversion of King Aethelberht of Kent.

19 *Vita S. Sadlabergae abbatissae*, cap. 11–12, ed. Bruno Krusch, *MGH SS rer. Merov.* 5, pp. 55–6. *Vita S. Gertrudis virginis A*, cap. 2, ed. Bruno Krusch, *MGH SS rer. Merov.* 2, pp. 455–6.

20 In his fifth century *Regula sanctarum virginum*, cap. 7, 18 (*PL* 67, cols 1108, 1109–10), Bishop Caesarius of Arles prescribed that novices entering monasteries should donate their property, and he anticipated that the recipient would be the monastery into which a novice had been accepted.

old kin members lost their role as inheritors of property and traditions and the kin groups were alienated from at least part of the material basis of their existence.[21] To the young, the Church also offered an alternative way of learning, namely the absorption of knowledge through the reading of written texts. Young children would enter church institutions for the purpose of being taught by the clergy, sometimes monks and nuns, how to read and to write.[22] Thus learning to read and to write implied a departure from the orally transmitted kin-group traditions and a switch towards the work and the rules of the clergy. There are several pieces of evidence which show that clashes occurred between parents and children when the latter wanted to learn how to read and to write. In these cases, the parents tried to resist their children's wishes or agreed to such plans only under the condition that, after becoming literate, the children would return to the authority of their kin group. These cases concerned boys and girls alike.[23] Initially, the kin groups reacted by involving church institutions in rituals for the care of the soles of deceased kin members. Their names were registered in the so-called *libri memoriales*, that is, books which were kept in monasteries from the ninth to the twelfth centuries and contained the names of donors and their relatives. Monasteries became the recipients of donations under the condition that the monks and nuns would continuously have to say prayers for the souls of the deceased donors. Thus the *libri memoriales* reflected an attempt at the preservation of kin tradition in a monastic environment and under the authority of the Church. Rulers and members of the higher aristocracy were included in the ranks of these donors.[24]

But these policies could only retard the eventual fragmentation of the kin groups. At the latest with the falling from use of the *libri memoriales* in the twelfth century, kin groups as larger non-resident groups lost their competence for the revering of the old as the transmitters of group-bound oral traditions and for educating the young through the authoritative transmission of these traditions. Under these conditions, children grew up to become embedded in a network of bonds and ties represented by various persons at different places. The variety of these persons ranged far beyond the members of a three-generation nuclear family, namely parents and grandparents and would include not only collateral relatives, but also age cohorts. Adolescents could join such age cohorts if they were dissatisfied or if they could approach

21 Early records are extant among the St Gall charters, ed. Hermann Wartmann, *Urkundenbuch der Abtei Sanct Gallen*, part 1 (Zurich, 1863), No. 1. The *Vita S. Rusticulae*, cap. 5 (see note 16), p. 342, referred to the difficulties for old kin members had no one to devise and bequeath their property to if their children opted for monastic life.

22 Caesarius of Arles (see note 20), cap. 5, col. 1108, prescribed that novices in monasteries should learn how to read and to write.

23 Bruno Krusch, Wilhelm Levison, ed., *MGH SS rer. Merov.* 7, p. 9. *MGH SS* 15, p. 68 (a report about Gregory of Utrecht who wanted to follow St Boniface).

24 See, for example, Karl Schmid, ed., 'Die Verbrüderungsbücher', in Schmid, Michael Borgolte, Dieter Geuenich, eds, *Subsidia Sangallensia*, vol. 1, St Galler Kultur und Geschichte XVI (St Gall, 1986), pp. 81–276.

relatives at different places. Remarkably, age cohorts of 'young retainers' were a means for the articulation of protest and for conflict resolution within the kin groups.[25] On the other hand, education could be regarded as a cooperative task of a variety of resident and non-resident kin-group members as well as of other persons living in a given household. Particularly, the practice of having babies fed by wet-nurses seems to have been quite common during the early Middle Ages up to the tenth century, while the earliest bans against this practice are recorded from the eleventh century.[26]

Allowing movements and the formulation of wishes and desires: the old and the young in the high and late Middle Ages and in the sixteenth century

Within the residential three-generation nuclear families as the novel type of kin group, the temporal aspect of order was redefined. Within these smaller residential families, the children were fully exposed to the authority of their parents who were the only kin members responsible for the education of their children. These responsibilities began at birth. Although nursing continued to be a widespread practice throughout and beyond the Middle Ages, various arguments were adduced with the goal of inducing mothers to feed their children themselves. Indeed, babies were given some equivalent to a right to be fed by their mothers; for example, the late eleventh-century *Life of St Peter Damian* (1007–72) by John of Lodi referred to the mother's breast as the 'property' of the child.[27] And this 'right' was soon expanded into a right to proper education to be provided by the parents and specific teaching institutions referred to as schools. The professional lay faculty working in the schools began to replace the monastic or other clerical teachers of young children. This change took place most rapidly in the urban communities of towns and cities, where 'grammar' schools spread for the teaching of Latin from the thirteenth century. It was not only in these urban communities but also in aristocratic families that parents saw to it that their children received proper schooling.[28]

---

25 E.g. *Continuatio Reginonis*, s. a. 953, in ed. Friedrich Kurze, *MGH SS rer. Germ.* (50), p. 166. Even in the thirteenth century, Wolfram of Eschenbach let his youthful hero Parzival be educated by his mother in the woods in order to keep him away from what she regarded as the ugly distractions of the knightly world. But, after spending a while in the woods, Parzival managed to escape from his seclusion and joined a band of young knights. See Wolfram von Eschenbach, *Parzival*, book 2, 112, book 3, 119–21, 154–9, 6th edn by Karl Lachmann (Berlin, Leipzig ,1926), pp. 39, 47–8, 53–5.

26 Avicenna, *Canon medicinae* (Basle, 1536), p. 107.

27 John of Lodi, *Life of St. Peter Damian* (PL 144, 1853, col. 115). New edn in Klaus Arnold, *Kind und Gesellschaft in Mittelalter und Renaissance* (Paderborn, 1980), p. 101.

28 Giovanni Villani, *Chronica*, cap. II/94, ed. F. G. Dragomanni, vol. 3 (Florence, 1845; repr. Frankfurt, 1969), p. 324. For the aristocracy see: Vincent of Beauvais, *De eruditione filiorum nobilium*, cap. XVI–XXIV, ed. Arpad Steiner, Mediaeval Academy of America Publication XXXII (Cambridge, Mass., 1938; repr. New York, 1970), pp. 58–88.

Swaddling was a common practice throughout the Middle Ages. However, during the thirteenth century, theorists of education began to argue that swaddling stood against the ancient Greek and Roman practice of exercising children so that they could acquire physically strong bodies. Egidius Romanus (1243–1316), perhaps the leading educational theorist of his time, quoted Aristotle when, in his mirror for magistrates, he recommended physical education for young aristocrats.[29] At the turn of the fourteenth century, Conrad of Megenberg seconded this,[30] and Bernard Gordon (dec. after 1308), who taught medicine at the University of Montpellier, demanded that boys should be allowed to decide about their future lives by themselves at the age of twelve.[31]

The later fourteenth and the fifteenth centuries abounded with educational tracts and treatises whose dominant tone recast parents' obligation to look after their children with love and devotion. Leon Battista Alberti (1404–72), a foremost educational reformer of his time, demanded that parents should treat their children with love in return for 'a solid rest in times of old age and for a comfortable place during one's final days'.[32] The late Middle English poem *Dives and Pauper* agreed with Alberti and repeated the biblical demand that children should honour their parents.[33] But scepticism that parents' efforts to educate their children could remain unrewarded was also vocal. The twelfth-century authors of the *Prose Salernitan Questions* argued that parents should love their children because children contain their parents' substance, but insisted that the reverse was not the case.[34]

Nevertheless, parents took to observing the gestures and other movements of their children for the purpose of detecting their current moods and attitudes. Beating children for the purpose of forcing them to abide by certain norms and rules became discredited. Instead, Alberti described fathers discussing among themselves the tricks which they used for testing how their children interacted with others and for understanding their inarticulate wishes and desires. Others considered education as if it were a process of hedging. Already in the twelfth century, the education of children had explicitly been compared with the growing of trees and plants,[35] and this analogy

---

29 Egidius Romanus, *De regimine principum III*, cap. II/2, 5 (Rome, 1607; repr. Aalen, 1967). New edn in Arnold (see note 27), p. 140. This author also used the physical-education prescripts suggested by the Roman military theorist Vegetius in the late fourth century.

30 Conrad of Megenberg, *Yconomica*, ed. Sabine Krüger, MGH Staatsschriften III, 5 (Stuttgart, 1973), pp. 89–92.

31 Bernard Gordon, *De conservatione vitae humanae* (Leipzig, 1570), pp. 29–30.

32 Leon Battista Alberti, *Della famiglia*, ed. Arnold (see note 27), p. 147.

33 *Dives and Pauper*, ed. Priscilla Heath Barnum, vol. 1, Early English Text Society, Original Series CCLXXV (London, New York, Toronto, 1976), pp. 305–30.

34 *The Prose Salernitan Questions*, q. 101, ed. Brian Lawn (Oxford, 1979), p. 47.

35 Eadmer, *Life of St Anselm*, ed. Richard William Southern (London, 1962), pp. 37–9. The saint was revered for having condemned the beating of children, and instead having demanded freedom for children for the reason that they are like trees which require space for their growth.

was later successively used by Egidius Romanus[36] and Pope Pius II. However, the use of the analogy changed during the later Middle Ages. The twelfth-century sources emphasised the freedom with which plants can grow in an uncontrolled physical environment and thus used the analogy in an argument against the excessive control of children through their educators. In contrast, later sources stressed educational guidance and control and intended to show that education resembles measures for the straightening up and budding of young trees. Pius II made the latter desire explicit when he addressed King Ladislaus V Postumus of Hungary (1440–57) in a letter written in 1450:

> It is the task of the teacher to hedge you with sound and moral principles and admonitions towards orderly life in the same way as the farmers hedge young trees, so that upright sprouts of sound morality grow up. For true discipline is the source and root of orderly life. However, your teachers shall not beat you, but they shall admonish you.[37]

The text amply displays the ambivalence of such educational practice. On the one hand there was the desire to let children grow up to become physically strong, while on the other it was believed necessary to subject them to rigorous methods of moral education. Frequently the latter dominated, and beating continued despite the warnings by educationalists. In consequence, school attendance was not always popular among children, and differences existed between school teachers and parents in their choice of educational methods. Thus Johannes Butzbach (1478–1516), a Benedictine monk and scholar born in Frankfurt, wrote in his early sixteenth-century autobiography how much he had hated school and how he had tried his best to avoid going there. When it was discovered that he had not attended school, but had hidden in a punt on the river Main, his teacher had him beaten, while his mother had defended him and requested the Frankfurt town government that beating in schools should be stopped.[38]

Alberti's demands also made explicit the change that was occurring in the relationship between the old and the young during the late Middle Ages. While, until the eleventh century, the order governing the relations between the old and the young had been focused on the transmission of group-bound traditions from time immemorial to the unforeseeable future, the new order resembled a contract among the members of a residential three-generation family according to which education was to be provided for the young as a kind of prepayment in exchange for the obligations of the young to care for

---

36 Egidius Romanus (see note 29), p. 140.
37 Enea Silvio Piccolomini, *Der Briefwechsel*, No. 40, II. Abt., ed. Rudolph Wolkau, Fontes rerum Austriacarum II, 67 (Vienna, 1912), pp. 103–58. Arnold (see note 27), p. 157. Similarly, Albrecht von Eyb, *Ehebüchlein*, ed. K. Herrmann, *Deutsche Schriften des Albrecht von Eyb*, vol. 1, Schriften zur Germanischen Philologie IV (Berlin, 1890), pp. 19–25.
38 Johannes Butzbach, [*Odeporicon*, 1506] *Chronika eines fahrenden Schülers oder Wanderbüchlein*, cap. 3, ed. Damian Joseph Becker (Ratisbon, 1869). Another edition by Andreas Beriger (Frankfurt, 1993). New edn by Arnold (see note 27), p. 168.

Fig. 43 Michelangelo, *The Battle of Cascina*, 1505. Holkham Hall, Holkham, Wells, Norfolk, UK. Reprinted by permission.

the old at a later stage. However, the contract was one-sided in that the obligations of the old preceded those of the young while the reverse obligations frequently remained unfulfilled. Even if the contract was fulfilled, its provisions were far from watertight. After the young received their education and established their own households, the old would remain as a potential and frequently manifest burden when frail and incapable of caring for themselves. Moreover, as the new age-grade scheme inserted adulthood as the intermittent grade between the old and the young, caring for the old became the task of adults rather than of the young. Hence, the young could take for granted that they could postpone the fulfilment of the generational contract until they reached adulthood. Under these conditions, the stereotype of the old as frail, ill and dependent could replace the early medieval ideal of the old as the vigorous transmitters of normative oral traditions. If the contract remained unfulfilled the old were left with the choice of entering church institutions for their care or of securing for themselves a place in one of the so-called 'hospitals' where they could await their death. Joining a monastery became a common fate for widows. Twelfth-century theological tracts contained advice about the conditions under which widows should be allowed to become nuns. A common rule was that young widows who could earn their own living and had a kin group to care for them should not be admitted.[39] Admission to these institutions could, however, be purchased through donations. The

[39] Peter Cantor (dec. 1197). Peter Lombard (dec. 1160). Herveus of Bourgdieu (dec. c. 1150). Ed. Sprandel (see note 3), pp. 108–12, 153.

Fig. 44 Maximilian learns a martial art, early sixteenth century. From Maximilian, *Weisskunig* (Vienna, 1775), plate 31. Reprinted by permission of the Sächsische Landesbibliothek – Staats-und Universitätsbibliothek, Dresden. Dezernat Deutsche Fotothek. Photographer: R. Richter.

popularity of the 'hospitals' during the later Middle Ages, particularly in the urban communities of towns and cities, seems to reflect the growing difficulty of the urban old to enforce the generational contract, whereas, in the countryside, the old continued to be needed as long as they could sustain their ability to work.

The desire to develop children's personalities and bodily strength was not limited to specific social groups. From the middle of the fifteenth century, the style of depicting nude men with strong muscles and well-trained bodies was used to represent human beings *per se*, as the cartoon by Michelangelo

Fig. 45 Children enjoy playing at jousting with wooden toy horses, early sixteenth century. From Maximilian I, *Weisskunig* (Vienna, 1775), plate 10. Reprinted by permission of the Sächsische Landesbibliothek – Staats- und Universitäts- bibliothek, Dresden. Dezernat Deutsche Fotothek. Photographer: R. Richter.

(1475–1564) in Figure 43 shows. Among the aristocracy, training the young in physical exercise was part of the educational scheme, even though not every aristocrat will have been as active as Emperor Maximilian I, who proudly filled pages of his autobiographical writings with accounts of the exercises he had done and the *techniques du corps* which he had learned when he was young.

The practice of aristocratic tournaments, well recorded from the fifteenth and sixteenth centuries, supports the conclusion that what Maximilian did was not exceptional.[40] Likewise, the practice of physical education is confirmed by the number of sports playgrounds and fencing halls in towns and cities as well as by the several printed training manuals for a variety of martial arts, such as wrestling and fencing.[41] The manuals displayed fighters in dual combat taking equilibrium positions through which they could obtain firm stands and could bend, push and strike into many different directions. These fighters needed the self-confidence that their own bodily energies would allow them to overcome the resistance posed by their opponents and to do so by themselves without external assistance. Because schools for fencing and wrestling were frequent in the urban communities of towns and cities it is safe to assume that such self-confidence was acquired through education.

Moreover, it can be surmised that this desire also included the peasant farming population, although few direct records exist about this population group. It was from the peasant farming population that Maximilian recruited his highly mobile and vigorously individualistic fighting force, the lansquenets. Pictorial battle scenes depict bands of warriors with few defensive weapons in an equilibrium position from of which warriors could push and strike strongly into many different directions. Again, in order to be able to execute such movements warriors had to give priority to the use of the energies contained in their own bodies over the reliance on the coordination of movements in larger groups of infantrymen. Hence the peasant farming population must have been receptive to Maximilian's ideals of bodily movements.

However, there were critics for whom such efforts towards the advancement of physical education did not reach far enough. One of them was Roger Ascham (1515–68), who, in 1545, published an educational tract for the purpose of urging the young of his time to continue exercising their bodies, and he recommended the then traditionally English practice of shooting with longbows.[42] But there were other critics who believed that excessive movements, such as dancing, were unbecoming, and they argued that children should be warned not to commit themselves to such practices in order to preserve their moral integrity.[43] Nevertheless, the moveable strong body was the ideal of the young during the later fifteenth and the sixteenth centuries. They used this ideal to distinguish themselves from the old with their weak and immobile bodies, and they developed new preferences which required

---

40 Maximilian, *Freydal*, ed. Quirin von Leitner, 3 vols (Vienna, 1880–82). See also Georg Rüxner, *Von Anfängen, Ursachen, Ursprung und Herkommen der Thurnier im heyligen Römischen Reich Teutscher Nation* [1530], ed. Sigmund Feyerabend (Frankfurt, 1566).

41 See, among others, Albrecht Dürer, *Hoplodidaskalia* [1512], ed. Franz Dörnhöffer, *Jahrbuch der Kunstsammlungen des Allerhöchsten Kaiserhauses* XXVII (1907–09), pp. XXVIII–LXXXI. Christian Egenolff, *Der altenn Fechter anfengliche Kunst* (Frankfurt, 1531; repr. in Flugschriften-Sammlung Gustav Freytag. Mikrofiche ed., No. X/1422). Georg Bender, *Kurzer Underricht dess lobwürdigen . . . Ballen-Spiels* (Nuremberg, 1680).

42 Roger Ascham, *Toxophilus* (London, 1545; repr. Menston, 1971).

43 Florian Daul, *Tanzteuffel* (Frankfurt, 1569) (repr., ed. Kurt Petermann, Documenta choreologica VIII [Leipzig, 1978]).

Fig. 46 Two fencers in action. From Christian Egenolff, *Die Ritterliche, Mannliche Kundt vnd Handarbeyt des Fechtens vnd Kempffens* (Frankfurt, 1558), plate 1.

mobility and the use of physical strength. Among these preferences, the lust for war was, perhaps, most prominent, as can be gleaned from the multifarious military campaigns which usually attracted large numbers of professional warriors, mainly young men from the lower ranks of urban and peasant farming populations. Another was the desire to travel to far away places and to experience something new. Both desires became prominent during the second half of the fifteenth century and continued throughout the sixteenth century. The high degree of appreciation of long distances, the risk of ocean-crossing voyages and the increasing attraction of the novelties and expected riches of 'new' worlds, frequently coupled with the lust for war, stood behind the several daring overseas expeditions which were conducted and highly esteemed throughout the period.[44]

All of these attitudes had the consequences that the gap between the old and the young widened and that it became more difficult to maintain order in the generation change in the urban communities of towns and cities. When more of the young emigrated to distant places without any intention of returning – and this was the case, particularly in the Iberian peninsula during the sixteenth century – it became harder to fulfil the contract between the generations and, consequently, the care for the old developed into a social

---

[44] Christopher Columbus, [Letter to the Catholic Kings of Spain, 22 February 1498], Columbus, *Lettere e scritti*, vol. 2, ed. Paolo Emilio Taviani, Consuelo Varela (Rome, 1993), pp. 62–83.

problem. When church institutions, such as monasteries, were closed in areas where the Reformation took roots, old-age alms had to be provided for in hospitals run by urban or territorial governments. When the old were in dependent positions and could no longer work with sufficient energy, they were to become a cause of expenditure. They would be forced into unpaid retirement, except if they had a benevolent partner or an affluent employer who honoured them for their life-long service and granted them a reduced pay without charging them with work. Among the peasant farming population, the management of the generation change was perhaps easiest, if the owner of a farm was the elder of a residential family and could reserve for himself a part of the estate when handing the rest of it on to his son. Yet, in all these cases, agreements were made on a case-by-case basis, pending the specific conditions in which the transition of power from generation to generation could occur. Instead, the general rule was that the old would have to care for themselves after their retirement, using their own fortunes, where these were available, or depending on public alms. Under these conditions, the time span between retirement from active work and death was usually short. Even in the case of a ruler who did not have to face economic austerity, such as Emperor Charles V (1500–58), his life lasted little more than two years after he had abdicated all his offices and retired to life in the vicinity of a monastery.

Conclusion

Until about 1600, the importance of the European kin groups in the shaping of the generational contract was reduced in consequence of two major interventions into their autonomy: first, in the eleventh and twelfth centuries they ceased to exist as the authoritative transmitters of group-bound traditions between the old and the young and kin groups began to be reduced to three-generation residential nuclear families; second, at around AD 1500, the power transition from the old to the young within residential families was disassociated from its previous connection with the divinely willed order of the world as represented by the world ages and became subject to the control of human-made institutions. The result was that the generational contract between the old and the young was no longer determined by the continuing existence of the kin groups but by the willingness and capability of the young to carry out their obligations *vis-à-vis* the old.

XIII

Images of Order II:
Rule and Representation

> Secunda autem ratio regis erat interrogatio quid unusquisque ex
> illa parte regni qua veniebat dignum relatu vel retractu secum
> afferret*
>
> — Hinkmar, Archbishop of Rheims

Introduction

Following descriptions of the principles and concepts by which order has
been maintained in space and through time, this chapter deals with the maintenance of order within and among groups. Since the nineteenth century, it
has mostly been taken for granted that the establishment, maintenance and
enforcement of order is equal to the enforcement of law through lasting and
legitimate institutions of government within the boundaries of territorially
unified sovereign states and upon a purportedly or manifestly homogeneous
population.[1] The subsumption of the establishment, maintenance and
enforcement of order within the legitimate tasks of the governments of sovereign states has been justified with the arguments, first, that legitimate government is government based on the rule of law, second, that the legitimacy of
governments is derived from some degree of consent by the governed, and
third, that a core reason why the governed give their consent to the existence
and the work of governments is that the governments are expected by the
governed to procure security through the establishment, maintenance and
enforcement of order.

From the point of view of conceptual history, there are three major problems with this complex of theories of the state. The first problem is that the
theories of the state are operable only as long as this definition of the state is
applicable. However, empirically, not all states fulfil these conditions and the

---

* It has been a further occupation of the king to inquire with anyone about whatever was
  worth reporting and deliberating from that part of the realm where he came from.
[1] The triad of the unities of government, territory and population has been a standard
  element in definitions of the state since Georg Jellinek, *Allgemeine Staatslehre*, 3rd edn,
  7th printing (Bad Homburg, 1960), pp. 394–434 (first published Berlin, 1900).

demand that they should do so has been in existence only since the end of the eighteenth century. The implication is that, for the purposes of conceptual history, theories of the state must rest on a variety of changing concepts of order.

The second problem is that the theories are based on the assumption that the population groups of states regard themselves as homogeneous so that they can act as the legitimisers of sovereign states. Again, not all population groups living in sovereign states have empirically regarded themselves as homogeneous, and the demand that they should do so has been in existence only since the eighteenth century. Consequently, for the purposes of conceptual history, theories of the state must be grounded on a variety of changing concepts of legitimacy.

The third problem is that theories of the state take into account only one type of government, namely government as a set of lasting interconnected bureaucratic institutions which can act as the executors of the law beyond the lifetime of a person. However, the identification of government as a set of lasting interconnected bureaucratic institutions is far from self-evident before the eighteenth century in most parts of Europe. If so, for the purposes of conceptual history, theories of the state must cover a variety of changing concepts of rule as the ways and means of establishing, maintaining and enforcing order.

In short, the conceptual history of the establishment, maintenance and enforcement of order within and among groups deals with the various ways in which rulers or ruling institutions to which these tasks have been entrusted can act as representatives of those who have entrusted these tasks to rulers or ruling institutions.[2] The conceptual history of representation then is the core part of the conceptual history of the establishment, maintenance and enforcement of order; it deals with the changing criteria by which is defined the nature of representation, who are the represented and who the representers.

For the purpose of avoiding misunderstandings, a specific descriptive terminology will be applied in this chapter. First, whenever the entire complex of the establishment, maintenance and enforcement of order is referred to as a whole, the term 'socio-political environment' will be used. By contrast, whenever the various aspects of establishing, maintaining and enforcing order are referred to separately, the population groups will be referred to by the term 'ruled', the institutions of government will be referred to by the term 'rulers', and the space in which order is established, maintained and enforced will be referred to by the term 'territorial administrative unit'. It is hoped that, with the help of this terminology, the conceptual changes of representation in association with changes of the establishment, maintenance and enforcement of order can be described and analysed. There have been two main concepts of representation. First, representation can have been understood as representation of the ruled by the ruler *vis-à-vis* the divinity, and, second, representation can have been understood as representation of the ruled in the ruler.

2   See Nicholas Greenwood Onuf, *World of Our Making* (Columbia, S.C., 1989).

Establishing, maintaining and enforcing order in the divinely ordained socio-political environment: the early Middle Ages

The modern English word *order,* equivalents of which are current in many other European languages, contains no more than a few of those connotations which its Latin root *ordo* covered during the Middle Ages. The medieval *ordo* embraced a wide variety of hierarchical arrangements, stratified social groups and behavioural norms. The word *ordo* could be used for descriptions of the world as a divinely created hierarchical order, but it could also stand for certain types of monastic brotherhood or for large-scale social groups. Its derivative *ordinatio* meant ordering commands issued by high ranking rulers,[3] but it could also denote the humble human activity of putting things in an order.[4] One element, however, was consistently present in all these meanings, namely the conviction that what was in order was stable. The stability of the socio-political environment was recognised as being divinely willed, as in the case of descriptions of the world whose order was taken to be beyond human interference.[5] Thus all changes which were indeed brought about in the world in consequence of human action took place against the background of the belief that, ultimately, human beings had been created bereft of the essential possibility of changing the world to any significant degree.

The demand to maintain the socio-political environment in a stable lasting order through human activity was expressed in the ninth century with the formulae 'status totius regni' and 'communis societas et status'.[6] These expressions could easily fuse in a single phrase the three main dimensions of the socio-political environment, namely time, in the sense that *status* may have stood for the steady condition of the order, space, in the sense that *regnum* seems to have vaguely connoted the spatial dimension as a word for some area within which the order was perceived to be establishable, maintainable and enforceable (including the world at large), and groups, in the sense that *communis* as well as *societas* appear to have included references to the groups upon whom the order was established, maintained and enforced. However, the difficulty is that during the early Middle Ages these three aspects of the socio-political environment were not clearly and explicitly separated. Instead, a large number of technical terms, frequently in use at the time, defy unequivocal definition with regard to all three dimensions of the socio-political environment. Among others, this is the case for the antecedents of the modern English and modern High German words *rich, reich* and *Reich* together with their Latin analogues, namely *rex, regnum* and *regalis,* as well as

---

3 Louis the Pious, *Ordinatio Imperii* (817), ed. Alfred Boretius, *MGH Capit.* 1, No. 136, pp. 270–1.

4 Walahfrid Strabo, *Libellus de exordiis et incrementis quarundam in observationibus ecclesiasticis rerum,* cap. 31–2, ed. Alfred Boretius, Viktor Krause, *MGH Capit.* 2, p. 514.

5 Hinkmar of Rheims, *De ordine palatii,* cap. IV–VII, ed. Thomas Gross, Rudolf Schieffer, *MGH Fontes iuris Germ. ant.* 3, pp. 57–97.

6 Louis the Pious, *Ordinatio imperii* (see note 3), cap. 14, p. 305.

imperator, imperium and *imperialis.* These words simultaneously denoted powerful people, an area, and the competence of establishing, maintaining and enforcing order over groups and areas as well as, finally, certain institutions continuing beyond the lifetime of a person. Similarly, the Latin words *potens* and *potestas* and their derivatives in Romance languages could be used in reference to rich as well as powerful people. The comprehensiveness of the meaning of these words was suitable to a concept of the socio-political environment in which rulers and some of the ruled were interconnected mainly through a variety of personal bonds and ties and not through many institutional relationships. Likewise, because the ruled had to have their residences in spaces of daily experience and because the rulers also had to demarcate their spheres of influence, the personal bonds and ties between the ruled and the rulers had to rest upon some at least vaguely defined territorial administrative unit as a substrate of space, and they had to be perceivable as outlasting the lifetime of a person. The tenth-century legal formula 'lant ioh liuti'[7] gave expression to the interconnectedness of the concepts of group and of space within the socio-political environment and described rule as rule over land and people as a lasting condition of the socio-political environment. As, within the context of conceptual history, the dimension of time is self-evident, it does not need to be discussed specifically. Instead, the focus will be directed towards the changing interconnectedness of the dimensions of space and group to both of which the formula referred.

That ties between rulers and ruled were considered to be personal is attested in many early medieval sources. Every free person, that is, everyone who was not subject to the protection or commands of someone else could enter into personal ties with rulers. These ties could be bonds of kinship (*consanguinitas*), of neighbourhood (*familiaritas*) or contract (*amicitia*) as a mid-ninth-century legal record explicitly stated.[8] In consequence, it was difficult for contemporaries to devise a generic terminology for the socio-political environment as long as the ruled could join various types of group. Specifically, generic terms for the ruled were rare other than those in use for under-privileged or unfree persons who were dependent upon the protection offered

---

7　Notker Labeo, *Die Schriften Notkers und seiner Schule*, ed. Paul Piper, vol. 2. (Freiburg, 1883), p. 237. The gloss cast into diction the interconnectedness of these two dimensions of the socio-political environment which were combined already in the late seventh century. At this time, an English name list, the so-called 'Tribal Hidage', contained names of population groups and area names side by side, and placed population groups as well as areas under the joint rule of the kings of Mercia. See Wendy Davies, Hayo Vierck, 'The Contexts of Tribal Hidage', *Frühmittelalterliche Studien* VIII (1974), pp. 230–4.

8　*Conventus in villa Colonia* [Treaty of Coulaines] 843, ed. Alfred Boretius, Viktor Krause, *MGH Capit.* 2, No. 254, pp. 253–5. The treaty listed the three regular types of bond because it stipulated a specific convention according to which a ruler (the Frankish king, Charles the Bald) had entered into a general contract with the ruled so as to preclude partial relations between himself and the ruled. But such conventions remained exceptional at the time.

or the commands issued by others. The most common terms for the ruled were ethnic and kin-group names or names for contractual groups. Hence the diversity of types of groups living under the control of a ruler reduced, but did not annihilate, the significance of spatial boundaries and limited the competence which a ruler could exercise over the ruled.

Consequently, the rulers' task of maintaining the socio-political environment in a stable order could be executed only under two mutually supplementary conditions, first, that the rulers were to be respected by the ruled and, second, that the ruled consented to the rulers with the proviso that the rulers executed their tasks with legitimacy and justice. The first condition became explicit in a variety of different contexts in which such rulers' virtues as *sapientia* and *fortitudo* were referred to. The frequent combination of these two virtues illustrated the joint quests for wisdom or fairness on the side of the rulers and fright or terror on the side of the ruled.[9] The former virtue was considered to be a necessary qualification for rulers and the latter one was described as the divine gift to the rulers who were empowered to use force in order to subdue evildoers and disobedient subjects as well as to protect the rightful and loyal.[10] Consequently, rulers were regarded as having received their power to rule from the divinity with the implication that it was not possible for rulers to be everyone's friend.[11]

However, rulers who acted unwisely and overused terror were to face resistance or at least received criticism and a bad reputation. Such could – and frequently did – happen in the case of controversies about succession when two or more pretenders competed for the same office and involved groups of ruled in their struggles. Such campaigns could appear as incompatible with the rulers' task of maintaining the socio-political environment in a stable order. The *Anglo-Saxon Chronicle* contains the record of an incident which illustrates this point. This is the account of the death of King Cynewulf (to which reference was made in Chapter Seven).[12] His anonymous ninth-century chronicler harshly criticised him for neglecting his duties as king towards his retainers in the midst of a dispute over succession. Cynewulf's action was regarded as unwise and an abuse of his divinely ordained power. This negative report, however, upheld the ideal of the relationship between rulers and ruled as one in which rulers exercised their divinely ordained power for the benefit of the ruled and the maintenance of a stable socio-political environment.

This portrait can be confirmed by a consideration of the second condition for the stability of the socio-political environment, namely the consent by the

---

9 *De XII abusivis saeculi*, ed. Siegmund Hellmann, Texte und Untersuchungen zur Geschichte der altchristlichen Literatur XXXIV (Leipzig, 1909), pp. 43–4.

10 Alcuin, Ep. 252, ed. Ernst Dümmler, *MGH Epp. Karol.* 2, p. 414.

11 Thietmar of Merseburg, *Chronicon*, cap. I/5, ed. Robert Holtzmann, *MGH SS rer. Germ. N. S.* 9, pp. 8–9.

12 *The Anglo-Saxon Chronicle: A Collaborative Edition*, vol. 3: MS A, s. a. 755, ed. Janet M. Bately (Cambridge, 1986), pp. 36–8.

ruled to the ruler. Early medieval sources abound with references to acts of consent by the ruled to legal and other acts of the rulers. Bede, for one, remarked in his obituary of King Aethelberht of Kent that this ruler had wisely enacted laws for the ruled 'with the consent of the wise', that is, those among the ruled who were knowledgeable in legal affairs.[13] Likewise, insular charters recording or enforcing transactions of land tenure regularly included the subscriptions of those who had witnessed or were considered to have to consent to the transactions or who had been responsible for the making of the charter. Some eighth- and ninth-century continental sources referred to gatherings of rulers with some of the ruled when they jointly discussed such matters as the enactment of general laws, the holding of judicial trials and the making of contracts between rulers. These matters were considered to involve counselling of the rulers and consent by the ruled.[14] Remarkably, unlike in later periods, the requirement of consent by the ruled commonly remained unjustified, but sources abound with phrases according to which rulers and ruled should be closely related together and that the ruled were able to manifest themselves as political groups solely under the condition that they stood under a ruler.[15] Moreover, extant early medieval genealogies confirm an early sixth-century statement by Cassiodore who claimed that rulers with a long and distinguished ancestry could act more forcefully in the accomplishment of their tasks.[16] Hence the mutual dependence of rulers and ruled also had a temporal dimension in the sense that rulers were considered to be eligible mainly from specifically respectable kin groups of long standing whose members had previously qualified themselves through their capability of ruling with *sapientia* and *fortitudo*.

In summary, the stability of the socio-political environment during the early Middle Ages was described as the enactment of the divinely willed command for the maintenance of order within and among groups of ruled. Political theorists were aware of the consequence that the task of rulers to maintain the socio-political environment in a stable order would generate inequalities between the ruler and the ruled.[17] In the fifth century, St Augustine associated the concept of the socio-political environment with his concept of peace by saying that the latter was an ordered concord according to which the rulers command and the ruled obey.[18] He justified the inequality

---

[13] Bede, *Historia ecclesiastica gentis Anglorum*, cap. II/5, ed. Bertram Colgrave, R. A. B. Mynors (Oxford, 1969), p. 150.

[14] *MGH Capit.* 1, No. 82, ed. Alfred Boretius, p. 30. *MGH Capit.* 2, No. 205, ed. Alfred Boretius, Viktor Krause, p. 74, No. 284, p. 368, No. 300, p. 451.

[15] Salvian, 'De gubernatione Dei libri VIII', cap. V/15, in *Salviani presbyteri Massiliensis libri qui supersunt*, ed. Karl Hahn, *MGH AA* 1,1, p. 58. Jordanes, *Getica*, cap. 249, ed. Theodor Mommsen, *MGH AA* 5,1, p. 122. Bede (see note 13), cap. II/14, III/7, pp. 186–8, 232.

[16] Cassiodore, *Variarum libri XII*, cap. XI/1, 10, ed. Åke J. Fridh, CCSL XCVI (Turnhout, 1973), p. 424.

[17] Atto of Vercelli, *Polypticum* (*PL* 134, cols 881–3).

[18] Augustine, *De civitate Dei*, cap. XIX/13, CCSL XLVIII (Turnhout, 1955), pp. 678–82.

with the diversity of interests and capabilities among human beings which, he thought, had come into existence as a consequence of the Fall. The conclusion was that it was in accordance with divine will that the prudent should rule the less prudent and that they should do so with justice and legitimacy.[19]

Thus the early medieval concept of order brought about a hierarchy in which the ruler was the entrusted guarantee of peace as a stable condition of relations among groups and territorial administrative units and was placed in proximity to the divinity. In this respect the medieval concept of order was informed and influenced by the political structure of the Roman Empire of Antiquity wherein the emperor had occupied a sacral position. In *De civitate Dei*, St Augustine[20] accommodated the sacral position of the Roman Emperor with the Christian faith and thereby provided the authoritative text on which perceptions of the ruler as the intermediary between the divinity and the ruled could be based. But Augustine tried to limit the ruler's position by imposing constraints against wilfulness and exuberance. Using the model of the kin group, Augustine insisted on the reciprocity of the relations between the ruler and the ruled:

A man has a responsibility for his own household – obviously, both in the order of nature and in the framework of human society, he has easier and more immediate contact with them; he can exercise his concern for them. That is why the Apostle says, 'Anyone who does not take care of his own people, especially those in his own household, is worse than an unbeliever – he is a renegade.' This is where domestic peace starts, the ordered harmony about giving and obeying orders among those who are concerned for the interests of others; thus the husband gives orders to the wife, parents to children, masters to servants. While those who are the objects of this concern obey orders; for example, wives obey husbands, the children obey their parents, the servants their masters. But in the household of the just man who lives on the basis of faith and who is still on pilgrimage, far from that Heavenly City, even those who give orders are the servants of those whom they appear to command. For they do not give orders because of a lust for domination, but from a dutiful concern for the interests of others, not with pride in taking precedence over others, but with compassion in taking care of others.[21]

The world had thus been ordered by the divinity so as to have a ruler who ruled for the benefit of the ruled, not for his own benefit. Augustine was aware of attempted infringements against the divine order of the world, but, nevertheless, insisted that such manifest infringements did not tell against the principle as such, for, in the last resort, the divinity would not allow the world order to be turned upside down and subjected to wilful human control. The conceptualisation of just rule as divinely willed rule for the benefit of the

---

19 Gregory I, *Moralia*, cap. XXI/15, XXVI/26, ed. Marcus Adriaen, CCSL CXLIII (Turnhout,1985), pp. 1081–3, 1298–1303.
20 Augustine (see note 18), CCSL XLVII, cap. V/21, pp. 157–8.
21 Augustine (see note 18), cap. XIX/14, pp. 680–2. The quotation in the quotation is from 1 Timothy 5: 8.

Fig. 47 Emperor Charles the Bald communicating with Christ, ninth century.
Prayerbook of Charles the Bald, Munich, Residenz, Schatzkammer, Kat. 4, fol. 38 verso–
39 recto.

ruled contained an ideology which placed a ruler in the position of an intermediary between the ruled and the divinity. This ideology was strong enough
to establish an ecclesiastical image according to which the ruler had gained his
or her power from the divinity for the purpose of transmitting it to the ruled
as a group of believers. This image was made explicit in the early eleventh
century in a poem which Bishop Adalbero of Laon (dec. after 1030) addressed
to King Robert of France (in office 996–1031). The king, Adalbero wrote, had
the sacral ability of being an *orator*, that is a preacher, who could say prayers
on behalf of the ruled although he was a layman. According to Adalbero the
king should use his priestly powers to preserve unity among the believers.[22]
This image of the ruler as the highest preacher suggests that the human world
of Christian believers was understood as the church, with the ruler being its
highest and most visible representative before the divinity and overarching
the particularisms of the competing groups and types of groups. This meant
that sacral rulers were also entitled to exercise control over the ordained
clergy. The same image was visualised in book illuminations in which the
ruler was depicted as the highest representative of the ruled before the
divinity and, at the same time, as the transmitter of divine orders towards the
ruled. In other words, just secular rule as rule over the Church could be
conceptualised as the divinely willed establishment, maintenance and
enforcement of order in the stable socio-political environment through the
commands of a ruler for the benefit of the ruled.

Whereas pre-Christian ideologies of sacral rulership seem to have been
based on the belief that rulers were descendants of divinities, and pre-
Christian sacrality had been heritable through certain outstanding kin groups
and needed to be ascertained by recognisable signs of membership in such kin
groups, the Christian concept of divinely ordained rulership was informed by
the ideology that the divinity had placed the ruler in control of the ruled as
the church regardless of their particularist traditions. This ideology was made
explicit through rituals and a verbal expression which was used in certain
formulae during coronation rituals and in legal documents: 'Dei gratia' (by
the grace of God). The ruler thus represented before the divinity the ruled as
the entirety of the people living on the lands under the control of the ruler.

The concept of representation as intermediation between the ruled and the
divinity is also contained in the dedication picture shown in Figure 48. This
tenth-century book illumination depicts a ruler who interacts with the
divinity. The picture is the dedication frontispiece to a charter which King
Edgar of England (943–75) had issued to the benefit of the church and
monastery of New Minster, Winchester, in 966. In the lower part of the

---

22 Adalbero of Laon, *Carmen ad Rodbertum regem*, vv. 366–8, ed. Claude Carozzi, Adalbéron of Laon, *Poème au Roi Robert*, Les classiques de l'histoire de France au Moyen Age
XXXII (Paris, 1979), p. 28. See also Aelfric of Eynsham, *Die Hirtenbriefe Aelfrics*, ed.
Bernhard Fehr, Bibliothek der angelsächsischen Prosa IX (Hamburg, 1914), p. 223
(repr., ed. Peter Clemoes [Darmstadt, 1966]). In this passage, the Benedictine abbot of
Eynsham argued early in the eleventh century that the *oratores* should mediate between
the divine and the human worlds.

Fig. 48 King Edgar offering the charter for New Minster, Winchester, to Christ, late tenth century. New Minster Charter, London, British Library, Ms. Cotton Vespasian A VIII, fol. 2 verso. Reprinted by permission of The British Library.

picture, Edgar, with his left hand, offers the charter to Christ who appears in a mandorla which is carried by four angels in the upper part of the picture. The crowned king is flanked by two bishop–saints whose gestures indicate their support for him. The upward looking king is placed slightly above the two bishops for whose benefit he acts. Thus the king is placed in a position where, at the instigation of the bishops, he mediates between the human world and the divinity.

The opposite relationship is expressed in the eleventh-century picture in Figure 49 showing King Cnut and Queen Emma presenting a cross to New Minster, Winchester. In this picture, the king and the queen appear being crowned by angels at the command by the divinity. Following the divine command, they present the cross to the church and the monastery whose monks are depicted in a row at the bottom of the picture. Taken together, all three pictures portrayed rulers as intermediaries between the human world and the divinity.

Coronation orders can be adduced in support of the argument that this pictorial style was neither exceptional nor idiosyncratic. Coronations took place in church buildings and involved high-ranking office holders of the Church. Moreover, the coronation orders contained formulae which made explicit the fact that the newly installed king was to act in fulfilment of divine commands and in the interests of the ruled.[23] Thus, even if it remained unspecified in these sources who the ruled were, rule itself was perceived as overarching the particularisms of competing groups. In this capacity, rulers represented the ruled as the Church before the divinity and, vice versa, acted as the executors of divine commands among the ruled as the Church in the lands under their control.

Desacralising the socio-political environment: the high and late Middle Ages

Because the extant early medieval pictures of rulers as the sacral representatives of the human world before the divinity all came from church institutions, it is necessary to assume that this image of rulership was then considered to be in full agreement with church doctrines, even though, on occasion, aspects of papal participation in the installation of emperors seems to have been contested.[24] But the sacrality of the rulers and their competence

---

23 Percy Ernst Schramm, ed., 'Promissio regis', in Schramm, *Kaiser, Könige und Päpste*, vol. 2 (Stuttgart, 1968), p. 211. Also in Felix Liebermann, ed., *Die Gesetze der Angelsachsen*, vol. 1 (Halle, 1903), pp. 214–16.

24 Einhard (*Vita Karoli Magni*, cap. 28, ed. Oswald Holger-Egger, *MGH SS rer. Germ.* [25], pp. 32–3) objected to aspects of the installation of Charlemagne as emperor in the church of St Peter in Rome in 800, and Widukind of Corvey (*Rerum gestarum Saxonicarum*, cap. III/44–8, ed. Paul Hirsch, Hans-Eberhard Lohmann, *MGH SS rer. Germ.* [60], pp. 123–9) remained conspicuously silent about the installation of Otto I as emperor in Rome in 962.

Fig. 49 King Cnut and Queen Emma (Aelfgifu) present a cross to New Minster, Winchester, c. 1031. London, British Library, Ms. Stowe 944, fol. 6 recto. Reprinted by permission of The British Library.

as representers of the human world as the Church remained unchallenged up until the eleventh century,[25] when ordained clergy began to challenge their subordination to secular rulers. During the second half of the eleventh century, the papacy, supported by several reform-minded bishops, began to criticise the premise that high-ranking secular rulers could and ought to be able to exercise some degree of legitimate control over the clergy and act as its representatives before the divinity. This criticism gained steam in response to doubts which had been expressed about the previous conviction that secular rulers could be sacral. In a curiously radical text probably composed late in 1076, Pope Gregory VII expressed these doubts and expanded them into a position which amounted to nothing less than the statement that the then traditional subordination of the clergy under the authority of rulers should be reversed and that sacrality should be denied the latter.[26] Subsequently, the Church was conceptually separated from the secular world with which the socio-political environment became identified. A controversy arose between the pope and the emperor as the highest representatives of the Church and the secular world. The Church succeeded in desacralising rulership and in confining the work of rulers to the *temporalia* as secular affairs, whereas it established itself as the sole institution in charge of *spiritualia* as religious matters. The separation of *temporalia* and *spiritualia* had the ultimate consequence that rulers could no longer derive their legitimacy from their position as intermediaries between the ruled and the divinity. Once the controversy had been played out, after 1125, secular rulers had to discover other sources of their legitimacy, ultimately seeking to derive it from non-religious sources.

Not surprisingly, rulers turned more readily towards secular administrative as well as military tasks. In pursuit of such tasks, they strove to accomplish manifest records of success in battle, to establish themselves as manifest leaders of powerful clienteles and to create nascent bureaucracies whose members, although tied to rulers through oaths of fidelity, could act with some degree of autonomy as administrators of more precisely demarcated territorial administrative units.

Since the twelfth century, these newly emerging territorial administrative units were frequently described by a concept of sovereignty (although not the word) which was expressed through the metaphor of the human body. This metaphor of the body politic had been part of the legacy of Antiquity and was supported by phrases from the New Testament, most notably I Corinthians 12:12.[27] Beginning in the fourth century, commentators on this epistle

---

25 *Die Texte des Normannischen Anonymus*, ed. Karl Pellens, Veröffentlichungen des Instituts für Europaische Geschichte Mainz XLII (Wiesbaden, 1966). Another edition is by Heinrich Böhmer, *MGH Libelli de lite* 3, pp. 642–87.

26 Gregory VIII, *Dictatus papae* (1076), ed. Erich Caspar, *Das Register Gregors VII*, No. 55a, *MGH Epp. Sel.* 2, 1, pp. 201–8.

27 'For as the body is one, and hath many members, and all the members of that one body, being many, are one body: so also is Christ' (King James version).

described socio-political environments, first and foremost the Roman Empire, with this metaphor.[28] But during the entire early Middle Ages, little use was made of the metaphor although there were contemporary commentaries on I Corinthians written on the basis of the fourth-century texts.[29] Instead of using the body metaphor in descriptions of the pluralism of particularistic territorial administrative units, early medieval legal and political texts contained references to bodies (*corpora*) when the socio-political environment as a totality was mentioned.[30] But in the twelfth century, the late Roman usage was restored and immediately achieved great prominence. Elaborate schemes were devised according to which the constitutive parts of territorial administrative units were likened to the several parts of the human body and their relations were described in terms of bodily behaviour.[31] Thus the spreading of the metaphor of the body politic seems to reflect the fragmentation of the socio-political environment into a pluralism of antagonistic territorial administrative units the rulers of which strove to establish for themselves the exclusive right of control over the people and the lands under their rule.

However, during a transitional period in the twelfth and thirteenth centuries, some rulers, notably emperors Frederick I, Henry VI and Frederick II, temporarily strove to stem the tide of territorialisation. As the secularised heads of the Holy Roman Empire, so called since 1157, they attempted to pose as the representatives of universal rule, just as the Roman emperors of Antiquity and Charlemagne and his successors had. They used the Crusades to Palestine for the purpose of demonstrating their ability to act as universal rulers. However, these attempts failed cataclysmically. Frederick I, in fact the only invested and legitimate emperor to head a crusade, died in its course in 1190. His son Henry VI pledged to renew his father's effort, but died before another Crusade got on its way. Frederick II, Henry's son, was forced to conduct a Crusade as a banned emperor and, although he had himself crowned as King of Jerusalem in 1229, his success was temporary in that he lost control over the city in 1244. Thus the failure of the imperial Crusades only precipitated the downfall of the emperors as the claimants of universal rule, and this meant that, although, until the sixteenth century, some emperors continued to uphold the claim towards the universality of their rule, in practice, they had to compete with other rulers about control over land and people. After the thirteenth century, this was an open contest, and it was uncertain whether at all and, if so, to what extent the emperors would be the

---

28 Ambrosiaster (*PL* 17, col. 261).
29 Raban Maur, *Enarrationes in Epistolas Beati Pauli liber nonus* (*PL* 112, cols 9–160). Haimo of Auxerre, *Enarratio in Epistolam I ad Corinthos* (*PL* 117, cols 1507–1606). Atto of Vercelli, *Expositio in Epistolas Pauli* (*PL* 134, cols 125–834).
30 E. g. *Divisio regnorum* (806), *MGH Capit.* 1, No. 45, p. 9.
31 John of Salisbury, *Policraticus*, cap. V/6, VI/1–21, ed. C. J. Webb (Cambridge 1909; repr. New York, 1979), pp. 548d–554a, 587d–620a.

winners of the struggle. For their rivals were not only those rulers who had established themselves outside the emerging boundaries of the Holy Roman Empire, notably the Roman emperors at Byzantium as well as the kings of France and England, but also within the Holy Roman Empire a number of territorial rulers, such as the kings of Bohemia, dukes of Bavaria, or the landgraves of Thuringia, began, in the thirteenth century, to carve out territories which they tried to keep immune from the reach of the emperors.

Moreover, the desacralisation of rulers was not confined to emperors. Other rulers also had their grasp on church institutions reduced, namely the kings of England and, less so, the kings of France. Hence, the *Dei gratia* formula, although continuing to be in use, lost its realistic background and became fossilised as a relic of traditionalism. In consequence, late medieval rulers could no longer derive their legitimacy from the belief that they were incumbents of a divinely ordained office and the ruled could no longer perceive the rulers as their representatives before the divinity. Instead, the practical demand for the secular recasting of ideologies of representation arose among rulers and ruled alike.

Demands for the new type of representation among the ruled became manifest during revolts in the fourteenth and fifteenth centuries, first and foremost during the great English Rebellion of June 1381. According to the author of the Anglo-Norman *Anonimalle Chronicle*, the revolting 'commoners' welcomed King Richard II as 'Our Lord King Richard' at Mile End, east of the City of London, on Friday, 14 June 1381, assured him that 'we will not have any other king but you', and then presented the following demands to him:

> That the king would suffer them to take and deal with all the traitors against him and the law; . . . that henceforth no man should be a serf nor make homage or any type of service to any lord, but should give four pence for an acre of land; . . . that no one should serve any man except at his own will and by means of regular covenant.[32]

These demands posited the ruler as the executor of the will of the ruled and they were rested upon the expectation that the ruler would rule under, act in accordance with, as well as establish, maintain and enforce the law. According to this source, the king was approached as the ruler of the common people, neither as their representative *vis-à-vis* the divinity nor as the incumbent of a divinely ordained office. Moreover, the commoners, namely peasants and urban artisans, were demanding that he should act as their true representative against those who, in their view, had infringed upon the law and imposed themselves as lords of the commoners. Specifically, they were infuriated by their personal dependence upon the will of secular as well as ecclesiastical lords, specifically the Archbishop of Canterbury, whom they killed during the rising. Finally, the commoners claimed that the king should act on their

---

32 *Anonimalle Chronicle*, s. a. 1381, ed. Vivian Hunter Galbraith, Publications of the University of Manchester, History Series XLV (Manchester, 1927), pp. 144–5.

behalf for the purpose of improving their rights and conditions of life under a general concept of inalienable equality and freedom which was derived from the body of thought that was then known as 'natural law'.

In his late thirteenth-century commentaries, St Thomas Aquinas applied Aristotle's distinction between rule over free persons and rule over slaves. Slaves were defined as living tools in service to other persons, and, therefore, St Thomas concluded that rule over slaves could not have been divinely willed because the divine creation had established all human beings as equals. However, like other late medieval political theorists, he accepted rule over free persons as based on reason because of the natural diversity of human capabilities and the assumed necessity that the more capable should guide the less capable. St Thomas's conclusion was that rule over free persons was just as long as it did not deteriorate into rule over slaves. In order to distinguish between these two forms of rule, St Thomas applied a concept of law, which he assumed was unchangeable, inalienable and could be derived directly from the divine will and which could thereby be applied to all humankind, including slaves. It was this concept of law which served as the basis for the law of conflict in contexts of domestic strife as well as of inter-group violence and which has most commonly been referred to as 'natural law'.[33]

In agreement with 'natural law', the rebellious commoners requested the abolishment of serfdom and the commutation of manual labour services into the payment of taxes directly to the ruler. In short, according to the rebelling commoners of 1381, the king was to be the guardian of 'natural law' as well as the executor of statutory law to the benefit of the ruled, and rule was just if and as long as the ruled could recognise themselves as represented directly in the ruler without the intercession of ecclesiastical institutions or secular lords. Put differently, the commoners articulated their claim that they were willing to accept the ruler as legitimate under the condition that rule was direct, subject to the law and in accordance with their own interests.[34] In this respect, the rebellious commoners made explicit a sense of belonging together as the subjects of their ruler who was understood to be their representative within one and the same territorial administrative unit.

Needless to say that, after an initially positive response by the king, the rebellion, which received its momentum from local protest among neighbourhood groups, eventually failed facing the military resistance of the ruling élites.[35] However, the rebellion was a successor to the granting of privileges of

---

33 Thomas Aquinas, *In quattuor libros sententiarum*, I/2, dist. 44, qu. I, ar. 3., ed. Roberto Busa, *Sancti Thomae Aquinatis Opera omnia*, vol. 1 (Stuttgart, 1980), p. 255. Cf. Thomas Aquinas, *Sententia libri politicorum*, cap. III/3, ed. Roberto Busa, *Sancti Thomae Aquinatis Opera omnia*, vol. 4 (Stuttgart, 1980), pp. 251–2.

34 For twelfth-century parallels, specifically a rising against the pope in Rome, see *Codice diplomatico del Senato Romano dal MCXLIV al MCCCXLVII*, No. 5, vol. 1, ed. Francesco Bertolini, Fonti per la storia d'Italia LXXXVII (Rome, 1948), pp. 3–6.

35 See John Cleveland, *The Rustick Rampart: Or Rurall Anarchy Affronting Monarchy* (London, 1658), pp. 75–96, 114–21. The account is drawn on contemporary records but takes the point of view of the aristocracy.

self-rule to the urban communities of towns and cities during and after the eleventh century, predominantly in northern Italy, the Netherlands and areas in the Empire, as it was contemporaneous with urban unrest and civil-protest movements among artisans against the rule of urban patriciates.[36] It was also paralleled – at least inside the Empire – with the establishment of some form of communal organisation of the rural settlements of the peasant farming population. Such communalism initially pursued the goal of simplifying the collection of food rents and taxes in such a way that the entire community of villagers was made responsible for the delivery of rents and taxes, rather than the individual farming household. Eventually, however, communalism became an ideology supporting demands for the limited self-rule of villagers and the payment of taxes directly to the territorial rulers instead of local seigneurial lords. Thus communalism reduced the authority of local seigneurial lords and created a consciousness among the peasant farming population that they shared certain political interests and had the potential of participating in a political group. Likewise, communalism promoted the idea of coalitions between the peasant farming population and the lower ranks of the urban artisans. One case of such a coalition ushered in the English Rebellion of 1381.

The ideological basis for the establishment of communal self-rule was the belief in the validity of a legal contract into which the inhabitants of a settlement as a community entered and the goal of which was to install a government for the benefit of the ruled. These contracts were the foundations upon which governments in towns and cities operated once these urban communities had been granted the privilege of self-rule.[37] The contracts resulted from statutory law and, moreover, established a specific legal framework for rule which, among others, stipulated the principle that the ruled were to be represented in the rulers, mainly urban ruling councils. Henceforth, ruling councils would derive their legitimacy solely through the secular instrument of willed agreements among the resident population in the urban settlement over which they had been entrusted rule. In the case that the ruling councils were recognised as having broken the contract, dissent arose among those who were dissatisfied with the ruling councils, and such dissent could, and frequently did, become the ferment for open violence and revolt.

Finally, in the territorial administrative units where most of the farming villages and some towns were located the relationship between a ruler, the seigneurial lords and the peasant farmers under their control came to be understood in terms of a contract. The contract drew on the belief that the ruler provided protection for the ruled in return for service by the ruled and was made explicit in oaths of allegiance which the ruled swore to the ruler on the occasion of his public inauguration. It was held that the contract was

---

[36] See J. Dumolyn, *De Brugse opstand van 1436–1438* (Kortrijk, 1997).

[37] *Nürnberger Polizeiordnungen aus dem XIII. bis XV. Jahrhundert*, ed. Joseph Baader, Bibliothek des Litterarischen Vereins in Stuttgart LXIII (Tübingen, 1861; repr. Amsterdam, Atlanta, 1966).

invalidated if the ruler failed to provide protection, for example in the case of a lost war, or if the ruled refused to provide service, such as in consequence of a rebellion. The contract was to be concluded after the ruler was ceremonially inaugurated. It was considered to be theoretically possible that the ruled could refuse to enter into the contract. In practice there were cases where inaugurations of rulers were contested and when rulers' inaugurations were used as opportunities for the articulation of dissent and protest. In the course of the later Middle Ages, ever more seigneurial lords among the lesser aristocracy were included in these contracts between rulers and ruled. Perhaps in consequence of economic difficulties and lack of legitimate successors, they renounced their positions of independence and swore oaths of allegiance to a territorial ruler in their vicinity. The establishment of a hierarchy at the top of which were the rulers, as the highest representatives of the territorial administrative units under their control, enhanced the territorialisation of rule and replaced the early medieval principle of uniting rulers and ruled through various bonds and ties of personal relationships.

From the fourteenth century, territorial rulers could avail themselves of an emerging secular political theory which was informed by the practical philosophy of Aristotle. According to Aristotle, rulership was neither derived from nor justified through divine will but grew out of a natural willingness of human beings to accept existing hierarchies. Within such a secular justification of rule, the early medieval concept of representation had to be recast into a concept according to which the ruler no longer acted as the intermediary between the human world and the divinity but became the executor of the will of the ruled. In other words, the new concept which was advocated by fourteenth-century political theorists denoted representation as the rulers' activity of identifying, coordinating and implementing the will of the ruled.[38]

Late medieval political theory thus supported the establishment of a multitude of particularist and antagonistic socio-political environments which, as a rule, overlapped with territorial administrative units. During the fourteenth century, several political theorists devoted themselves to the problem of justifying these units. They observed that, although humankind had been created as one, such original unity had become fragmented after the Fall because human ineptitudes had unleashed rivalries, divisiveness and diversity and had thus promoted particularism. Whereas in the early Middle Ages the Fall had been accepted as the occasion through which rule had entered the world, fourteenth-century and later political theorists regarded human sinfulness as the reason for the fragmentation of humankind and the establishment of particularist, diverse and antagonistic territorial administrative units.[39]

---

38 Engelbert of Admont, 'De ortu et fine Romani imperii', cap. 2, ed. Melchior Goldast, *Politica imperialia* (Frankfurt, 1614), p. 755.

39 Engelbert of Admont (see note 38), cap. 10–11, pp. 759–61. Bartolus of Sassoferato, In *secvndvm Digesti noui partem commentaria*, ad dig. XLIX/15, 22, Bartolus, *Opera*, vol. 6 (Venice, 1570–71), pp. 227–8. Enea Silvio Piccolomini [Pope Pius II], 'De ortu et auctoritate imperii Romani [1 March 1446]', in Piccolomini, *Der Briefwechsel*, part II: *Briefe*

Abbot Engelbert of Admont (c. 1250–1332) was one of the first to derive rule from a hypothetical covenant (*pactum*) between the ruled and the ruler. He believed that, at some time after the Flood (*primae aetatis*), human beings had voluntarily agreed among themselves to establish a government which they would obey for their own safety and salvation, and he assumed that this covenant was irrevocable. The theory implied that the contracting human beings had been constituted as a political group already before the contract could have been concluded. Hence Engelbert explicitly acknowledged that the group which was subjecting itself to the control of a ruler was residential, lived within established boundaries and had the same language and customs.[40] Understandably, Engelbert regarded the conclusion of the contract as a single event which he took to have occurred once in sacred history after the Flood. Hence Engelbert's contractualism was an element of speculative political theory for which its author sought no practical application.

Another branch of fourteenth-century contractualist theory arrived at equally speculative results. Proponents of this theory, namely John of Paris (dec. 1306) and Marsilius of Padua (c. 1290–before 1343),[41] maintained that a contract had been concluded between the ruled and the ruler but that this contract was not a covenant. Instead, these theorists insisted that the contract consisted in a mere concession by which rule had temporarily been entrusted to the ruler. According to this theory, the ruled retained their sovereignty and reserved for themselves the right to cancel the contract if the ruler was unjust or incapable. Later proponents of this theory saw to it that it was applied in practice.[42]

But the most powerful brand of contractualism resulted from the widening application from the thirteenth century of the Justinian legal formula that 'whatever is of equal concern to everyone needs to be approved by everyone' (*quod omnes similiter tangit ab omnibus comprobetur*).[43] The formula was transmitted in the context of canon law but was used only from the thirteenth century as the justification for participation in political decision-making. Whereas early medieval authors had passed over it in silence, fourteenth-century political theorists such as Marsilius of Padua employed it in the context of their contractualist justifications of rule.[44] And, in the fifteenth

---

als Priester und als Bischof von Trient, ed. Rudolph Wolkau, Fontes rerum Austriacarum II, 67 (Vienna, 1912), pp. 7–8.

40 Engelbert of Admont (see note 38).

41 Johannes Quidort of Paris, *De potestati regia et papali*, cap. 1, ed. Fritz Bleienstein, Frankfurter Studien zur Wissenschaft von der Politik IV (Stuttgart, 1969), pp. 75–8. Marsilius of Padua, *Defensor pacis*, dictio I, cap. XX/6–7, ed. Richard Scholz, *MGH Fontes iuris Germ. ant.* 7, pp. 66–8.

42 The theory was applied in the late fourteenth century on the occasion of the deposition of King Wenzel of Germany in 1400. See Julius Weizsäcker, ed., *Deutsche Reichstagsakten unter König Wenzel*, No. 204–5, vol. 3 (Göttingen, 1956), pp. 260–4.

43 *Corpus iuris civilis* 5, LIX/5 (various editions).

44 Marsilius of Padua (see note 41).

century, theorists of the conciliar movement declared that decrees issued by ecclesiastical councils ought to be given priority over legislation by the pope.[45]

Thus, at the beginning of the fourteenth century, secular political theory emerged as a veritable ideology not only for the fragmentation of the socio-political environment but also for the desacralisation of rule. Rule over territorial administrative units came to be categorised as resulting not from divine will but from human needs and desires. Both processes had fundamental consequences for the stability of the socio-political environment: first, that the antagonistic territorial administrative units in themselves contained potential for rifts and controversies; and second, that the derivation of rule from human needs and desires in itself contained potential for change and upheaval. Early in the fourteenth century, theorists were aware of these consequences and tried to fend them off. Some jurists, such as Bartolus of Sassoferato (1314–57), focused on the conditions by which Roman emperors could defend their claims towards the universality of their rule against the rulers of the particularist territorial administrative units. Bartolus categorised the Roman Empire as an overarching socio-political environment which not only extended across the *ecumene* but also remained one of the four eschatological world empires which spanned the periods between the Fall and Judgement Day. He tried to reconcile the claim for the universality of the Roman Empire with the particularism of the existing territorial administrative units by admitting four types of such units: namely, units which were inhabited by groups (*gentes*) of Roman origin abiding by Roman rule; units which were inhabited by groups living under Roman law without necessarily abiding by Roman rule; units inhabited by groups which neither abided by Roman rule nor lived according to Roman law but were of Roman origin; and units inhabited by groups which neither abided by Roman rule nor lived under Roman law, were not of Roman origin and claimed to be independent of Roman rule on the grounds of some privilege of immunity which they had previously received from a Roman emperor. Because Bartolus admitted no more than these four groups in the *ecumene*, the Roman emperor exercised a suzerainty which, at the very least, consisted in his exclusive capability of granting privileges of immunity and thereby imposing limits on his own rule.[46]

Alternatively, several early fourteenth-century political theorists simultaneously expressed their concerns for the stability of the fragmented socio-political environment without a universal ruler. Among them, Engelbert of Admont, Dante Alighieri (1265–1321) and Pierre Dubois (c. 1250–c. 1320)[47]

---

45 Nicholas of Cusa, *De concordantia catholica*, liber III, ed. Gerhard Kallen, Cusa. *Opera omnia*, vol. 14 (Hamburg, 1959–65). Jean Gerson, *Opera*, ed. Ellies du Pin (Antwerp, 1706), vol. 2, p. 850.

46 Bartolus (see note 39).

47 Engelbert (see note 38). Dante Alighieri, 'De monarchia', book I, cap. XI/2–3, Dante, *Opere minori*, ed. Bruno Nardi, vol. 2 (Milan, Naples, 1979), pp. 328–30. Pierre Dubois, *De recuperatione terrae sanctae*, cap. 13, 116, ed. Charles-Victor Langlois (Paris, 1891), pp. 12–13, 103–5. See also Piccolomini (see note 39), pp. 6–24.

insisted that a universal socio-political environment was required for the purpose of safeguarding stability, and they devised a utopian theory in the early years of the fourteenth century according to which the Roman emperors or any other king or secular ruler had to act as the ultimate guarantors of the stability of the socio-political environment. Engelbert of Admont was most explicit in attaching this theory to the eschatological world empires and concluded from these references that a universal ruler had been invested by the divinity and that, consequently, the universal empire could not be abolished by human intervention.[48] Evidently Engelbert's theory of the socio-political environment was in conflict with his theory of the covenant between the ruled and the rulers of territorial administrative units, because he had the ruler of the universal empire invested directly by the divinity. But Engelbert made no attempt to reconcile these two doctrines. Hence he made manifest the widening gap between the conventionalism of theories on the universal socio-political environment, on the one hand and, on the other, the pragmatism of theories of the particularist territorial administrative units. The touch of utopia inherent in the universal theories displayed his concern for the static quality of the socio-political environment. Where particularist territorial administrative units could come and go, a solid ground had to be found in utopian theory where one could plant the roots of stability in the universal socio-political environment.

In summary, between the thirteenth and the fifteenth centuries, representation was transformed from a type of order through which the ruled were linked to the divinity by the ruler into a type of order through which the ruled could find their interests and their identities represented in the ruler. Under the government of the latter type of representation, rulers could be perceived as legitimate, apt and acceptable if and as long as they could be judged to be using their competence in accordance with the interests, and in service to the identities, of the ruled. In consequence, the static concept of divinely willed order which had been dominant in the early and high Middle Ages became increasingly desacralised. Henceforth, the belief increased in strength that human actors could and should use their own energies for the purpose of exerting their influence upon the world under goal of creating new orders.

Conclusion

Nevertheless, during the later Middle Ages, much of the traditional concept of the divine right of monarchs continued to inform governmental practice as well as rulers' ceremonial practice. For example, the coronation orders continued to be composed in accordance with early medieval precedents, although with some adjustments, and the coronations would conventionally be regarded as religious ceremonies taking place inside church buildings.

---

48 Engelbert (see note 38).

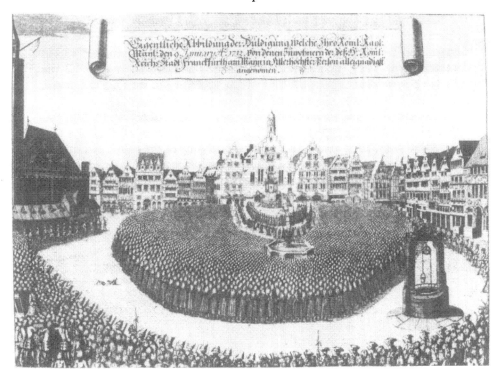

Fig. 50 The public oath of allegiance sworn to Emperor Charles VI on the day of his coronation at Frankfurt on 9 January 1712. From the eighteenth-century Frankfurt *Festbücher*, Frankfurt, Historical Museum, Inv.-No. C 2219.

However, there were also radical departures from this practice, leading to attempts at the construction of new secular rituals. In 1508, the Roman King and Emperor-elect, as well as heir to the Habsburg territories, Maximilian I, for the first time, staged his own imperial coronation without the assistance of the pope, and, eventually, in 1562, a custom was instigated such that the Holy Roman Emperor was no longer to be crowned in Italy, nor even in a church building, but the secular environment of the city hall of the Free Imperial City of Frankfurt. The transfer of the coronation place was of highly symbolic significance. First, the pope, who since the later fourteenth century had no longer been involved in imperial elections, ceased to be involved in imperial coronations. Second, the coronation of the emperor as the highest ranking monarch in Europe was performed in a place without a monarchical government, as the emperors, even though they held suzerainty rights over imperial cities, did not interfere in their self-rule. Third, the coronation itself ceased to be an exclusively religious ceremony and became part of a public festival.

On the occasion of these festivals, the new rulers were literally presented to the ruled by being visually exposed to groups which they were expected to represent. Hence the coronation ceremonies, not only for the emperors, but also for other types of monarchs, acquired the novel task of making manifest the bonds and ties between the ruler and the ruled. Finally, factions of the Reformation movements, namely those lead by John Calvin (1509–64) in Geneva and by Heinrich Bullinger (1504–75) in Zurich emphatically used contractualism. They claimed that the relations between the ruled and the ruler were equivalent to the Covenant which, according to the Old Testament, had existed between the divinity and believers since the time of creation.[49]

The essential condition upon which the new concept of representation was applicable was that the representative tasks of the ruler were all-inclusive and that a given population group, as a political grouping of the ruled, was subject to no more than a single ruler or ruling council. Hence, if the ruled were to accept their ruler as the representative of their own interests and identities, it was mandatory that only one ruler could act as such a representative at a time and that the territorial administrative unit could be understood as the area wherein a population group with common interests resided.

49 Heinrich Bullinger, *De testamente seu foedere Dei unico et aeterno* (Zurich, 1534). John Calvin, *L. Annei Senecae libri duo De clementia* [Commentary] (Paris, 1532).

Conclusion – Change and changes

Cultural change has been approached descriptively in this book; why-questions have rarely been asked, and explanations have rarely been provided. This approach is liable to the criticism of being utterly conventional and empiricist. The criticism is sound and irrefutable in the last resort, for descriptions of change remain incomplete if they are not supplemented by explanations. My justification for confining myself to the descriptive approach is that, to me, change is endemic to culture in general and in medieval culture in particular. I have considered it advisable to focus on description rather than explanation because change as a constitutive part of medieval culture demands careful description before lending itself to explanation and many of the described conceptual changes warrant cross-cultural comparisons before explanations can be provided. These comparisons would have to be conducted with regard to the categories of action, interaction and order. In the first stage of the comparisons, it would have to be ascertained whether these categories are universal and stable and can thus extend beyond the confines of medieval culture. Then, appropriate objects would have to be selected for the comparison. I took it to be beyond the range of this book to include cross-cultural comparisons with regard to these matters.

Another criticism is that the book presents medieval culture in segments described separately, one after the other, and without a coherent narrative. Again, this criticism is fair. It suggests that no effort has been made to display the interconnectedness of the features making up medieval culture and that, more importantly, the Middle Ages may appear as a single systemic unit. My justification for choosing this arrangement against these odds is drawn on the interactionist model of change to which I adhere. The model suggests that change is hardly ever identical with a sudden and fundamental break that sharply separates two subsequent periods or cultures, but that it overlaps with continuities and, moreover, proceeds at unequal speeds. Hence I take the view that the changes described with regard to one cultural feature lead to a periodisation which may not be the same as the periodisations which emerges from descriptions of change in other features. Therefore, I have located descriptions of change not at the systemic level of medieval culture as a whole but at the level of the various concepts to which reference has been made in this book.

In summary, conceptual changes regarding the following general, as well as specific, features have been described.

Generalities: time, space, body, groups, men and women

With regard to time, we observe the waning dualism of the group-oriented experience of time versus universal time. The dualism was dominant throughout the early Middle Ages and well into the twelfth century. Universal time was experienced in accordance with Biblical eschatology and was expected to end after the coming of the Antichrist. The primary units of the measurement of group-oriented time followed the rhythms of the physical environment or were identical with the solar and the lunar cycles or parts of them, namely the year, the season, the month, the day and the hour. Units longer than a year came into use only among specific types of group and were defined in terms of periods during which rulers held their offices. Within the Church, such units were measured for specific purposes, such as the determination of the dates of Easter. Dating by the universal AD chronology spread only gradually after the beginning of the eighth century. The twelfth and thirteenth centuries marked the breakthrough of the reception, first among intellectuals, of the Aristotelian concept of infinite astronomical time, which reduced the validity of the particularist group-oriented experiences of time, and called into question the eschatological hope for a world without time after the coming of the Antichrist. The practical application of the Aristotelian concept of time ushered in the building of complex and complicated mechanical chronometers for the simultaneous measurement of many different units of time. The earliest of these chronometers appeared in monasteries during the second half of the thirteenth century. From the fourteenth century, time was experienced as infinite in the urban communities of towns and cities where artisans and merchants used it for the organisation of production and distribution.

With regard to space, we find the distinction between space as the world, the space of regular communication, and space as the property of a group or a person in operation throughout the Middle Ages. However, the ways of conceptualising the three categories of space changed. In the early Middle Ages, as far as we know, space as the world seems to have been conceptualised in eschatological terms whereby the world as a universal totality was mainly the object of theological speculation about the end of time. Space as the space of regular communication was hardly distinguished from the space of daily experience. Neither category of space was defined in abstract terms, but by the groups within and among which regular communication occurred. The space of regular communication was composed of finite numbers of units which were distinguished by their various qualities. As with the experience of time, a fundamental reorientation of the concept of space took place during the twelfth and thirteenth centuries. While space as the world continued to be perceived mainly in universal eschatological terms (although, from the twelfth century, merchant traders and other long-distance travellers made efforts to experience the world as a concrete reality), the space of regular communication became defined in precise terms as the measurable distance between persons and objects. From the twelfth century, groups no longer defined space, but space formed the basis of group identity. Eventually, by the fourteenth century, space began to be experienced also as permeable, continuous and uniform, and persons as well as groups ceased to associate qualities with sections of space. The same process of territorialisation took place with regard to the space of daily experience as the property of persons or groups. In the latter case, however, the practice of defining relations among persons through rights in landed property had already begun in the eighth century. The process of the reorientation of the entire concept of space was completed when space as the world was de-eschatologised in the fifteenth century.

With regard to the body, we recognise a continuing awareness of the interaction between the human body and its environments, whereas the perception of that interaction changed. In the early Middle Ages, the interaction was perceived in the form of heterodynamic impacts flowing onto a person from the physical environment and/or from other persons. One consequence of this perception was that the ordinary person was seen as receiving his or her essential energies from other agents, that is, from sources outside his or her body. By contrast, a person with power or high status was expected to act as a source of energy of others, which meant in practice that he or she had to act as the giver of wealth and to provide protection against evil forces in the physical environment and hostilities emerging form other groups. Likewise, everyone was seen as capable of seeking protection and tapping sources of energy from the physical environment, specifically supernatural or divine agencies. In this way, it was perceived to be possible to overcome manifest obstacles posed by the physical environment or resistance from other persons or groups through concerted actions. From the eleventh century, however, the emerging hilltop castles and urban communities of towns and cities created small segments whose inhabitants were expected to act autodynamically as individuals, and they were regarded as capable of relying more on their own bodily energies than on the assistance or protection of others. The autodynamic perception of the interaction between persons and the physical environment had immediate impacts on the conceptualisation of action in towns and cities as well as among the aristocracy. But the larger part of the farming population retained their heterodynamic attitudes up until the fifteenth century.

With regard to groups, we become aware of a continuous process of the reduction of coexisting types of group offering a declining number of options for membership and affiliations to their members. In the early Middle Ages, there were kin groups, neighbourhood groups, groups by contract, political groups, as well as social groups. They coexisted and created multiple networks of partly conflicting, partly complementary interrelations. From the point of view of a person, there were a number of options, for instance, between membership in a large double-descent kin group or membership in a contractual group, and both kinds of membership were not mutually exclusive. The process of the decline of the number of the types of group began in the later early Middle Ages with a reduction in the competence and size of kin groups and the simultaneous waning of the neighbourhood groups. It gained further significance with the stigmatisation of some contractual groups as allegedly lawless bands of men from the eleventh century. At this time, rulers began to make efforts to integrate these contractual groups into political groups under their control. Moreover, some contractual groups turned into groups of settlers in the newly establishing urban communities of towns and cities. At the same time, political groups became territorialised and began to compete with the non-territorial hierarchically stratified social groups and with the equally non-territorial but vertically arrayed kin groups. By the fifteenth century, territorial rulers became strong enough to enact territory-wide oaths of allegiance to be sworn by their subjects, and they could also enforce a uniform legislation to which all permanent residents in their territories ought to be subject.

With regard to the relations between men and women, we trace a fundamental transformation of the kinship structure. Kinship in the early Middle Ages was based on double descent through which women received a status equal to men as inheritors of kin traditions. Matrilinear descent could convey power and raise ranks, and marital affiliations between high-ranking women and lower-ranking men were common in ruling kin groups. However, double descent militated against the preference for patrilinear descent which the Catholic Church inherited from Roman Antiquity. Therefore, the Church supported all attempts to exclude succession rights drawn on matrilinear descent. Early cases of ecclesiastical intervention against double descent in ruling kin groups are recorded in the British Isles around AD 700, while on the continent the most prominent case was the support granted by the Church to the ousting of the Merovingians from Frankish kingship in AD 751. Yet the major attack on large kin groups was launched between the tenth and the twelfth centuries. During this period, in the aristocracy, matrilinear descent ceased to be relevant to succession to high office whenever descendants in direct male lines were available. Moreover, in the newly establishing urban communities of towns and cities, contractual groups of settlers were constituted whose members had frequently cut their traditional kin ties. In the urban communities as well as in the aristocracy, adherence to the traditional double descent was difficult because the novel type of the three-generation residential family emerged as the standard-type kin group, being defined in terms of residence rather than in accordance with kin traditions of descent. This novel type of kin group reduced the status of women through whom descent was traced only in cases where male lines had died out.

Action, interaction and order

With regard to action, we recognise a remarkable similarity between the changes which effected the various kinds of action. In the case of production and distribution, early medieval group-centred action gave way to market-centred action between the tenth and the twelfth centuries, which in turn was conducted under the auspices of the newly formed abstract concepts of time and space from the thirteenth century. The diversification of local markets into product markets with various spatial extensions occurred from the twelfth century, and product markets expanded across the tri-continental *ecumene*. Moreover, political groups represented the dominant type of groups engaged in long-distance trade between the eighth and the tenth centuries, whereas from the eleventh century contractual groups of professional traders took charge of this trade. In the case of war, early medieval group-centred strategies of warfare for the purpose of the acquisition or maintenance of status began to compete with strategies of territorial conquest in the twelfth century, and the latter strategies began to dominate warfare in the sixteenth century. In the case of thinking, the early medieval comprehensiveness of synthetically thinking the world as a whole was replaced in the twelfth century by analytical means of investigation, with controversial discourses about the world as the sum of its parts. In all cases, groups experienced a declining significance as the foci of action during the high and late Middle Ages.

With regard to interactions, we can record the addition to group-centred interaction of transpersonal interaction through the use of technology. Early medieval communication was carried out in integrated processes of communicative action about complex matters within and between groups in which the use of writing was possible but not essential. Between the twelfth and the fifteenth centuries, these integrated processes of communicative action became fragmented, and communication by means of writing about specific matters became standard. Likewise, communication across time as a means to link the past with the future became disconnected from the transmission of particular group traditions. The Catholic mission helped to absorb particularist group traditions into the universalist concept of world history enshrined in the Bible. Hence, the universalisation of historical time became dominant over the particularist histories of kin and other types of group. Finally, there were changes in the way movements of persons took place. In the early Middle Ages, the major form of movement was migration in mostly larger groups, even though solitary migration did occur. It was possible, on principle, for migrants to determine the targets of their migration and the location of their eventual settlements. During the high and late Middle Ages, migration in large groups became exceptional whereas solitary migration became a common phenomenon, often prescribed for members of certain professional groups. At this time, migration was normally regarded to be in-migration into already existing spaces of regular communication. Thus migrants were, as a rule, neither free to determine the targets of their migration nor to lay out the spaces of their settlements.

With regard to the establishment and maintenance of order, we sense a proliferation of normative and institutional control of the actions and interactions within and among groups. In the case of the order of time, manifest in the succession of generations, the large double-descent kin groups provided the organisation for the maintenance of security for the old and for the education of the young in the early Middle Ages. From the point of view of its members, the kin group was the manifestation of a pre-existent and, to a substantial degree, predetermined and unchangeable order because no single member could unilaterally change such matters as determinants of kinship or succession rules or the behavioural codes specific in each kin group. But, with the reduction of the order-maintaining capabilities of the kin groups between the later tenth and the twelfth centuries and the successive emergence of the three-generation residential family, the needs of the education of the young and the care of the old were difficult to meet from the resources of these smaller groups. Consequently, specifically in urban communities of towns and cities, ecclesiastical and lay institutions were established for the provisions of these services. In the case of the order of the socio-political environment, administrative institutions were usually represented by monarchs with a touch of sacrality in the early Middle Ages. In this capacity, rulers could act as outstanding persons providing protection for ordinary people in the same way as they could act as the representatives of the ruled before the divinity. However, with the emergence of the urban communities of towns and cities in the eleventh century, the mainly contractual groups of settlers in these communities established a novel perception of the order of the socio-political environment, namely the perception that this order should be purposefully established through human efforts and explicitly willed by the ruled and that it was to be maintained for their practical benefit.

Overview of the changes

Overlooking the conceptual changes in European culture, we can identify a fundamental transformation of heterodynamic and group-centred actions and interactions towards autodynamic as well as space- and time-centred actions and interactions. At the same time, images of order which were considered as impacting upon or as being imposed upon the human world were altered into images of order which were more or less rigorously subjected to human control. This transformation began in the period between the late tenth and the twelfth centuries and was paralleled by simultaneous changes in the general concepts of time, space, the body, groups and female–male relationships. The consequences of the latter changes were the reorientation of the experience of time and the concepts of space from groups to perceived objective, though abstract, realities, the reduction of the significance and size of certain types of group, and the waning of the heterodynamic as well as the increase of autodynamic perceptions of the body. In short, the fundamental transformation of concepts in the Middle Ages shifted European culture from a group-centred system of comprehensive and synthetic concepts towards a space- and time-centred system of partial and analytic concepts. Much of this shift was accomplished by the thirteenth century. At this time, action became oriented towards the accomplishment of preconceived goals, the attainment of which was regarded as the manifestation of the human capability of adapting to or even provoking change. The shift promoted the acceptance of the new experience of time as an infinite universal entity beyond human control, and in the course of the fourteenth, fifteenth and sixteenth centuries supported the conceptualisation and depiction of space as continuous, uniform and permeable.

In conclusion, it is fair to say that, in the cultural history of medieval Europe, change was endemic but unequally distributed. There were some features of remarkable stability in this process, mainly the concept of space as the world. These features justify the use of the term 'Middle Ages' as a label tagged on the sum of the years between the gradual transformation of the Mediterranean Sea from an inland lake to a border zone and the abrupt abandonment of the image of the world as the tri-continental *ecumene*. During the Middle Ages, periods of accelerated and condensed change alternated with periods of relative stability. It is difficult to date the periods with any degree of precision as conceptual changes are generally elusive and defy being dated to the year. But it is arguable that the period between the late tenth and the thirteenth centuries was the period which witnessed most of the fundamental changes which were crucial in the history of European culture as a whole. That is to say that European culture in the early tenth century and European culture in the late thirteenth century betrayed more differences than continuities, and did so despite the strong concerns for the maintenance of stability which prevailed throughout the Middle Ages.

But change was not only unequally distributed in time. Its effects on European culture also differed with regard to the dimensions of space and group. One reason why the changes defy precise dating was the fact that whatever changes took place did not take place everywhere at the same time. Specifically, the process of territorialisation launched late in the early Middle Ages and enhanced during and after the twelfth century contributed to the widening diversity of spaces of regular communication in European culture. Not only was there a widening gap among the several regions making up the continent but also between the rural countryside and the urban communities of towns and cities. Last but not least, cultural change proceeded unevenly with regard to the various types of group. Most importantly, the rising significance of social groups *vis-à-vis* kin groups and neighbourhood groups made possible the contemporary as well as retrospective perception that social groups could enforce upon their members different degrees of willingness to adapt to change. Most notably, the social group of peasant farmers obtained a reputation for a willingness to preserve existing conditions of life and to resist change. This perception has a good deal of positive evidence to support it, but that does not mean that peasant farmers were necessarily and always unwilling or unable to adapt themselves to change.

Recognition of the changeability of the conditions of life and of the modes of reflection on it promoted cultural self-alienation. During the Middle Ages, Europeans learned to perceive the more remote past of their own culture as different, if not strange and imperfect. Yet the more the old attitudes, customs, habits, norms, values, traditions, material objects and, last but not least, concepts were recognised as having fallen from use, the more vocal became the demand that architectural as well as archaeological artefacts, pieces of art and music, as well as the wealth of records of written and oral tradition which had, by intention or not, survived the changes of the past, should be preserved and handed over to the custody of libraries, archives and museums. The 'hotness' of the European vision of history was complementary to the 'coldness' of living memories and repetitively re-enacted traditions. Therefore, in European culture, the ubiquity of change has been the cause of both a profound sense of history and a loss of genuine tradition.

References: A Select List

The following list of titles contains a selection of secondary literature which may be helpful as a way into the Middle Ages. Preference is given to publications other than handbooks and to recently published research work when they provide further references. The arrangement of this list follows the course of the argument in each chapter.

Introduction/Generalities

General work on the Middle Ages

Borst, Arno: *Lebensformen im Mittelalter* (Frankfurt, Berlin, 1979; first published Frankfurt, Berlin, 1973).

Braudel, Fernand: *The Structures of Everyday Life* (Berkeley, Los Angeles, 1992; first published Paris, 1979).

Favier, Jean, ed.: *XIVe et XVe siècles. Crises et genèses* (Paris, 1996).

Fichtenau, Heinrich: *Living in the Tenth Century* (London, 1991; reprinted London, 1993; first published, Monographien zur Geschichte des Mittelalters XXX, Stuttgart, 1984).

Gurevich, Aaron Yakovlevich: *Categories of Medieval Culture* (London, 1985; first published Moscow, 1972).

Le Goff, Jacques: *The Medieval Imagination* (Chicago, London, 1988; reprinted Chicago, London, 1992; first published Paris, 1985).

Le Goff, Jacques: *Medieval Civilization 400–1500* (Oxford, 1990; first published Paris, 1972; new edn Paris, 1997).

Le Goff, Jacques, ed.: *Der Mensch des Mittelalters* (Frankfurt, 1996; first published Rome, Bari, 1987).

Riché, Pierre: *La vie quotidienne dans l'empire Carolingien* (Paris, 1963).

Schultz, Alwin: *Das häusliche Lebe der europäischen Kulturvölker vom Mittelalter bis zur zweiten Hälfte des 18. Jahrhunderts* (Munich, 1903; reprinted Munich, 1985).

The concept of Europe

Fischer, Jürgen: *Oriens–Occidens–Europa: Begriff und Gedanke 'Europa' in der späten Antike und im frühen Mittelalter*, Veröffentlichungen des Instituts für Europäische Geschichte Mainz XV (Wiesbaden, 1957).

Hay, Denys: *Europe: The Emergence of an Idea*, Edinburgh University Publications. History, Philosophy and Economics VII (Edinburgh, 1957).

Leyser, Karl: 'Concepts of Europe in the Early and High Middle Ages', *Past and Present* CXXXVII (1992), pp. 25–47.

Wallach, Richard: *Das abendländische Gemeinschaftsbewußtsein im Mittelalter*, Beiträge zur Kulturgeschichte des Mittelalters und der Renaissance XXXIV (Leipzig, 1928).

Methodological problems of conceptualising culture

Comaroff, Jean, John Comaroff: *Ethnography and Historical Imagination* (Boulder, San Francisco, Oxford, 1992).

Foucault, Michel: *Archéologie du savoir* (Paris, 1969).

Koselleck, Reinhart: *Vergangene Zukunft: Zur Semantik geschichtlicher Zeiten*, 5th edn (Frankfurt, 1986; first published Frankfurt, 1978).

Muchembled, Robert: *Popular Culture and Elite Culture in France 1400–1750* (Baton Rouge, London, 1985; first published Paris. 1978).

Rosen, Robert: 'On a Theory of Transformations of Cultural Systems', in Colin Renfrew, Michael J. Rowlands, Barbara Abbott Segraves, eds, *Theory and Explanation in Archaeology* (London, 1982), pp. 301–13.

Time

Concepts and experiences of time

Dilg, Peter, Gundolf Keil, Dietz-Rüdiger Moser, eds: *Rhythmus und Saisonalität* (Sigmaringen, 1998).

Duhem, Pierre Maurice Marie: 'Le temps et le mouvement selon des scholastiques', *Revue de philosophie* 23 (1913), pp. 453–78; 24,1 (1914), pp. 5–15, 136–49, 225–41, 361–80, 470–88; 24,2 (1914), pp. 104–51.

Flasch, Kurt: *Was ist Zeit? Augustinus von Hippo: Das XI. Buch der Confessiones* (Frankfurt, 1993).

Fraser, Julius Thomas, ed.: *Voices of Time* (London, New York, 1968).

Fraser, Julius Thomas, N. Lawrence, eds: *The Study of Time*, vol. 2 (Berlin, Heidelberg, New York, 1975).

Jeck, Udo: *Aristoteles contra Augustinum: Zur Frage nach dem Verhältnis von Zeit und Seele bei den antiken Aristoteleskommentatoren, im arabischen Aristotelismus und im 13. Jahrhundert* (Amsterdam, Philadelphia, 1994).

Le Goff, Jacques: 'Temps de l'Eglise et temps du marchand', *Annales* XV (1960), pp. 417–33. Reprinted in Le Goff, *Pour un autre Moyen Age* (Paris, 1977), pp. 46–65.

Le Goff, Jacques: 'Le temps du travail dans la "crise" du XIVe siècle', *Le Moyen Age* 69 (1963), pp. 597–615.

Le Goff, Jacques: *Time, Work and Culture in the Middle Ages* (Chicago, London, 1982).

Lepenies, Wolf: *Das Ende der Naturgeschichte* (Munich, 1976).

Leroux, J.-M., ed.: *Le temps chrétien de la fin de l'Antiquité au Moyen Age* (Paris, 1981).

Smoller, Laura Ackerman: *History, Prophecy and the Stars: The Christian Astrology of Pierre d'Ailly 1350–1420* (Princeton, 1994).

Temps, mémoire et tradition au Moyen Age. Actes du 13e congrès de la Société des historiens médiévistes (Aix-en-Provence, 1983).

Measurement of time

Bilfinger, Gustav: *Die mittelalterlichen Horen und die modernen Stunden* (Stuttgart, 1892; repr. Vaduz, 1985).

Borst, Arno: *The Ordering of Time* (Chicago, London, 1993). First published in *Deutsches Archiv für Erforschung des Mittelalters* XLIV (1988), pp. 1–82. 2nd edn (Berlin , 1990).

Cipolla, Carlo Maria: *Clocks and Culture 1300–1700* (New York, 1967).

Dohrn-van Rossum, Gerhard: *The History of the Hour* (Chicago, London, 1997; first published Munich, Vienna, 1992).

Landes, David Saul: *Revolution in Time: Clocks and the Making of the Modern World* (Cambridge, Mass., London, 1984).

Maurice, Klaus, Otto Mayr: *The Clockwork Universe: German Clocks and Automata 1550–1650* (Bristol, 1980; also published Munich, 1980).

Zinner, Ernst: *Aus der Frühzeit der Räderuhr*, Deutsches Museum. Abhandlungen und Berichte XXII, 3 (Munich, Düsseldorf 1954).

Chronology, world ages

Bodmann, Gertrud: *Jahreszahlen und Weltalter: Zur Grundlegung von Zeit- und Raumvorstellungen in der mittelalterlichen Chronistik* (Frankfurt, New York, 1992).

Carozzi, Claude: *Weltuntergang und Seelenheil: Apokalyptische Visionen im Mittelalter* (Frankfurt, 1996).

Emmerson, Richard Kenneth: *Antichrist in the Middle Ages* (Seattle, 1981).

Fried, Johannes: 'Endzeiterwartung um die Jahrtausendwende', *Deutsches Archiv für Erforschung des Mittelalters* XLV (1989), pp. 381–473.

Haber, Francis C.: *The Age of the World: Moses to Darwin* (Baltimore, 1966; first published Baltimore, 1959; reprinted Des Plaines, 1978).

Konrad, Robert: *De ortu et tempore Antichristi. Antichristvorstellungen und Geschichtsbild des Abtes Adso von Montier-en-Der*, Münchener historische Studien, Abteilung Mittelalterliche Geschichte I (Kallmünz, 1964).

McGinn, Bernard: *Visions of the End* (New York, 1979).

Rauh, Horst Dieter: *Das Bild des Antichrist im Mittelalter: Von Tyconius zum Deutschen Symbolismus*, 2nd edn, Beiträge zur Geschichte der Philosophie und Theologie des Mittelalters N. F. IX (Münster, 1978; first published Münster, 1973).

Rossi, Paolo: *The Dark Abyss of Time: The History of the Earth and the History of Nations from Hooke to Vico* (Chicago, London, 1984; first published Milan, 1979).

Rudwick, Martin John Spencer: *The Meaning of Fossils,* 2nd edn (Chicago, London 1985; first published London, 1972).

Tristram, Hildegard L. C.: *Sex aetates mundi: Die Weltzeitalter bei den Angelsachsen und den Iren,* Anglistische Forschungen CLXV (Heidelberg, 1985).

Verbeke, Werner, Daniel Verhelst, Andries Welkenhuysen, eds: *The Use and Abuse of Eschatology in the Middle Ages,* Mediaevalia Lovaniensia, Series I, vol. XV (Louvain, 1988).

Verhelst, Daniel: 'Préhistoire des conceptions d'Adson concernant l'Antichrist', *Recherches de théologie ancienne et médiévale* LX (1973), pp. 52–103.

Verhelst, Daniel: 'Adso van Montier-en-Der en de angst voor het jaar Duizend', *Tijdschrift voor geschiedenis* XC (1977), pp. 1–10.

Wilcox, Donald J.: *The Measurement of Time: Pre-Newtonian Chronologies and the Rhetoric of Relative Time* (Chicago, London, 1987).

Space

Concepts and experiences of space

Davies, Wendy, Paul Fouracre, eds: *The Settlement of Disputes in Early Medieval Europe* (Cambridge, 1986). Reprinted (Cambridge, 1998).

Dupront, A.: 'Espace et humanisme', *Bibliothèque d'Humanisme et Renaissance* VIII (1946), pp. 7–104.

Fèbvre, Lucien: *La terre et l'évolution humaine* (Paris, 1970; first published Paris, 1922).

Gautier Dalché, Patrick: *Géographie et culture: La représentation de l'espace du VIe au XIIe siècle,* Variorum Collected Studies Series DXCII (Aldershot, 1997).

Gellrich, Jesse M.: 'The Semiology of Space in the Middle Ages: On Manuscript Painting, Sacred Architecture, Scholasticism, and Music', in Gellrich, *The Idea of the Book in the Middle Ages* (Ithaca, London, 1986), pp. 51–93.

Graf, Klaus: 'Das "Land" Schwaben im späten Mittelalter', in Peter Moraw, ed., *Regionale Identität und soziale Gruppen im deutschen Mittelalter,* Zeitschrift für Historische Forschung. Beiheft XIV (Berlin, 1992), pp. 127–64.

Moraw, Peter, ed.: *Raumerfassung und Raumbewußtsein im späteren Mittelalter,* Protokolle des Konstanzer Arbeitskreises für Mittelalterliche Geschichte CCCLXVII (Constance, 1995).

Rosenwein, Barbara H.: *Negotiating Space: Power, Restraint, and Privileges of Immunity in Early Medieval Europe* (Ithaca, London, 1999).

Woodward, David: 'Reality, Symbolism, Time, and Space in Medieval World Maps', *Annals of the Association of American Geographers* LXXV (1985), pp. 510–21.

Cartography

Arentzen, Jörn-Geerd: *Imago mundi cartographica: Studien zur Bildlichkeit mittelalterlicher Welt- und Ökumenekarten unter besonderer Berücksichtigung eines Zusammenwirkens von Text und Bild*, Münsterische Mittelalter-Schriften LIII (Munich, 1984).

Black, Jeremy: *Maps and Politics* (London, 1997).

Börner, Klaus: *Auf der Suche nach dem irdischen Paradies* (Frankfurt, 1984).

Brincken, Anna-Dorothee von den: *Fines Terrae*, MGH Schriften XXXVI (Hanover, 1992).

Gautier Dalché, Patrick: *La 'Descriptio Mappae Mundi' de Hugues de Saint Victor* (Paris, 1988).

Grimm, Reinhold: *Paradisus coelestis, paradises terrestris: Zur Auslegungsgeschichte des Paradieses im Abendland bis um 1200*, Medium Aevum XXXIII (Munich, 1977).

Harley, John Brian, David Woodward, eds: *The History of Cartography*, vol. 1 (Chicago, London, 1987).

Kugler, Hartmut, Eckhard Michael, eds: *Ein Weltbild vor Columbus* (Weinheim, 1991).

Marshall, Peter James, Glyndwr Williams: *The Great Map of Mankind* (London, 1982).

Randles, William Graham Lester: *De la terre plate au globe terrestre* (Paris, 1980).

Russell, Jeffrey Burton: *Inventing the Flat Earth: Columbus and Modern Historians* (New York, Westport, London, 1997; first published New York, 1991).

Simek, Rudolf: *Altnordische Kosmographie*, Ergänzungsbände zum Reallexikon für Germanische Altertumskunde IV (Berlin, New York, 1990).

Woodward, David, ed.: *Art and Cartography* (Chicago, London, 1987).

Houses, settlements

Beck, Heinrich, Heiko Steuer, eds: *Haus und Hof in ur- und frühgeschichtlicher Zeit. Gedenkschrift für Herbert Jankuhn*, AAWG CCXVIII (Göttingen, 1997).

Davies, Wendy, Hayo Vierck: 'The Contexts of Tribal Hidage: Social Aggregates and Settlement Patterns', *Frühmittelalterliche Studien* VIII (1974), pp. 223–93.

Devroey, Jean-Pierre: *Etudes sur le grand domaine carolingien*, Variorum Collected Studies Series CCCXCI (Aldershot, 1993).

Hooke, Della: 'The Organization of the Country', in Hooke, *The Landscape of Anglo-Saxon England* (London, Washington, 1998), pp. 39–104.

Jankuhn, Herbert: 'Terra . . . silvis horrida (zu Tactus, Germanica, cap. 8)', *Archaeologia geographica* X, 1 (1961/63), pp. 19–37.

Kroeschell, Karl: *Haus und Herrschaft im frühen deutschen Recht*, Göttinger Rechtswissenschaftliche Studien LXX (Göttingen, 1968).

Kyll, Nikolaus: *Tod, Grab, Begräbnisplatz, Totenfeier: Zur Geschichte ihres Brauchtums im Trierer Lande und in Luxemburg unter besonderer Berücksichtigung des Visitationshandbuchs des Regino von Prüm*, Rheinisches Archiv LXXXI (Bonn, 1972).

Oexle, Otto Gerhard: 'Mahl und Spende im mittelalterlichen Totenkult', *Frühmittelalterliche Studien* XVIII (1984), pp. 401–20.

Oexle, Otto Gerhard: 'Haus und Ökonomie im früheren Mittelalter', in Gerd Althoff, Dieter Geuenich, Otto Gerhard Oexle, Joachim Wollasch, eds, *Person und Gemeinschaft im Mittelalter. Festschrift für Karl Schmid* (Sigmaringen, 1988), pp. 101–22.

Sawyer, Peter Hayes, ed.: *Medieval Settlement* (London, 1976).

Territories, polities

Algazi, Gadi: *Herrengewalt und Gewalt der Herren im späten Mittelalter*, Historische Studien XVII (Frankfurt, New York, 1996).

Brunner, Otto: *Land and Lordship* (Philadelphia, 1984; first published, VIÖG I, Baden, 1939).

Jäckenhövel, Albrecht, ed.: *Bergbau, Verhüttung und Waldnutzung im Mittelalter*, VSWG. Beiheft CXXI (Stuttgart, 1996).

Janssen, Wilhelm: '. . . na gesetze unser lande: Zur territorialen Gesetzgebung im späten Mittelalter', in Dietmar Willoweit, ed., *Gesetzgebung als Faktor der Staatsentwicklung*, Der Staat. Beiheft VII (Berlin, 1984), pp. 7–40.

Kießling, Rudolf: *Die Stadt und ihr Umland*, Städteforschung Reihe A, vol. XXIX (Cologne, Vienna, 1989).

Maitland, Frederic William: *Domesday Book and Beyond* (Cambridge, 1897; reprinted Cambridge, 1988).

Oexle, Otto Gerhard: 'Sozialgeschichte–Begriffsgeschichte–Wissenschaftsgeschichte: Anmerkungen zum Werk Otto Brunners', *VSWG* LXXI (1984), pp. 305–41.

Welti, Max: 'Der Begriff des Landes bei Otto Brunner und seine Rezeption durch die verfassungsgeschichtliche Forschung', *Zeitschrift der Savigny-Stiftung für Rechtsgeschichte, Germanistische Abteilung* CVII (1990), pp. 339–76.

Willoweit, Dietmar: *Rechtsgrundlagen der Territorialgewalt: Landesobrigkeit, Herrschaftsrechte und Territorium in der Rechtswissenschaft der Neuzeit* (Cologne, Vienna, 1975).

Wolf, Armin: *Gesetzgebung in Europa 1150–1500* (Munich, 1996).

The Body – Modes of Behaviour

Perceptions of the body

Bernath, Klaus: *Anima forma corporis: Eine Untersuchung über die ontologischen Grundlagen der Anthropologie des Thomas von Aquin*, Abhandlungen zur Philosophie, Psychologie und Pädagogik XXXVII (Bonn, 1969).

Buisson, Ludwig: *Der Bildstein Ardre VIII auf Gotland: Göttermythen, Heldensagen und Jenseitsglaube der Germanen im 8. Jahrhundert nach Christus*, AAWG CII (Göttingen, 1976).

Dinzelbacher, Peter: *Vision und Visionsliteratur im Mittelalter*, Monographien zur Geschichte des Mittelalters XXIII (Stuttgart, 1981).

Eichberg, Henning: *Body Cultures: Essays on Sport, Space and Identity*, ed. John Bale (London, New York, 1998).

Fehrer, Michael, ed.: *Fragments of the History of the Human Body* (New York, 1989).

Huizinga, Johan: *Homo ludens* (Hamburg, 1956).

Krause, Burkhard: 'Hermeneutische Aspekte der Körpererfahrung im Mittelalter', in Joachim Kuolt, Harald Kleinschmidt, Peter Dinzelbacher, eds, *Das Mittelalter – Unsere fremde Vergangenheit*, Flugschriften der Volkshochschule Stuttgart N. F. VI (Stuttgart, 1990), pp. 71–115.

Muchembled, Robert: *L'invention de l'homme moderne: Culture et sensibilités en France du XVe au XVIIIe siècle*, 2nd edn (Paris, 1994; first published Paris, 1988).

Nitschke, August: *Körper in Bewegung* (Stuttgart, 1989).

Schreiner, Klaus, Norbert Schnitzler, eds: *Gepeinigt, begehrt, vergessen: Symbolik und Sozialbezug des Körpers im späten Mittelalter und in der frühen Neuzeit* (Munich, 1992).

Zur Lippe, Rudolf: *Vom Leib zum Körper: Naturbeherrschung am Menschen in der Renaissance* (Reinbek, 1988).

Crucifixes

Hürkey, Edgar J.: *Das Bild des Gekreuzigten im Mittelalter* (Worms, 1983).

Cults of saints

Abou-el-Haj, Barbara: *The Medieval Cult of Saints* (Cambridge, 1995).

Angenendt, Arnold: *Monachi peregrini: Studien zu Pirmin und den monastischen Vorstellungen des frühen Mittelalters*, Münsterische Mittelalter-Schriften VI (Munich, 1972).

Goodich, Michael: *Vita perfecta: The Ideal of Sainthood in the Thirteenth Century*, Monographien zur Geschichte des Mittelalters XXV (Stuttgart, 1982).

Kemp, Eric Waldram: *Canonization and Authority in the Western Church* (London, 1948).

Quinn, Patricia A.: *Better than the Sons of Kings: Boys and Monks in the Early Middle Ages* (New York, 1989).

Ridyard, Susan J.: *The Royal Saints of Anglo-Saxon England*, Cambrige Studies in Medieval Life and Thought Fourth Series, vol. IX (Cambridge, 1988).

Scholz, Sebastian: *Transmigration und Translation: Studien zum Bistumswechsel der Bischöfe von der Spätantike bis zum hohen Mittelalter*,

Kölner historische Abhandlungen XXXVII (Cologne, Weimar, Vienna, 1992).

Schulenburg, Jane Tibbetts: *Forgetful of Their Sex: Female Sanctity and Society c. 500–1100* (Chicago, London, 1997).

Powerful lay people and experiences of powerlessness

Deshman, Robert: 'The Exalted Servant: The Ruler Theology of the Prayer-book of Charles the Bald', *Viator* XI (1980), pp. 385–417.

Delumeau, Jean: *Le peche et la peur: La culpibilisation en Occident* (Paris, 1983).

Graus, František: *Pest, Geißler, Judenmorde: Das 14. Jahrhundert als Krisenzeit*, VMPIG LXXXVI (Göttingen, 1987).

Individualism

Aertsen, Jan A., Andreas Speer, eds: *Individuum und Individualität im Mittelalter*, Miscellanea Mediaevalia XXIV (Berlin, New York, 1996).

Gurevich, Aaron Yakovlevich; 'Die Darstellung von Persönlichkeit und Zeit in der mittelalterlichen Kunst und Literatur', *Archiv für Kulturgeschichte* LXXI (1989), pp. 1–44.

MacFarlane, Alan: *The Origins of English Individualism* (Oxford, 1989; first published Oxford, 1978).

Misch, Georg: *Geschichte der Autobiographie*, 3rd edn, vol. 2, 3, 4 (Frankfurt, 1955–1969; first published Leipzig, 1907).

Rühl, Joachim K.: 'Wesen und Bedeutung von Kampfansagen und Trefferzahlskizzen für die Geschichte des spätmittelalterlichen Turniers', in Giselher Spitzer, Dieter Schmidt, eds, *Sport zwischen Eigenständigkeit und Fremdbestimmung. Festschrift für Hajo Bernett* (Bonn, 1986), pp. 86–112.

Groups

Kin groups

Althoff, Gerd: *Adels- und Königsfamilien im Spiegel ihrer Memorialüberlieferung: Studien zum Totengedenken der Billunger und Ottonen*, Münstersche Mittelalter-Schriften XLVII (Munich, 1984).

Bouchard, Constance B.: 'Consanguinity and Noble Marriages in the Tenth and Eleventh Century', *Speculum* LVI (1981), pp. 268–87.

Bouchard, Constance B.: 'Structure and Family Consciousness among the Aristocracy in the 9th to 11th Centuries', *Francia* XIV (1986), pp. 639–58.

Brunner, Heinrich: 'Sippe und Wergeld nach niederdeutschem Recht', *Zeitschrift der Savigny-Stiftung für Rechtsgeschichte, Germanistische Abteilung* III (1882), pp. 1–101. Edited in Brunner, *Abhandlungen zur Rechtsgeschichte*, ed. Karl Rauch, vol. 1 (Weimar, 1931), pp. 104–208. Reprinted (Leipzig, 1965).

Duby, Georges: *Hommes et structures du Moyen Age* (The Hague, Paris, 1973).

Ewig, Eugen: 'Studien zur merowingischen Dynastie', *Frühmittelalterliche Studien* VIII (1974), pp. 15–59.

Fehring, Günter Peter: 'Missions- und Kirchenwesen in archäologischer Sicht', in Herbert Jankuhn, Reinhard Wenskus, eds, *Geschichtswissenschaft und Archäologie*, VuF XXII (Sigmaringen, 1979), pp. 547–91.

Geary, Patrick J.: *Living with the Dead in the Middle Ages* (Ithaca, London, 1994).

Hauck, Karl: 'Geblütsheiligkeit', *Liber floridus. Festgabe für Paul Lehmann* (St. Ottilien, 1950), pp. 187–240.

Hauck, Karl: 'Lebensnormen und Kultmythen in germanischen Stammes-und Herrschergenealogien', *Saeculum* VI (1955), pp. 186–223.

Heers, Jacques: *Family Clans in the Middle Ages* (Amsterdam, 1978; first published Paris, 1974).

Hennebicque, Régine: 'Structures familiales et politiques au IXe siècle: Un group familial de l'aristocratie franque', *Revue historique* CCLXV (1981), pp. 289–333.

Herlihy, David: 'Land, Family and Women in Continental Europe 700–1200', *Traditio* XVIII (1962), pp. 89–120.

Meyer, Ulrich: *Soziales Handeln im Zeichen des 'Hauses': Zur Ökonomik in der Spätantike und im früheren Mittelalter*, VMPIG CXL (Göttingen, 1998).

Murray, Alexander Callander: *Germanic Kinship Structure*, Pontifical Institute of Medieval Studies. Texts and Studies LXV (Toronto, 1983).

Mitterauer, Michael: *Ahnen und Heilige: Namengebung in der europäischen Geschichte* (Munich, 1993).

Oexle, Otto Gerhard: 'Memoria und Memorialüberlieferung im früheren Mittelalter', *Frühmittelalterliche Studien* X (1976), pp. 70–95.

Pader, E.-J.: *Symbolism, Social Relations and the Interpretation of Mortuary Remains*, BAR, International Series CXXX (Oxford, 1982).

Patlagean, Evelyne: 'Une représentation de la patenté et ses origines occidentales', *L'homme* VI (1966), pp. 159–81.

Rollason, David: 'The Shrines of Saints in Later Anglo-Saxon England: Distribution and Significance', in L. A. S. Butler, R. K. Morris, eds, *The Anglo-Saxon Church. Papers on History, Architecture and Archaeology in Honour of Dr Harold McCarter Taylor*, Council for British Archaeology. Research Report LX (London, 1986), pp. 32–43.

Rollason, David: *Saints and Relics in Anglo-Saxon England* (Oxford, Cambridge, Mass., 1989).

Schmid, Karl, Joachim Wollasch: 'Die Gemeinschaft der Lebenden und Verstorbenen in Zeugnissen des Mittelalters', *Frühmittelalterliche Studien* I (1967), pp. 365–405.

Schmid, Karl: *Gebetsgedenken und adliges Selbstverständnis im Mittelalter* (Sigmaringen, 1983).

Schuler, Peter Johannes, ed.: *Die Familie als sozialer und historischer Verband* (Sigmaringen, 1987).

Stutz, Ulrich: *Die Eigenkirche als Element des mittelalterlich-germanischen Kirchenrechts* (Berlin 1895; reprinted, Libelli XXVIII, Darmstadt, 1955).

Tanz, Sabine: *Jean d'Arc: Spätmittelalterliche Mentalität im Spiegel eines Weltbildes*, Forschungen zur mittelalterlichen Geschichte XXXIII (Weimar, 1991).

Wenskus, Reinhard: *Sächsischer Stammesadel und fränkischer Reichsadel*, AAWG XCIII (Göttingen, 1976).

Neighbourhood groups

Arnold, Klaus: *Niklashausen 1476*, Saecvla spiritalia III (Baden-Baden. 1980).

Blickle, Peter, ed.: *Revolte und Revolution in Europa*, Historische Zeitschrift. Beiheft N. F. IV (Munich, 1975).

Blickle, Peter, Peter Bierbrauer, C. Ullrich, eds: *Aufruhr und Empörung? Studien zum bäuerlichen Widerstand im Alten Reich* (Munich, 1980).

Chibnall, Albert Charles: *Sherington* (Cambridge, 1965).

Dobson, Richard Barrie: *The Peasants' Revolt of 1381* (London, 1970).

Hilton, Rodney Howard: *Bond Men Made Free: Medieval Peasant Movements and the English Rising of 1381*, A Series on Popular Risings II (London, 1973).

Lüdtke, Alf, Thomas Lindenberger, eds: *Physische Gewalt: Studien zur Geschichte der Neuzeit* (Frankfurt, 1995).

Phythian-Adams, Charles: *Rethinking English Local History*, University of Leicester. Department of English Local History. Occasional Papers Fourth Series I (Leicester, 1987).

Rösener, Werner: *Peasants in the Middle Ages* (Urbana, Chicago, 1993; first published Munich, 1985).

Rösener, Werner, ed.: *Grundherrschaft und bäuerliche Gesellschaft im Hochmittelalter*, VMPIG CXV (Göttingen, 1995).

Schulz, Knut: *'Denn sie lieben die Freiheit so sehr': Kommunale Erhebungen in mittelalterlichen Städten* (Darmstadt, 1992).

Contractual groups

Althoff, Gerd: 'Zur Frage nach der Organisation der sächsischen Coniurationes in der Ottonenzeit', *Frühmittelalterliche Studien* XVI (1982), pp. 129–42.

Brogliolo, G. P.: 'Ideas of the Town in Italy during the Transition from Antiquity to the Middle Ages', in G. P. Brogiolo, Bryan Ward-Perkins, eds, *The Idea and Ideal of the Town between Late Antiquity and the Early Middle Ages* (Leiden, Boston, Cologne, 1999), pp. 99–146.

Classen, Carl Joachim: *Die Stadt im Spiegel der descriptiones und laudes urbium in der antiken und mittelalterlichen Literatur bis zum Ende des zwölften Jahrhunderts*, Beiträge zur Altertumswissenschaft II (Hildesheim, New York, 1986).

De Minicis, Elisabetta, Enrico Guidoni, eds: *Case e torri medievali. Atti del 2o*

Convegno di studi 'La città e le case: Tessuti urbani, domus e case-torri nell'I-talia communale (secc. XI–XV)' (Rome, 1996).

Dilcher, Gerhard: *Bürgerrecht und Stadtverfassung im europäischen Mittelalter* (Cologne, Weimar, Vienna, 1996).

Dollinger, Philippe: *La Hanse*, 2nd edn (Paris, 1988; first published Paris, 1970).

Fleckenstein, Josef, Karl Stackmann, eds: *Über Bürger, Stadt und städtische Literatur im Spätmittelalter*, AAWG CXXI (Göttingen, 1980).

Frugoni, Chiara: *A Distant City: Images of Urban Experience in the Medieval World* (Princeton, 1991; first published Turin, 1983).

Geuenich, Dieter: 'Zur Landnahme der Alemannen', *Frühmittelalterliche Studien* XVI (1982), pp. 25–44.

Gierke, Otto von: *Das deutsche Genossenschaftsrecht*, vol. 3 (Berlin 1881; reprinted Graz, 1954).

Hammel-Kiesow, Rolf, ed.: *Wege zur Erforschung städtischer Häuser und Höfe: Beiträge zur fachübergreifenden Zusammenarbeit am Beispiel Lübecks im Spätmittelalter und in der frühen Neuzeit* (Neumünster, 1993).

Head, Thomas, Richard Landes, eds: *The Peace of God: Social Violence and Religious Response in France around the Year 1000* (Ithaca, London, 1992).

Irsigler, Franz, Neithard Bulst, Jochen Hoock, eds: *Bevölkerung, Wirtschaft und Gesellschaft: Stadt-Land-Beziehungen in Deutschland und Frankreich: 14. bis 19. Jahrhundert* (Trier, 1983).

Keller, Hagen: *Adelsherrschaft und städtische Gesellschaft in Oberitalien 9.–12. Jahrhundert*, Bibliothek des Deutschen Historischen Instituts in Rom LII (Tübingen, 1979).

Knowles, David: *The Monastic Order in England*, 2nd edn (Cambridge, 1963; first published Cambridge, 1940).

Kottje, Raymund, Helmut Maurer, eds: *Monastische Reformen im 9. und 10. Jahrhundert*, VuF XXXVIII (Sigmaringen, 1989).

Kruse, Holger, Werner Paravicini, Andreas Ranft, eds: *Ritterorden und Adelsgesellschaften im spätmittelalterlichen Deutschland: Ein systematisches Verzeichnis*, Kieler Werkstücke. Reihe D, vol. I (Frankfurt, Bern, New York, 1991).

Les libertés urbaines et rurales du XIe au XIVe siècles, Pro civitate: Collection histoire in 8o XIX (Brussels, 1968).

Les métiers au Moyen Age: Aspects économiques et sociaux (Louvain-la-Neuve, 1994).

Oexle, Otto Gerhard: *Forschungen zu monastischen und geistlichen Gemein-schaften im westfränkischen Bereich*, Münsterische Mittelalter-Schriften XXXI (Munich, 1978).

Oexle, Otto Gerhard: 'Gilden als soziale Gruppen in der Karolingerzeit', in Herbert Jankuhn, Walter Janssen, Ruth Schmidt-Wiegand, Heinrich Tiefenbach, eds, *Das Handwerk in vor- und frühgeschichtlicher Zeit*, AAWG CXXII (Göttingen, 1981), pp. 284–354.

Oexle, Otto Gerhard: 'Gilde und Kommune', in Peter Blickle, Elisabeth

Müller-Luckner, eds, *Theorien kommunaler Ordnung in Europa*, Schriften des Historischen Kollegs. Kolloquien XXXVI (Munich, 1996), pp. 75–97.

Padberg, Lutz von: *Mission und Christianisierung* (Stuttgart, 1995).

Ranft, Andreas: *Adelsgesellschaften, Gruppenbildungen und Genossenschaften im spätmittelalterlichen Reich*, Kieler historische Studien XXXVIII (Sigmaringen, 1994).

Reininghaus, Wilfried: *Die Entstehung der Gesellengilden im Spätmittelalter*, VSWG. Beiheft LXXI (Stuttgart, 1981).

Schlesinger, Walter: *Beiträge zur deutschen Verfassungsgeschichte des Mittelalters*, 2 vols (Göttingen, 1963).

Schwineköper, Berent, ed.: *Gilden und Zünfte, kaufmännische und gewerbliche Genossenschaften im frühen und hohen Mittelalter*, VuF XXIX (Sigmaringen, 1985).

Stoob, Heinz: *Die Hanse* (Graz, 1995).

Werner, Ernst: *Stadtluft macht frei: Frühscholastik und bürgerliche Emanzipation in der ersten Hälfte des 12. Jahrhunderts*, Sitzungsberichte der Sächsischen Akademie der Wissenschaften, Philol.-Hist. Kl. CXVIII,5 (Leipzig, 1976).

Political groups

Beaune, Colette: *Naissance de la nation* (Paris, 1985).

Brunner, Karl, Brigitte Merta, eds: *Ethnogenese und Überlieferung*, VIÖG XXXI (Vienna, 1994).

Ehlers, Joachim: 'Mittelalterliche Voraussetzungen für nationale Identität in der Neuzeit', in Bernhard Giesen, ed., *Nationale und kulturelle Identität* (Frankfurt, 1991), pp. 77–99.

Forde, Simon, Lesley Johnson, Alan V. Murray, eds: *Concepts of National Identity in the Middle Ages*, Leeds Texts and Monographs N. S. XIV (Leeds 1995).

Fried, Johannes: 'Gens und *regnum*: Wahrnehmungs- und Deutungskategorien politischen Wandels im früheren Mittelalter', in Jürgen Miethke, Klaus Schreiner, eds, *Sozialer Wandel im Mittelalter* (Sigmaringen, 1994), pp. 73–104.

Goffart, Walter: *Barbarians and Romans A.D. 418–584* (Princeton, 1980).

Hellmuth, Doris: *Frau und Besitz: Zum Handlungsspielraum von Frauen in Alemannien (700–940)*, VuF. Sonderband XLII (Sigmaringen, 1998).

Kahl, Hans-Dietrich: 'Einige Beobachtungen zum Sprachgebrauch von natio im mittelalterlichen Latein', in Helmut Beumann, Werner Schröder, eds, *Aspekte der Nationenbildung im Mittelalter*, Nationes I (Sigmaringen, 1978), pp. 63–107.

Pohl, Walter, ed.: *Kingdoms of the Empire: The Integration of Barbarians in Late Antiquity* (Leiden, Boston, Cologne, 1997).

Schröker, Alfred: *Die deutsche Nation: Beobachtungen zur politischen Propaganda des ausgehenden 15. Jahrhunderts*, Historische Studien CDXXVI (Lübeck, 1974).

Wenskus, Reinhard: *Stammesbildung und Verfassung*, 2nd edn (Cologne, Vienna, 1977; first published Cologne, Graz, 1961).

Wolfram, Herwig, Walter Pohl, eds: *Typen der Ethnogenese unter besonderer Berücksichtigung der Bayern*, 2 vols (Vienna, 1990).

Social groups

Bloch, Marc: *Feudal Society*, 2 vols. (London, New York, 1989; first English edition London, 1961–62; first published Paris, 1939).

Bois, Guy: *The Crisis of Feudalism* (Cambridge, Paris, 1984; first published Paris, 1981).

Bosl, Karl: *Die Sozialstruktur der mittelalterlichen Residenz- und Fernhandelsstadt Regensburg*, Abhandlungen der Philos.-Hist. Klasse der Bayerischen Akademie der Wissenschaften N. F. LXIII (Munich, 1966).

Bosl, Karl: *Die Grundlagen der modernen Gesellschaft im Mittelalter*, 2 vols., Monographien zur Geschichte des Mittelalters IV (Stuttgart, 1972).

Duby, Georges: *The Three Orders* (Chicago, London, 1980; first published Paris, 1978).

Frantzen, Allen J., Douglas Moffat, eds: *The Work of Work: Servitude, Slavery and Labor in Medieval England* (Glasgow, 1994).

Hilton, Rodney Howard: *Class Conflict and the Crisis of Feudalism* (London, Ronceverte, 1985).

Karras, Ruth M.: *Slavery and Society in Medieval Scandinavia* (New Haven, London, 1988).

Koselleck, Reinhart, Klaus Schreiner, eds: *Bürgerschaft: Rezeption und Innovation der Begrifflichkeit vom hohen Mittelalter bis ins 19. Jahrhundert*, Sprache und Geschichte XXII (Stuttgart, 1994).

Meier, Ulrich: *Mensch und Bürger: Die Stadt im Denken spätmittelalterlicher Theologen, Philosophen und Juristen* (Munich, 1994).

Mindermann, Arend: *Adel in der Stadt des Spätmittelalters: Göttingen und Stade 1300 bis 1600*, Veröffentlichungen des Instituts für Historische Landesforschung der Universität Göttingen XXXXV (Bielefeld, 1996).

Oexle, Otto Gerhard: 'Die funktionale Dreiteilung als Deutungsschema der sozialen Wirklichkeit in der ständischen Gesellschaft des Mittelalters', Winfried Schulze, Helmut Gabel, eds, *Ständische Gesellschaft und soziale Mobilität*, Schriften des Historischen Kollegs. Kolloquien XII (Munich, 1988), pp. 19–51.

Pelteret, David A. E.: *Slavery in Early Medieval England* (Woodbridge, 1995).

Polívka, Miloslav: 'The Self-Consciousness of the Czech Nobility against the Background of Czech–German Relations at the End of the Hussite Period', *Historica* S. N. II (1995), pp. 75–100.

Powell, Timothy E.: 'The "Three Orders" of Society in Anglo-Saxon England', *Anglo-Saxon England* XXIII (1994), pp. 103–32.

Schreiner, Klaus, Ulrich Meier, eds: *Stadtregiment und Bürgerfreiheit: Handlungsspielräume in deutschen und italienischen Städten des späten Mittelalters und der frühen Neuzeit*, Bürgertum VII (Göttingen, 1994).

Schreiner, Klaus: 'Religiöse, historische und rechtliche Legitimation spätmit-telalterlicher Adelsherrschaft', in Otto Gerhard Oexle, Werner Paravicini, eds, *Nobilitas: Funktion und Repräsentation des Adels in Alteuropa*, VMPIG CXXXIII (Göttingen 1997), pp. 376–430.

Wenskus, Reinhard, Herbert Jankuhn, Klaus R. Grinda, eds: *Wort und Begriff 'Bauer'*, AAWG XCIII (Göttingen, 1976).

Zimmermann, Albert, ed.: *Soziale Ordnungen im Selbstverständnis des Mittelalters*, Miscellanea Mediaevalia XII (Berlin, New York, 1979).

Men and Women

Perceptions of the relations between the sexes in the early Middle Ages

Affeldt, Werner, ed.: *Frauen in Spätantike und Frühmittelalter* (Sigmaringen, 1989).

Ebel, Else: *Der Konkubinat nach altwestnordischen Quellen: Philologische Studien zur sogenannten 'Friedelehe'*, Ergänzungsbände zum Reallexikon für Germanische Altertumskunde VIII (Berlin, New York, 1993).

Enright, Michael Joseph: *Lady with a Mead-Cup: Ritual, Prophecy and Lord-ship in the European Warband from LaTene to the Viking Age* (Dublin, 1996).

Fell, Christine Elizabeth, Cecily Clark: *Women in Anglo-Saxon England and the Impact of 1066* (London, 1984).

Fischer, Andreas: *Engagement, Wedding and Marriage in Old English*, Anglis-tische Forschungen CLXXVI (Heidelberg, 1986).

Flandrin, Jean-Louis: *Familles, parenté, maison, sexualité dans l'ancienne société* (Paris, 1976).

Goetz, Hans-Werner, ed.: *Weibliche Lebensgestaltung im frühen Mittelalter* (Cologne, Weimar, Vienna, 1991).

Goetz, Hans-Werner: *Frauen im Mittelalter: Frauenbild und Frauenleben im fränkischen Reich* (Cologne, Weimar, Vienna, 1995).

Nitschke, August: 'Frauen und Männer im Mittelalter', in Jochen Martin, Renate Zoepffel, eds, *Aufgaben, Rollen und Räume von Mann und Frau*, Veröffentlichungen des Instituts für Historische Anthropologie IV (Freiburg, Munich, 1989), pp. 677–707.

Stafford, Pauline A.: *Queens, Concubines, and Dowagers: The King's Wife in the Early Middle Ages* (Athens, London, 1983; reprinted London, Washington, 1998).

Stafford, Pauline A.: 'Women and the Norman Conquest', *Transactions of the Royal Historical Society* Sixth Series, IV (1994), pp. 221–49.

Wemple, Suzanne Fonay: *Women in Frankish Society: Marriage and the Cloister 500 to 900* (Philadelphia, 1985).

Perceptions of the relations between the sexes in the high and late Middle Ages

Duby, Georges: *The Knight, the Lady and the Priest* (Harmondsworth, 1985; re-edited Chicago, London, 1993; first published Paris, 1981).

Duby, Georges, Michelle Perrot, eds: *A History of Women*, vols 1–3 (Cambridge, Mass., London, 1992–93; first published Rome, Bari, 1990–91).

Ennen, Edith: *The Medieval Women* (Oxford, 1989; first published Munich, 1984).

La Femme, 2 vols, Recueils de la Société Jean Bodin XI–XII (Brussels, 1959–62).

Herlihy, David: *Medieval Households* (Cambridge, Mass., London, 1985).

Howell, Martha: *Women, Production and Patriarchy in Late Medieval Cities* (Chicago, London, 1988).

Klapisch-Zuber, Christiane: *Les Toscans et leurs familles* (Paris, 1978).

Opitz, Claudia: *Frauenalltag im Mittelalter*, Ergebnisse der Frauenforschung V (Weinheim, Basle, 1985).

Ozment, Steven: *When Fathers Ruled: Family Life in Reformation Europe* (Cambridge, Mass., London, 1983).

Rosenthal, Joel T., ed.: *Medieval Women and the Sources of Medieval History* (Athens, Ga., London 1990).

Schuster, Beate: 'Frauenhandel und Frauenhäuser im 15. und 16. Jahrhundert', *VSWG* LXXVIII (1991), pp. 172–89.

Shahar, Shulamith: *The Fourth Estate: History of Women in the Middle Ages* (London, 1983).

Wensky, Margret: *Die Stellung der Frau in der stadtkölnischen Wirtschaft im Spätmittelalter*, Quellen und Darstellungen zur hansischen Geschichte N. F. XXVI (Cologne, Vienna, 1980).

Women as transmitters of knowledge

Grundmann, Herbert: 'Die Frauen und die Literatur im Mittelalter', *Archiv für Kulturgeschichte* XXVI (1936), pp. 129–61.

McNamara, Jo-Ann, Suzanne Fonay Wemple: 'The Power of Women through Family in Medieval Europe', in Mary S. Hartman, Lois W. Banner, eds, *Clio's Consciousness Raised: New Perspectives on the History of Women* (New York, 1974), pp. 103–18.

Nelson, Janet Laughland: 'Reconstructing a Royal Family: Reflections on Alfred, from Asser, cap. 2', in Ian Wood, Niels Lund, eds, *People and Places in Northern Europe 500–1600: Essays in Honour of Peter Hayes Sawyer* (Woodbridge, 1991), pp. 47–66.

Nolte, Cordula: *Conversio und Christianitas: Frauen in der Christianisierung vom 5. bis 8. Jahrhundert*, Monographien zur Geschichte des Mittelalters XLI (Stuttgart, 1995).

Sexual taboos

Brundage, James A.: *Sex, Law and Marriage in the Middle Ages*, Variorum Collected Studies Series CCCXCVII (Aldershot, 1993).

Frantzen, Allen J.: *The Literature of Penance in Anglo-Saxon England* (New Brunswick, 1986).

Payer, Pierre J.: *Sex and the Penitentials* (Toronto, 1984).

Consensual marriage

Brundage, James A.: *Sex, Law and Christian Society in the Middle Ages* (Chicago, London, 1990).

Duby, Georges: *Medieval Marriage*, The Johns Hopkins Symposia in Comparative History IX (Baltimore, London, 1978; reprinted Baltimore, London, 1992).

Freisen, Joseph: *Geschichte des canonischen Eherechts bis zum Verfall der Glossenliteratur*, 2nd edn (Paderborn, 1893; reprinted Paderborn, 1963; first published Tübingen, 1888).

Sheehan, Michael M., K. Scardellato: *Family and Marriage in Medieval Europe* (Toronto, 1976).

Sheehan, Michael M.: 'The Bishop of Rome to a Barbarian King on the Rituals of Marriage', in Steven B. Bowman, Blanche E. Cody, eds, *Studies on Canon Law in Memory of Schafer Williams* (Cincinatti, 1991), pp. 187–99.

Theory of love

Dallapiazza, Michael: *Minne, hûsêre und das ehlich leben: Zur Konstitution bürgerlicher Lebensmuster in spätmittelalterlichen und frühhumanistischen Didaktiken* (Frankfurt, Bern, 1981).

Glier, Ingeborg: *Artes amandi: Untersuchung zu Geschichte, Überlieferung und Typologie der deutschen Minnereden*, Münchener Texte und Untersuchungen zur deutschen Literatur des Mittelalters XXXIV (Munich, 1971).

Jaeger, C. Stephen: *The Origin of Courtliness* (Philadelphia, 1985).

Karnein, Alfred: *De Amore in volkssprachlicher Literatur: Untersuchungen zur Andreas-Capellanus-Rezeption in Mittelalter und Renaissance* (Heidelberg, 1985).

Schnell, Rüdiger: *Causa amoris* (Bern, Munich, 1985).

Feminism

Kottenhoff, Margarete: *'Du lebst in einer schlimmen Zeit': Christine de Pizans Frauenstadt zwischen Sozialkritik und Utopie* (Cologne, Weimar, Vienna, 1994).

Rigaud, Rose: *Les idées féministes de Christine de Pisan* (Geneva, 1972; first published Neuchatel, 1911).

Willard, Charity Cannon: *Christine de Pizan* (New York, 1984).

Production and Distribution

Techniques of agricultural production and work ethics

Astill, Grenville, John Langdon, eds: *Medieval Farming and Technology: The Impact of Agricultural Change in Northwest Europe*, Technology and Change in History I (Leiden, Boston, Cologne, 1997).

Böhme, Horst Wolfgang, ed.: *Siedlungen und Landesausbau zur Salierzeit*, 2 vols, 2nd edn, Römisch-Germanisches Zentralmuseum Mainz, Forschungsinstitut für Vor- und Frühgeschichte. Monographien XXVII–XXVIII (Sigmaringen, 1992).

Bolens, Lucie: *Les méthodes culturales au Moyen Age d'après les traités d'agronomie andalous* (Geneva, 1974).

Ciriacono, Salvatore: *Acque e agricoltura* (Milan, 1994).

Hanning, Jürgen: 'Ars donandi: Zur Ökonomie des Schenkens im früheren Mittelalter', in Richard van Dülmen, ed., *Armut, Liebe, Ehre* (Frankfurt, 1987), pp. 11–37.

Hamesse, Jacqueline, Colette Muraille-Samaran, eds: *Le travail au Moyen Age* (Louvain-la-Neuve, 1990).

Janssen, Wilhelm, Dieter Lohrmann, eds: *Villa, curtis, grangia: Landwirtschaft zwischen Loire und Rhein von der Römerzeit zum Hochmittelalter*, Beihefte der Francia XXI (Sigmaringen, 1982).

Lavorare nel medioevo (Naples, 1983).

Rackham, James, ed.: *Environment and Economy in Anglo-Saxon England*, Council for British Archaeology. Research Report LXXXIX (London, 1994).

Reynolds, Terry S.: *'Stronger than a Hundred Men': A History of the Vertical Water Wheel* (Baltimore, London, 1983).

Seibt, Ferdinand: *Glanz und Elend des Mittelalters* (Berlin, 1987).

Slicher van Bath, Bernard Hendrik: *Yield Ratios 810–1210*, Landbouwhogeschool, Afdeling Agrarische Geschiedenis. Bijdragen X (Wageningen, 1963).

Slicher van Bath, Bernard Hendrik: 'The Yields of Different Crops (Mainly Cereals) in Relation to the Seed c. 810–1820', *Acta historica neerlandica* II (1967), pp. 26–106.

Webster, James Carson: *The Labors of the Month in Antique and Medieval Art to the End of the 13th Century*, Princeton Monographs in Art and Archaeology XXI = Northwestern University Studies in the Humanities IV (Princeton, Evanston, 1938).

Wolff, Philippe, ed.: *Histoire générale du travail*, vol. 2 (Paris, 1960).

Urban communities of towns and cities in the early Middle Ages

Astill, Grenville: 'Archaeology, Economics and Early Medieval Europe', *Oxford Journal of Archaeology* IV (1985), pp. 215–31.

Brachmann, Hansjürgen, Joachim Herrmann, eds: *Frühgeschichte der europäischen Stadt*, Schriften zur Ur- und Frühgeschichte XLIV (Berlin, 1991).

Christie, Neil, S. T. Loseby, eds: *Towns in Transition: Urban Evolution in Late Antiquity and the Early Middle Ages* (Aldershot, 1996).

Howard B. Clarke, Anngret Simms, eds: *The Comparative History of Urban Origins in non-Roman Europe*, BAR, International Series LXXXII (Oxford, 1985).

Jankuhn, Herbert: *Typen und Formen vor- und frühwikingerzeitlicher Handelsplätze im Ostseegebiet*, Sitzungsberichte der Österreichischen Akademie der Wissenschaften, Philos.-Hist. Kl. CCLXXIII,5 (Vienna, 1971).

Jankuhn, Herbert, et al., eds: *Vor- und Frühformen der europäischen Stadt im Mittelalter*, 2 vols, AAWG LXXXIII–LXXXIV (Göttingen, 1975).

Kossack, Georg, K.-E. Behre, Peter Schmid, eds: *Archäologische und naturwissenschaftliche Untersuchungen an ländlichen und frühstädtischen Siedlungen im deutschen Küstengebiet vom 5. Jahrhundert vor Christus bis zum 11. Jahrhundert nach Christus*, 2 vols (Weinheim, 1984).

Mercati e mercanti nell' alto medioevo, 2 vols, Settimane di studio del Centro Italiano di Studi sul' Alto Medioevo XL (Spoleto, 1993).

Müller-Boysen, Carsten: *Kaufmannschutz und Handelsrecht im frühmittelalterlichen Nordeuropa* (Neumünster, 1990).

Russo, Daniel G.: *Town Origins and Development in Early England, c.400–950 A.D.*, Contributions to the Study of World History LVIII (Westport, Conn., London, 1998).

Verhulst, Adriaan, ed.: *La fortune historiographique des thèses d'Henri Pirenne*, Archives et Bibliothèques de Belgique, XXVII, numéro spécial (Brussels, 1986).

Verhulst, Adriaan: 'The Origins of Towns in the Low Countries and the Pirenne Thesis', *Past and Present* CXXII (1989), pp. 3–35.

Verhulst, Adriaan: *Rural and Urban Aspects of Early Medieval North-West Europe*, Variorum Collected Studies Series CCCLXXXV (Aldershot, 1992).

Verhulst, Adriaan, ed.: *Anfänge des Städtewesens an Schelde, Maas und Rhein bis zum Jahre 1000*, Städteforschung Reihe A, vol. XL (Cologne, Weimar, Vienna, 1996).

Urban communities of towns and cities in the high and late Middle Ages

Blokmans, Wim P.: 'Stadt, Region und Staat', in Ferdinand Seibt, Winfried Eberhard, eds, *Europa um 1500: Integrationsprozesse im Widerstreit* (Stuttgart, 1987), pp. 211–26.

Dirlmeier, Ulf: *Untersuchungen zu Einkommensverhältnissen und Lebenshaltungskosten in oberdeutschen Städten des Spätmittelalters*, Abhandlungen der Heidelberger Akademie der Wissenschaften, Philos.-Hist. Kl. 1978,1 (Heidelberg, 1978).

Ennen, Edith: *Die europäische Stadt des Mittelalters*, 2nd edn (Munich, 1975; first published Göttingen, 1972).

Irsigler, Franz: 'Kaufmannsmentalität im Mittelalter', in Cord Meckseper, Elisabeth Schraut, eds, *Mentalität und Alltag im Spätmittelalter* (Göttingen, 1985), pp. 53–75.

Jenks, Stuart: 'Die *Carta Mercatoria*: Ein "Hansisches" Privileg', *Hansische Geschichtsblätter* (1990), pp. 45–86.

Johanek, Peter, Heinz Stoob, eds: *Europäische Messen und Märktesysteme in Mittelalter und Neuzeit*, Städteforschung Reihe A, vol. XXXIX (Cologne, Weimar, Vienna, 1996).

Maschke, Erich: 'Das Berufsbewußtsein des mittelalterlichen Fernkaufmanns', in Paul Wilpert, ed., *Beiträge zum Berufsbewußtsein des mittelalterlichen Menschen*, Miscellanea Mediaevalia III (Berlin, New York, 1964), pp. 306–35. Reprinted in Maschke, *Städte und Menschen*, VSWG. Beiheft LXVIII (Wiesbaden, 1980), pp. 380–419.

Mitterauer, Michael: *Markt und Stadt im Mittelalter: Beiträge zur historischen Zentralitätsforschung*, Monographien zur Geschichte des Mittelalters XXI (Stuttgart, 1980).

Pirenne, Henri: *Medieval Cities* (London, Princeton, 1925).

Local and long distance trade

Abu-Lughod, Janet Lippman: *Before European Hegemony* (New York, Oxford, 1989).

Adam, Hildegard: *Das Zollwesen im fränkischen Reich und das spätkarolingische Wirtschaftsleben*, VSWG. Beiheft CXXVI (Stuttgart, 1996).

Bleiber, Waltraut: *Naturalwirtschaft und Ware-Geld-Beziehungen zwischen Somme und Loire während des 7. Jahrhunderts*, Forschungen zur mittelalterlichen Geschichte XXVII (Berlin, 1981).

Bolin, Sture: 'Mohammed, Charlemagne and Ruric', *Scandinavian Economic History Review* I (1953), pp. 5–39.

Claude, Dietrich: *Der Handel im westlichen Mittelmeer während des Frühmittelalters*, AAWG CXLIV (Göttingen, 1985).

Düwel, Klaus, Herbert Jankuhn, Harald Siems, Dieter Timpe, eds: *Untersuchungen zu Handel und Verkehr der vor- und frühgeschichtlichen Zeit in Mittel- und Nordeuropa*, vol. 1, AAWG CXLIII (Göttingen, 1985).

Endemann, Traute: *Markturkunde und Markt in Frankreich und Burgund vom 9. bis 11. Jahrhundert* (Constance, 1964).

Fryde, Natalie: *Ein mittelalterlicher deutscher Großunternehmer: Terricus Teutonicus de Colonia in England 1217–1247*, VSWG. Beiheft CXXV (Stuttgart, 1997).

Grierson, Philip: 'Commerce in the Darl Ages', *Transactions of the Royal Historical Society* Fifth Series IX (1959), pp. 123–40. Reprinted in Grierson, *Dark Age Numismatics* (London, 1979), No. III.

Hatz, Gerd: *Handel und Verkehr zwischen dem Deutschen Reich und Schweden in der späten Wikingerzeit: Die deutschen Münzen des 10. und 11. Jahrhunderts in Schweden* (Uppsala, 1974).

Herrmann, Joachim: *Wikinger und Slawen* (Neumünster, 1982).

Hodges, Richard: *Dark Age Economics* (London, 1982).

Hodges, Richard, David Whitehouse: *Mohammed, Charlemagne and the Origins of Europe* (London, 1983).

Hodges, Richard, Brian Hobley, eds: *The Rebirth of Towns in the West A.D. 700–1050,* Council for British Archaeology. Research Report LXVIII (London, 1988).

Irsigler, Franz: 'Divites und pauperes in der Vita Meinwerci', *VSWG* LVII (1970), pp. 449–99.

Jellema, Dirk: 'Frisian Trade in the Dark Ages', *Speculum* XXX (1955), pp. 15–26.

Jones, S. R. H.: 'Transaction Costs, Institutional Change, and the Emergence of a Market Economy in Later Anglo-Saxon England', *Economic History Review* XLVI (1993), pp. 658–78.

Lebecq, Stéphane: *Marchands et navigateurs Frisons au haut Moyen Age,* 2 vols (Lille, 1983–84).

Lloyd, T. H.: *Alien Merchants in England in the High Middle Ages* (New York, London, 1982).

Maddicott, J. R.: 'Trade, Industry and the Wealth of King Alfred', *Past and Present* CXXIII (1989), pp. 11–26.

Noonan, Thomas S.: *The Islamic World, Russia and the Vikings 750–900,* Variorum Collected Studies Series DXCV (Aldershot, 1998).

Seiffert, Dieter: *Kompagnons und Konkurrenten: Holland und die Hanse im späten Mittelalter,* Quellen und Darstellungen zur hansischen Geschichte N. F. XLIII (Cologne, Weimar, Vienna, 1997).

Tracy, James D., ed.: *The Rise of the Merchant Empires* (Cambridge, 1990).

Yamada, Masahiko: 'Le mouvement des foires en Flandre avant 1200', *Villes et campagnes au Moyen Age. Mélanges Georges Despy* (Louvain-la-Neuve, 1991), pp. 773–88.

Migrant producers

Axboe, Morten: 'The Scandinavian Gold Bracteates', *Acta Archaeologica* LII (Copenhagen, 1981), pp. 1–100.

Bakka, Egil: 'On the Beginning of Salin's Style I in England', *Universitetet i Bergen Årbok* (1958), pp. 1–83.

Bakka, Egil: 'Scandinavian-Type Gold Bracteates in Kentish and Continental Grave Finds', in Vera I. Evison, ed., *Angles, Saxons and Jutes: Essays Presented to John Nowell Linton Myers* (Oxford, 1981), pp. 11–35.

Hawkes, Sonia Chadwick, Marc Pollard: 'Gold Bracteates from Sixth-Century Graves in Kent', *Frühmittelalterliche Studien* XV (1981), pp. 317–70.

König, Gerd G.: 'Schamane und Schmied, Medicus und Mönch', *Helvetica archaeologica* LI–LII (1982), pp. 75–174.

Bookkeeping and banking

Buck, Mark: *Politics, Finance and the Church in the Reign of Edward III* (Cambridge, 1983).

Coleman, Janet: 'The Civic Culture of Contracts and Credit', *Comparative Studies in Society and History* XXVIII (1986), pp. 778–84.

Gilchrist, John: *The Church and Economic Activity in the Middle Ages* (London, 1969).

L'impresa. Industria, commercio, banca, sec. XXIII–XVIII (Florence, 1991).

Lane, Frederic Chapin: *Money and Banking in Medieval and Renaissance Venice*, vol. 1 (Baltimore, 1985).

North, Michael, ed.: *Kredit im spätmittelalterlichen und frühneuzeitlichen Europa*, Quellen und Darstellungen zur hansischen Geschichte N. F. XXXVII (Cologne, Vienna, 1991).

Roover, Raymond de: 'The Development of Accounting prior to Luca Pacioli according to the Account-Books of Medieval Merchants', in A. C. Littleton, Basil S. Yamey, eds, *Studies in the History of Accounting* (London, 1956), pp. 114–74.

Siems, Harald: *Handel und Wucher im Spiegel frühmittelalterlicher Rechtsquellen*, MGH Schriften XXXV (Hanover, 1992).

Yamey, Basil S.: 'Scientific Bookkeeping and the Rise of Capitalism', *Economic History Review* Second Series, vol. I (1949), pp. 99–113.

War

Attitudes toward war and peace

Bachrach, Bernard S.: *Armies and Politics in the Early Medieval West*, Variorum Collected Studies Series CDV (Aldershot, 1993).

Hasenfratz, Hans-Peter: 'Krieg und Frieden bei den alten Germanen', in Gerhard Binder, Bernd Effe, eds, *Krieg und Frieden im Altertum* (Trier, 1989), pp. 204–18.

Busse, Wilhelm G.: 'Kriegerfürst oder Bruder der Mönche? Zum Wandel des Herrscherbildes in England im 10. Jahrhundert', in Hans Hecker, ed., *Der Herrscher* (Düsseldorf. 1990), pp. 121–39.

Delbrück, Hans: *Geschichte der Kriegskunst im Rahmen der politischen Geschichte*, vol. 3, 3rd edn (Berlin, 1923; reprinted Berlin, 1962; first published Berlin, 1907).

Duby, Georges: *Guerriers et paysans* (Paris, 1978).

Erdmann, Carl: *The Origin of the Idea of the Crusades* (Princeton, 1977; first published, Forschungen zur Kirchen- und Geistesgeschichte VI, Stuttgart 1935).

Hale, John Rigby: *Renaissance War Studies* (London, 1983).

Halsall, Guy, ed.: *Violence and Society in the Early Medieval West* (Woodbridge, 1998).

Keen, Maurice Hugh, ed.: *Medieval Warfare* (Oxford, 1999).

Kottje, Raymund: *Die Tötung im Kriege: Ein moralisches und rechtliches Problem im frühen Mittelalter* (Barsbüttel, 1990).

Kurze, Dietrich: 'Krieg und Frieden im mittelalterlichen Denken', in Heinz Duchhardt, ed., *Zwischenstaatliche Friedenswahrung in Mittelalter und Früher Neuzeit*, Münsterische historische Forschungen I (Cologne, Vienna, 1991), pp. 1–44.

Oman, Charles William Chadwick: *A History of the Art of War in the Middle Ages*, 2nd edn (London, 1924; first published London, 1898; reprinted Ithaca, 1960; another reprint London, 1978).

Schaufelberger, Walter: *Der alte Schweizer und sein Krieg* (Zurich, 1966).

Smail, Raymond Charles: *Crusading Warfare 1097–1192*, 2nd edn, Cambridge Studies in Medieval Life and Thought N. S. III (Cambridge, 1972; first published Cambridge, 1956).

Tattershill, Jill: 'Anthropophagi and Eaters of Raw Flesh in French Literature of the Crusades Period', *Medium Aevum* LVII (1988), pp. 240–53.

Verbruggen, Jan Frans: *The Art of War in Western Europe*, Europe in the Middle Ages. Selected Studies I (Amsterdam, New York, 1977; first published, Koninklijke Vlaamse Academie vor Wetenschappen, Letteren en Schone Kunsten, Klasse der Letteren. Verhandelingen XX, Brussels, 1954).

Wallace-Hadrill, John Michael: 'War and Peace in the Earlier Middle Ages', *Transactions of the Royal Historical Society* Fifth Series XXV (1975), pp. 157–74.

Wright, N. A. R.: 'The Tree of Battles of Honoré Bouvet and the Law of War', in Christopher T. Allmand, ed., *War, Literature and Politics in the Later Middle Ages [Essays for George W. Coopland]* (Liverpool, 1976), pp. 12–31.

Military organisation, strategy

Abels, Richard P.: *Lordship and Military Obligation in Anglo-Saxon England* (Berkeley, Los Angeles, 1988).

Ayton, Andrew: *Knights and Warhorses: Military Service and the English Aristocracy under Edward III* (Woodbridge, 1994; reprinted Woodbridge, 1999).

Bachrach, Bernard S.: *Merovingian Military Organization* (Minneapolis, 1972).

Bennett, Matthew: 'The Medieval Warhorse Reconsidered', in Stephen Church, Ruth Harvey, eds, *Medieval Knighthood*, vol. 5: Papers from the Sixth Hill Conference 1994 (Woodbridge, 1995), pp. 19–40.

Bodmer, Jean-Pierre: *Der Krieger der Merowingerzeit und seine Welt*, Geist und Werk der Zeiten II (Zurich, 1957).

Contamine, Philippe: *Guerre, état et société à la fin du Moyen Age* (Paris, The Hague, 1972).

Davis, Ralph Henry Carless: *The Medieval Warhorse* (London, 1989).

DeVries, Kelly Robert: *Infantry Warfare in the Early Fourteenth Century* (Woodbridge, 1996).

Eltis, David: *The Military Revolution in the Sixteenth Century* (London, 1995).

Hobohm, Martin: *Machiavellis Renaissance der Kriegskunst*, 2 vols (Berlin, 1913).

Lynn, John A., ed.: *Feeding Mars: Logistics in Western Warfare from the Middle Ages to the Present* (Boulder, San Francisco, 1993).

Mallett, Michael: *Mercenaries and Their Masters* (London, Sydney, Toronto, 1974).

Pieri, Piero: *Guerra e politica negli scrittori italiani* (Milan, Naples, 1955; reprinted Milan, 1975).

Powicke, Michael: *Military Obligation in Medieval England* (Oxford, 1962).

Prestwich, Michael: *Armies and Warfare in the Middle Ages* (New Haven, London, 1996).

Puddu, Rafaele: *Eserciti e monarchie nazionali nei secoli XV e XVI* (Florence, 1975).

Werner, Karl Ferdinand: 'Heeresorganisation und Kriegsführung im deutschen Königreich des 10. und 11. Jahrhunderts', *Settimane di studio del Centro Italiano di studi sull' alto medioevo di Spoleto* XV (1968), pp. 791–843.

Emergence of the cavalry, chivalry

Bumke, Joachim: *Höfische Kultur*, 8th edn (Munich, 1997; first published 1986).

Cardini, Franco: *Alle radici della cavalleria medievale* (Florence, 1981).

Fleckenstein, Josef: 'Zum Problem der Abgrenzung des Ritterstandes', in Helmut Beumann, ed., *Festschrift für Walter Schlesinger* (Cologne, Vienna, 1974), pp. 252–71.

Flori, Jean: *L'idéologie du glaive: Préhistoire de la chevalerie* (Geneva, 1983).

Hooper, Nicholas: 'The Aberlemno Stone and Cavalry in Anglo-Saxon England', *Northern History* XXIX (1993), pp. 188–96.

Keen, Maurice Hugh: *Chivalry* (New Haven, London, 1984).

Lyon, Bryce: *The Role of Cavalry in Medieval Warfare*, Koninklijke Academie voor Wetenschappen, Letteren en Schone Kunsten van België. Mededelingen XLIX, 2 (Brussels, 1987).

Paravicini, Werner: *Die ritterlich-höfische Kultur des Mittelalters* (Munich, 1994).

Vale, Juliet: *Edward III and Chivalry* (Woodbridge, 1982).

Vale, Malcolm Graham Allan: *War and Chivalry* (London, 1981).

Law of war

Hehl, Ernst-Dieter: *Kirche und Krieg im 12. Jahrhundert: Studien zu kanonischem Recht und politischer Wirklichkeit*, Monographien zur Geschichte des Mittelalters XIX (Stuttgart, 1980).

Keen, Maurice Hugh: *The Laws of War in the Late Middle Ages* (London, 1965).

Tournaments

Barber, Richard, Juliet Barker: *Tournaments: Jousts, Chivalry and Pageants in the Middle Ages* (Woodbridge, 1989).

Barker, Juliet: *The Tournament in England 1100–1400* (Woodbridge, 1986).

Fleckenstein, Josef, ed.: *Das ritterliche Turnier im Mittelalter*, 2nd edn, VMPIG LXXXVI (Göttingen, 1986; first published Göttingen, 1985).

Van den Neste, E.: *Tournois, joutes, pas d'armes dans les villes de Flandre à la fin du Moyen Age* (Paris, 1996).

Castles, fortresses

Kenyon, John R.: *Medieval Fortifications* (Leicester, New York, 1991).

Patze, Hans, ed.: *Die Burgen im deutschen Sprachraum*, 2 vols, VuF XIX (Sigmaringen, 1976).

Pepper, Simon, Nicholas Adams: *Firearms and Fortifications: Military Architecture and Siege Warfare in Sixteenth-Century Siena* (Chicago, London, 1986).

Pounds, Norman G.: *The Medieval Castle in England and Wales* (Cambridge, 1991; reprinted Cambridge, 1994).

Thompson, Michhael Welman: *The Decline of the Castle* (Cambridge, 1988).

Thompson, Michael Welman: *The Rise of the Castle* (Cambridge, 1991).

Military technology, military science

DeVries, Kelly Robert, ed.: *Medieval Military Technology* (Peterborough, Ont., Lewiston, N.Y., 1992).

Hagenmeyer, Christa: 'Kriegswissenschaftliche Texte des ausgehenden 15. Jahrhunderts', *Leuvense Bijdragen* LVI (1967), pp. 169–97.

Hall, Bert S.: *The Technological Illustrations of the So-called 'Anonymous of the Hussite Wars'* (Wiesbaden, 1979).

Hardy, Richard: *The Longbow* (London, 1976; reprinted London, 1992).

Jähns, Max: *Geschichte der Kriegswissenschaften vornehmlich in Deutschland*, 3 vols, Geschichte der Wissenschaften in Deutschland XXI (Munich, Leipzig, 1889–91; reprinted Hildesheim, New York, 1966).

Rathgen, Bernhard: *Das Geschütz im Mittelalter* (Berlin 1928).

Webb, Henry Jameson: *Elizabethan Military Science: The Books and the Practice* (Madison, Milwaukee, London, 1967).

Lansquenets

Baumann, Reinhard: *Die Landsknechte* (Munich, 1994).

Kurzmann, Gerhard: *Maximilian I. und das Kriegswesen der österreichischen Länder und des Reiches*, Militärgeschichtliche Dissertationen österreichischer Universitäten V (Vienna, 1985).

Nell, Martin: *Die Landsknechte*, Historische Studien CXXIII (Berlin, 1914; reprinted Vaduz, 1965).

Wohlfail, Rainer, Traudl Wohlfail: 'Das Landsknechtsbild als geschichtliche Quelle', in Peter Blickle, ed., *Bauer, Reich und Reformation. Festschrift für Günther Franz* (Stuttgart, 1982), pp. 104–19.

Wollbrett, Alphonse, ed.: *La guerre des paysans*, Société d'histoire et d'archéologie de Saverne. Etudes alsatiques CXIII, No. supplémentaire (Saverne, 1975).

Thinking

Hermeneutics, theory of language

Biser, Eugen: *Theologische Sprachtheorie und Hermeneutik* (Munich, 1970).

Borst, Arno: *Der Turmbau von Babel*, 5 vols (Stuttgart, 1957–63).

Brinkmann, Hennig: *Mittelalterliche Hermeneutik* (Tübingen, 1980).

Fried, Johannes, ed.: *Kommunikation im Mittelalter: Dialektik und Rhetorik im frühen Mittelalter*, Schriften des Historischen Kollegs. Kolloquien XXVII (Munich, 1996).

Goody, Jack: *The Domestication of the Savage Mind* (Cambridge, 1978).

Hallpike, Christopher Robert: *The Foundations of Primitive Thought* (Oxford, 1979).

Janson, Tore: *Prose Rhythm in Medieval Latin from the 9th to the 13th Century*, Acta Universitatis Stockholmiensis XX (Stockholm, 1975).

Law, Vivian: *Insular Latin Grammarians* (Woodbridge, 1981).

Lévi-Strauss, Claude: *The Savage Mind* (Chicago, 1968; first published Paris, 1968).

Pinborg, Jan: *Die Entwicklung der Sprachtheorie des Mittelalters*, 2nd edn, Beiträge zur Geschichte der Philosophie und Theologie des Mittelalters XLII, 2 (Münster, 1985; first published Münster, 1967).

Radding, Charles M.: *A World Made by Men: Cognition and Society 400–1200* (Chapel Hill, London, 1985).

Sturges, Robert S.: *Medieval Interpretation: Models of Reading in Literary Narrative 1100–1500* (Carbondale, Edwardsville, 1990).

Concepts of magic

Burnett, Charles: *Magic and Divination in the Late Middle Ages*, Variorum Collected Studies Series DLVII (Aldershot, 1996).

Flint, Valerie Irene Jean: *The Rise of Magic in Early Medieval Europe* (Princeton, 1991).

Harmening, Dieter: *Superstitio: Überlieferungs- und theoriegeschichtliche Untersuchungen zur kirchlich-theologischen Aberglaubensliteratur des Mittelalters* (Berlin, 1979).

Hoffmann, Hartmut, Rudolf Pokorny: *Das Dekret des Bischofs Burchard von Worms*, MGH Hilfsmittel XII (Munich, 1991).

Kieckhefer, Richard: *Magic in the Middle Ages* (Cambridge, 1989; reprinted Cambridge, 1990).

Kieckhefer, Richard: 'The Specific Rationality of Medieval Magic', *American Historical Review* XCIX (1994), pp. 813–36.

Tambiah, Stanley Jeyaraja: *Magic, Science, Religion and the Scope of Rationality* (New York, 1990).

Thorndyke, Lynn: *The History of Magic and Experimental Science*, 8 vols (New York, 1923–58).

Ward, Benedicta: *Miracles and the Medieval Mind* (London, 1982).

Trinitarian doctrines

Chevalier, I.: 'La théorie augustinienne des relations trinitaires', *Divus Thomas* XVIII (1940), pp. 317–84.

Dürig, Walter: *Imago: Ein Beitrag zur Terminologie und Theologie der römischen Liturgie*, Münchener theologische Studien Reihe II, vol. V (Munich, 1952).

Kretschmar, G.: *Studien zur frühchristlichen Trinitätstheologie*, Beiträge zur historischen Theologie XXI (Tübingen, 1956).

Paissac, Henry: *Théologie du verbe: Saint Augustin et Saint Thomas* (Paris, 1951).

Perler, Othmar: *Der Nus bei Plotin und das Verbum bei Augustinus als vorbildliche Ursache der Welt*, Studia Friburgensia (Fribourg, 1931).

Prestige, George Leonard: *God in Patristic Thought*, 2nd edn (London, 1952; first published London, Toronto, 1936).

Regnon, Théodore de: *Etudes de théologie sur la sainte Trinité*, 4 vols (Paris, 1892–98).

Schmaus, Michael: *Die Denkform Augustins in seinem Werke De trinitate*, Sitzungsberichte der Bayerischen Akademie der Wissenschaften, Philos.-Hist. Kl. 1962, 6 (Munich, 1962).

Schurr, Viktor: *Die Trinitätslehre des Boethius im Lichte der 'skythischen Kontroversen'*, Forschungen zur christlichen Literatur- und Dogmengeschichte XVIII, 1 (Paderborn, 1935).

Stohr, A.: 'Die Hauptrichtungen der spekulativen Trinitätslehre in der Theologie des 13. Jahrhunderts', *Theologische Quartalschrift* XLIX (1925), pp. 113–35.

Concepts of the person

Altheim, Franz: 'Persona', *Archiv für Religionswissenschaft* XXVII (1929), pp. 35–52.

Andresen, Carl: 'Zur Entstehung und Geschichte des trinitarischen Personenbegriffes', *Zeitschrift für neutestamentliche Wissenschaft* LII (1961), pp. 1–39.

Boigelot, R.: 'Le mot "personne" dans les écrits trinitaires de Saint Augustin', *Nouvelle revue théologique* LVII (1930), pp. 5–16.

Gurevich, Aaron Yakovlevich: 'Die Darstellung von Persönlichkeit und Zeit in der mittelalterlichen Kunst', in Friedrich Möbius, Ernst Schubert, eds, *Architektur des Mittelalters* (Weimar, 1983), pp. 87–104.

Hirzel, Rudolf: *Die Person,* Sitzungsberichte der Bayerischen Akademie der Wissenschaften, Philos.-Hist. Kl. 1914, 10 (Munich, 1914).

Platelle, H.: 'Erreur sur la personne', *Universitas* XXXIV (1977, Special Issue), pp. 117–45.

Rheinfelder, Hans: *Das Wort 'Persona',* Zeitschrift für Romanische Philologie. Beiheft LXXVII (Halle, 1928).

Trendelenburg, Adolf: 'Zur Geschichte des Wortes Person', *Kant-Studien* XIII (1908), pp. 1–17.

Wilde, Arie de: *De persoon: Over de granslagen van het personalistisch denken,* van Gorcums's Theologische Bibliotheek XX (Assen, 1951).

Articles

Amos, Ashley Crandell: *Linguistic Means of Determining the Dates of Old English Literary Texts,* Mediaeval Academy Books XC (Cambridge, Mass., 1980).

Kramský, Jiří: *The Article and the Concept of Definiteness in Language,* Janua Linguarum. Series minor CXXV (Paris, The Hague, 1972).

Lichtenheld, Adolf: 'Das schwache Adjektiv im Altenglischen, *Zeitschrift für deutsches Altertum und deutsche Literatur* XVI (1873), pp. 325–93.

Sarrazin, Gregor: 'Zur Chronologie und Verfassserfrage angelsächsischer Dichtungen', *Englische Studien* XXXVIII (1907), pp. 145–95.

Mnemotechnics

Carruthers, Mary J.: *The Book of Memory* (Cambridge, 1992).

Carruthers, Mary J.: *The Craft of Thought,* Cambridge Studies in Medieval Literature XXXIV (Cambridge, 1998).

Hajdu, Helga: *Das mnemotechnische Schrifttum des Mittelalters* (Vienna, 1936).

Haverkamp, Anselm, Renate Lachmann, eds: *Gedächtniskunst* (Frankfurt, 1991).

Rossi, Paolo: *Clavis universalis: Arti della memoria e logica combinatoria da Lullo a Leibniz* (Bologna, 1983).

Roy, Bruno, Paul Zumthor, eds: *Jeux de mémoire* (Montreal, Paris, 1985).

Volkmann, Ludwig: 'Ars memorativa', *Jahrbuch der Kunsthistorischen Sammlungen in Wien* N. F. XXX (1929, Supplementary Volume), pp. 111–203.

Yates, Frances Amelia: *The Art of Memory* (London, 1966).

Ziliotto, Baccio: 'Fratre Lodovico Pirano e le sue regole memoriae artificialis', *Atti e memorie della Società Istriana di archeologia e storia patria* XLIX (1927), pp. 189–224.

Communication

Oral traditions, art of speaking

Althoff, Gerd: 'Verformung durch mündliche Tradition', in Hagen Keller, Norbert Staubach, eds, *Iconologia sacra [Essays for Karl Hauck]* (Munich, 1994), pp. 438–50.

Bjork, Robert E.: 'Speech as Gift in Beowulf', *Speculum* LXXIX (1994), pp. 993–1018.

Clanchy, Michael T.: *From Memory to Written Record* (Oxford, 1992).

Foley, Miles: *Oral Tradition in Literature* (Columbia, Miss., 1986).

Kühnel, Harry, ed.: *Kommunikation und Alltag in Spätmittelalter und früher Neuzeit*, Sitzungsberichte der Österreichischen Akademie der Wissenschaften, Philos.-Hist. Kl. DXCVI = Veröffentlichungen des Instituts für Realienkunde des Mittelalters und der frühen Neuzeit XV (Vienna, 1992).

O'Keeffe, Katherine O'Brien: *Visible Song: Transitional Literacy in Old English Verse* (Cambridge, 1990).

Ong, Walter J., S. J.: *Orality and Literacy: The Technologizing of the Word*, 2nd edn (London, 1990; first published London, 1982).

Schaefer, Ursula, ed.: *Vokalität: Altenglische Dichtung zwischen Mündlichkeit und Schriftlichkeit*, Scriptoralia XXXIX (Tübingen, 1992).

Wenzel, Horst: *Hören und Sehen* (Munich, 1995).

Significance of letters and the book

Assmann, Aleida, Jan Assmann, Christof Hardmeier, eds: *Schrift und Gedächtnis*, Archäologie der literarischen Kommunikation I (Munich, 1983).

Düwel, Klaus: 'Buchstabenmagie und Alphabetzauber', *Frühmittelalterliche Studien* XXII (1988), pp. 70–110.

Ganz, Peter, ed.: *The Role of the Book in Medieval Culture*, 2 vols, Bibliologia III–IV (Turnhout, 1985).

Ganz, Peter, Malcolm Parkes, eds: *Das Buch als magisches und als Repräsentationsobjekt*, Wolfenbütteler Mittelalter-Studien V (Wiesbaden, 1992).

Gellrich, Jesse M.: *The Idea of the Book in the Middle Ages* (Ithaca, London, 1986).

Keller, Hagen: 'Vom heiligen Buch zur "Buchführung"', *Frühmittelalterliche Studien* XXVI (1992), pp. 1–31.

McKitterick, Rosamond: *The Carolingians and the Written Word* (Cambridge, 1989; reprinted Cambridge, 1995).

McKitterick, Rosamond, ed.: *The Uses of Literacy in Early Medieval Europe* (Cambridge, 1989; reprinted Cambridge, 1995).

Nystrom, Staffan, ed.: *Runor och ABC: Elva forelasningar fran et symposium i Stockholm varen 1995* (Stockholm, 1997).

Schaefer, Ursula, ed.: *Schriftlichkeit im frühen Mittelalter*, Scriptoralia LIII (Tübingen, 1993).

Schenda, Rudolf: *Von Mund zu Ohr: Bausteine zu einer Kulturgeschichte des volkstümlichen Erzählens* (Göttingen, 1993).

Stevick, Robert D.: *The Earliest Irish and English Bookarts: Visual and Poetic Forms before A.D. 1000* (Philadelphia, 1994).

Stock, Brian: *The Implications of Literacy: Written Language and Models of Interpretation in the Eleventh and Twelfth Centuries* (Princeton, 1983).

Wormald, Patrick: 'The Uses of Literacy in Anglo-Saxon England and its Neighbours', *Transactions of the Royal Historical Society* Fifth Series XXVII (1977), pp. 95–114.

Reading and writing

Borst, Arno: *Das Buch der Naturgeschichte: Plinius und seine Leser im Zeitalter des Pergaments*, Abhandlungen der Heidelberger Akademie der Wissenschaften, Philol.-Hist. Kl. 1994, 2 (Heidelberg, 1994).

Fichtenau, Heinrich: *Mensch und Schrift im Mittelalter*, VIÖG V (Vienna, 1946).

Goody, Jack: *The Logic of Writing and the Organization of Society* (Cambridge, 1986).

Goody, Jack: *The Interface between the Written and the Oral* (Cambridge, 1987).

Grundmann, Herbert: 'Literatur und illiteratus im Mittelalter', *Archiv für Kulturgeschichte* XL (1958), pp. 1–65.

Günther, Hartmut, Otto Ludwig, eds: *Schrift und Schriftlichkeit/ Writing and its Use*, vol. 1 (Berlin, New York, 1994).

Illich, Ivan: *In the Vineyard of the Text* (Chicago, London, 1993; first published Paris, 1990).

Leclercq, Jean: *The Love of Learning and the Desire for God* (New York, 1982).

Wattenbach, Wilhelm: *Das Schriftwesen im Mittelalter*, 3rd edn (Leipzig, 1896). Reprinted (Graz, 1958; first published Leipzig, 1871).

Concepts of authorship

Andersen, Elizabeth, ed.: *Autor und Autorschaft im Mittelalter* (Tübingen, 1998).

Beer, Jeannette, ed.: *Translation Theory and Practice in the Middle Ages* (Kalamazoo, 1997).

Cerquiglini, Bernard: *Eloge de la variante* (Paris, 1989).

Stackmann, Karl: 'Neue Philologie?', in Joachim Heinzle, ed., *Modernes Mittelalter*, 2nd edn (Frankfurt, Leipzig, 1999), pp. 398–427. (First published Frankfurt, Leipzig, 1994.)

Minnis, Alastair J.: *Medieval Theory of Authorship*, 2nd edn (Philadelphia, 1988; first published Berkeley, 1984).

Pragmatic writing

Blum, R.: 'Bibliographia', *Archiv für Geschichte des Buchwesens* X (1970), col. 1010–1234.

Boehm, Laetita: 'Artes mechanicae und artes liberales im Mittelalter', in Karl Schnith, Roland Pauer, eds, *Festschrift für Eduard Hlawitschka* (Kallmünz, 1993), pp. 419–44. Reprinted in Boehm, *Geschichtsdenken, Bildungsgeschichte, Wissenschaftsorganisation*, ed. Gert Melville, Rainer A. Müller, Winfried Müller, Historische Forschungen LVI (Berlin, 1996), pp. 493–516.

Bruguière, Marie-Bernadette: *Littérature et droit dans la Gaule au VI siècle* (Paris, 1974).

Classen, Peter: *Kaiserreskript und Königsurkunde*, Byzantina keimena kai meletai XV (Thessalonica, 1977).

Classen, Peter, ed.: *Recht und Schrift im Mittelalter*, VuF XXIII (Sigmaringen, 1977).

Keller, Hagen, Klaus Grubmüller, Nikolaus Staubach, eds: *Pragmatische Schriftlichkeit im Mittelalter*, Münsterische Mittelalter-Schriften LXV (Munich, 1992).

Pitz, Ernst: *Papstreskripte im frühen Mittelalter*, Beiträge zur Geschichte und Quellenkunde des Mittelalters XIV (Sigmaringen, 1990).

Steinwenter, Artur: 'Die Deponierung von Privaturkunden in öffentlichen Archiven', Steinwenter, *Beiträge zum öffentlichern Urkundenwesen der Römer* (Graz, 1915), pp. 58–92.

Theory and practice of the forgery

Bagnani, G.: 'On Fakes and Forgeries', *Phoenix* XIV (1960), pp. 228–44.

Constable, Giles: 'Forgery and Plagiarism in the Middle Ages', *Archiv für Diplomatik, Siegel- und Wappenkunde* XXIX (1983), pp. 1–41. Reprinted in Constable, *Culture and Spirituality in Medieval Europe*, Variorum Collected Studies Series DXLI (Aldershot, 1996), No. I.

Fälschungen im Mittelalter, 5 vols, MGH Schriften XXXIII (Hanover, 1988).

Fuhrmann, Horst: 'Die Fälschungen im Mittelalter', *Historische Zeitschrift* CXCVII (1963), pp. 529–54.

Grafton, Anthony: *Forgers and Critics* (Princeton, 1990).

Leo, P. de: *Richerche sui falsi medievali*, Università degli studi di Calabria. Studi e documenti I (Reggio di Calabria, 1974).

Tout, Thomas Frederick: 'Medieval Forgers and Forgeries', *Bulletin of the John Rylands Library* V (1918/20), pp. 208–34.

Manuscript trade and printing by movable types

Chartier, Roger, ed.: *The Cultural Use of Printing in Early Modern France* (Princeton, 1987; first published Paris, 1985).

Chartier, Roger, ed.: *The Culture of Print* (Princeton, 1989).

Chrisman, Miriam Usher: *Lay Culture, Learned Culture: Books and Social Change in Strasbourg 1480–1599* (New Haven, London, 1982).

Eisenstein, Elizabeth L.: *The Printing Press as an Agent of Social Change*, 2 vols (Cambridge, 1979).

Fèbvre, Lucien, Henri-Jean Martin: *The Coming of the Book: The Impact of Printing 1450–1800*, 2nd edn (London, 1979; first English edn London, 1976; first published Paris, 1958).

Giesecke, Michael: *Der Buchdruck in der frühen Neuzeit: Eine historische Fallstudie über die Durchsetzung neuer Informations- und Kommunikationstechnologien*, 2nd edn (Frankfurt, 1998; first published Frankfurt, 1990).

Kirchhoff, Albrecht: *Die Handschriftenhändler des Mittelalters* (Leipzig, 1853; reprinted Osnabrück, 1966).

Kock, Thomas, Rita Schlusemann, eds: *Laienlektüre und Buchmarkt im späten Mittelalter* (Frankfurt, Bern, New York, 1997).

Rück, Peter, ed.: *Rationalisierung der Buchherstellung*, Elementa diplomatica II (Marburg, 1994).

History

Forms of collective memory, politics of history

Assmann, Jan: *Das kulturelle Gedächtnis* (Munich, 1992).

Coreth, Anna: 'Dynastisch-politische Ideen Kaiser Maximilians I.', *Mitteilungen des Österreichischen Staatsarchivs* III (1950), pp. 81–105.

Eggert, Wolfgang, Barbara Pätzold: *Wir-Gefühl und Regnum Saxonum bei frühmittelalterlichen Geschichtsschreibern*, Archiv für Kulturgeschichte. Beiheft XXI (Cologne, Vienna 1985).

Graus, František: *Volk, Herrscher und Heiliger im Reich der Merowinger* (Prague, 1961).

Mertens, Dieter: 'Geschichte und Dynastie', in Kurt Andermann, ed., *Historiographie am Oberrhhein im späten Mittelalter und in der Frühen Neuzeit*, Oberrheinische Studien VII (Sigmaringen, 1988), pp. 121–53.

Müller, Jan-Dirk: *Gedechtnus: Literatur und Hofgesellschaft um Maximilian I.*, Forschungen zur Geschichte der älteren deutschen Literatur II (Munich, 1982).

Nelson, Janet Laughland: *Politics and Ritual in Early Medieval Europe* (London, Ronceverte, 1986).

Oexle, Otto Gerhard, Dieter Geuenich, eds: *Memoria in der Gesellschaft des Mittelalters*, VMPIG CXXI (Göttingen, 1995).

Schmid, Karl, Joachim Wollasch, eds: *Memoria: Der geschichtliche Zeugniswert des liturgischen Gedenkens im Mittelalter*, Münsterische Mittelalter-Schriften XLVIII (Munich, 1984).

Weddige, Hilbert: *Heldensage und Stammessage: Iring und der Untergang des Thüringerreiches in Historiographie und Dichtung* (Tübingen, 1989).

Speculative approaches to world history

Brincken, Anna-Dorothee von den: 'Universalkartographie und geographische Schulkenntnisse im Inkunabelzeitalter', in Karl Stackmann, Bernd Moeller, Hans Patze, eds, *Studien zum städtischen Bildungswesen*, AAWG CXXXVII (Göttingen, 1983), pp. 398–429.

Goetz, Hans-Werner: *Das Geschichtsbild Ottos von Freising*, Archiv für Kulturgeschichte. Beiheft XIX (Cologne, Vienna, 1984).

Häusler, Martin: *Das Ende der Geschichte in der mittelalterlichen Weltchronistik*, Archiv für Kulturgeschichte. Beiheft XII (Cologne, Vienna, 1980).

Hanning, Robert William: *Visions of History in Early Britain* (New York, 1966).

Tersch, Harald I.: *Unruhe im Weltbild: Darstellung und Deutung des zeitgenössischen Lebens in deutschsprachigen Weltchroniken des Mittelalters* (Cologne, Weimar, Vienna, 1996).

Concepts of history

Boehm, Laetita: 'Der wissenschafttheoretische Ort der historia im früheren Mittelalter', in Clemens Bauer, Max Müller, eds, *Speculum historiae [Essays for Johannes Spörl]* (Freiburg, Munich, 1965), pp. 663–93.

Graus, František: *Lebendige Vergangenheit: Überlieferung im Mittelalter und die Vorstellungen vom Mittelalter* (Cologne, Vienna, 1975).

Seifert, Arno: 'Historia im Mittelalter', *Archiv für Begriffsgeschichte* XXI (1977), pp. 226–84.

Genealogies

Althoff, Gerd: 'Studien zur habsburgischen Merowingersage', *Mitteilungen des Instituts für Österreichische Geschichtsforschung* LXXXVII (1979), pp. 71–100.

Angenendt, Arnold: 'Der eine Adam und die vielen Stammväter', in Peter Wunderli, ed., *Herkunft und Ursprung: Historische und mythische Formen der Legitimation* (Sigmaringen, 1994), pp. 27–52.

Dumville, David N.: 'Kingship, Genealogies and Regnal Lists', in Peter Hayes Sawyer, Ian N. Wood, eds, *Early Medieval Kingship* (Leeds, 1977), pp. 72–104. Reprinted in Dumville, *Histories and Pseudo-histories of the Insular Middle Ages*, Variorum Collected Studies Series CCCXVI (Aldershot, 1990), No. XV.

Krag, Claus: *Ynglingatal og Ynglingasaga*, Studia humaniora II (Oslo, 1991).

Laschitzer, Simon: 'Die Heiligen aus der "Sipp-, Mag- und Schwagerschaft" des Kaisers Maximilian I.', *Jahrbuch der Kunsthistorischen Sammlungen des Allerhöchsten Kaiserhauses* IV (1886), pp. 70–287, V (1887), pp. 117–261.

Laschitzer, Simon: 'Die Genealogie des Kaisers Maximilian I.', *Jahrbuch der Kunsthistorischen Sammlungen des Allerhöchsten Kaiserhauses* VII (1888), pp. 1–199.

Scheibelreiter, Georg: 'Zur Typologie und Kritik genealogischer Quellen', *Archivum* XXXVII (1992), pp. 1–26.

Spiegel, Gabrielle M.: *Romancing the Past: The Rise of Vernacular Prose Historiography in Thirteenth-century France* (Berkeley, Los Angeles, Oxford, 1993).

Turville-Petre, J.: 'The Genealogist and History', *Saga Book of the Viking Society for Northern Research* XX (1978/79), pp. 1–23.

Theory and practice of historiography and hagiography

Fouracre, Paul: 'Merovingian History and Merovingian Hagiography', *Past and Present* CXXVII (1990), pp. 3–38.

Galbraith, Vivian Hunter: *Chroniclers and Historians* (London, Ronceverte, 1982).

Goetz, Hans-Werner: *Geschichtsschreibung und Geschichtsbewußtsein im hohen Mittelalter* (Berlin, 1999).

Goffart, Walter: *Narrators of Barbarian History (A.D. 550–800)* (Princeton, 1988).

Gransden, Antonia: *Historical Writing in England*, 2 vols (London, 1974–82).

Holdsworth, Christopher, T. P. Wiseman, eds: *The Inheritance of Historiography*, Exeter Studies in History XII (Exeter, 1986).

Jones, Charles William: *Bede, the Schools and the Computus*, Variorum Collected Studies Series CDXXXVI (Aldershot, 1994).

Nie, Giselle de: *Views from a Many-windowed Tower*, Studies in Classical Antiquity VII (Amsterdam, Atlanta, 1987).

Rücker, Elisabeth: *Die Schedelsche Weltchronik: Das größte Buchunternehmen der Dürer-Zeit*, Bilder aus der deutschen Vergangenheit XXXIII (Munich, 1973).

Scharer, Anton, Georg Scheibelreiter, eds: *Historiographie im frühen Mittelalter*, VIÖG XXXII (Munich, Vienna, 1994).

Schmale, Franz Josef: *Funktion und Formen mittelalterlicher Geschichtsschreibung* (Darmstadt, 1985).

Sider, Gerald, Gavin Smith, eds: *Between History and Histories* (Toronto, 1996).

Sims-Williams, Patrick: *Religion and Literature in Western England 600–800*, Cambridge Studies in Anglo-Saxon England III (Cambridge 1990).

Spiegel, Gabrielle M.: *The Past as Text* (Baltimore, London 1997).

Thomson, Rodney: *William of Malmesbury* (Woodbridge, 1987).

Wallace-Hadrill, John Michael: 'Gregory of Tours and Bede', *Frühmittelalterliche Studien* II (1968), pp. 31–44. Reprinted in Wallace-Hadrill, *Early Medieval History* (Oxford, 1975), pp. 96–114.

Wright, Neil: *History and Literature in Late Antiquity and the Early Medieval West*, Variorum Collected Studies Series DIII (Aldershot, 1995).

Historical research

Gransden, Antonia: 'Antiquarian Studies in Fifteenth-century England', *Antiquaries Journal* LX (1980), pp. 75–97. Reprinted in Gransden, *Legends, Traditions and History in Medieval England* (London, Ronceverte, 1992), No. I.

Grössling, Helmut: 'Johannes Stabius: Ein Oberösterreicher im Kreis der Humanisten um Kaiser Maximilian I.', *Mitteilungen des Oberösterreichischen Landesarchivs* IX (1968), pp. 239–64.

Lhotsky, Alphons: *Aufsätze und Vorträge*, vol. 2, ed. Hans Wagner, Heinrich Koller (Munich, Vienna, 1971).

Migration and Travel

Group migration

Comba, Rinaldo, Gabriella Piccini, Giuliano Pinto, eds: *Strutture familiari, epidemie, migrazioni nell'Italia medievale*, Nouve richerche di storia II (Naples, 1984).

Jaritz, Gerhard, Albert Müller, eds: *Migration in der Feudalgesellschaft*, Studien zur Historischen Sozialwissenschaft VIII (Frankfurt, New York, 1988).

Le migrazioni in Europa secc. XIIII–XVIII: Atti della 20a Settimana di studi, Istituto di storia economica 'Francesco Datini' (Prato, 1994).

Müller-Wille, Michael, Reinhard Schneider, eds: *Ausgewählte Probleme europäischer Landnahmen des Früh- und Hochmittelalters*, 2 vols, VuF XLI (Sigmaringen, 1993–94).

O'Murchadha, Diarmuid: 'Nationality Names in the Irish Annals', *Nomina* XVI (1982/3), pp. 49–70.

Penners, Th.: 'Fragen der Zuwanderung in den Hansestädten des späten Mittelalters', *Hansische Geschichtsblätter* LXXXIII (1965), pp. 12–45.

Reininghaus, Wilfried: 'Die Migration der Handwerksgesellen in der Zeit der Entsehung ihrer Gilden', *VSWG* LXVIII (1981), pp. 1–21.

Vogel, Bernard, ed.: *Les migrations de l'Antiquité à nos jours* (Strasbourg, 1996).

Wissel, Rudolf: *Des alten Handwerks Recht und Gewohnheit*, vol. 1, 2nd edn by Ernst Schraepler, Einzelveröffentlichungen der Historischen Kommission zu Berlin VII (Berlin, 1971; first published Berlin, 1929).

Wolfram, Herwig, Alexander Schwarcz, eds: *Anerkennung und Integration*, Denkschriften der Österreichischen Akademie der Wissenschaften CXCIII (Vienna, 1988).

Solitary migration

Andre, Elsbeth: *Ein Königshof auf Reisen: Der Kontinentaufenthalt Edwards III. von England 1338–1340*, Archiv für Kulturgeschichte. Beiheft XLI (Cologne, Weimar, Vienna, 1995).

Schmugge, Ludwig: 'Mobilität und Freiheit im Mittelalter, in Johannes Fried, ed., *Die abendländische Freiheit vom 10. zum 14. Jahrhundert,* VuF XXXIX (Sigmaringen, 1991), pp. 307–49.

Group travel

Erfen Irene, Karl-Heinz Spieß, eds: *Fremdheit und Reisen im Mittelalter* (Stuttgart, 1997).

Labarge, Margaret Wade: *Medieval Travellers: The Rich and the Restless* (London, 1982).

Moraw, Peter, ed.: *Unterwegssein im Spätmittelalter,* Zeitschrift für Historische Forschung. Beiheft I (Berlin, 1985).

Ohler, Norbert: *Reisen im Mittelalter* (Munich, Zurich, 1986).

Paravicini, Werner: 'Von der Heidenfahrt zur Kavalierstour: Über Motive und Formen adligen Reisens im späten Mittelalter', in Horst Brunner, ed., *Wissensliteratur im Mittelalter und in der frühen Neuzeit* (Wiesbaden, 1993), pp. 91–130.

Solitary travel

Baaken, Gerhard, Roderich Schmidt: *Königtum, Burgen und Königsfreie: Königsumritt und Huldigung in ottonisch-salischer Zeit,* 2nd edn, VuF VI (Sigmaringen, 1981; first published Constance, 1961).

Bernhardt, I. W.: *Itinerant Kingship and Royal Monsteries in Early Medieval Germany,* Cambridge Studies in Medieval Life and Thought Fourth Series, vol. XXI (Cambridge, 1993).

Brühl, Carlrichard: 'Die Herrscheritinerare', *Settimane di studio del Centro Italiano di studi sull' alto medioevo di Spoleto* XIX (1985), pp. 615–45.

Ewert, Christian: 'Itinerar und Herrschaft im Spätmittelalter: Ein wirtschaftstheoretischer Ansatz und empirische Ergebnisse für die burgundischen Herzöge im 15. Jahrhundert (1419–1477)', *Historical Social Research* XXI (1996), pp. 89–114.

Müller-Mertens, Eckhard: *Die Reichsstruktur im Spiegel der Herrschaftspraxis Ottos des Großen,* Forschungen zur mittelalterlichen Geschichte XXV (Berlin, 1980).

Müller-Mertens, Eckhard, Wolfgang Huschner: *Reichsintegration im Spiegel der Herrschaftspraxis Kaiser Konrads II.,* Forschungen zur mittelalterlichen Geschichte XXXV (Weimar, 1992).

Peyer, Hans Conrad: *Von der Gastfreunschaft zum Gasthaus,* MGH Schriften XXXI (Hanover, 1987).

Schlauch, Margaret: 'Widsith, Vithförull, and Some Other Analogues', *Publications of the Modern Language Association of America* XLVI (1931), pp. 969–87.

Pilgrimages

Aronstam, Robin Ann: 'Penintential Pilgrimages to Rome in the Early Middle Ages', *Archivum historiae pontificiae* XIII (1973), pp. 65–83.

Herbers, Klaus: *Der Jakobsweg* (Tübingen, 1986).

Moore, Wilfrid J.: *The Saxon Pilgrims to Rome and the Schola Saxonum* (Fribourg, 1937).

Stancliffe, Claire: 'Kings Who Opted out', in Patrick Wormald, Donald Bullough, Roger Collins, eds, *Ideal and Reality in Frankish and Anglo-Saxon Society: Studies Presented to John Michael Wallace-Hadrill* (Blackwell, 1983), pp. 134–67.

Webb, Diana: *Pilgrims and Pilgrimage in the Medieval West* (London, New York, 1999).

Means of transportation and road condition

Bautier, Anne-Marie: 'Contribution à l'histoire du cheval au Moyen Age', *Bulletin philologique et historique du Comité des travaux historiques et scientifiques* (1976), pp. 209–49.

Harrison, D. F.: 'Bridges and Economic Development 1300–1800', *Economic History Review* XLV (1992), pp. 240–61.

Langdon, John: *Horses, Oxen, and Technological Innovation* (Cambridge, 1986).

Ludwig, Friedrich: *Untersuchungen über die Reise-und Marschgeschwindigkeit im 12. und 13. Jahrhundert* (Berlin, 1897).

Pelteret, David A.: 'The Roads of Anglo-Saxon England', *Wiltshire Archaeological and Natural History Magazine* LXXIX (1985), pp. 155–63.

Reuter, Timothy: 'Die Unsicherheit auf den Straßen im europäischen Früh- und Hochmittelalter: Täter, Opfer und ihre mittelalterlichen und modernen Beobachter', in Johannes Fried, ed., *Träger und Instrumentarien des Friedens im hohen und späten Mittelalter*, VuF XLIII (Sigmaringen, 1996), pp. 169–201.

Stenton, Frank Merry: 'The Road System of Medieval England', *Economic History Review* VII (1936(38), pp. 7–21. Reprinted in Stenton, *Preparatory to Anglo-Saxon England*, ed. Doris Mary Stenton (Oxford, 1970), pp. 234–51.

Travel literature, travel reports

Bennett, Josephine Walters: *The Rediscovery of Sir John Mandeville*, Modern Language Association of America. Monograph Series XIX (New York, 1954).

Ertzdorff, Xenia von, Dieter Neukirch, eds: *Reisen und Reiseliteratur im Mittelalter und in der frühen Neuzeit*, Chloe XIII (Amsterdam, Atlanta, 1992).

Esch, Arnold: 'Gemeinsames Erlebnis – individueller Bericht: Vier Parallelberichte aus einer Reisegruppe von Jerusalempilgern 1480', *Zeitschrift für*

Historische Forschung XI (1984), pp. 385–416. Reprinted in Esch, *Zeitalter und Menschenalter: Der Historiker und die Erfahrung vergangener Gegenwart* (Munich, 1994), pp. 189–216.

The Old and the Young

Age grades

Ghellinck, J. S. J.: 'Iuventus, gravitas, senectus', *Studia medievalia in honorem R. J. Martin* (Bruges, 1948), pp. 39–59.

Goodich, Michael: *From Birth to Old Age: The Human Life Cycle in Medieval Thought 1250–1350* (New York, 1989).

Hofmeister, Adolf: 'Puer, iuvenis, senex', in Albert Brackmann, ed., *Papsttum und Kaisertum. Festschrift für Paul Fridolin Kehr zum 65. Geburtstag* (Munich, 1926), pp. 287–316. (Reprint Aalen, 1973.)

Die Lebenstreppe: Bilder der menschlichen Lebensalter, Schriften des Rheinischen Museumsamtes XXIII (Pulheim, 1983).

Wackernagel, Wilhelm: *Die Lebensalter* (Basle, 1862).

Education of children

Arnold, Klaus: *Kind und Gesellschaft in Mittelalter und Renaissance*, Sammlung Zebra. Reihe B, vol. II (Paderborn, 1980).

L'enfant, Recueils de la Société Jean Bodin XXXVI (Brussels, 1976).

Garin, Eugenio: *L'educazione in Europa (1400–1600)*, Biblioteca di cultura moderna DXXXI (Bari, 1957).

Jussen, Bernhard: *Patenschaft und Adoption im frühen Mittelalter*, VMPIG XCVIII (Göttingen, 1991).

Levi, Giovani, Jean-Claude Schmitt, eds: *Ancient and Medieval Rites of Passage*, vol. 1 (Cambridge, Mass., London, 1997).

Lynch, Joseph H.: *Godparents and Kinship in Early Medieval Europe* (Princeton, 1986).

Riché, Pierre: 'L'enfant dans le haut Moyen Age', *Annales de démographie historique* (1973), pp. 75–98.

Schwarz, Heinz W.: *Der Schutz des Kindes im Recht des frühen Mittelalters*, Bonner historische Forschungen LVI (Siegburg, 1993).

Shahar, Shulamith: *Childhood in the Middle Ages*, 2nd edn (London, New York, 1992; first published London, 1980).

Schools

Courtenay, William J.: *Schools and Scholars in Fourteenth-century England* (Princeton, 1988).

Fried, Johannes ed.: *Schulen und Studium im sozialen Wandel des hohen und späten Mittelalters*, VuF XXX (Sigmaringen, 1986).

Orme, Nicholas: *English Schools in the Middle Ages* (London, 1973).

Orme, Nicholas: 'The Culture of Children in Medieval England', *Past and Present* CXLVIII (1995), pp. 48–88.

Riché, Pierre, *Daily Life in the World of Charlemagne* (Philadelphia, 1978; first published Paris, 1963.)

Riché, Pierre: *Education et culture dans l'Occident*, 3rd edn (Paris, 1973; first published, Patristica Sorbonensia IV, Paris, 1962).

Riché, Pierre: *Instruction et vie religieuse dans le haut Moyen Age* (London, 1981).

Riché, Pierre: *Education et culture dans l'Occident médiéval*, Variorum Collected Studies Series CDXX (Aldershot, 1993).

Aging

Borscheid, Peter: *Geschichte des Alters*, 2nd edn (Munich, 1989; first published Münster, 1987).

Sheehan, Michael M.: *Aging and the Ages in Medieval Europe* (Toronto, 1990).

Sprandel, Rolf: *Altersschicksal und Altersmoral: Die Geschichte der Einstellungen zum Altern nach der Pariser Bibelexegese des 12.–16. Jahrhundert*, Monographien zur Geschichte XXII (Stuttgart, 1981).

Death and Burial

Boase, Thomas Scherrer Ross: *Death in the Middle Ages* (London, 1972).

Braet, Herman, Werner Verbeke, eds: *Death in the Middle Ages* (Louvain, 1983).

Daniell, Christopher: *Death and Burial in Medieval Europe* (London, 1996).

Kölmer, Lothar, ed.: *Der Tod des Mächtigen: Sterben, Tod und Begräbnis spätmittelalterlicher Herrscher* (Paderborn, 1997).

Ohler, Norbert: *Sterben und Tod im Mittelalter* (Munich, 1990).

Sutto, Claude, ed.: *Le sentiment de la mort au Moyen Age* (Montreal, 1979).

Taylor, Jane H. M., ed.: *Dies illa: Death in the Middle Ages* (Liverpool, 1984).

Vovelle, Michel: *La mort et l'occident de 1300 à nos jours* (Paris, 1983).

Rule and Representation

Concepts of rule

Althoff, Gerd: 'Königsherrschaft und Konfliktbewältigung im 10. und 11. Jahrhundert', *Frühmittelalterliche Studien* XXIII (1989), pp. 265–90.

Althoff, Gerd: *Verwandte, Freunde und Getreue: Zum politischen Stellenwert der Gruppenbindungen im früheren Mittealter* (Darmstadt, 1990).

Althoff, Gerd: *Amicitia und Pacta: Bündnis, Einung, Politik und Gebetsgedenken im beginnenden 10. Jahrhundert*, MGH Schriften XXXVII (Hanover, 1992).

Anton, Hans Hubert: *Fürstenspiegel und Herrscherethos in der Karolingerzeit*, Bonner historische Forschungen XXXII (Bonn, 1968).

Born, Lester Kruger: 'The Perfect Prince: A Study in Thirteenth- and Fourteenth-century Ideals', *Speculum* III (1928), pp. 470–504.

Courtenay, William: *Capacity and Causality: A History of the Distinction between Absolute and Ordained Power* (Bergamo, 1990).

Green, Dennis Howard: *The Carolingian Lord* (Cambridge, 1965).

Holenstein, André: *Die Huldigung der Untertanen: Rechtskultur und Herrschaftsordnung (800–1800)*, Quellen und Forschungen zur Agrargeschichte XXXVI (Stuttgart, New York, 1991).

Jackson, William Thomas Hobdell: 'The Conflict between Hero and King', in Jackson, *The Hero and the King* (New York, 1982), pp. 1–111.

Kaske, Robert E.: '*Sapientia et fortitudo* as the Controlling Theme in *Beowulf*', *Studia Neophilologica* LV (1958), pp. 423–56.

Kern, Fritz: *Gottesgnadentum und Widerstandsrecht im früheren Mittelalter* (Leipzig, 1914; reprinted Darmstadt, 1973).

Leyerle, John: 'Beowulf, the Hero and the King', *Medium Aevum* XXXIV (1965), pp. 89–102.

Manz, Luise: *Der Ordo-Gedanke*, VSWG. Beiheft XXXIII (Stuttgart, 1937).

Seebold, Elmar: 'Die ae. Entsprechungen von lat. sapiens und prudens', *Anglia* XCII (1974), pp. 291–333.

Weinacht, Paul-Ludwig: *Staat: Studien zur Bedeutungsgeschichte des Wortes von den Anfängen bis ins 19. Jahrhundert*, Beiträge zur Politischen Wissenschaft II (Berlin, 1968).

Concepts of representation

Althoff, Gerd, Ernst Schubert, eds: *Herrschaftsrepräsentation im ottonischen Sachsen*, VuF XLVI (Sigmaringen, 1998).

Blockmans, Wim P.: 'A Typology of Representative Institutions in Late Medieval Europe', *Journal of Medieval History* IV (1978), pp. 189–215.

Blockmans, Wim P.: 'Representation (since the Thirteenth Century)', *The New Cambridge Medieval History*, vol. 7, ed. Christopher T. Allmand (Cambridge, 1998), pp. 29–64.

Classen, Peter: 'Die Verträge von Coulaines und Verdun 843 als Grundlagen des westfränkischen Reiches', *Historische Zeitschrift* CXCVI (1963), pp. 1–35.

Höß, Irmgard: 'Parlamentum: Zur Verwendung des Begriffes im Sprachgebrauch der spätmittelalterlichen Reichskanzlei', in Helmut Beumann, ed., *Historische Forschungen für Walter Schlesinger* (Cologne, Vienna, 1974), pp. 570–83.

Hofmann, Hasso: *Repräsentation: Studien zur Wort- und Begriffsgeschichte von der Antike bis ins 19. Jahrhundert*, Schriften zur Verfassungsgeschichte XXII (Berlin, 1974).

Ragotzky, Helga, Horst Wenzel, eds: *Höfische Repräsentation* (Tübingen, 1990).

Stafford, Pauline A.: 'The Laws of Cnut and the History of Anglo-Saxon Royal Promises', *Anglo-Saxon England* X (1978), pp. 173–90.

Zimmermann, Albert, ed.: *Der Begriff repraesentatio im Mittelalter,* Miscellanea Mediaevalia VIII (Berlin, New York, 1972).

The problem of sovereignty

David, Michel: *La souveraineté et les limites principales du pouvoir* (Paris, 1954).

Knabe, Lotte: *Die gelasianische Zweigewaltentheorie bis zum Ende des Investiturstreits,* Historische Studien CCXCII (Berlin, 1936; reprinted Vaduz, 1965).

Quaritsch, Helmut: *Souveränität,* Schriften zur Verfassungsgeschichte XXXVIII (Berlin, 1986).

Ullmann, Walter: 'Zur Entwicklung des Souveränitätsbegriffs im Spätmittelalter', in Louis Carlen, Fritz Steinegger, eds, *Festschrift für Nikolaus Grass zum 60. Geburtstag,* vol. 1 (Innsbruck, 1974), pp. 9–27.

Wilks, Michael: *The Problem of Sovereignty in the Later Middle Ages,* Cambridge Studies in Medieval Life and Thought N. S. IX (Cambridge, 1964).

Political theory and philosophy

Arquillière, Henri-Xavier: *L'Augustinisme politique: Essai sur la formation des théories politiques du Moyen Age,* 2nd edn, Colloque L'Eglise et l'Etat au Moyen Age II (Paris, 1955; first published Paris, 1934).

Bernheim, Ernst: *Mittelalterliche Zeitanschauungen in ihrem Einfluß auf Politik und Geschichtsschreibung* (Tübingen, 1918).

Burns, James Henderson: *Lordship, Kingship, and Empire: The Idea of Monarchy 1400–1525* (Oxford, 1992).

Canning, Joseph: *The Political Thought of Baldus de Ubaldis,* Cambridge Studies in Medieval Life and Thought Fourth Series VI (Cambridge, 1987).

Canning, Joseph, Otto Gerhard Oexle, eds: *Political Thought and the Realities of Power in the Middle Ages/ Politisches Denken und die Wirklichkeit der Macht im Mittelalter,* VMPIG CXLVII (Göttingen, 1998).

Fowler, George Bingham: *Intellectual Interests of Engelbert of Admont,* Studies in History, Economics and Public Law DXXX (New York, 1947; reprinted New York, 1967).

Goez, Werner: *Translatio imperii: Ein Beitrag zur Geschichte des Geschichtsdenkens und der politischen Theorie im Mittelalter und in der frühen Neuzeit* (Tübingen, 1958).

Hamm, Marlies: 'Engelbert von Admont als Staatstheoretiker', *Studien und Mitteilungen zur Geschichte Benediktinerordens und seiner Zweige* LXXXV (1974), pp. 343–495.

Holtzmann, Robert: 'Dominium mundi und imperium merum', *Zeitschrift für Kirchengeschichte* LXI (1942), pp. 191–200.

Kantorowicz, Ernst Hartwig: *The King's Two Bodies: A Study of Medieval Political Theology* (Princeton, 1957).

Miethke, Jürgen: 'Politische Theorie in der Krise der Zeit', in Gert Melville, ed., *Institutionen und Geschichte, Norm und Struktur* I (Cologne, Weimar, Vienna, 1992), pp. 157–86.

Nederman, Cary J., Kate Langdon Forsham, eds: *Medieval Political Theory: The Quest for the Body Politic 1100–1400* (London, 1993).

Schramm, Percy Ernst: *Kaiser, Rom und Renovatio*, Studien der Bibliothek Warburg XVII (Leipzig, 1929; reprinted Darmstadt, 1962).

Struve, Tilman: *Die Entwicklung der organologischen Staatsauffassung im Mittelalter*, Monographien zur Geschichte des Mittelalters XVI (Stuttgart, 1978).

Stürner, Wolfgang: *Peccatum und potestas: Der Sündenfall und die Entstehung der herrschaftlichen Gewalt im mittelalterlichen Staatsdenken*, Beiträge zur Geschichte und Quellenkunde des Mittelalters XI (Sigmaringen, 1986).

Wilks, Michael, ed.: *The World of John of Salisbury*, Studies in Church History. Subsidia III (Oxford, 1984).

Woolf, Cecil Nathan Sidney: *Bartolus of Sassoferato: His Position in the History of Medieval Political Thought* (Cambridge, 1913).

Ceremonies and symbols of rulership

Biehl, Ludwig: *Das liturgische Gebet für Kaiser und Reich*, Görres-Gesellschaft zur Pflege der Wissenschaften im katholischen Deutschland. Veröffentlichungen der Sektion für Rechts- und Staatswissenschaft LXXV (Paderborn, 1937).

Bloch, Marc: *The Royal Touch* (New York, 1990; first published, Publications de la Faculté des Lettres de l'Université de Strasbourg XIX, Strasbourg, 1924).

David, Michel: 'Le serment de sacre du IXe au XVe siècle', *Revue du Moyen Age Latin* VI (1950), pp. 5–272.

Eichmann, Eduard: *Die Kaiserkrönung im Abendland*, 2 vols (Würzburg, 1942).

Enright, Michael Joseph: *Iona, Tara, and Soissons: The Origins of the Royal Anointing Ritual*, Arbeiten zur Frühmittelalterforschung XVII (Berlin, New York, 1985).

Hellmann, Manfred, ed.: *Corona regni*, Wege der Forschung III (Darmstadt, 1961).

McCormick, Michael: *Eternal Victory: Triumphal Rulership in Late Antiquity, Byzantium and the Early Medieval West* (Cambridge, 1985; reprinted Cambridge, 1987).

Prodi, Paolo: *Das Sakrament der Herrschaft: Der politische Eid in der Verfassungsgeschichte des Okzidents*, Schriften des Italienisch–Deutschen Historischen Instituts in Trient XI (Berlin, 1997).

Schmitz, Karl: *Ursprung und Geschichte der Devotionsformeln bis zu ihrer Aufnahme in die fränkische Königsurkunde*, Kirchenrechtliche Abhandlungen LXXXI (Stuttgart, 1913).

Schramm, Percy Ernst: *Herrschaftszeichen und Staatssymbolik*, 3 vols, MGH Schriften XII (Stuttgart, 1954–56).

Staats, Reinhart: *Theologie der Reichskrone*, Monographien zur Geschichte des Mittelalters XIII (Stuttgart, 1976).

Staubach, Nikolaus: *Rex christianus: Hofkultur und Herrschaftspropaganda im Reich Kalrs des Kahlen*, vol. 2, Pictura et poesis II,2 (Cologne, Weimar, Vienna 1992).

Wolf, Gunther G.: *Die Wiener Reichskrone*, Schriften des Kunsthistorischen Museums I (Vienna, 1995).

Contractualism

Blockmans, Wim P.: 'Du contrat féodal à la souveraineté du peuple', *Assemblee di stati e istituzioni rappresentative nella storia del pensiero politico moderno* (Rimini, 1983), pp. 135–50.

Congar, Yves Marie-Joseph: 'Quod omnes tangit ab omnibus tractari et approbari debet', *Revue historique de droit français et étranger* XXXVI (1958), pp. 210–59. Reprinted in Heinz Rausch, ed., *Die geschichtlichen Grundlagen der modernen Volksvertretung*, vol. 1, Wege der Forschung CXCVI (Darmstadt, 1980), pp. 115–82.

Courtenay, William: *Covenant and Causality in Medieval Thought*, Variorum Collected Studies Series CCVI (Aldershot, 1984).

Hamm, Bernd: *Promissio, Pactum, Ordinatio: Freiheit und Selbstbindung Gottes in der scholastischen Gnadenlehre*, Beiträge zur Historischen Theologie LIV (Tübingen, 1977).

Hanning, Jürgen: *Consensus fidelium: Frühfeudale Interpretationen des Verhältnisses von Königtum und Adel am Beispiel des Frankenreiches*, Monographien zur Geschichte des Mittelalters XXVII (Stuttgart, 1982).

McCoy, Charles S., J. Wayne Baker: *Fountainhead of Federalism: Heinrich Bullinger and the Covenantal Tradition* (Louisville, KY, 1991).

Marongiu, Antonio: 'Das Prinzip der Demokratie und der Zustimmung', in Heinz Rausch, ed., *Die geschichtlichen Grundlagen der modernen Volksvertretung*, vol. 1, Wege der Forschung CXCVI (Darmstadt, 1980), pp. 183–221. First published in *Studia Gratiana* VIII (1962), pp. 555–75.

Näf, Werner: 'Herrschaftsverträge und Lehre vom Herrschaftsvertrag', *Schweizerische Beiträge zur allgemeinen Geschichte* VII (1949), pp. 26–52.

Oakley, Francis: *Natural Law, Conciliarism and Consent in the Late Middle Ages*, Variorum Collected Studies Series CLXXXIX (London, 1984).

Oestreich, Gerhard: *Neostoicism and the Early Modern State*, eds. Brigitta Oestreich, Helmuth Georg Koenigsberger (Cambridge, 1982).

Post, Gaines: 'A Romano-canonical Maxim "Quod omnes tangit" in Bracton', *Traditio* IV (1946), pp. 197–251.

Post, Gaines: 'A Roman Legal Theory of Consent', *Wisconsin Law Review* (1950), pp. 66–78.

Tierney, Brian: *Church Law and Constitutional Thought in the Middle Ages*, Variorum Collected Studies Series XC (London, 1979).

Structure and development of institutions of rule

Black, Antony J.: *Monarchy and Community: Political Ideas in the Later Conciliar Controversy 1430–1450*, Cambridge Studies in Medieval Life and Thought Third Series, vol. II (Cambridge, 1970).

Blokmans, Wim P., Jean-Philip Genet, eds: *Visions sur le développement des états européens*, Collection de l'Ecole Française de Rome CLXXI (Rome, 1993).

Cheyette, Fredric L., ed.: *Lordship and Community in Medieval Europe* (New York, 1968).

Dam, Raymond van: *Leadership and Community in Late Antique Gaul* (Berkeley, Los Angeles, 1985).

Englberg, Johann: *Gregor VII. und die Investiturfrage*, Passauer historische Forschungen IX (Cologne, Weimar, Vienna 1996).

Fleckenstein, Josef: *Die Hofkapelle der deutschen Könige*, vol. 1, MGH Schriften XVI (Stuttgart, 1959).

Gernhuber, Josef: *Die Landfriedensbewegung in Deutschland bis zum Mainzer Landfrieden*, Bonner rechtwissenschaftliche Abhandlungen XLIV (Bonn, 1952).

Head, Thomas, Richard Landes, eds: *The Peace of God: Social Violence and Religious Response in France around the Year 1000* (Ithaca, London, 1992).

Krynen, Jacques: *L'Empire du roi: Idées et croyances en France: XIIe–XVe siècles* (Paris, 1993).

Lindow, John: *Comitatus, Individual and Honor: Studies in North Germanic Institutional Vocabulary*, University of California Publications in Linguistics LXXXIII (Berkeley, Los Angeles, London, 1976).

Mayer, Theodor, ed.: *Das Königtum*, 4th edn, VuF III (Sigmaringen, 1973; first published Constance, 1956).

Patze, Hans, ed.: *Der deutsche Territorialstaat im 14. Jahrhundert*, 2 vols, VuF XIII–XIV (Sigmaringen, 1970).

La Regalità sacra, Studies in the History of Religions. Supplements to Numen IV (Leiden, 1959).

Reynolds, Susan: *Kingdoms and Communities in Western Europe 900–1300* (Oxford, New York, Toronto 1984).

Santifaller, Leo: *Zur Geschichte des ottonisch-salischen Reichskirchensystems*, Sitzungsberichte der Österreichischen Akademie der Wissenschaften, Philos.-Hist. Kl. CCXXIX, 1 (Vienna, 1954; 2nd edn Vienna, 1964).

Schlesinger, Walter: *Die Entstehung der Landesherrschaft*, 2nd edn (Darmstadt, 1964; reprinted Darmstadt, 1983; first published, Sächsische Forschungen zur Geschichte I, Dresden, 1941).

Schramm, Percy Ernst: *Kaiser, Könige und Päpste*, 4 vols (Stuttgart, 1968–70).

Wallace-Hadrill, John Michael: *Early Germanic Kingship in England and on the Continent* (Oxford, 1971).

Structure and reform of the Holy Roman Empire and of the Papacy

Angermeier, Heinz: *Das alte Reich in der deutschen Geschichte* (Munich, 1991).

Black, Antony J.: *Council and Commune: The Conciliar Movement and the Fifteenth-century Heritage* (London, 1980).

Cuming, Geoffrey John, Derek Baker, eds: *Councils and Assemblies* (Cambridge, 1971).

Folz, Robert: *L'idée de l'Empire en Occident du Ve au XIVe siècle* (Paris, 1953).

Heinig, Paul-Joachim, ed.: *Kaiser Friedrich III. (1440–1493) in seiner Zeit,* Forschungen zur Kaiser- und Papstgeschichte des Mittelalters. Beihefte zu J. F. Böhmer, Regesta Imperii II (Cologne, Weimar, Vienna, 1993).

Heinig, Paul-Joachim: *Kaiser Friedrich III. (1440–1493): Hof, Regierung und Politik,* 3 vols, Forschungen zur Kaiser- und Papstgeschichte. Beiheft zu J. F. Boehmer, Regesta Imperii XVII (Cologne, Weimar, Vienna, 1997).

Kuttner, Stephan: *Mediaeval Councils, Decretals and Collections of Canon Law,* Collected Studies Series CXXVI (London, 1980).

Michaud-Quantin, Pierre: *Universitas: Expression du mouvement communautaire dans le Moyen Age,* Collection L'Eglise et l'Etat au Moyen Age XIII (Paris, 1970).

Schubert, Ernst: *König und Reich,* VMPIG LXIII (Göttingen, 1979).

Index

Index